STRE|

Essex

Chelmsford, Colchester, Harlow, Southend-on-Sea

CW00411018

www.philips-maps.co.uk

First published in 2003 by

Philip's, a division of
Octopus Publishing Group Ltd
www.octopusbooks.co.uk
2-4 Heron Quays, London E14 4JP
An Hachette Livre UK Company

Second edition 2008
First impression 2008
ESXBA

ISBN-13   978-0-540-09196-6 (pocket)

© Philip's 2008

This product includes mapping data licensed from
Ordnance Survey® with the permission of the
Controller of Her Majesty's Stationery Office.
© Crown copyright 2008. All rights reserved.
Licence number 100011710.

Data for the speed cameras provided by
PocketGPSWorld.com Ltd.

Ordnance Survey and the OS Symbol are
registered trademarks of Ordnance Survey, the
national mapping agency of Great Britain

Printed and bound in Spain
by Cayfosa-Quebecor

Contents

Digital Data

The exceptionally high-quality mapping found in this atlas is available as digital data in TIFF format, which is easily convertible to other bitmapped (raster) image formats.

The index is also available in digital form as a standard database table. It contains all the details found in the printed index together with the National Grid reference for the map square in which each entry is named.

For further information and to discuss your requirements, please contact james.mann@philips-maps.co.uk

Mobile speed cameras

The vast majority of speed cameras used on Britain's roads are operated by safety camera partnerships. These comprise local authorities, the police, Her Majesty's Court Service (HMCS) and the Highways Agency.

This table lists the sites where each safety camera partnership may enforce speed limits through the use of mobile cameras or detectors. These are usually set up on the roadside or a bridge spanning the road and operated by a police or civilian enforcement officer. The speed limit at each site (if available) is shown in red type, followed by the approximate location in black type.

A12
Braintree, Overbridge nr Kelvedon Interchange

A13
30 Castle Point, High St (Hadleigh twds London)
30 Leigh on Sea, London Rd
Southend, Bournes Green Chase
Southend, North Shoebury
Southend, Southchurch Boulevard

A1016
30 Chelmsford, Waterhouse Lane

A1017
30 Sible Hedingham, Swan St
30 Witham / Braintree, Rickstone Rd

A1023
30 Brentwood, Chelmsford Rd
30 Brentwood, London Rd
30 Brentwood, Shenfield Rd

A1025
40 Harlow, Second Avenue
40 Harlow, Third Avenue

A1060
Little Hallingbury, Lower Rd

A1090
30 Purfleet, London Rd
30 Purfleet, Tank Hill Rd

A1124
30 Colchester, Lexden Rd

A113
30 Epping, High Rd

A1158
30 Westcliff on Sea, Southbourne Grove

A1168
30 Loughton, Rectory Lane

A1169
40 Harlow, Southern Way

A120
Little Bentley, Pellens Corner
Wix, Harwich Rd nr Colchester Rd

A1205
40 Harlow, Second Avenue

A121
30 Epping, High Rd
30 Loughton, Goldings Hill (j/w Monkchester Close)
Loughton, High Rd

Waltham Abbey, Farm Hill Rd
Waltham Abbey, Sewardstine Rd

A126
30 Grays, London Rd
30 Tilbury, Montreal Rd

A128
Chipping Ongar, High St
30 Ingrave/Herongate, Brentwood Rd
40 Kelvedon Hatch, Ongar Rd

A129
30 Basildon, Crays Hill
Billericay, Southend Rd
Rayleigh, London Rd
30 Wickford, London Rd
Wickford, Southend Rd

A130
30 Canvey Island, Long Rd
South Benfleet, Canvey Way

A133
30 Elmstead Market, Clacton Rd
Little Bentley, Colchester Rd

A134
40 Great Horkesley, Nayland Rd

A137
30 Lawford, Wignall St

B170
Chigwell, Chigwell Rise
Loughton, Roding Lane

B172
Theydon Bois, Coppice Row

B173
Chigwell, Lambourne Rd

B184
40 Great Easton, Snow Hill

B186
30 South Ockendon, South Rd

B1002
30 Ingatestone, High St

B1007
30 Billericay, Laindon Rd
30 Billericay, Stock Rd
40 Chelmsford, Stock Rd

B1008
30 Chelmsford, Broomfield Rd

B1013
30 Hawkwell, High Rd
30 Hawkwell, Main Rd
30 Hockley/Hawkwell, Southend Rd
Rayleigh, High Rd

B1014
30 South Benfleet, Benfleet Rd

B1018
30 Latchingdon, The St
30 Maldon, The Causeway

B1019
30 Hatfield Peveral, Maldon Rd
30 Witham, Powers Hall End

B1021
Burnham on Crouch, Church Rd

B1022
30 Colchester, Maldon Rd
30 Heckfordbridge, Maldon Rd
30 Maldon, Colchester Rd
30 Tiptree Heath, Maldon Rd

B1027
30 Clacton-on-Sea, Valley Rd/Old Rd
30 St Osyth, Pump Hill
40 Wivenhoe, Brightlingsea Rd

B1028
30 Wivenhoe, Colchester Rd
30 Wivenhoe, The Avenue

B1033
30 Kirby Cross, Frinton Rd

B1335
40 South Ockendon, Stifford Rd

B1352
Harwich, Main Rd

B1383
30 Newport, London Rd Stansted Mountfitchet, Cambridge Rd

B1389
30 Witham, Colchester Rd
30 Witham, Hatfield Rd

B1393
30 Epping, Palmers Hill

B1441
30 Clacton-on-Sea, London Rd
Tendring, Clacton Rd

B1442
30 Clacton-on-Sea, Thorpe Rd

B1464
30 Bowers Gifford, London Rd

UNCLASSIFIED
40 Alresford, St Osyth Rd
30 Aveley, Purfleet Rd
Aveley, Romford Rd
30 Barstable, Sandon Rd
30 Basildon, Ashlyns
Basildon, Clay Hill Rd
40 Basildon, Cranes Farm Rd (j/w Honywood Rd)
30 Basildon, Felmores
Basildon, London Rd, Wickford
30 Basildon, Vange Hill Drive
30 Basildon, Whitmore Way
30 Basildon, Wickford Avenue
30 Billericay, Mountnessing Rd
30 Bowers Gifford, London Rd
30 Braintree, Coldnailhurst Avenue
30 Brentwood, Eagle Way (nr j/w Clive Rd twds Warley Rd)

30 Brentwood, Eagle Way
30 Buckhurst Hill, Buckhurst Way/Albert Rd
30 Canvey Island, Dovervelt Rd
30 Canvey Island, Link Rd
30 Canvey Island, Thorney Bay Rd
Chadwell St Mary, Brentwood Rd
30 Chadwell St Mary, Linford Rd
30 Chadwell St Mary, Riverview
30 Chelmsford, Baddow Rd
30 Chelmsford, Chignall Rd
30 Chelmsford, Copperfield Rd
Chelmsford, Galleywood Rd
30 Chelmsford, Longstomps Avenue
30 Clacton-on-Sea, St Johns Rd
30 Clacton, Kings Parade
30 Clacton, Marine Parade East
30 Colchester, Abbots Rd
30 Colchester, Avon Way
30 Colchester, Bromley Rd
Colchester, Ipswich Rd
30 Colchester, Old Heath Rd
30 Colchester, Shrub End Rd
30 Corringham, Southend Rd
30 Corringham, Springhouse Rd
Danbury, Maldon Rd
30 Daws Heath, Daws Heath Rd
30 Eastwood, Green Lane j/w Kendal Way
30 Eastwood, Western Approaches j/w Rockall
30 Grays, Blackshots Lane
30 Grays, Lodge Lane
Grays, London Rd (nr Angel Rd)
Grays, London Rd (nr Bransons Way)
30 Hainault, Fencepiece Rd
40 Harlow, Abercrombie Way, twds Southern Way
40 Harlow, Howard Way
30 Hawkwell, Rectory Rd
30 Hockley, High Rd
30 Hullbridge, Coventry Hill
30 Laindon, Durham Rd
30 Laindon, High Rd
30 Laindon, Nightingales
30 Laindon, Wash Rd
Langdon Hills, High Rd
30 Leigh on Sea, Belton Way East
30 Leigh on Sea, Belton Way West
30 Leigh on Sea, Blenheim Chase
30 Leigh on Sea, Grand Parade/Cliff Parade
30 Leigh on Sea, Hadleigh Rd
30 Leigh on Sea, Highlands Boulevard
30 Leigh on Sea, Manchester Drive
30 Leigh on Sea, Mountdale Gardens
30 Leigh on Sea, Western Rd
30 Loughton, Alderton Hill
30 Loughton, Loughton Way
Loughton, Valley Hill
30 Maldon, Fambridge Rd
30 Maldon, Holloway Rd
30 Maldon, Mundon Rd
30 Pitsea, Rectory Rd

30 Prittlewell, Kenilworth Gardens
30 Prittlewell, Prittlewell Chase
30 Rayleigh, Bull Lane
Rayleigh, Downhall Rd
30 Rayleigh, Trinity Rd, nr Church Rd
30 Rochford, Ashingdon Rd
30 Rochford, Rectory Rd
Rush Green, St Osyth Rd
30 Shoeburyness, Ness Rd
30 South Woodham Ferrers, Hullbridge Rd
30 South Woodham Ferrers, Inchbonnie Rd
30 Southend on Sea, Lifstan Way
Southend, Bournemouth Park Rd
30 Southend, Hamstel Rd
Southend on Sea, Bournemouth Park Rd
Southend, Western Esplanade/Westcliff on Sea
30 Springfield, New Bowers Way
30 Stanford le Hope, London Rd
30 Tendring, Burrs Rd, Clacton
30 Tendring, Frinton Rd, Frinton
Tendring, Harwich Rd, Wix Arch Cottages to Cansey Lane
30 Tendring, Osyth Rd, Rush Green
Theydon Bois, Piercing Hill
30 Thorpe Bay, Barnstaple Rd
30 Thorpe Bay, Thorpe Hall Avenue
Waltham Abbey, Paternoster Hill
Weeley Heath, Clacton Rd
Weeley Heath, Clacton Rd
30 West Thurrock, London Rd
30 Westcliff on Sea, Chalkwell Avenue
30 Westcliff on Sea, Kings Rd
30 Wickford, London Rd
30 Wickford, Radwinter Avenue
30 Witham, Powers Hall End
30 Witham, Rickstones Rd

Key to map symbols

III

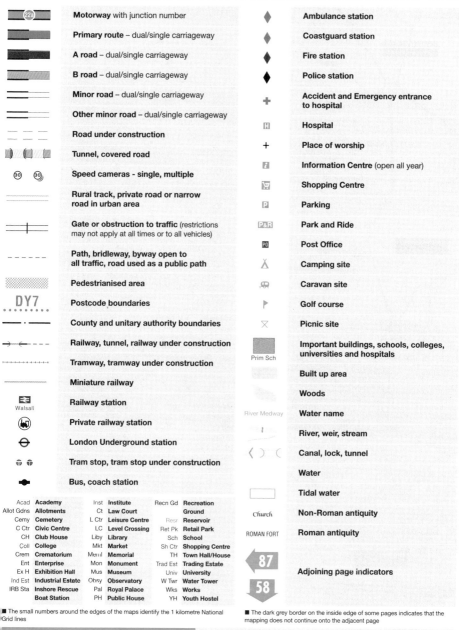

Motorway with junction number	Ambulance station
Primary route – dual/single carriageway	Coastguard station
A road – dual/single carriageway	Fire station
B road – dual/single carriageway	Police station
Minor road – dual/single carriageway	Accident and Emergency entrance to hospital
Other minor road – dual/single carriageway	Hospital
Road under construction	Place of worship
Tunnel, covered road	Information Centre (open all year)
Speed cameras - single, multiple	Shopping Centre
Rural track, private road or narrow road in urban area	Parking
Gate or obstruction to traffic (restrictions may not apply at all times or to all vehicles)	Park and Ride
Path, bridleway, byway open to all traffic, road used as a public path	Post Office
Pedestrianised area	Camping site
Postcode boundaries	Caravan site
County and unitary authority boundaries	Golf course
Railway, tunnel, railway under construction	Picnic site
Tramway, tramway under construction	Important buildings, schools, colleges, universities and hospitals
Miniature railway	Built up area
Railway station	Woods
Private railway station	Water name
London Underground station	River, weir, stream
Tram stop, tram stop under construction	Canal, lock, tunnel
Bus, coach station	Water
	Tidal water

DY7

Walsall

Prim Sch

River Medway

Church

ROMAN FORT

87

58

Acad	Academy	Inst	Institute	Recn Gd	Recreation Ground	Non-Roman antiquity
Allot Gdns	Allotments	Ct	Law Court			Roman antiquity
Cemy	Cemetery	L Ctr	Leisure Centre	Resr	Reservoir	
C Ctr	Civic Centre	LC	Level Crossing	Ret Pk	Retail Park	
CH	Club House	Liby	Library	Sch	School	
Coll	College	Mkt	Market	Sh Ctr	Shopping Centre	Adjoining page indicators
Crem	Crematorium	Meml	Memorial	TH	Town Hall/House	
Ent	Enterprise	Mon	Monument	Trad Est	Trading Estate	
Ex H	Exhibition Hall	Mus	Museum	Univ	University	
Ind Est	Industrial Estate	Obsy	Observatory	W Twr	Water Tower	
IRB Sta	Inshore Rescue Boat Station	Pal	Royal Palace	Wks	Works	
		PH	Public House	YH	Youth Hostel	

■ The small numbers around the edges of the maps identify the 1 kilometre National Grid lines

■ The dark grey border on the inside edge of some pages indicates that the mapping does not continue onto the adjacent page

The scale of the maps on the pages numbered in blue is 4.2 cm to 1 km • 2⅔ inches to 1 mile • 1: 23810

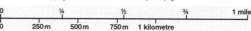

0	¼	½	¾	1 mile
0	250 m	500 m	750 m	1 kilometre

IV

Great Shelford
Sawston

Cambridgeshire STREET ATLAS

Cavendish 1

Hinxton 3 Hadstock 4 5 Shudy Camps 6 7 Haverhill 8 9 Boyton End 10 11 Clare Pentlow
Ickleton Ashdon Sturmer Drapers Green Stoke by Clare 12 13
Great Chesterford

Heydon Little Walden Helions Bumpstead Birdbrook Belchamp Walter
Royston 19 20 21 22 23 24 25 Steeple 26 27 Ridgewell 28 29 30 31 Gestingthorpe
Chrishall Littlebury Saffron Walden Hempstead Bumpstead

Duddenhoe End Wendens Ambo Radwinter Cornish Hall End Toppesfield Audley End
Nuthampstead 39 40 41 42 43 44 45 46 47 48 49 50 51 52
Langley Arkesden Newport Elder Street Great Sampford Gainsford End Sible Hedingham

Baldock Wicken Bonhunt Debden Little Sampford Finchingfield Southey Green
64 65 66 67 68 69 70 71 72 73 74 75 76
Brent Pelham Clavering Quendon Cutlers Green Thaxted Great Bardfield Wethersfield Blackmore End Halstead

Buntingford Rickling Green Henham Richmond's Green 98 99 Shalford Gosfield
92 93 94 95 96 97 100 101 102 103 Beazley End High Garrett
Manuden Broxted Duton Hill Lindsell Bardfield Saling

Stevenage Stansted Mountfitchet Molehill Green Great Easton Stebbing Panfield Stisted
Hertfordshire STREET ATLAS 118 119 120 121 122 123 124 125 126 127 128 129
Birchanger Church End Stebbing Green Rayne Braintree Bradwell End

Bishop's Stortford Takeley Street Takeley Great Dunmow Felsted Great Notley Cressing
145 146 147 148 149 150 151 152 153 154 155 156
Great Hallingbury Great Canfield Barnston Willows Green White Notley Silver End

Little Hallingbury Taverners Green Ford End Great Leighs Church End
172 173 174 175 176 177 178 179 180 181 182 183
Sawbridgeworth Hatfield Heath High Easter Pleshey Howe Street Terling Witham

Ware Hunsdonbury Gilston Sheering White Roding Leaden Roding Great Waltham Little Waltham Hatfield Peverel
197 198 199 200 201 202 203 204 205 206 207 208 209 210 211
Hertford Stansted Abbotts Roydon Harlow Matching Green Abbess Roding Mashbury Broomfield

Hoddesdon Tye Green Tilegate Green High Laver Roxwell Boreham Woodham Walter
221 222 223 224 225 226 227 228 229 230 231 232 233 234 235
Lower Nazeing Roydon Hamlet Hastingwood Moreton Fyfield Willingale Writtle Chelmsford Little Baddow

Cheshunt Bumble's Green North Weald Bassett Bobbingworth Widford Great Baddow Danbury
243 244 245 246 247 248 249 250 251 252 253 254 255 256 257
Aimes Green Waltham Abbey Epping Chipping Ongar Norton Heath Loves Green Howe Green Cock Clarks

Potters Bar Ivy Chimneys Fiddlers Hamlet Stanford Rivers Blackmore Mill Green Margaretting East Hanningfield
Holdbrook 265 266 267 268 269 270 271 272 273 274 275 276 277 278 279
Theydon Bois Stapleford Tawney Kelvedon Hatch Doddinghurst Ingatestone West Hanningfield Woodham Ferrers

Enfield High Beach Abridge Navestock Heath Mountnessing 298 299 South Woodham Ferrers
287 288 289 290 291 292 293 294 295 296 297 300 301
East Barnet Loughton Stapleford Abbotts Bentley Pilgrims Hatch Billericay Ramsden Heath Runwell Hullbridge
Chingford Shenfield

Southgate Chingford Hatch Chigwell Chigwell Row South Weald Brentwood South Green Wickford Rawreth
Edmonton 309 310 311 312 313 314 315 316 317 318 319 320 321 322 323
Wood Green Tottenham Woodford Harold Hill Ingrave Dunton Wayletts Nevendon Shotgate Rayleigh
Walthamstow Great Warley

Golders Green Barkingside Romford West Horndon Laindon Basildon Thundersley
Stoke Newington 332 333 334 335 336 337 338 339 340 341 342 343 344 345
London STREET ATLAS Wanstead Goodmayes Cranham Langdon Hills Vange Hadleigh
Ilford Upminster

Camden Town Becontree Elm Park Corbets Tey Bulphan 360 361 Winter Gardens 364
Islington Hackney Stratford 352 353 354 355 356 357 358 359 362 363 Canvey Island
Finsbury Shoreditch Bow West Ham Dagenham North Ockendon Horndon on the Hill Fobbing
Paddington Barking Rainham South Ockendon Stanford-le-Hope
City of London Poplar Wennington Aveley Orsett
Westminster London City 369 370 371 372 373 374 375 Kent STREET ATLAS
Chelsea Bermondsey Erith Little Thurrock Chadwell St Mary
Battersea Deptford Greenwich Purfleet Grays Tilbury East Tilbury
Camberwell Woolwich 376 377 378 379 380
Clapham Lewisham Swanscombe Northfleet
Eltham Bexley Dartford Gravesend Strood Rochester
Streatham Sidcup Crayford
Wimbledon Penge Bromley Chislehurst Swanley
Mitcham

V

Needham Market

Woodbridge

Stanstead
Glemsford
2
Foxearth   Long Melford
14   15
Borley Sudbury
Bulmer   Great Cornard
32 33 34
Middleton

Wickham St Paul
54   55
53   Alphamstone Bures
Pebmarsh
Mount Bures 80 81
77 Colne 78 79 Little Horkesley
Engaine
Wormingford

A1124 Earls
Colne
104 105

Hadleigh

Whitton
Ipswich   Rushmere St Andrew
16 17 18
Sproughton
Stoke
Rose Hill
Washbrook Belstead Wherstead
35 36 37 38
Capel St Mary Freston   Woolverstone

Stoke-by-Nayland 58 59 Tattingstone
56 57 East Bergholt Bentley Holbrook
Thorington Street Stratford St Mary 60 61 62 63 Chelmondiston
Nayland Dedham Brantham Trimley St Mary
Boxted 82 83 84 85 86 87 Harkstead Shotley Gate 384
Langham Mistley 88 89 Wrabness 90 91
Great Horkesley Great Horksley Manningtree Ramsey Parkeston Harwich

Wakes Colne 108 109 A12 Ardleigh Little Bromley Wix
106 107 West Bergholt 110 111 112 113 114 A120 115 Little Oakley
Fordham Heath Mile End Parson's Heath Great Bromley Tendring Heath 116 117
Great Oakley

Aldham Eight Ash Green Greenstead Elmstead Beaumont
130 131 132 133 134 135 136 137 Market Tendring 140 141 142 143 144
Coggeshall Marks Colchester A133 138 139 Weeley Thorpe- Kirby-
Tey Wivenhoe Frating Green le-Soken le-Soken

Feering A12 Easthorpe Blackheath Alresford Great Bentley Weeley Heath Walton-on-the-Naze
157 158 159 160 161 162 163 High Park Corner 166 167 168 169 170 171
Messing Birch Green Malting 164 165 St Osyth Heath Little Clacton Frinton-on-Sea
Kelvedon Green Abberton Great Holland

Rivenhall End Tiptree Peldon Brightlingsea 196
184 185 186 187 188 189 190 191 192 193 194 195 Holland-on-Sea
Great Braxted Tolleshunt Great Little East Mersea St Osyth Clacton-
Knights Wigborough Wigborough on-Sea

Wickham Bishops Tolleshunt D'Arcy West Mersea Seawick
212 213 214 215 216 217 218 219 220 Jaywick
Great Totham Tolleshunt Major Tollesbury

Langford Goldhanger
Heybridge 238 239 240 241 242 382
236 237 Bradwell Waterside
Maldon Bradwell-on-Sea

258 259 260 261 St Lawrence 264 382
Purleigh Maylandsea Steeple 262 263 Tillingham

Cold Norton Mayland Asheldham
280 281 Latchingdon 282 283 284 285 286 383
Stow Maries Althorne Southminster

North Ostend Burnham- Montsale
Fambridge 304 305 on-Crouch 308 383
302 303 Canewdon 306 307

Hockley 326 327 Paglesham Churchend
324 325 Great Eastend 330 331
Rochford Stambridge 328 329

Southend Barling 350 351
346 347 Little Wakering
Leigh-on-Sea 348 349 Great Wakering
365 366 367 368
Southend-on-Sea Shoeburyness

Sheerness
Minster

Leysdown-on-Sea

Margate
Birchington

Key to map pages

| 220 | Map pages at 2⅔ inches to 1 mile |

Scale
0   5   10   15   20 km
0   5   10 miles

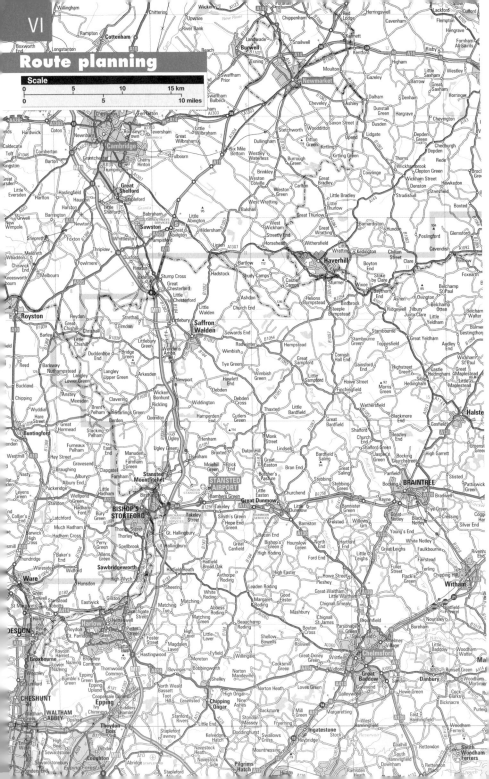

Route planning

Scale

0   5   10   15 km
0   5   10 miles

Major administrative and Postcode boundaries

County and unitary authority boundaries
District boundaries
Postcode boundaries
Area covered by this atlas

Scale
0   5   10   15km
0   5   10 miles

Cambridgeshire
Suffolk
Hertfordshire
Essex
Colchester
Braintree
Chelmsford
Brentwood
Uttlesford
Epping Forest
Basildon
Castle Point
Rochford
Maldon
Southend-on-Sea
London
Kent
Medway

Haverhill
Glemsford
Sudbury
Bures
Clare
Great Chesterford
Saffron Walden
Newport
Clavering
Stansted Mountfitchet
Bishop's Stortford
Sawbridgeworth
Harlow
Waltham Abbey
Chingford
Loughton
Abridge
Epping
Chipping Ongar
Thaxted
Great Sampford
Great Bardfield
Stebbing
Great Dunmow
Hatfield Heath.
Elsenham
Belchamp St Paul
Castle Hedingham
Halstead
Earls Colne
Coggeshall
Braintree
Witham
Great Leighs
Tye Green
Broomfield
Chelmsford
Stock
Billericay
Brentwood
Ingrave
Upminster
Romford
Barking
Tilbury
Stanford-le-Hope
Basildon
Rayleigh
Wickford
East Hanningfield
Danbury
Hatfield Peverel
Tiptree
Tollesbury
Maldon
Cold Norton
Tillingham
Southminster
Burnham-on-Crouch
Great Wakering
Canvey Island
Southend-on-Sea
Canewdon
Steeple Bumpstead
West Mersea
Brightlingsea
St Osyth
Clacton-on-Sea
Frinton-on-Sea
Walton-on-the-Naze
Harwich
Great Oakley
Manningtree
Wivenhoe
Ardleigh
East Bergholt
Holbrook
Ipswich
Felixstowe
Layer-de-la-Haye
Colchester

CB1 CB9 CB10 CB11
CM0 CM1 CM2 CM3 CM4 CM5 CM6 CM7 CM8 CM9 CM10 CM11 CM12 CM13 CM14 CM15 CM16 CM17 CM18 CM19 CM20 CM21 CM22 CM23 CM24 CM77
CO1 CO2 CO3 CO4 CO5 CO6 CO7 CO8 CO9 CO10 CO11 CO12 CO13 CO14 CO15 CO16
DA1 DA2 DA8 DA9 DA10 DA11 DA12 DA17 DA18
E4 E6 E7 E11 E12 E17 E18
EN3 EN9 EN10 EN11
IG1 IG2 IG3 IG4 IG5 IG6 IG7 IG8 IG9 IG10 IG11
IP1 IP2 IP3 IP4 IP5 IP7 IP8 IP9 IP10 IP11 IP29
RM1 RM2 RM3 RM4 RM5 RM6 RM7 RM8 RM9 RM10 RM11 RM12 RM13 RM14 RM15 RM16 RM17 RM18 RM19 RM20
SG8 SG9 SG12
SS0 SS1 SS2 SS3 SS4 SS5 SS6 SS7 SS8 SS9 SS11 SS12 SS13 SS14 SS15 SS16 SS17
TL TM TQ TR

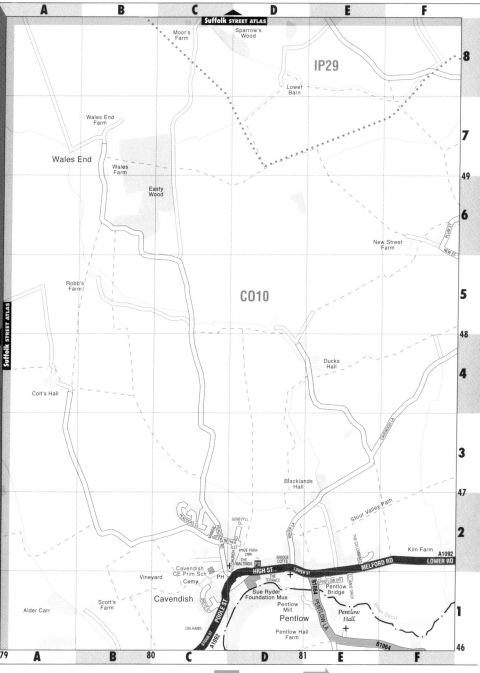

Suffolk STREET ATLAS

A   B   C   D   E   F

8

IP29

Moor's Farm

Sparrow's Wood

Lower Barn

7

Wales End Farm

49

Wales End

Wales Farm

Easty Wood

6

New Street Farm

PLUM ST

NEW ST

Robb's Farm

CO10

5

48

Ducks Hall

4

Colt's Hall

CAVENDISH LA

3

47

Blacklands Hall

Stour Valley Path

2

GENEVYLL CL

WATER LA

THE COLUMBINES

Kiln Farm

A1092

FACTORY CL

MANOR RD

HYDE PARK CNR

BRIDGE COTTS

MELFORD RD   LOWER RD

NETHER RD

CHURCH ST

THE MALTINGS

HIGH ST

LOWER ST

PENTLOW DR

CLUNIE ORCH

PO

PH

Cavendish CE Prim Sch

Cemy

THE TERRACE

Pentlow Bridge

B1064

PENTLOW LA

Vineyard

Scott's Farm

Cavendish

GREEN ST

Sue Ryder Foundation Mus

Pentlow Mill

Pentlow

Pentlow Hall

River Stour

Alder Carr

DALHAMS

PIDLEY ST

STOUR ST

A1092

Pentlow Hall Farm

B1064

1

46

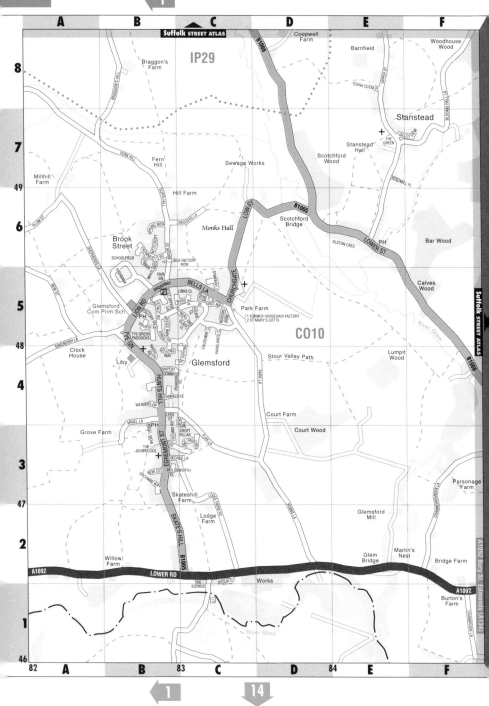

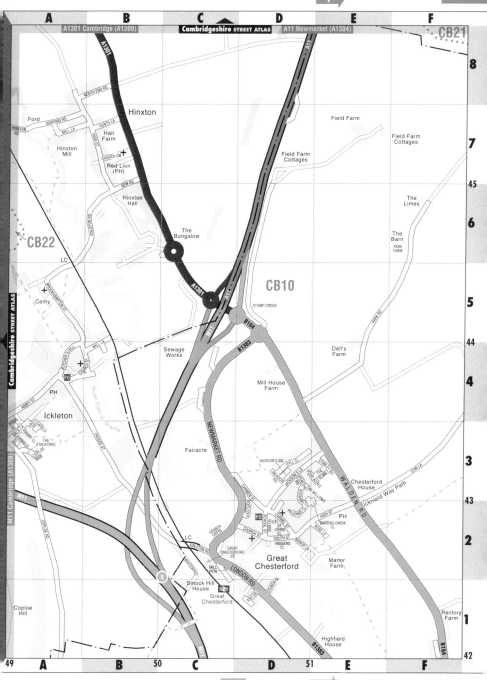

A B C D E F

A1301 Cambridge (A1309)   A11 Newmarket (A1304)   CB21

8

Hinxton

NORTH END RD

Ford   DUXFORD RD   HURTS LA   Field Farm

HINXTON RD   MILL LA   Hall Farm

HIGH ST

Hinxton Mill   CHURCH GN   Field Farm Cottages

Red Lion (PH)

NEW RD   Field Farm Cottages   7

45

Hinxton Hall   The Limes

CB22   ICKLETON RD   The Bungalow   6

LC   The Barn   PARK FARM

Cemy   BROCKHAMPTON ST   CB10   PARK RD   5

STUMP CROSS

BUTCHER'S HILL   MILL LA   B184   44

PO   Sewage Works   B1383   Dell's Farm   4

PH   River Cam or Granta   TROGGS ST   Mill House Farm

ABBEY ST   NEWMARKET RD

Ickleton   GOLD ST   WALDEN RD

FROGGE ST   Fairacre   JACKSON'S SQ   HYLL CL   Chesterford House

THE STACKYARD   MEAD WY   STANLEY CL   Ickmield Way Path   3

ELMS CL   COW LA

CARMEL ST   HIGH ST   PH   43

EASTDALE   PO   BARTHOLOMEW CL   ROSE LA

JOHN'S CL   Sch   CHURCH ST   SOUTH ST

M11 Cambridge (A1309)   GRANTA COTTS   HAGGERS CL   MANOR LA   2

LC   ICKLETON RD   GREAT CHESTERFORD CT   Great Chesterford   Manor Farm

WALDENSIDE   MILL VIEW   LONDON RD   GRANTA SIDE

Smock Hill House   Great Chesterford   AGG ST

Coploe Hill   Highfield House   Rectory Farm   1

B1383   B184   42

49   A   B   50   C   D   51   E   F

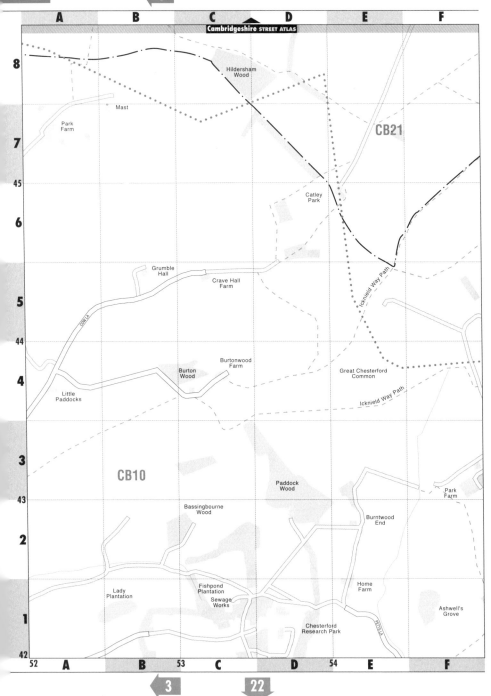

Cambridgeshire STREET ATLAS

8

Hildersham
Wood

Mast

Park
Farm

CB21

7

45

6

Catley
Park

Grumble
Hall

Crave Hall
Farm

Icknield Way Path

5

44

Burtonwood
Farm

Burton
Wood

Great Chesterford
Common

4

Little
Paddocks

Icknield Way Path

3

CB10

Paddock
Wood

Park
Farm

43

Bassingbourne
Wood

Burntwood
End

2

Lady
Plantation

Fishpond
Plantation

Sewage
Works

Home
Farm

Ashwell's
Grove

1

Chesterford
Research Park

42

52   A   B   53   C   D   54   E   F

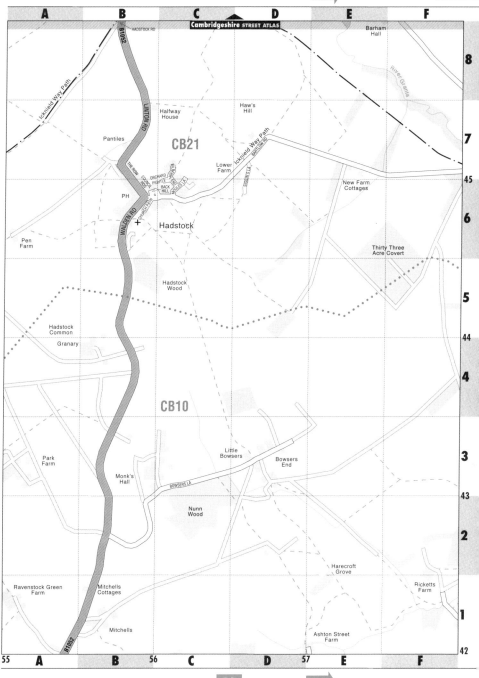

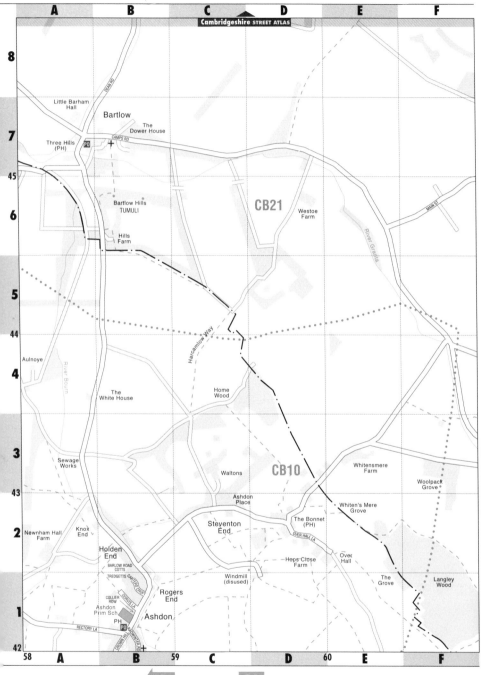

Cambridgeshire STREET ATLAS

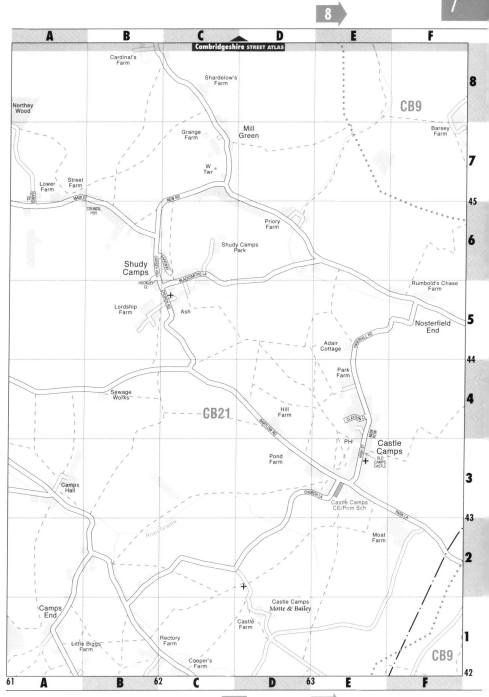

Cambridgeshire STREET ATLAS

| A | B | C | D | E | F |

Cardinal's Farm

Shardelow's Farm

Northey Wood

CB9

Barsey Farm

8

Mill Green

Grange Farm

7

W Twr

Lower Farm

Street Farm

BANKS CL

MAIN ST

NEW RD

COUNCIL HOS

45

Priory Farm

6

Shudy Camps Park

Shudy Camps

CARDEL HILL

NEWPORT

BLACKSMITHS LA

HOCKLEY CL

CHURCH LA

Rumbold's Chase Farm

Lordship Farm

Ash

Nosterfield End

5

Adair Cottage

MAURHILL RD

44

Park Farm

Sewage Works

GB21

BARTLOW RD

Hill Farm

CLAYDON CL

4

HIGH ST

BREW ROW

Castle Camps

PH

X

OLD CAMPS CASTLE

Pond Farm

3

Camps Hall

CHURCH LA

Castle Camps CE/Prim Sch

PARK LA

43

River Granta

Moat Farm

2

Camps End

Castle Camps Motte & Bailey

CB9

1

Little Biggs Farm

Rectory Farm

Castle Farm

Cooper's Farm

61 | A | B | 62 | C | D | 63 | E | F | 42

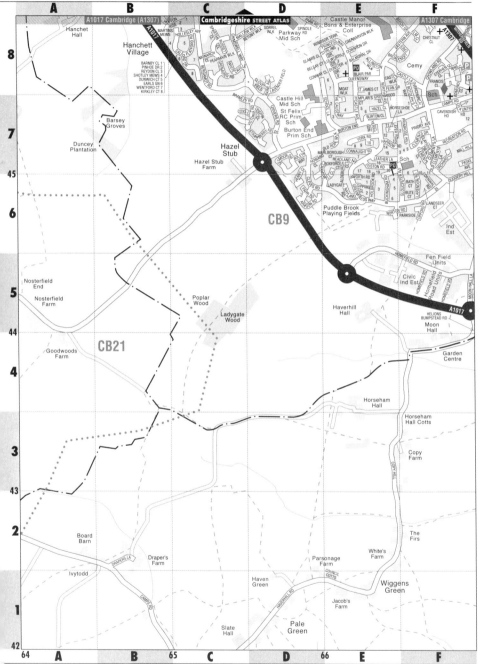

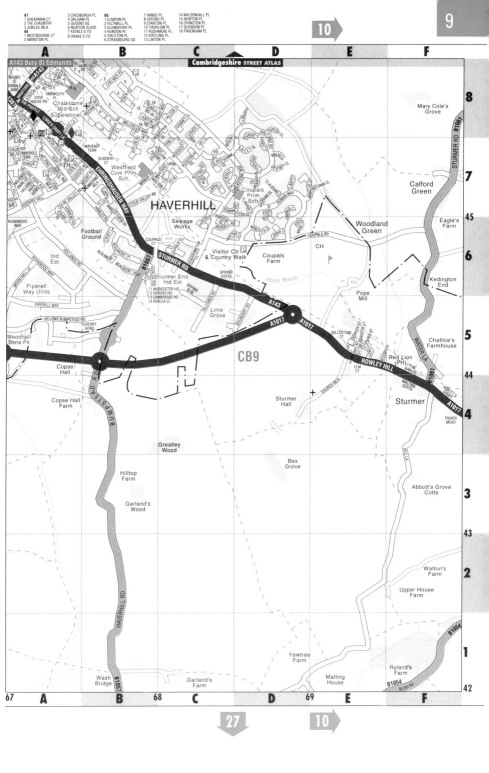

10

A7
1 SHEARMAN CT
2 THE CHAUNTRY
3 JUBILEE WLK
A8
1 WESTBOURNE CT
2 ABINGTON PL

3 CHEDBURGH PL
4 DALHAM PL
5 QUEENS SQ
6 MURTON SLADE
7 KEEBLE'S YD
8 DRAKE'S YD

B8
1 ELMDON PL
2 FELTWELL PL
5 GLEMSFORD PL
4 HUNDON PL
6 ICKLETON PL
6 STRASBOURG SQ

7 VANGE PL
8 UFFORD PL
9 STANTON PL
10 THURLOW PL
11 RUSHMERE PL
12 KIRTLING PL
13 LINTON PL

14 MILDENHALL PL
15 NEWTON PL
16 OVINGTON PL
17 QUENDON PL
18 PAKENHAM PL

A143 Bury St Edmunds Cambridgeshire STREET ATLAS

HAVERHILL

CB9

Mary Cole's Grove

Calford Green

Eagle's Farm

Kedington End

Woodland Green

Challice's Farmhouse

Sturmer

Friars Mead

Abbott's Grove Cotts

Walton's Farm

Upper House Farm

Ryland's Farm

Yewtree Farm

Malting House

Copse Hall

Copse Hall Farm

Greatley Wood

Hilltop Farm

Garland's Wood

Wash Bridge

Garland's Wood

Moonhall Bsns Pk

Piperell Way Units

Ind Est

Rookwood Way

Football Ground

Sewage Works

Coupals Prim Sch

Visitor Ctr & Country Walk

Coupals Farm

Sturmer End Ind Est
1 WORCESTER HO
2 OXFORD HO
3 CAMBRIDGE HO
4 ASHLEA CL

Lime Grove

Spring Cotts

Pope Mill

Red Lion (PH)

Rowley Hill

Sturmer Hall

Bex Grove

Chalkstone Mid-Sch

Superstore

Westfield Com Prim Sch

Duddery Ct

Waveney Terr

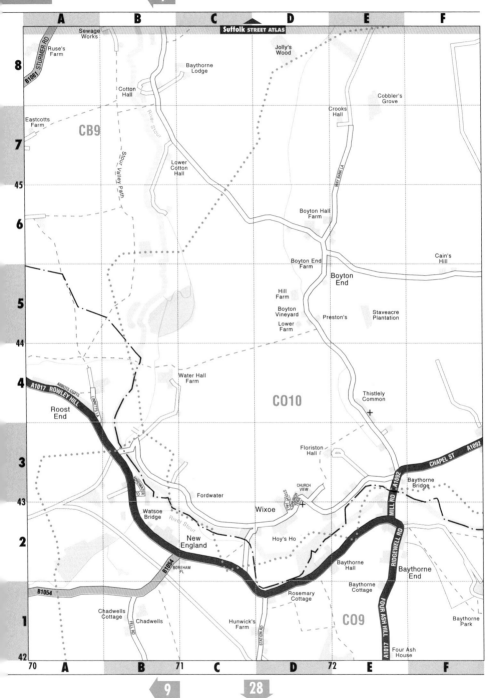

9

Suffolk STREET ATLAS

Ruse's Farm
Sewage Works
STURMER RD B1061
Eastcotts Farm
CB9
Baythorne Lodge
Cotton Hall
Jolly's Wood
River Stour
Stour Valley Path
Lower Cotton Hall
Crooks Hall
Cobbler's Grove
HALL BAKER LA
Boyton Hall Farm
Boyton End Farm
Cain's Hill
Boyton End
Hill Farm
Boyton Vineyard
Lower Farm
Preston's
Staveacre Plantation
Water Hall Farm
CO10
Thistlely Common
ABBOTS COTTA
A1017 ROWLEY HILL
Roost End
Floriston Hall
CHAPEL ST A1092
Baythorne Bridge
A1092
CHURCH VIEW
MILL RD
Fordwater
Watsoe Bridge
River Stour
Wixoe
Hoy's Ho
Baythorne Hall
RIDGEWELL RD
Baythorne End
New England
B1054 BOREHAM PL
Rosemary Cottage
Baythorne Cottage
FOUR ASH HILL A1017
B1054
Chadwells Cottage
FELL RD
Chadwells
Hunwick's Farm
STATION RD
CO9
Baythorne Park
Four Ash House

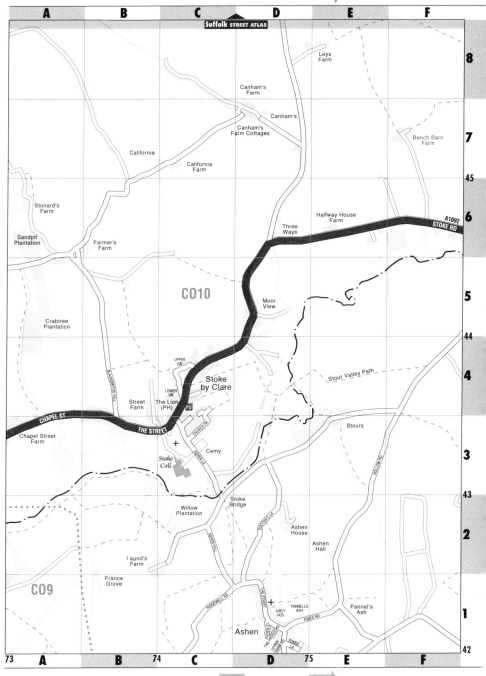

Suffolk STREET ATLAS

Leys Farm

Canham's Farm

Canham's

Canham's Farm Cottages

Bench Barn Farm

California

California Farm

Stonard's Farm

Halfway House Farm

A1092 STOKE RD

Three Ways

Sandpit Plantation

Farmer's Farm

CO10

Moor View

Crabtree Plantation

UPPER GN

Stoke by Clare

Stour Valley Path

River Stour

LOWER GN

Street Farm

The Lion (PH)

PO

Stours

BLACKSMITHS HILL

CHAPEL ST

THE STREET

CHURCH PK

Chapel Street Farm

ASHEN LA

Cemy

Stoke Coll

HOLLOW RD

Willow Plantation

Stoke Bridge

Ashen House

Ashen Hall

Laund's Farm

ASHEN HILL

OXFORDS LA

CO9

France Grove

RIDGEWELL RD

Pannel's Ash

PANNELLS ASH

FOXES RD

THE STREET

AIREY HOS

Ashen

THE ASHEN LA

UPPER FROST RD

FOXES LA

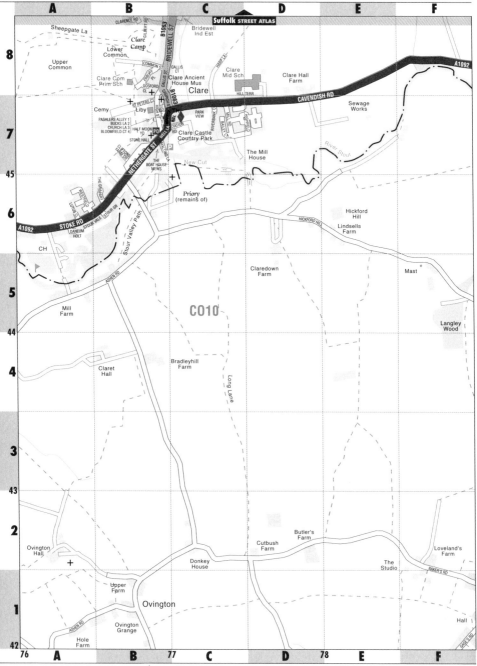

Suffolk STREET ATLAS

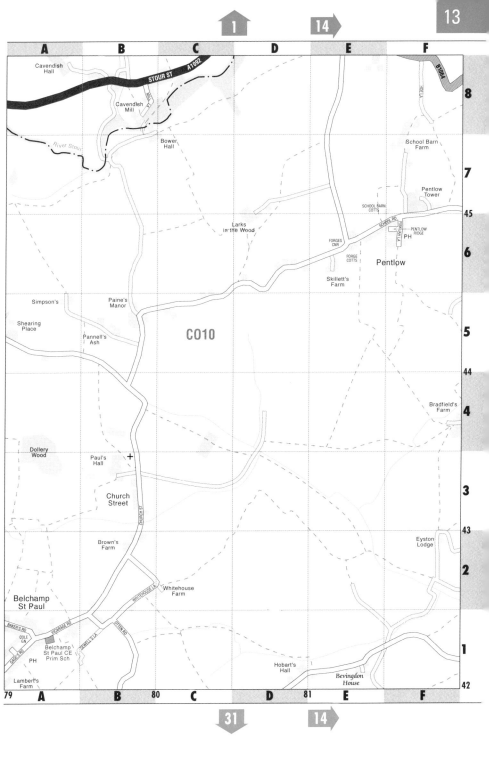

8
7
45
6
5
44
4
3
43
2
1
42

A B C D E F

Cavendish Hall

STOUR ST A1092

Cavendish Mill

River Stour

Bower Hall

School Barn Farm

Pentlow Tower

SCHOOL BARN COTTS

SCHOOL RD

Larks in the Wood

FORGES CNR

PENTLOW RIDGE

PH

PINKUAH LA

FORGE COTTS

Pentlow

Skillett's Farm

Simpson's

Paine's Manor

Shearing Place

Pannell's Ash

CO10

Bradfield's Farm

Dollery Wood

Paul's Hall

Church Street

Eyston Lodge

Brown's Farm

Belchamp St Paul

WHITEHOUSE LA

Whitehouse Farm

VICARAGE RD

BAKER'S RD

COLE GN

OTTEN RD

SEWELL'S LA

PH

Belchamp St Paul CE Prim Sch

Hobart's Hall

Bevingdon House

Lambert's Farm

79 A B 80 C D 81 E F

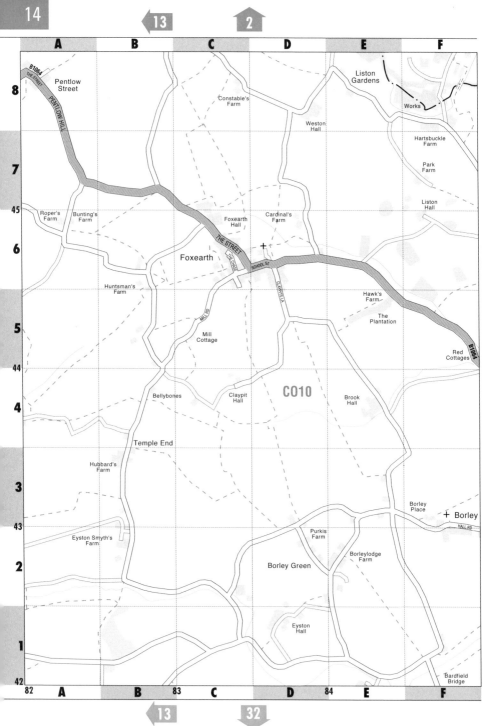

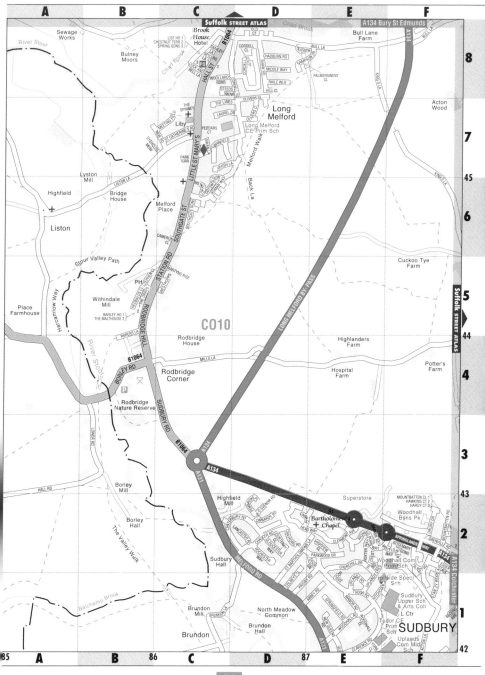

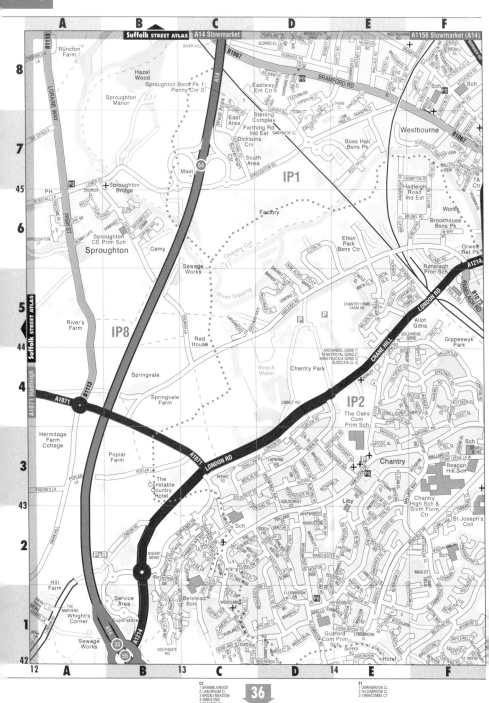

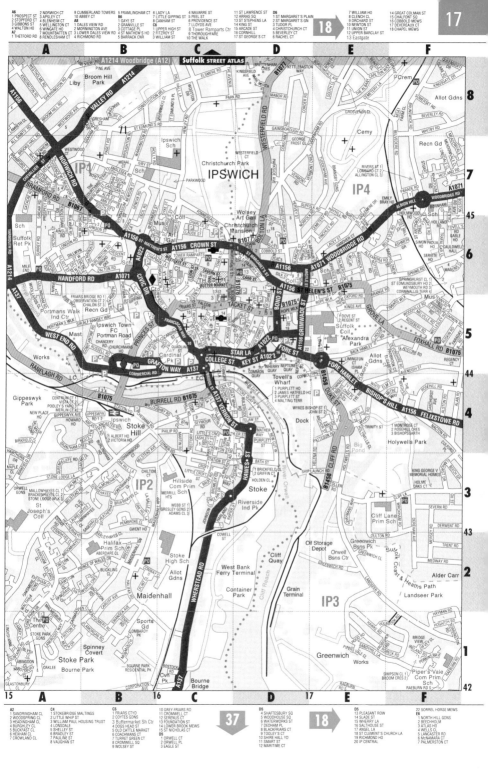

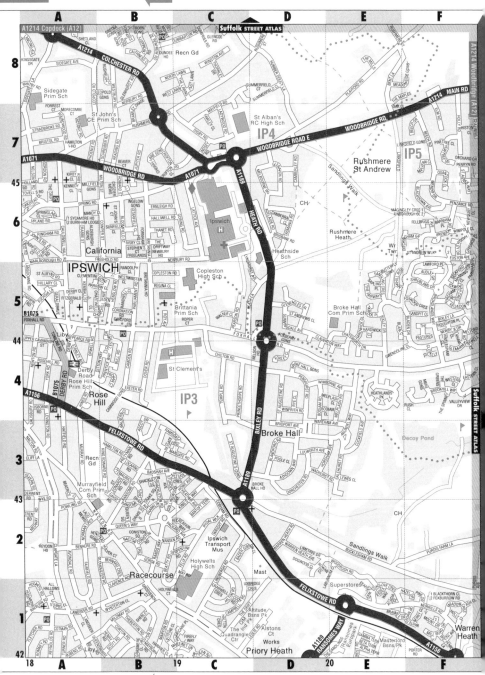

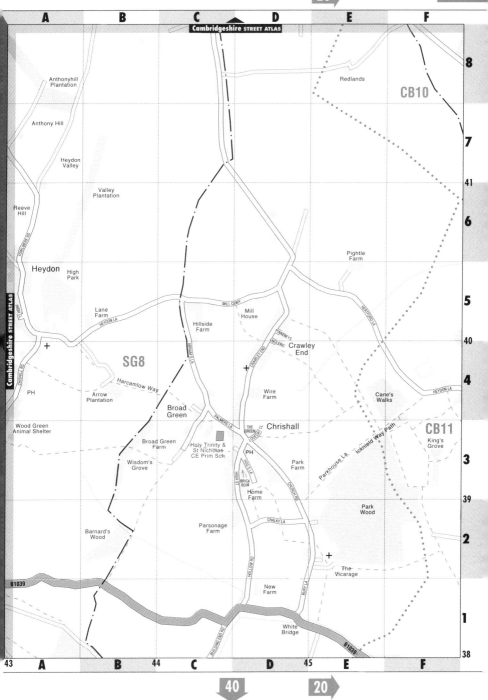

Cambridgeshire STREET ATLAS

CB10

CB11

SG8

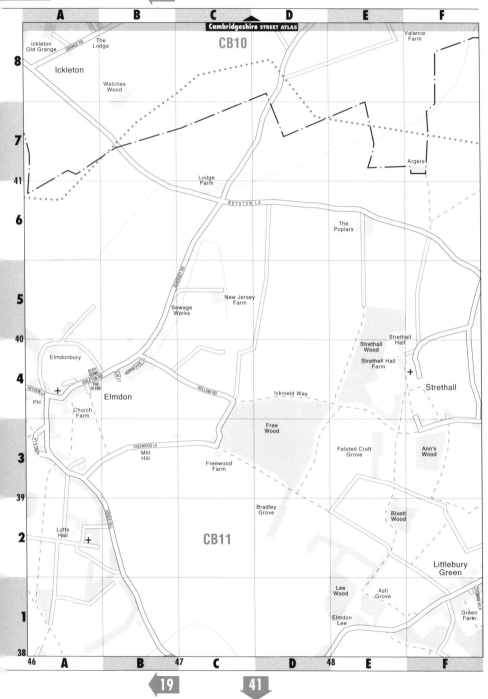

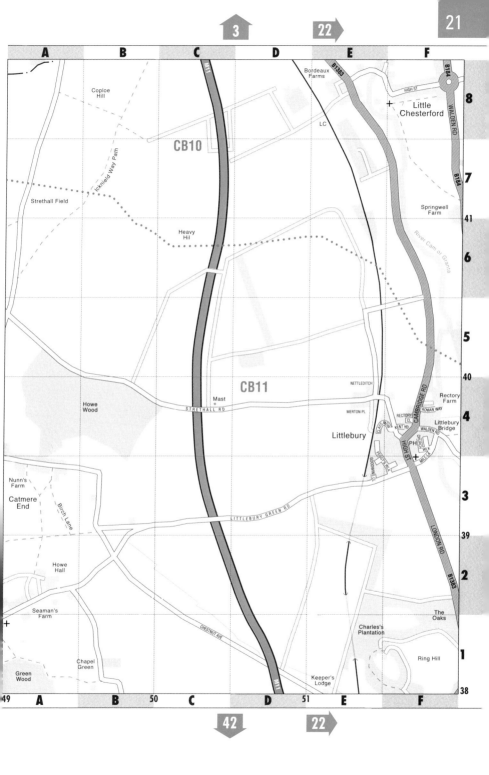

CB10

CB11

Emanuel Cott
Emanuel Wood
Four Acre Grove
Little Walden
PH
PETLANDS
The Hall Farm
Bell Cotts
Stone Bridge
Stonebridge Farm
Grimsditch Wood
Joseph Farm
Springwell
High Balks
Protection Plantation
Rowley Hill Farm
Westley Wood
Mead Hall
Byrds Farm
Westley Farm
WESTLEY LA
John's Acre
Brown's Plantation
Northend Farm
Northend
Northend Lodge
The Vineyard
SAFFRON WALDEN
Spring Wood
WINDMILL HILL
Obelisk
Duck Street
Home Farm
Tea Bridge
Nursery
Stable Bridge
Sir William's Plantation
Sewage Works
Place Pond
Audley Park
Audley End House & Gardens

1 DODDENHILL CL
2 CORNWALLIS PL
3 WYNYARD RD
4 COLYN PL

St Mary's CE Prim Sch
Castle (rems of)
The Common
EASTACRE 1
BEECHO 2
HATHERLEY CT 3

JOHNSONS RD 1
MARKET PL 2
MARKET ST 3
ROSE & CROWN WLK 4
MERCERS ROW 5
MARKET WLK 6
BUTCHER ROW 7
MARKET ROW 8
CENTRAL ARC 9

CHURCH PATH 10
BARNARDS CT 11
MYDDYLTON PL 12
EDWARD BAWDEN CT 13
KING EDWARD VI'S RLMHOUSES 14
THE MALTINGS 15
BARNARDS ROW 16
INGLESIDE CT 17
AUDLEY CT 18
BARLEY CT 19
SAFFRON CT 20

RA Butler Jun & Inf Schs
Cemy
Shire Hill Ind Est
Medina Bsns Ctr
Saffron Bsns Ctr

E1
1 NEWCROFT
2 ALPHA PL
3 JORDAN CL
4 FARMADINE CT
5 JOHN DANE PLAYER CT
6 FARMADINE HO

F2
1 BRADLEY MEWS
2 NIGHTINGALE MEWS
3 HAMILTON MEWS
4 HADLEIGH CT
5 ST JAMES CT
6 LAVENDER FIELD
7 THE SPIKE
8 CAVENDISH CT

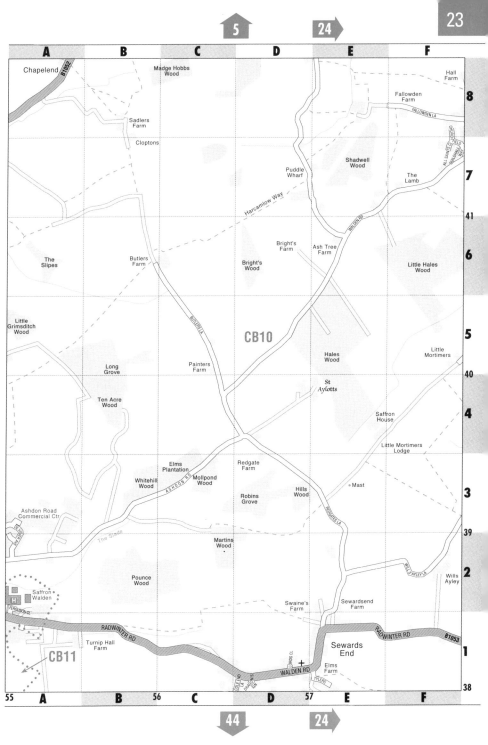

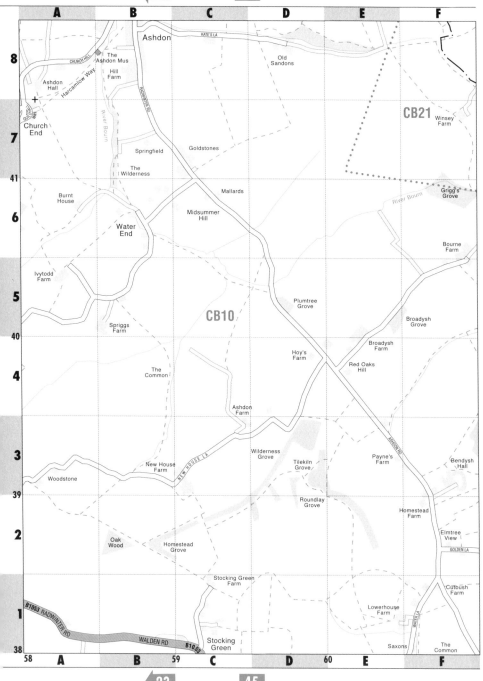

A   B   C   D   E   F

8

Ashdon
KATE'S LA
Old Sandons

The Ashdon Mus
CHURCH HILL
Hill Farm

Harcamlow Way
Ashdon Hall

CB21
Winsey Farm

7
Church End

River Bourn
Springfield

Goldstones

41
The Wilderness

Mallards

River Bourn
Grigg's Grove

Burnt House

6
Midsummer Hill

Water End

Bourne Farm

Ivytodd Farm

5
Plumtree Grove

CB10

Broadysh Grove

Spriggs Farm

40
Broadysh Farm

Red Oaks Hill

4
The Common

Hoy's Farm

ASHDON RD

Ashdon Farm

Wilderness Grove

Payne's Farm

Bendysh Hall

3
New House Farm

NEW HOUSE LA

Tilekiln Grove

Woodstone

Roundlay Grove

Homestead Farm

39

2
Oak Wood

Homestead Grove

Elmtree View
GOLDEN LA

WATER LA

Stocking Green Farm

Cutbush Farm

1
B1053 RADWINTER RD

Lowerhouse Farm

WALDEN RD   B1053

Stocking Green

Saxons

The Common

38

58   A   B   59   C   D   60   E   F

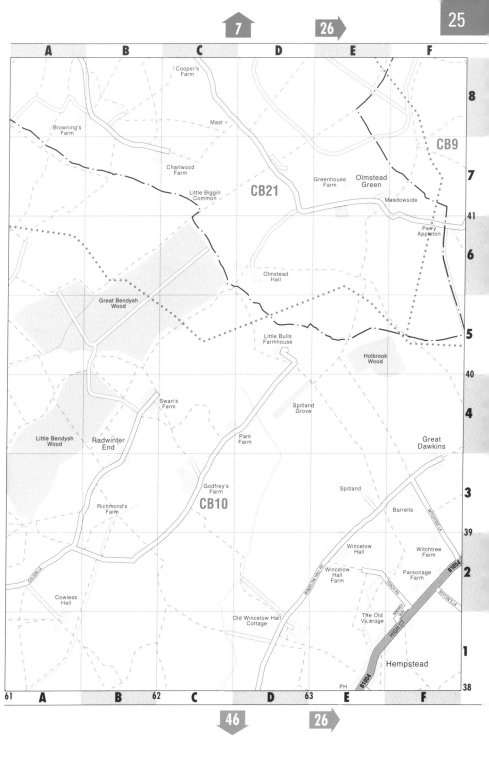

Cooper's Farm

Browning's Farm

Mast

Charlwood Farm

Little Biggin Common

CB21

Greenhouse Farm

Olmstead Green

Meadowside

Perry Appleton

Great Bendysh Wood

Olmstead Hall

Little Bulls Farmhouse

Holbrook Wood

Swan's Farm

Spitland Grove

Little Bendysh Wood

Radwinter End

Park Farm

Great Dawkins

Godfrey's Farm

CB10

Spitland

Richmond's Farm

Barrells

Wincelow Hall

Witchtree Farm

Parsonage Farm

Cowless Hall

Wincelow Hall Farm

Old Wincelow Hall Cottage

The Old Vicarage

HIGH ST

B1054

Hempstead

PH

A B C D E F

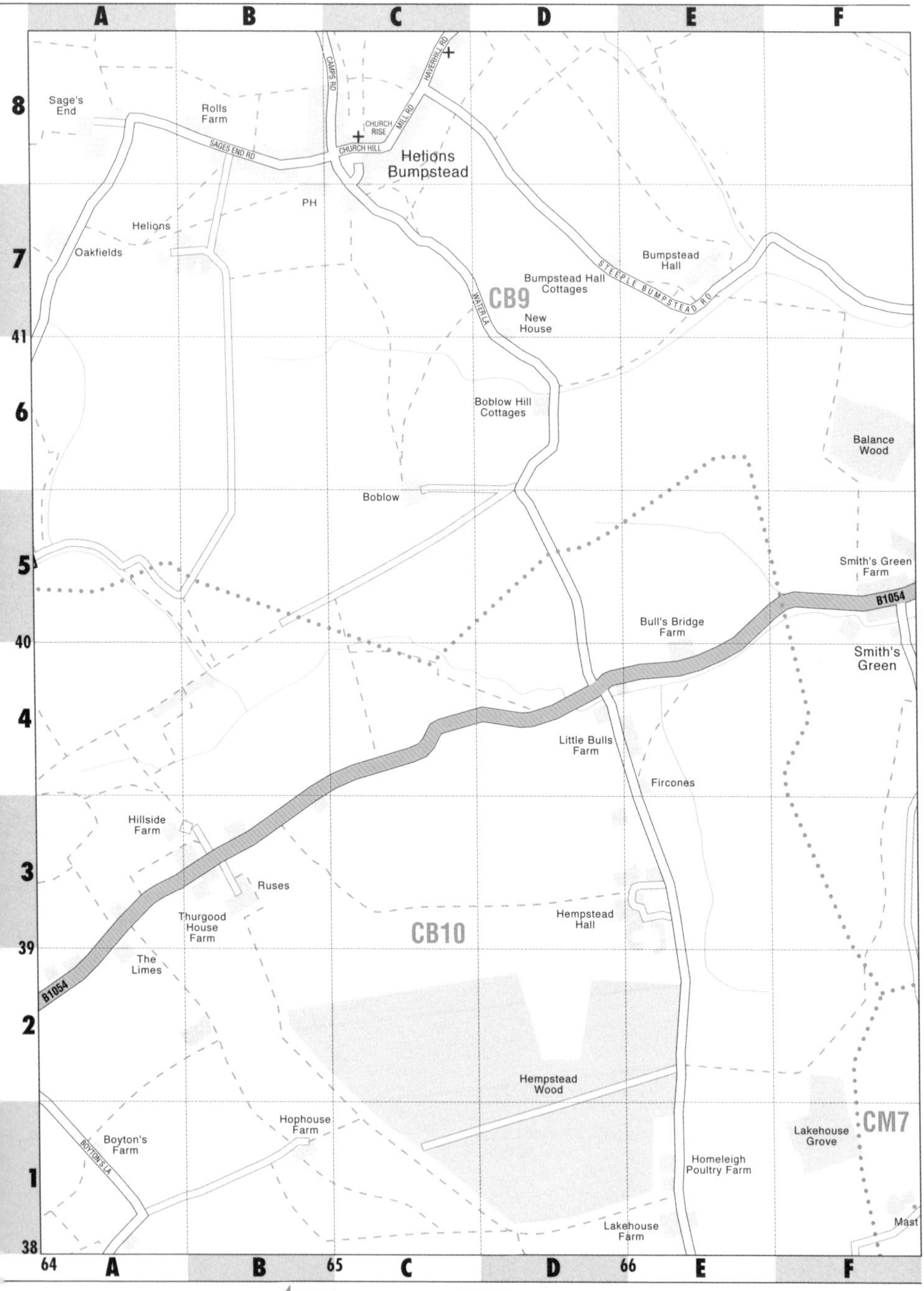

8
Sage's End
Rolls Farm
SAGES END RD
Helions
Oakfields
PH
CAMPS RD
IMPERIAL RD
CHURCH RISE
MILL RD
CHURCH HILL
Helions Bumpstead
7
41
Bumpstead Hall
STEEPLE BUMPSTEAD RD
Bumpstead Hall Cottages
WATER LA
CB9
New House
6
Boblow Hill Cottages
Balance Wood
Boblow
5
40
Smith's Green Farm
B1054
Bull's Bridge Farm
Smith's Green
4
Little Bulls Farm
Fircones
Hillside Farm
3
Ruses
Thurgood House Farm
CB10
Hempstead Hall
39
The Limes
B1054
2
Hempstead Wood
Boyton's Farm
BOYTON'S LA
Hophouse Farm
Lakehouse Grove
CM7
1
38
64
Homeleigh Poultry Farm
Lakehouse Farm
Mast

A B C D E F

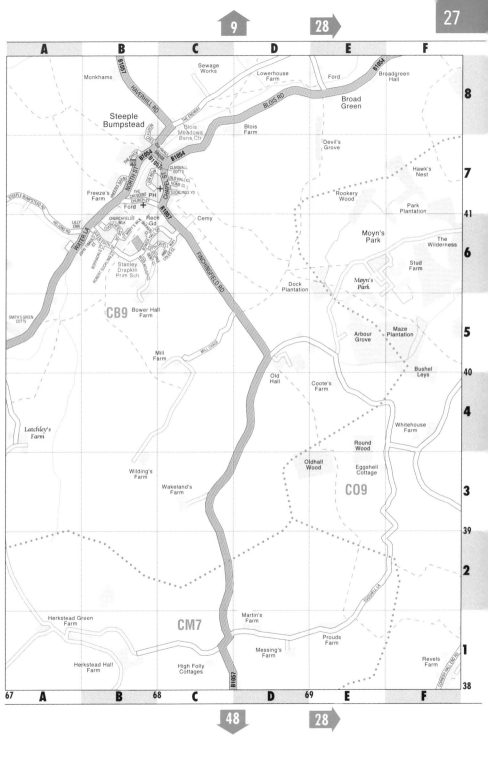

A B C D E F

Monkhams

HAVERHILL RD

B1057

Sewage Works

Lowerhouse Farm

Ford

Broadgreen Hall

B1054

8

BLOIS RD

Broad Green

Steeple Bumpstead

Blois Meadows Bsns. Ctr

Blois Farm

THE CAUSEWAY

Devil's Grove

7

Hawk's Nest

B1054
B1057
CHAPEL ST

CLAYWALL COTTS
OLD HALL CL
HOME CL
SUCKLINGS YD

Rookery Wood

Park Plantation

NORTH ST
CAUSTON MDW

STEEPLE BUMPSTEAD RD

Freeze's Farm

THE CRESCENT
CHURCH ST
Ford
PH

Cemy

41

HELIONS RD

LILLY CNR

WATER LA

CHURCHFIELDS WLK
ST MARY'S WY
RATNER CT

Recn Gd

Moyn's Park

The Wilderness

6

Stud Farm

JOHN BIRD
ROBERT SUCKLING CT
BORDEALE CT
TOFTS DE
BOWER HALL WY
COLES GN
AMOS
HALL

Stanley Drapkin Prim Sch

Moyn's Park

Dock Plantation

SMITH'S GREEN COTTS

CB9

Bower Hall Farm

Arbour Grove

Maze Plantation

5

Bushel Leys

40

FINCHINGFIELD RD

Mill Farm

MILL CHASE

Old Hall

Coote's Farm

Whitehouse Farm

4

Latchley's Farm

Round Wood

Oldhall Wood

Eggshell Cottage

CO9

3

Wilding's Farm

Wakeland's Farm

39

EGGSHELL LA

2

Herkstead Green Farm

CM7

Martin's Farm

Prouds Farm

Revels Farm

1

Herkstead Hall Farm

High Folly Cottages

B1057

Messing's Farm

CORNISH HALL END RD

38

67 A B 68 C D 69 E F

A B C D E F

8

Moyn's
Wood
CB9

A1017
FOUR ASH HILL

THE CAUSEWAY

Causeway
Hall

A1017

7

Birdbrook

STATION RD

Whitley
House

MOAT RD

Birdbrook
Hall
The Plough
(PH)
FELL RD
THE STREET
DAM ST
MOAT
FARM

41

Churchfield
Grove

6

Paddock
Belt
SCHOOLFIELD
The
Rectory

Wash
Bridge

Carter's
Bridge

Wash
Farm

Stubland's
Farm
Wash
Farm

Woodview

CO9

Three Chimneys
Wood

STAMBOURNE RD

5

Highfield
Clump
Finkle
Green
Bailey Hill
Farm
Bailey
Hill

Three Chimneys
Farm

Essex Hall

Pettyfield La

40

4

Park
Wood

WESLEY END RD

Wesley End

3

Warren
Farm
BIRDBROOK RD

Little Collin's
Farm
MILL RD
Hill
Farm

Stambourne

CHURCH RD

Stambourne
Hall

39

Chapel End Way
PO
Chapelend
Way
Oldhouse
Farm

2

Slough
Farm

Stambourne
Grange

Greenfield's
Farm

Mill
Farm

CORNISH HALL END RD

DYERS RD

1

Moat Hall
Farm
Stambourne
Green

Dyer's
End

Elm's
Farm

38

Great Tagley
Farm
FINCHINGFIELD RD

70 A B 71 C D 72 E F

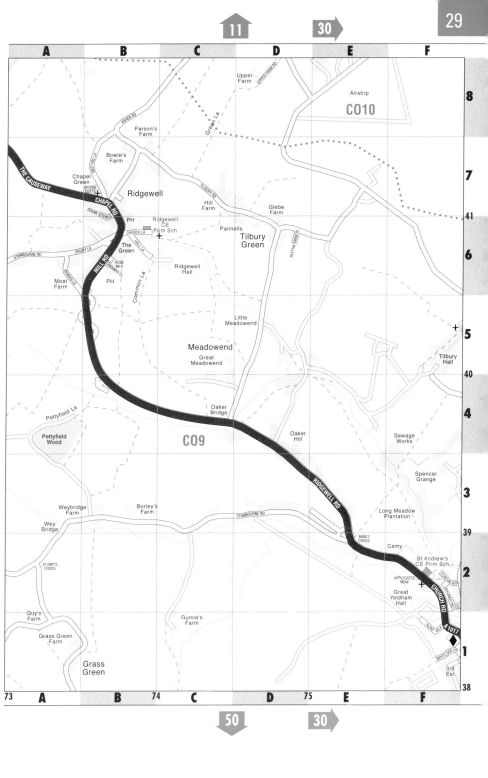

8
CO10
Airstrip

7
41

6

5
40

4
CO9

3
39

2

1
38

THE CAUSEWAY
ASPEN RD
Parson's Farm
Upper Farm
UPPER FARM RD
Green La
Bowle's Farm
MEETING LA
Chapel Green
BRIDGE COTTS
CHAPEL RD
Ridgewell
COLNE SPRINGS
Hill Farm
TILBURY RD
Glebe Farm
PH
Ridgewell CE Prim Sch
CHURCH LA
Pannells
Tilbury Green
STAMBOURNE RD
DRURY LA
The Green
TAN LA
Ridgewell Hall
ALETHA FARM PL
MILL RD
ROSE WLK
ORCHARD CL
Moat Farm
SPAINS LA
PH
Common La
Little Meadowend
Meadowend
Great Meadowend
Tilbury Hall
Pettyfield La
Oaker Bridge
Oaker Hill
Sewage Works
Pettyfield Wood
CO9
RIDGEWELL RD
Spencer Grange
Weybridge Farm
Borley's Farm
STAMBOURNE RD
Long Meadow Plantation
Wey Bridge
MAN'S CROSS
STUMP'S CROSS
Cemy
St Andrew's CE Prim Sch
DUNCAN RISE
APPLEGATES MDW
CHURCH RD
Quy's Farm
Gunce's Farm
Great Yeldham Hall
CHURCH DRI
Grass Green Farm
STONE WLK
A1017
Grass Green
WHITLOCK DR
Ind Est

73   74   75

A B C D E F

8

CO10

Silver End

Rowan Bank House

Knowl Green

Gage's House

Hole Farm

Wakeshall Farm

Cherry Tree (PH)

7

Lodge Farm

Park Farm

WAKESHALL LA

Marshy La

Wood Barns Farm

41

Mashay Farm

Marshy Wood

6

Tilbury Cottage

Twelve Acre Wood

5

Tilbury Juxta Clare

BELCHAMP RD

Red Barn

Jay's La

MASHY RD

40

Tilbury Court

Red House

4

Hyde Wood

CO9

Little Yeldham

CHURCH GN

Lodge

The Hyde

HYDEWOOD RD

SCHOOL RD

Bendysh House

3

MILL LA

Brook Farm

The Hyde Farm

LITTLE YELDHAM RD

Hall Green

North End

NORTH END RD

39

TILBURY RD

PH

2

ARMSTRONG WAY

HIGH FIELDS

LITTLE HYDE CL

CLOCKHOUSE WAY

NORTHFIELD

THE COURT

OAK LN

LEATHER LA

Upper Yeldham Hall

GREAT OAK PH

BUTLERS WAY

Highlands Farm

1

A1017 HIGH ST A1017

BRIDGE ST

WHITLOCK DR

POPLAR CL

Great Yeldham

Spayne's Hall

Hunt's Wood

Priestfields Farm

MARKET GR

38

76 A B 77 C D 78 E F

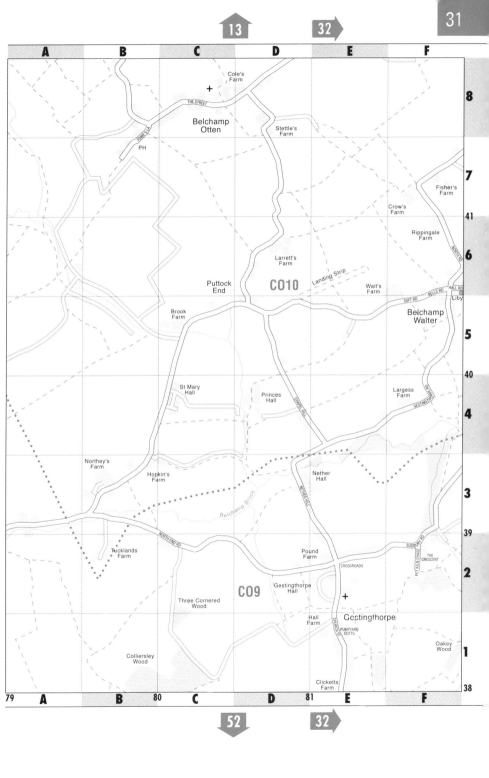

31
14

	A	B	C	D	E	F

8

The Rookery

Newbon

Clark's Farm

7

Smeetham Hall

Heaven Wood

41

Smeetham Hall Cottages

SMEETHAM HALL LA

6

HALL RD

+

Belchamp Hall

Belchamp Brook

SUDBURY RD

Springgate Farm

5

New Barns

Goldingham Hall

CO10

THE STREET

Blackhouse Farm

VICAR'S ORCH

SWAINS CROFT

Bulmer

Grigg's Farm

40

PO

BULMER ST

LINCOLN'S RISE

CHURCH MDW

+

SANDY LA

Auberies

4

Lower Houses

Brakey Hill

CHURCH RD

SUDBURY RD

St Andrew's CE Prim Sch

3

UPPER HOUSES

OLD CHURCH LA

39

Hill Farm

New Barn

Hilltop Farm

Bulmer Tye

OLD CHURCH LA

PARK LA

A131

CO9

2

Jenkins Farm

PH

Wiggery Wood

TYE CNR

BLACKSMITHS LA

Parsonage Wood

1

Wesborough Hill

Tyecorner Farm

A131

38

Hole Farm

HEDINGHAM RD

82	A		B	83	C		D	84	E		F

31
53

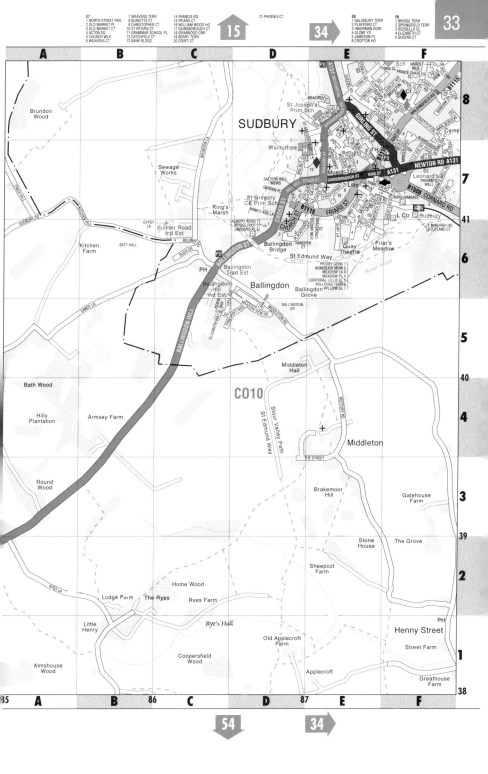

Suffolk STREET ATLAS

SUDBURY

A134 Bury St. Edmunds

Chilton Rd Ind Est

Chilton Ind Est

Grange Farm

Valley Farm

Cemy

South Suffolk Bsns Ctr

NEWTON RD

Cornard Tye

The Elms

Lawn Farm

Water Tower

Tye Farm

A134 Sudbury Rd

Pot Kiln Sch

Cemy

Languidic

Abbas Hall

Abbas Hall Wood

CO10

Great Cornard

Little Greys Farm

Wells Hall Com Prim Sch

Great Cornard Upper Sch & Tech Coll

Great Cornard Mid Sch

Prospect Hill Farm

Greys Hall

Moor's Farm

Brook Farm

PH

Little Mere

Blackhouse Farm

Great Cornard Country Park

Prospect Hill

Little Cornard

Cornard Mere

Nature Trail

WILLOWMERE CVN PK

Holly Lodge

Peacock Hall

Stone Farm

Sewage Works

Shalford Meadow

Casefields Farm

Costens Hall

River Stour

BURES RD

B1508

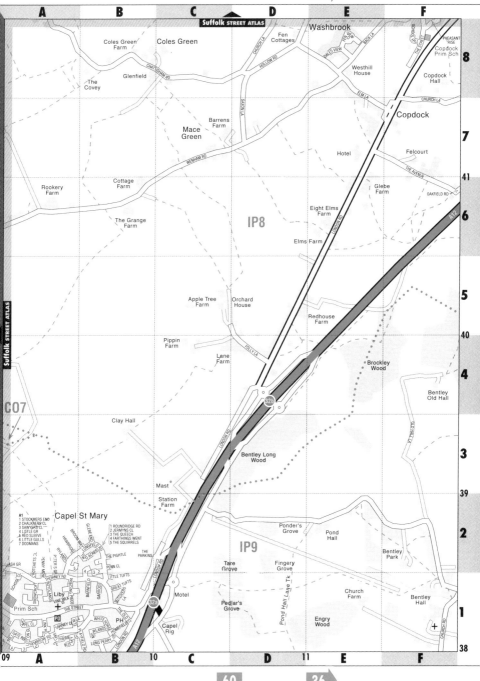

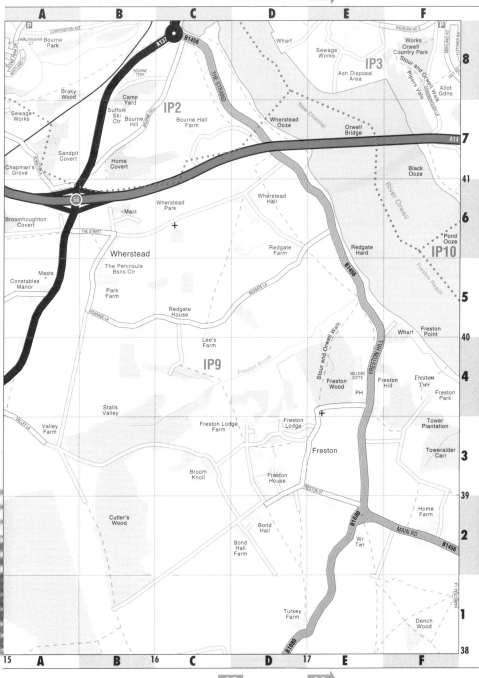

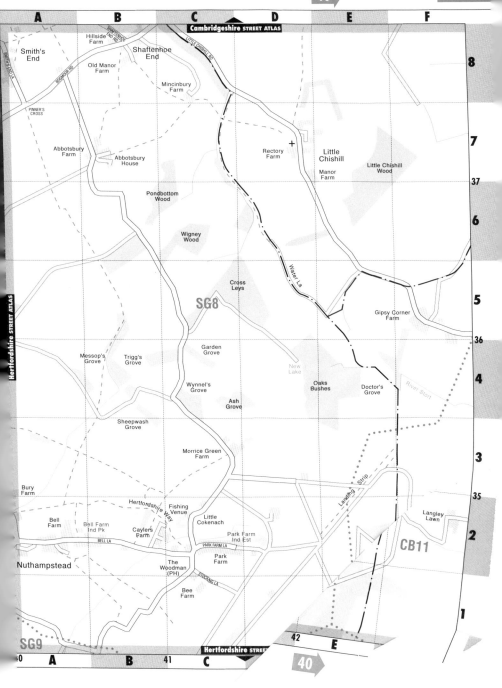

A	B	C	D	E	F

Smith's End

Hillside Farm

Shaftenhoe End

Old Manor Farm

Mincinbury Farm

PINNER'S CROSS

Abbotsbury Farm

Abbotsbury House

Rectory Farm

Little Chishill

Manor Farm

Little Chishill Wood

Pondbottom Wood

Wigney Wood

Cross Leys

Water La

SG8

Gipsy Corner Farm

Garden Grove

Messop's Grove

Trigg's Grove

New Lake

Wynnel's Grove

Oaks Bushes

Doctor's Grove

River Start

Ash Grove

Sheepwash Grove

Morrice Green Farm

Landing Strip

Bury Farm

Hertfordshire Way

Fishing Venue

Little Cokenach

Langley Lawn

Bell Farm

Bell Farm Ind Pk

Caylers Farm

Park Farm Ind Est

CB11

BELL LA

PARK FARM LA

Nuthampstead

The Woodman (PH)

Park Farm

STOCKING LA

Bee Farm

SG9

A	B	C	D	E	

42

40

A B C D E F

8

7

37

6

5

36

4

35

3

2

1

34
43

Monkshole Wood

B1039

B1039

Lower Pond Street

Building End RD

Lower Farm

Chiswick Hall

Hope Farm House

Building End

Upper Farm

COMMON LA

BUILDING END RD

SG8

Mead Bushes Wood

Upper Pond Street

SCHOOL LA

Harcamlow Way

Wicken Water

Duddenhoe End Farm

Hall

B1038

Common La

Pickerton Green

High Wood

Roughway Wood

White Friars Farm

Chrishall Common

Oldfield Grove

Killem's Green

Lorking's La

Grange Farm

River Stort

Hall Grove

Duddenhoe Grange

CB11

Cosh Farm

PARK LA

The Hall

Harcamlow Way

Church Farm

THE CAUSEWAY

Upper Green

Hall

THE KANGELS

LONG LEY

BULL LA

Langley

HIGH ELMS

The Bull (PH)

Lower Green

Bury Farm

WATERPITS LA

Roper's La

New Farm

A B D 45 E F

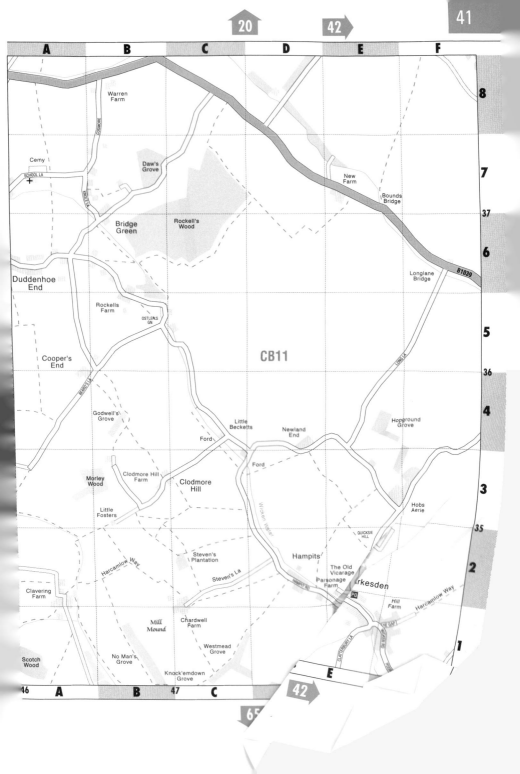

A **B** **C** **D** **E** **F**

8

Bush Pasture Grove

Cups Grove

The Triangle

Strawberry Close Belt

CHESTNUT AVE

The Willows

B1383

Cornwallis Hill

Mast

7

Neville Hill

LONDON RD

Red Leg Plantation

37

6

WALDEN RD

PH

The Old Vicarage

Wenden Place Farm

MILL LA

THE BEECHES

RAILWAY COTTS

STATION RD

B1039

SILVER ROW

B1039

ROYSTON RD

PH

Mutlow Farm

Audley End

Mutlow Hall

MUTLOW HILL

5

CB11

FUNNEL LA

Wenden Hall

Bearwalden Bsns Pk

Wendens Ambo

Clanverend Farm

Clanverend Bridge

Norton End

Rookery Farm

ROOKERY LA

36

Mill Farm

LC

4

Duckantose La

Bulse Farm

Mill Hill

LONDON RD

B1383

3

35

Harcamlow Way

Long Plantation

Whiteditch Farm

Tudhope Farm

WHITEDITCH LA

2

Newport Free Gram Sch

BURY WATER LA

Nursery

BURYWATER COTTS

CENTERFIELDS

BURY WATER LA

GACE ACRE

SCHOOL LA

GIBEL LA

1

Severals Farm

B1038

WICKEN RD

A **B** **C** **D** **E** **F**

51

B1059

	A	B	C	D	E	F

8

Ridley's Wood

Delvyn's Lane

Delvyn's Farm

Audley End

Edeys Farm

PH

Rectory Farm

7

37

Parkgate Farm

Crouch House

Great Lodge Farm

DELVYN'S LA

Branwhite's Grove

The Moat

6

Lawrence's Farm

C09

5

Pannells Ash Farm

SUDBURY RD

Odewells

Rosemary Farm

36

ROSEMARY LA

Pantile Cottage

Kendallscroft Grove

Little Chelmshoe House

4

ST JAMES'S ST

Byham Hall

Little Lodge Farm

Chelmshoe House Farm

New Barn

3

Monks Lodge Farm

Monks Lodge

35

Hosden's Farm

MONKS LODGE RD

2

St Giles CE Prim Sch

Link Hills

Hopwell's Farm

ST GILES CE

STONE COTTS

Great Maplestead

+

Lucking Street

Luckinghouse Farm

CHURCH ST

1

Little Lodge Farm

34

Purls Cottage

Barrett's Hall

79	A	B	80	C	D	81	E	F

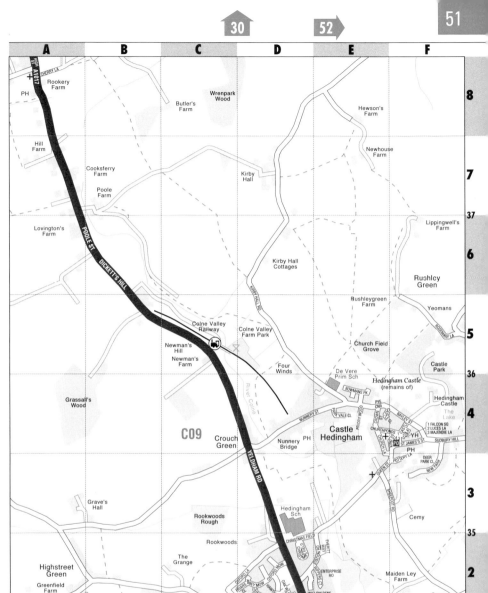

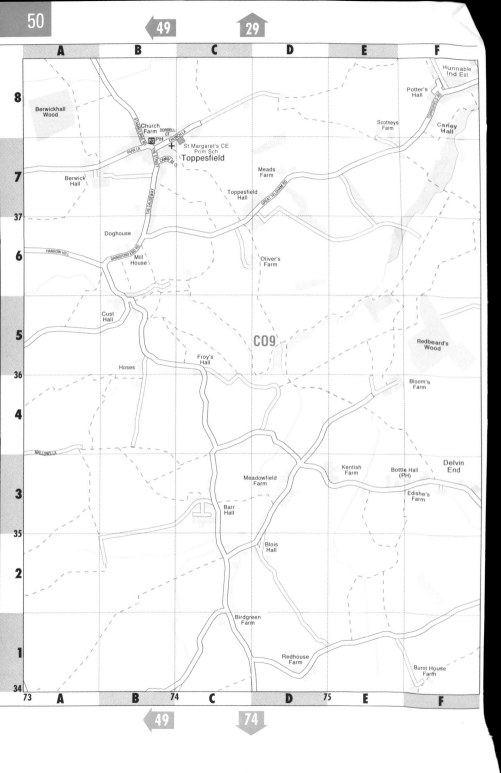

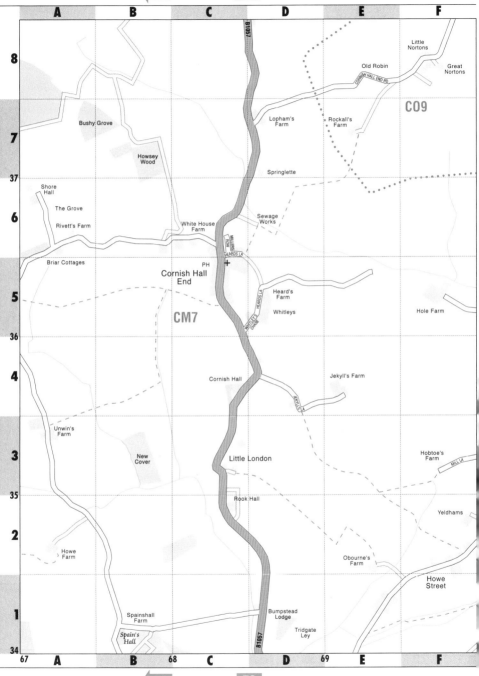

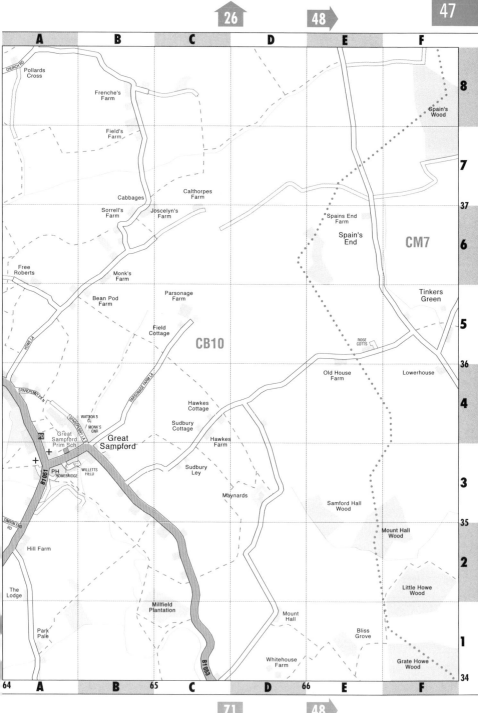

45 25

| A | B | C | D | E | F |

WINCELOW HALL RD
HILL RD
B1054
HIGH ST
Church Farm
CHURCH RD
Shelland's Farm
Hill Farm
B1054
LONGCROFT
B1055

8

Equestrian Ctr
+
B1054
Pant Brook House
Prentice's Farm

Sharp Crofts Wood

PH
B1053

7

Hill Farm
Moss's Farm

37

Anso Corner Farm
B1053
B1055
Howses

6

Anser Gallows Farm

Long Thatch

Mortlock's Farm
Clay Wood
River Pant
CB10

5

36

B1053

Sparrow's Hall
Moor End Farm

4

Little Brockholds Farm
Different Part Grove

Great Brockholds
Goddards Farm
Ivytodd's Farm
Barleyfields

3

Byeball's Farm

35

Giffords Farm

Longmead
TINDON END ROAD
Broadfields

2

Collins Cross
The Dovehouse
Blacklands Farm
B1051
Bush Cottage
Mill Farm House
Mast
South Fields

Grassy Grove
Tindon End
Tindon Manor
Bush Farm
Hole Farm

1

Market Farm
Broadcroft Grove
B1051

34

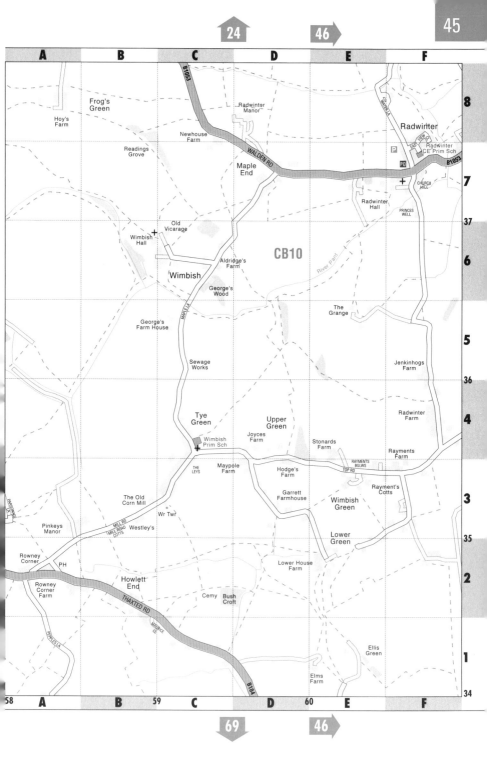

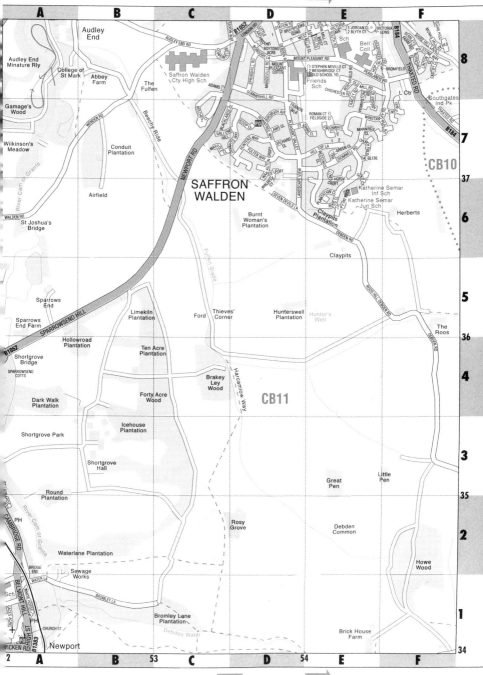

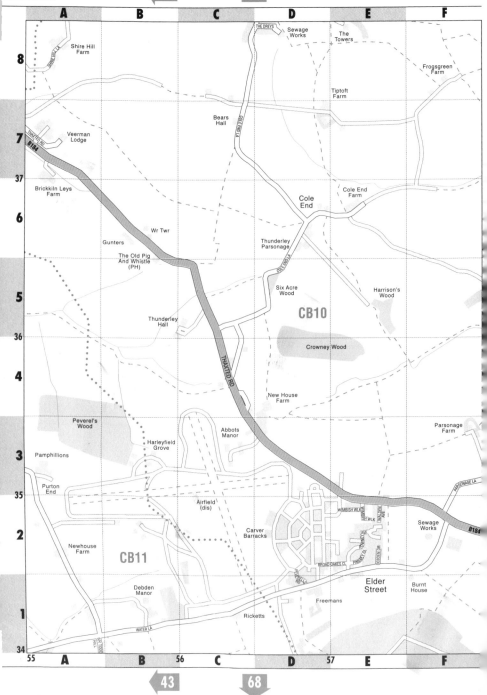

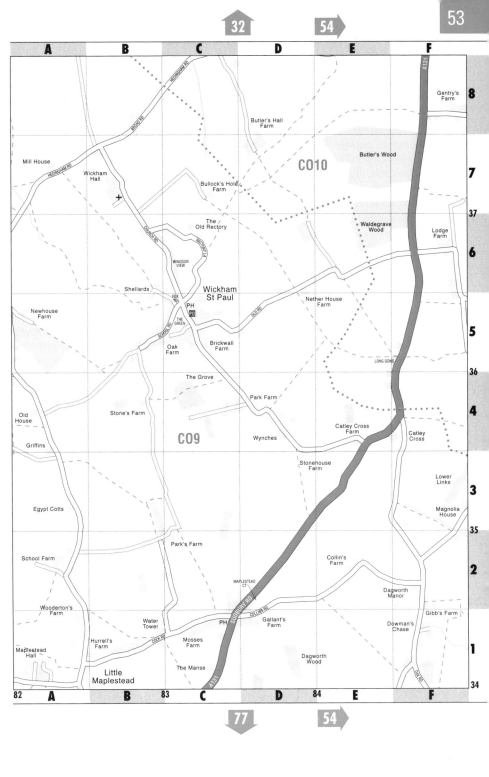

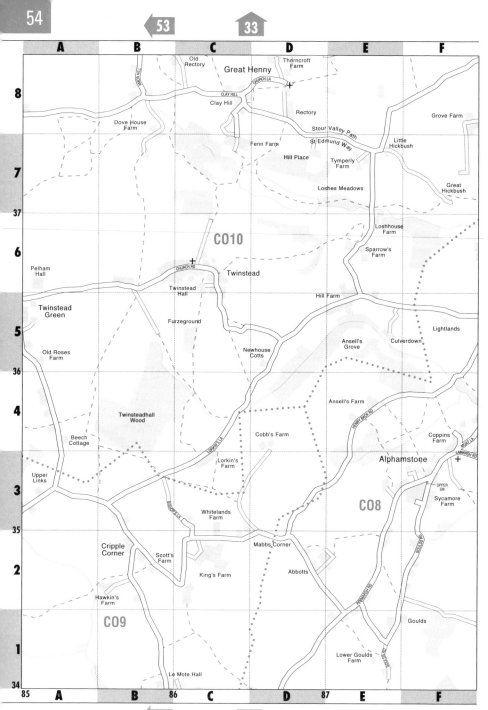

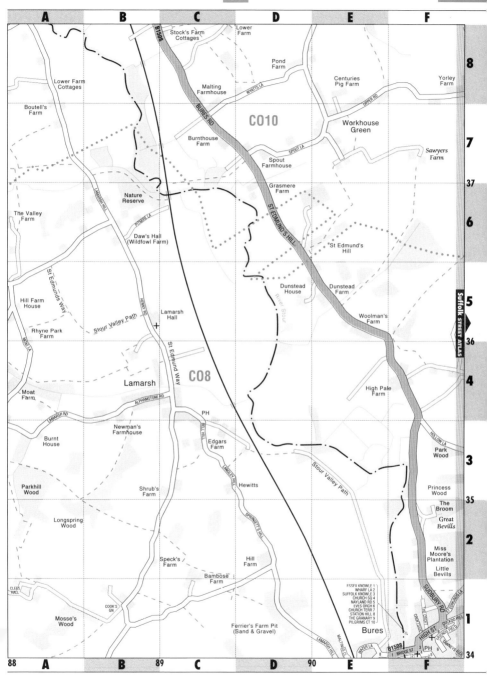

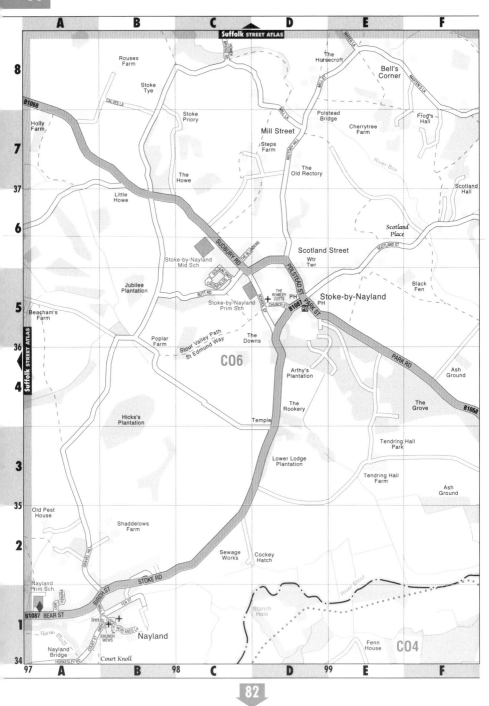

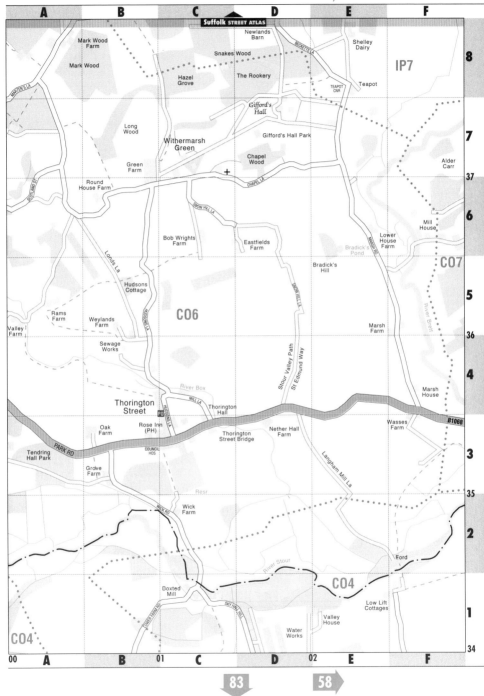

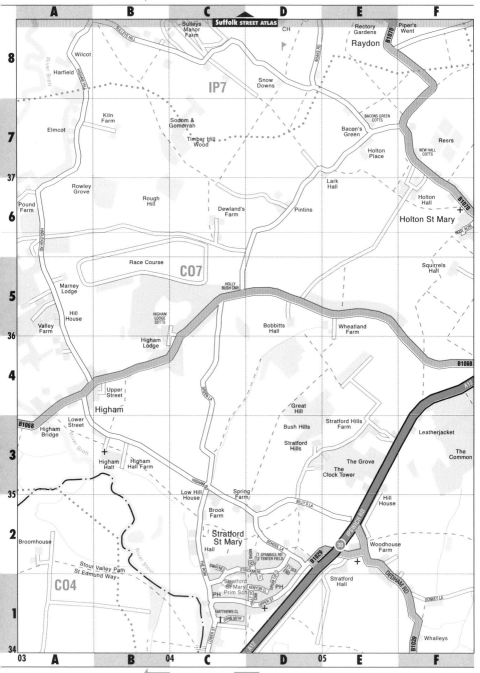

Suffolk STREET ATLAS

8

7

37

6

5

36

4

3

35

2

1

34

A   B   03   C   04   D   05   E   F

River Brett

Wilcot

Harfield

Sulleys Manor Farm

CH

Rectory Gardens

Piper's Went

Raydon

IP7

Snow Downs

Kiln Farm

Elmcot

Sodom & Gomorrah

Timber Hill Wood

Bacons Green Cotts

Bacon's Green

Resrs

NEW HALL COTTS

Holton Place

Rowley Grove

Rough Hill

Dewland's Farm

Pintins

Lark Hall

Holton Hall

Holton St Mary

Pound Farm

HADLEIGH RD

ROSE ACRE

B1070

B1070

Race Course

CO7

HOLLY BUSH CNR

Squirrels Hall

Marney Lodge

Hill House

HIGHAM LODGE COTTS

Bobbitts Hall

Wheatland Farm

Valley Farm

Higham Lodge

B1068

Upper Street

Higham

GREEN LA

Great Hill

Bush Hills

Stratford Hills Farm

Leatherjacket

The Common

B1068

Higham Bridge

Lower Street

River Brett

Higham Hall

Higham Hall Farm

Low Hill House

Spring Farm

Stratford Hills

The Grove

The Clock Tower

Hill House

A12

Broomhouse

Brook Farm

Stratford St Mary

Hall

BILLY'S LA

Woodhouse Farm

IPSWICH RD

Stour Valley Path St Edmund Way

River Stour

SCHOOL LA

SPANBIES RD

TENTER FIELD

MILL END

THE ROW

SWAYNES

STRICKMERE

KENYON CL

PH

Stratford St Mary Prim Sch

PH

UPPER ST

Stratford Hall

30

B1029

DEDHAM RD

DONKEY LA

CO4

MATTHEWS CL

BRAM MDW

LOWER ST

A12

Whalleys

B1029

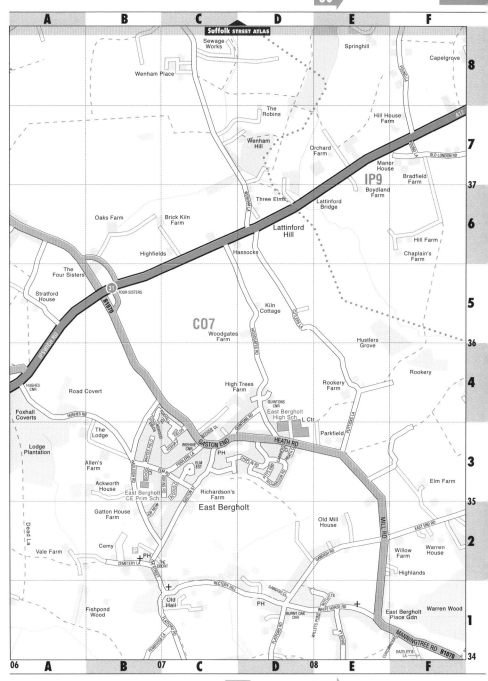

Suffolk STREET ATLAS

8

Sewage Works

Springhill

Capelgrove

Wenham Place

The Robins

Hill House Farm

7

Wenham Hill

Orchard Farm

Manor House

Old London Rd

IP9

Bradfield Farm

37

Three Elms

Lattinford Bridge

Boydland Farm

Oaks Farm

Brick Kiln Farm

6

Lattinford Hill

Hill Farm

Highfields

Hassocks

Chaplain's Farm

The Four Sisters

Kiln Cottage

5

Stratford House

FOUR SISTERS

CO7

Woodgates Farm

Hustlers Grove

36

Rookery

Road Covert

High Trees Farm

Rookery Farm

4

Foxhall Coverts

HUGHES CNR

QUINTONS CNR

East Bergholt High Sch

L Ctr

Parkfield

Lodge Plantation

The Lodge

GASTON END

HEATH RD

3

Allen's Farm

BEEHIVE CNR

PH

ELM EST

Ackworth House

East Bergholt CE Prim Sch

CHAPLIN RD

Elm Farm

Richardson's Farm

35

Gatton House Farm

East Bergholt

Old Mill House

2

Dead La

Vale Farm

Cemy

PH

THE COURT

Willow Farm

Warren House

CEMETERY LA

GANDISH RD

Highlands

RECTORY HILL

1

Fishpond Wood

Old Hall

PH

WHITE HORSE RD

East Bergholt Place Gdn

Warren Wood

BURNT OAK CNR

MANNINGTREE RD   B1070

DAZELEY'S LA

34

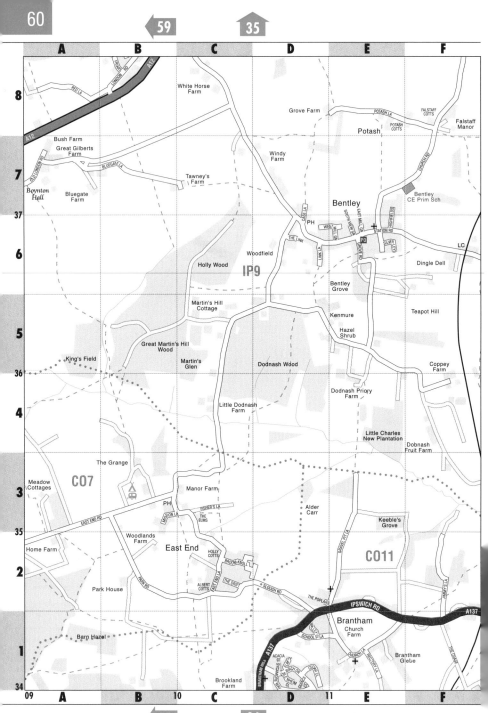

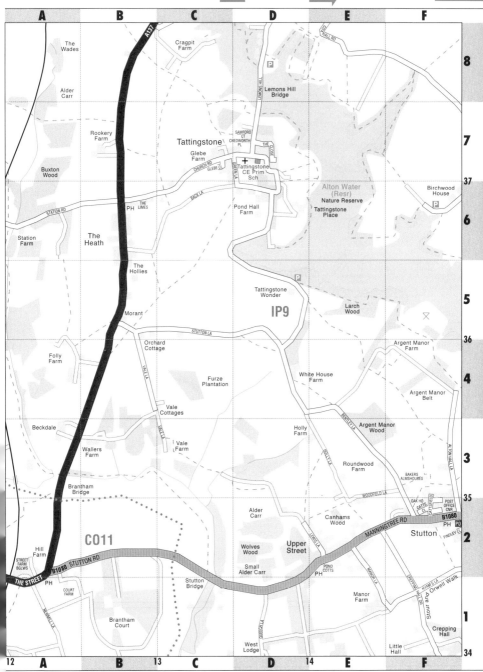

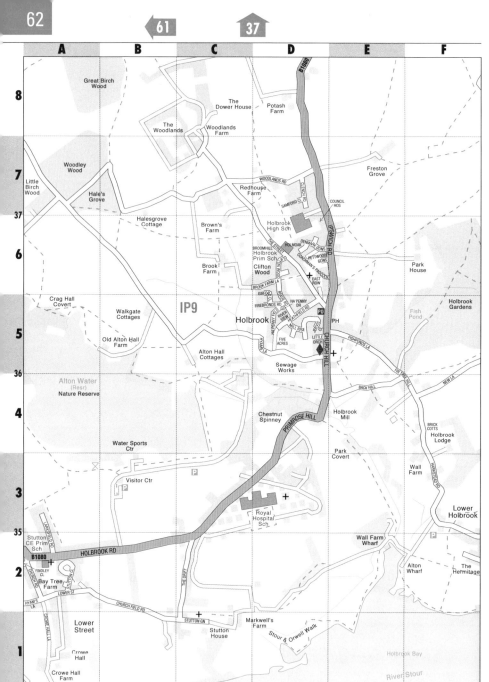

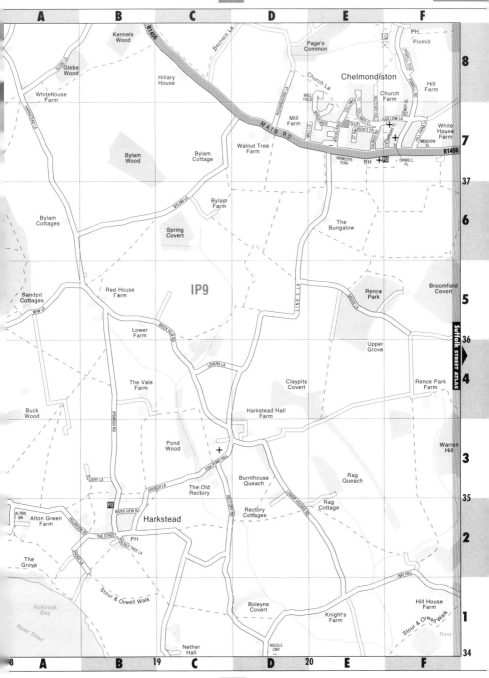

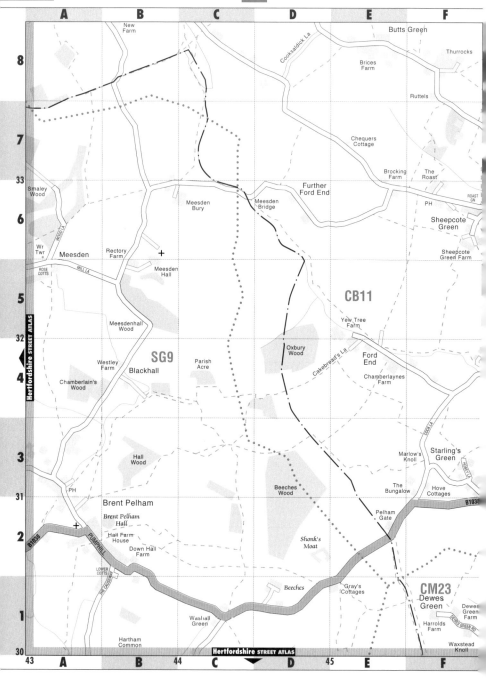

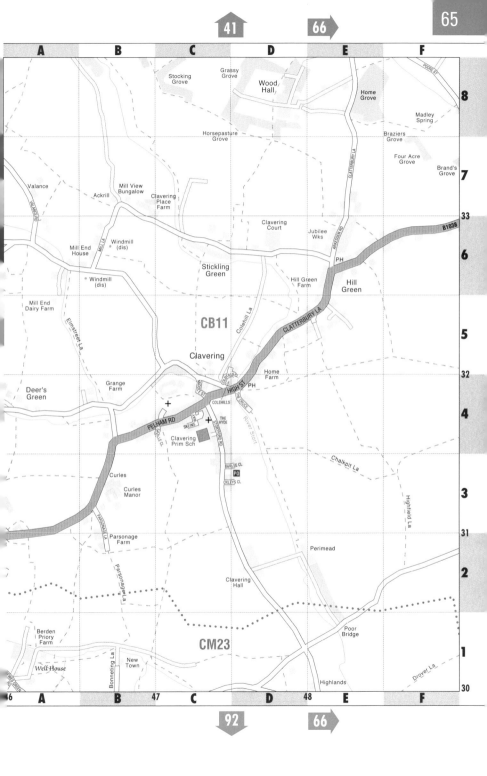

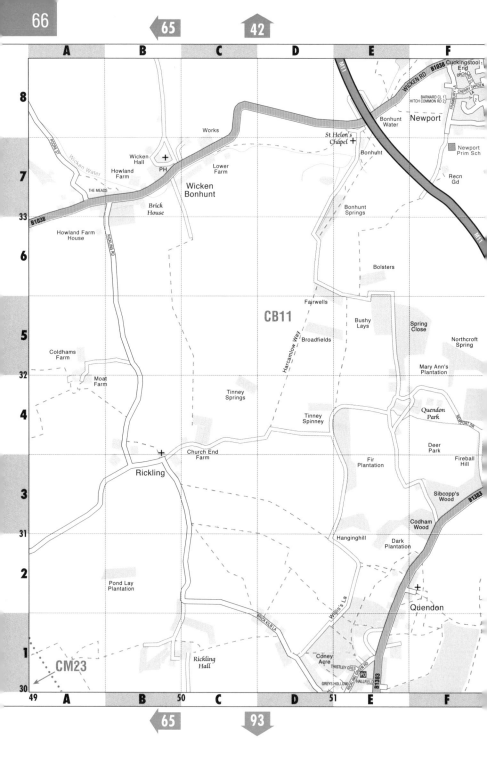

A **B** **C** **D** **E** **F**

B1383
HIGH ST
BULLFIELDS
POND CROSS FARM
STATION RD
Newport
1 CHERRY GARDEN LA
2 CHESTNUT CT
3 CHAPEL LA
4 POND CROSS WAY
5 POND CROSS COTTS
6 FRAMBURY LA

DEBDEN RD
Harcamlow Way
Ringers Barn
Ringers Farmhouse
Ringers
Dean's Grove
Hanging Grove

8

Chalk Farm
Newport Pond

Harcamlow Way
Debden Park

7

THE SPINNEY
LONDON RD

Pig's Parlour
Horseley Wood

33

Waldgraves
Cabbage Wood
Yewtree Plantation

6

CB11

Shiptons Farm
Park Wood
Dunstables
HOPE END LA

5

River Cam or Granta
Mast
LC
Springhill
WELLS MEAD

32

Prior's Hall Barn
Widdington Hall
Widdington
Swaynes Hall

CHURCH LA
PH
Martins Farm
THE SQUARE
HAMEL WAY
HIGH ST

4

CRABTREE HILL
HOLLOW RD
HOLLOW RD
HOLLOW RD
NORTH HALL RD
WOOD END
Newlands Farm
Wr Twr
CORNELLS LA
MOLE HALL LA
Mole Hall Wildlife Park

3

31

Broom Wood
London Jack Wood
LC
High Wood
Brickclamp Spring

2

Prior's Wood

M11
Jock Farm
Little Henham Hall
Little Henham Lodge

1

North Hall
Little Henham
River Cam or Granta
CM22

30

A **B** **C** **D** **E** **F**

2 53 54

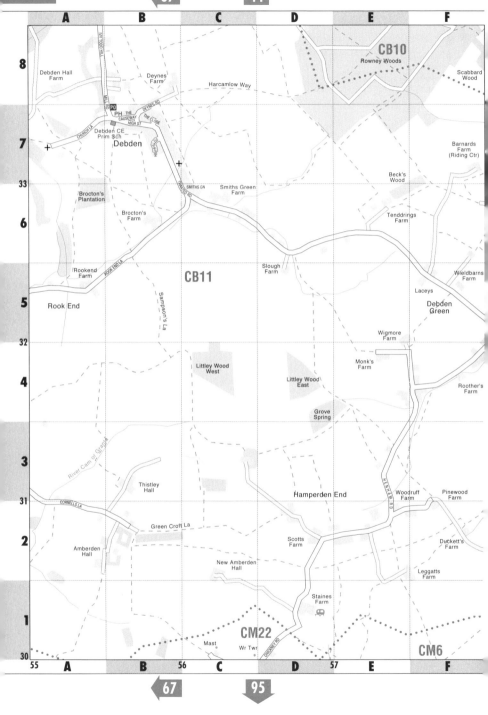

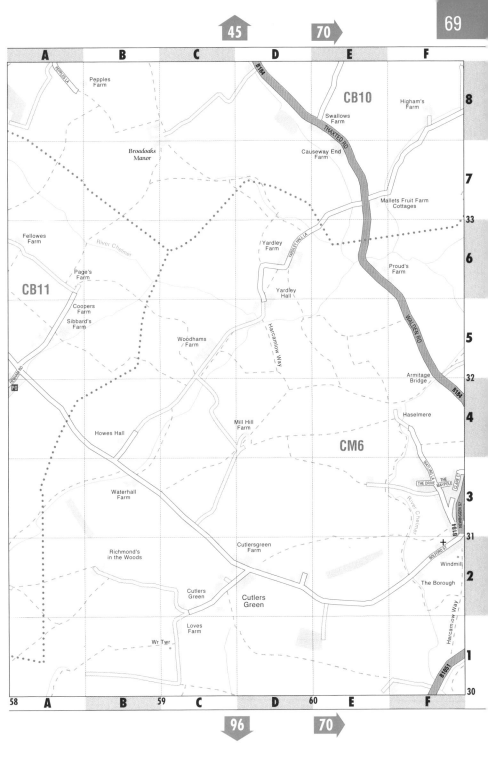

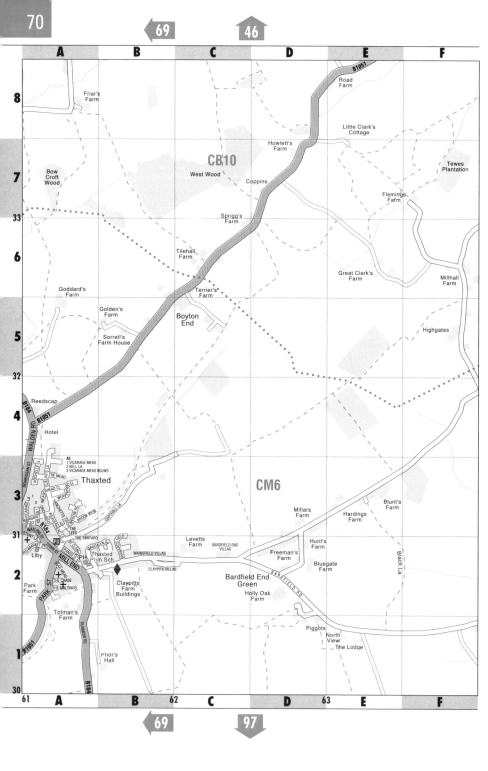

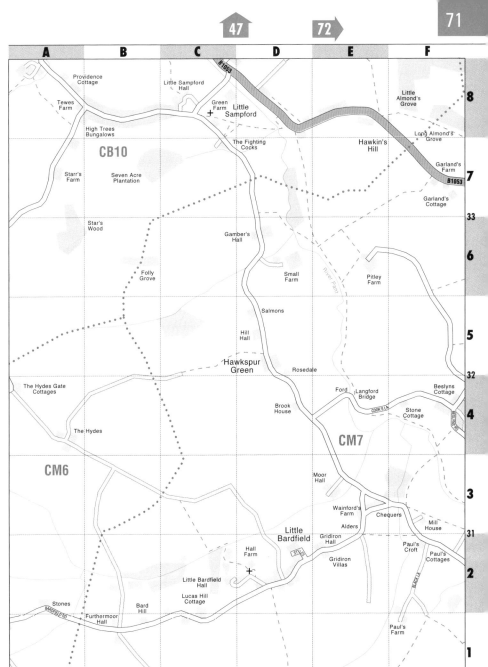

A   B   C   D   E   F

8

Providence
Cottage

Tewes
Farm

Little Sampford
Hall

Little Almond's
Grove

High Trees
Bungalows

Green
Farm

Little
Sampford

Long Almond's
Grove

CB10

The Fighting
Cocks

Hawkin's
Hill

Garland's
Farm

B1053

7

Starr's
Farm

Seven Acre
Plantation

Garland's
Cottage

33

Star's
Wood

Gamber's
Hall

6

Folly
Grove

Small
Farm

River Pant

Pitley
Farm

Salmons

5

Hill
Hall

Hawkspur
Green

Rosedale

32

The Hydes Gate
Cottages

Ford

Langford
Bridge

Beslyns
Cottage

Brook
House

COOK'S LA.

Stone
Cottage

BESLYNS RD.

4

The Hydes

CM7

CM6

Moor
Hall

3

Wainford's
Farm

Chequers

Mill
House

Alders

31

Little
Bardfield

Gridiron
Hall

Paul's
Croft

Paul's
Cottages

Hall
Farm

STY. RD.

Gridiron
Villas

BLACK LA.

2

Little Bardfield
Hall

Stones

Lucas Hill
Cottage

BARDFIELD RD.

Bard
Hill

Furthermoor
Hall

Paul's
Farm

1

Marks
Wood

64   A   B   65   C   D   66   E   F

30

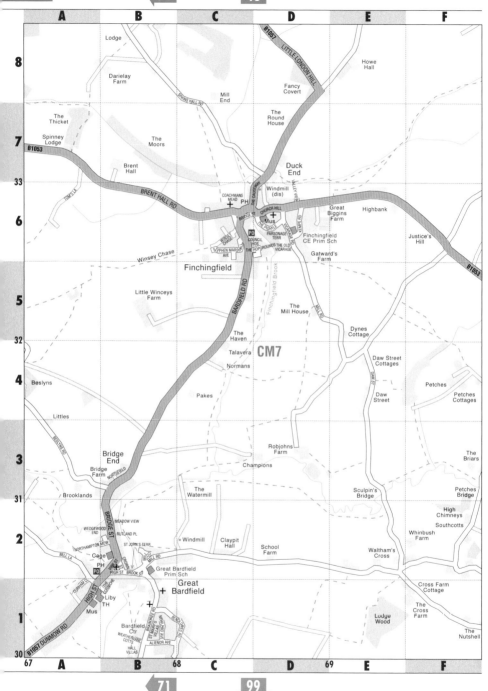

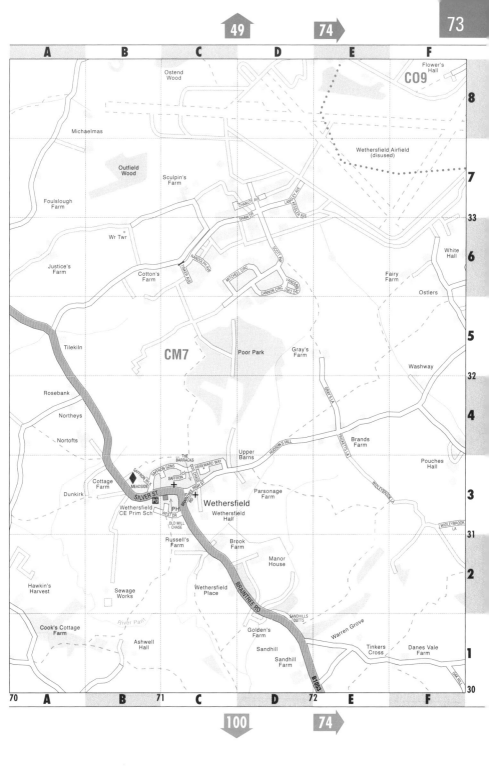

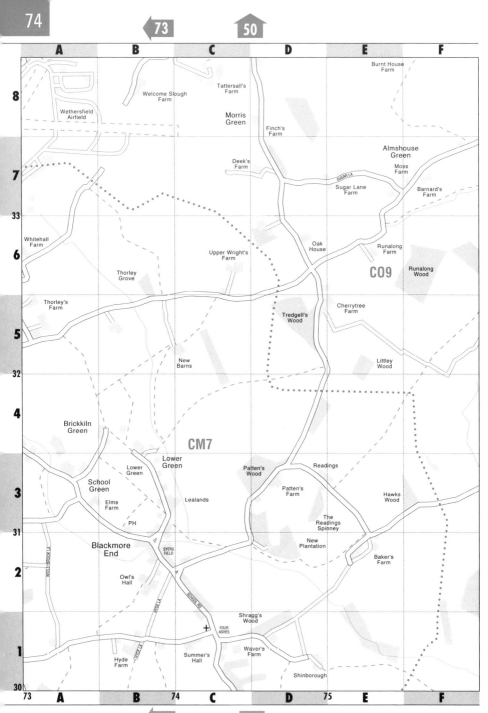

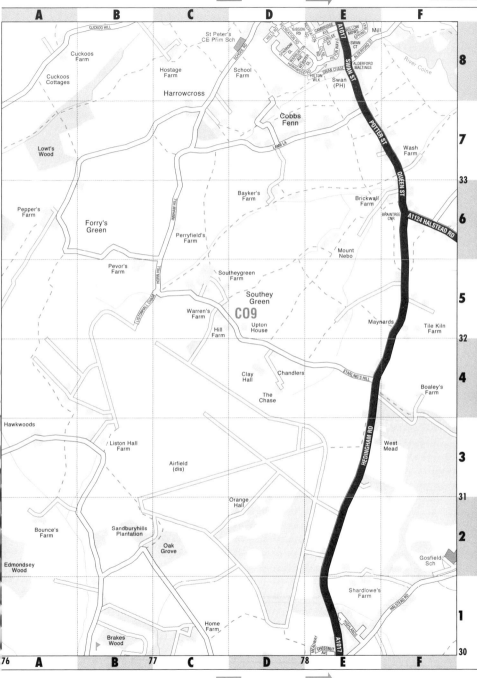

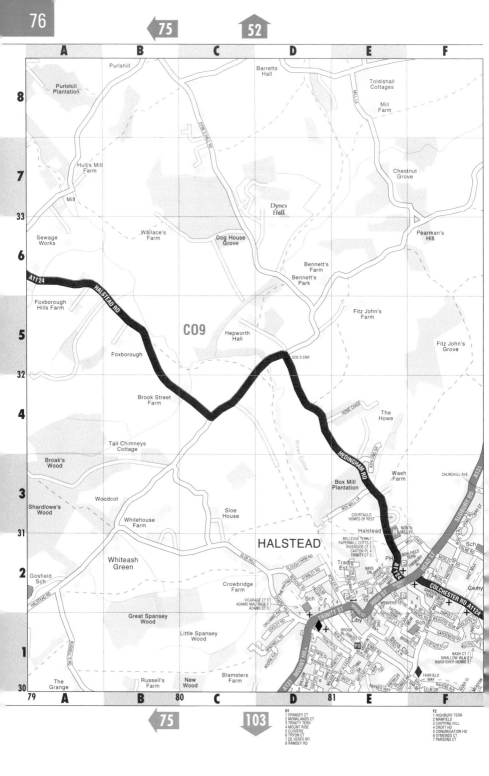

D1
1 SPANSEY CT
2 MONKLANDS CT
3 TRINITY TERR
4 MOUNT RISE
5 CLOVERS
6 TRYON CT
7 DE VERES RD
8 RAMSEY RD

F2
1 HIGHBURY TERR
2 MANFIELD
3 CHIPPING HILL
4 CROFT HO
5 CONGREGATION HO
6 SYMONDS CT
7 PARSONS CT

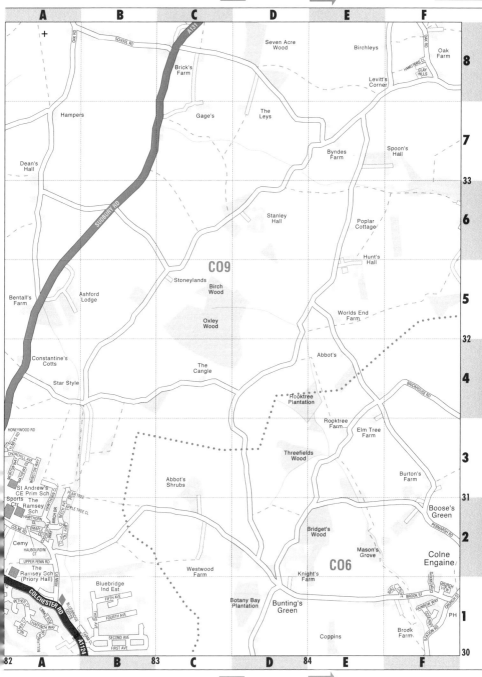

53
78
104
78

A131

SUDBURY RD

SCHOOL RD

Seven Acre Wood

Birchleys

Oak Farm

HAMSTERS CL

CLAY HILLS

OAK RD

Levitt's Corner

Brick's Farm

Hampers

Gage's

The Leys

Byndes Farm

Spoon's Hall

Dean's Hall

Stanley Hall

Poplar Cottage

CO9

Hunt's Hall

Bentall's Farm

Ashford Lodge

Stoneylands

Birch Wood

Worlds End Farm

Oxley Wood

Constantine's Cotts

The Cangle

Abbot's

BROOKHOUSE RD

Star Style

Rooktree Plantation

Rooktree Farm

Elm Tree Farm

HONEYWOOD RD

Abbot's Shrubs

Threefields Wood

Burton's Farm

St Andrew's CE Prim Sch

CHURCHILL AVE

MORTON WAY

MATHEWS RD

WINSTON WAY

THRIFT RD

Sports Ctr

The Ramsey Sch

PEAR TREE CL

Boose's Green

PERRMARSH RD

APPLE TREE CL

BIRCH DR

HAWTHORN

Bridget's Wood

Mason's Grove

Colne Engaine

MAPLE CL

Cemy

HAUBOURDIN CT

UPPER FENN RD

CO6

Knight's Farm

SHEEP COTT

BROOK ST

CHURCH VIEW

RAINBOW WAY

The Ramsey Sch (Priory Hall)

FENN RD

PH

COLCHESTER RD

A1124

BLUEBRIDGE COTTS

Bluebridge Ind Est

FIFTH AVE

THIRD AVE

FOURTH AVE

Westwood Farm

Botany Bay Plantation

Bunting's Green

Brook Farm

STATION RD

CHURCHILL

RAM CL

SECOND AVE

FIRST AVE

Coppins

82   83   84   30   31   32   33

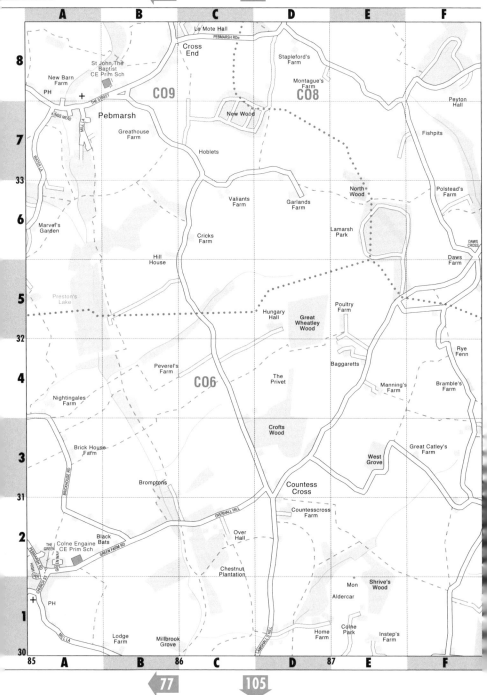

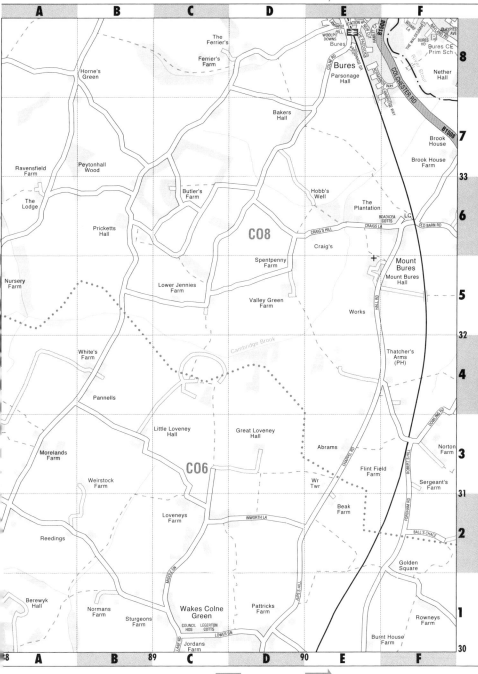

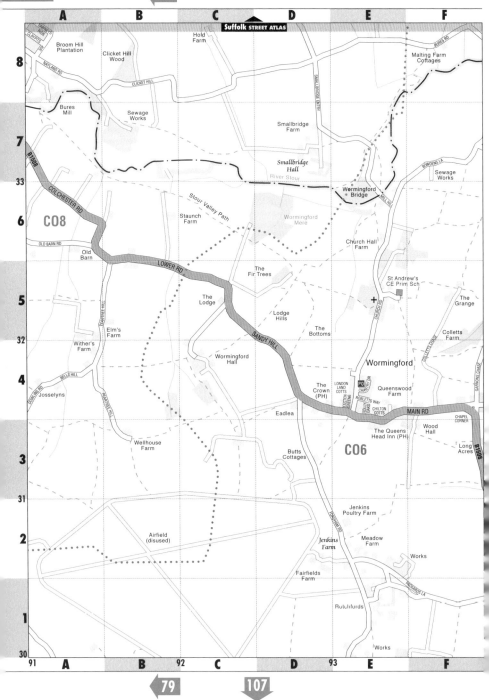

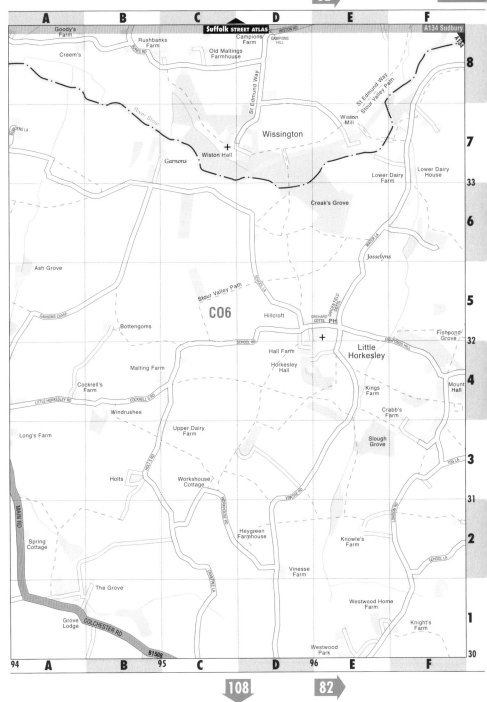

Suffolk STREET ATLAS

A134 Sudbury

Goody's
Farm

Rushbanks
Farm

Campions
Farm

Campions
Hill

Creem's

Old Maltings
Farmhouse

St Edmund Way

Stour Valley Path

8

River Stour

Wissington

Wiston
Mill

7

Wiston Hall

Garnons

Lower Dairy
Farm

Lower Dairy
House

33

Creak's Grove

6

Ash Grove

Josselyns

Stour Valley Path

5

CO6

Hillcroft

Orchard
Cotts

Garden Field
Cotts

PH

Garnons Chase

Fishpond
Grove

32

Bottengoms

School Rd

Fishponds Hill

Hall Farm

Little
Horkesley

Malting Farm

Horkesley
Hall

Cockrell's
Farm

Cockrell's Rd

Kings
Farm

Mount
Hall

4

Little Horkesley Rd

Windrushes

Crabb's
Farm

Long's Farm

Upper Dairy
Farm

Slough
Grove

Holts Rd

Log La

3

Holts

Workshouse
Cottage

31

Main Rd

Spring
Cottage

Heygreen
Farmhouse

Knowle's
Farm

Vinesse Rd

London Rd

School La

2

Workshouse Rd

Chapel La

The Grove

Vinesse
Farm

Westwood Home
Farm

Grove
Lodge

Colchester Rd

Knight's
Farm

1

B1508

Westwood
Park

30

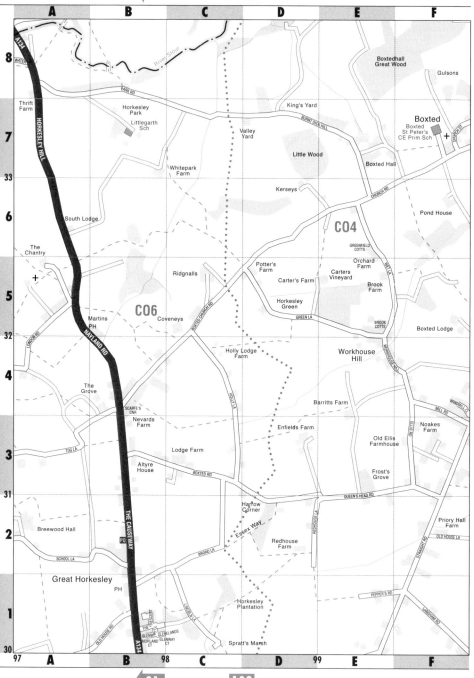

81
56

A B C D E F

8

WATER LA

AT34

Thrift
Farm

HORKESLEY HILL

7

33

6

The
Chantry

5

32

4

3

31

2

30

97 A B 98 C D 99 E F

Park Rd

River Stour

Horkesley
Park

Littlegarth
Sch

South Lodge

CO6

NAYLAND RD

Martins
PH

The
Grove

SCARFE'S
CNR

Nevards
Farm

TOG LA

Altyre
House

THE CAUSEWAY

PO

Breewood Hall

SCHOOL LA

Great Horkesley

PH

THE CHURCH

GLENWAY
MORLAND
CT

GLEBELANDS
GLENWAY
CT

OLD HOUSE RD

AT34

Whitepark
Farm

Ridgnalls

Coveneys

BOXTED CHURCH RD

Holly Lodge
Farm

Lodge Farm

BOXTED RD

HALL LA

Harrow
Corner

Essex Way

BROAD LA

LUCAS LA

Horkesley
Plantation

Spratt's Marsh

Valley
Yard

King's Yard

BURNT DICK HILL

Little Wood

Kerseys

Potter's
Farm

Carter's Farm

Horkesley
Green

GREEN LA

Barritts Farm

Enfields Farm

Frost's
Grove

QUEEN'S HEAD RD

Redhouse
Farm

REDHOUSE LA

Boxtedhall
Great Wood

Boxted
St Peter's
CE Prim Sch

Boxted

Boxted Hall

CHURCH RD

CO4

GREENFIELD
COTTS

Orchard
Farm

Carters
Vineyard

Brook
Farm

BROOK
COTTS

Workhouse
Hill

WORKHOUSE HILL

Old Ellis
Farmhouse

WELL LA

Gulsons

CHUCKLEY

Pond House

Boxted Lodge

MILL RD

WINDMILL LA

Noakes
Farm

ELLIS RD

STRAIGHT RD

Priory Hall
Farm

OLD HOUSE LA

PEPPER'S RD

CANDSAM RD

81
109

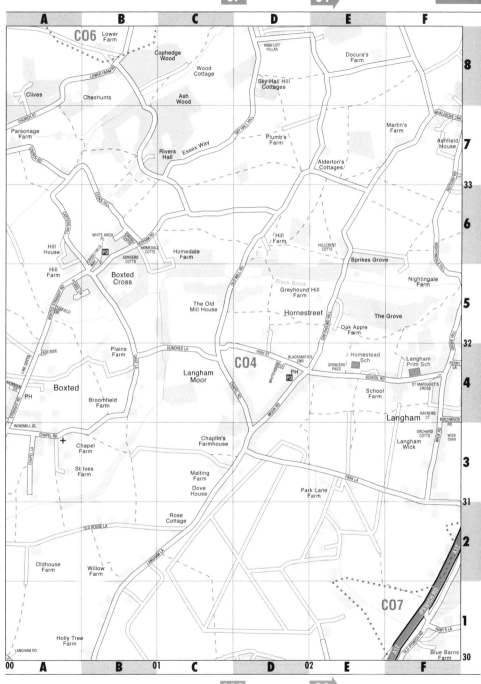

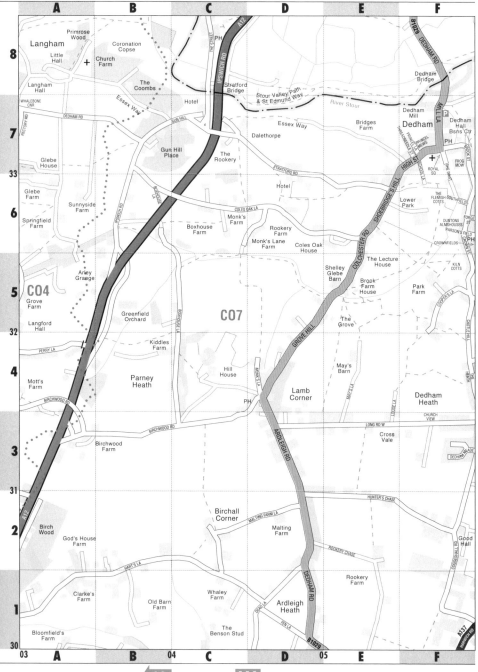

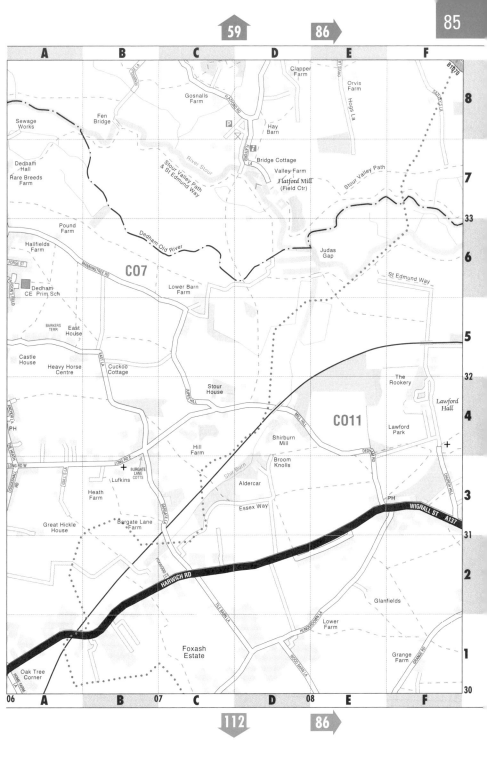

59
86

A | **B** | **C** | **D** | **E** | **F**

B1070

8

Clapper
Farm

Orvis
Farm

Gosnalls
Farm

Hay
Barn

Hogs La

Sewage
Works

Fen
Bridge

River Stour

Stour Valley Path
& St Edmund Way

Bridge Cottage

Valley Farm

Stour Valley Path

7

Dedham
Hall

Rare Breeds
Farm

Flatford Mill
(Field Ctr)

33

Pound
Farm

Dedham Old River

Judas
Gap

6

Hallfields
Farm

FORGE ST

MANNINGTREE RD

CO7

St Edmund Way

Dedham
CE Prim Sch

Lower Barn
Farm

BARKERS
TERR

East
House

5

Castle
House

Heavy Horse
Centre

Cuckoo
Cottage

FAST LA

Stour
House

The
Rookery

32

Lawford
Hall

LONG RD W

PH

CO11

DEDHAM RD

Lawford
Park

4

Hill
Farm

Shirburn
Mill

BURGATE
LANE
COTTS

Lufkins

Broom
Knolls

Shir Burn

CHURCH HILL

Heath
Farm

Aldercar

PH

3

Great Hickle
House

Bargate Lane
Farm

Essex Way

WIGNALL ST **A137**

31

HARWICH RD

FOXWOOD LA

Glanfields

2

ILLEIGH LA

HUNGERDOWN LA

Lower
Farm

GRANGE RD

Grange
Farm

Foxash
Estate

Oak Tree
Corner

HOME FARM

30

A | **B** | **C** | **D** | **E** | **F**

06 | 07 | 08

112
86

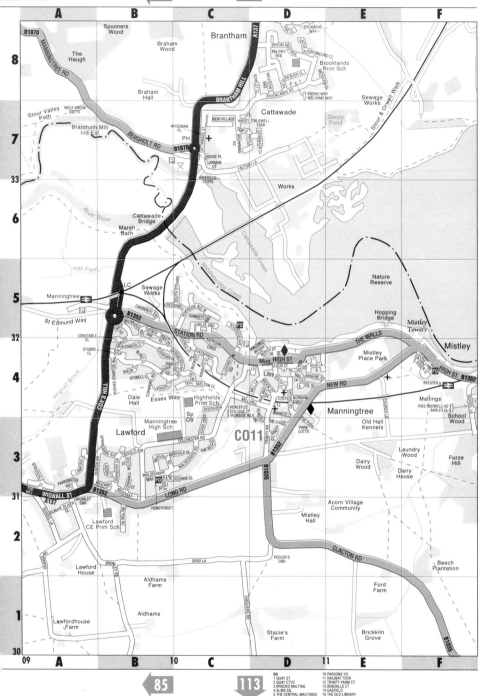

← 85
↑ 60

← 85
↓ 113

D4
1 QUAY ST
2 QUAY CTYD
3 BROOKS MALTING
4 ALMA SQ
5 THE CENTRAL MAILTINGS
6 ST MICHAELS CT
7 YORK ST
8 FALKLANDS DR
9 REGENT ST
10 PARSONS YD
11 RAILWAY TERR
12 TRINITY FARM CT
13 BENDALLS CT
14 GASFIELD
15 THE OLD LIBRARY
16 COMPASS CT

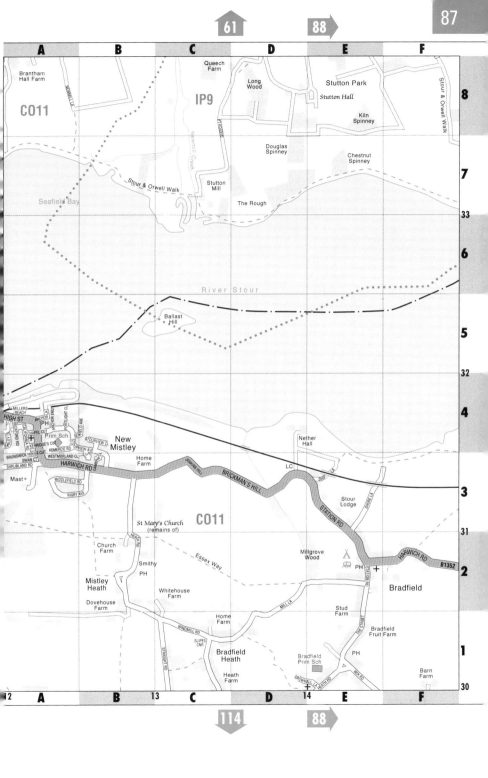

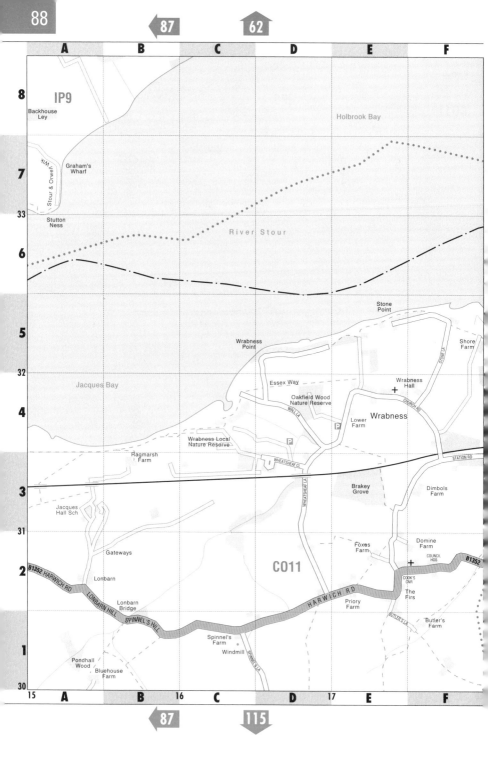

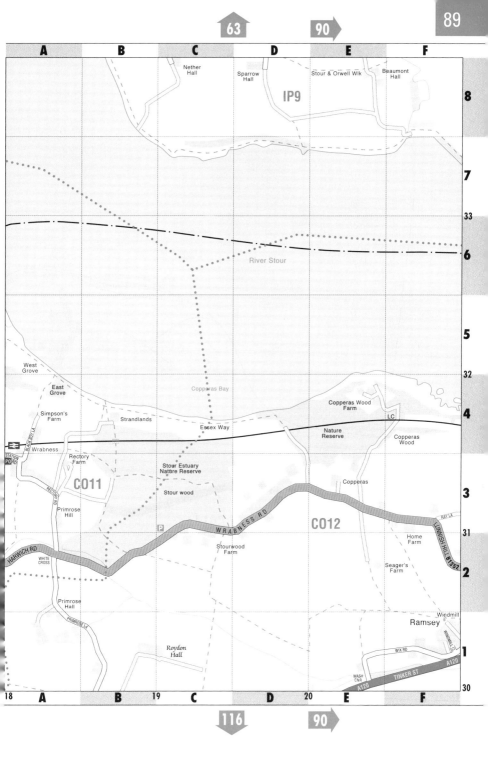

A **B** **C** **D** **E** **F**

8

7

33

6

IP9

Nether
Hall

Sparrow
Hall

Stour & Orwell Wlk

Beaumont
Hall

River Stour

5

32

West
Grove

East
Grove

Copperas Bay

Copperas Wood
Farm

4

Simpson's
Farm

Strandlands

Essex Way

Nature
Reserve

LC

Copperas
Wood

BLACK BOY LA

Wrabness

Rectory
Farm

Stour Estuary
Nature Reserve

Stour wood

Copperas

STATION RD

RECTORY RD

CO11

Primrose
Hill

W R A B N E S S   R D

CO12

BAY LA

Copperas

Home
Farm

LUNNISH HILL B1352

3

31

HARWICH RD

WHITE
CROSS

Stourwood
Farm

Seager's
Farm

2

Primrose
Hall

PRIMROSE LA

Windmill

Ramsey

WINDMILL LA

1

30

Roydon
Hall

WIX RD

WASH
CNR

A120

TINKER ST

A120

18

19

20

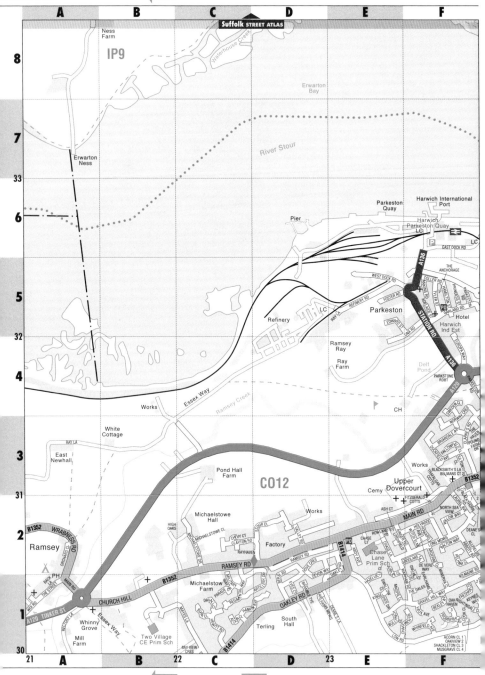

Suffolk STREET ATLAS

A **B** **C** **D** **E** **F**

8

IP9

Ness Farm

Waterhouse Creek

Erwarton Bay

7

River Stour

33

Erwarton Ness

6

Parkeston Quay

Harwich International Port

Pier

Harwich Parkeston Quay LC

P

LC

EAST DOCK RD

THE ANCHORAGE

A136

WEST DOCK RD

COLLER RD

5

Refinery

LC

REFINERY RD

FOSTER RD

Parkeston

EDWA

STATION RD

Hotel

Harwich Ind Est

32

Ramsey Ray

Ray Farm

Delf Pond

A136

PARKESTONE RDBT

A120

4

Essex Way

Ramsey Creek

CH

Works

3

White Cottage

RAY LA

Works

A120

B1352

East Newhall

Pond Hall Farm

CO12

Upper Dovercourt

Cemy

BLACKSMITH'S LA 1
BELMANS CT 2

31

Michaelstowe Hall

Works

FITZGERALD COTTS

ASH CT

MAIN RD

NORTH SEA VIEW

2

B1352

WRABNESS RD

HIGH OAKS

Michaelstowe Hall

MICHAELSTOWE CL

CHEVY CT
CLAYTON RD

Factory

RAMSEY CRES

CHASE CT

ROWLAND CL

Chase Lane Prim Sch

DE VERNE WAY

DEANE

Ramsey

BACK PH LA

THE STREET

MAIN RD

CHURCHGATE

RAMSEY RD

B1352

Michaelstow Farm

OAKLEY RD

B1414

South Hall

Terling

1

A120 TINKER ST

CHURCH HILL

Essex Way

Whinny Grove

Mill Farm

Two Village CE Prim Sch

RAY VIEW CRES

B1414

ACORN CL 1
OAKVIEW 2
SHACKLETON CL 3
MUSGRAVE CL 4

30

21 **A** **22** **B** **C** **23** **D** **E** **F**

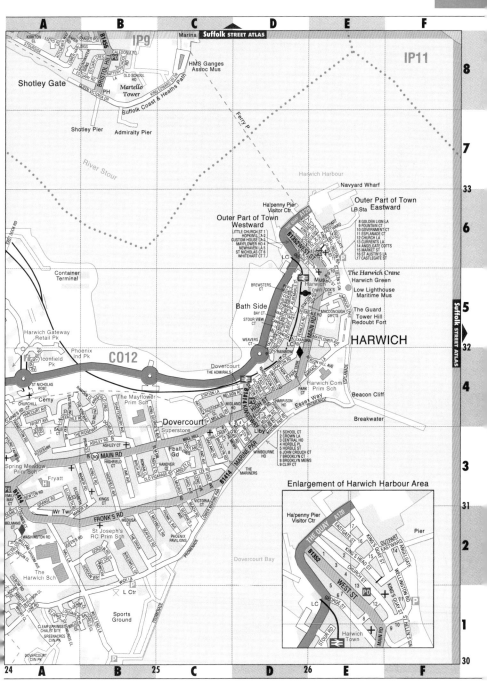

IP9

IP11

Shotley Gate

Martello Tower

Marina

HMS Ganges Assoc Mus

Shotley Pier

Admiralty Pier

Suffolk Coast & Heaths Path

Ferry P

River Stour

Harwich Harbour

Navyard Wharf

Ha'penny Pier Visitor Ctr

Outer Part of Town Westward
LITTLE CHURCH ST 1
HOPKING LA 2
CUSTOM HOUSE LA 3
MAYFLOWER HO 4
NEWHAVEN LA 5
ST NICHOLAS CT 6
WHITEHART CT 7

Outer Part of Town Eastward
LB Sta

8 GOLDEN LION LA
9 FOUNTAIN CT
10 GOVERNMENT CT
11 ESPLANADE CT
12 CHURCH LA
13 CURRENTS LA
14 ANGELGATE COTTS
15 MARKET ST
16 ST AUSTIN'S LA
17 CASTLEGATE ST

Container Terminal

BREWSTERS CT

Mus
Harwich Town
Cox's

The Harwich Crane
Harwich Green
Low Lighthouse
Maritime Mus

Bath Side

BAY CT
STOUR VIEW

WEAVERS CT

MACDONOUGH COTTS

The Guard
Tower Hill
Redoubt Fort

HARWICH

Harwich Gateway Retail Pk

Iconfield Pk

CO12

Phoenix Ind Pk

Dovercourt
THE ADMIRALS

Harwich Com Prim Sch

Beacon Cliff

Breakwater

St Nicholas Rdbt
Cemy

The Mayflower Prim Sch

STATION LA
NELSON RD

Essex Way
PROMENADE

Dovercourt
Superstore

MILL HILL

Liby

1 SCHOOL CT
2 CROWN CT
3 CENTRAL HO
4 HORDLE PL
5 HORDLE ST
6 JOHN CROUCH CT
7 BROOKLYN CT
8 BROOKLYN MEWS
9 CLIFF CT

Fball Gd

HANOVER

WIMBOURNE HO

THE MARINERS

Spring Meadow Prim Sch

Fryatt

MAIN RD

HIGHFIELD

Victoria

Wr Twr

FRONK'S RD

MEDUSA

PHOENIX PAVILIONS

KINGS CT

St Joseph's RC Prim Sch

Belmans Ct

Washington Rd

The Harwich Sch

L Ctr

Sports Ground

DOVERCOURT CVN PK

Dovercourt Bay

Enlargement of Harwich Harbour Area

Ha'penny Pier Visitor Ctr

THE QUAY

B1352

WEST ST

EASTGATE ST

KING'S HEAD ST

CHURCH ST

GEORGE ST

STOUR RD

LC

Harwich Town

King's Quay St

OUTPART EASTWARD

ANGELGATE

WELLINGTON RD

KING'S QUAY ST

ST HELEN'S GN

Pier

MAIN RD

24   25   26

30   31   32   33

1   2   3   4   5   6   7   8

A   B   C   D   E   F

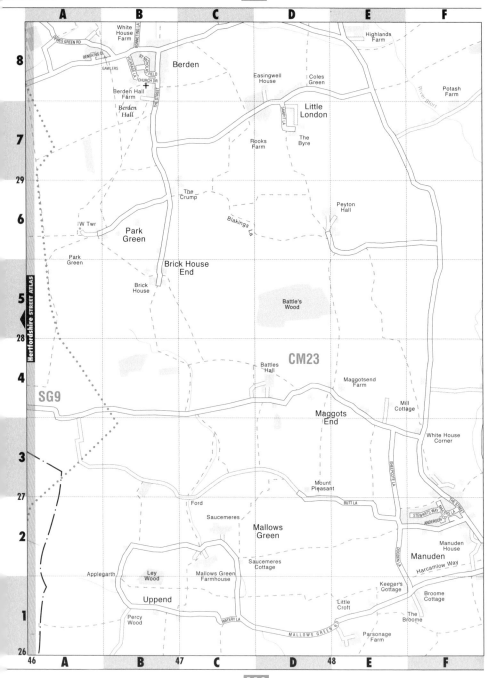

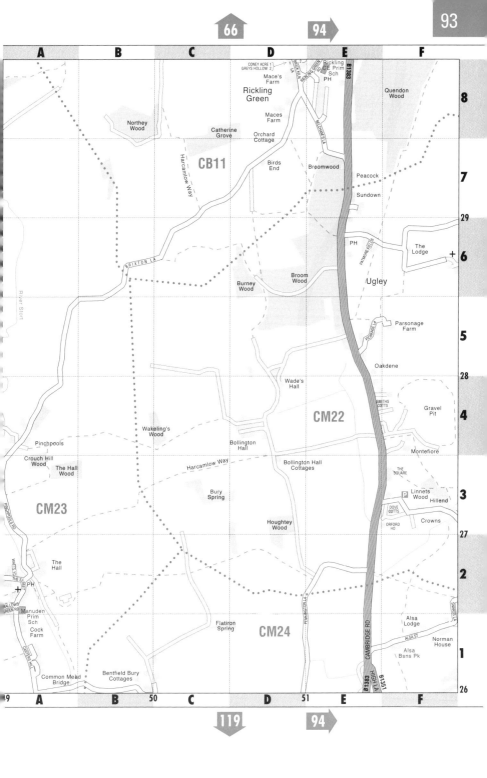

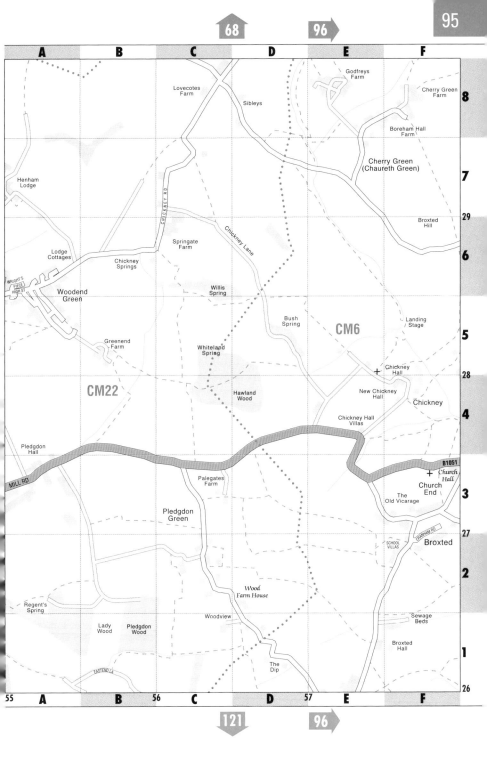

A B C D E F

Godfreys Farm
Cherry Green Farm
Lovecotes Farm
Sibleys
8

Boreham Hall Farm
Henham Lodge
Cherry Green (Chaureth Green)
7

CHICKNEY RD
Broxted Hill
29

Springate Farm
Chickney Lane
Lodge Cottages
Chickney Springs
6

WRIGHT'S PIECE HIGH ST
Woodend Green
Willis Spring
Bush Spring
CM6
Landing Stage
5

Greenend Farm
Whiteland Spring
Chickney Hall
28

CM22
Hawland Wood
New Chickney Hall
Chickney Hall Villas
Chickney
4

Pledgdon Hall
B1051
Church Hall
Church End
3

MILL RD
Palegates Farm
The Old Vicarage

Pledgdon Green
27
DUNMOW RD
SCHOOL VILLAS
Broxted
2

Regent's Spring
Wood Farm House
Woodview
Sewage Beds

Lady Wood
Pledgdon Wood
Broxted Hall
1

EASTEND LA
The Dip
26

55 A B 56 C D 57 E F

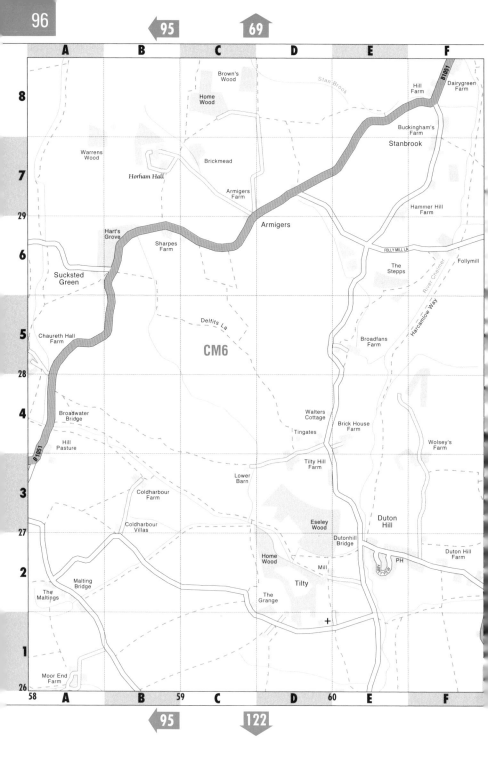

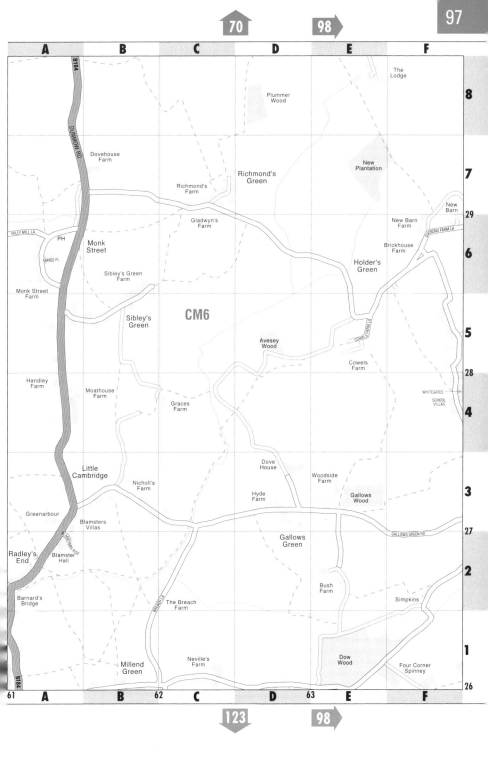

The Lodge

8

Plummer
Wood

New
Plantation

7

29

Dovehouse
Farm

Richmond's
Green

New
Barn

B184

DUNMOW RD

Richmond's
Farm

New Barn
Farm

RUCKEND FARM LA

FOLLY MILL LA

Gladwyn's
Farm

Brickhouse
Farm

6

PH

Monk
Street

Holder's
Green

MAYES PL

Sibley's Green
Farm

Monk Street
Farm

CM6

5

Sibley's
Green

Avesey
Wood

COWEL FARM LA

28

Cowels
Farm

Handley
Farm

Moathouse
Farm

Graces
Farm

WHITEGATES

SCHOOL
VILLAS

4

Dove
House

Little
Cambridge

Nicholl's
Farm

Woodside
Farm

3

Hyde
Farm

Gallows
Wood

Greenarbour

Blamsters
Villas

GALLOWS GREEN RD

27

Radley's
End

Blamster
Hall

CASTERN RISE

Gallows
Green

2

Barnard's
Bridge

Bush
Farm

Simpkins

BEGGRLA

The Breach
Farm

Neville's
Farm

Dow
Wood

Four Corner
Spinney

1

Millend
Green

26

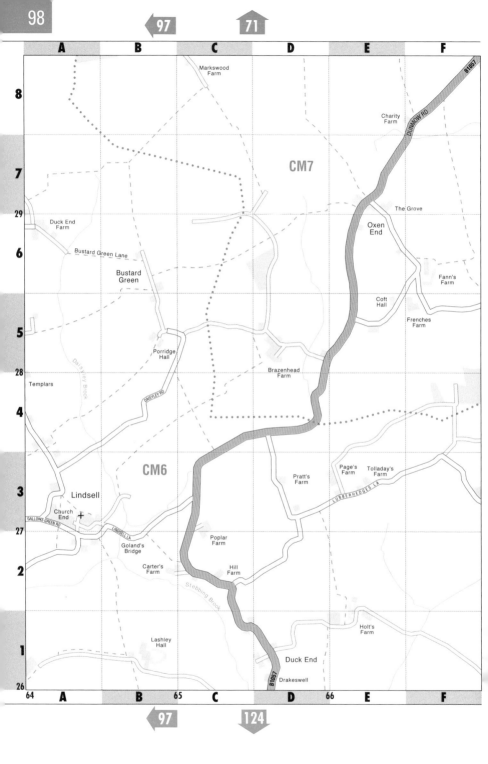

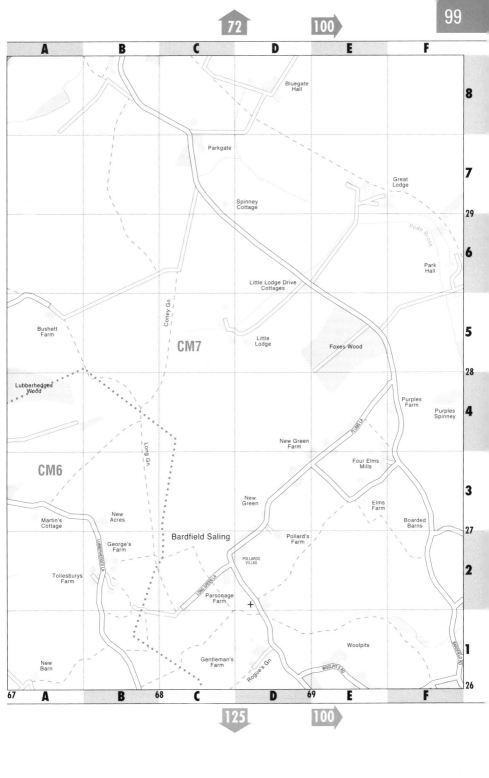

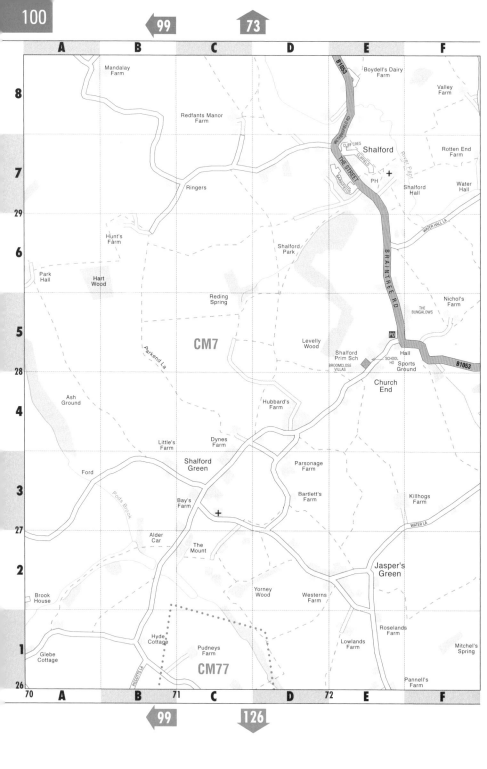

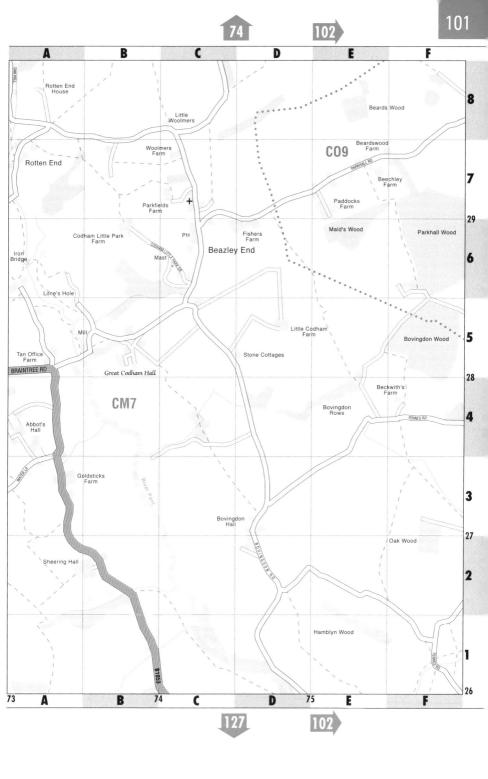

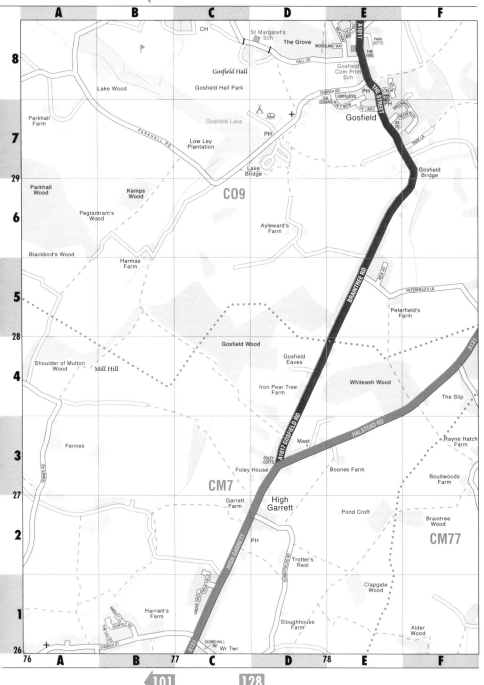

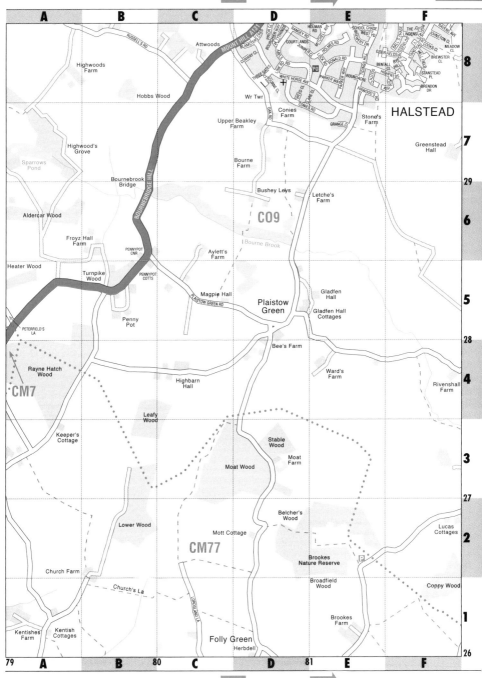

HALSTEAD

CO9

CM7

CM77

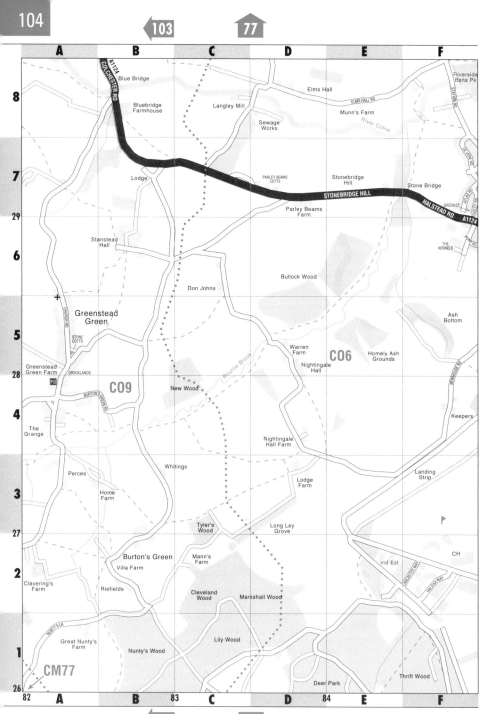

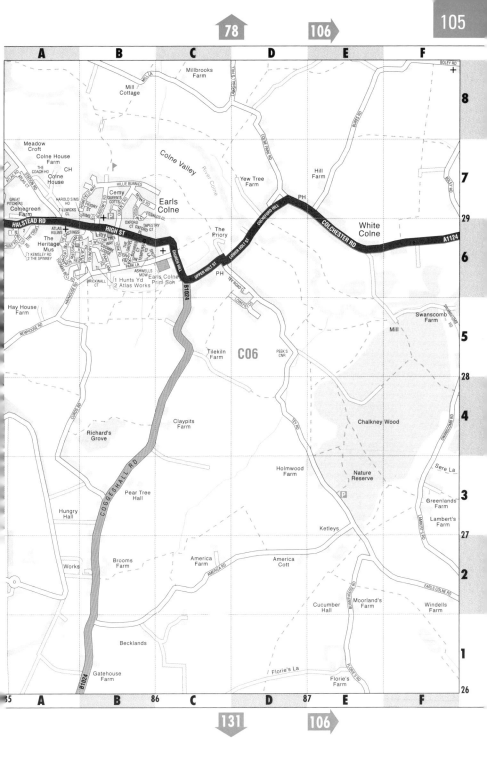

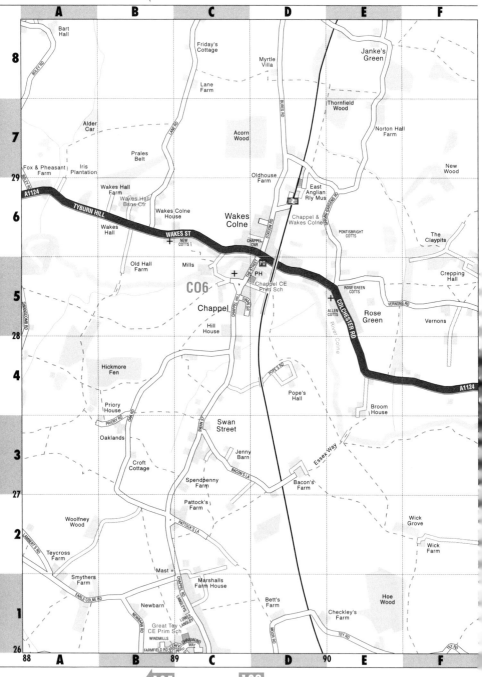

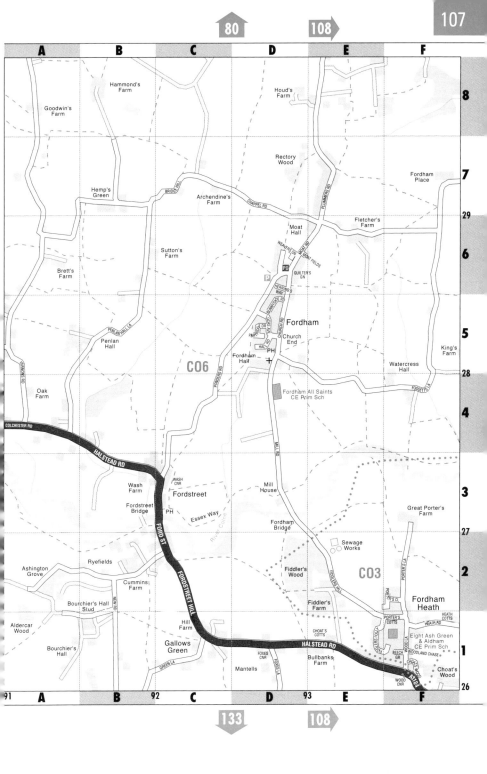

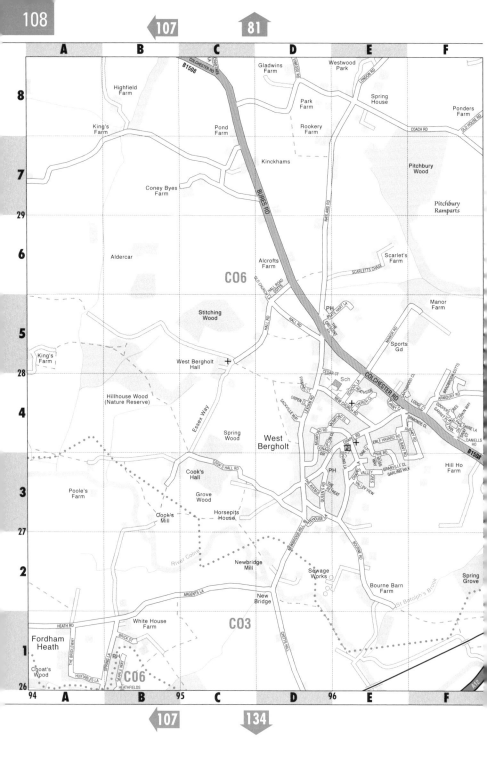

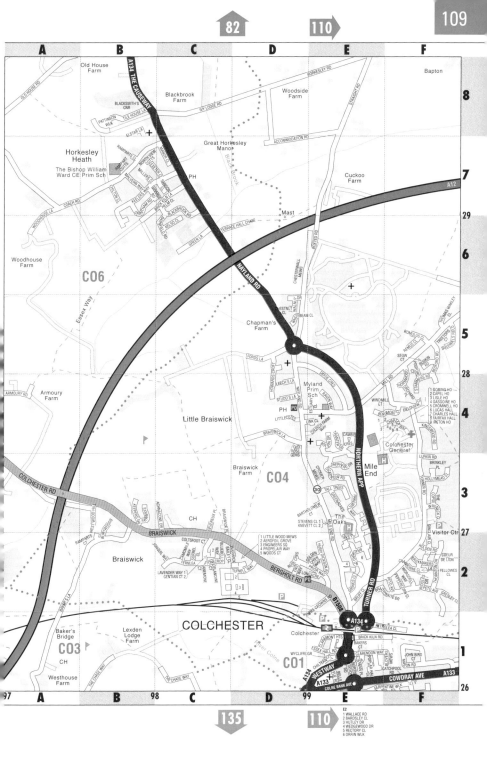

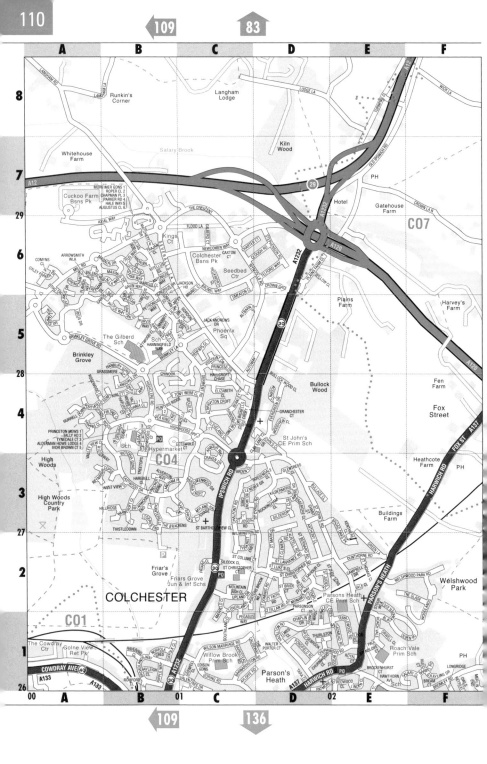

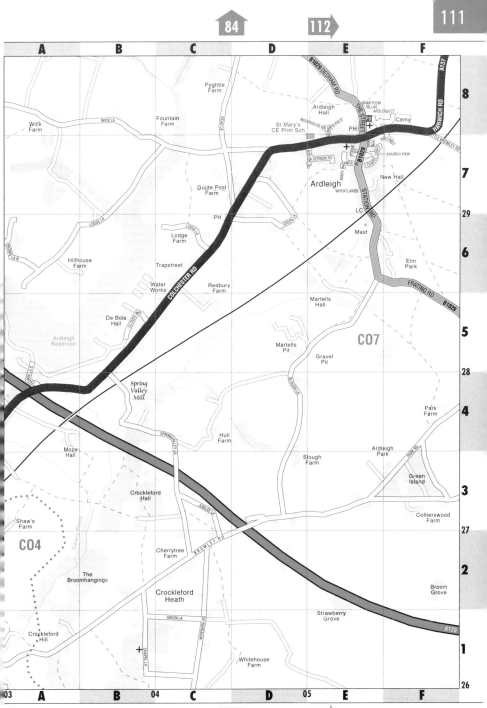

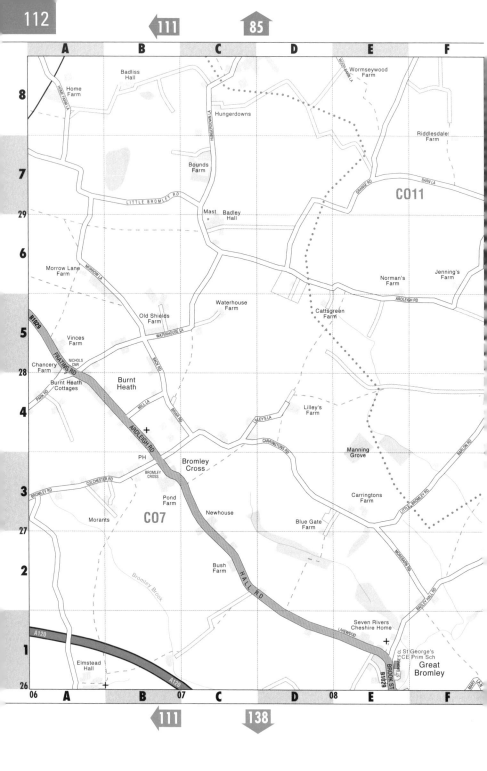

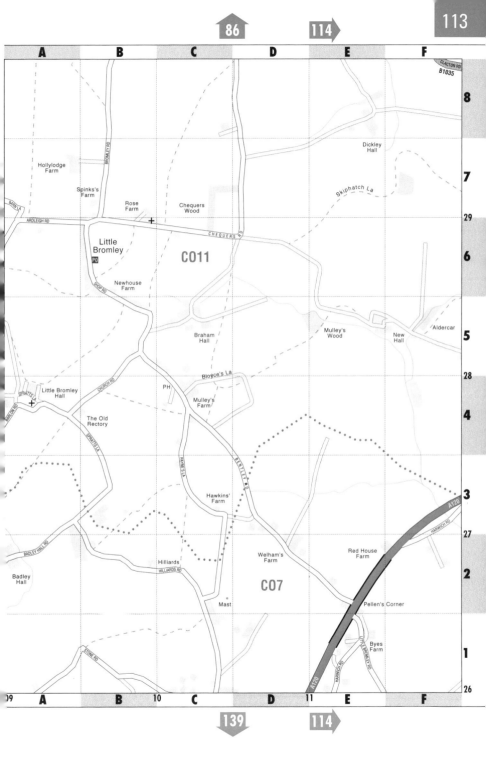

113
87

| A | B | C | D | E | F |

8

B1035

Old Mount

Steam Mill Corner

KING ST

DUNNING CL

Bradfield Heath

KING ST PH

PO

STEAM MILL RD

STRAIGHT RD

IMBRAYS RD

HEATH RD

Mast

Mayfield Cottages

7

Bradfield Hall

Dairy House

DARTHOUSE LA

WIX RD

29

CANSEY LA

6

Goldenferry

CLACTON RD

Horsleycross Street

PH

CO11

Wix Lodge

5

Rosemary Cottage

Bradfield Lodge

Lipstone

A120

28

Crossman's Farm

CANSEY LA

Burrow's Farm

4

Arch Cottages

COLCHESTER RD

Baker's Farm

Spring Farm

HOLLYBUSH LA

Wr Twr

Abbott's Hall

PH

Burnt Ash Farm

Goose Green

3

A120

HORSLEY CROSS

HARWICH RD

Hempstall's Farm

CO12

Kellys Farm

27

New House Farm

Greentrees Fruit Farm

STOKES GREEN RD

2

Knight's Farm

CO16

Brockett's Hall

Holland Brook

LITTLE BENTLEY RD

HEATH RD

PH

Tendring Heath

1

CO07

Chy

Old Hall Farm

B1035

PARSONAGE LA

WOLVES HALL LA

26

| 12 | A | B | 13 | C | D | 14 | E | F |

113
140

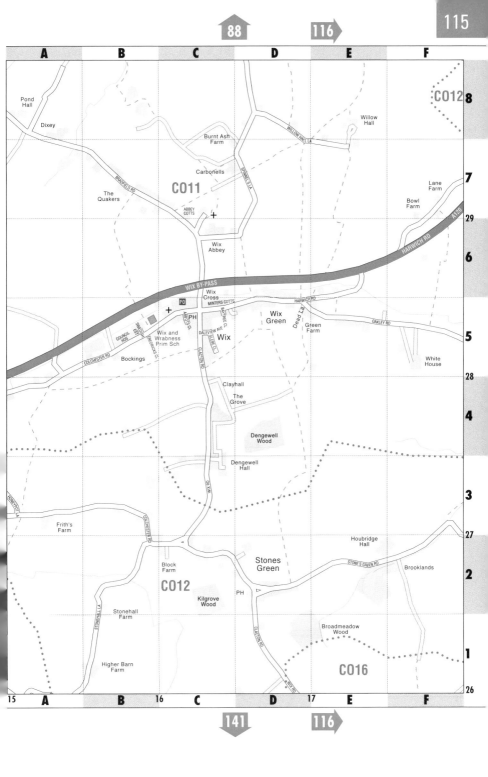

CO12

Pond Hall

Dixey

Burnt Ash Farm

Willow Hall

Carbonells

CO11

The Quakers

BRADFIELD RD

SPINKE'S LA

WILLOW HALL LA

Lane Farm

Bowl Farm

ABBEY COTTS

Wix Abbey

A120

HARWICH RD

WIX BY-PASS

Wix Cross

MINTERS COTTS

PO

PH

ABBOTS CL

BATCHEL CL

HARWICH RD

Wix Green

Dead La

Green Farm

OAKLEY RD

COUNCIL HOS

SWIFTS CNR

MEADOWS CL

DALEVIEW AVE

GLEBE CL

Wix

COLCHESTER RD

Wix and Wrabness Prim Sch

Bockings

White House

Clayhall

The Grove

Dengewell Wood

OLD RD WIX

Dengewell Hall

Frith's Farm

STANDLEY LA

Block Farm

COLCHESTER RD

CO12

Kilgrove Wood

PH

Stones Green

Houbridge Hall

27

STONE'S GREEN RD

Brooklands

Stonehall Farm

STONEHALL LA

Higher Barn Farm

CLACTON RD

Broadmeadow Wood

CO16

WIX RD

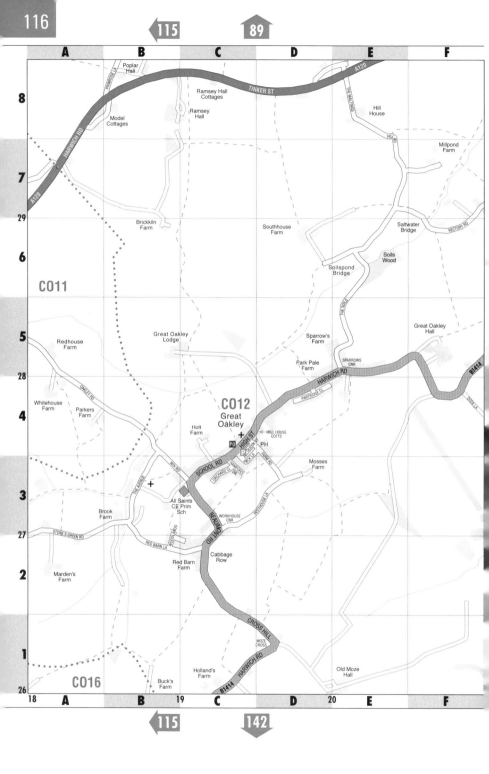

90

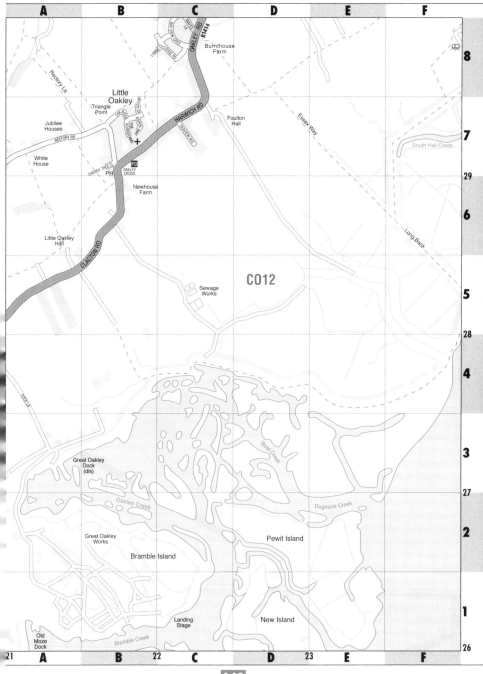

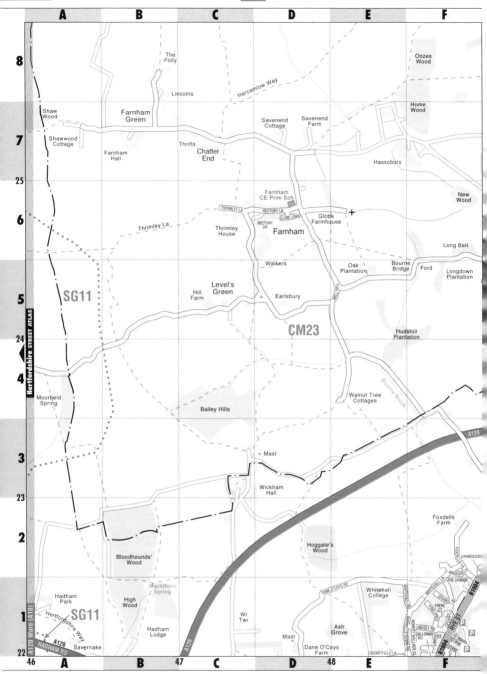

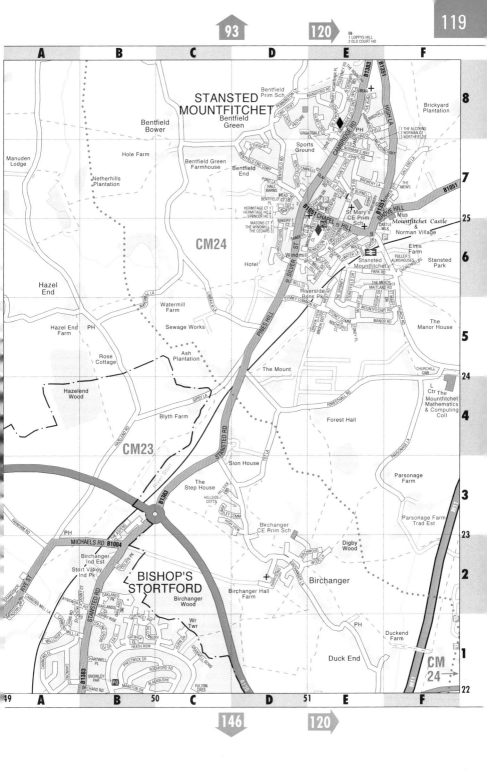

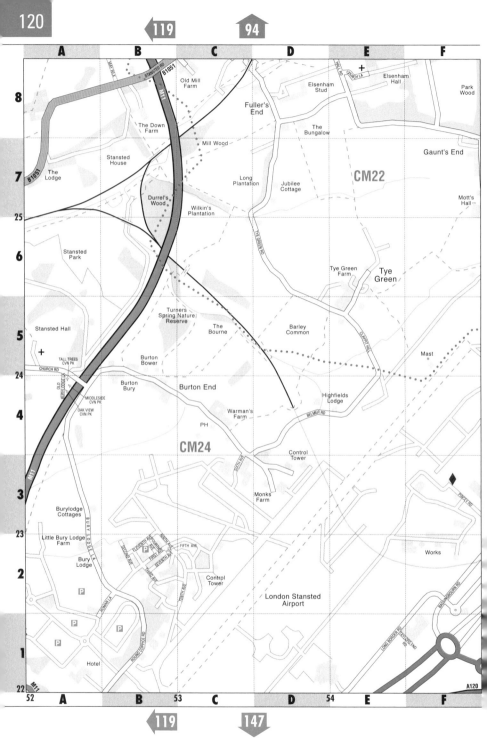

119
94

A   B   C   D   E   F

8

Old Mill
Farm

B1051
STANSTED RD
M11

Fuller's
End

Elsenham
Stud

CHURCH LA

Elsenham
Hall

Park
Wood

7

The Down
Farm

Mill Wood

The
Bungalow

Gaunt's End

The
Lodge
B1051

Stansted House

Long
Plantation

Jubilee
Cottage

CM22

25

Durrel's
Wood

Wilkin's
Plantation

Mott's
Hall

6

Stansted
Park

TYE GREEN RD

Tye Green
Farm

Tye
Green

5

Stansted Hall

Turners
Spring Nature
Reserve

The
Bourne

Barley
Common

CLAVERT HILL

Mast

24

CHURCH RD
TALL TREES
CVN PK

Burton
Bower

Burton
Bury

Burton End

Highfields
Lodge

OLD BURY LODGE LA

MIDDLESIDE
CVN PK

Warman's
Farm

BELMER RD

4

OAK VIEW
CVN PK

PH

CM24

Control
Tower

PINCEY RD

3

Burylodge
Cottages

Monks
Farm

BURY LODGE LA

23

Little Bury Lodge
Farm

ELEVENTH AVE
NINTH AVE
SEVENTH AVE
FIFTH AVE
FIRST AVE

Works

Bury
Lodge

SECOND AVE
SIXTH AVE
FOURTH AVE

LONG BORDER RD
TAYLOR'S END

2

P

THIRD AVE

Control
Tower

BASSINGBOURN RD

London Stansted
Airport

ROUNDCOPPICE RD
ROMAN LA

P

P

TENTH AVE

1

P

Hotel

22
M11

A120

52   A   B   53   C   D   54   E   F

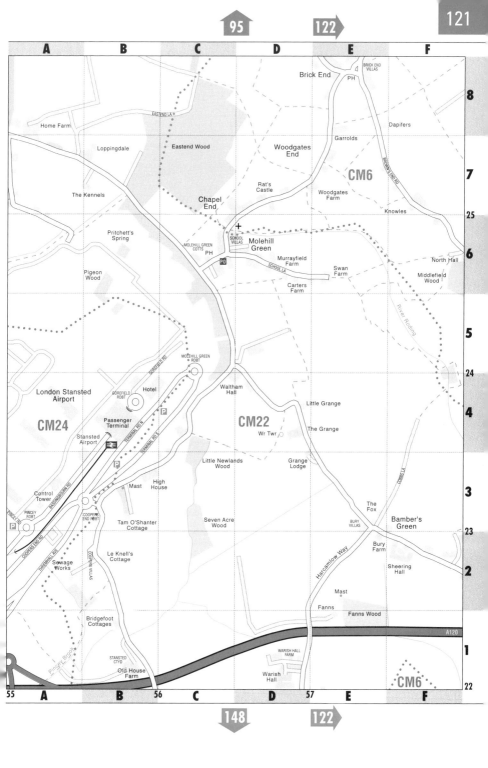

95
122

A B C D E F

8
Brick End
BRICK END VILLAS
PH
Home Farm
Dapifers
Loppingdale
Eastend Wood
Garrolds
Woodgates End
EASTEND LA
7
The Kennels
Chapel End
Rat's Castle
Woodgates Farm
CM6
Knowles
25
Pritchett's Spring
MOLEHILL GREEN COTTS
PH
SCHOOL VILLAS
Molehill Green
Murrayfield Farm
North Hall
6
Pigeon Wood
PO
SCHOOL LA
Swan Farm
Middlefield Wood
Carters Farm
River Roding
5
MOLEHILL GREEN RDBT
24
London Stansted Airport
ROGEFIELD RD
Hotel
Waltham Hall
BOREFIELD RDBT
Little Grange
CM24
TERMINAL RD N
Passenger Terminal
CM22
The Grange
4
CM24
Stansted Airport
TERMINAL RD S
Wr Twr
23
Control Tower
BASINGBOURNE RD
Little Newlands Wood
Grange Lodge
The Fox
3
PINCEY RDBT
COOPERS END RDBT
Mast
High House
Seven Acre Wood
BURY VILLAS
Bamber's Green
23
P
COOPERS END RD
COOPERS VILLAS
Tam O'Shanter Cottage
Bury Farm
THERMAL AVE
Sewage Works
Le Knell's Cottage
HATCAMLOW WAY
Sheering Hall
2
Bridgefoot Cottages
Mast
Fanns
Fanns Wood
A120
1
PINCEY BROOK
STANSTED CTYD
Old House Farm
WARISH HALL FARM
Warish Hall
CM6
22

55 A B 56 C D 57 E F

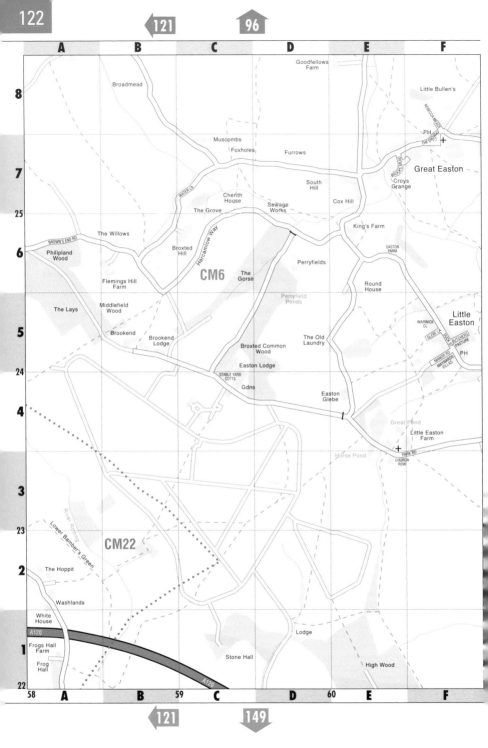

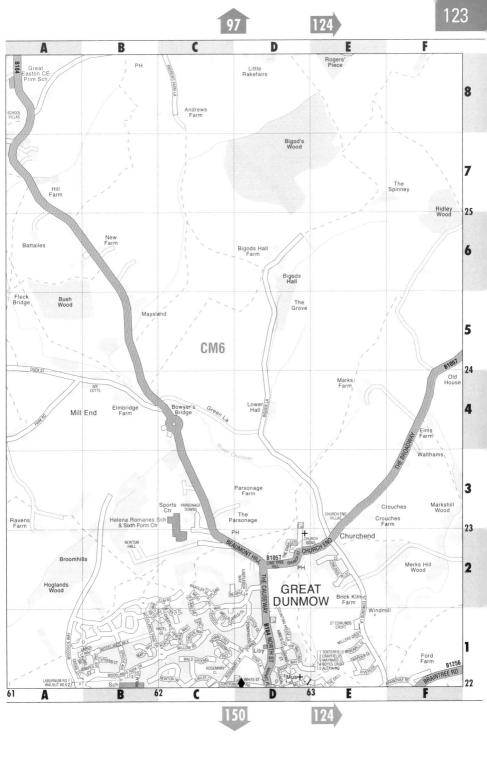

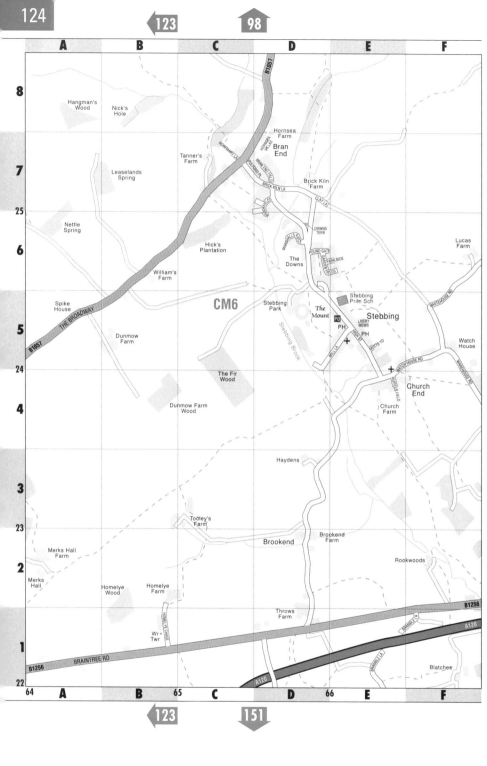

A B C D E F

8

Hangman's Wood
Nick's Hole

Hornsea Farm

Bran End

ROSEMARY LA

7

Tanner's Farm

Leaselands Spring

BRAN END TER

PUFORD ST

BRICK KILN LA

Brick Kiln Farm

CLAY LA

B1057

25

Nettle Spring

BACK LA

DOWNS TERR

MARSHALLS FIELD

Lucas Farm

6

Hick's Plantation

William's Farm

POUND GATE

The Downs

PARK SIDE
CURER FIELDS

Stebbing Prim Sch

WHITEHOUSE RD

Spike House

CM6

Stebbing Park

The Mount

PO
PH

LIVERY MEWS

Stebbing

PH

Watch House

THE BROADWAY

Dunmow Farm

Stebbing Brook

MILL LA

HIGH ST

POTTS YD

5

B1057

24

The Fir Wood

Church End

WATCH HOUSE RD

WARDHOUSE RD

Dunmow Farm Wood

RUFFELS FIELD

Church Farm

4

Haydens

3

Tooley's Farm

23

Merks Hall Farm

Brookend

Brookend Farm

Rookwoods

2

Merks Hall

Homelye Wood

Homelye Farm

HOMELYE LANE

Throws Farm

B1256

BRAMBLE LANE

A120

1

Wr Twr

BRAMBLE LA

Blatches

B1256

BRAINTREE RD

A120

22

64 A B 65 C D 66 E F

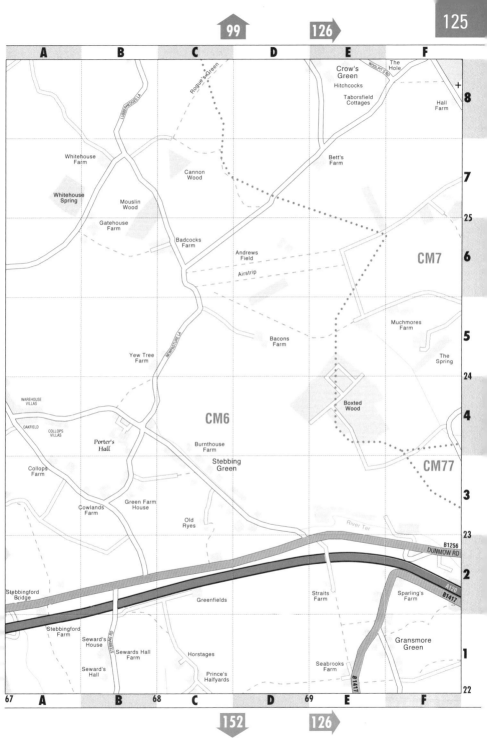

99
126

| A | B | C | D | E | F |

8

The Hole

Crow's Green

Hitchcocks

WOOLPIT'S RD

Taborsfield Cottages

Hall Farm

Whitehouse Farm

Bett's Farm

7

Cannon Wood

LUBBERHEDGES LA

Whitehouse Spring

Mouslin Wood

Gatehouse Farm

25

Badcocks Farm

Andrews Field

CM7

6

Airstrip

Yew Tree Farm

NEWPASTURE LA

Bacons Farm

Muchmores Farm

5

The Spring

24

WAREHOUSE VILLAS

Boxted Wood

4

OAKFIELD

COLLOPS VILLAS

CM6

Porter's Hall

Burnthouse Farm

Stebbing Green

CM77

Collops Farm

3

Cowlands Farm

Green Farm House

Old Ryes

River Ter

23

B1256
DUNMOW RD

Stebbingford Bridge

A120

2

Straits Farm

Sparling's Farm

B1417

Stebbingford Farm

Greenfields

Seward's House

STEBBING RD

Sewards Hall Farm

Horstages

Gransmore Green

1

Seward's Hall

Seabrooks Farm

B1417

Prince's Halfyards

22

67

| A | B | C | D | E | F |

68

69

152
126

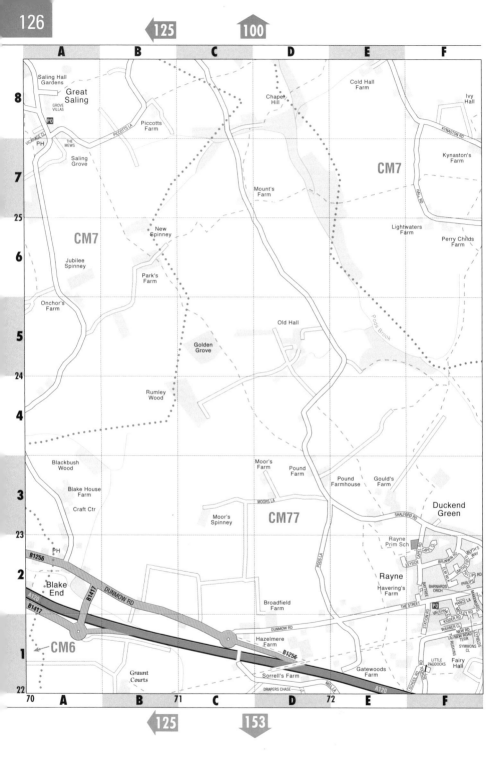

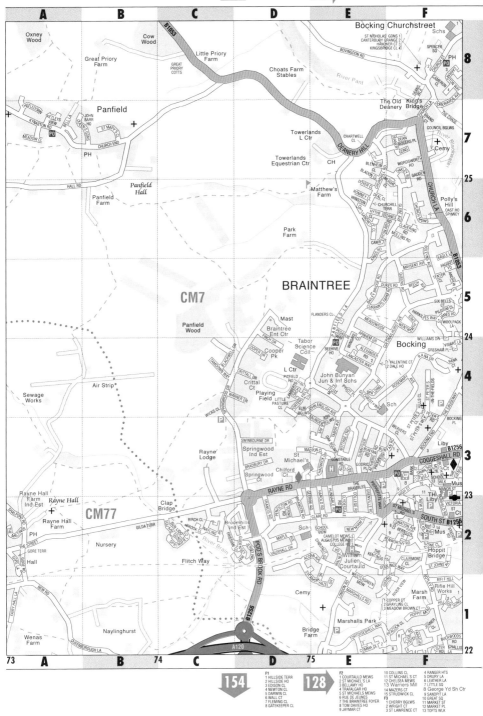

101
128

Bocking Churchstreet

BRAINTREE

Bocking

CM7

CM77

154
128

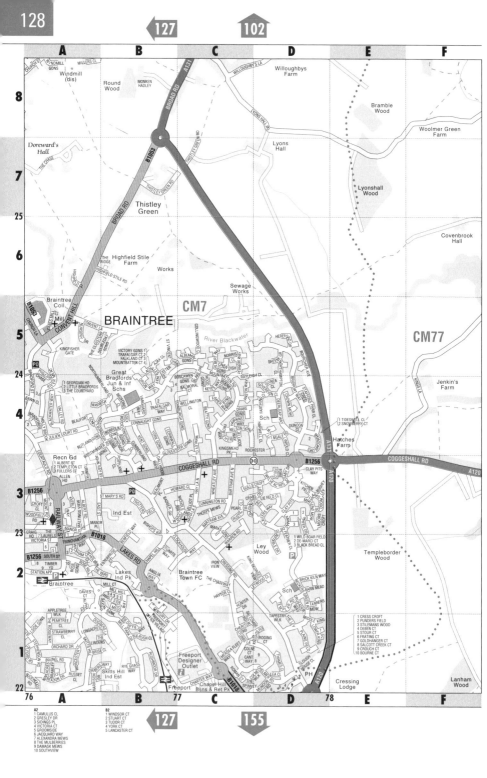

Windmill (dis)

Round Wood

MONKEN HADLEY

WILLOUGHBYS LA

Willoughbys Farm

BROAD RD

A131

B1053

Doreward's Hall

THE CHASE

Lyons Hall

Bramble Wood

Woolmer Green Farm

Lyonshall Wood

Covenbrook Hall

THISTLEY GREEN RD

Thistley Green

THE RIDGE

Highfield Stile Farm

HIGHFIELD STILE RD

Works

Sewage Works

CM7

Braintree Coll.

Mill

CONVENT HILL

BRAINTREE

River Blackwater

CM77

Jenkin's Farm

Kingfisher Gate

Recn Gd

1 ALBERT ST
2 TEMPLETON CT
3 FULLERS CT

ALLEN HO

B1256

CROFT RD

WOODFIELD RD

CRAIG HO

THE LAURELS

VICTORIA ST

B1256   SOUTH ST

TIMBER YD

STATION APP

Braintree

RAILWAY ST

LAKES RD

B1018

Ind Est

MANOR HO

MANOR RD

Lakes Ind Pk

ANGLIA WAY

Braintree Town FC

IRON VIEW

THE CHASEWAY

HAYTOR CT

Ley Wood

COGGESHALL RD

30

B1256

A120

COGGESHALL RD

A120

CLAY PITS WAY

1 WILD BOAR FIELD
2 DE-MARCI CT
3 BLACK BREAD CL

Templeborder Wood

Hatches Farm

1 TIDESWELL CL
2 SNOWBERRY CT

Sch

A120

Sch

BRICK KILN WAY

BARN MEAD

TAYNERS MDW

1 CRESS CROFT
2 PUNDERS FIELD
3 STILEMANS WOOD
4 DEBEN CT
5 STOUR CT
6 FRATING CT
7 GOLDHANGER CT
8 SALCOTT CREEK CT
9 CROUCH CT
10 BOURNE CT

APPLETREE WLK

PEARTREE CL

STRAWBERRY CL

ORCHARD DR

BRUNEL RD

RUSSET CT

THE LINDENS

BRISK WAY

RYE GRASS WAY

Freeport Designer Outlet

Skitts Hill Ind Est

CHARTER WAY

Freeport

Chapel Hill Bsns & Ret Pk

B1018

THE SPINNEY

COLNE CT

CANT WAY

A1201

PH

Cressing Lodge

Lanham Wood

A2
1 CAMULUS CL
2 GRESLEY DR
3 SIDINGS PL
4 VICTORIA CT
5 GROOMSIDE
6 JACQUARD WAY
7 ALEXANDRA MEWS
8 THE MULBERRIES
9 DAMASK MEWS
10 SOUTHVIEW

B2
1 WINDSOR CT
2 STUART CT
3 TUDOR CT
4 YORK CT
5 LANCASTER CT

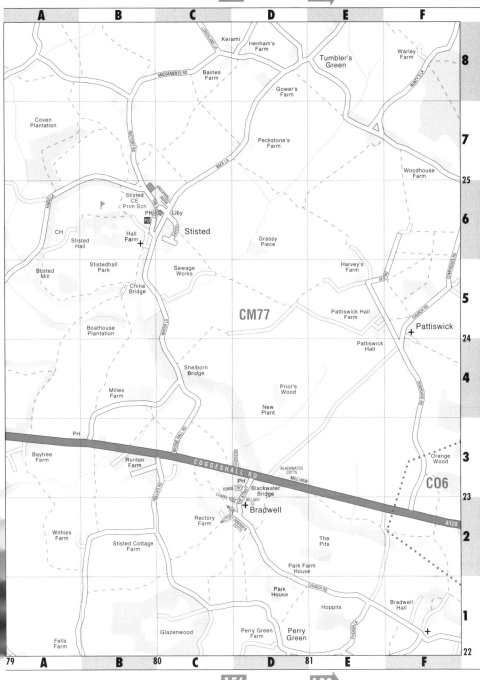

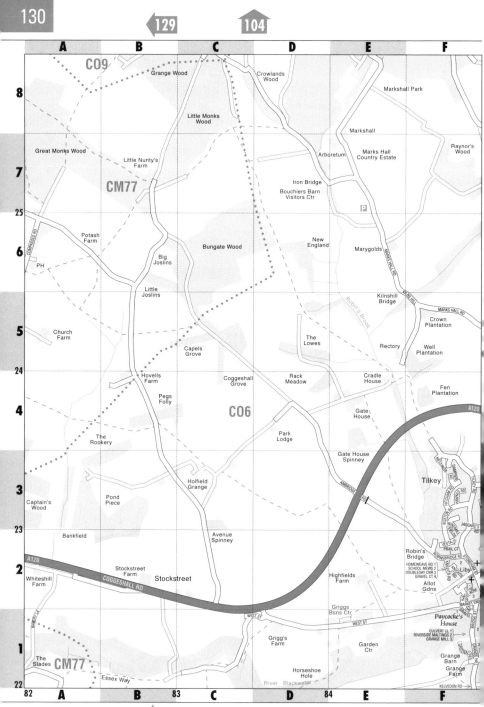

CO9

Grange Wood

Crowlands Wood

Markshall Park

Little Monks Wood

Markshall

Great Monks Wood

Little Nunty's Farm

Arboretum

Marks Hall Country Estate

Raynor's Wood

CM77

Iron Bridge

Bouchiers Barn Visitors Ctr

Potash Farm

New England

Marygolds

Bungate Wood

Big Joslins

Kilnshill Bridge

Little Joslins

MARKS HALL RD

Church Farm

The Lowes

Crown Plantation

PH

Capels Grove

Rectory

Well Plantation

Hovells Farm

Coggeshall Grove

Rack Meadow

Cradle House

Fen Plantation

Pegs Folly

CO6

Gate House

A120

The Rookery

Park Lodge

Gate House Spinney

Captain's Wood

Pond Piece

Holfield Grange

Tilkey

AMBRIDGE RD

Bankfield

Avenue Spinney

Robin's Bridge

Liby

Whiteshill Farm

A120

COGGESHALL RD

Stockstreet Farm

Stockstreet

Highfields Farm

Allot Gdns

Paycocke's House

WEST ST

Griggs Bsns Ctr

WEST ST

The Slades

CM77

Grigg's Farm

Garden Ctr

Grange Barn

Grange Farm

Essex Way

Horseshoe Hole

River Blackwater

KELVEDON RD

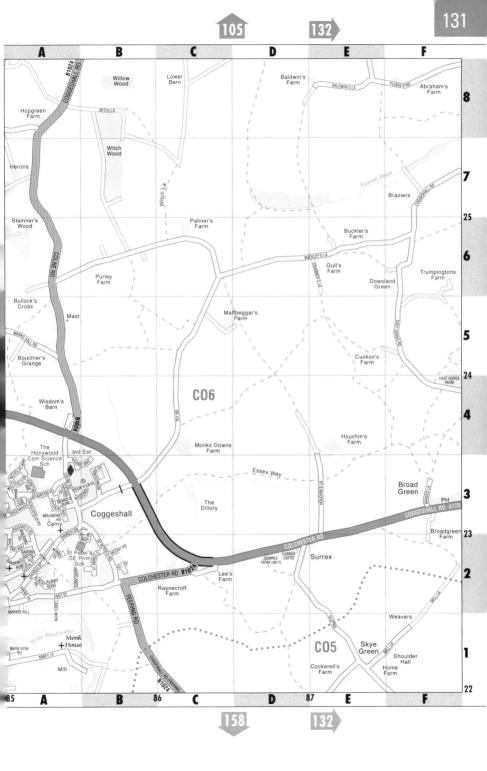

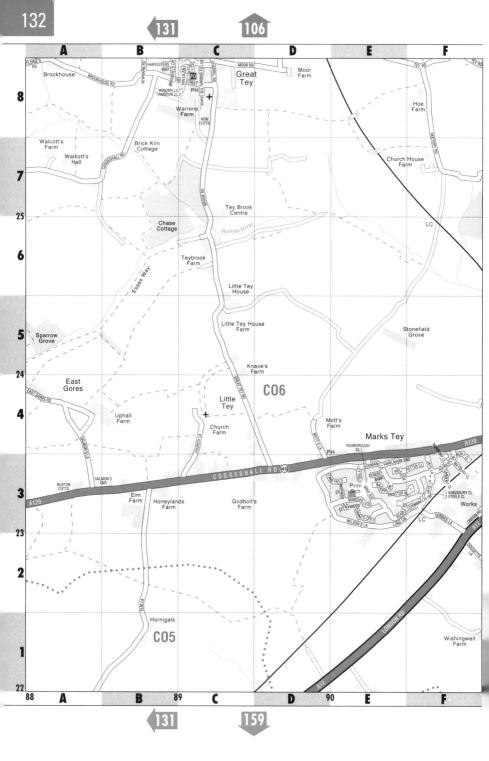

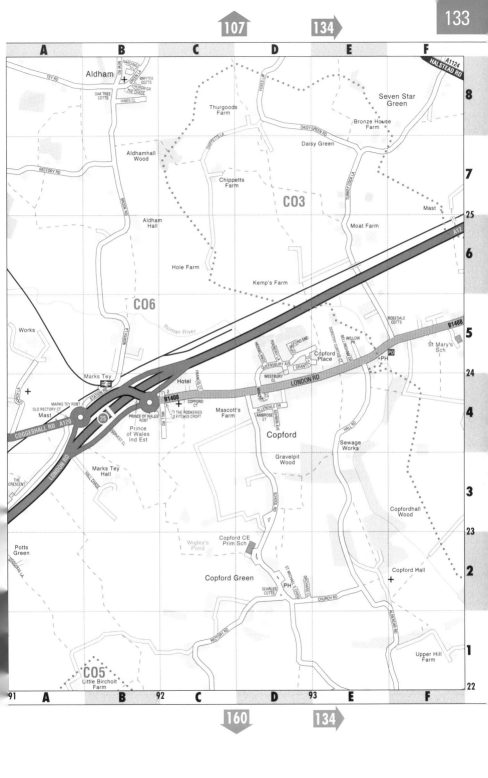

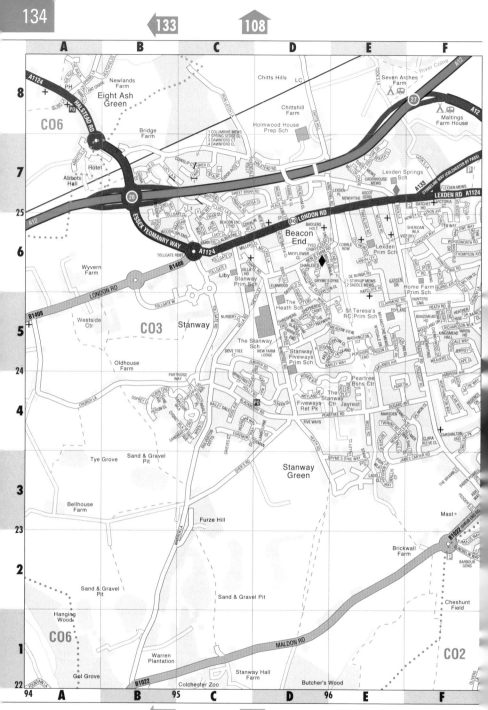

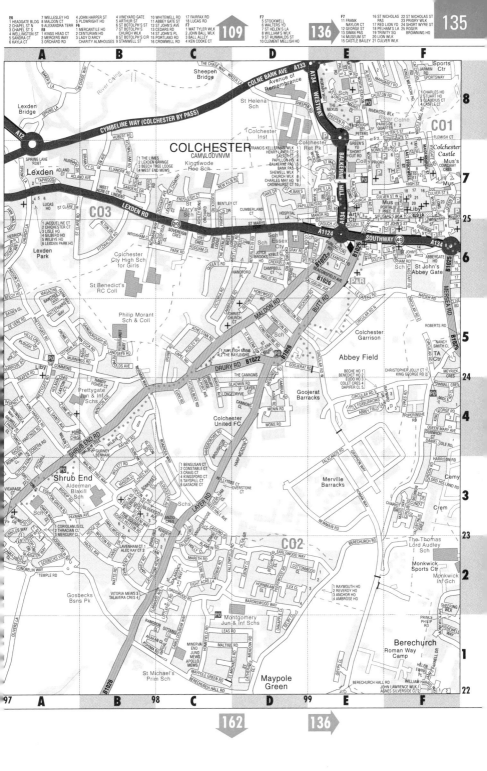

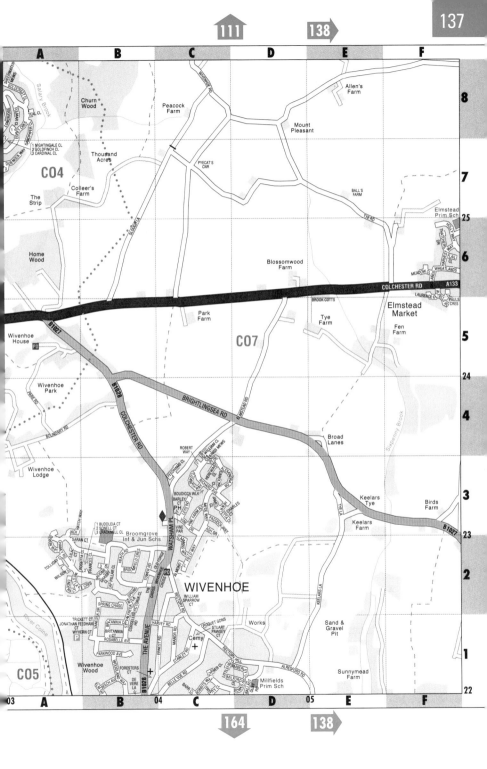

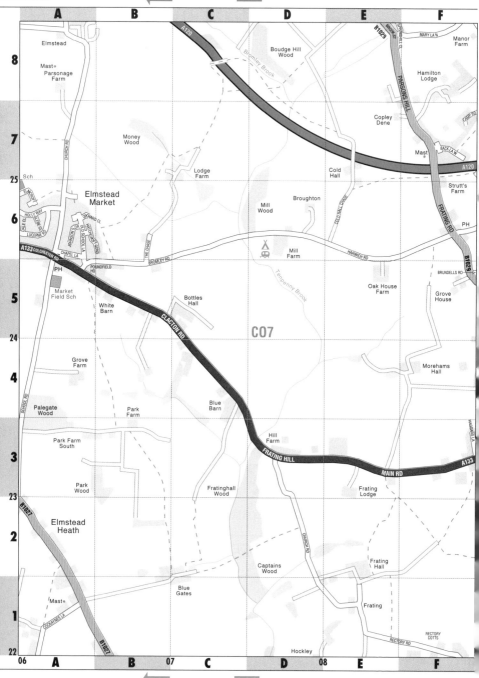

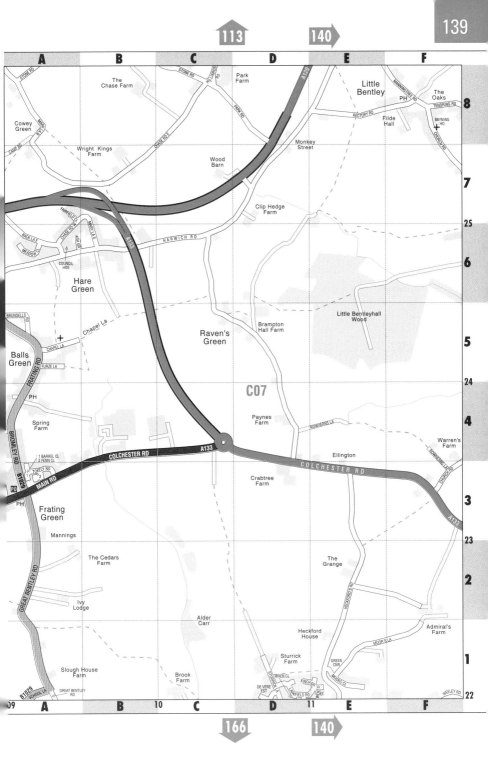

A | B | C | D | E | F

8

Pump Fram
Malting Farm
Brook Cottages
TENDRING RD
PARSONAGE LA
B1035
Wolves Hall Farm
Tendring Green
CHAPEL LA
Glebe Farm
HEATH RD
Mill Green
PILCOX HALL LA
Grange Farm
Pilcox Wood

7
Redhouse Farm
Woodfield Farm
Pond Farm
Goose Green
Pilcox Hall
Church Farm
LODGE LA

25
PO
Tendring Prim Sch

6
Little Bentley Hall
SCHOOL RD

CO16
Tendring
The Grange

5
CO7
Holland Brook
The Hall
THE STREET
THORPE RD
B1035
Brookmead Cottages
PO
HOLLYVIEW CL

24
Hill Farm
New Hall
New Hall Farm
The Mill

4
Gurnhams
CRUMP LA
Home Wood
Hillands Wood

3
Brett's Hall
Shair Wood
Hawk Farm
Pestles Hall

23
A133
High Barn
Chiltern Farm
CRUMP LA

2
Fisher's Farm
COLCHESTER RD
SHAIR LA
Elizabeth Cottage
Crem
PH
KATE DANIELS HO
THORPE RD
B1033

1
The Woodlands
A133
B1033
Saxon Lodge
PH
Service Area
WHITE LANES RD
WOODLANDS RD
HILLTOP RD
COLCHESTER RD
B1441 WEELEY BY-PASS RD
Mast
1 THORNBERRY AVE
2 ALEXANDRA RD
FIRST AVE
ST ANDREWS RD
SECOND

22
SWALLOW'S ROW
Green Lane Farm
A133
Weeley

12 | A | B | 13 | C | D | 14 | E | F

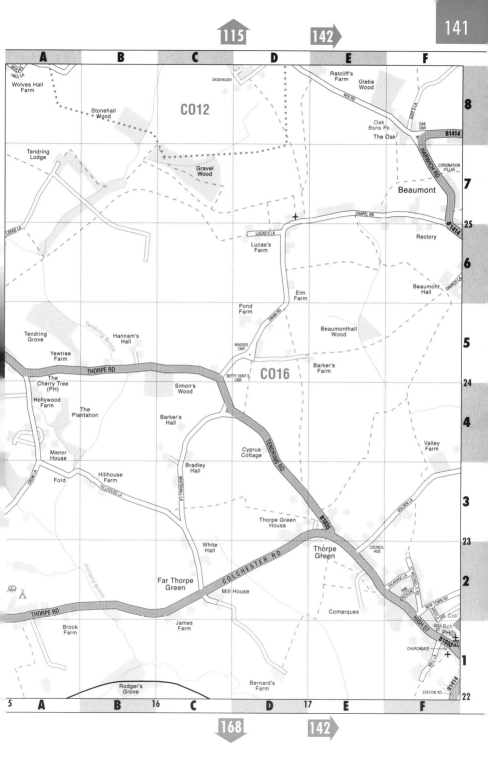

141
116

| | A | B | C | D | E | F |

8

Oldhouse Farm

Glebe Farm

Potland

B1414

HARWICH RD

B1414

The Horseshoes

New Moze Hall

CO12

Maze Creek

7

25

B1414

HARWICH RD

Northfield Farm

CHURCH LA

6

THORPE RD

LOWER BARN FARM

Landermere Creek

5

Quay Farm

Quay (dis)

Beaumont Cut

QUAY LA

24

Beaumont Bridge

Beaumont Quay

CO16

White House

GULL COTTS

4

GOLDEN LA

Landermere Hall

Landermere

3

Thorpe Lodge

New Hall

Kentshill Farm

WALTON RD

23

CO13

LANDERMERE RD

2

NEW TOWN RD

PALMERS RD

SPENCER RD

LONGDALE RD

ARGYLL RD

WENDWORTH RD

FITZROLPH CL

THE STREET

BELGAMS CL

Dale Hill Farm

DAMANT'S FARM LA

Damont's Farm

Coll

ABBEY

B1414

Thorpe-le-Soken

OAK CL

ELM FARM CVN PK

BYNG HO

BYNG CL

Folly Farm

WYRE LODGE

Sneating Hall

SNEATING HALL LA

B1034

1

ABBEY ST

B1033

FRINTON RD

B1033

B1034

B1034

22

| **18** | A | | B | **19** | C | | D | **20** | E | | F |

141
169

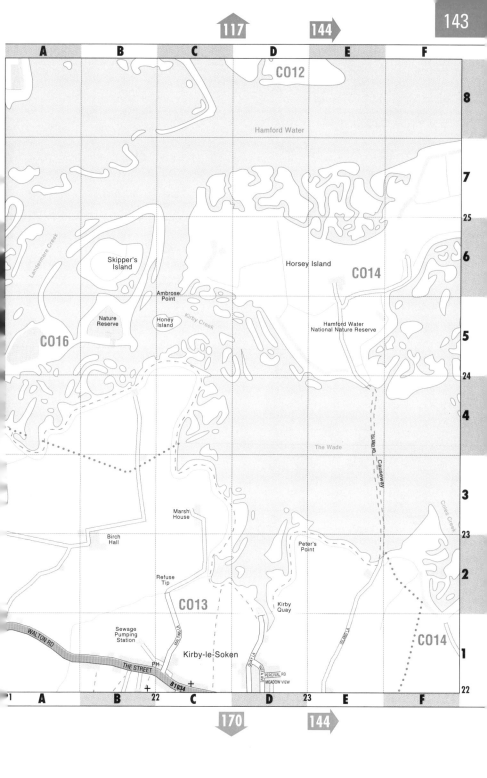

143

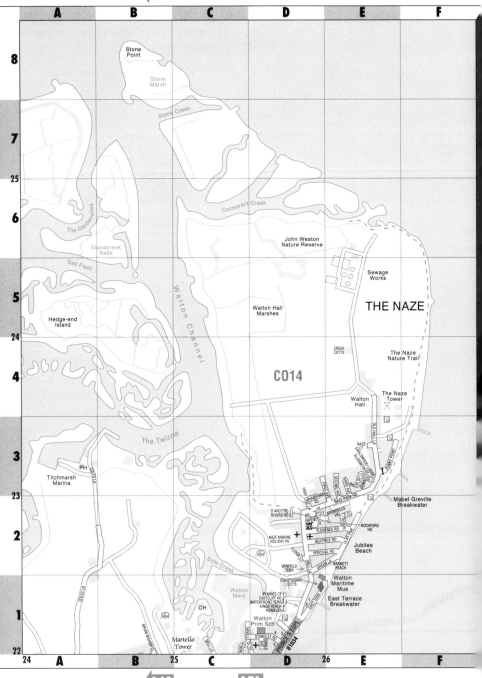

8 Stone Point

Stone Marsh

Stone Creek

7

25

Cormorant Creek

The Dardenelles

6

Standcreek Salts

John Weston Nature Reserve

Salt Fleet

Sewage Works

5 Walton Channel

Walton Hall Marshes

THE NAZE

Hedge-end Island

24

CREEK COTTS

The Naze Nature Trail

4 CO14

The Naze Tower

Walton Hall

OLD HALL LA

The Naze Tower P

3 The Twizzle

NAZE CT
EARLSWOOD LODGE
ELIZABETH LODGE
THIRD AVE

SUNNY POINT

PH

ODESEA

Titchmarsh Marina

HIGHFIELD AVE
FIRST AVE
SECOND AVE
NAZE PARK RD

P

Mabel Greville Breakwater

23

D'ARCY RD
RIVERS HO

SPENDELLS
HO

SPENCE
DE

ROCHFORD HO

2

NAZE MARINE HOLIDAY PK.

FLORENCE RD
BEATRICE RD
PERCIVAL RD

Jubilee Beach

CLIFF PAR

Sole Creek

WINFIELD TERR

FLOOR LA
GREEN LA

BARNETT REACH

1 Walton Mere

COASTGUARD COTTS

PENRICE CT
EASTCLIFF HO
WATERFRONT TERR
KINGS REACH
HOMELEAS

Walton Maritime Mus

East Terrace Breakwater

CH

STANDLEY RD

Walton Prim Sch

P

22 Martello Tower

GILES LA

BRIAN BISHOP CL

NEWGATE ST LA

PRINCE S ESPL

B1034

24 **A** **B** **25** **C** **D** **26** **E** **F**

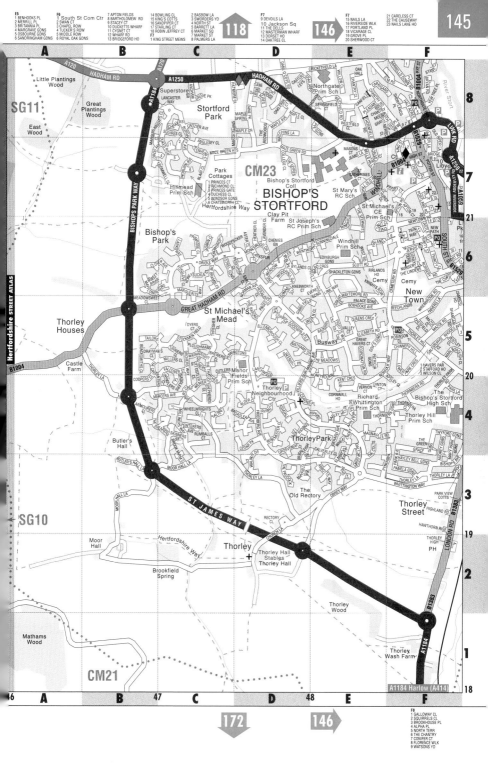

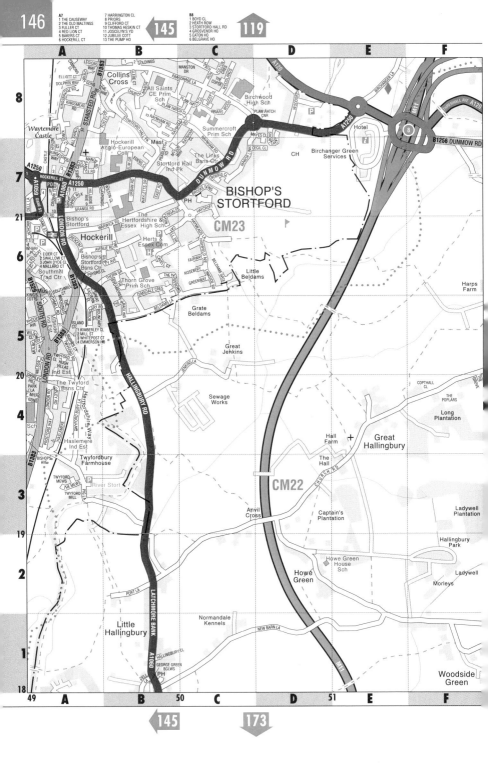

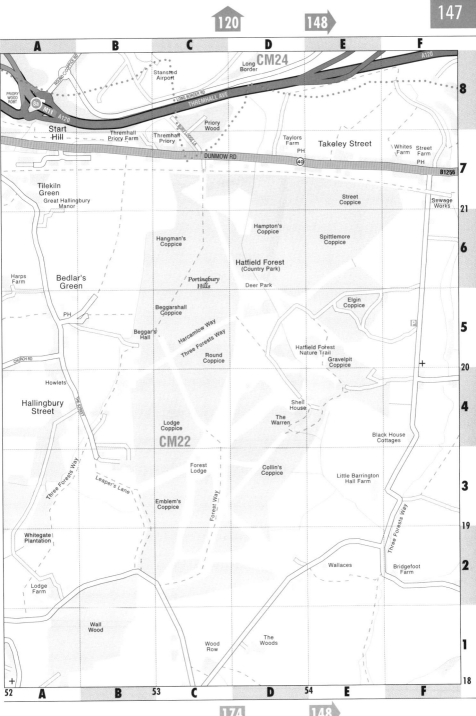

120
148

A B C D E F

CM24

Long Border

A120

Stansted Airport

ROUND COPPICE RD

8

PRIORY WOOD RDBT

8a

MT1 A120

Long Border Rd

THREMHALL AVE

Priory Wood

Start Hill

Thremhall Priory Farm

Thremhall Priory

BURY LODGE LA

DUNMOW RD

49

Taylors Farm PH

Takeley Street

Whites Farm

Street Farm PH

7

B1256

Tilekiln Green

Great Hallingbury Manor

Street Coppice

Sewage Works

21

Hampton's Coppice

Hangman's Coppice

Spittlemore Coppice

6

Harps Farm

Bedlar's Green

Portingbury Hills

Hatfield Forest (Country Park)

Deer Park

Beggarshall Coppice

PH

Beggar's Hall

CHURCH RD

Harcamlow Way

Three Forests Way

Round Coppice

Elgin Coppice

P

5

Hatfield Forest Nature Trail

Gravelpit Coppice

20

Howlets

Hallingbury Street

THE STREET

Shell House

The Warren

Black House Cottages

4

Lodge Coppice

CM22

Forest Lodge

Collin's Coppice

Little Barrington Hall Farm

3

Three Forests Way

Leaper's Lane

Emblem's Coppice

Forest Way

19

Whitegate Plantation

Wallaces

Bridgefoot Farm

2

Three Forests Way

Lodge Farm

Wall Wood

Wood Row

The Woods

1

18

52 A B 53 C D 54 E F

174
148

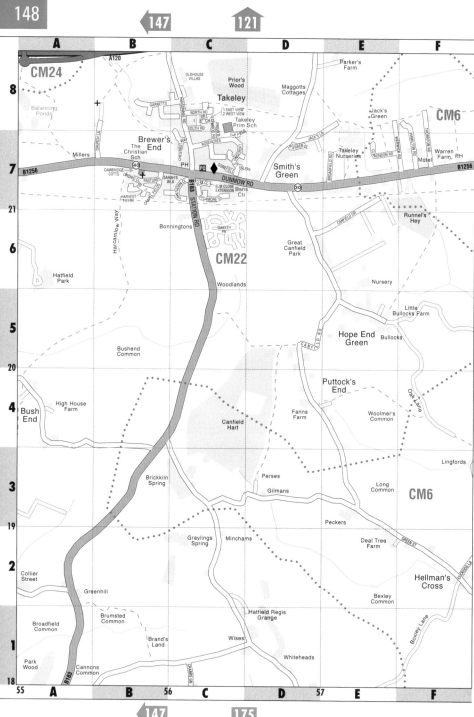

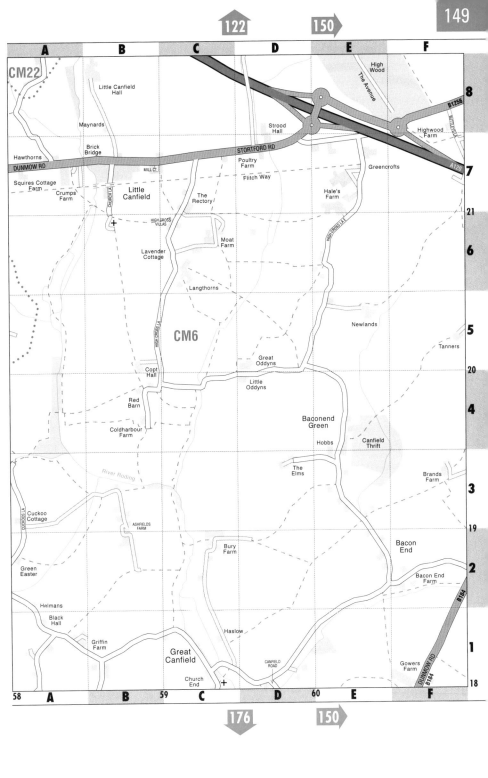

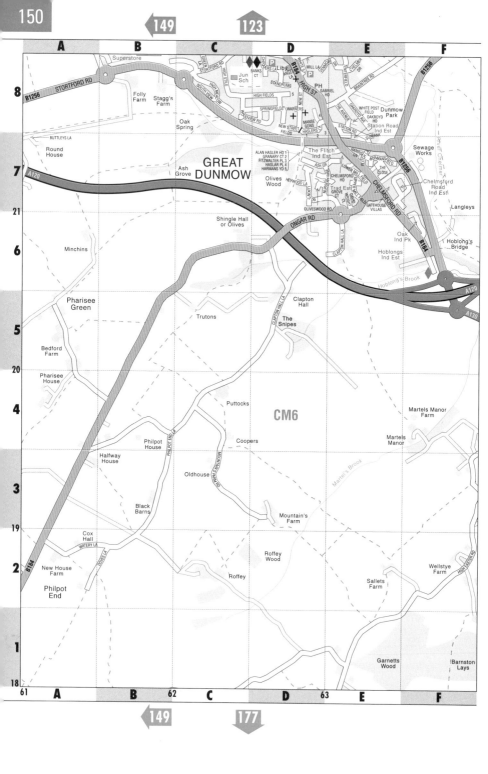

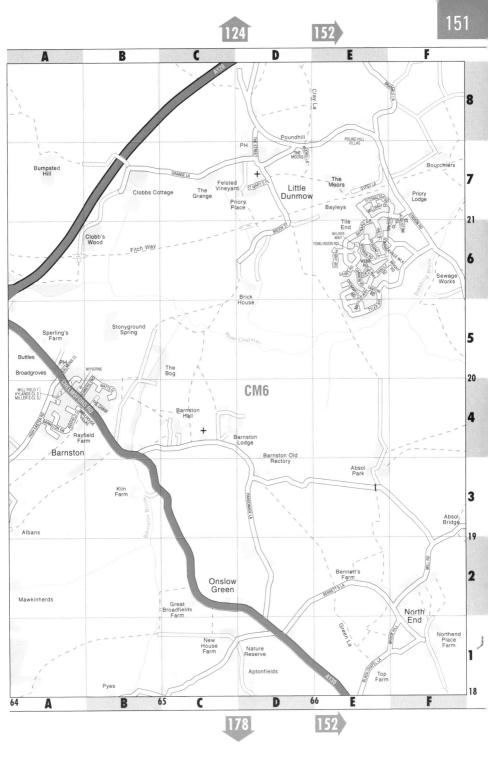

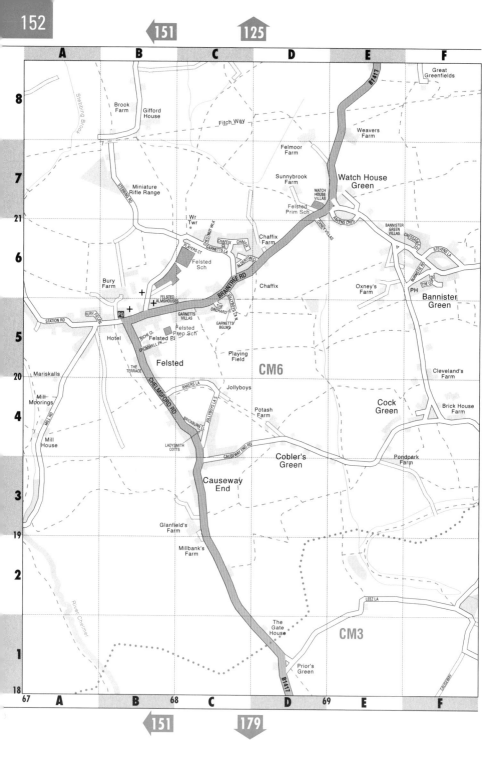

151
125

A B C D E F

8

Stebbing Brook

Brook Farm

Gifford House

Fitch Way

Great Greenfields

7

Miniature Rifle Range

Felmoor Farm

Sunnybrook Farm

Weavers Farm

Watch House Green

21

Wr Twr

CHESTNUT WLK

CHAFFIX

CHAG

Chaffix Farm

WATCH HOUSE VILLAS

Felsted Prim Sch

RAVENS CRES

JOBYS VILLAS

BANNISTER GREEN VILLAS

CRESSING RD

STEVENS LA

6

PLAYERS CT

GARNETTS LA

Felsted Sch

ALDINGTON CL

BRAINTREE RD

Chaffix

Oxney's Farm

BARNFIELD RD

THE OR

PH

Bannister Green

Bury Farm

FELSTED ALMSHOUSES

GARNETTS VILLAS

THE ORCHARD

SCHOOLHOUSE LA

5

STATION RD

BURY LODGE

PO

BIRCH CL

CROMWELL PK

Felsted Pl

Felsted Prep Sch

GARNETTS BGLWS

Playing Field

CM6

Cleveland's Farm

Hotel

Felsted

THE TERRACE

20

Mariskalls

CHELMSFORD RD

BAKERS LA

Jollyboys

Cock Green

Brick House Farm

4

Mill Moorings

MILL RD

BROOKBURN CL

ALDINGTON LA

Potash Farm

Cobler's Green

Pondpark Farm

Mill House

LADYSMITH COTTS

CAUSEWAY END RD

3

Glanfield's Farm

Causeway End

19

Millbank's Farm

CM3

2

River Chelmer

LEEZ LA

1

The Gate House

Prior's Green

18

B1417

CAUSEWAY

67 A B 68 C D 69 E F

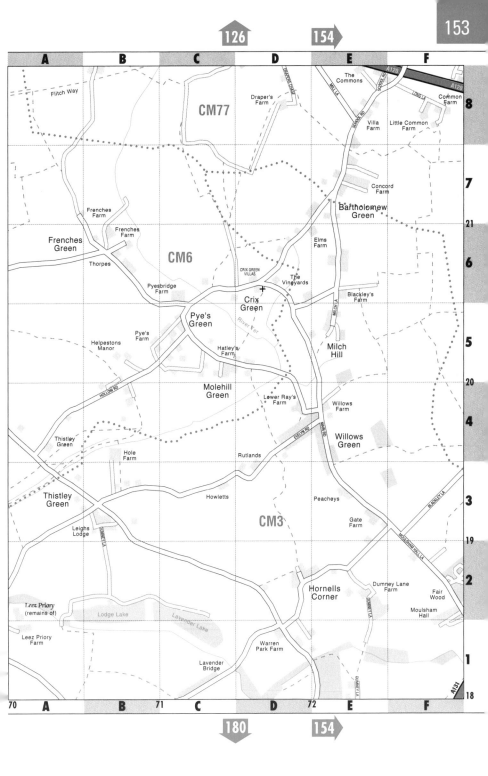

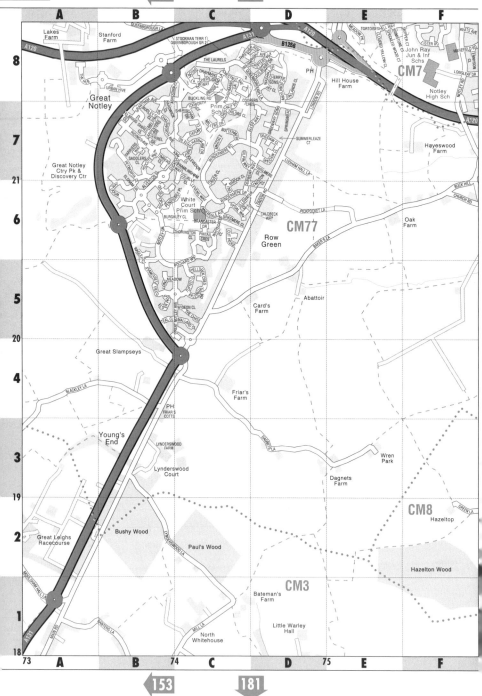

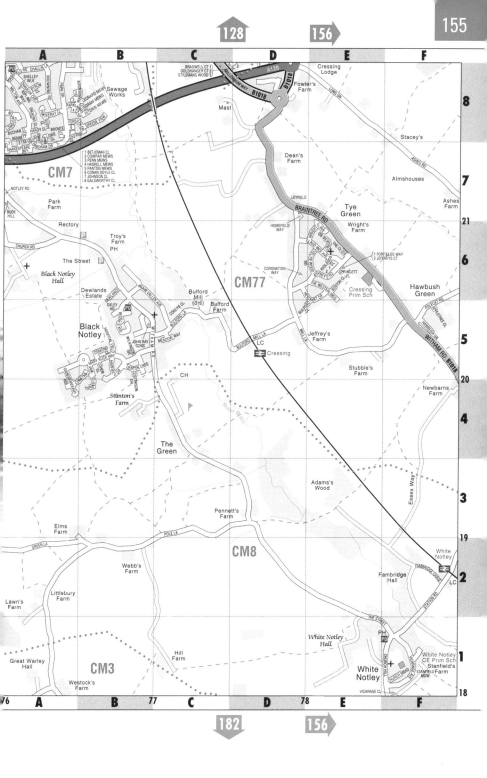

155
129

	A	B	C	D	E	F

8

Lanham Manor Farm

Sand & Gravel Pit

LANHAM FARM RD

Wr Twr

Lanham Green

Jubilee Plantation

LINK RD

Clapdog Green

Gosling's Farm

7

Ashes Farm

PH

LANHAM GREEN RD

ASHES RD

Link's Farm

Link's Wood

Schills Farm

Essex Way

21

Wright's Farm

THE STREET

6 Cressing

POLECAT RD

Egypts Farm

BORES YRD RD

Rolphs Farmhouse

ROLPHS COTTS

Mast

Airfield (disused)

Sheepcotes Farm

Shardloes Bsns Pk

CHURCH RD

5 CM77

COMFIELD

THE GOSLINGS

WEAVERSFIELD

FRANCIS CT

RUNNACLES ST

BROADWAY

BRAINTREE RD

SHEEPCOTES LA

20

COUNCIL HOUSES

MANOR WAY

FRANCIS WAY

SILVER ST

+

Silver End

4

B1018

PETTIT LA

New House

MANOR WAY

Liby
PO
THE SHOPS
Hotel

Works

JOSEPH GDNS

Bower Hall

WESTERN RD

3

STATION RD

Sheepcote Wood

WITHAM RD

TEMPLE LA

MAGDALEN CRES

VALENTINE WAY

LISTER RD

STRETFORD CT

BRISTOL CT

SCHOOL RD

Silver End Prim Sch

PH

WESTERN RD

CM8

Park House

19

Rivenhall Place

2

Cressing Temple

Cressing Temple Barns

Old Court Room

P

Essex Way

1

Sewage Works

B1018

Hungry Hall

Rivenhall Thicks

18

79	A	80	B	C	81	D	E	F

155
183

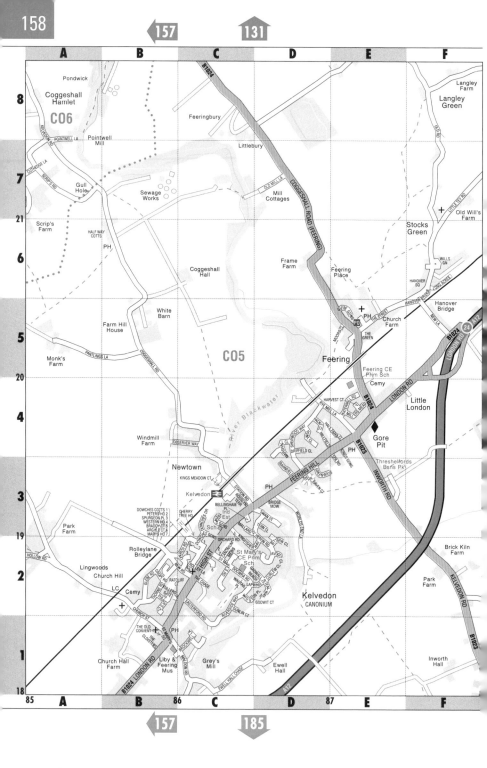

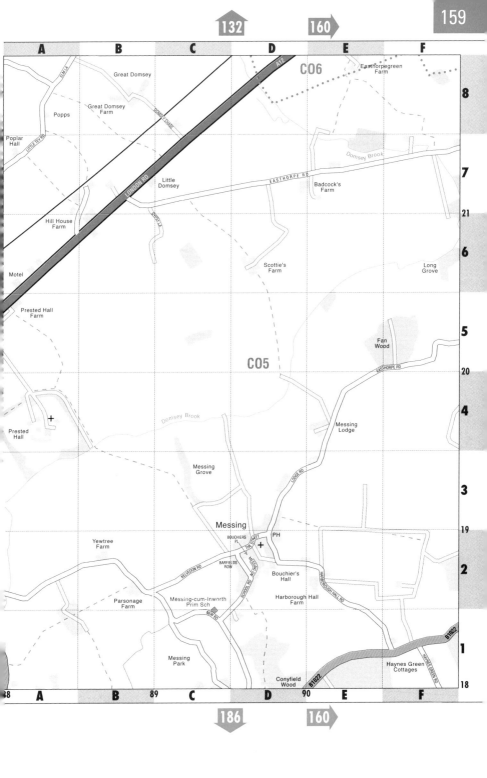

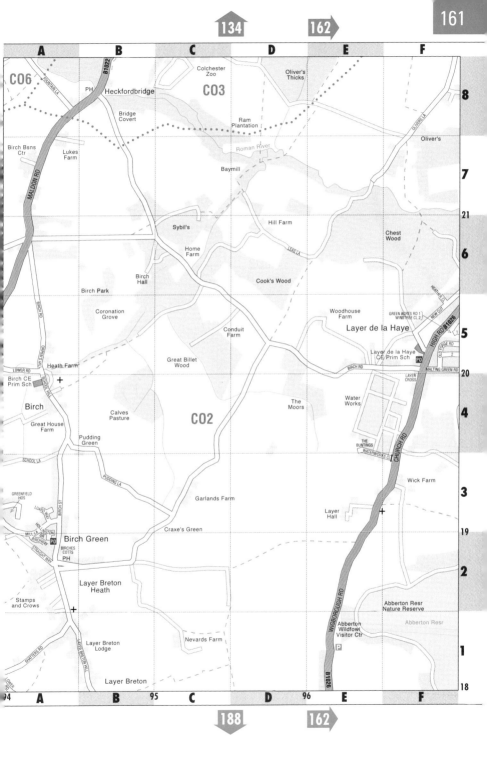

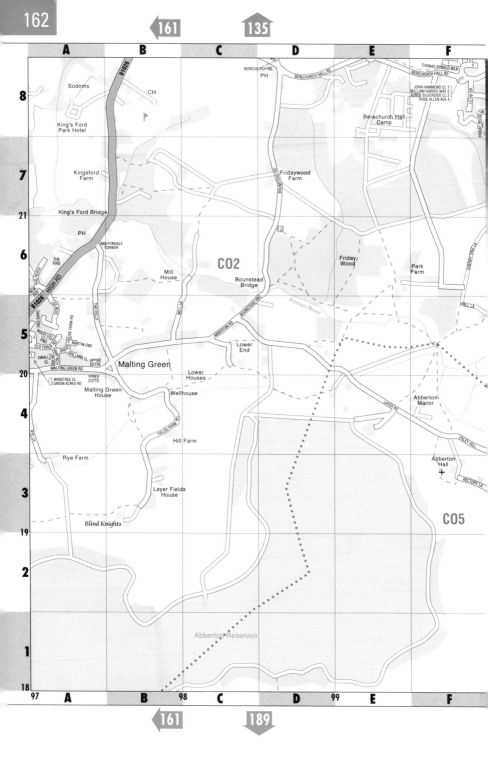

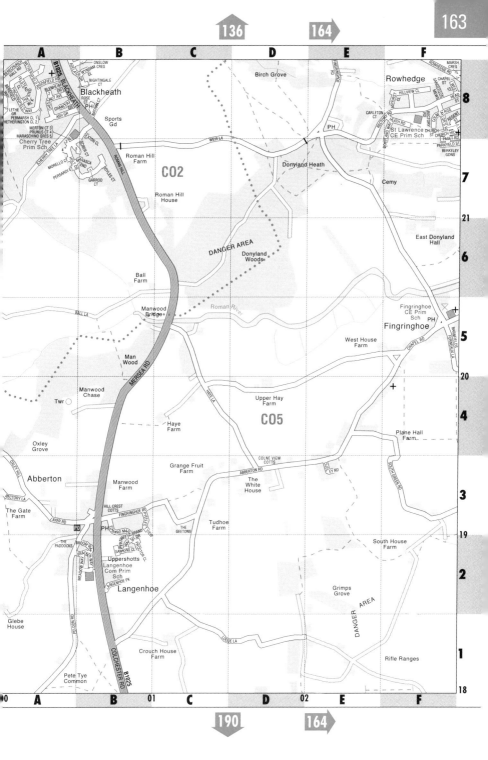

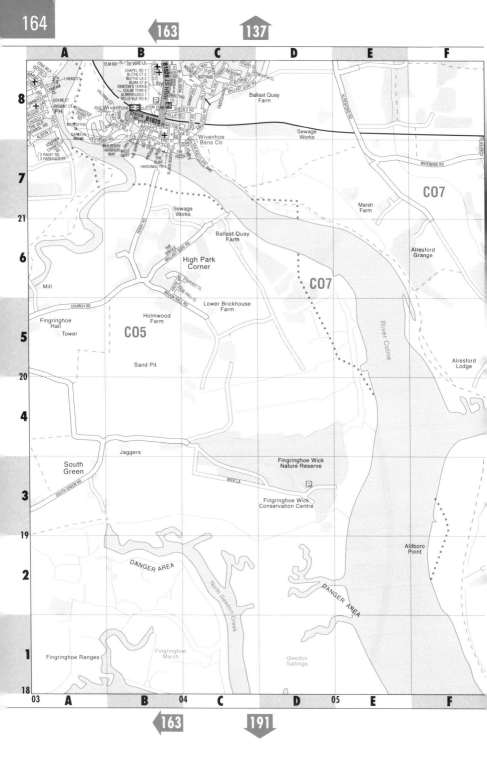

	A	B	C	D	E	F

8

ELM RD
DE VERE LA
CHAPEL RD 1
BLYTHE CT 2
BLYTHE LA 3
ALMA ST 4
DENTON'S TERR 5
COLNE TERR 6
ALMSHOUSES 7
BELLE VUE RD 8
FRIARS CL
DENHAM
KESWORTH CL

IONA WLK
CLYTHA CT
MAY...
1 HEAD ST

Ballast Quay
Farm

Wivenhoe

CLIFTON TERR

QUEEN'S RD

PHILLIP RD

HAMILTON RD

B1028

Wivenhoe
Bsns Ctr

Sewage
Works

Wivenhoe Rd

CO7

7

21

Sewage
Works

Ballast Quay
Farm

Marsh
Farm

Alresford
Grange

6

FERRY RD

THE DINGLE

BALLAST QUAY RD

High Park
Corner

CO7

5

Fingringhoe
Hall

Tower

CHURCH RD

Holmwood
Farm

BROOK HALL RD

Lower Brickhouse
Farm

CO5

Alresford
Lodge

20

Mill

Sand Pit

River Colne

4

Jaggers

3

South
Green

SOUTH GREEN RD

WICK LA

Fingringhoe Wick
Nature Reserve

Fingringhoe Wick
Conservation Centre

19

DANGER AREA

Aldboro
Point

2

North Geedon Creek

DANGER AREA

1

Fingringhoe Ranges

Fingringhoe
Marsh

Geedon
Saltings

18

03	A	B	04	C		D	05	E		F

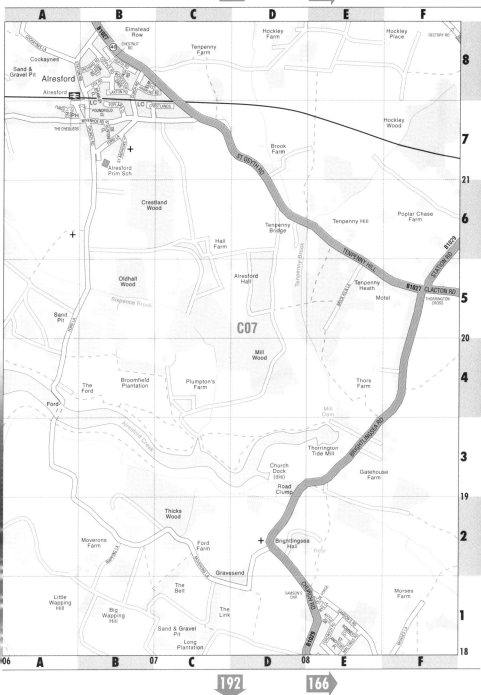

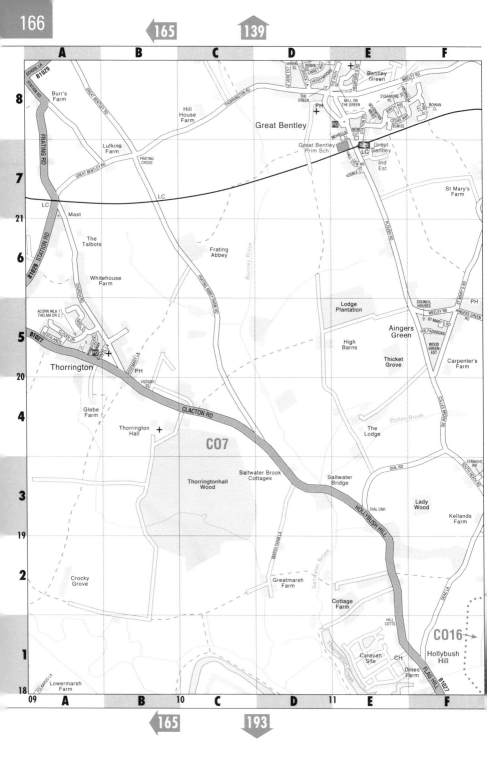

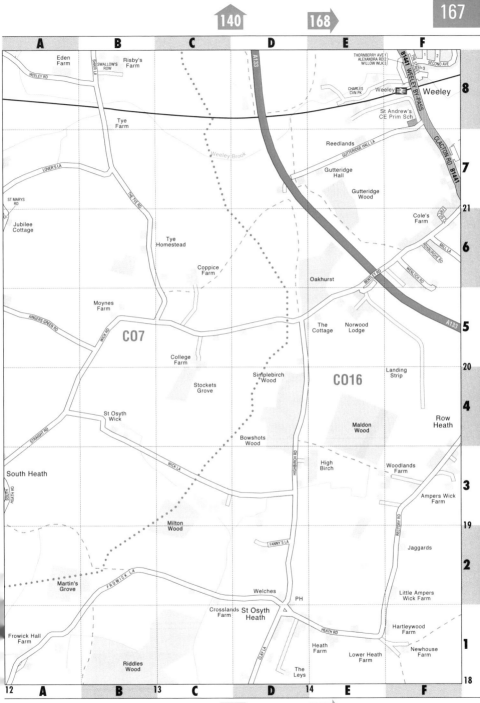

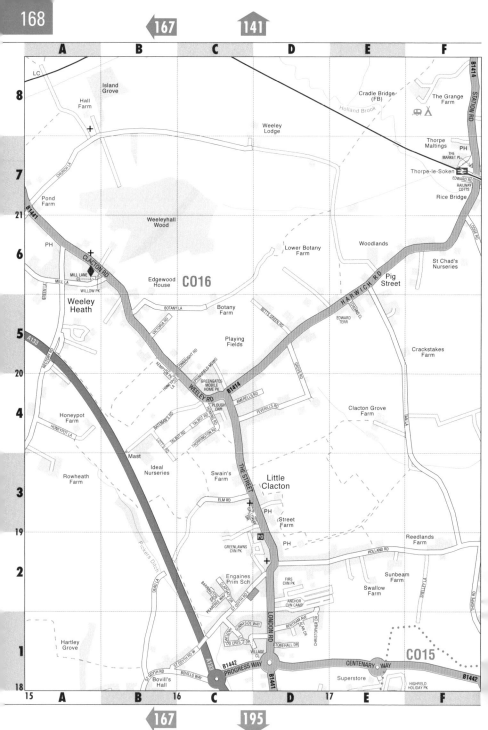

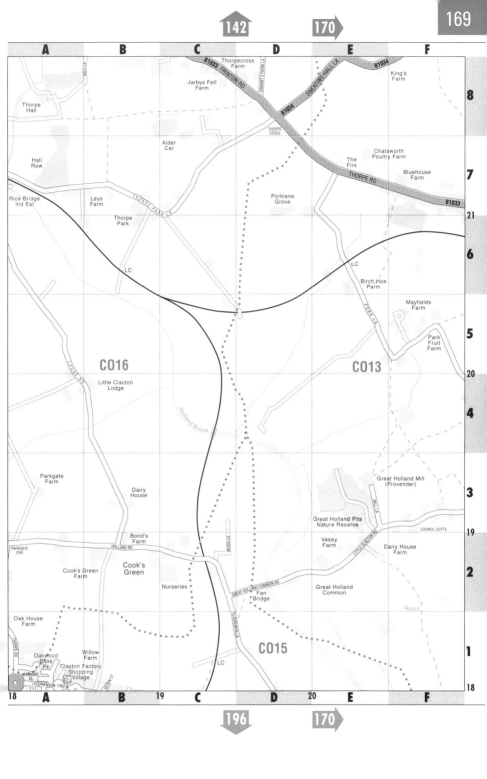

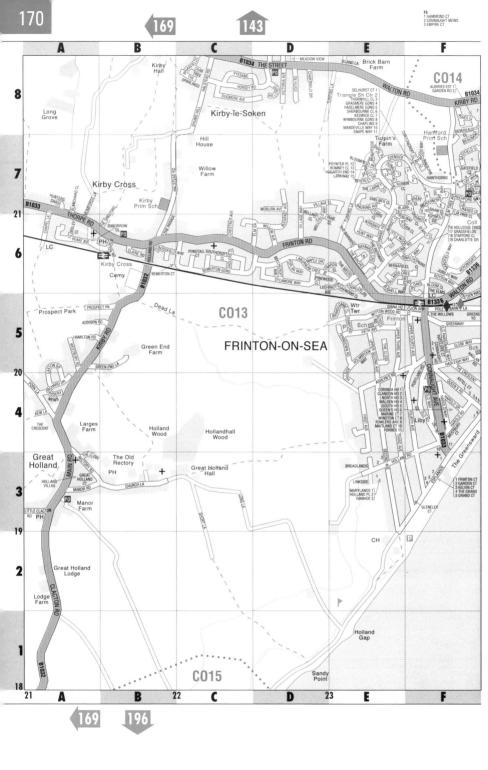

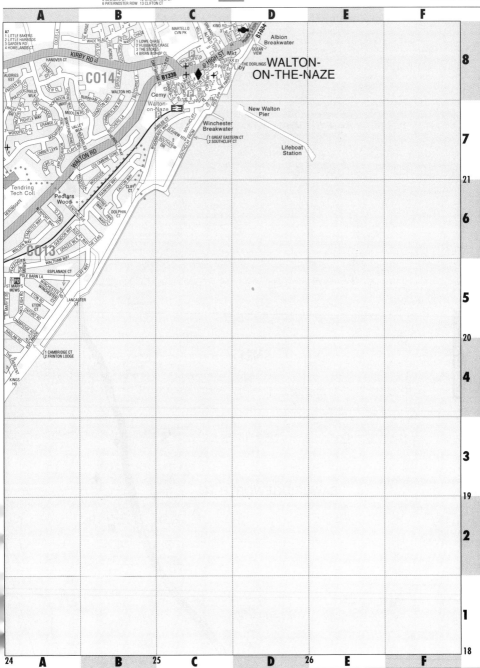

144

C8
1 MARINA MEWS
2 VICARAGE LA
3 HAVENCROFT CT
4 STRATFORD PL
5 NEWGATE ST
6 PATERNOSTER ROW

7 NEW PIER ST
8 MARTELLO RD
9 AGAR RD
10 AGAR ROAD APP
11 ST BOTOLPH'S TERR
12 CHURCHVIEW CT
13 CLIFTON CT

14 MARINE BLDGS

A7
1 LITTLE BAKERS
2 LITTLE HARRODS
3 GARDEN RD
4 HOMELANDS CT

C014

WALTON-ON-THE-NAZE

Albion Breakwater

MARTELLO CVN PK

OCEAN VIEW

New Walton Pier

Winchester Breakwater
1 GREAT EASTERN CT
2 SOUTHCLIFF CT

Lifeboat Station

Tendring Tech Coll

Pedlars Wood

C013

1 LOWE CHASE
2 HUBBARDS CHASE
3 THE STOKES
4 BRIAN BISHOP CL

KIRBY RD

WALTON RD

Cemy
Walton-on-Naze

1 CAMBRIDGE CT
2 FRINTON LODGE

Lancaster Ct

KINGS HO

ESPLANADE CT

POLE BARN LA

WALTHAM WAY

DOLPHIN CT

A B C D E F

24 A   25 C   26 E   F

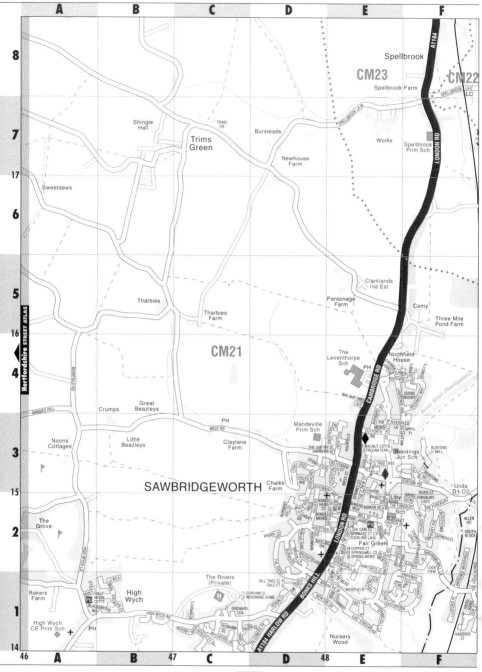

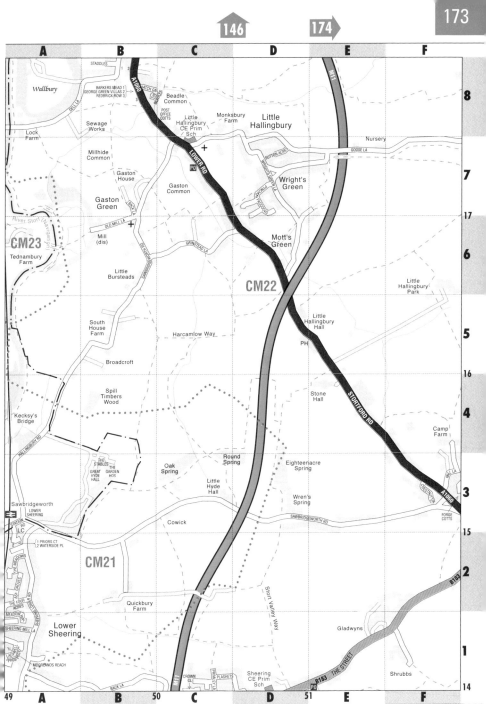

| A | B | C | D | E | F |

8
WOODSIDE GN
Woodfold
Monk's Wood
Wallis's Spring
Forest Hall
Forest Farm
Footpath Common

7
Harcamlow Way
GOOSE LA
RYES LA
Child's Common
The Marsh
Three Forests Way
The Park

17
Ryes Farm

6
Forest Way
Copperfields
Lang Bridge
FEATHERS HILL
PO PH
HIGH ST
BROAD ST
DUNMOW RD
B183
St Mary's CE Prim Sch
CADES PINCH
MEAD
MEAD
CANNONS VILLAS
CANNONS 1

5
The Round Lodge
OLD STREET HILL
CM22
Town Farm
Town Farm
Mus Brook
CAGE END
CAGE END CL
NEW BURY MDW
Hatfield Broad Oak

16
Corringales
Pincey Brook

4
Town Grove

Lea Green
LEA HALL BGLWS
Lea Hall

3
Ongars
LITTLE HEATH
THE CLOSE
COX LEY
Hatfield Heath Com Prim Sch
WOD HEDGE
WEST HAYES
THE OAK
Hatfield Heath
BEEHIVE CT
PO PH
B183

15
STORTFORD RD
CHELMSFORD RD
Stone Bridge
Lancasters

2
PARK GN
Peggerells
BENTLEYS
MATCHING RD
BENTLEY VILLAS
Bentley Common
Muchfield Common
Lancaster's Spring
Hill Farm
BARLEYS
The Paddocks

1
Heath Common
YEWLANDS
Ardley End
Friars
Pooles Cottages
Grange Farm Riding Stables
CM6
SPARROWS LA
A1060

14
Sewage Works
Gibsons
Hatfield Grange

| 52 | A | B | 53 | C | D | 54 | E | F |

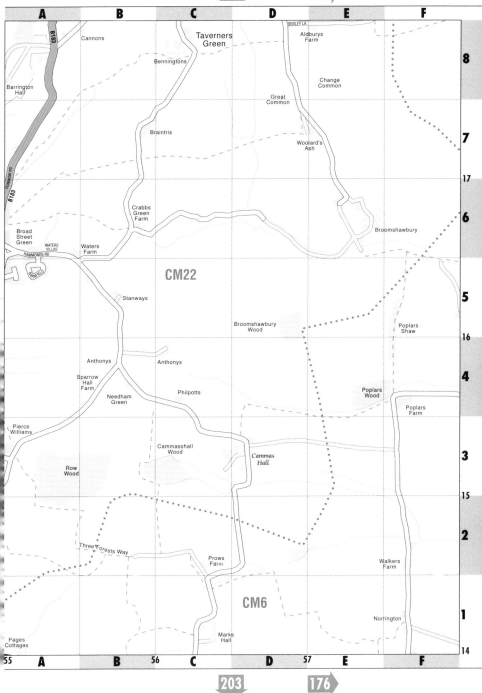

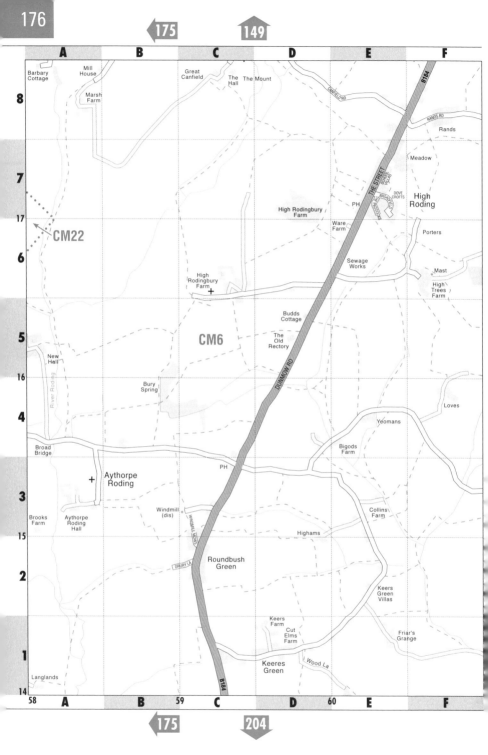

175
149

A **B** **C** **D** **E** **F**

Barbary
Cottage

Mill
House

Great
Canfield

The
Hall

The Mount

CANFIELD RD

B184

8

Marsh
Farm

RANDS RD

Rands

THE STREET

Meadow

THE PADDOCKS

DOVE
CROFTS

High
Roding

7

PH

17

High Rodingbury
Farm

Porters

CM22

Ware
Farm

6

Sewage
Works

Mast

High
Trees
Farm

High
Rodingbury
Farm

Budds
Cottage

5

CM6

The
Old
Rectory

DUNMOW RD

New
Hall

16

River Roding

Bury
Spring

Loves

4

Yeomans

Broad
Bridge

Bigods
Farm

PH

Collins
Farm

3

Aythorpe
Roding

Windmill
(dis)

WINDMILL MEWS

Highams

Brooks
Farm

Aythorpe
Roding
Hall

15

DRURY LA

Roundbush
Green

Keers
Green
Villas

2

Keers
Farm

Cut
Elms
Farm

Friar's
Grange

1

Langlands

Keeres
Green

Wood La

B184

14

58 **A** **B** 59 **C** **D** 60 **E** **F**

175
204

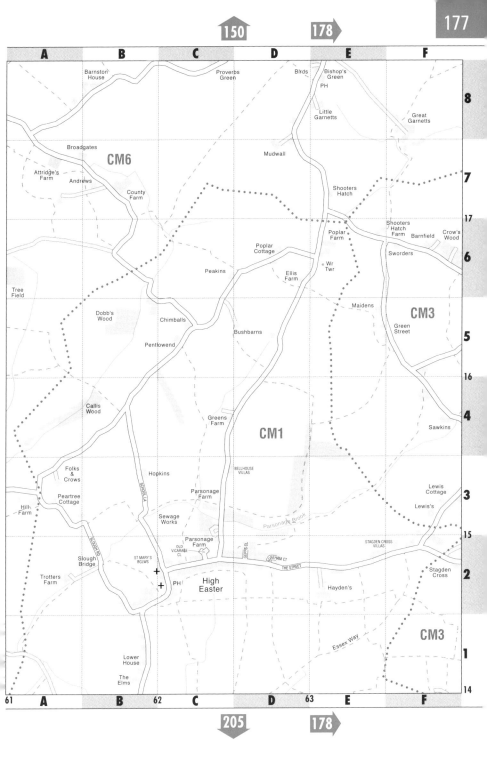

150
178

A B C D E F

8
7
17
6
5
16
4
3
15
2
1
14

Barnston House
Proverbs Green
Birds
Bishop's Green
PH
Little Garnetts
Great Garnetts

Broadgates
CM6
Mudwall
Shooters Hatch

Attridge's Farm
Andrews
County Farm
Shooters Hatch Farm
Barnfield
Crow's Wood
Sworders

Tree Field
Dobb's Wood
Poplar Cottage
Peakins
Ellis Farm
Poplar Farm
Wr Twr
Maidens
CM3
Green Street

Chimballs
Bushbarns
Pentlowend

Callis Wood
Greens Farm
CM1
Sawkins

Folks & Crows
Hopkins
BELLHOUSE VILLAS
Lewis Cottage
Lewis's

Peartree Cottage
Parsonage Farm
Parsonage Brook
STAGDEN CROSS VILLAS

Hill Farm
Sewage Works
Parsonage Farm
OLD VICARAGE CL
DEHAM CT
THE STREET
Stagden Cross

SLOUGH RD
SCHOOL LA
ST MARY'S BGLWS
Slough Bridge
Trotters Farm
PH
High Easter
Hayden's

Lower House
Essex Way
CM3

The Elms

61 A B 62 C D 63 E F

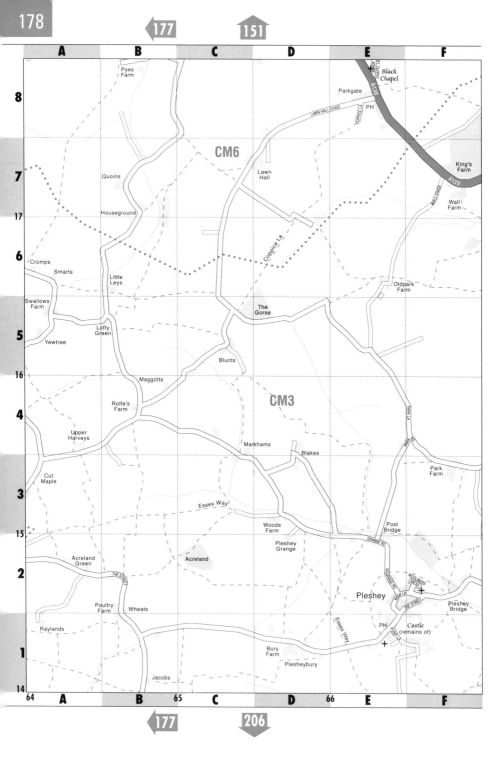

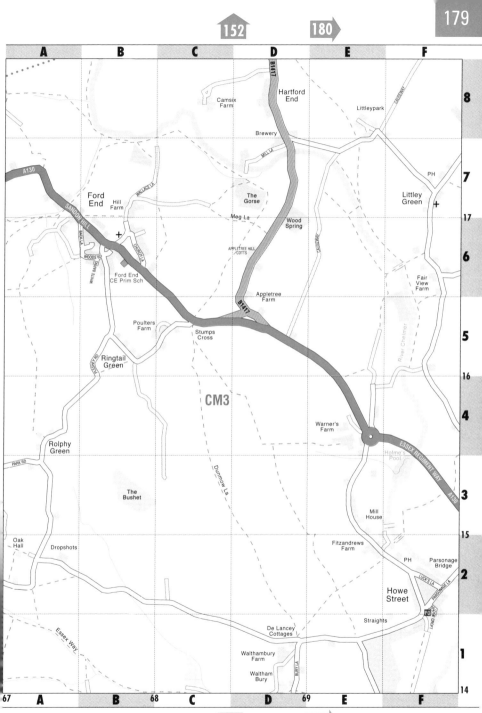

152

180

A B C D E F

8

Camsix
Farm

Hartford
End

Littleypark

B1417

CAUSEWAY

Brewery

7

A130

Ford
End

Hill
Farm

WALLACE LA

The
Gorse

Meg La

MILL LA

Wood
Spring

PH

Littley
Green

17

SANDON HILL

CHURCH LA

+

APPLETREE HILL
COTTS

CAUSEWAY

6

BACK LA

WOODS RD

WHITE BARNS RD

Ford End
CE Prim Sch

Appletree
Farm

B1417

Fair
View
Farm

Poulters
Farm

Stumps
Cross

River Chelmer

5

PLESHEY RD

Ringtail
Green

16

CM3

4

Warner's
Farm

ESSEX REGIMENT WAY

Holme's
Pool

Rolphy
Green

PARK RD

Dunmow La

The
Bushet

Mill
House

A130

3

15

Oak
Hall

Dropshots

Fitzandrews
Farm

PH

Parsonage
Bridge

LUCK'S LA

2

PARSONAGE LA

Howe
Street

BURY CROFT

Essex Way

De Lancey
Cottages

Straights

1

Walthambury
Farm

Waltham
Bury

BURY LA

14

67 A 68 B C 69 D E F

207

180

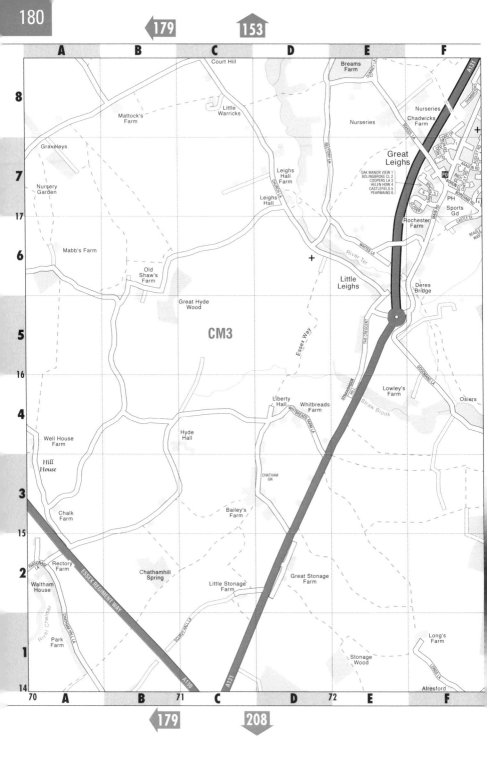

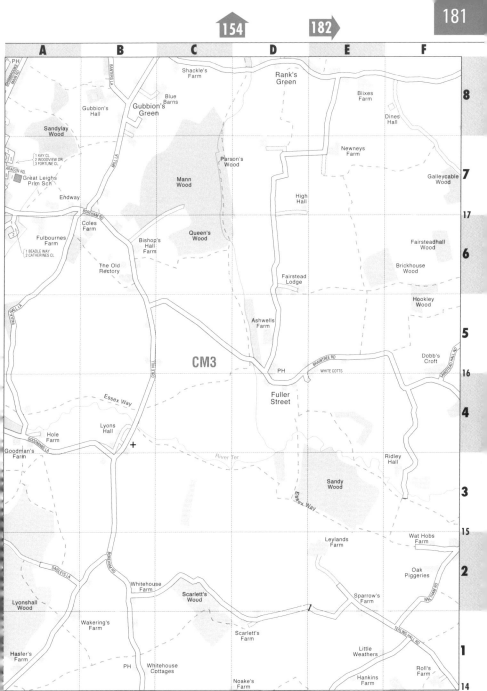

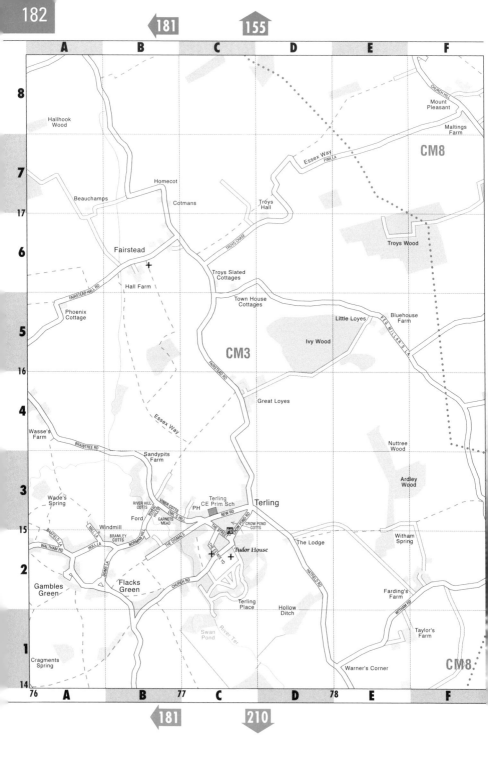

181
155

A   B   C   D   E   F

8

Hallhook
Wood

Mount
Pleasant

Maltings
Farm

CM8

7

Homecot

Beauchamps

Cotmans

Troys
Hall

Essex Way

PINK LA

17

CHURCH HILL

Fairstead

Troys Wood

Troys Slated
Cottages

TROYS CHASE

6

Hall Farm

Phoenix
Cottage

Town House
Cottages

Little Loyes

Bluehouse
Farm

PYE MILLAR'S LA

5

CM3

Ivy Wood

FAIRSTEAD RD

16

Great Loyes

4

Wasse's
Farm

Essex Way

Nuttree
Wood

BRAINTREE RD

Sandypits
Farm

Ardley
Wood

3

Wade's
Spring

Terling
CE Prim Sch

Terling

RIVER HILL
COTTS

LINES COTTS

OWL'S HILL

PH

NEW RD

Ford

GARNETS
MEAD

CROW RD

CROW POND
COTTS

THE STREET

Windmill

BELL LA

RIVER HILL

PO

The Lodge

Witham
Spring

15

HATFIELD LA

BELL LA

BRAMLEY
COTTS

MORNING

THE DIDMALS

THE WALNUT TD

Tudor House

WALTHAM RD

DUNN LA

2

Gambles
Green

Flacks
Green

CHURCH RD

Terling
Place

Hollow
Ditch

HATFIELD RD

Farding's
Farm

WITHAM RD

Taylor's
Farm

Swan
Pond

River Ter

CM8

1

Cragments
Spring

Warner's Corner

14

76   A   B   77   C   D   78   E   F

181
210

156

184

A B C D E F

8

Essex Way
Whiteways
Godfry's
Farm

Whitehead's Farm

7

Hole Farm

Tarecroft
Wood

Oak Farm
Grove
Cottages

CHURCH HILL

Faulkbourne

Hill Farm

B1018

17

COURT ONE 1
COURT TWO 2
COURT THREE 3
COURT FOUR 4
COURT FIVE 5
COURT SIX 6
COURT SEVEN 7
COURT EIGHT 8
COURT NINE 9
COURT TEN 10
COURT ELEVEN 11
COURT TWELVE 12
COURT THIRTEEN 13
COURT FOURTEEN 14
COURT FIFTEEN 15
COURT SIXTEEN 16
COURT SEVENTEEN 17
COURT EIGHTEEN 18
COURT NINETEEN 19
COURT TWENTY 20

The Rickstones
Sch

6

CRESSING RD

Southview
Sch

Elm Hall
Farm

Troys
Farm

Faulkbourne
Hall

Home
Farm

River Brain

The Old
Rectory

Warren
Farm

Dorothy
Sayers Dr

Templars
Inf & Jun
Schs

5

WITHAM

16

CM8

LAVENDER CL 1
PRIMROSE PL 2
BUTTERCUP WLK 3
COVERDALE 4

4

BELLMILLSTONE

Chipping Hill

Sch

B1018

Resr

SPEEDWELL
CL

FOXGLOVE
CL

CALAMINT RD

SAMPHIRE CL

Powers Hall
End

Powers Hall
Inf & Jun Schs

P

PH

3

The
Grove
CM3

Powers
Hall

TERLING RD

EDEN CT

P

15

MILL VALLEY LA

CROMWELL WA4

GIMSON

2

PODSBROOK HO 1
CHITHAVON CT 2
RBX MOTT CT 3
OLD PARSONAGE CT 4
MILL VALE LO 5

NICHOLAS
CT

LOCKRAM LA

Dancing Dicks
Cottages

Wheeler's

Sports
Gd

BLUNTS HALL RD

BLUNT'S HALL DR

Blunt's
Hall

STEVENS RD

The Bungalows 6
NEWLAND CT 7

The
John Bramston
Sch Sports Ctr

ST GEORGES CT 3
DARNFIELD PL 4
MOORFIELD CT 5

1

PHILIP
RD

HALCYON CL 1
RICHARDS CL 2

BRIDGE
CT

B1389

14

9 A B 80 C D 81 E F

211 184

| A | B | C | D | E | F |

8

Rivenhall CE Prim Sch

Rivenhall

Tarecroft Wood

Hoo Hall

Hare Lodge

Hole Farm

7

Stovern's Hall

17

Rickstone's Farm

CH

Durwards Hall

Rivenhall Bridge

6

Glebe Farm

The Old Rectory

HENRY DIXON RD

Rivenhall End

Hotel

Sewage Works

Rose Cottage

Appleford Farm

5

1 WIMSEY CT
2 VANE CT
3 HAWTHORNE RISE

Whitelands

The Matchyn's

CM8

Appleford Bridge

16

Cemy

PO

Waterside Bsns Pk

Colemans Resr

4

Superstore

CRITTALL CT

Eastways Ind Est

1 Enterprise Ct
2 Europa Pk
3 Swanbridge Ind Pk

Coleman's Bridge

River Blackwater

Commodity Ctr

Workhouse Plantation

Hall Broad House

CHURCH CHASE

3

Witham Junction

Witham

COLCHESTER RD

Coleman's Farm

Elm Springs

15

Swan Vale Ind Est

MOSS RD

Cromwell Ctr

1 KYNASTON PL
2 RICHARDSON WLK

Lea Lane Wood

2

Liby

NEWLAND ST

Little Braxted

Hall

Lea Lane Fruit Farm

Broomfield's Farm

1

TH

The Grove Ctr

Wheater Ind Est

PERRY WAY

Briarsford Ind Est

B1018

MALDON RD

Sewage Works

14

82 A B 83 C D 84 E F

A2
1 GROVE COTTS
2 FOSTER CT
3 DU CANE PL
4 HORNER PL
5 FREEBOURNES CT
6 HEWITT WLK
7 LOCKRAM LA
8 NEWLANDS PREC
9 PENHALIGON CT

10 COACH HOUSE WAY
11 GUITHAVON ST

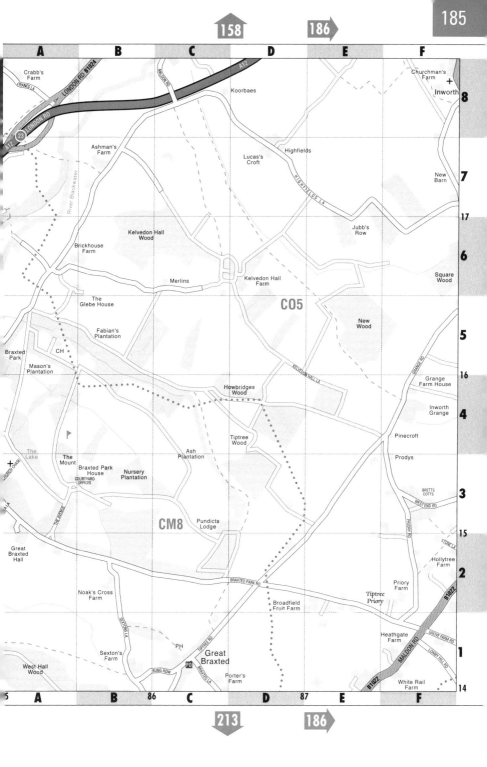

A   B   C   D   E   F

8   PH
THE STREET
Hill House
B1023
HAPPY GDNS
Hill Farm
Perry's Wood
KELVEDON RD
Baynard's Prim Sch
Hill Wood
WATERWORKS COTTS
GRANGE RD
Vine Farm
Windmill Hill

Messing Park Farm
Bishops Cottage
The Elms
PH
COLCHESTER RD
Woodview Farm
EATON COTTS
OAK RD
CEDAR AVE
SIMONS FLATS
MAYTREE CT
Thurstable Sch
SPINNEYFIELDS
HEATON WAY
Milldene Prim Sch
BARBROOK LA
MAYPOLE RD

Pods Wood
Napiers Farm
CO5
Poyston
Haynes Green
The Rampart
Viners Farm
Ransome's Grove
1 DOWNTON WLK
2 ST JEAN WLK
3 ELEANOR WLK
4 TALISMAN WLK
5 GLOBE WLK
6 ELTON WLK
1 BROCK CV
2 OLLEY WLK
Sewage Works
Viners Farm
BLENHEIM WAY

7

17

6   Tiptree Windmill
KINGSWAY
QUEENSWAY
HARRINGTON CL
MEADOW CL
BLUE RD
PERRY RD
PENNSYLVANIA LA
THE CUT
HOLLY WALK
RANSOM RD
GREEN LA
CHURCH RD

5   Tiptree
Bryanita
NEW RD
THYME CL
ROSEMARY CRES
Liby
Sch
ROSEMARY
ST LUKES CHASE
BROOK MEAD
SAGE WLK
CLARKES MEAD
SAFFRON WLK
CHERRY CL
LARKSPUR
The Centre
ELEVENTHORN CL
NEWBRIDGE RD

16

4   Sand & Gravel Pit
MALDON RD
PH
STATION RD
Birch Wood
Gate House
Factory
Tiptree Mus
FACTORY HILL
Brook Hall

3   WEST END RD
SAMPSONS LA
PH
Tiptree Heath Prim Sch
ORCHARD LODGE
GORSE LA
Layer Brook
BROOK CL
STRAWBERRY LA
KNIGHTS
BROOK RD
THE FORT
D'ARCY RD
PH

15   Manor House Farm
STONE LA
Villa Farm
P
Tiptree Heath
TIPTREE HALL LA
Tolleshunt Knights

2   B1026
Tiptree Hall
Venn Farm
Oxley Farm

1   GROVE FARM RD
CM9
Hawthorn Farm
Wilkin's Grove
Elmwood Farm
Wr Twr
CM9

14   88   A   B   89   C   D   90   E   F

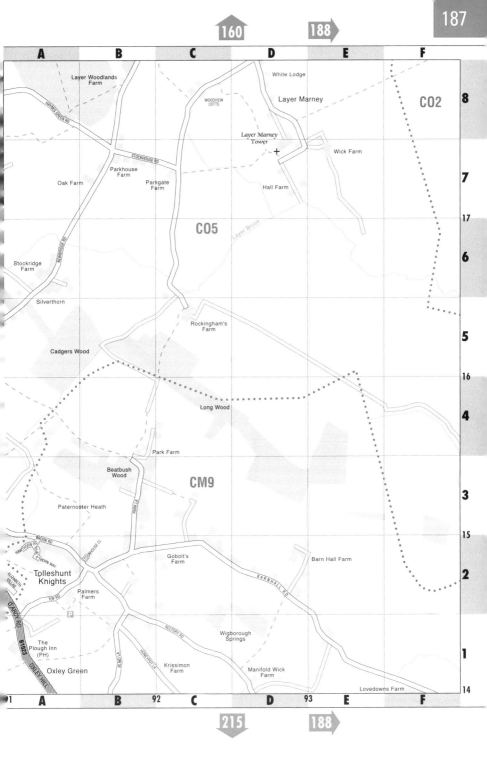

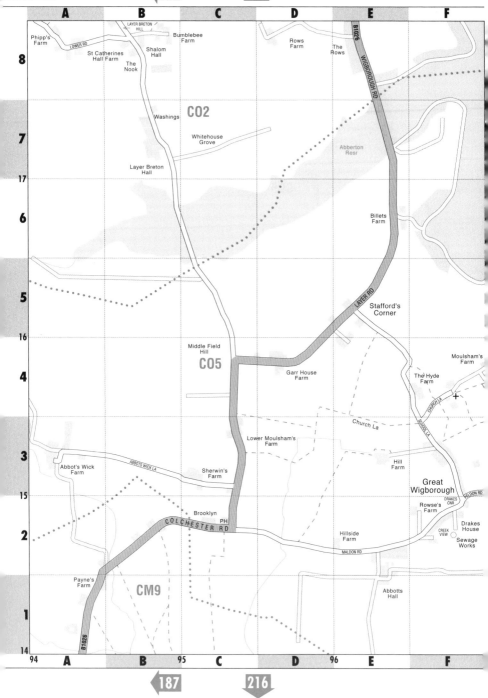

A B C D E F

Phipp's Farm
LOWER RD
St Catherines Hall Farm
The Nook
LAYER BRETON HILL
Shalom Hall
Bumblebee Farm

8

Rows Farm
The Rows
B1026
WIGBOROUGH RD

CO2

7

Washings

Whitehouse Grove

Abberton Resr

17

Layer Breton Hall

6

Billets Farm

5

LAYER RD

Stafford's Corner

16

Middle Field Hill
CO5

Garr House Farm

Moulsham's Farm
The Hyde Farm
CHURCH LA

4

Church La

Lower Moulsham's Farm

Hill Farm

3

Abbot's Wick Farm
ABBOTS WICK LA
Sherwin's Farm

Great Wigborough

15

Rowse's Farm
DRAKES CNR
FELDON RD

Brooklyn
PH
COLCHESTER RD

CREEK VIEW
Drakes House

2

Hillside Farm
MALDON RD

Sewage Works

Payne's Farm

CM9

Abbotts Hall

1

B1026

14

94 A 95 C D 96 E F

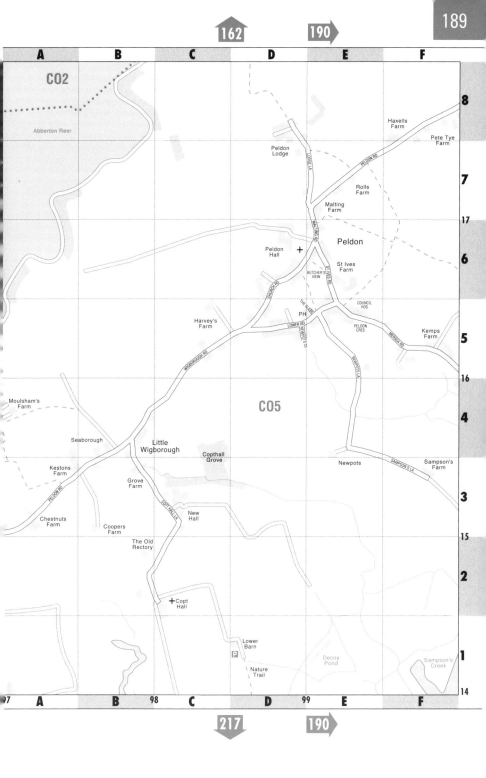

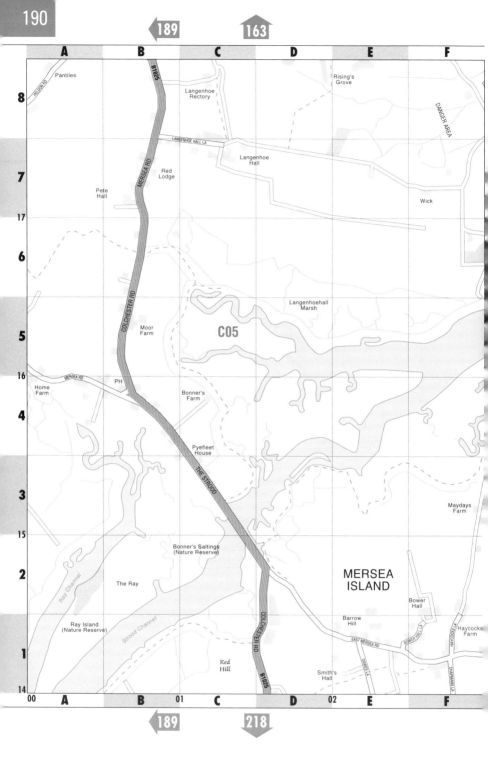

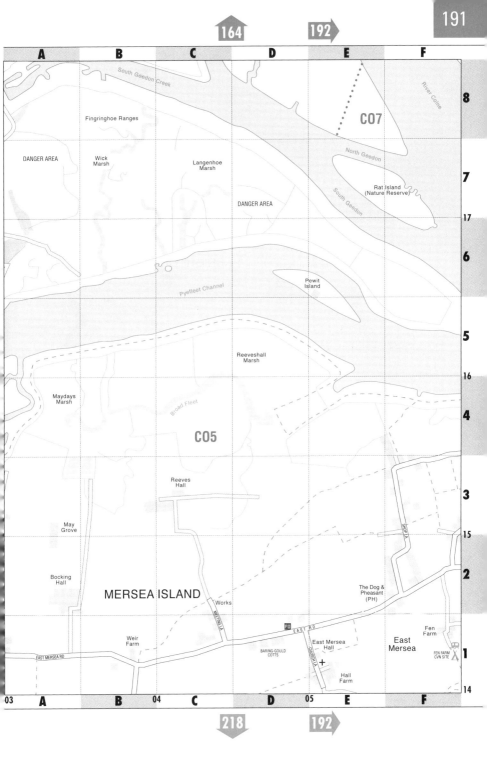

164
192

	A	B	C	D	E	F

South Geedon Creek

CO7

River Colne

8

Fingringhoe Ranges

North Geedon

DANGER AREA

Wick Marsh

Langenhoe Marsh

7

Rat Island (Nature Reserve)

South Geedon

DANGER AREA

17

6

Pyefleet Channel

Pewit Island

5

Reeveshall Marsh

16

Maydays Marsh

Broad Fleet

4

CO5

Reeves Hall

3

May Grove

15

Bocking Hall

2

The Dog & Pheasant (PH)

MERSEA ISLAND

Works

Fen Farm

Weir Farm

East Mersea Hall

East Mersea

PO EAST RD

FEN FARM CVN SITE

EAST MERSEA RD

BARING-GOULD COTTS

Hall Farm

1

14

MEETING LA

CHURCH LA

SHOP LA

218
192

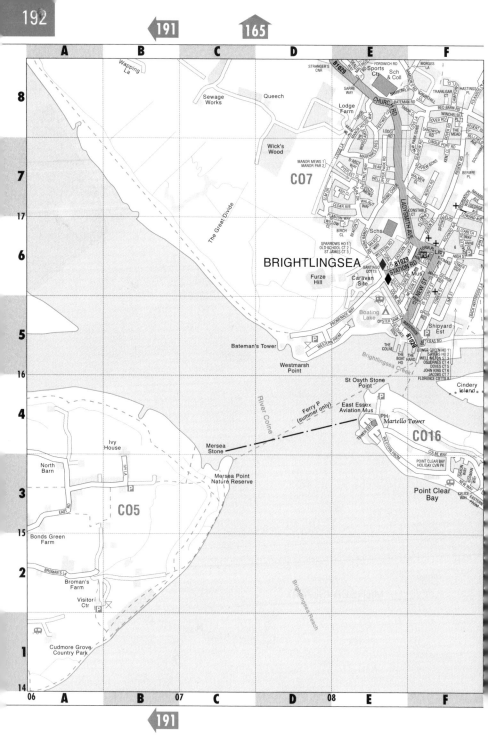

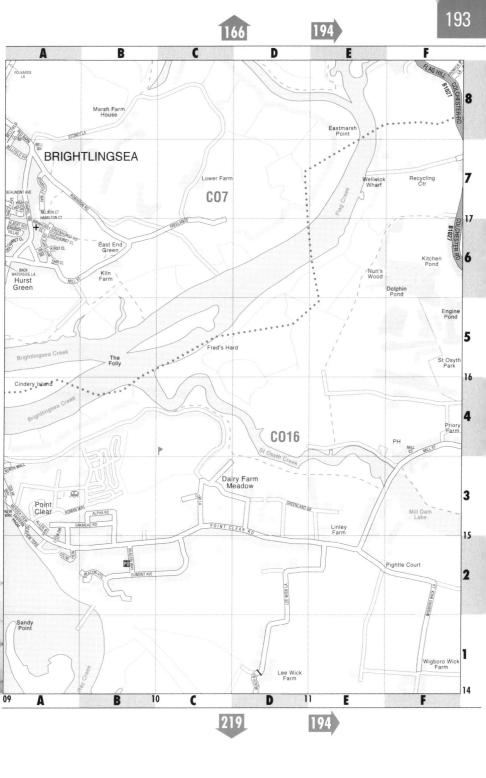

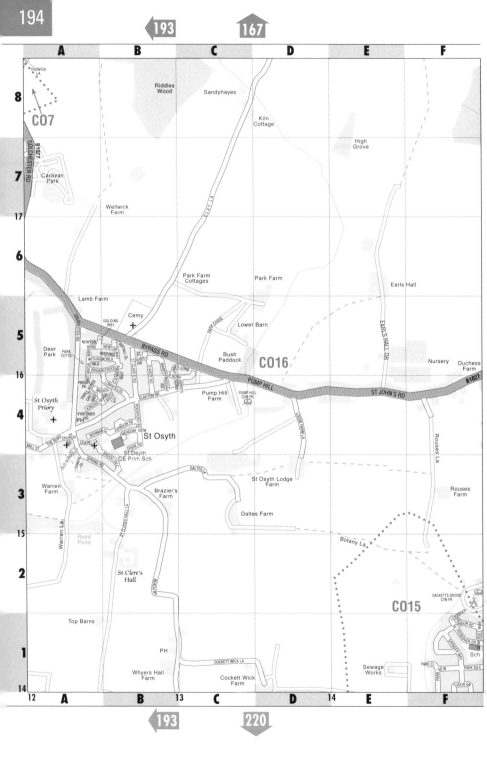

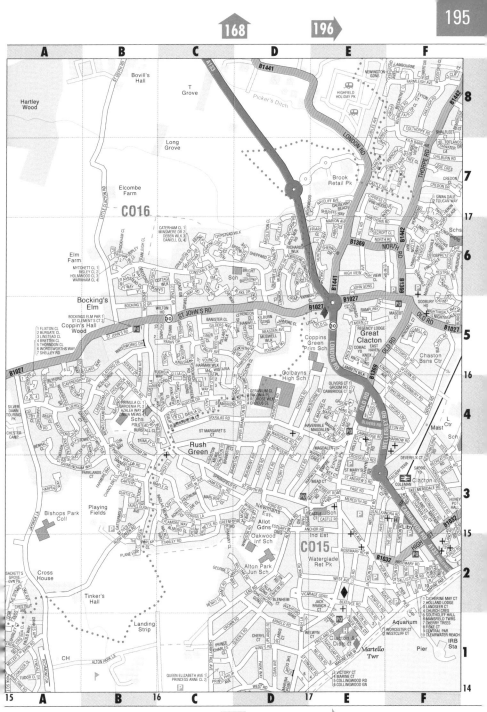

Hertfordshire STREET ATLAS

| | A | | B | | C | | D | | E | | F | |

Widburyhill Farm — Widbury Wood — Mead Wood — The Dairy Farm — The Bournes — Harcamlow Way

8

Easneye Wood

Easneye Wood — Newgate Wood

Easneye

River Ash

HOLLYCROSS RD

Easneye Cottage — Ballard's Wood

7

Thirsty Spring

13

Sheepcote Farm — LC

6

Amwell

Little Briggens

B180

SG12

PH — CHURCH LA — St Johns La

St John the Baptist CE Prim Sch

Limes Farm

Hill House — Newlands — Home Farm Ind Pk

5

Hillside Farm

LC — Swing Bridge

HUNSDON RD

HUNSDON ROAD COTTS

PEPPER HILL

St Margarets

A414 Hertford (A10)

A1170 Ware

B181

A414

ABBOTTS CT — PO

WOODHAM WAY — St Margarets — P

ABBOTTS WK — CHAPTER CT

St Andrew's CE Prim Sch — Stanstead Abbotts

12

Cat's Hill — Coldharbour Wood

4

STATION RD — HIGH ST — The Maltings Ind Est — HORSESHOE CT — P — THELE EST — ROYDON RD

Coldharbour Farm

Amwell View Sch

SG13

LAKES CT — SPRINGWELL CT — LEE CL — RUSH CL — LAWNS CL

Marina — KINGFISHER CL — NETHERFIELD CT — Works — Netherfield House

Nursery — Ryegate Farm — Terbets Hill — Stanstead Bury

A414

B181

3

The Wilderness

ROBIN CL — SWIFT CL

11

HODDESDON

THE GRANARY

New River Way — River Lea Navigation

EN11

Rye Meads

2

ST MARGARET'S RD — CHELSEA FIELDS — CHESTNUT GR — LC

The John Warner Sch — CRANBOURNE HO

Toll

The Coppings — BRIDLE WAY (N) — CRANBOURNE RD

Sewage Works

River Stort — Harcamlow Way

1

A1170 WARE RD — CHRISTIAN — Works — RYE RD

CM19

10

A1
1 BOREHAM MEWS
2 PLOMER AVE
3 CATHROW MEWS
4 BEYERS RIDE
5 BRIDLE WAY
6 BEYERS GDNS

B1
1 WESTERN TERR
2 SOUTHERN TERR
3 PARKLAND CL
4 ESTFELD CL
5 CHITTENDEN CL

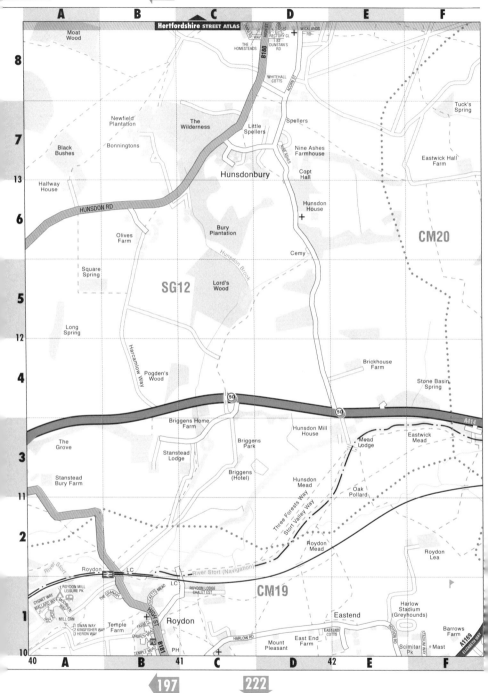

Hertfordshire STREET ATLAS

Moat Wood

WICKLANDS RD

THE HOMESTEADS

ST DUNSTAN'S RD

RECTORY CL

WHITEHALL COTTS

Newfield Plantation

The Wilderness

Little Spellers

Spellers

Nine Ashes Farmhouse

Bonningtons

Black Bushes

Hunsdonbury

Copt Hall

Halfway House

HUNSDON RD

Hunsdon House

CM20

Olives Farm

Bury Plantation

Cemy

Square Spring

SG12

Lord's Wood

Hunsdon Brook

Long Spring

Harcamlow Way

Pogden's Wood

Brickhouse Farm

Stone Basin Spring

50

50

A414

Briggens Home Farm

Hunsdon Mill House

Eastwick Mead

The Grove

Stanstead Lodge

Briggens Park

Mead Lodge

Stanstead Bury Farm

Briggens (Hotel)

Hunsdon Mead

Oak Pollard

Three Forests Way

Stort Valley Way

Roydon Mead

Roydon Lea

River Stort

Roydon

LC

River Stort (Navigation)

LC

Roydon Lodge Chalet Est

CM19

Eastend

Harlow Stadium (Greyhounds)

Barrows Farm

ROYDON MILL LEISURE PK

CYGNET WAY

MALLARD WAY

MOORHEN

SWAN WAY

KINGFISHER WAY

HERON WAY

MILL CRN

THE GRANARY

COCKETTS MEAD

Temple Farm

HIGH ST

Roydon

FARM CL

CHURCH LEYS

TEMPLE MEAD

B181

PH

HARLOW RD

Mount Pleasant

East End Farm

EASTEND COTTS

Eastend

STADIUM WAY

Scimitar Pk

Mast

SCIMITAR WAY

ELIZABETH WAY

A1169

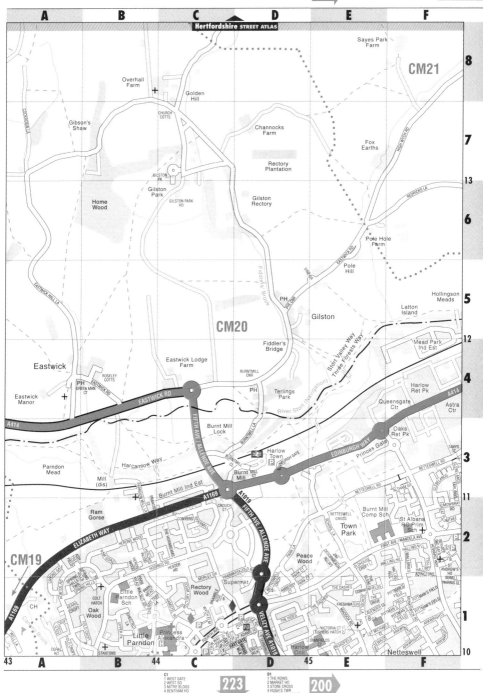

C1
1 WEST GATE
2 WEST SQ
3 MITRE BLDGS
4 BENTHAM HO
5 THE ANGLE
6 AMHERST LO

D1
1 THE ROWS
2 MARKET HO
3 STONE CROSS
4 HUGH'S TWR
5 NETTESWELL TWR

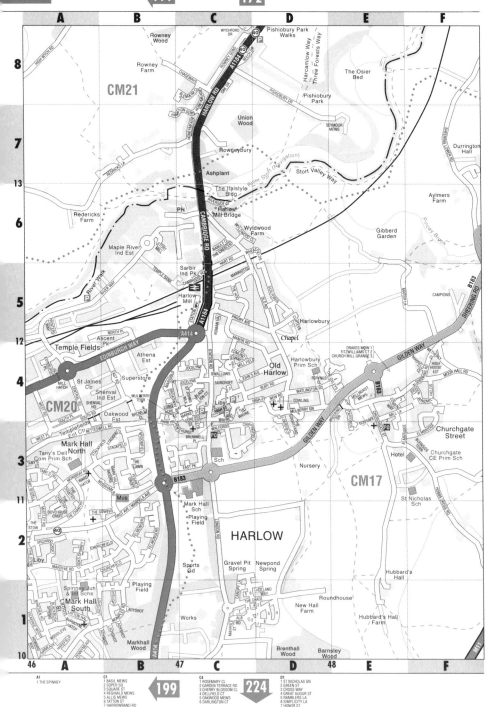

A1
1 THE SPINNEY

C1
1 BASIL MEWS
2 SOPER SQ
3 SQUARE ST
4 REGINALD MEWS
5 ALLIS MEWS
6 TATTON ST
7 HARROWBAND RD

C4
1 ROSEMARY CL
2 GARDEN TERRACE RD
3 CHERRY BLOSSOM CL
4 DELLFIELD CT
5 OAKWOOD MEWS
6 DARLINGTON CT

D1
1 ST NICHOLAS GN
2 GREEN ST
3 CROSS WAY
4 GREAT AUGUR ST
5 RAMBLERS LA
6 SIMPLICITY LA
7 HONOR ST

199

224

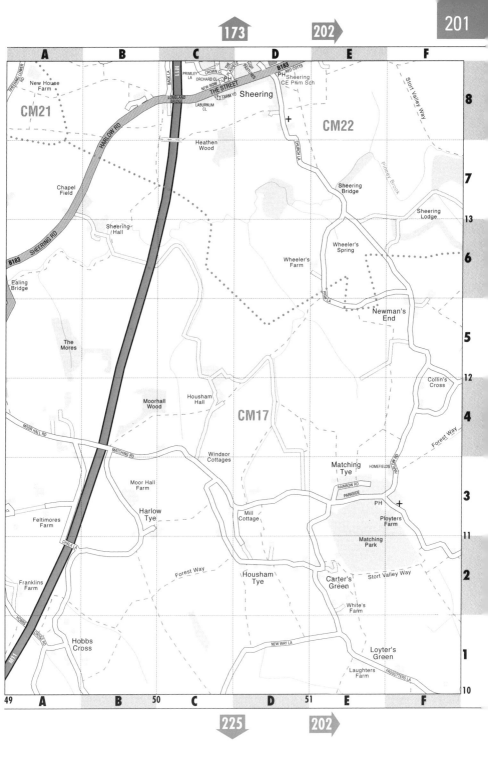

173
202

A   B   C   D   E   F

8
7
13
6
5
12
4
3
11
2
1
10

CM21

New House Farm

SHEERING RD LOWER

HARLOW RD

Chapel Field

SHEERING RD

B183

Ealing Bridge

The Mores

MOOR HALL RD

MATCHING RD

Feltimores Farm

CHALK LA

M11

HOBBS CROSS RD

Franklins Farm

Hobbs Cross

M11

LONGLAND BRIDGE

VT BDY

PRIMLEY LA
ORCHARD CL
NEW ROW
THE FIELDS
CROWN CL
LABURNUM CL
THE STREET
D TARM YD
PH

Sheering

B183
RED COTTS
PH
Sheering CE Prim Sch

CM22

Heathen Wood

Sheering Hall

CHURCH LA

Wheeler's Farm

Wheeler's Spring

Sheering Bridge

HIGH LA

Pincey Brook

Stort Valley Way

Sheering Lodge

Newman's End

CM17

Moorhall Wood

Housham Hall

Windsor Cottages

Moor Hall Farm

Harlow Tye

Mill Cottage

Forest Way

Housham Tye

Matching Tye

RAINROW RD
PARKSIDE
PH
HOMEFIELDS

Ployters Farm

Matching Park

Carter's Green

Stort Valley Way

White's Farm

NEW WAY LA

Collin's Cross

Forest Way

Loyter's Green

Laughters Farm

FAGGOTTERS LA

49   A   B   50   C   D   51   E   F

225
202

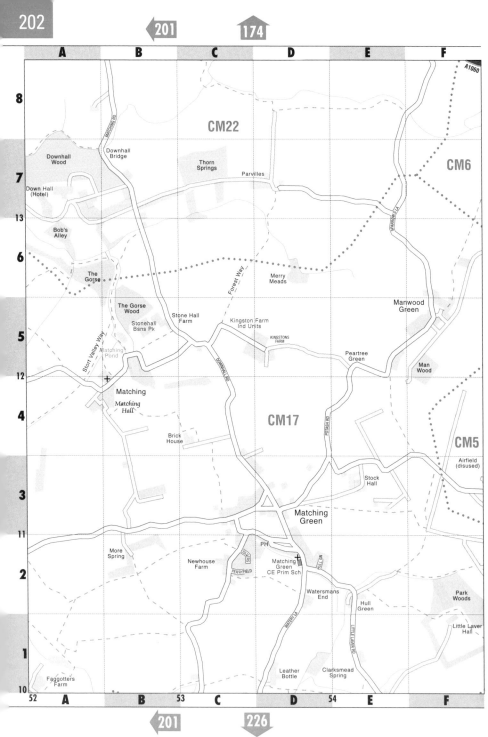

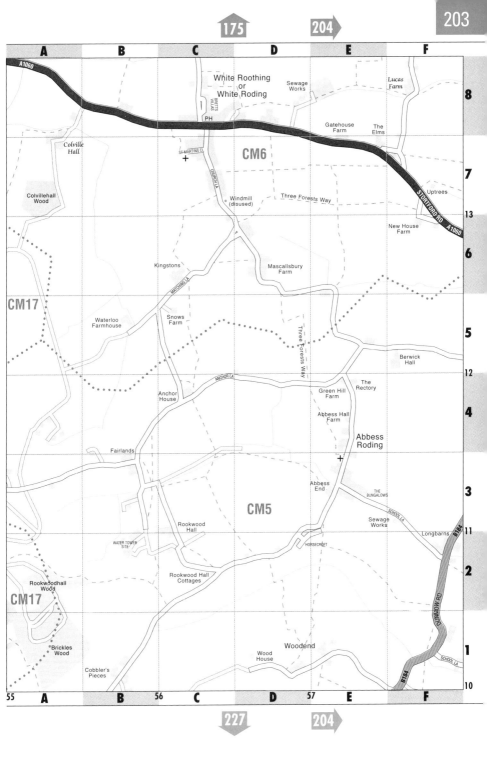

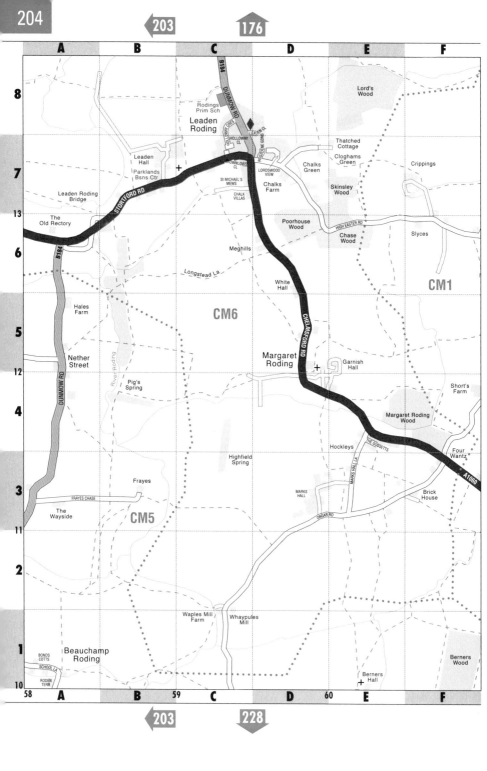

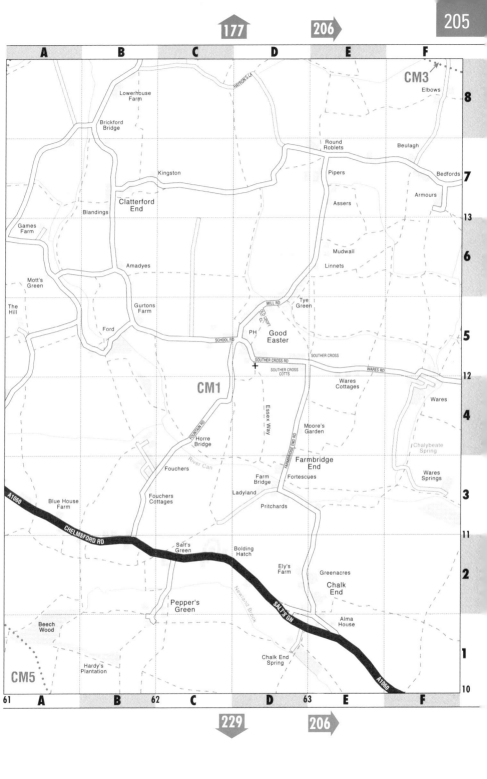

A B C D E F

8

CM3

Elbows

Lowerhouse
Farm

Brickford
Bridge

Round
Roblets

Beulagh

7

Kingston

Pipers

Bedfords

Clatterford
End

Assers

Armours

13

Blandings

Games
Farm

Mudwall

6

Amadyes

Linnets

Mott's
Green

Gurtons
Farm

MILL RD

Tye
Green

The
Hill

OLD CROFT CL

Ford

SCHOOL RD

PH

Good
Easter

5

SOUTHER CROSS RD

SOUTHER CROSS

WARES RD

12

CM1

SOUTHER CROSS
COTTS

Wares
Cottages

Wares

4

Essex Way

Moore's
Garden

FOUNTAIN RD

Horre
Bridge

FARMBRIDGE END RD

Chalybeate
Spring

River Can

Farmbridge
End

Fouchers

Fortescues

Wares
Springs

Farm
Bridge

3

A1060

Blue House
Farm

Fouchers
Cottages

Ladyland

Pritchards

11

CHELMSFORD RD

Salt's
Green

Bolding
Hatch

Ely's
Farm

Greenacres

2

Chalk
End

Pepper's
Green

Navland Brook

SALT'S GN

Beech
Wood

Alma
House

1

CM5

Hardy's
Plantation

Chalk End
Spring

A1060

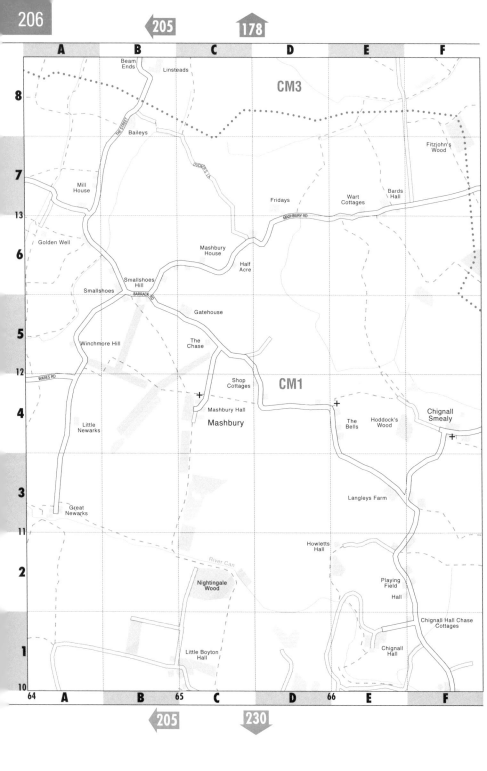

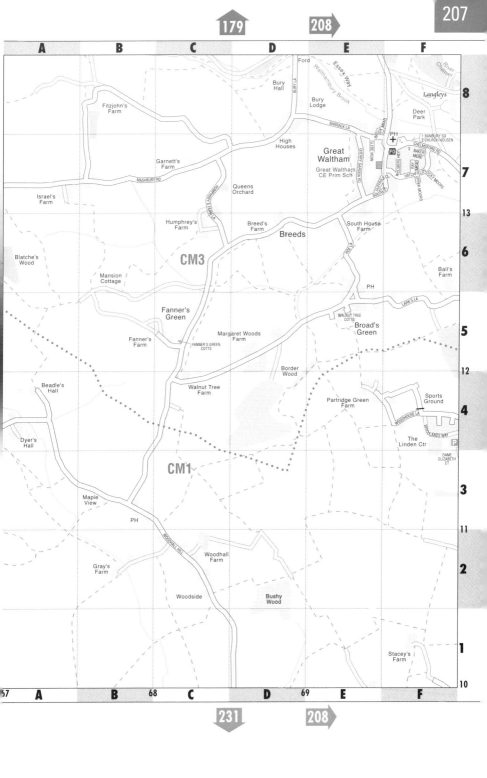

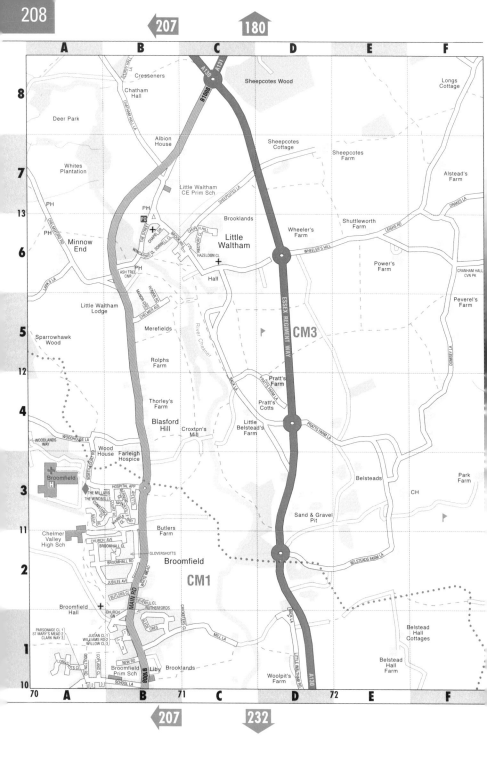

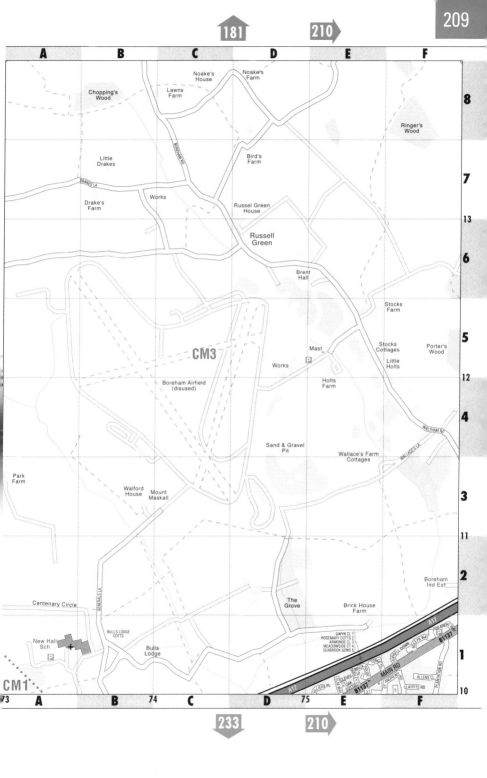

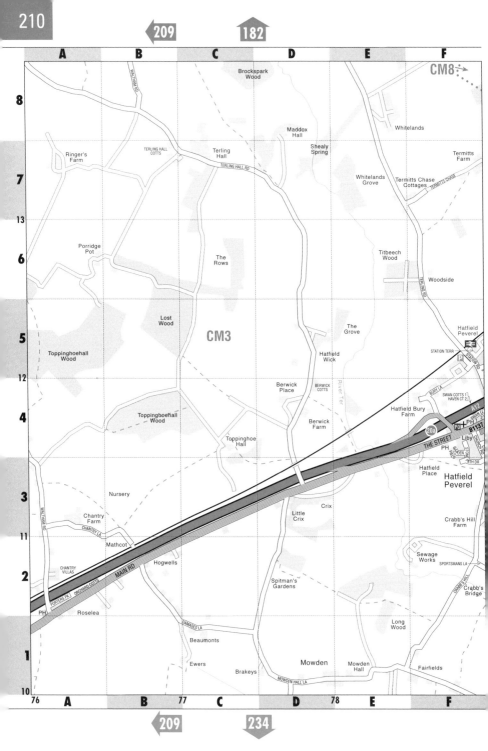

CM8

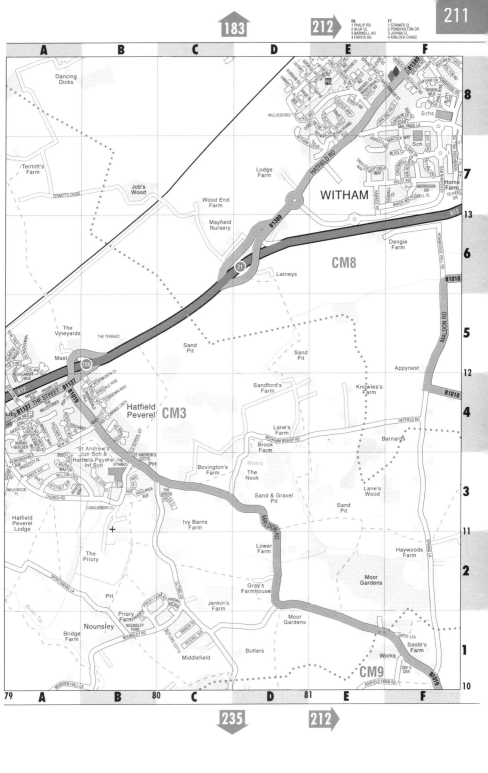

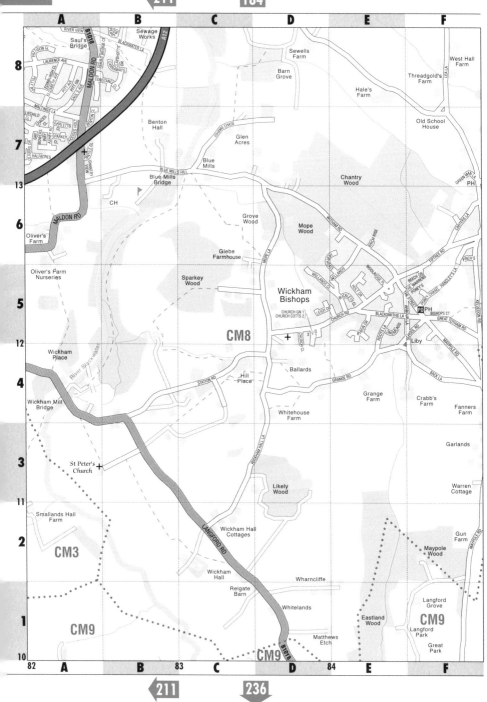

213
186

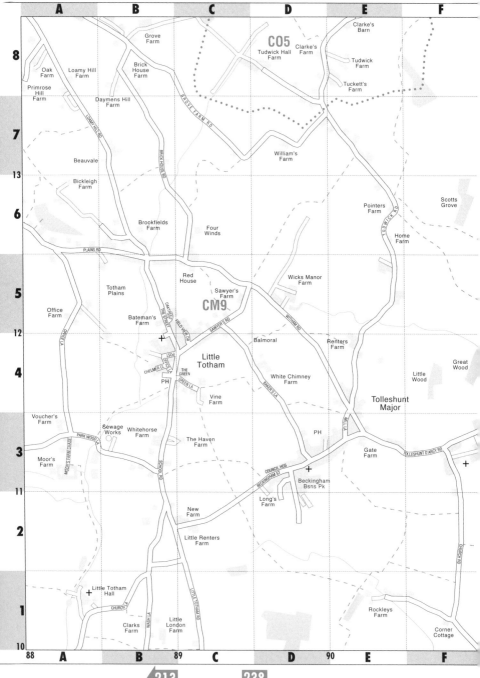

213
238

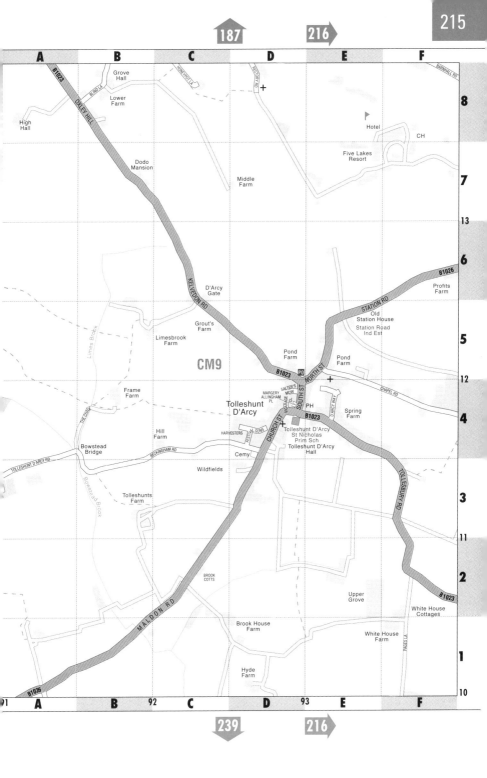

187
216

A **B** **C** **D** **E** **F**

B1023

Grove Hall

BLIND LA

OXLEY HILL

Lower Farm

HONEYPOT LA

RECTORY RD

BARNHALL RD

8

High Hall

Hotel

Five Lakes Resort

CH

7

Dodo Mansion

Middle Farm

13

KELVEDON RD

D'Arcy Gate

B1026

Profits Farm

6

STATION RD

Old Station House

Station Road Ind Est

Grout's Farm

Limesbrook Farm

Limes Brook

5

CM9

Pond Farm

Pond Farm

CHAPEL RD

12

Frame Farm

B1023

PO

NORTH ST

SOUTH ST

Tolleshunt D'Arcy

MARGERY ALLINGHAM PL

SALTER'S MDW

VICARAGE CL

PH

D'ARCY WAY

Spring Farm

4

THE CHASE

Hill Farm

BECKINGHAM RD

HARVESTERS

THE STREET

AL GDNS

CHURCH ST

Tolleshunt D'Arcy St Nicholas Prim Sch

Tolleshunt D'Arcy Hall

Bowstead Bridge

Cemy

TOLLESHUNT D'ARCY RD

Bowstead Brook

Wildfields

TOLLESBURY RD

11

Tolleshunts Farm

3

BROOK COTTS

Upper Grove

2

MALDON RD

Brook House Farm

White House Farm

PAGES LA

White House Cottages

B1023

1

Hyde Farm

B1026

10

239
216

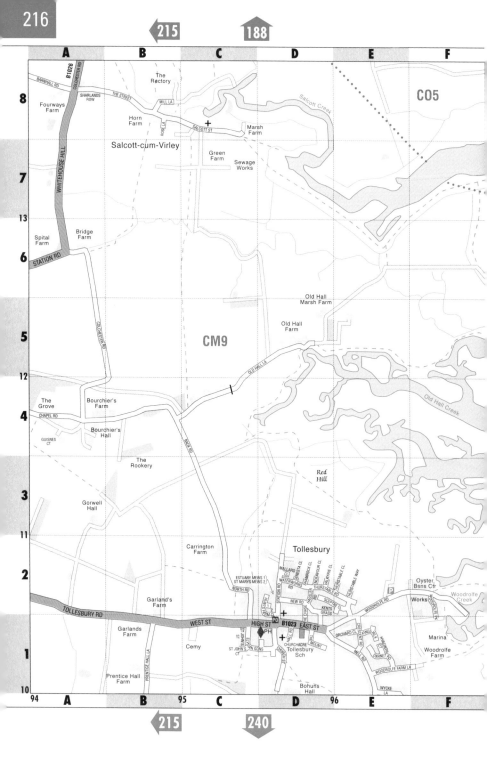

A B C D E F

8

7

13

6

5

12

4

3

11

2

1

10

94 A B 95 C D 96 E F

B1026
BARNHALL RD
COLCHESTER RD
WHITEHOUSE HILL
SHARLANDS ROW
THE STREET
The Rectory
MILL LA
Salcott Creek
CO5
Fourways Farm
Horn Farm
RIDE LA
SALCOTT ST
Marsh Farm
Salcott-cum-Virley
Green Farm
Sewage Works
Spital Farm
Bridge Farm
STATION RD
COLCHESTER RD
Old Hall Marsh Farm
Old Hall Farm
CM9
OLD HALL LA
Old Hall Creek
The Grove
CHAPEL RD
Bourchier's Farm
Bourchier's Hall
GUISNES CT
The Rookery
BACK RD
Red Hill
Gorwell Hall
Carrington Farm
Tollesbury
MALLARD CL
GENESTA CL
SHAMROCK CL
SHEARWATER CL
VALKYRIE CL
THURSTABLE CL
TURNTABLE WAY
Oyster Bsns Ctr
Woodrolfe Creek
ESTUARY MEWS 1
ST MARYS MEWS 2
WATERWORKS RD
NORTH RD
STATION RD
NEW RD
THE CHASE
NASSEE
SCEPTRE CL
KENTS GRASS
WOODROLFE RD
Works
P
Garland's Farm
TOLLESBURY RD
WEST ST
HIGH ST
PH
B1023
EAST ST
PO
GYM LA
CHURCH RD
CHURCHACRE
Tollesbury Sch
ORCHARD CL
CRESCENT RD
KINGS WICK
MOUNT
MELL RD
DARNET RD
VINERS CL
Marina
Woodrolfe Farm
Garlands Farm
Cemy
ST JOHNS RD
ST JOHN'S CT
N GDNS
Bohun's Hall
WOODROLFE FARM LA
WYCKE LA
Prentice Hall Farm
PRENTICE HALL LA

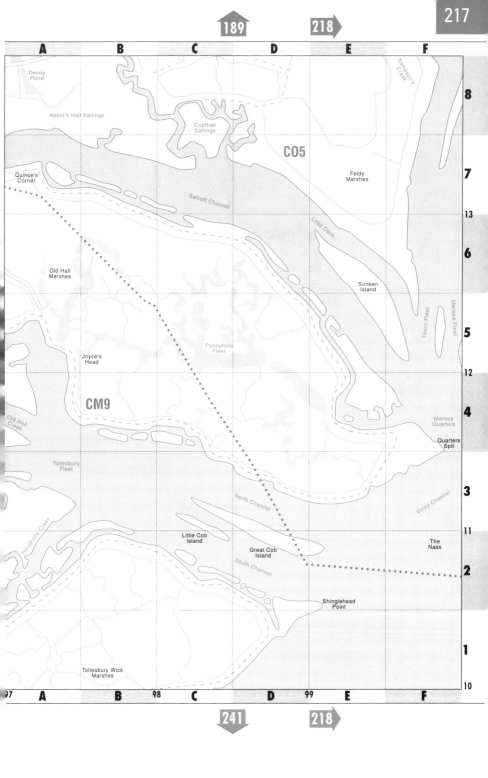

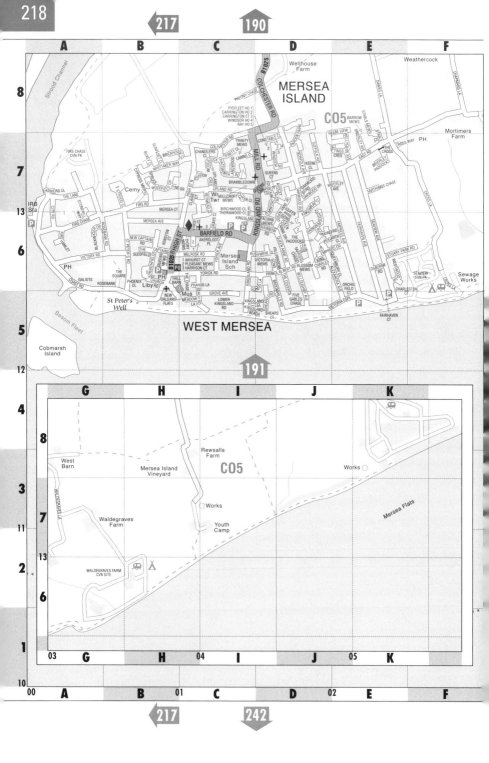

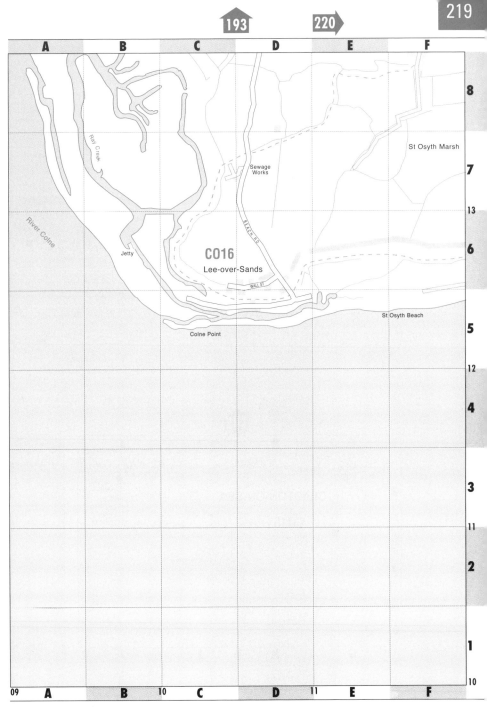

A B C D E F

8

St Osyth Marsh

7

13

River Colne

Ray Creek

Sewage Works

BEACH RD

6

Jetty

CO16
Lee-over-Sands

WALL ST

St Osyth Beach

Colne Point

5

12

4

3

11

2

1

10

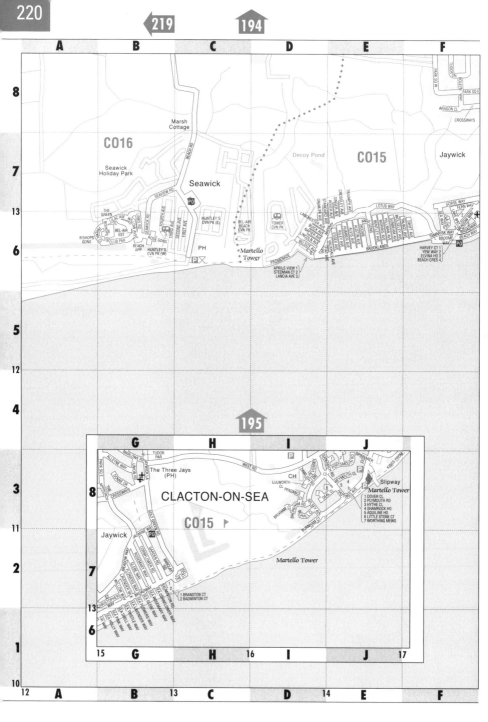

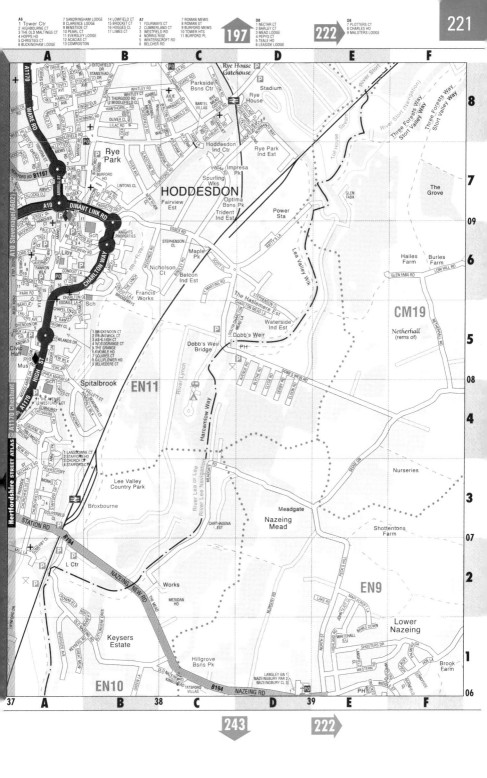

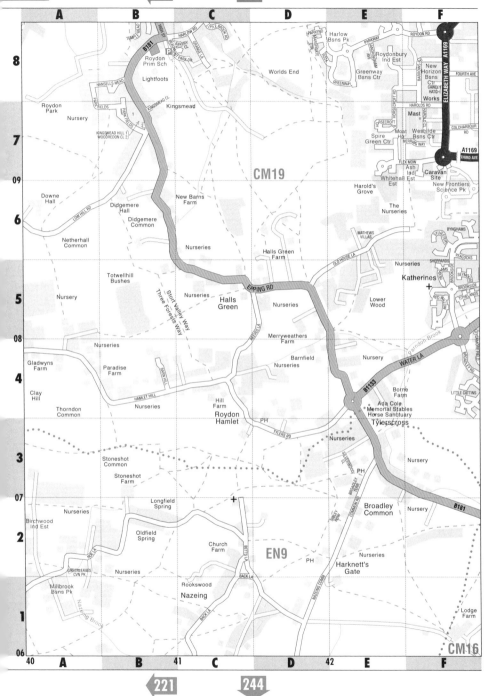

CM19

EN9

CM16

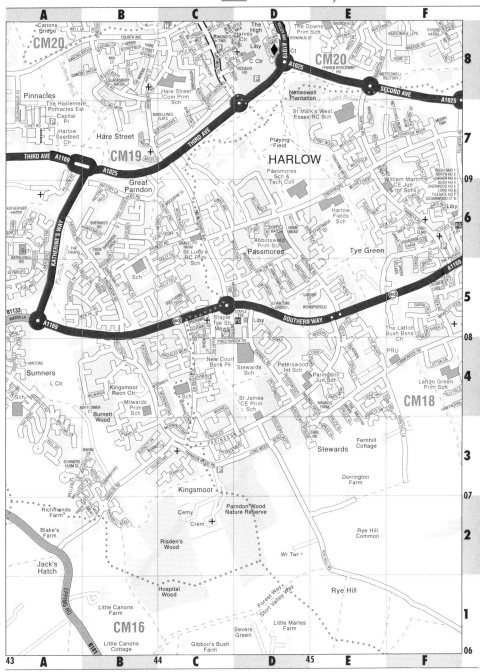

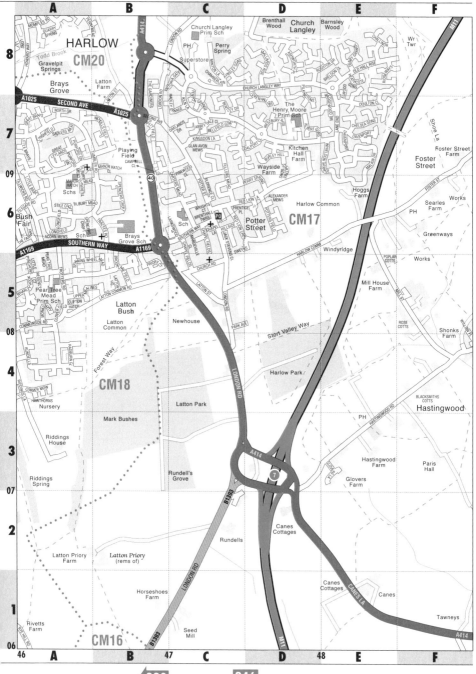

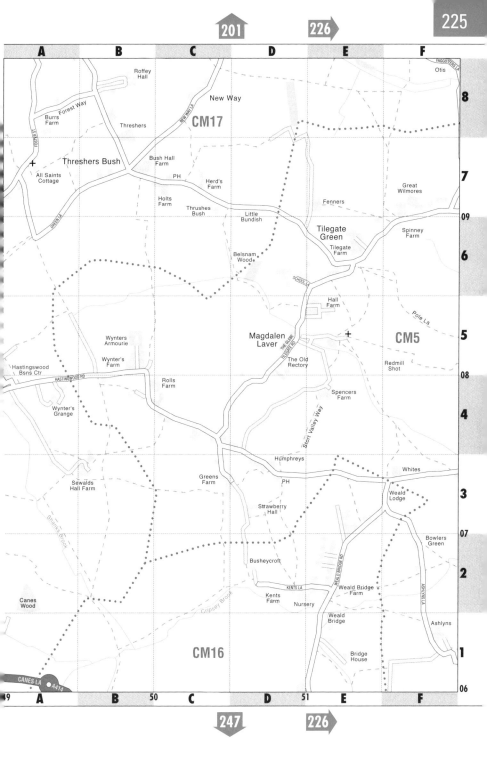

Otis
FAGGOTERS LA

Roffey
Hall

New Way

CM17

Forest Way

Burrs
Farm

Threshers

8

Threshers Bush

Bush Hall
Farm

Great
Wilmores

+
All Saints
Cottage

PH

Herd's
Farm

7

Fenners

Holts
Farm

Spinney
Farm

Thrushes
Bush

Little
Bundish

09

Tilegate
Green

GREEN LA

NEW BELL LA

Belsnam
Wood

Tilegate
Farm

6

SCHOOL LA

Pole La

Hall
Farm

Wynters
Armourie

Magdalen
Laver

CM5

5

THE GLEBE

TILEGATE RD

Wynter's
Farm

The Old
Rectory

+

Hastingwood
Bsns Ctr

HASTINGWOOD RD

Rolls
Farm

Redmill
Shot

08

Wynter's
Grange

Spencers
Farm

4

Stort Valley Way

Shanks Brook

Sewalds
Hall Farm

Greens
Farm

Humphreys

Whites

PH

Weald
Lodge

3

Strawberry
Hall

WEALD BRIDGE RD

07

Bowlers
Green

Busheycroft

2

Canes
Wood

Cripsey Brook

KENTS LA

Kents
Farm

Weald Bridge
Farm

ASHLYNS LA

Nursery

Ashlyns

CM16

Weald
Bridge

Bridge
House

1

CANES LA

A414

06

A   B   50   C   D   51   E   F

49

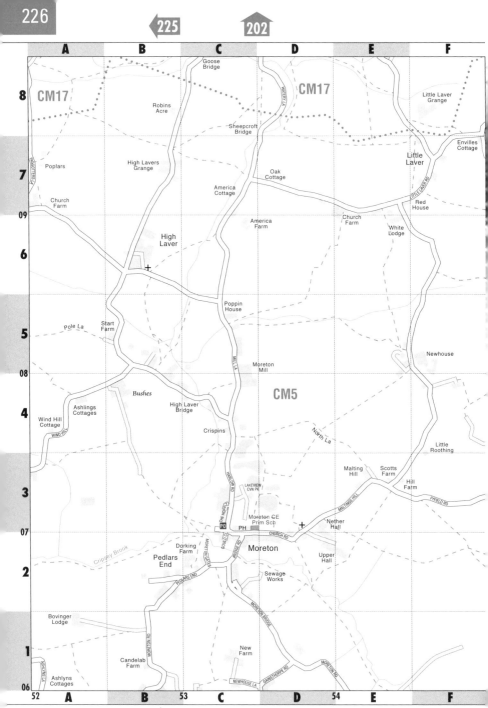

225
202

CM17

8

7

09

6

5

08

4

3

07

2

1

06

A   B   C   D   E   F

Goose Bridge

Robins Acre

Sheepcroft Bridge

CM17

Little Laver Grange

Little Laver

Envilles Cottage

Poplars

High Lavers Grange

Oak Cottage

America Cottage

Church Farm

Red House

High Laver

America Farm

Church Farm

White Lodge

Poppin House

Newhouse

Pole La

Start Farm

Moreton Mill

MILL LA

CM5

Bushes

High Laver Bridge

Crispins

Wind Hill Cottage

Ashlings Cottages

WIND HILL

North La

Little Roothing

Malting Hill

Scotts Farm

Hill Farm

FYFIELD RD

LAKEVIEW CVN PK

Moreton CE Prim Sch

THE HYDE

P

PH

MALTINGS HILL

Nether Hall

HIGH LAVER RD

MORETON CENTRE

BRIDGE ST

CHURCH RD

Moreton

Dorking Farm

Pedlars End

Upper Hall

Sewage Works

Cripsey Brook

PEDLARS END

MORETON BRIDGE

Bovinger Lodge

MORETON RD

Candelab Farm

New Farm

GAINSTHORPE RD

MORETON RD

Ashlyns Cottages

ASHLING LA

NEWHOUSE LA

52   A   B   53   C   D   54   E   F

225
248

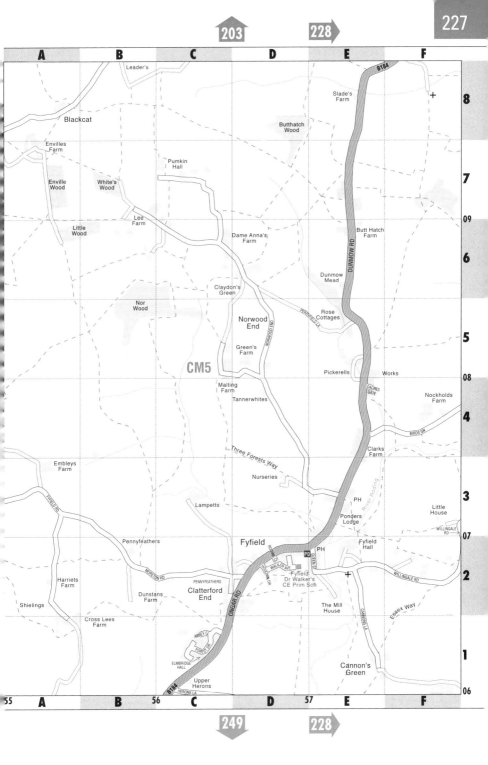

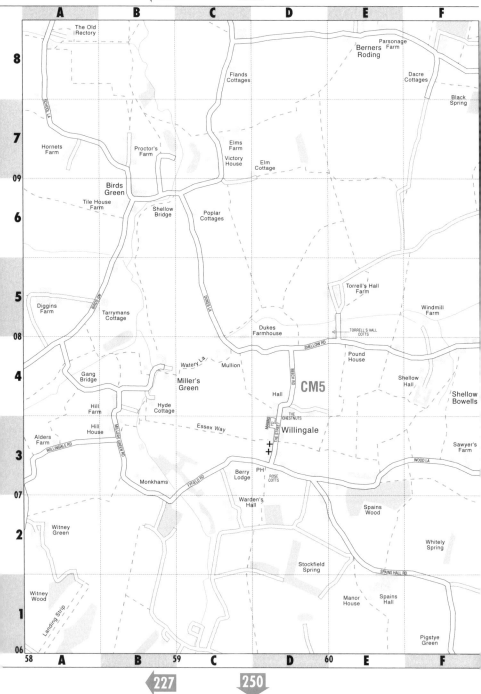

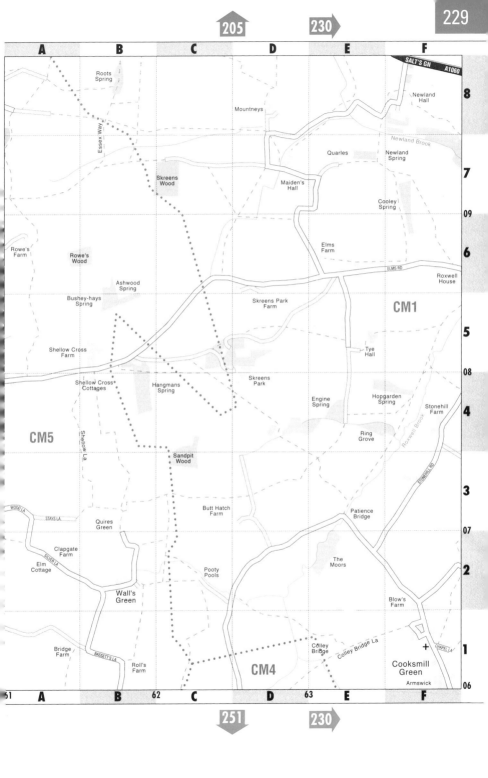

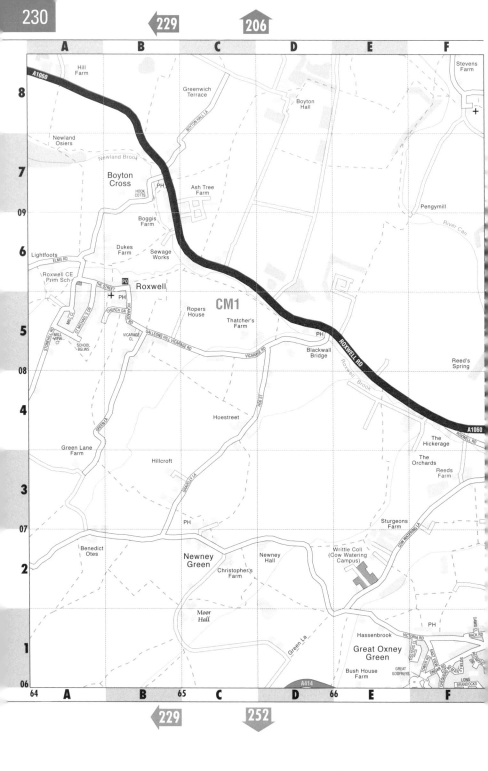

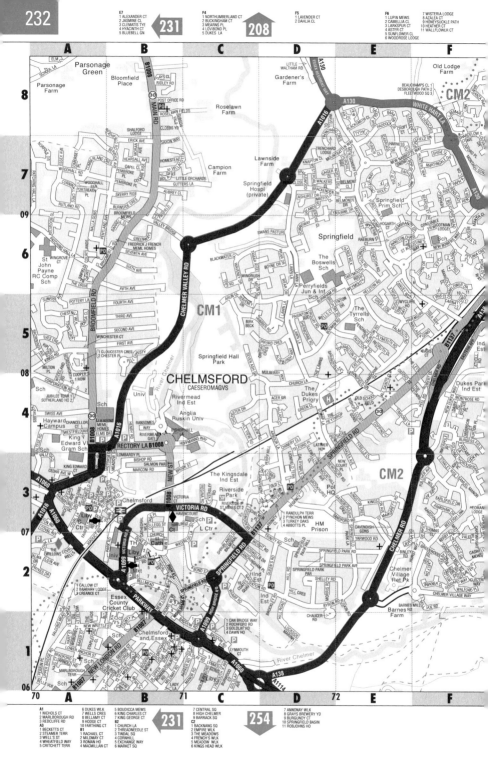

A B C D E F

8

Rickstones

MOWDEN HALL LA

Gardener's Farm

Culverts Cottages

Brakey Wood

Botter's Farm

7

Mulberries

Culvert's Farm

Belstead Cottages

World's End Cottage

Multum in Parvo

Chelmer & Blackwater Navigation

09

Weir

Paper Mill Lock

Paper Mill Bridge

Bassett's Farm

6

River Chelmer

New Wood

Brickwell Wood

TOFTS CHASE

5

Coleraines

VICA COTTS

SPRING CL

WICKHAY COTTS

JARVIS FIELD

NORTH HILL

Walters Cottage

Tofts

Holybreds Wood

08

PH

THE VALE

Bassett's Wood

Little Baddow Hall

The Hoppet

Cuckoos

Holybreds Farm

HOLYBREAD LA

CM3

Warren Farm

Scrub Wood

4

PECH RD

Little Baddow

Mount Pleasant

PO

MOUNT PLEASANT

The Warren

Gibbs

CHAPEL LA

COLAM LA

Burghfields Farm

HIGH PASTURES

Duke's Orchard

SPRING ELMS LA

3

HURRELLS LA

Waterhall

Belle Vue Farm

THE BURY FIELD

PH

MILL LA

POSTMANS LA

Birch Wood

07

NEW LODGE CHASE

New Lodge

Blake's Wood

Elm Green Prep Sch

PARSONAGE LA

OAKLANDS WAY

2

Long Spring Wood

Old Riffhams

Long Wood

THE RIDGE

COMMON LA

Pheasanthouse Wood

Nature Reserve

RIFFHAMS CHASE

GRACES LA

1

Great Graces

The White House

Ling Wood

FIR TREE LA

CHANTRY

CHEST NUT WK

WOODSIDE

Poors' Piece Nature Trail

Hall Wood

Great Graces Farm

Riffhams

RIFFHAMS LA

06

76 A 77 C 78 E F

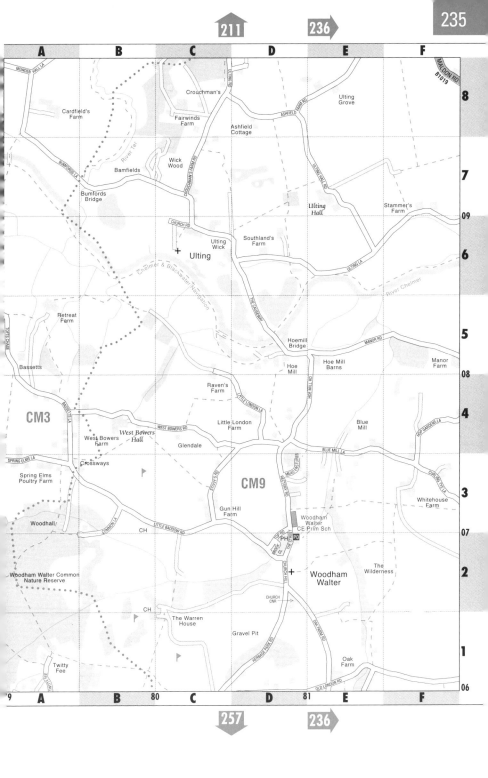

235
212

	A	B	C	D	E	F

The Elms

MALDON RD
B1019

Stock Hall
Farm

LITTLE
HILLS

B1018
LANGFORD RD

CM8

Langford
Park

8

Beavis Hall

River Blackwater

Little Park

HATFIELD RD

WITHAM RD
B1018

Langford
Hall

MAPLE RD

Depot

Fords
Farmhouse

7

BILTING LA

Langford
Bridge

B1019
MALDON RD

Langford

09

Mus of
Power

Langford Cut

Sewage
Wks

LANGFORD RD
B1018

Resr

Resrs

Chelmer & Blackwater Navigation

6

HOLLOWAY RD

RAINBOW MEWS 1
TEN ACRE APP 2

CRESCENT
CT

HEYBRIDGE APP

Beeleigh Falls
House

5

Guy's
Farm

Woodlands

CM9

Beeleigh Grange
Farm

CH

River Chelmer

ROMAN CL

A414

08

HKP GARDENS LA

LEADER RD

Beeleigh
Abbey

ABBEY TURNING

BEELEIGH CHASE

B1018

4

CUT-A-THWART LA

Northall
Cottages

Ind
Est

CROMWELL

COACH LA 1
THE KINGS HEAD CTR 2
EDWARDS WLK 3

3

Little Beeleigh
Farm

Great Beeleigh
Farm

Curling Tye
Green

CURLING TYE LA

LONDON RD

BEELEIGH RD

WEST SQ

Sch

THE
COURT
YARD

HIGH
A414

Ashman's
Farm

Cemy

CYRIL
DOWSETT

Sch

St Peter's

H

COOPER

Plum
Sch

07

Brook Farm

ST GILES CRES

2

Bog
Wood

GREEN
WAYS

WOOD CNR

Maldon Hall
Farm

PO

Sch

1

Cvn
Pk

Green Rd

OLD LONDON RD

West
Station
Ind Est

SPITAL RD

A414

Maldon
Hall

CUMBERLAND
AVE

DORSET
RD

06

82	A		B	83	C		D	84	E		F

235
258

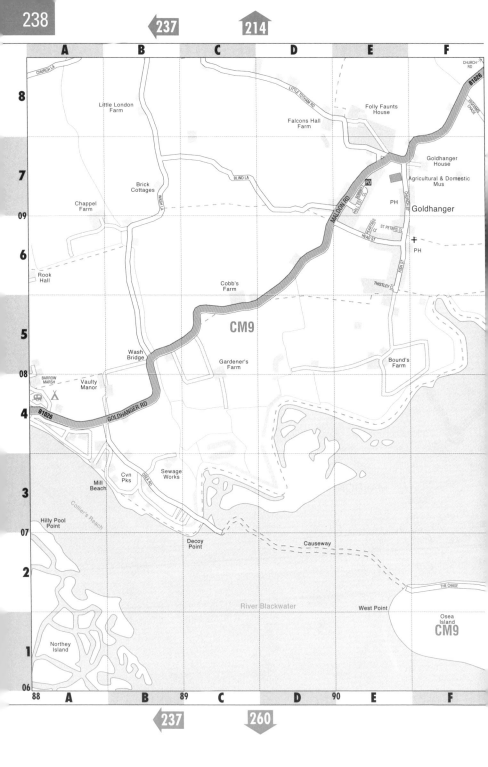

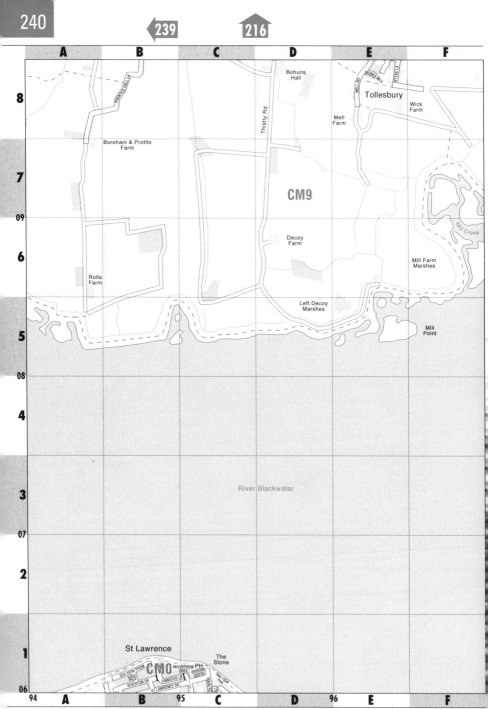

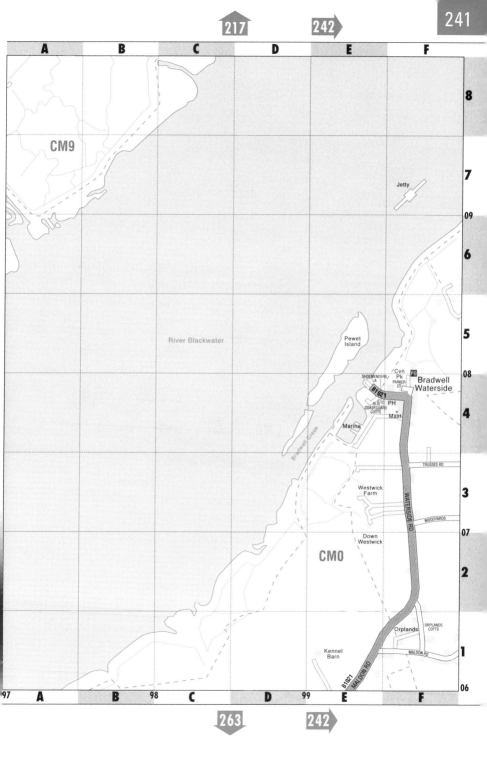

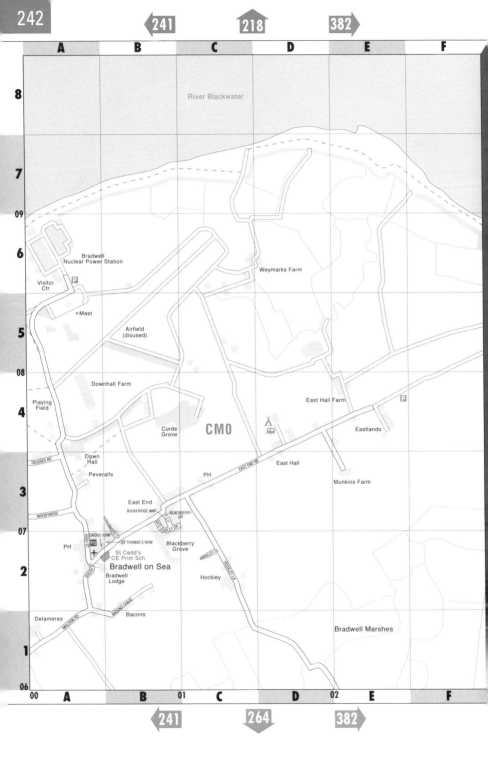

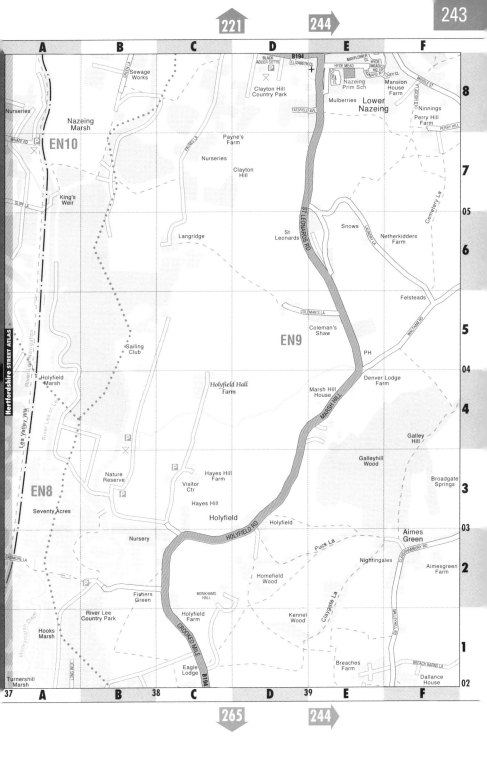

A B C D E F

8

7

05

6

5

04

4

3

03

2

1

02

Nurseries

Nazeing Marsh

EN10

BWHARF RD

King's Weir

SLIPE LA

GREEN LA

Sewage Works

PAYNE'S LA

Payne's Farm

Nurseries

Clayton Hill

Langridge

Clayton Hill Country Park

BLACK ADDER COTTS

ELIZABETH CL

B194

St Leonards

ST LEONARDS RD

Snows

Netherkidders Farm

Cemetery La

MAYFLOWER CL

HYDE MEAD

Nazeing Prim Sch

Mulberries

Lower Nazeing

Mansion House Farm

Ninnings

Perry Hill Farm

PERRY HILL

MIDDLE ST

OLD HOUSE LA

COLEMAN'S LA

Coleman's Shaw

EN9

Felsteads

WALTHAM RD

LAUNDS LA

PH

Denver Lodge Farm

River Lee Navigation

Sailing Club

Holyfield Marsh

River Lea or Lee

Lea Valley Wlk

EN8

Holyfield Hall Farm

Marsh Hill House

MARSH HILL

Galley Hill

Galleyhill Wood

Broadgate Springs

Seventy Acres

Nature Reserve

Visitor Ctr

Hayes Hill Farm

Hayes Hill

Holyfield

HOLYFIELD RD

Holyfield

Aimes Green

Nightingales

Aimesgreen Farm

CLAVERHAMBURY RD

Nursery

Hoozymash Ditch

River Lee Country Park

Hooks Marsh

CADMORE LA

Fishers Green

LONG WLK

MONKHAMS HALL

Holyfield Farm

CROOKED MILE

Eagle Lodge

B194

Homefield Wood

Kennel Wood

Puck La

Claygate La

GALLEYHILL RD

Breaches Farm

BREACH BARNS LA

Dallance House

Turnershill Marsh

Herfordshire STREET ATLAS

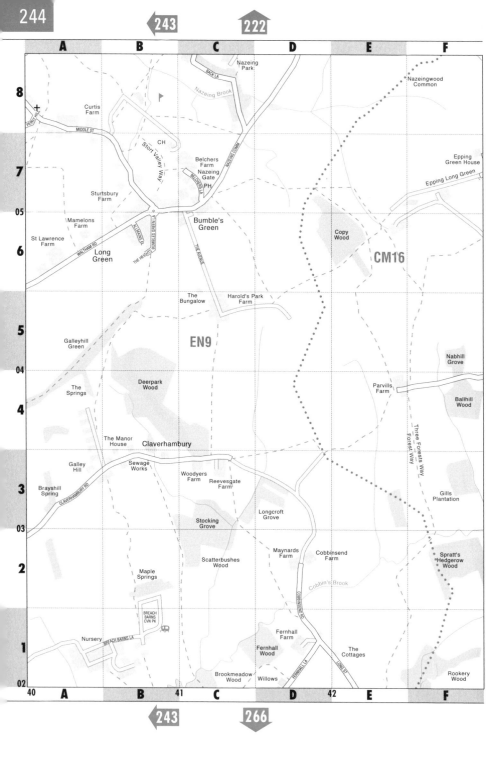

243
222

Nazeingwood
Common

Nazeing
Park

BACK LA

Nazeing Brook

Epping
Green House

Curtis
Farm

MIDDLE ST

CH

Stort Valley Way

Belchers
Farm
Nazeing
Gate
PH

Epping Long Green

Sturtsbury
Farm

Mamelons
Farm

Bumble's
Green

Copy
Wood

CM16

St Lawrence
Farm

WALTHAM RD

Long
Green

THE AVENUE

BUMBLES GREEN RD

THE HEIGHTS

ST JAMES CL

The
Bungalow

Harold's Park
Farm

Galleyhill
Green

EN9

Nabhill
Grove

The
Springs

Deerpark
Wood

Parvills
Farm

Balihill
Wood

The Manor
House

Claverhambury

Galley
Hill

Sewage
Works

Three Forests Way
Forest Way

CLAVERHAMBURY RD

Woodyers
Farm

Reevesgate
Farm

Gills
Plantation

Brayshill
Spring

Stocking
Grove

Longcroft
Grove

Maynards
Farm

Cobbinsend
Farm

Spratt's
Hedgerow
Wood

Maple
Springs

Scatterbushes
Wood

COBBINSEND RD

Cobbin's Brook

BREACH
BARNS
CVN PK

Nursery

BREACH BARNS LA

Fernhall
Farm

Fernhall
Wood

The
Cottages

FERNHALL LA

LONG LEYT

Rookery
Wood

Brookmeadow
Wood

Willows

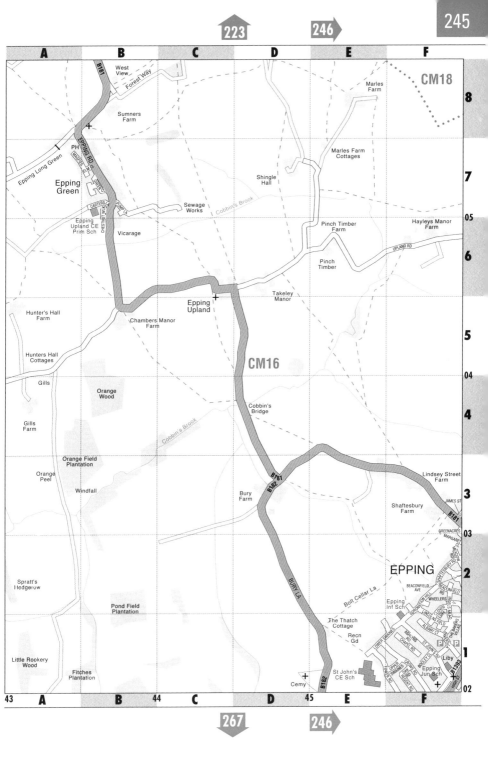

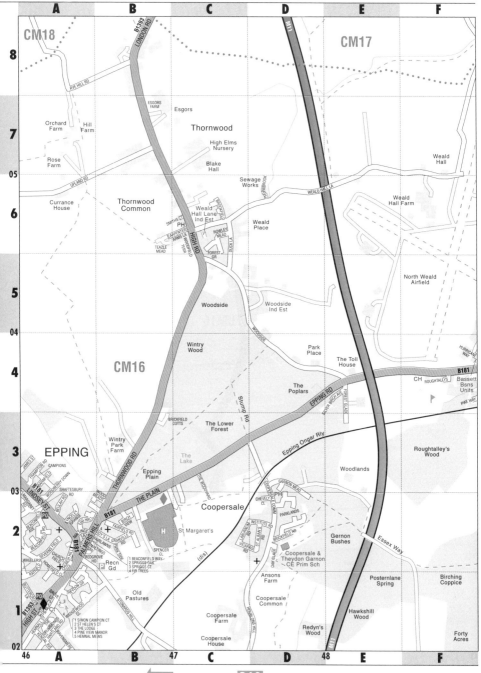

245
224

CM18

B1393 LONDON RD

CM17

8

ESGORS FARM

Esgors

Thornwood

Orchard Farm

Hill Farm

7

High Elms Nursery

Weald Hall

Rose Farm

Blake Hall

05

UPLAND RD

Sewage Works

Weald Hall Farm

Currance House

Thornwood Common

SMITHS CT

Weald Hall Lane Ind Est

Weald Place

Weald Hall

6

PH

CARPENTERS ARMS LA

ROWLEY MEAD

DUCK LA

HIGH RD

WOODFIELD

TERR

TEAZLE MEAD

FOREST GR

North Weald Airfield

5

Woodside

Woodside Ind Est

04

WOODSIDE

CM16

Wintry Wood

Park Place

The Toll House

HURRICANE WAY

B181

4

The Poplars

EPPING RD

FOREST GLADE

CH ROUGHTALLYS

Bassett Bsns Units

SILVER BIRCH AVE

PIKE WAY

BRICKFIELD COTTS

The Lower Forest

Stump Rd

Epping Ongar Rly

Roughtalley's Wood

3

EPPING

Wintry Park Farm

The Lake

Woodlands

JAMES ST

CRAMPTON RD

CAMPIONS

The Plain

THORNWOOD RD

THE WOODWARD

Epping Plain

GARNON MEAD

PH

VOSSEY DOWN

SHAFTESBURY RD

03

B181

LINDSEY ST

THE PLAIN

B181

COOPERSALE COMM

CHEVELY CL

PARKLANDS

PD

COOPERSALE RD

2

FAIRFIELD RD

GRASSELL RD

Coopersale

St Margaret's

INSTITUTE RD

ST ALBANS RD

Gernon Bushes

Essex Way

PALMERS HILL

SPENCER CL

H

BRICKFIELD RD

VICARAGE RD

Coopersale & Theydon Garnon CE Prim Sch

Recn Gd

1 BEACONFIELD WAY
2 SPRIGGS OAK
3 SPRIGGS CT
4 FIR TREES

OAK GLADE

Ansons Farm

Posternlane Spring

Birching Coppice

WHEELERS

CHURCH HILL

Old Pastures

Coopersale Common

Hawkshill Wood

PD

HIGH ST

B1393

STONARDS HILL

THEYDON GR

1

1 SIMON CAMPION CT
2 ST HELEN'S CT
3 THE LODGE
4 PINE VIEW MANOR
5 HEMNAL MEWS

Coopersale Farm

COOPERSALE HALL LA

Redyn's Wood

Forty Acres

02

Coopersale House

46

A

B

47

C

D

48

E

F

245
268

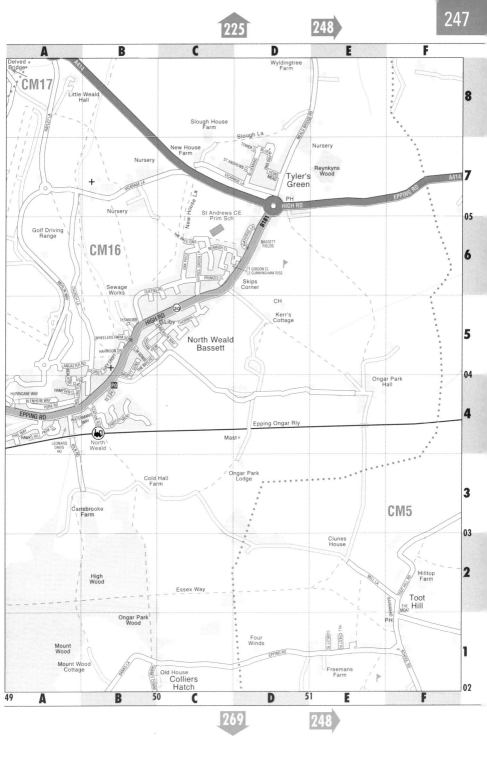

CM17

Delved
Bridge

Little Weald
Hall

Wyldingtree
Farm

Slough House
Farm

Slough La

New House
Farm

Nursery

Nursery

TOWER CL
BLUE LA

ST ANDREWS CL

VICARAGE LA

LHOWS
MEAD

NEALD BRIDGE RD

Nursery

Reynkyns
Wood

Tyler's
Green

PH
HIGH RD

EPPING RD

A414

Golf Driving
Range

CM16

Nursery

VICARAGE LA

New House La

St Andrews CE
Prim Sch

THE PAVILIONS

OAK PIECE

BEAMISH CL

SCHOOL GREEN LA

MARSH LA

PRINCES CL

B181

Bassett
Fields

1 GIBSON CL
2 CUNNINGHAM RISE

Skips
Corner

CH

Kerr's
Cottage

Sewage
Works

QUEENS RD

HIGH RD

Liby

LYSANDER
CT

THORNHILL

North Weald
Bassett

WHEELERS FARM RD

HARRISON DR

ELM GROVE

THE BIRCHES

Ongar Park
Hall

MERLIN HAW

CHURCH LA

LANCASTER RD

GEORGE

BASSETT

CLOSE

HAMPDEN CL

Hurricane Way

BLENHEIM WAY

YORK RD

EPPING RD

PIKE WAY

HAWK'S HILL

PARK CL

WATERMANS WAY

TEMPEST MEAD

SCOTTS MEAD

North
Weald

Mast

Epping Ongar Rly

LEONARD
DAVIS
HO

KILN RD

BARN LA

Cold Hall
Farm

Ongar Park
Lodge

CM5

Carisbrooke
Farm

Clunes
House

MILL LA

Hilltop
Farm

High
Wood

GARNANDO

HILL CREST RD

THE
MOAT

Toot
Hill

PH

SCHOOL RD

Essex Way

Ongar Park
Wood

BARN LA

WINDMILL

Four
Winds

COMET RD

EPPING RD

Freemans
Farm

Mount
Wood

Mount Wood
Cottage

Old House

Colliers
Hatch

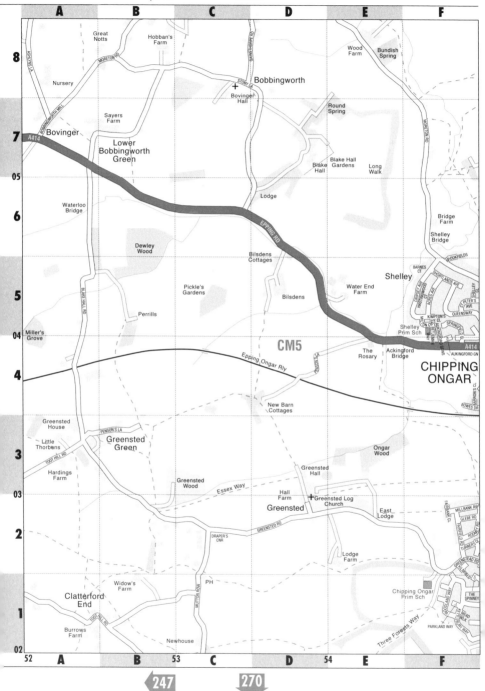

247
226

A   **B**   **C**   **D**   **E**   **F**

8

Great
Notts
Hobban's
Farm

Wood
Farm
Bundish
Spring

Nursery

MORETON RD

STONY LA

Bobbingworth

Round
Spring

Bovinger
Hall

7   A414   Bovinger

Sayers
Farm

Lower
Bobbingworth
Green

Blake Hall
Gardens
Blake
Hall

Long
Walk

05

Lodge

Waterloo
Bridge

6

Bridge
Farm

Shelley
Bridge

Dewley
Wood

Bilsdens
Cottages

BROOKFIELDS

EPPING RD

BARNES
CT

Shelley

SHORLANDS AVE

5

Pickle's
Gardens

Bilsdens

Water End
Farm

PETER'S
AVE

QUEENSWAY

Perrills

KIMPTON'S
CL

SPRING RD

04

Miller's
Grove

BLAKE HALL RD

Shelley
Prim Sch

AUKINGFORD GN

CM5

The
Rosary

Ackingford
Bridge

A414

**CHIPPING
ONGAR**

4

Epping Ongar Rly

PENSON'S LA

BOWES DR

New Barn
Cottages

Greensted
House

PENSON'S LA

Ongar
Wood

Little
Thorbens

TOOT HILL RD

Greensted
Green

Greensted
Hall

3

Hardings
Farm

Greensted
Wood

Essex Way

Greensted Log
Church

East
Lodge

PARLAND CL

MILLBANK AVE

GLEBE RD

Hall
Farm

Greensted

FAIRBANK CL

03

GREENSTEAD RD

ROOKES CL

TURNER'S CL

GREENSTEAD RD

2

DRAPER'S
CNR

Lodge
Farm

THE
SPINNEY

Chipping Ongar
Prim Sch

Widow's
Farm

PH

Clatterford
End

TOOT HILL RD

MUTTON RW

PARKLAND WAY

1

Burrows
Farm

Newhouse

Three Forests Way

02

52   **A**   **B**   53   **C**   **D**   54   **E**   **F**

247
270

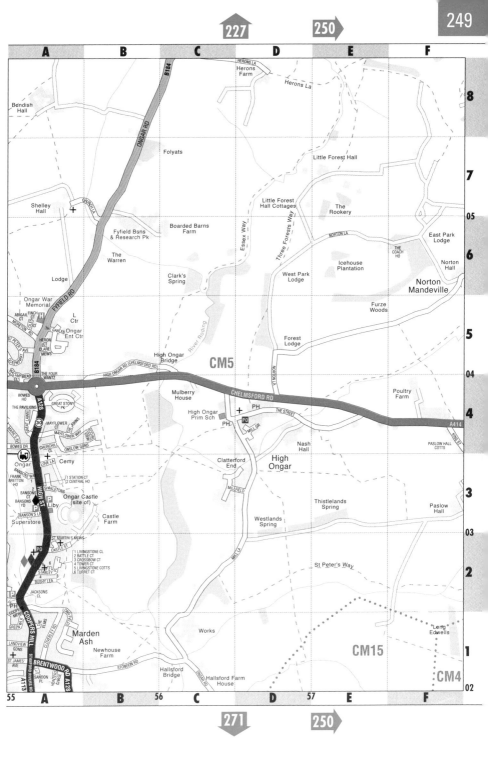

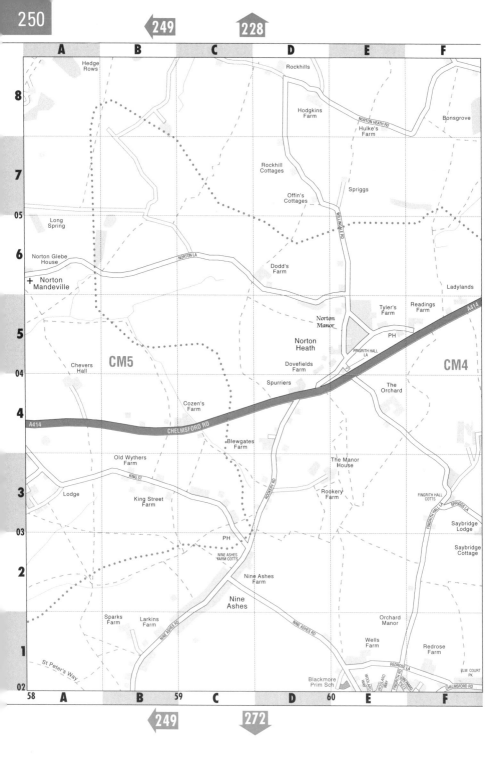

8

7

05

6

Norton Glebe
House

+ Norton
Mandeville

5

04

4 A414

3

Lodge

03

2

1

St Peter's Way

58 A B 59 C D 60 E F

A B C D E F

Hedge
Rows

Rockhills

Hodgkins
Farm

NORTON HEATH RD

Bonsgrove

Hulke's
Farm

Rockhill
Cottages

Spriggs

Offin's
Cottages

Long
Spring

NORTON LA

Dodd's
Farm

Ladylands

Norton
Manor

Tyler's
Farm

Readings
Farm

WILLINGALE RD

Norton
Heath

PH

Chevers
Hall

CM5

Dovefields
Farm

FINGRITH HALL
LA

CM4

Spurriers

The
Orchard

Cozen's
Farm

CHELMSFORD RD

Blewgates
Farm

The Manor
House

Old Wythers
Farm

FINGRITH HALL
COTTS

SPRINGS LA

KING ST

Rookery
Farm

FINGRITH HALL RD

Saybridge
Lodge

King Street
Farm

ROOKERY RD

Saybridge
Cottage

PH

NINE ASHES
FARM COTTS

Nine Ashes
Farm

Nine
Ashes

Orchard
Manor

Sparks
Farm

Larkins
Farm

NINE ASHES RD

NINE ASHES RD

Wells
Farm

Redrose
Farm

REDROSE LA

ELM COURT
PK

WOOLARD WAY

FINGRITH HALL
PLACE

Blackmore
Prim Sch

CHELMSFORD RD

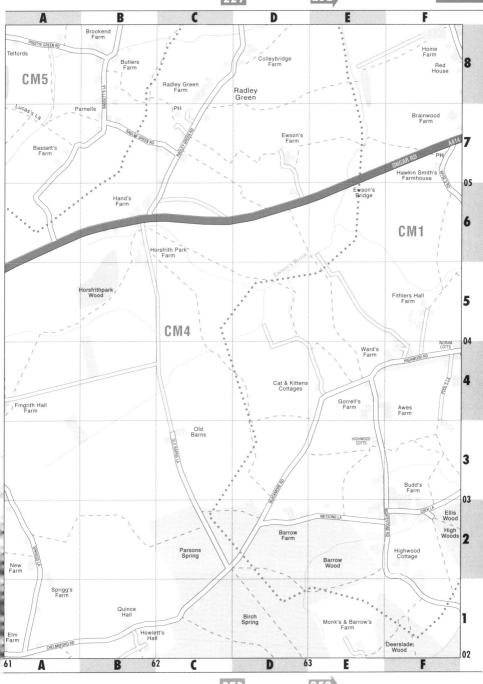

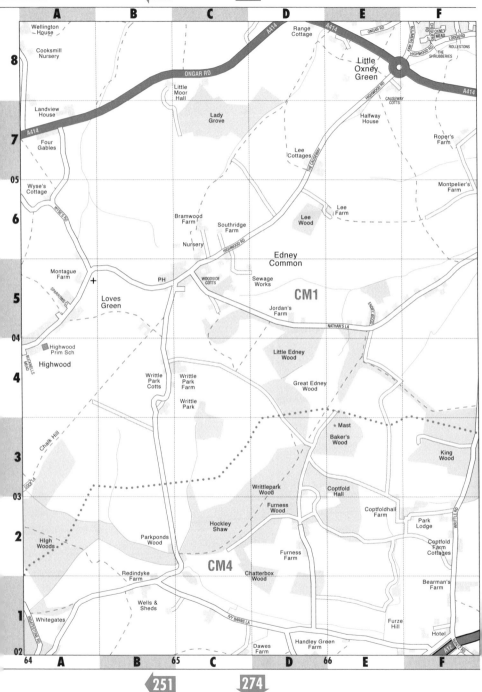

8

7

05

6

04

5

4

3

03

2

1

02

64   65   66

Wellington House
Cooksmill Nursery
Landview House
Four Gables
Wyse's Cottage
Montague Farm
Loves Green
Highwood Prim Sch
Highwood
High Woods
Whitegates
Redindyke Farm
Wells & Sheds
Parkponds Wood
Chalk Hill
Little Moor Hall
Lady Grove
Bramwood Farm
Southridge Farm
Nursery
PH
WOODSIDE COTTS
Writtle Park Cotts
Writtle Park Farm
Writtle Park
Hockley Shaw
Dawes Farm
ONGAR RD
A414
Range Cottage
Little Oxney Green
Lee Cottages
Lee Wood
Lee Farm
Edney Common
Sewage Works
Jordan's Farm
NATHAN'S LA
Little Edney Wood
Great Edney Wood
Mast
Baker's Wood
Writtlepark Wood
Furness Wood
Furness Farm
Chatterbox Wood
CM4
IVY BARNS LA
Handley Green Farm
Halfway House
Roper's Farm
Montpelier's Farm
CM1
Coptfold Hall
Coptfoldhall Farm
King Wood
Park Lodge
Coptfold Farm Cottages
Bearman's Farm
Furze Hill
Hotel
ONGAR RD
OXNEY MEAD
LODGE RD
ROLLESTONS
THE SHRUBBERIES
CAUSEWAY COTTS
HIGHWOOD RD
THE CAUSEWAY
HIGHWOOD RD
EDNEY WOOD
SPARROWS LA
WYSE'S RD
BURNELL'S MEAD
COCK LA
BLUESTONE RD
WRITTLE RD
A414
A414

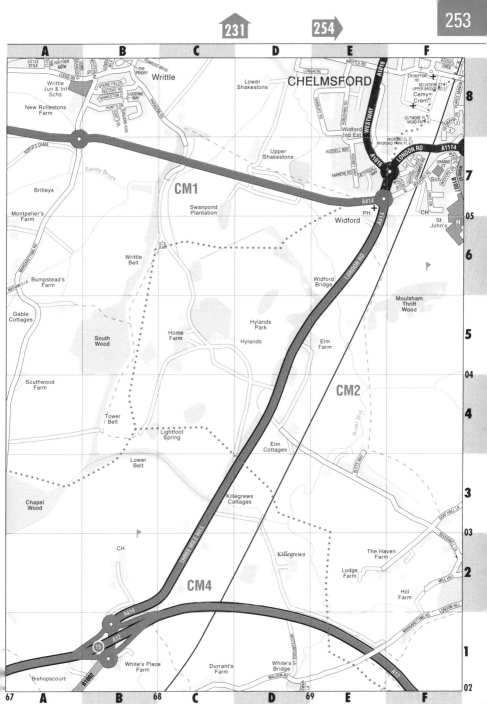

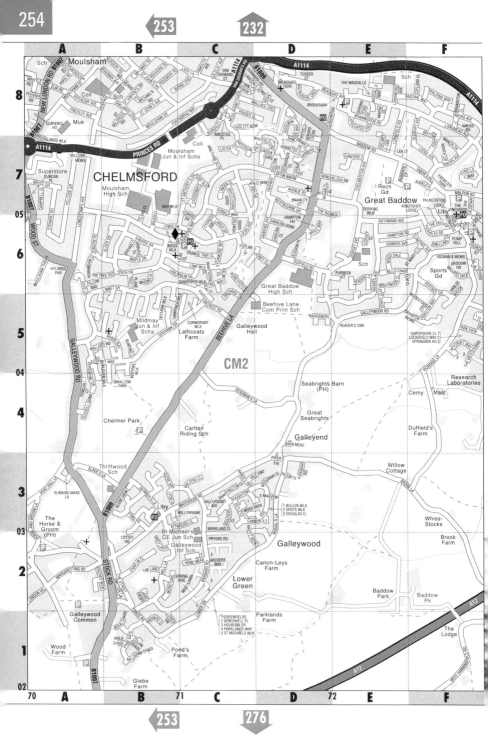

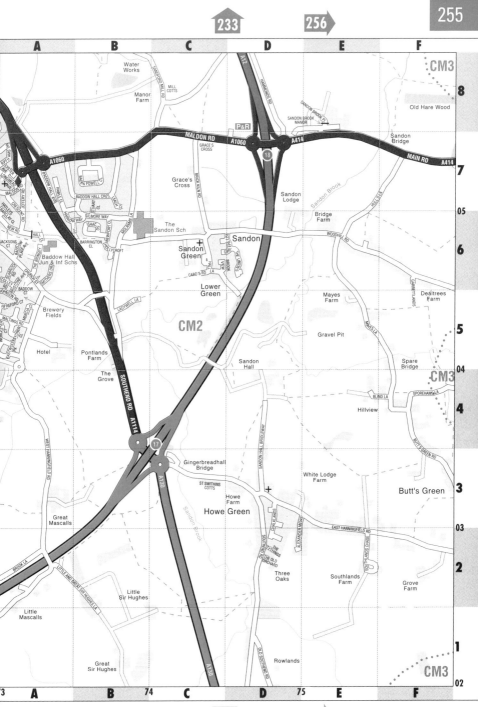

233
256

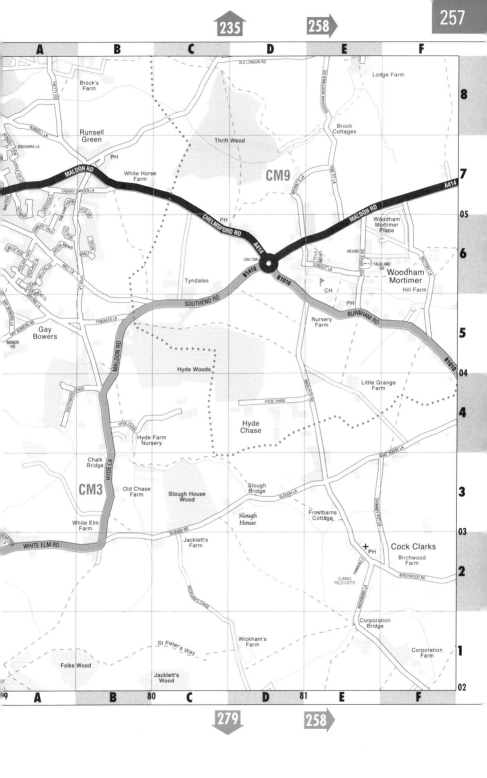

237
260
281
260

Northey
Island

Causeway

Southey Creek

Football
Gd

South House
Farm

SOUTH HOUSE CHASE

Halfway House
Farm

Lynbourne Creek

MALDON RD

Bramble Hall
Farm

Stud Hill
Bungalows

Garlands

Riding
Stables

Blackwater
Farm

Stud
Farm

White House
Farm

CM9

Copkitchen's
Farm

Mundon Wash

NEW HALL LA

Mundon Wash
Bridge

Purleigh Wash
Farm

BURNHAM LA

...AGE LA

Cammas
Farm

Mundon
Hall

FAMBRIDGE RD

PURLEIGH
WASH

B1018

PH

Mundon

St Mary's
Church

BARON'S LA   B1010

St Peter's Way

Sparrow
Wycke

WOODSIDE
WOODSIDE
COTTS
WEST CHASE

WESTFIELD
BGLWS

Eastcroft

B1010

Mundon
Furze

THE STREET

Clock House
Farm

Furze
Farm

WOOD LA

1 MASEFIELD RD
2 SHAKESPEARE DR
3 SHELLEY CL
4 CHAUCER CL
5 MIROSA REACH
6 FROBISHER CL

MILTON RD
LAMBOURNE
DR
MEMORY
LANE

CENTRAL AVE

LIMEBROOK WAY

PRIMROSE
WLK
KESTREL
CL
DARIN RD
PARK DR
TIDEWAY
OAK CL
BEAUMONT
WAY

8

7

05

6

5

04

4

3

03

2

1

02

A   B   C   D   E   F

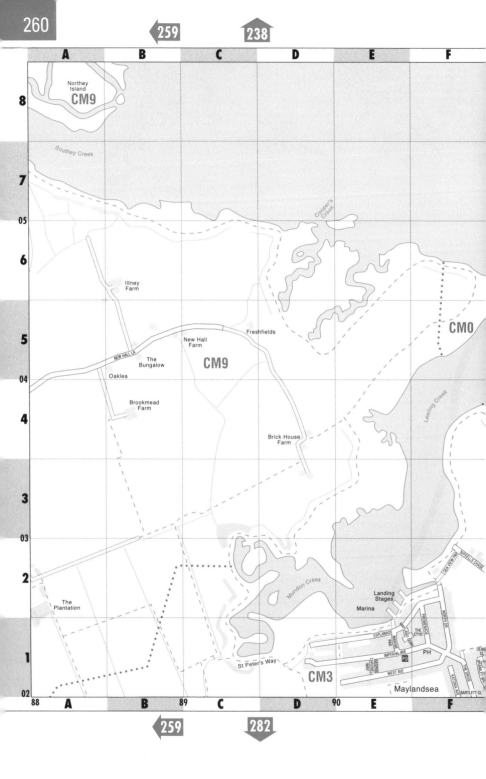

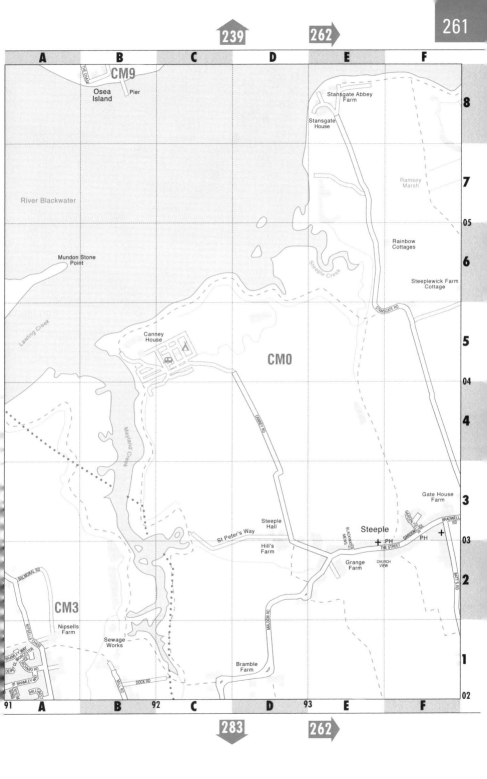

CM9

THE CAUSE

Osea
Island

Pier

Stansgate Abbey
Farm

Stansgate
House

8

Ramsey
Marsh

7

05

River Blackwater

Rainbow
Cottages

Mundon Stone
Point

6

Steeple Creek

Steeplewick Farm
Cottage

Lawling Creek

STANSGATE RD

5

Canney
House

CM0

04

4

Mayland Creek

Gate House
Farm

3

Steeple
Hall

St Peter's Way

BLACKWATER MEWS

GLADWIN RD

Steeple

+ PH

GARDENERS TCE

PH +

BRADWELL RD

03

Hill's
Farm

THE STREET

Grange
Farm

CHURCH
VIEW

BATT'S RD

2

CM3

Nipsells
Farm

BALMORAL RD

NIPSELLS CHASE

BRAMLEY WAY

WORCESTER

DERS

DR BRAMLEY RD

HILL CL

Sewage
Works

MALDON RD

DOCK RD

MILL RD

Bramble
Farm

1

02

91

A

B

92

C

D

93

E

F

261
240

A B C D E F

8

St Lawrence Bay

St Lawrence

BAY VIEW
WICK FARM
SEAWAY
HIGH VIEW
SUNNY WAY
MOUNTVIEW CRES
BEACHY QR
MOUNTNESSING RD

Ramsey Island

Caravan Park

PO

Ramsey Marsh

7

PH
ANCHORAGE VIEW
MEDLEY WY
CLOVERS
MAIN RD

Beacon Hill Leisure Park

05

Steeplewick Farm

Sewage Works

Beacon Hill Farm

6

BRADWELL RD

Mott's Farm

St Lawrence

5

CMO

ST LAWRENCE HILL

St Lawrence Hall

Wr Twr

Kings Farm

04

STEEPLE RD

4

Black House Court Farm

St Peter's Way

Brick House Farm

3

FOSSGATE RD
BRADWELL RD
IVY COTTS

Poplars Farm

SOUTHMINSTER RD

03

The Lodge

West Newlands

East Newlands

2

Asheldham Brook

Moynes Farm

Asheldham Grange

1

BATT'S RD

Batt's Farm

02

94 A 95 B C 96 D E F

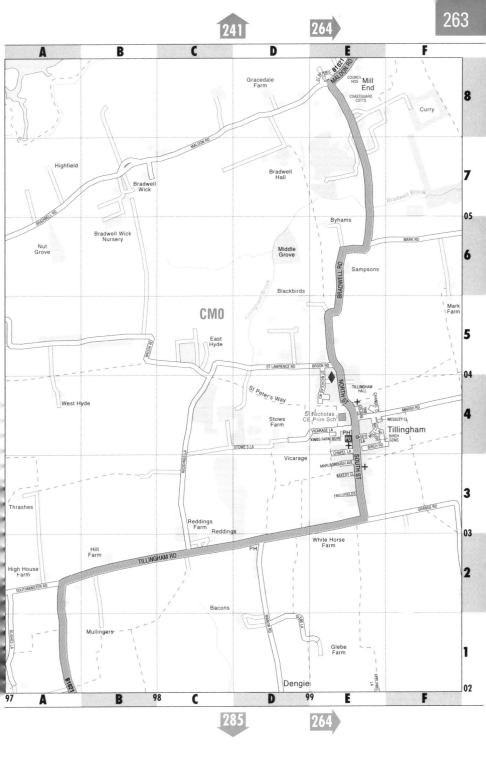

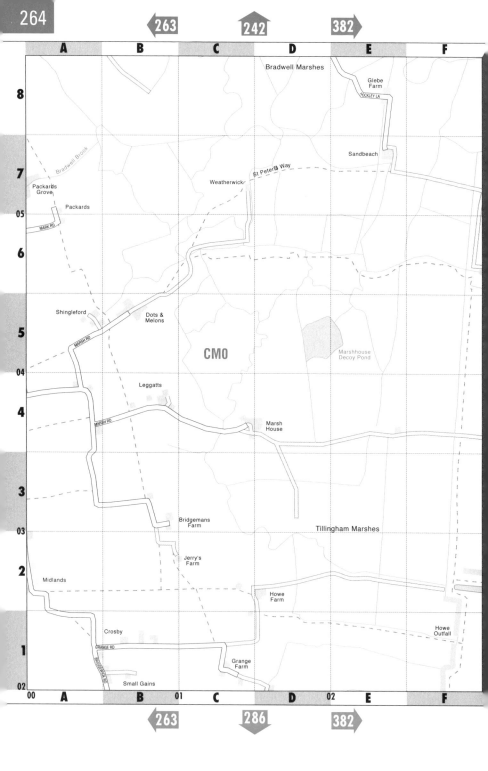

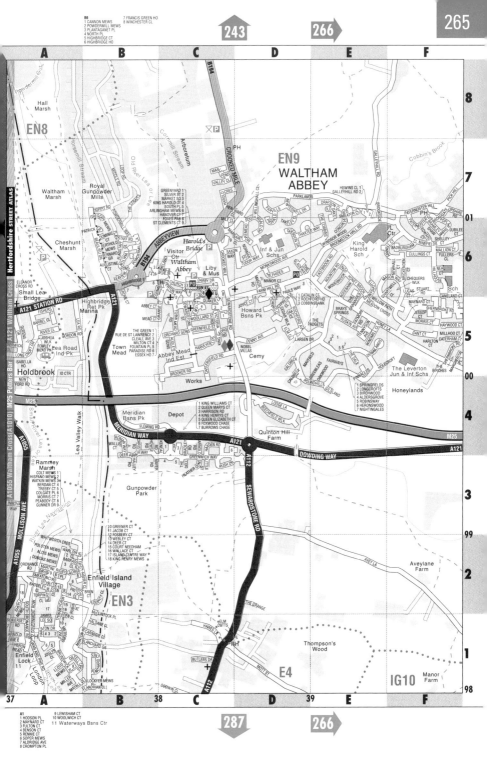

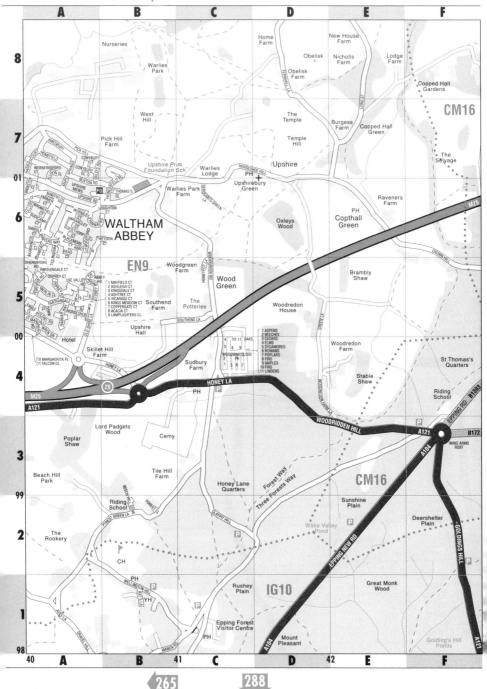

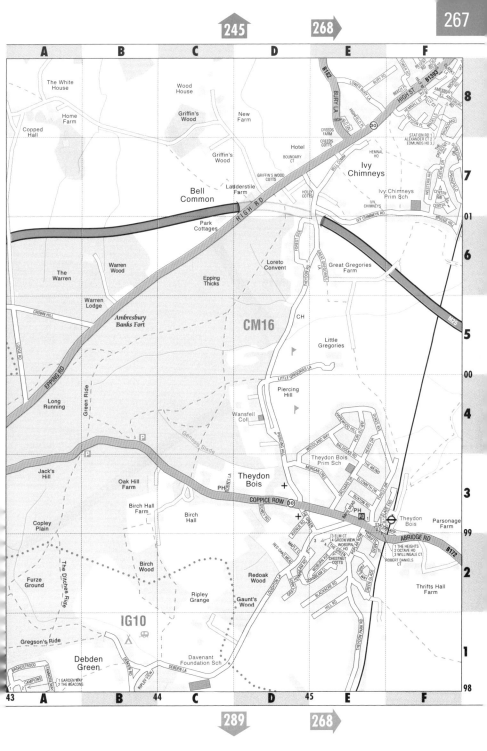

245
268
289
268

The White House

Wood House

Home Farm

Griffin's Wood

New Farm

Copped Hall

Griffin's Wood

Hotel

CREEDS FARM
CREEDS COTTS

HEMNAL HO

Ivy Chimneys

BOUNDARY CT

GRIFFIN'S WOOD COTTS

Ivy Chimneys Prim Sch

Bell Common

Ladderstile Farm

HOLLY COTTS

IVY CHIMNEYS

HIGH RD

Park Cottages

IVY CHIMNEYS RD

Warren Wood

The Warren

Epping Thicks

Loreto Convent

Great Gregories Farm

CM16

Warren Lodge

CROWN HILL

Ambresbury Banks Fort

CH

Little Gregories

LITTLE GREGORIES LA

Long Running

EPPING RD

Green Ride

Piercing Hill

Genesis Slade

Wansfell Coll

Theydon Bois Prim Sch

PIERCING HILL

WOODLAND WAY

Jack's Hill

Oak Hill Farm

PH

ROBIN'S LA

Theydon Bois

COPPICE ROW

MORGAN CRES

Theydon Bois

Parsonage Farm

Birch Hall Farm

Birch Hall

Copley Plain

PH
PO

Birch Wood

ABRIDGE RD

3 ELM CT
4 GREEN VIEW

1 THE HEIGHTS
2 OCTAVE HO
3 WILLINGALE CT

Furze Ground

The Ditches Ride

Ripley Grange

Redoak Wood

Gaunt's Wood

RED OAKS MEAD

WOBURN HO

CHESTNUT COTTS

ROBERT DANIELS CT

Thrifts Hall Farm

IG10

Gregson's Ride

Davenant Foundation Sch

DERDEN LA

Debden Green

BROADSTROOD

1 GARDEN WAY
2 THE BEACONS

CAMPIONS

B172

267
246

A B C D E F

RAVENSMERE

8

Stonards
Farm

PH

Lodge

Gaynes
Park

Mount
Quarter

Coopersale
Street

THEYDON
BOWER

1 AMESBURY RD
2 ST GREGORYS HO
3 BYBONS HO
4 TENNYSON HO
5 HARDING HO
6 CONISTON CT
7 HILLCREST WAY

Epping
P

BOWER
CT

Fiddlers
Hamlet

7

Bower Hill
Ind Est
SUNNYSIDE

Essex Way

Hornes
Farm

Mount
End

CHARLES ST
OAKLEIGH
RISE

Steward's
Green

Home
Farm

01

CALL NUTTS RD
INCHCAPE

PH

Searles
Hall

BROOK RD

STEWARDS GREEN RD

Masons Bridge
Farm

North
House

Sawkins
Farm

6

CH

Little Thorn
Hall

CM16

CH

Sewage
Works

Tarlins
Farm

HILLTOP
COTTS

Gardners
Farm

Coopersale
Hall Sch

North
Lodge

The Rough
Patch

5

M25

Long
Plantation

00

27

Peakes
Farmhouse

4

6

Garnish
Hall

Barber's
Wood

Hill Hall
(remains of)

HOBBS CROSS RD

The
Wilderness

Fiveponds
Wood

Hobbs
Cross

3

Theydon
Priory

Theydon
Garnon

HOBBS CROSS
COTTS

Hobbs Cross
Farm

Blunts
Farm

COOPERSALE LA

M25

99

Martins

Bartlemy
Grove

2

B172

Bush
Grove

Hobbscross
Cottages

CH

RM4

Hydes
Farm

Brook
House

1

Cemy

EPPING LA

Skinners Farm
Cottages

Three Forests
Way

98

M11

B172

46 A B 47 C D 48 E F

267
290

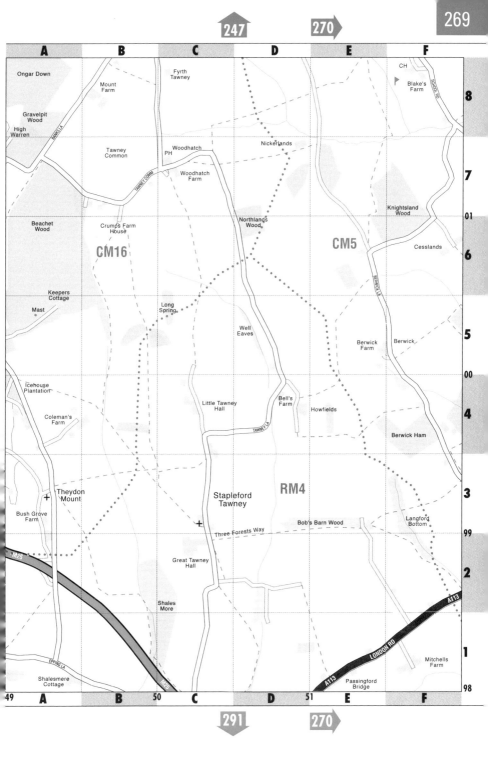

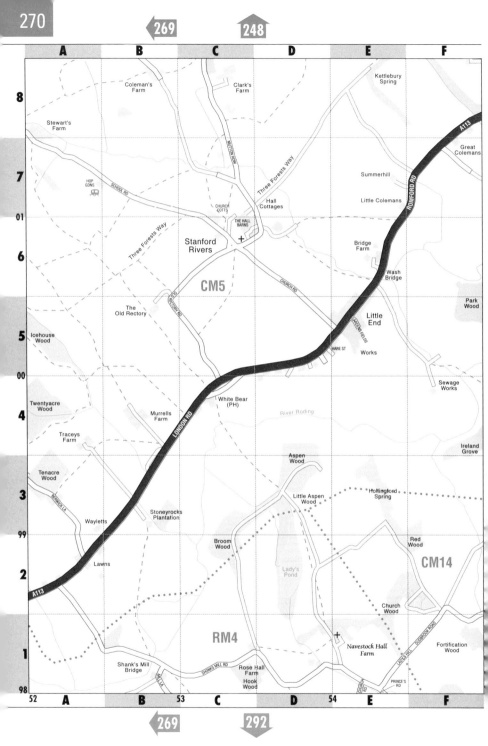

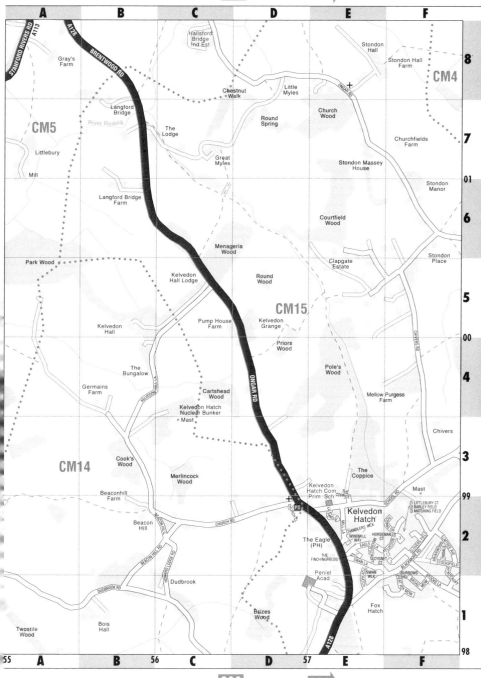

249
272
293
272

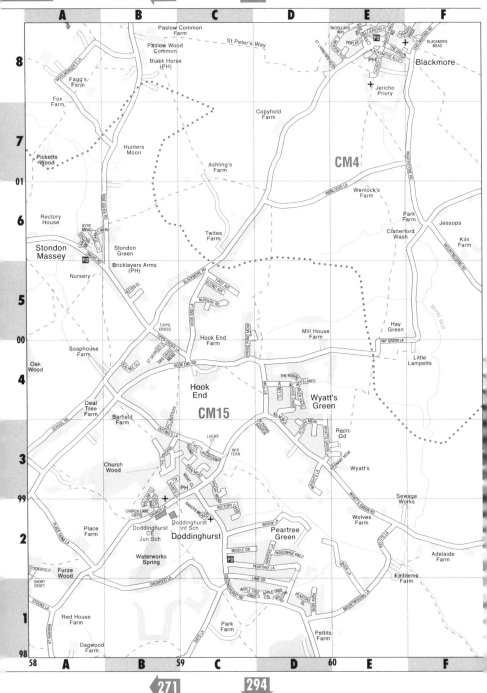

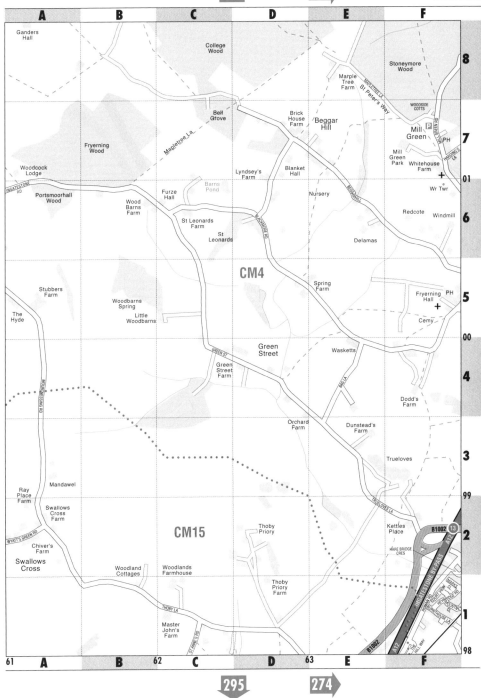

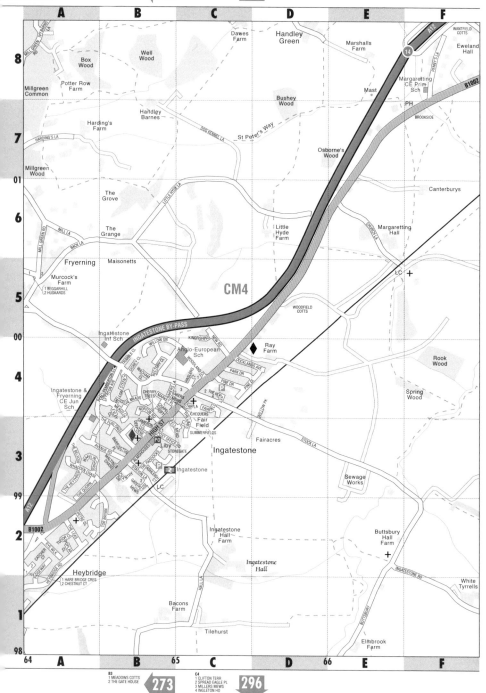

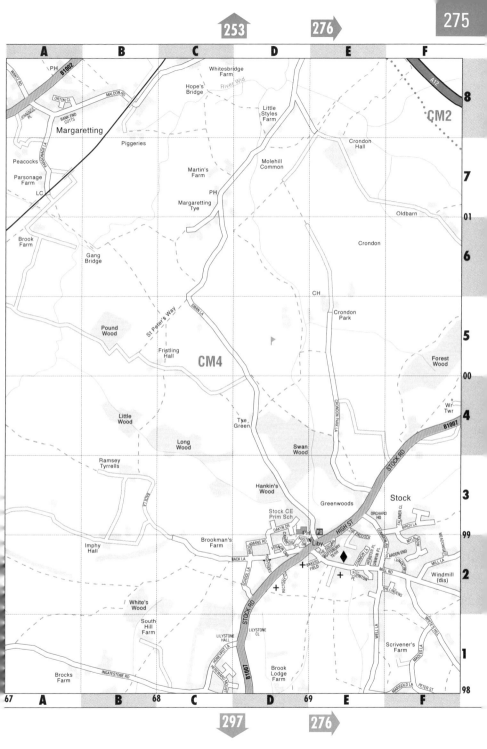

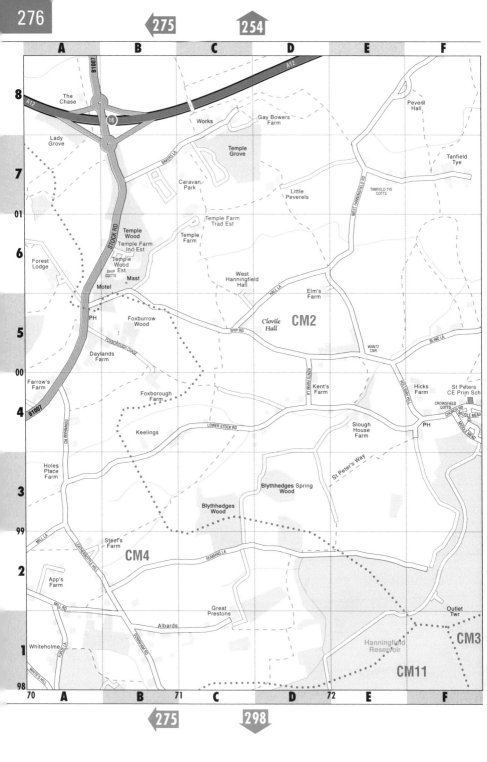

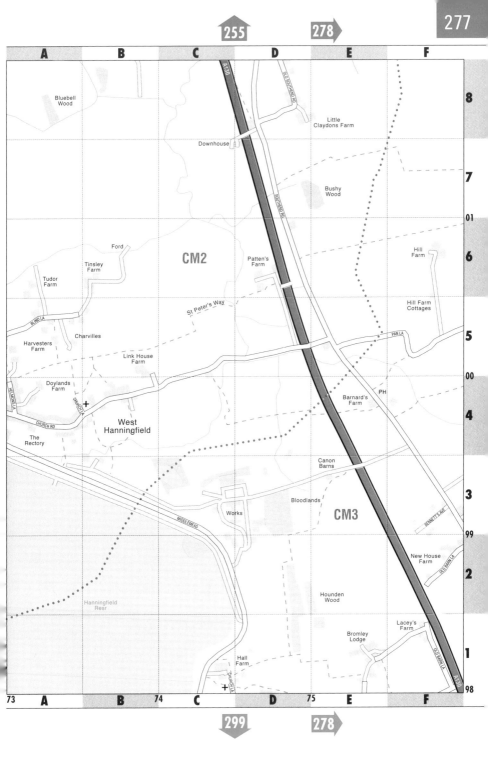

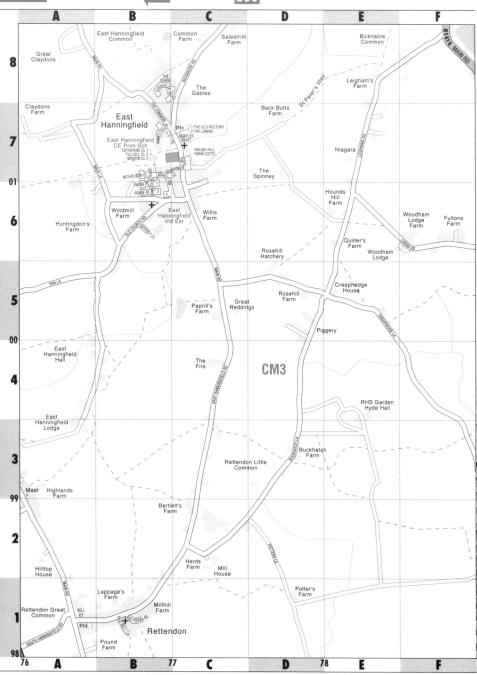

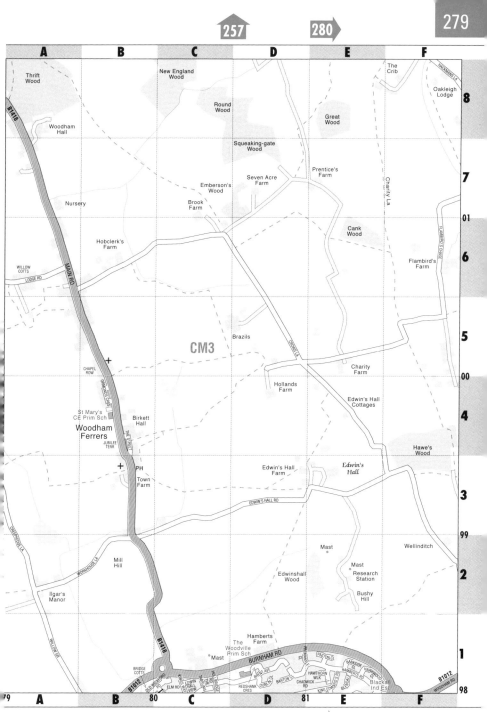

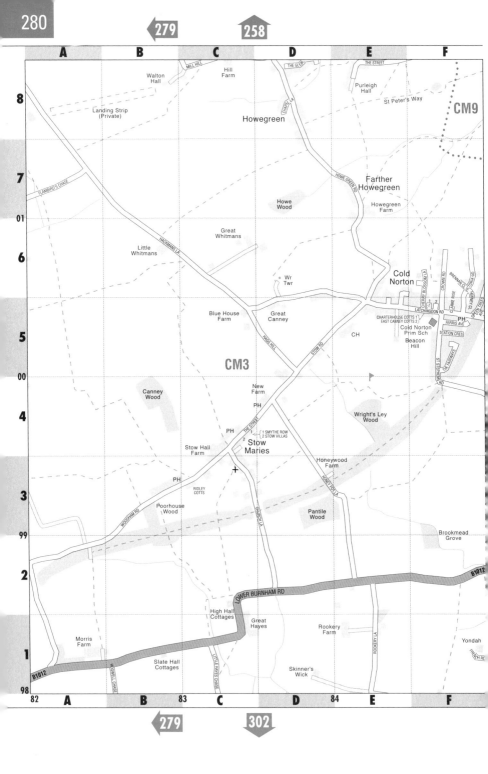

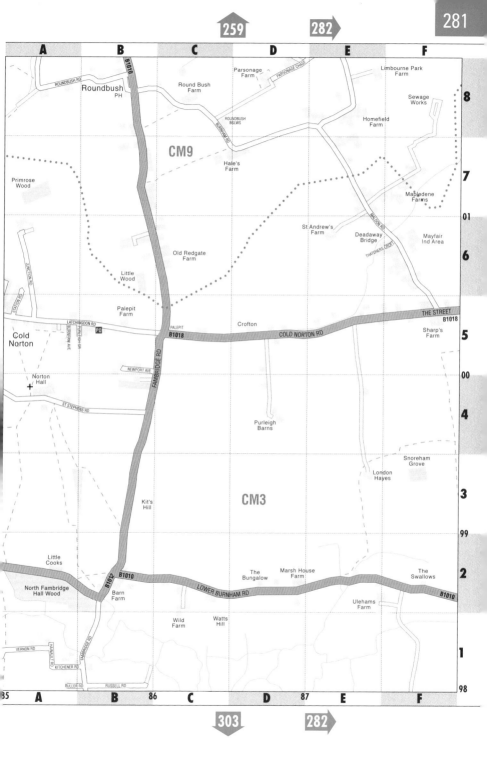

A B C D E F

8

Roundbush PH

Roundbush RD

B1010

Round Bush Farm

Parsonage Farm

PARSONAGE CHASE

Limbourne Park Farm

Sewage Works

CM9

ROUNDBUSH B&LWS

BURNHAM RD

Homefield Farm

7

Primrose Wood

Hale's Farm

01

MALDON RD

Mapledene Farms

St Andrew's Farm

Deadaway Bridge

Mayfair Ind Area

6

Old Redgate Farm

THATCHERS CROFT

JUNCTION RD

Little Wood

STATION RD

Palepit Farm

THE STREET

B1018

5

LATCHINGDON RD

BURNHAM AVE

ASHLEIGH GR

PO

PALEPIT

B1018

Crofton

COLD NORTON RD

Sharp's Farm

Cold Norton

FAMBRIDGE RD

NEWPORT AVE

00

Norton Hall

ST STEPHENS RD

4

Purleigh Barns

Snoreham Grove

3

Kit's Hill

CM3

London Hayes

99

Little Cooks

B1010

The Bungalow

Marsh House Farm

The Swallows

2

North Fambridge Hall Wood

Barn Farm

LOWER BURNHAM RD

B1010

Ulehams Farm

Wild Farm

Watts Hill

1

VERNON RD

FAMBRIDGE RD

CHANNEL RD

KITCHENER RD

BULLER RD

RUSSELL RD

98

35 A B 86 C D 87 E F

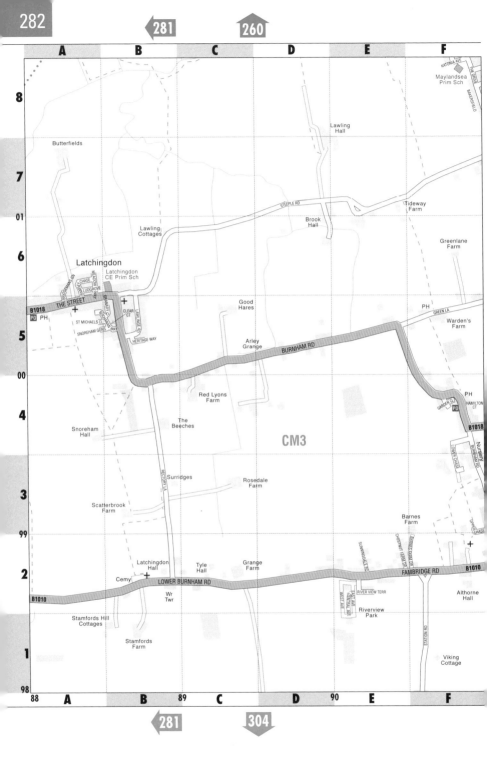

A B C D E F

8

KATONA AVE
THE DRIVE
BAKERSFIELD
Maylandsea
Prim Sch

Butterfields

Lawling
Hall

7

01

STEEPLE RD

Brook
Hall

Tideway
Farm

Lawling
Cottages

Greenlane
Farm

6

Latchingdon

Latchingdon
CE Prim Sch

MEADOW VW
CHASE
LUDGROVE
BROADWAY

THE STREET

B1018

CLEAR CT

Good
Hares

PH
GREEN LA

Warden's
Farm

PO PH

ST MICHAELS CL

SNOREHAM GDNS
WAY

HERITAGE WAY

LAWLING RD

5

Arley
Grange

BURNHAM RD

00

Red Lyons
Farm

PH

GARDEN CL
HAMILTON CT

PO

4

Snoreham
Hall

The
Beeches

CM3

B1018

LOWER CHASE

Nursey
BURNHAM RD

RECTORY LA

Surridges

Rosedale
Farm

3

Scatterbrook
Farm

Barnes
Farm

TIPPERS CHASE

99

Latchingdon
Hall

Tyle
Hall

Grange
Farm

SUNNINGDALE RD

CHESTNUT FERN DR

BARNES FARM DR

+

FAMBRIDGE RD

B1010

2

Cemy

LOWER BURNHAM RD

RIVER VIEW TERR

EAST AVE
CENTRAL AVE
WEST AVE

SOUTON RD

Althorne
Hall

B1010

Wr
Twr

Riverview
Park

Stamfords Hill
Cottages

Stamfords
Farm

1

Viking
Cottage

98

88 A B 89 C D 90 E F

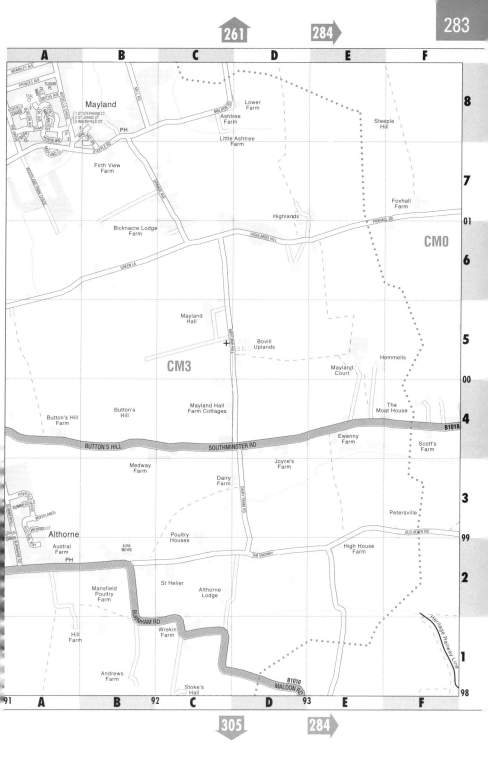

261
284
305
284

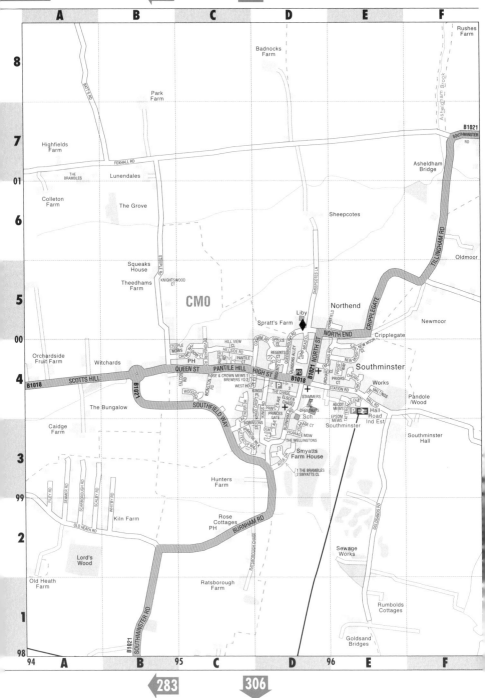

263
286

A **B** **C** **D** **E** **F**

Asheldham Pits
Nature Reserve

B1021

TILLINGHAM RD

END WAY
COTTS
SOUTHMINSTER RD

Asheldham

Asheldham
Hall

DALL RD

New Hall
Farm

MANOR RD

Dengie
Manor

Keelings

KEELINGS LA

KEELINGS RD

Cemy

Landwick
Farm

LANDWICK LA

Irrigation
Resr

Asheldham Brook

CMO

North
Wycke

Wraywick
Farm

Wraywick
Cottage

Broadward
Farm

Turncole Farm

8

7

01

6

5

00

4

3

99

2

1

98

A 98 **B** 98 **C** 99 **D** **E** **F**

97

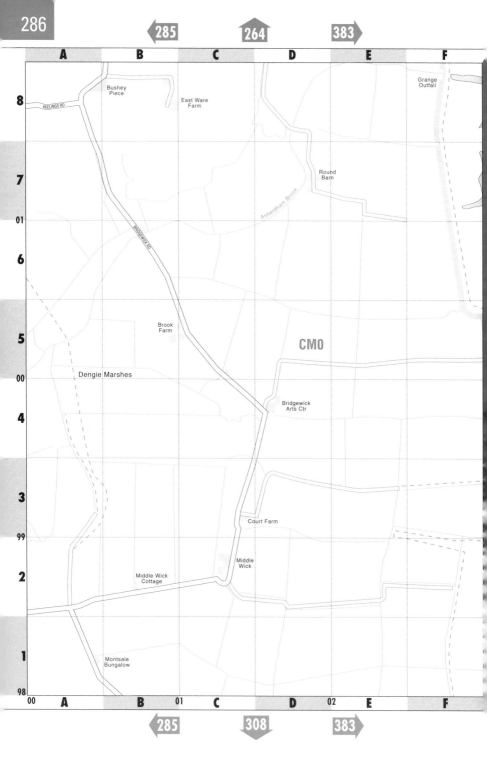

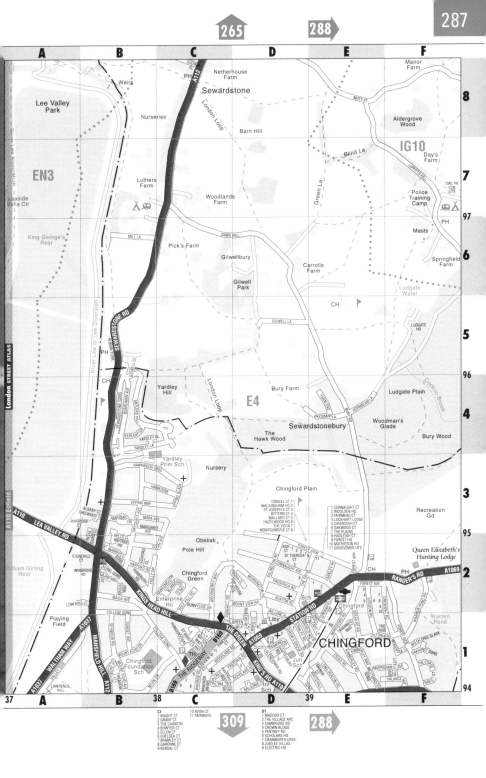

265 288 309 288

C1
1 KNIGHT CT
2 GRANT CT
3 THE CHANTRY
4 BOWYER CT
5 ELLEN CT
6 CHELSEA CT
7 BRAMLEY CT
8 GARENNE CT
9 KENDAL CT

10 AVON CT.
11 FAIRWAYS

D1
1 MADDOX CT
2 THE VILLAGE ARC
3 CAMBRIDGE RD
4 CROWN BLDGS
5 PENTNEY RD
6 SCHOLARS HO
7 CRANWORTH CRES
8 JUBILEE VILLAS
9 ELECTRIC HO

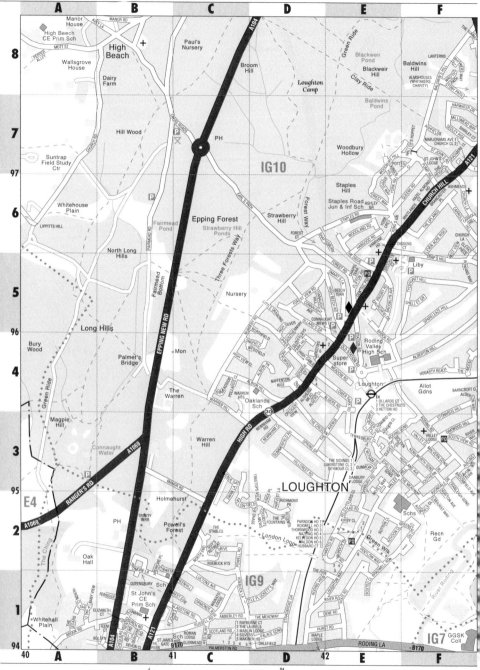

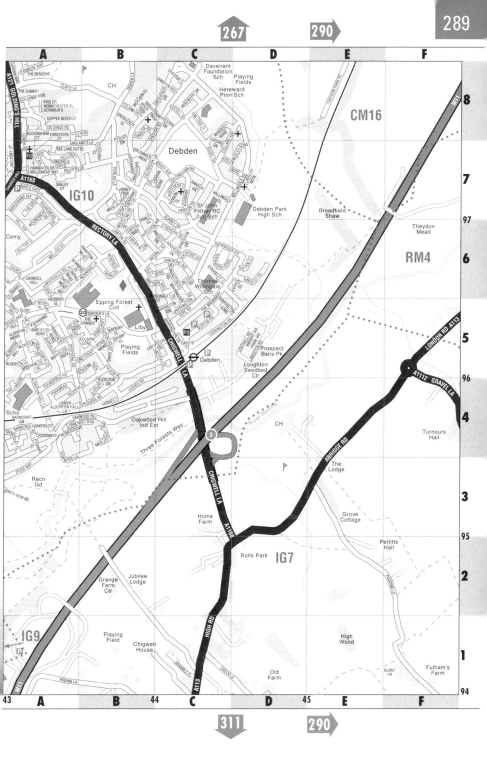

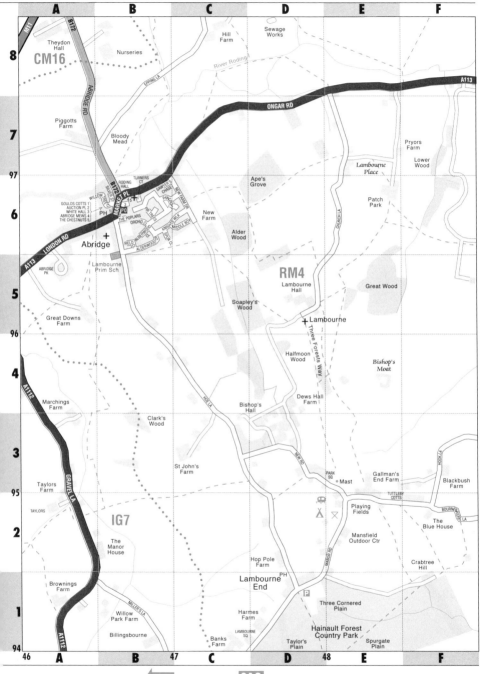

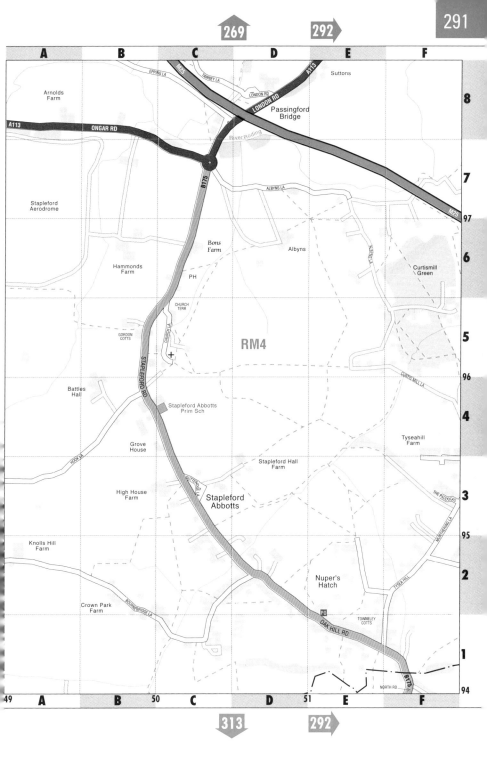

A B C D E F

8

Redgate Wood

Howletts Hall

Heronland Shaw

Strawberry Wood

Dabbs Farm

Yew Tree Farm

Navestock Heath

7

Randalls Farm

Marleys

97

PH

Sabine's Green

6

RM4

Loft Hall

Sabines Farm

Bower Farm

PH

Meadow View

Brook Farm

5

Horseman Side

PH

New Hall Farm

Sabines Farm

+

96

Jenkins Farm

Waterhales Farm

CM14

4

Lee Farm

Waterhales

Weald Brook

Spring Farm

Watton Farm

3

Watton's Green

Havering Plain

Wabbing's Plantation

95

Skips Corner Farm

CH

Navestock Common

Curtis Plantation

2

Asheton Farm

TYSEA HILL

GOATSWOOD LA

Sevenacre Plantation

Old MacDonald's Educational Farm Park

1

Sandpits Plantation

CHURCH RD

Pentowan Farm

RM3

94

LOWER NOKE CL.

52 A B 53 C D 54 E F

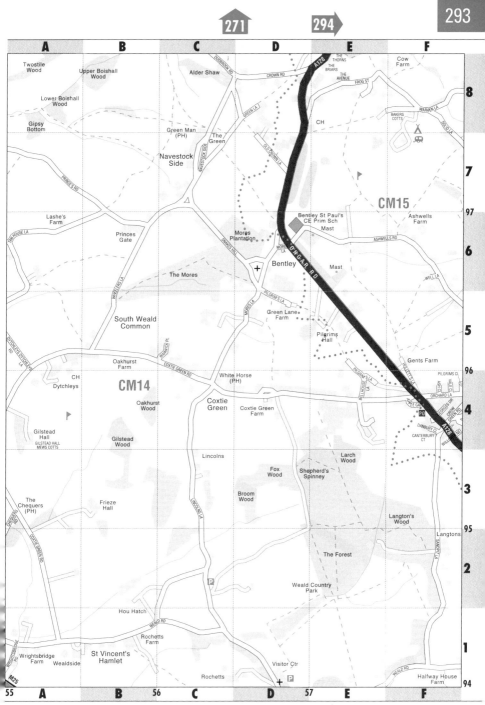

293
272

	A	B	C	D	E	F

8

Cowes Farm

Park Wood

America Farm

Heard's Farm

7

Wishfields Farm

Sumner's Farm

Rosecroft

97

Palmers Farm

Bennett's Farm

HALL LA

6

Howe's Farm

Days Farm

Brickhouse Farm

Brickhouse Wood

CM15

Crow Green

5

Canterbury Tye Hall

DODDINGHURST RD

96

Palmers

CROW GREEN LA

ORCHARD LA

Hatch Rd

4

Bishop's Hall Park

1 PEONY CL
2 ELIZABETH HO
3 MEADOW VIEW
4 WEALDEN HO

Shenfield Hall Farm

Pilgrims Hatch

The Brentwood Ctr

A12

3

Larchwood Prim Sch

Hall Wood

Shenfield Hall

CROSSWAYS

TUDOR CT
MARGARET AVE

St Mary's CE Prim Sch
SAWYERS CT

DOUNSELL CT
DARLINGTON CT

CHELMSFORD RD A1023

HUTTON RD

MISTLEIGH

95

High Wood

WARESCOT CL

St Helens RC Jun Sch

YORK RD

A1023

2

Calcott Hall Farm

ONGAR RD

KIMPTON AVE

ROBIN HOOD RD

1 DRUMMOND CT
2 GEARY CT
Sawyers Hall Coll

DODDINGHURST CT
YARROW

Convent of Mercy
St Thomas of Canterbury
CE Jun & Inf Schs

3 DUKE'S PL
4 INVERMAY CT
5 LAVENHAM CT
6 BURGESS CT
7 HIGHMEAD CT
8 ARGYLL CT
9 RAVENSCOURT

Shenfield

SHENFIELD RD

A129

COOMBE RISE

1

CM14

THE COURTYARD

MONTGOMERY

High Wood

HIGHLAND AVE

BURLAND RD

The Essex Nuffield

SHEN PLACE

HOLLY ALMSHOUSES

30

Brentwood Sch

94

CHAFFORD
CAPON CL
BLACK WATER
RODING

PARK VALE CT

WEALD RD

GREEN LA

WESTERN AVE

NORTH RD
NORTH ROAD AVE

A128

A1023

LIMES CT

HOMEHURST AVE

58 | **A** | **B** | **59** | **C** | **D** | **60** | **E** | **F**

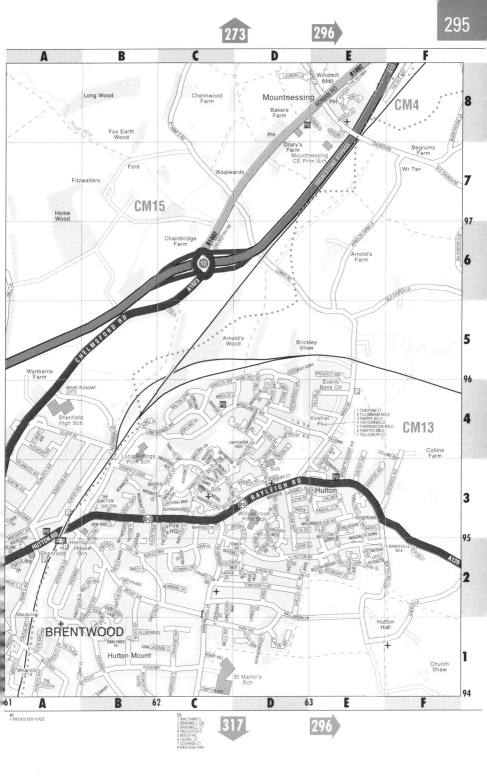

A B C D E F

8

Lodge Wood
Kitchen Wood
CM4
Little Farm
Shoulder Hall
CHURCH RD
HALL LA
PADHAM'S GREEN RD
BUTTERCUP
Bellman's Farm
Westlands Farm
Padham's Green

7
MARSH LA
Harespring Wood

97
BUCKWYNS CHASE
North Nook

6
Mountnessing Hall
OLD CHURCH LA
Wardroper's
Buckwyns Farm
Queens Park
MUNSTER CT

OLD CHURCH LA
Lawness
COLVILLE MEWS 1
BERESFORD CT 2
GRANVILLE CL 3
LORRIMORE EL 4
DOLPHIN GDNS 5
OAKLEIGH 6
QUEEN'S GATE MEWS 7
QUEENS PARK CT 8
TAVISTOCK DR 9
SLOANE MEWS 10
EDWARD CL 11
Recn Gd

5
River Rd
Brightside Prim Sch
BRIGHTSIDE CL

CM13
96

4
Cock Wood
Clapgate Wood
Sewage Works
Little Cowbridge Grange Farm
BLUEBELL WOOD
THE WARREN
UPLAND RD

THE FOXGLOVES 1
BUCKWYNS CT 2
HALLAM CT 3
UPLAND DR 4
COOMBES CL 5
PAVILLION PL 6
EARL MOUNTBATTEN DR 7
CRESCENT GDNS 8
CRESCENT CL 9
MAGENTA

3
Bushwood Farm
Great Cowbridge Grange Farm
CM12
LEIGHS RIFLEMAN 1
BRIDGE PAR 2
Lake Meadows Office Village 3
BRATHERTON CT 4
FORESTER CT 5
TRUMPETER CT 6
LEVELLER ROW 7
WARRINGTON SQ 8
Radford Bsns Ctr
WOODBRIDGE
CHARITY FARM CHASE

95
A129
Ellices Farm
RAYLEIGH RD
PH
BELLEVUE
STATION RD

2
CHURCH LA
Humes Farm
Martines Farm
Havering's Grove
WINTERS CHASE
Shipmans House
KENILWORTH CL
LONDON RD
BEAUFORT
ROSSLYN

FOKES GR
TALLY-HO DR
Shipmans Shaw
Greenleas Farm
WESTERN VIEW

1
Bfunts Wall Farm
Billericay Com H
A129
HILARY MEAD
HEATH CL
GILMOUR RD
ROMSEY RD
BOOTHAM
ABBEY RD

94
BLUNTS WALL RD

64 A 65 B C D 66 E F

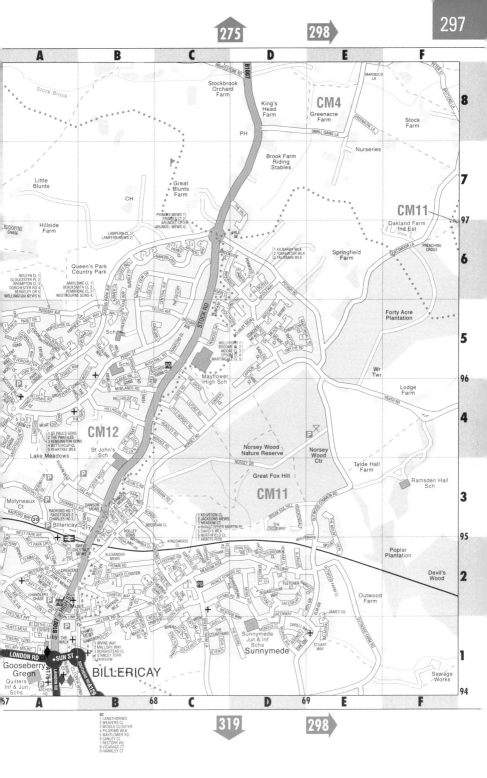

275
298

A   **B**   **C**   **D**   **E**   **F**

8

7

97

6

5

96

4

3

95

2

1

94

Stock Brook

Little Blunts

Hillside Farm

BUCKWYNS CHASE

Queen's Park Country Park

CH

Great Blunts Farm

Stockbrook Orchard Farm

King's Head Farm

PH

Brook Farm Riding Stables

CM4

Greenacre Farm

MARIGOLD LA

GREENACRE LA

SMALL GAINS LA

PETER ST

BRITTONS LA

Stock Farm

Nurseries

CM11

Oakland Farm Ind Est

PREACHING CROSS

COATSMOOR LA

Springfield Farm

Forty Acre Plantation

Wr Twr

Lodge Farm

HEATH RD

Tylde Hall Farm

Ramsden Hall Sch

PRINORS MEWS 1
PRINCES CL 2
ARUNDEL CR 3
ARUNDEL MEWS 4

LAMPERN CL 1
LAMPERN MEWS 2

THE DALE

VALE GR

1 KILBARRY WLK
2 FOXHUNTER WLK
3 TALISMAN WLK

BOLEYN CL 1
GLOUCESTER PL 2
BROMPTON CL 3
DORCHESTER RD 4
BERKELEY DR 5
WELLINGTON MEWS 6

MARLOWE CL 1
BEACKSMITH CL 2
PEMBROKE CL 3
WESTBOURNE GDNS 4

ROSEBAY AVE

PAGET DR

HOLLYFORD 1
BROOME CL 2
MOORE CL 3
EPSOM CL 4
MARTINGALE CL 5

Sch

Sch

PO

Mayflower High Sch

CM12

1 ST PAULS GDNS
2 THE PANTILES
3 KENSINGTON GDNS
4 BUTTERCUP CL
5 PEARTREE WLK

St John's Sch

Lake Meadows

Molyneaux Ct

Billericay

RADFORD HO 1
RADSTOCKS 2
CHARLES HO 3

WEST PARK AVE

Norsey Wood Nature Reserve

Norsey Wood Ctr

Great Fox Hill

CM11

BREAK EGG HILL

THE CROSSWAY

OUTWOOD COMMON RD

BRACKENDALE

WHITENAYS

THE MOUNT

OUTWOOD FARM RD

Poplar Plantation

Devil's Wood

1 KELVEDON CL
2 JACKSONS MEWS
3 MEADOW CT
4 CHRISTOPHER MARTIN PL
5 DAVID'S WLK
6 NORTHFIELD CL
7 ABBOTS RIDE

1 LANGTHORNES
2 WEAVERS CL
3 MIDDLE CLOISTER
4 PILGRIMS WLK
5 MAYFLOWER RD
6 GANLEY CL
7 RECTORY HO
8 VICARAGE CT
9 HAWKLEY CT

Alexander Mews

CROWN RD

LOWER CLOISTER

KINGSWOOD RD

SHALFORD RD

HOLBROOK CL

HILLWAY

FLETCHER HARBOUR

GASCOIGNE RD

SALESBURY

Outwood Farm

JAMES SQ

Sunnymede Jun & Inf Schs

Sunnymede

DARELL WAY

STUART WAY

MUS

LONDON RD

SUN ST

Gooseberry Green

Quilters Inf & Jun Schs

BILLERICAY

Sewage Works

319
298

57   **A**   68   **B**   **C**   69   **D**   **E**   **F**

A B C D E F

8

WHITE'S HILL
Bishop's Farm
Kiln Common
BRITTONS LA
Great Bishop's Wood
Whitelilies Farm

CM4

7

Broom Wood
Fremnells
DOWNHAM RD
BLACKMORE LA
CHATHAM LA
Visitor Ctr
P
HAWKSWOOD RD

97

Crowsheath Farm
DOMSETTS LA
MILL LA

6

Common Farm
Hilltop Nursery
Little Abbott's
Cock Wood
CROWSHEATH LA
Thrift Wood

Ramsden Back Common

5

TIPLERS BRIDGE
NORTON RD
KNS RD
BIRDS CL
STONEY HILLS
PENDELTON WLK
WILLOWMEADE
Nursery
PH
DOWNHAM RD
SCHOOL RD

96

PH
POST ST JOHNS PL
HEATH RD
PH
KNOWLE CL
DOVEDALE CL
1 BAKERS CT
2 FARRIER SQ
WINDSOR RD
OAK RD
DE
Windsor Trad Est
Greenacres Farm
Downham

4

Hunt's Farm
Ramsden Heath
CM11
Rectory Wood

Chitham's Farm
ROMA GDNS
ST JOHNS DR
BRABNER GDNS
SHORT LA
MEAD CL
MANOR CL
Downham CE Prim Sch
The Orchard Farm

3

Meepshole Wood
PARK LA
Cox Green
DE BEAUVOIR CHASE
De Beauvoir House
CASTLEDON RD

95

2

Crays Wood
Pump Hill
CHURCH RD
PH
ORCHARD AVE

Kent Hill
Barrenleys Wood
Claypitshills Wood
Ramsden Park Farm
RAMSDEN PARK RD

1

Ramsden Bellhouse
GLEBE RD

94

70 A B 71 C D 72 E F

Hanningfield Resr

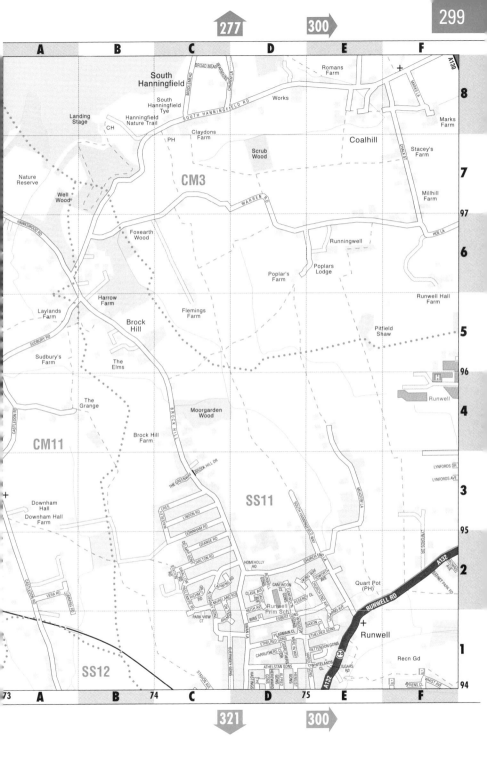

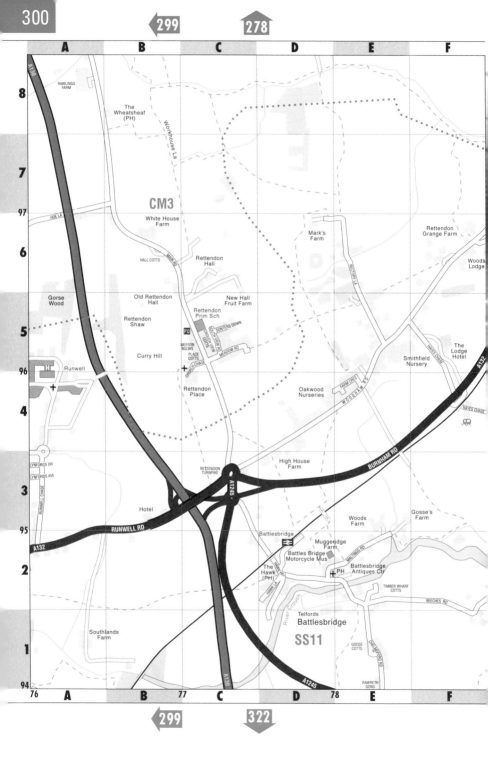

279

302

E7
1 AKENFIELD CL
2 WOODHAM CT
3 GUILD WAY
4 QUEEN ELIZABETH II SQ
5 CHIPPING ROW
6 TRINITY ROW

Tropical Wings
World of Wildlife

Fouracre Nursery

South
Woodham
Ferrers

Woodham Fen

Grange
Nurseries

Tabrum's
Farm

Sewage
Works

Eyotts
Farm

South
Woodham
Ferrers

Schs

Saltcoats Park &
Compass
Gardens

Sports
Gd

Liby

William
de Ferrers
Ctr

Elmwood
Prim Sch

CM3

Collingwood
Prim Sch

The
Chetwood
Prim Sch

Marsh Farm
Country Park

Visitor
Ctr

Hayes
Farm

SS11

Hayes
Farm
CVN PK

Long Reach

Slipway

HALCYON
CVN PK

River Crouch

Tower
Park

CROUCH

PH

QUEENS

POOLES LA

1 HIGHFIELD
2 POND CL
3 SUNSHINE CL
4 RIDGE WAY
5 THE GLEN
6 HIGH BANK
7 HORSESHOE LAWNS
8 HIGHVIEW
9 TOWER SIDE
10 POOLHURST WLK
11 ALMOND AVE
12 CENTRAL AVE

Riverside
Jun & Inf
Schs

SS5

Highlands

Pickerels
Farm

Maylons

Hullbridge

Cracknell's
Farm

Liby

Beeches
Farm

Boxes
Farmhouse

Sewage
Works

SS6

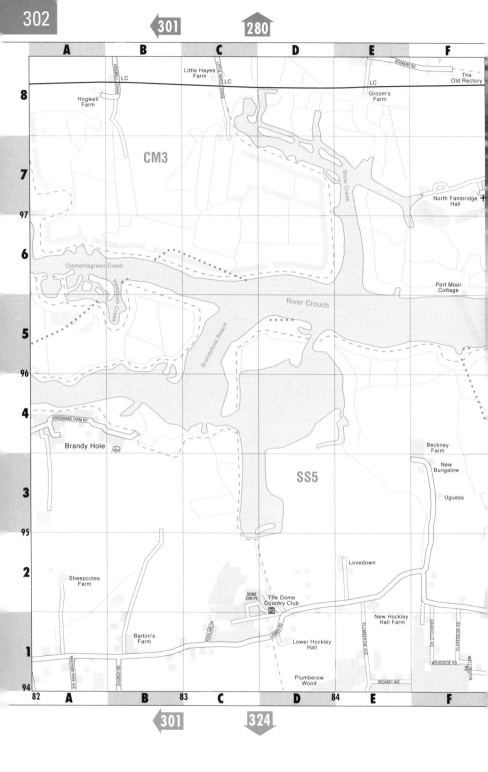

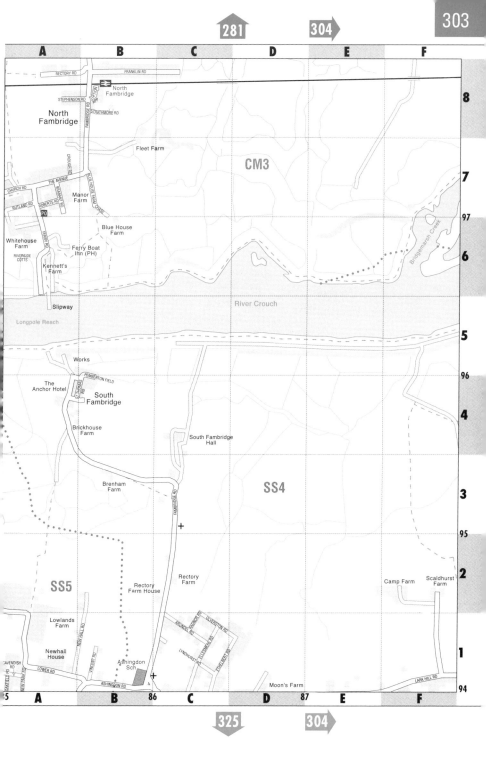

281
304

	A	B	C	D	E	F

8

RECTORY RD
FRANKLIN RD

North Fambridge

STEPHENSON RD
STRATHMORE RD

North
Fambridge

7

Fleet Farm

CM3

97

CHURCH RD
THE AVENUE
RUTLAND RD
BRAMBLE RD
ROBERTS RD

Manor
Farm

Blue House
Farm

6

Whitehouse
Farm

FERRY RD

Blue House Farm Chase
CROUCH RD

RIVERSIDE
COTTS

Ferry Boat
Inn (PH)

Kennett's
Farm

Bridgemarsh Creek

Slipway

Longpole Reach

River Crouch

5

Works

96

PEMBERTON FIELD
STAMBROS

The
Anchor Hotel

South
Fambridge

4

Brickhouse
Farm

South Fambridge
Hall

Brenham
Farm

FAMBRIDGE RD

SS4

3

+

95

SS5

Rectory
Farm

2

Camp Farm

Scaldhurst
Farm

NEW HALL RD

Lowlands
Farm

Rectory
Farm House

ASUNDEL RD
BADMINTON RD
ULVERSTON RD

Newhall
House

LYNDHURST RD
TILEHURST RD
ETHELBERT RD

CAVENDISH
RD
LOWER RD
NEW PARK RD
CORNFIELD RD

LYNDHURST RD

1

Ashingdon
Sch

+

LARK HILL RD

ASHINGDON RD

Moon's Farm

94

| 5 | A | B | 86 | C | D | 87 | E | F | 94 |

325
304

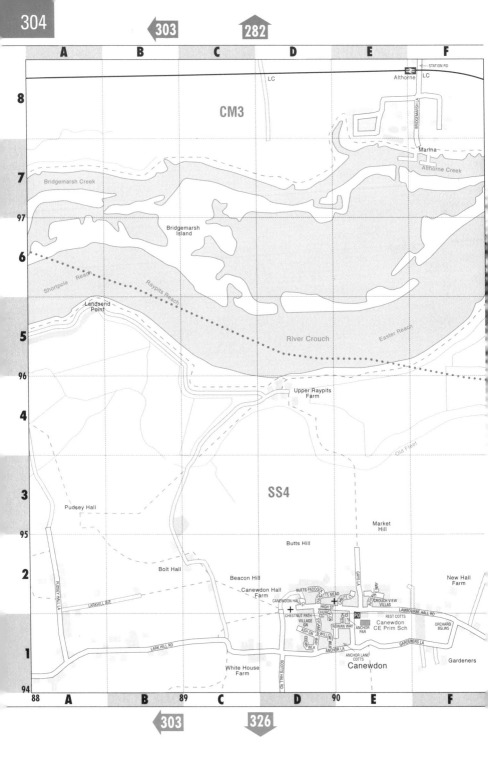

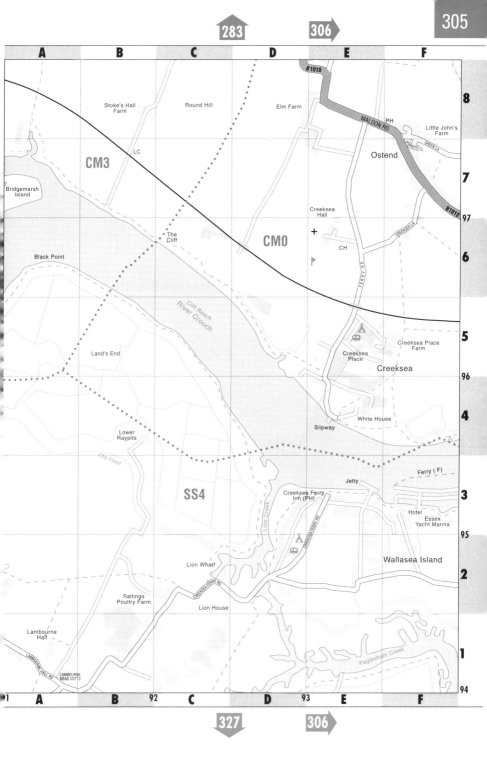

283
306

B1010

8

Stoke's Hall Farm

Round Hill

Elm Farm

MALDON RD

PH

Little John's Farm

GREEN LA

LC

CM3

Ostend

7

Bridgemarsh Island

Creeksea Hall

CREEKSEA LA

B1010

97

The Cliff

CM0

+

CH

FERRY RD

Black Point

6

Creeksea Place Farm

River Crouch

Cliff Reach

Creeksea Place

Creeksea

5

Land's End

96

Old Fleet

Lower Raypits

White House

4

Slipway

Ferry (F)

Jetty

SS4

Lion Creek

Creeksea Ferry Inn (PH)

Hotel

Essex Yacht Marina

3

95

Lion Wharf

CREEKSEA FERRY RD

Wallasea Island

2

Saltings Poultry Farm

Lion House

CREEKSEA FERRY RD

Lambourne Hall

Paglesham Creek

1

LAMBOURNE HALL RD

LAMBOURNE MEAD COTTS

94

327
306

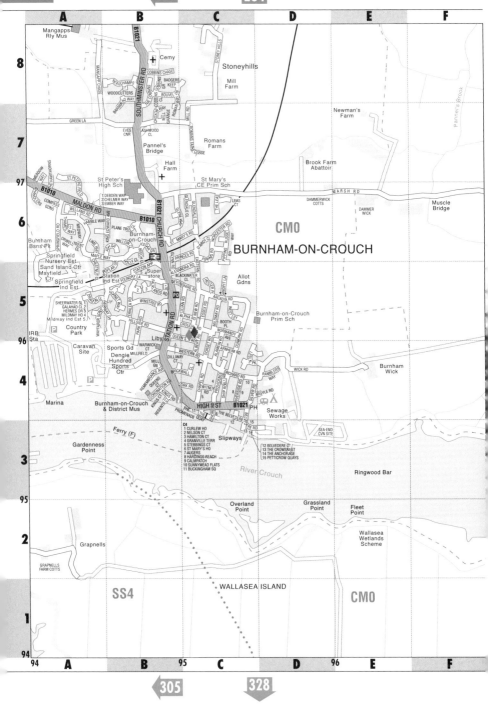

305
284

Mangapps
Rly Mus

A B C D E F

8

Cemy

Stoneyhills

Mill
Farm

SOUTHMINSTER RD

B1021

COBBINS CHASE

BADGERS
KEEP

BEAUCHAMPS

WOODCUTTERS

BOUVEL

Newman's
Farm

Pannel's Brook

GREEN LA

EVES
CNR

ASHWOOD
CL

7

Pannel's
Bridge

Romans
Farm

ROMANS TERR

CHASE

Brook Farm
Abattoir

Hall
Farm

St Peter's
High Sch

St Mary's
CE Prim Sch

MARSH RD

97

St Peter's RD

B1010

MALDON RD

1 DEBDEN WAY
2 CHELMER WAY
3 EMBER WAY

LEAS
CT

B1010

B1021 CHURCH RD

DAMMERWICK
COTTS

DAMMER
WICK

Muscle
Bridge

COMPASS
GDNS

HAMBLE WAY

PLANE TREE

Burnham-
on-Crouch

CM0

BURNHAM-ON-CROUCH

6

Burnham
Bsns Pk

Springfield
Nursery Est
Sand Island Ctr
Mayfield
Ctr

POPLARS

WILTON RD

ST MARY'S RD

WORCESTER RD

WAY

Springfield
Ind Est

Station
Ind Est

Super
store

ALEXANDRA RD

PRINCES RD

BLACKWATER
CL

Allot
Gdns

STATION APP

FOUNDRY LA

DEVONSHIRE RD

ARCADIA RD

WESLEY

ALPHA RD

Burnham-on-Crouch
Prim Sch

5

SHEERWATER DL 1
GALAHAD CL 2
HERMES DR 3
MILDMAY HO 4
Mildmay Ind Est 5

WINSTREE

HILLSIDE RD

FERNLEA RD

CROUCH

QUEEN'S

BOOTH
PL

NORMANDY
AVE

P

Country
Park

Liby
Sta

IRB
Sta

Caravan
Site

Sports Gd
Dengie
Hundred
Sports
Ctr

WARWICK
CT

MILLFIELD

MILL
GDN

DILLIWAY

Western RD

BRICKWALL

ARGYLE RD

Burnham
Wick

WICK RD

ARNHEIM RD

ORCHARD RD

RAMBLER
WAY

96

Marina

Burnham-on-Crouch
& District Mus

QUEENS

KINGS
LINES

REMEMBRANCE AV

WITNEY RD

LONDON RD

REGENT CL

HIGH ST

B1021

Sewage
Works

PH

4

Ferry (F)

Gardenness
Point

C4
1 CURLEW HO
2 NELSON CT
3 HAMILTON CT
4 GRANVILLE TERR
5 STEBBINGS CT
6 ST MARY'S HO
7 AUGERS
8 HARDINGS REACH
9 CALMPATCH
10 SUNNYMEAD FLATS
11 BUCKINGHAM SQ

Slipways

12 BELVEDERE CT
13 THE CROWSNEST
14 THE ANCHORAGE
15 PETTICROW QUAYS

SEA-END
CVN SITE

3

River Crouch

Ringwood Bar

95

Overland
Point

Grassland
Point

Fleet
Point

2

Grapnells

Wallasea
Wetlands
Scheme

GRAPNELLS
FARM COTTS

SS4

WALLASEA ISLAND

CM0

1

94

94 A B 95 C D 96 E F

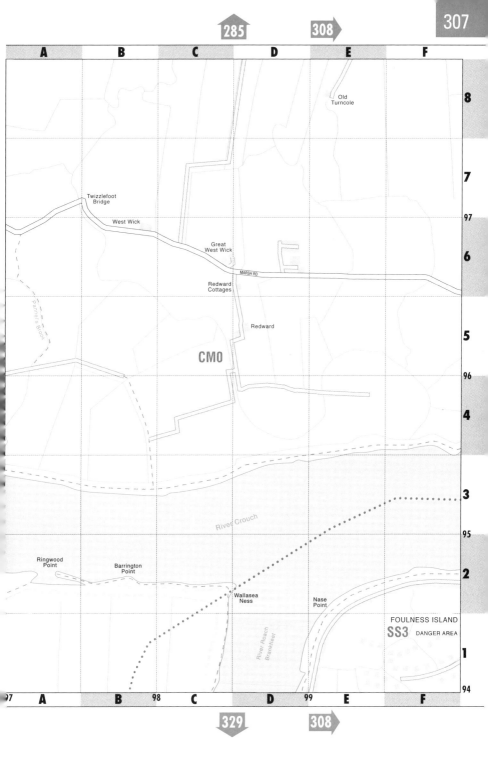

285
308

Old
Turncole

Twizzlefoot
Bridge

West Wick

Great
West Wick

MARSH RD

Redward
Cottages

Redward

CMO

River Crouch

Ringwood
Point

Barrington
Point

Wallasea
Ness

Nase
Point

River Roach
Branklfeet

FOULNESS ISLAND
SS3 DANGER AREA

329
308

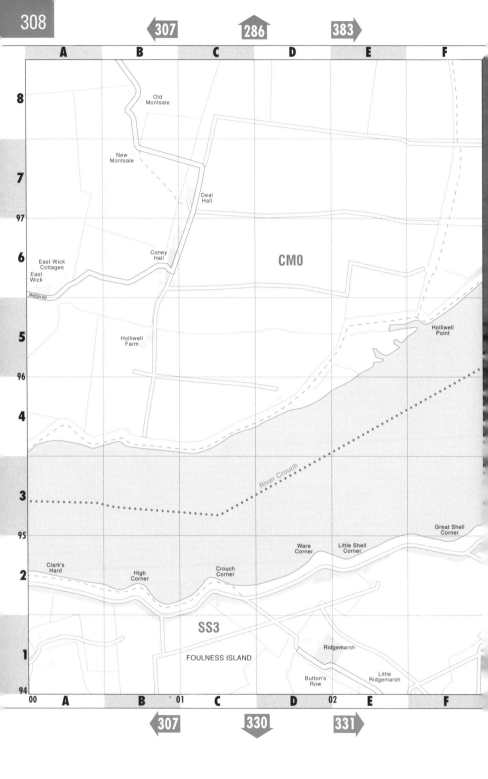

287
310

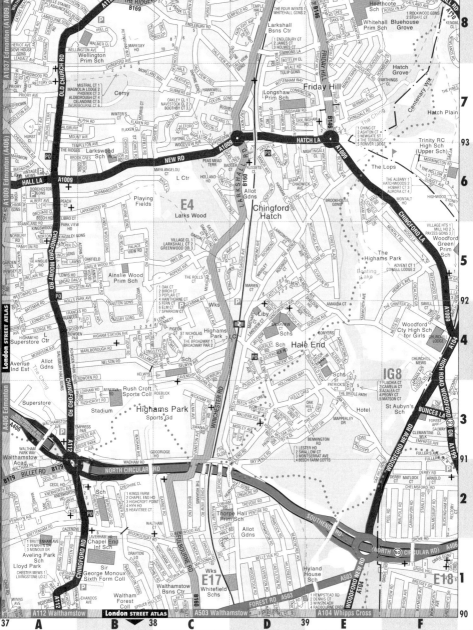

310

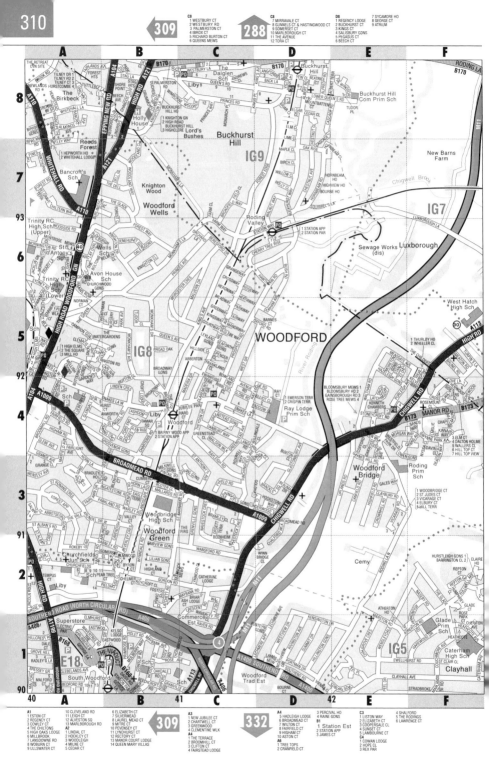

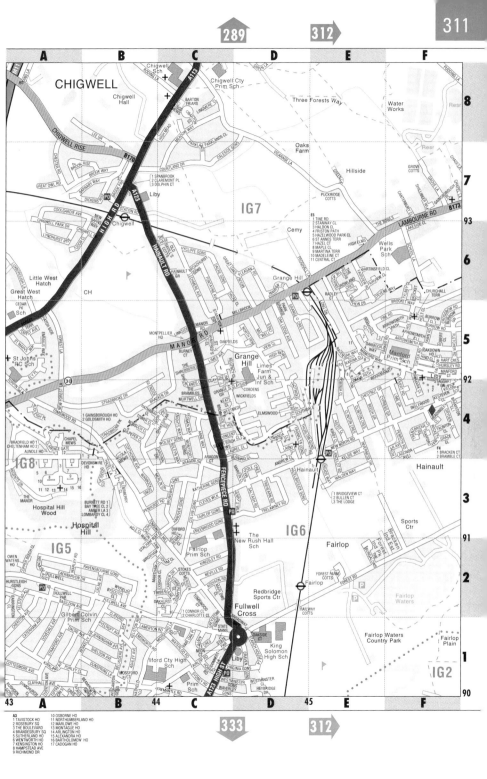

311
290

B6
1 THE RIDINGS
2 LARCHWOOD HO
3 HAWKESBURY CL
4 BUCKTHORNE HO

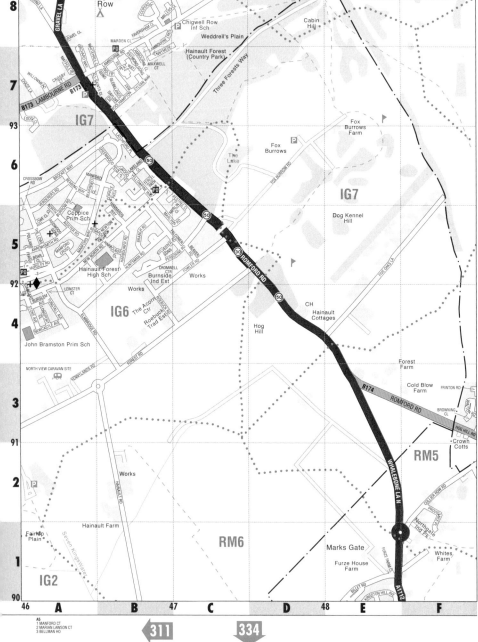

A B C D E F

RM4

Chigwell
Row

8

Chigwell Row
Inf Sch

Cabin
Hill

Weddrell's Plain

Three Forests Way

Hainault Forest
(Country Park)

MAXWELL
CT

7

B173

IG7

93

Fox
Burrows
Farm

Fox
Burrows

The
Lake

6

IG7

Coppice
Prim Sch

Dog Kennel
Hill

Manford

Hainault Forest
High Sch

5

ROMFORD RD

Cromwell
Burnside
Ind Est

Works

Works

CH
Hainault
Cottages

92

The Acorns
Ctr

IG6

Roebuck
Trad Est

Hog
Hill

John Bramston Prim Sch

Forest
Farm

NORTH VIEW CARAVAN SITE

Cold Blow
Farm

FRINTON RD

B174

ROMFORD RD

BROWNING
CL

3

91

HOG HILL RD

RM5

Crown
Cotts

Works

WHALEBONE LA N

2

Hainault Farm

Marks Gate

Northgate
Ind Pk

Fairlop
Plain

RM6

Furze House
Farm

Whites
Farm

1

IG2

A1112

90

46 A B 47 C D 48 E F

311
334

A5
1 MANFORD CT
2 MARIAN LAWSON CT
3 BELLMAN HO

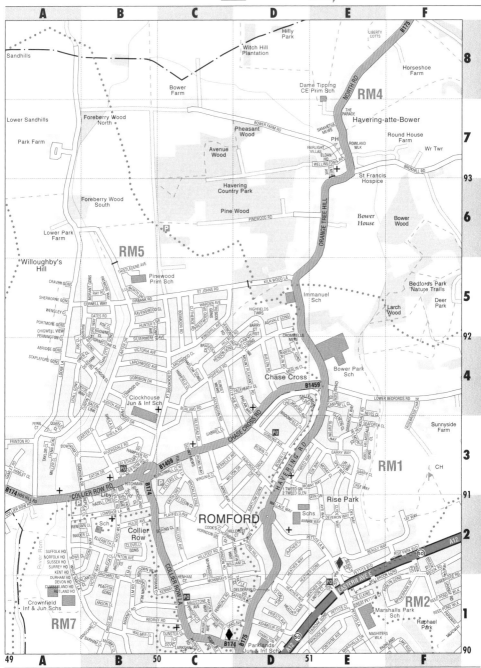

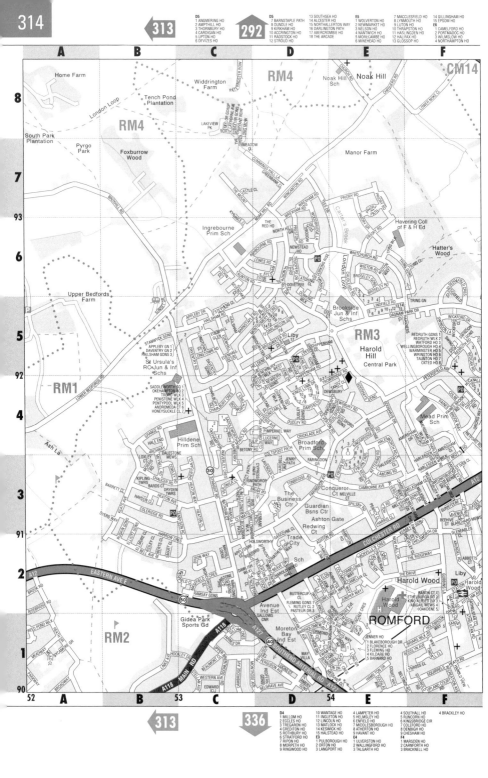

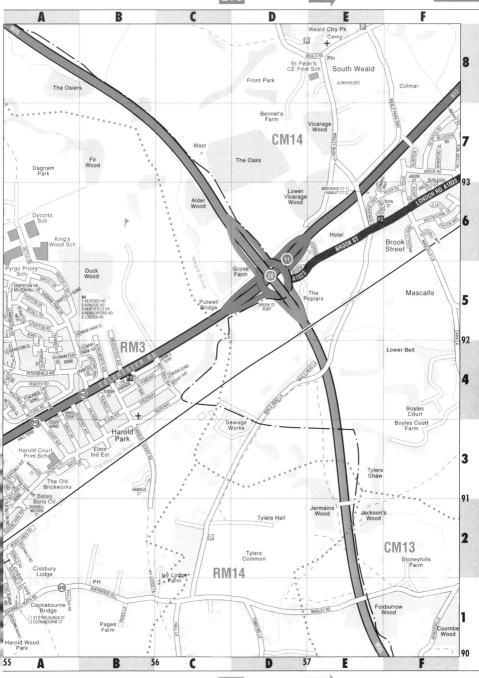

293
316

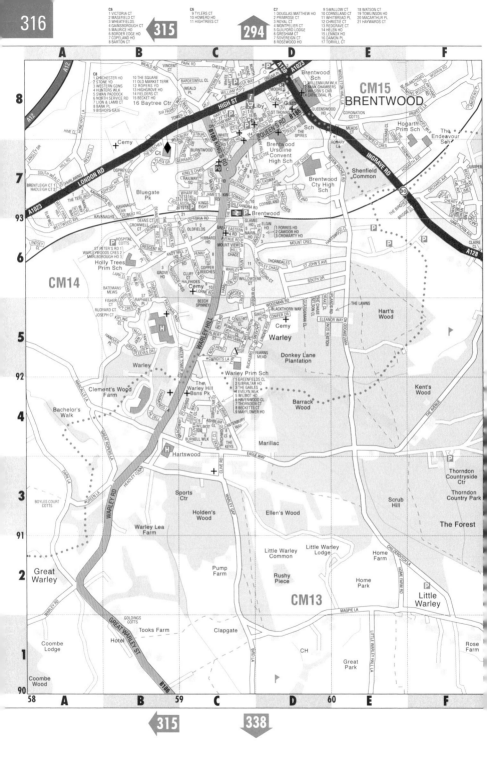

C6
1 VICTORIA CT
2 MASEFIELD CT
3 WHEATFIELDS
4 GAINSBOROUGH CT
5 MAURICE HO
6 BORDER EDGE HO
7 COPELAND HO
8 BARTON CT

C6
9 TYLERS CT
10 HOWERD HO
11 HIGHTREES CT

C7
1 DOUGLAS MATTHEW HO
2 PRIMROSE CT
3 ROYAL CT
4 MONTPELIER CT
5 GUILFORD LODGE
6 GRESHAM CT
7 SOVEREIGN CT
8 ROSEWOOD HO

9 SWALLOW CT
10 CORNSLAND CT
11 WHITBREAD PL
12 CHRISTIE CT
13 REDGRAVE CT
14 HELEN HO
15 LENNOX HO
16 DAMON PL
17 TORVILL CT

18 WATSON CT
19 TOMLINSON HO
20 MACARTHUR PL
21 HAYWARDS CT

C8
1 DORCHESTER HO
2 STONE YD
3 WESTERN GDNS
4 HUNTERS WLK
5 SWAN PADDOCK
6 NORTH SERVICE RD
7 LYON & LAMB CT
8 BANK PL
9 BISHOPS GATE
10 THE SQUARE
11 OLD MARKET TERR
12 ROPERS YD
13 HIGHGROVE HO
14 FIELDERS CT
15 BECKET HO
16 Baytree Ctr

295
318

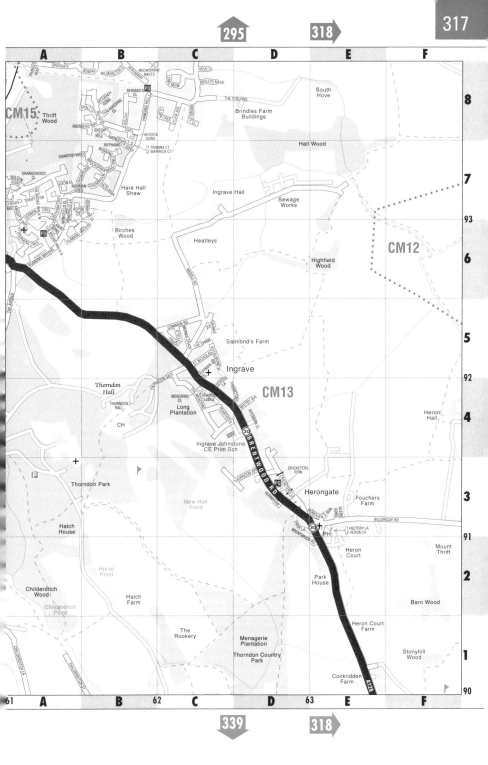

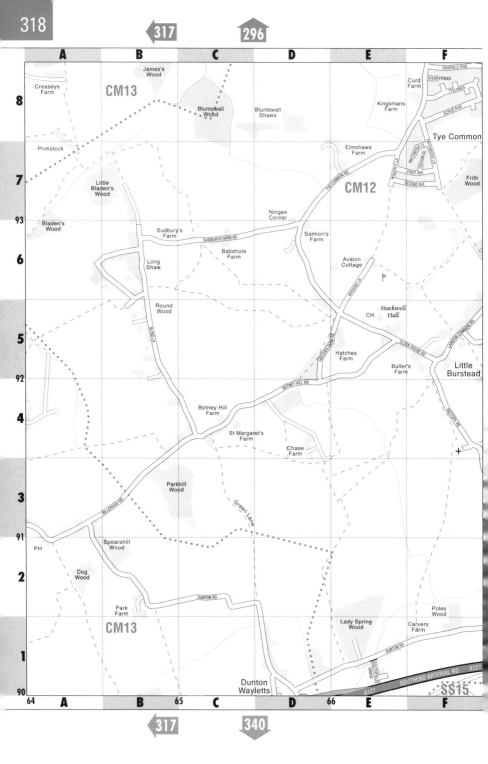

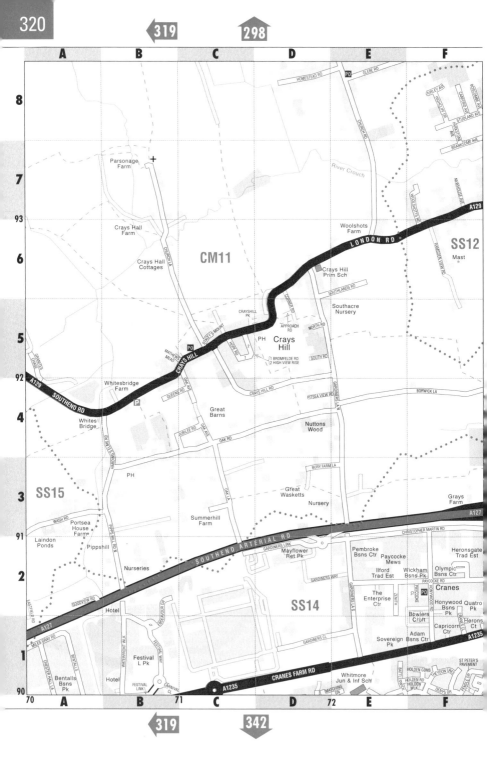

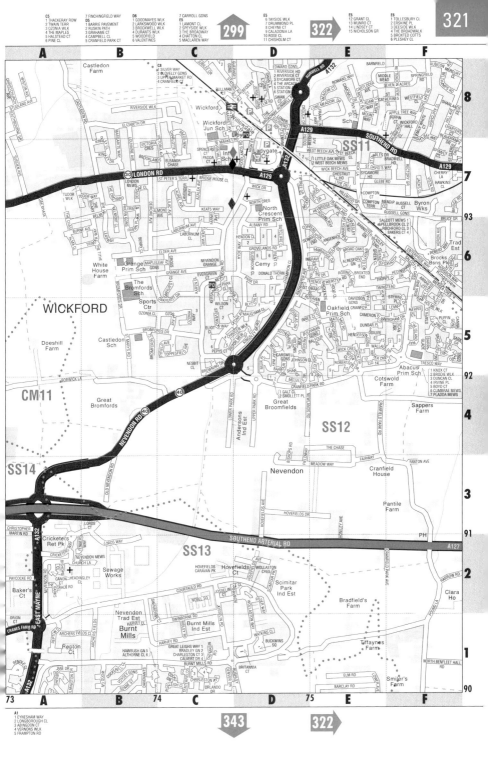

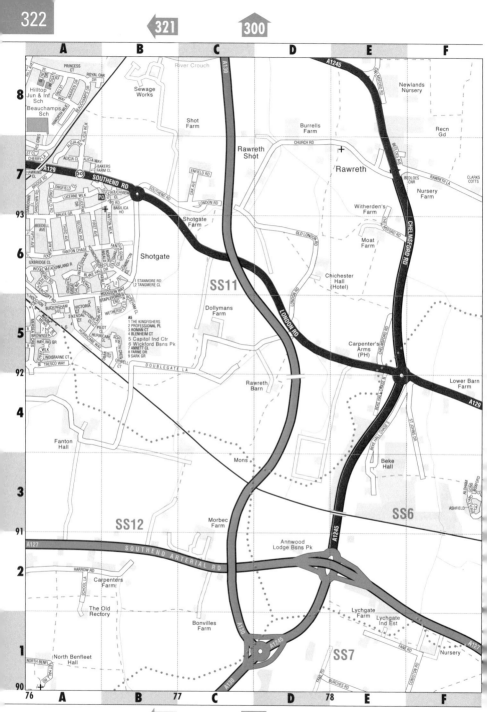

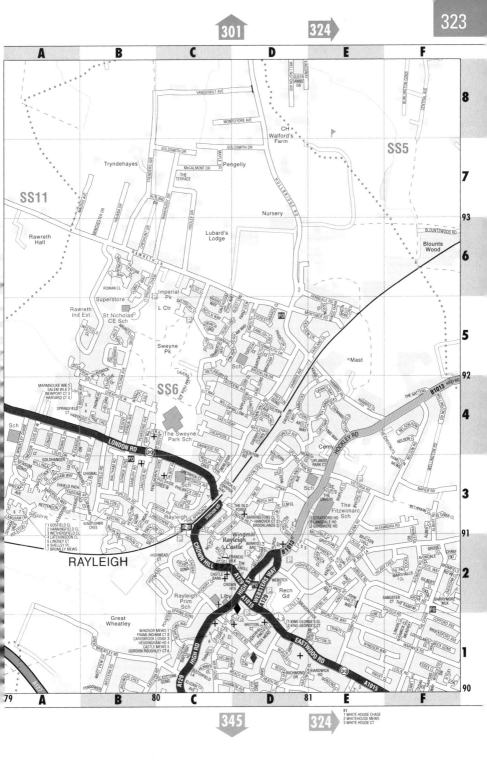

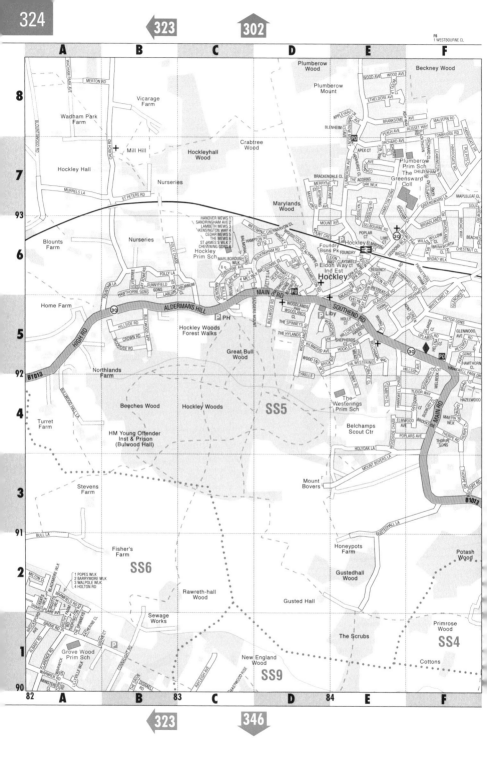

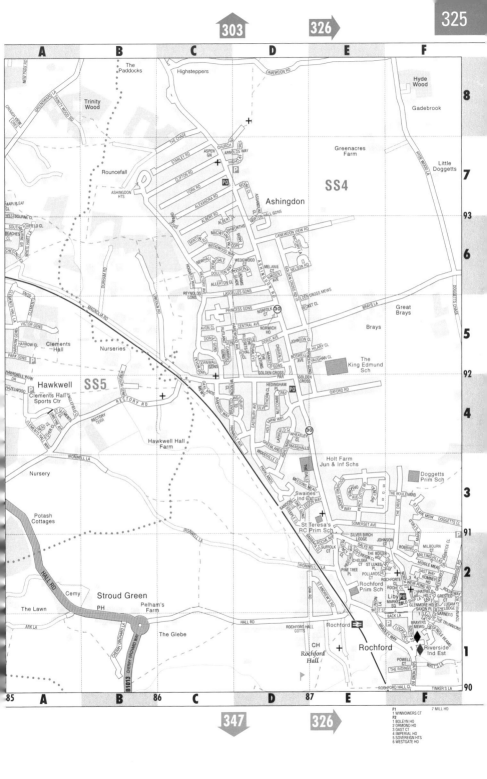

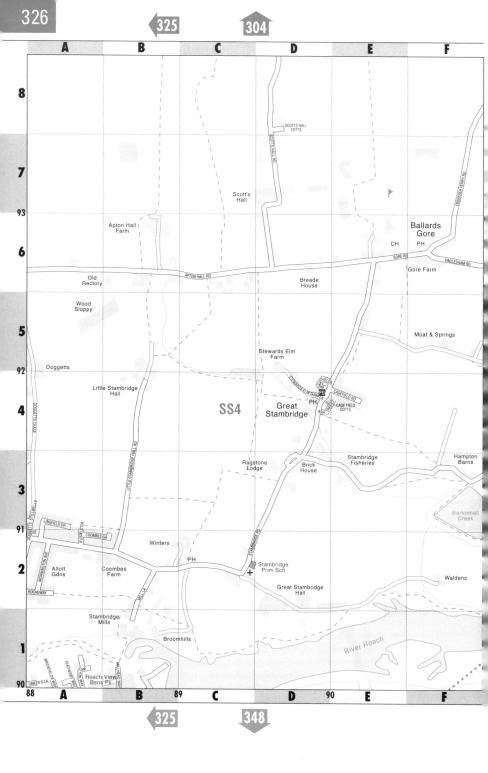

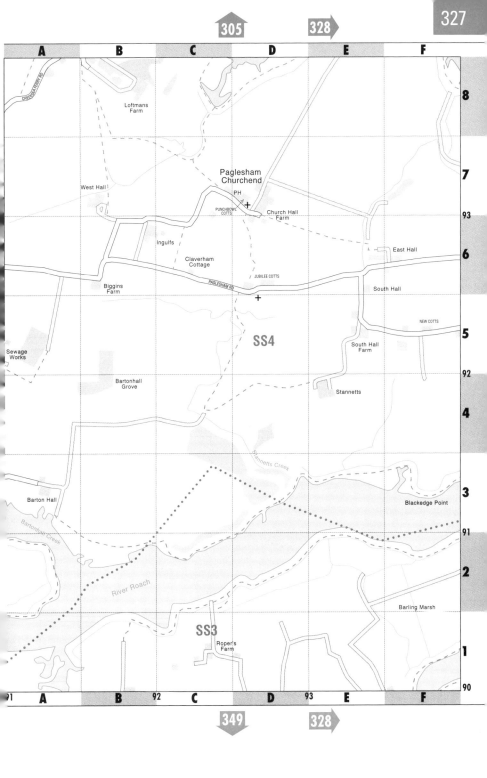

305
328

A   B   C   D   E   F

8

Loftmans
Farm

7

West Hall

Paglesham
Churchend

PH

PUNCHBOWL
COTTS

Church Hall
Farm

93

Ingulfs

East Hall

6

Claverham
Cottage

JUBILEE COTTS

Biggins
Farm

PAGLESHAM RD

South Hall

South Hall
Farm

NEW COTTS

5

SS4

Sewage
Works

92

Bartonhall
Grove

Stannetts

4

Stannetts Creek

Barton Hall

Blackedge Point

3

91

Bartonhall Creek

River Roach

2

Barling Marsh

SS3

Roper's
Farm

1

90

91   A   B   92   C   D   93   E   F

349
328

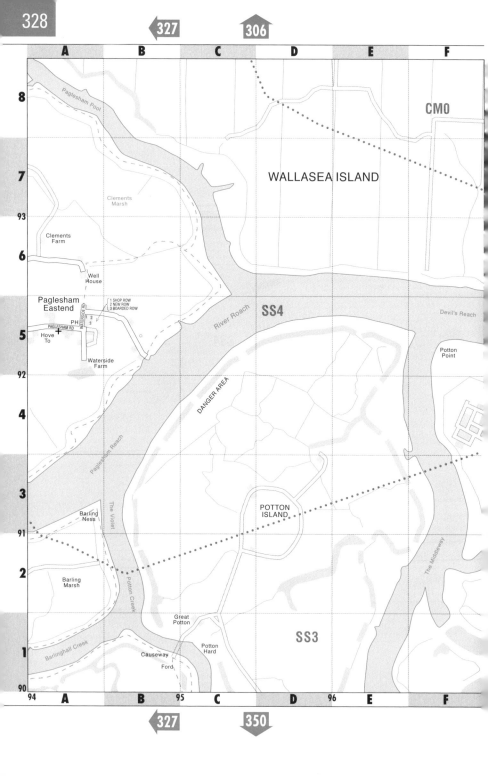

327
306

CM0

WALLASEA ISLAND

Paglesham Pool

Clements Marsh

Clements Farm

Well House

Paglesham Eastend

1 SHOP ROW
2 NEW ROW
3 BOARDED ROW

PH

PAGLESHAM RD

Hove To

Waterside Farm

River Roach

SS4

Devil's Reach

Potton Point

DANGER AREA

Paglesham Reach

The Violet

Barling Ness

Barling Marsh

Potton Creek

POTTON ISLAND

The Middleway

Great Potton

Potton Hard

Barlinghall Creek

Causeway

Ford

SS3

327
350

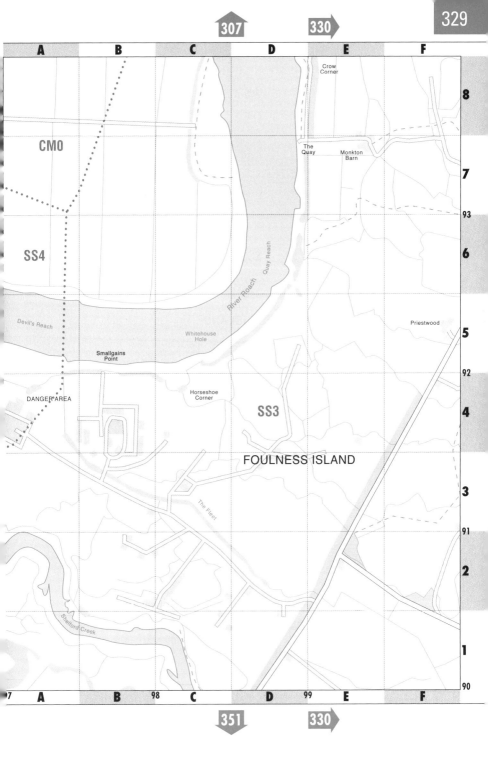

A B C D E F

8

CMO

The Quay
Crow Corner
Monkton Barn

7

93

SS4

6

Devil's Reach

River Roach

Quay Reach

Priestwood

5

Whitehouse Hole

Smallgains Point

92

DANGER AREA

Horseshoe Corner

SS3

4

FOULNESS ISLAND

3

The Fleet

91

2

Shelford Creek

1

90

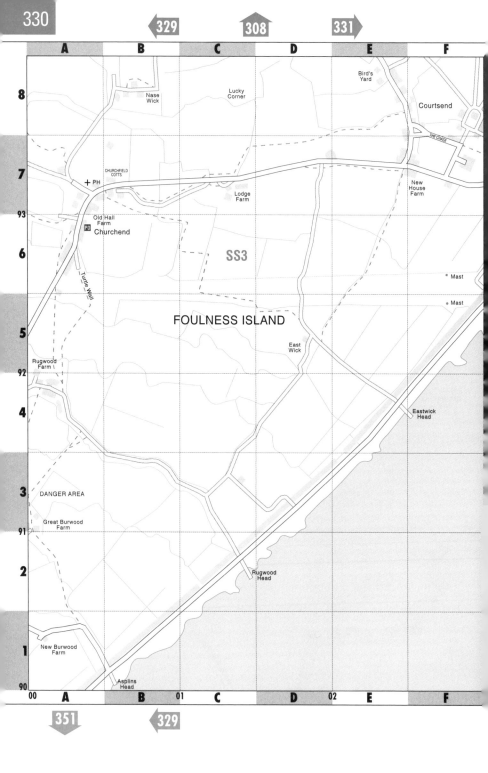

A   B   C   D   E   F

8

Bird's
Yard

Nase
Wick

Lucky
Corner

Courtsend

THE CHASE

7   + PH

CHURCHFIELD
COTTS

New
House
Farm

Lodge
Farm

93   Old Hall
Farm
PO   Churchend

SS3

6

• Mast

Turtle Wall

• Mast

FOULNESS ISLAND

5

East
Wick

Rugwood
Farm

92

4

Eastwick
Head

3   DANGER AREA

Great Burwood
Farm

91

2

Rugwood
Head

1   New Burwood
Farm

90

00   A   B   01   C   D   02   E   F

Asplins
Head

River Crouch

Foulness Point

East
Newlands

The Drift
(dis)

SS3

DANGER AREA

Masts

Mast

Northern
Corner

Fisherman's
Head

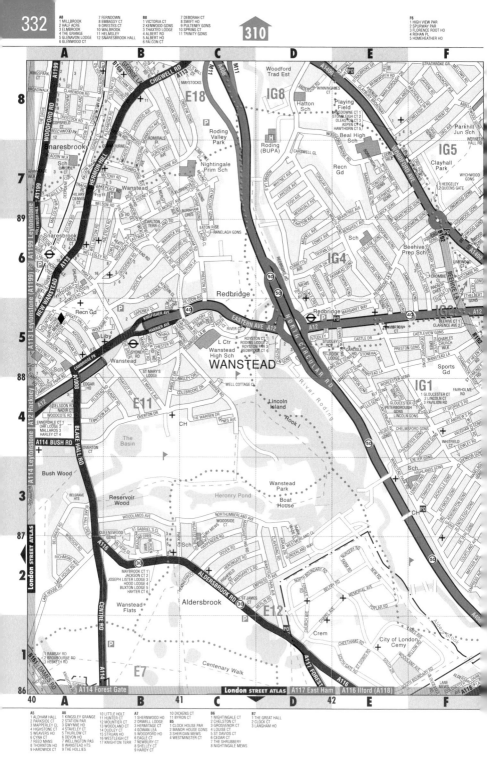

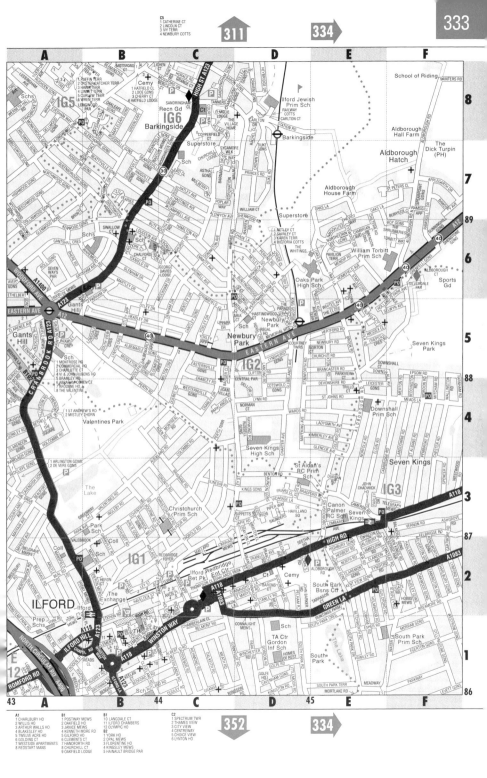

311
334

C5
1 CATHERINE CT
2 LINCOLN CT
3 IVY TERR
4 NEWBURY COTTS

A · B · C · D · E · F

8
7
89
6
5
88
4
3
87
2
87
1
86

IG5
IG6
Barkingside
School of Riding
PAINTERS RD
Aldborough
Hall Farm
The
Dick Turpin
(PH)
Aldborough
Hatch
Aldborough
House Farm
William Torbitt
Prim Sch
Ilford Jewish
Prim Sch
Barkingside
Superstore
Recn Gd
Superstore
Seven
Ways
Par
Gants
Hill
EASTERN AVE
Gants
Hill
Oaks Park
High Sch
Newbury
Park
Newbury
Park
EASTERN AVE
Seven Kings
Park
Valentines Park
IG2
Downshall
Prim Sch
Seven Kings
High Sch
St Aidan's
RC Prim
Sch
Seven Kings
IG3
Christchurch
Prim Sch
Canon
Palmer
RC Sch
John
Chadwick
The
Lake
St John's
Seven
Kings
Telegraph
IG1
HIGH RD
ILFORD
The
Exchange
Ilford Redbridge
Ret Ctr
Ilford
Cemy
South Park
Bsns Ctr
South Park
Prim Sch
South
Park
Prep
Schs
ROMFORD RD
NORTH CIRCULAR RD A406
ILFORD HILL
WINSTON WAY
TA Ctr
Gordon
Inf Sch
E
12

352
334

A1
1 CHARLBURY HO
2 WILLIS HO
3 ARTHUR WALLS HO
4 BLAKESLEY HO
5 TWELVE ACRE HO
6 GOLDING CT
7 WESTSIDE APARTMENTS
8 REDSTART MANS

B1
1 POSTWAY MEWS
2 OAKFIELD HO
3 JANICE MEWS
4 KENNETH MORE HO
5 GILFORD HO
6 CLEMENTS CT
7 HANDFORTH RD
8 CHURCHILL CT
9 OAKFIELD LODGE

B1
10 LANGDALE CT
11 ILFORD CHAMBERS
12 OLYMPIC HO

B2
1 YORK HO
2 OPAL MEWS
3 FLORENTINE HO
4 KINGSLEY MEWS
5 HAINAULT BRIDGE PAR

C2
1 SPECTRUM TWR
2 THAMES VIEW
3 CITY VIEW
4 CENTREWAY
5 CHOICE VIEW
6 LYNTON HO

43 · A · 44 · B · 44 · C · D · 45 · E · F · 86

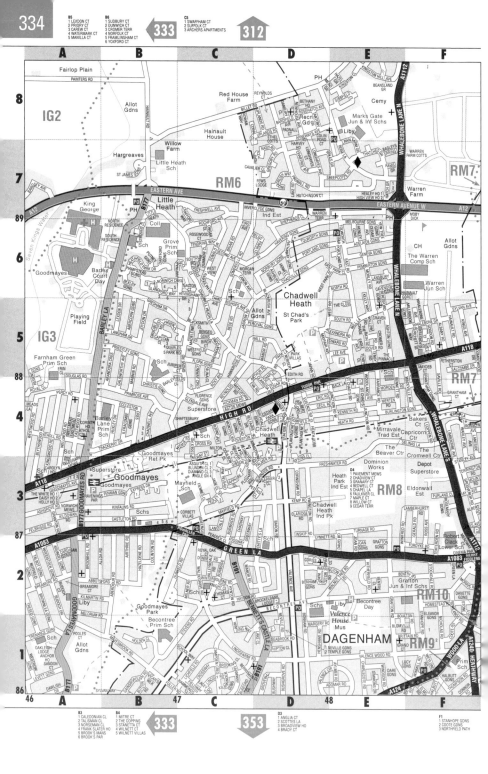

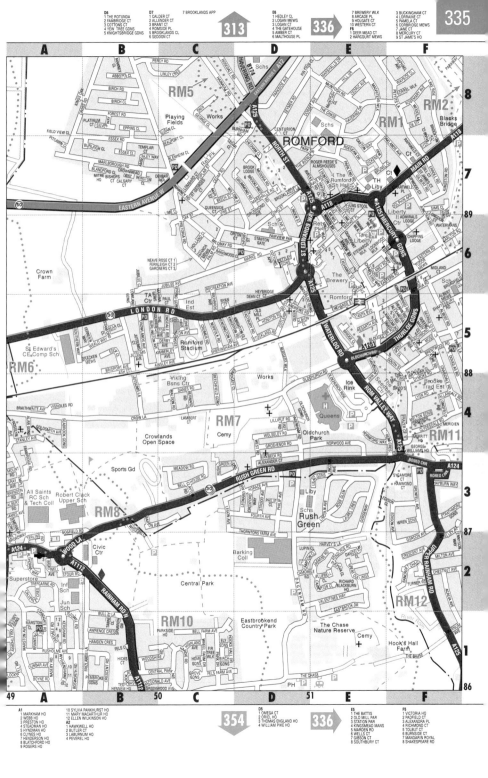

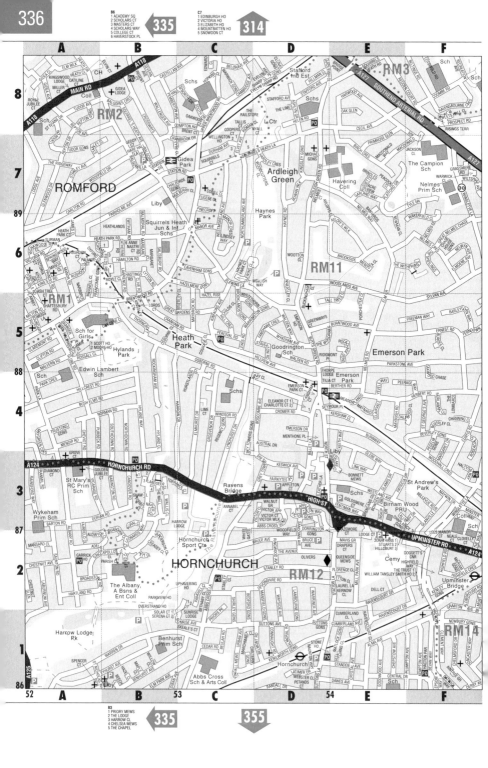

B6
1 ACADEMY SQ
2 SCHOLARS CT
3 MASTERS CT
4 SCHOLARS WAY
5 COLLEGE CT
6 HAVERSTOCK PL

335

C7
1 EDINBURGH HO
2 VICTORIA HO
3 ELIZABETH HO
4 MOUNTBATTEN HO
5 SNOWDON CT

314

B3
1 PRIORY MEWS
2 THE LODGE
3 HARROW CL
4 CHELSEA MEWS
5 THE CHAPEL

335

355

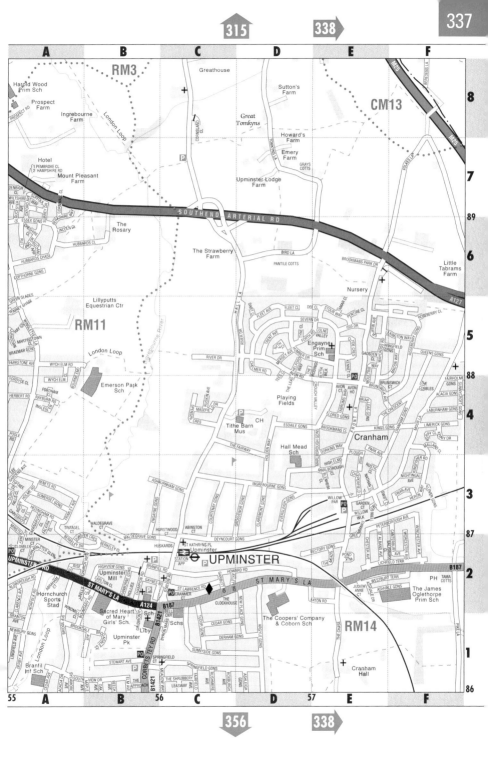

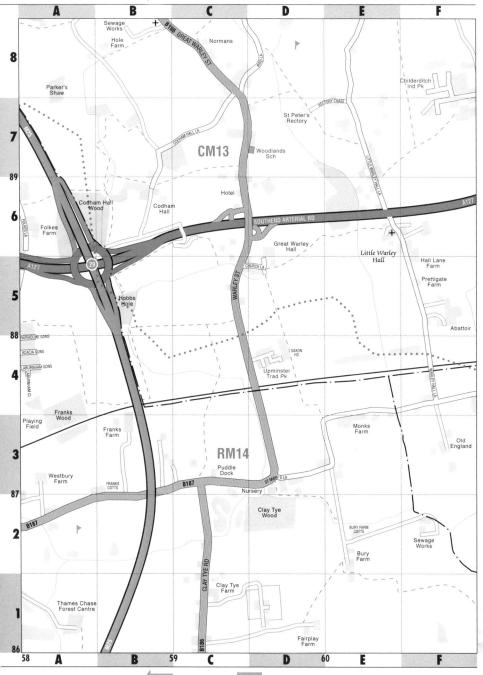

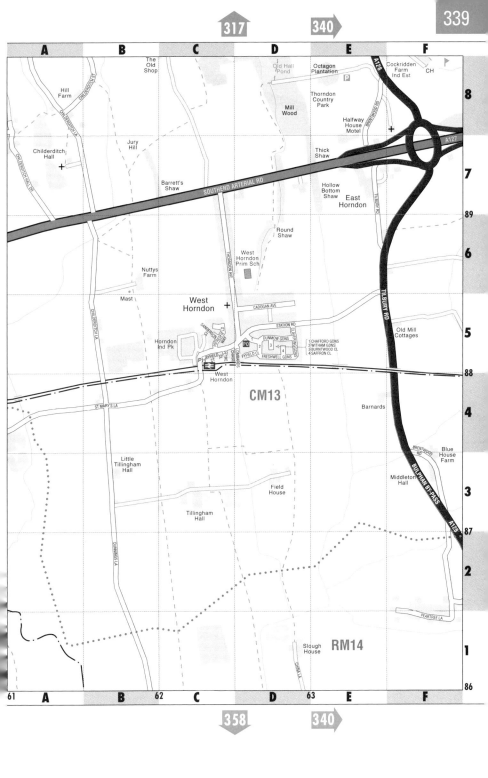

317 **340**

	A	B	C	D	E	F

Cockridden Farm Ind Est
CH

The Old Shop

Old Hall Pond

Octagon Plantation

8

Hill Farm

Thorndon Country Park

Mill Wood

Halfway House Motel

Jury Hill

Childerditch Hall

CHILDERDITCH LA

CHILDERDITCH ST

Thick Shaw

A127

7

Barrett's Shaw

SOUTHEND ARTERIAL RD

Hollow Bottom Shaw

East Horndon

89

TILBURY RD

Round Shaw

6

Nuttys Farm

Mast

West Horndon Prim Sch

West Horndon

CADOGAN AVE

Old Mill Cottages

5

THORNDON AVE

CHILDERDITCH LA

Horndon Ind Pk

STATION RD

DUNMOW GDNS
1 CHAFFORD GDNS
2 WITHAM GDNS
3 BURNTWOOD CL
4 SAFFRON CL
FRESHWELL GDNS
EYFIELD CL

West Horndon

88

CM13

ST MARY'S LA

Barnards

4

Little Tillingham Hall

Field House

Blue House Farm

Middleton Hall

BRENTWOOD RD

BULPHAN BY-PASS

A128

3

Tillingham Hall

DUNNINGS LA

87

2

PEARTREE LA

Slough House

RM14

DUNN LA

1

86

61	A	B	62	C	D	63	E	F

339
318

A   **B**   **C**   **D**   **E**   **F**

Dunton Wayletts

CM12

8

Eastlands Spring

Friern Manor Wood

SOUTHEND ARTERIAL RD

A127

Automobile Research Ctr

Green Meadows Nurseries

B148

SS15

7

Brookman's Farm

COMMERCIAL

CHRISTY CT

SYLVAN

SEAX WAY
ESSEX CT
ARGENT CT

Friern Manor

MERRYLANDS CHASE

CHRISTY WAY

HORNDON

FENTON WAY

Southfields

89

WEST MAYNE

BRAMSTON LINK

BRAMSTON WAY

SAFFRON CT

1 BROADWATER GN
2 WOODSTOCK CRES
3 WOODSTOCK GDNS
4 PRESIDENTS CT
5 HILLMORE CT

B148

6

Dunton Hills Farm

CM13

The Old Rectory

Westmayne Ind Pk

B1036

SUMPNERS LINK

BROOK AVE
NOB PK
PALATINE PK

KENNET

HELMORES

DUNHAM RD

FRASER

MANDEVILLE

BLACKMORES

5

+

Dunton Hall

CHURCH RD

ORCHARD VIEW
DUNTON PARK CVN PK
MAIN DR
BULPHAN VIEW

WAY

B1036

KENTON

NOTTINGHAM WAY

CHORLEY

READING

WORCESTER CL 1
SHREWSBURY CL 2
OSSULTEY DR 3
AMERSHAM AVE 4
MAHONIA DR 5
IPSWICH MEWS 6
ALNWICK CL 7
OXFORD CL 8
CAMBRIDGE CL 9
MONMOUTH MEWS 10

AYLESBURY DR

OAKHAM

HOLLY

88

Great Berry

WOODVIEW

DENEHURST GDNS

GLENWOOD GDNS

+

STAFFORD GN

WEST

MEADOWSIDE

MIMOSA

SUNNYSIDE

4

FIRST AVE

CENTRAL AVE

HIGH BANK 1
REEVES CL 2

FOREST GLADE

TORNEY

Great Berry Prim Sch

LAKE VIEW

SECOND AVE

THIRD AVE

FOURTH AVE

LONGREST AVE

WILDMAN CL

LAKE VIEW

3

Poultry Farm

Plotlands Mus

Langdon Conservation Ctr

SS16

87

Dunton Poultry Farm

Lower Dunton Hall

2

A128

RM14

BRENTWOOD RD

BULPHAN BYPASS

Motel   Garlesters

BRENTWOOD RD

Balgownie Farm

Noke Hall Farm

Doesgate Farm

Bentley Farm

OLD CHURCH HILL

1

DOESGATE LA

A128

86

Manor House

Little Malgraves

Little Malgraves Ind Est

64   **A**   **B**   65   **C**   **D**   66   **E**   **F**

339
359

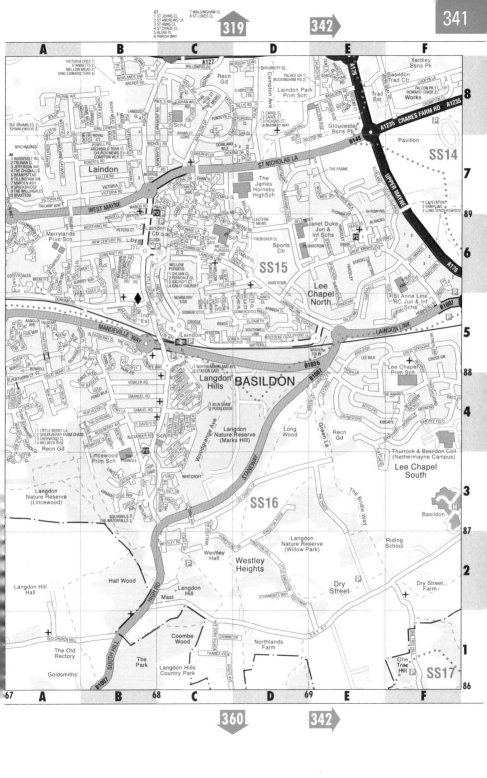

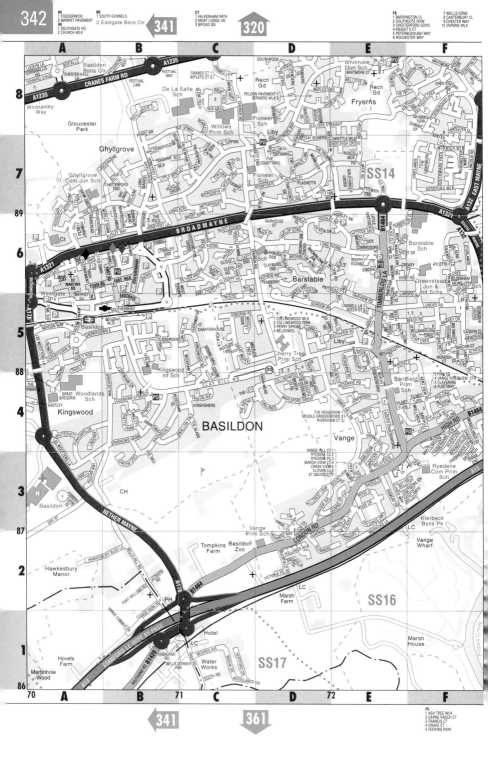

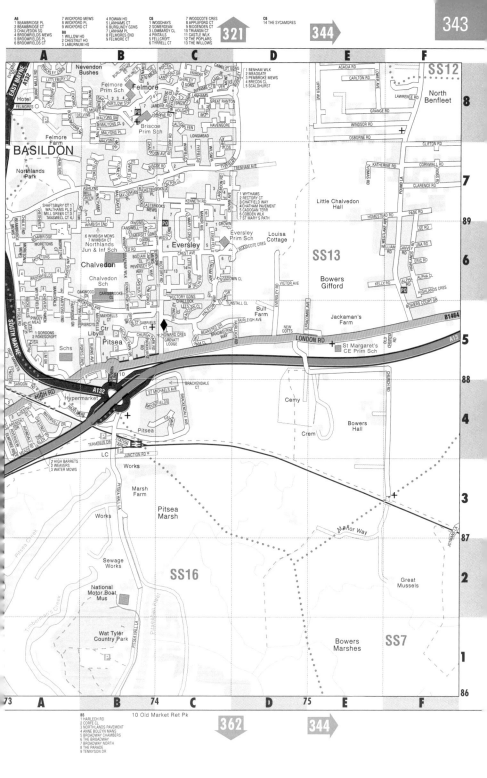

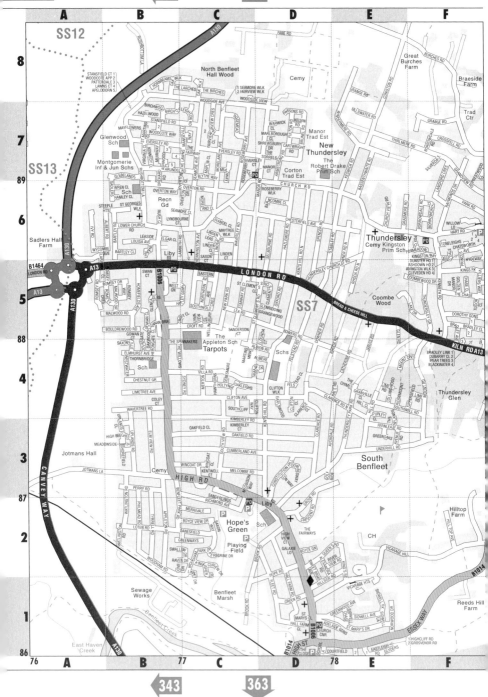

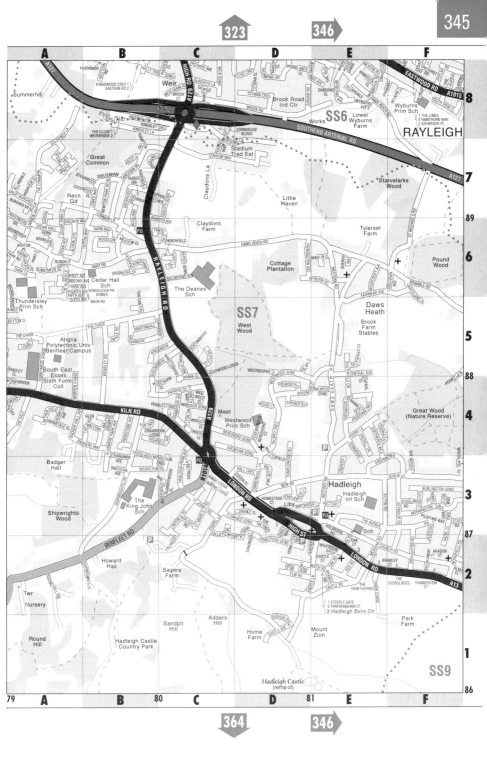

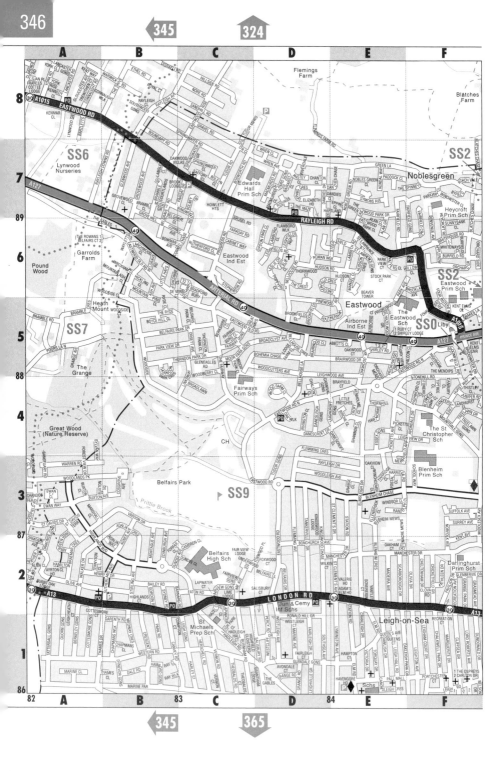

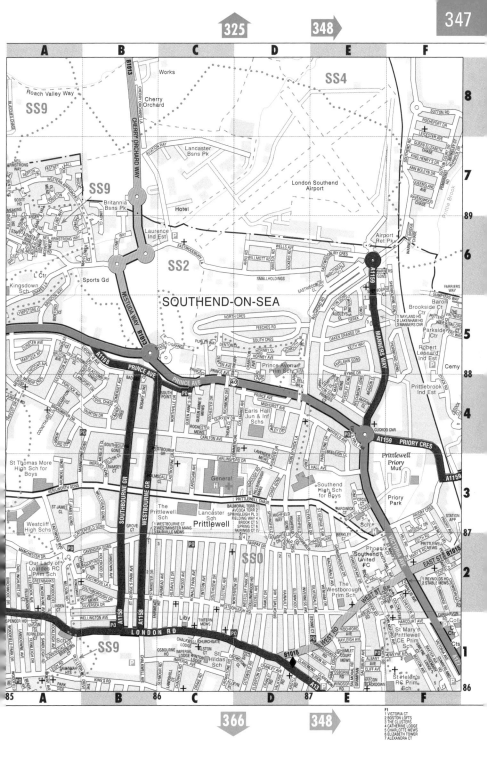

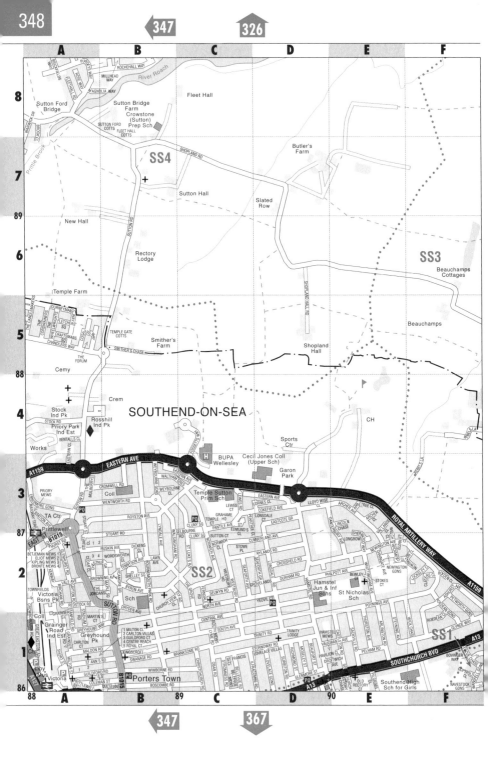

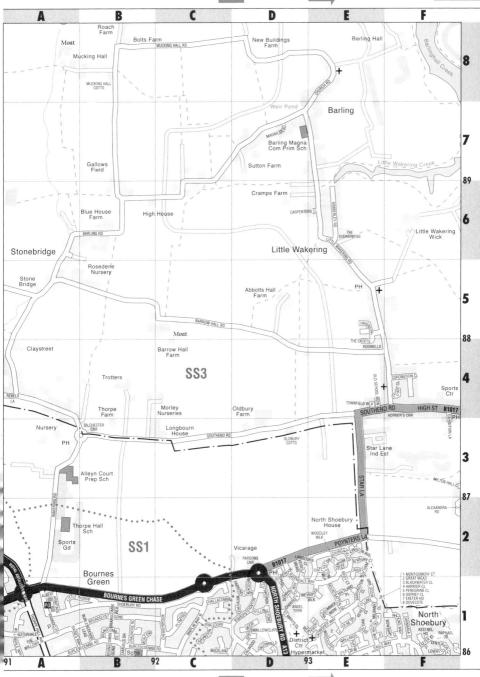

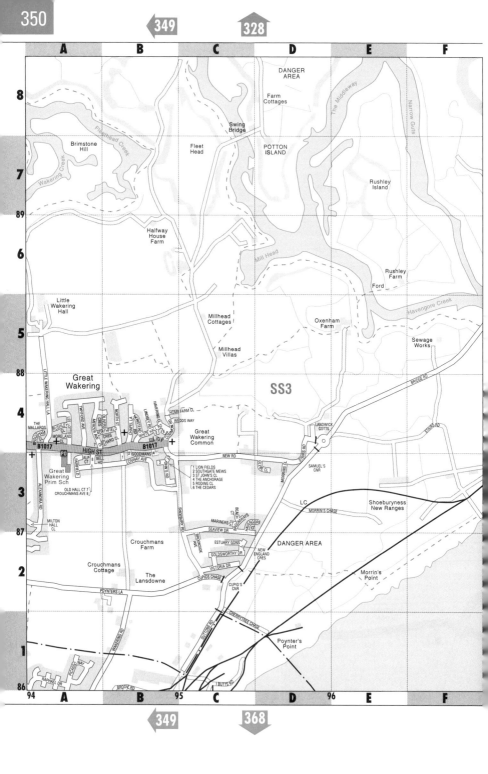

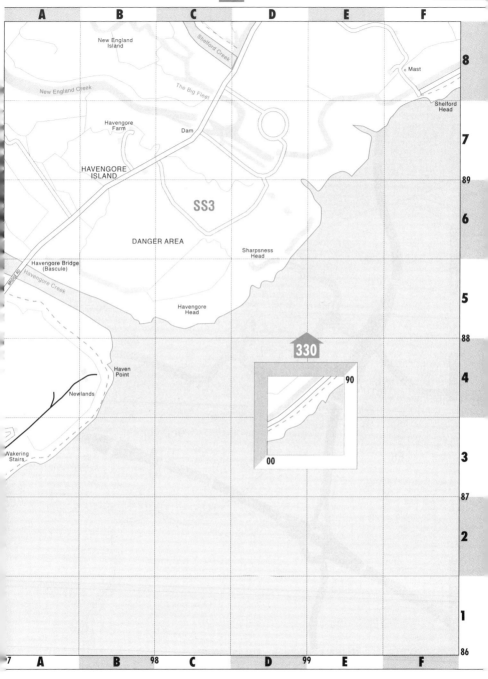

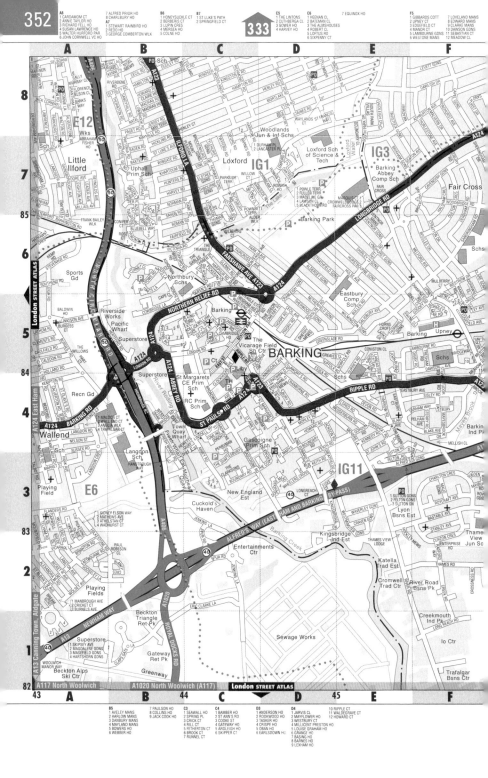

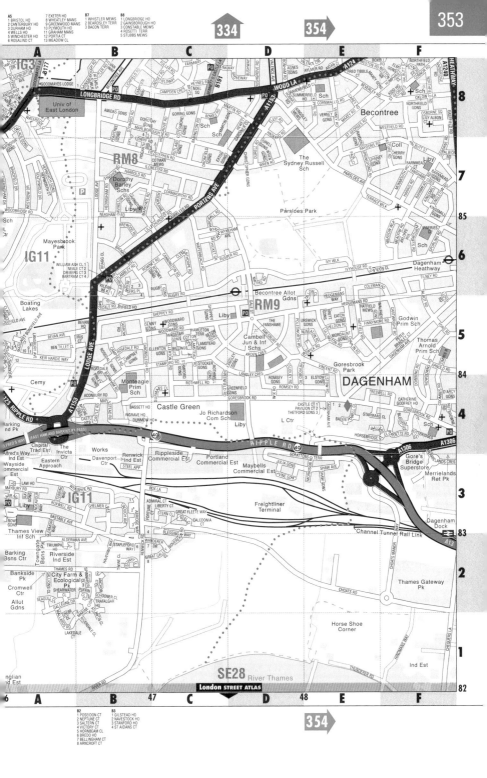

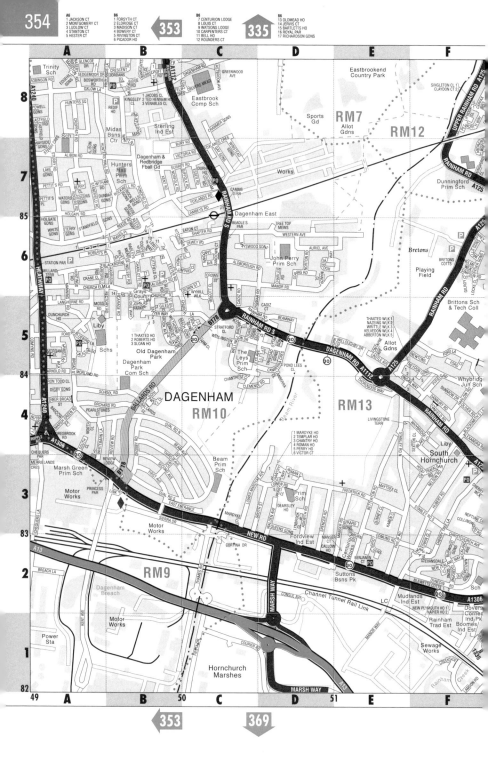

A **B** **C** **D** **E** **F**

Sch

ASPEN GA
SCARBROUGH AVE
LIME TREE WY
SYCAMORE AVE
OAK RD
POPLAR
GAYNES PARK RD
MAPLE AVE
OAK AVE
BEECH AVE
ELM AVE

PINE CT

LITTLE GAYNES LA
GROVE CT
MURFITT WAY

ALDER AVE

THE GROVE
CLAYTON AVE
CORBETS TEY RD
TAWNY AVE
GAYNES GDNS
LITTLE GAYNES GDNS

PARKLAND AVE

8

MEADOW AVE
LEASWAY
FAIRFIELD AVE
RUSHMERE AVE
ROXBURGH AVE
ASH LEA GDNS
ASH LEA

PARK DR
CONISTON AVE
CRANSTON PARK AVE

MELSTOCK AVE

Cranham Marsh
Nature Reserve

Spring Wood

Gaynes
Sch

FRESHFIELDS AVE
HACKETTS LA
FINCHINGFIELD
LONGWOOD CT
LONGWOOD CL
FORDALL RD
MEADOWSIDE RD
HUNTSMANS DR
THE GLADE
LANGMORE CL

Middle
Wood

Bonus
Wood

7

Crem
Cemy

Redcrofts
Farm

PO

Corbets Tey

Corbets
Tey Sch

BEARBLOCK
COTTS

B142

85

PARK FARM RD

P

HARWOOD HALL LA

Harwood
Hall

OCKENDON RD

Manor Farm

Lodge
Farm

Derham
House

Russell's
Lake

Stubbers
Outdoor Pursuits
Ctr

6

Central
Farm

Sullens
Farm

RM14

SUNNINGS LA
STUBBERS LA

5

Bush
Farm

Dennises
Cottages

DENNISES LA

84

LITTLE GERPINS
RD
Mast

Gerpins
Farm

GERPINS LA

Bramble
Farm

Freeman's
Shaw

4

FEN LA

BRAMBLE LA

P

Baldwins
Farm

3

HUNTS HILL
COTTS

Hunts Hill
Farm

Cockhide

83

RM13

WARWICK LA

White Post
Wood

Warwick
Wood

2

Belhus Woods
Country Park

Whitehall
Wood

P

RM15

ROMFORD RD

Running Water
Wood

Running Water Brook

Brickkiln
Wood

M25

1

82

A 55 **B** 56 **C** **D** 57 **E** **F**

M25

Hobbs Hole

Mast • Clay Tye Hill   Lowlands

Mast •

CRANHAM PL

OCKENDON RD   B1421

RM14

PH

CASTLE COTTS

North
Ockendon

Hall Farm

DENNISES LA

Kemps
Farm

PENNIS RD

CLAY TYE RD   B186

White Post
Farm

FEN LA

CH

The Grove

The
Wilderness

Groves
Cottages

Clay Pit

NORTH RD

CHEELSON RD

WILSMAN RD

NELSON RD

RM15

BENYON CT   OAK CT

South Ockendon
Hall

The Mount

Benyon
Prim Sch

PD

PH

1 DIDEA CL
2 THE GREEN
3 BENYON PATH

WEST RD

HALL LA

CANTERBURY
PAR

Recn
Gd

RM16 →

Factory

ROSEMARY
CL

CHURCH
CRES

COPPERS

BEECH

BIRCH CRES

KINGBEAM CHASE

UPPER DR

LAVENDER

ROSEWOOD CL

Ockendon

LARKSPUR
CL

BRANDON

HAZEL
DR

ASH WALK

CHERRY TREE

HOLLY DR

MAGNOLIA CL

VIOLA CL

CELANDINE
CL

TAMARISK AVE

LABURNUM GR

BIRCH CL

MAP LE DR

MEDLAR DR

Great Mollands
Farm

ARISDALE AVE

MAYFLOWER
CL

QUINCE TREE

GARTH RD

WOOD CHASE

POPLAR CL

AVONTAIR RD

NURSERY CL

SYCAMORE WAY

LAUREL

MOLLANDS CT

MOLLANDS LA

Little Mollands
Farm

Grange
Farm

LITTLE BUNYAN CL

DANIELS CT

AIRE DR

DAGLEN DR

ANTON RD

ARDMORE RD

ARDEN DR

AYRON RD

B186

SOUTH RD   B186

ALDER DR 1
CEDAR RISE 2

ARCANY RD

South Ockendon

MAR CL

8

85

7

6

5

84

4

3

83

2

1

82

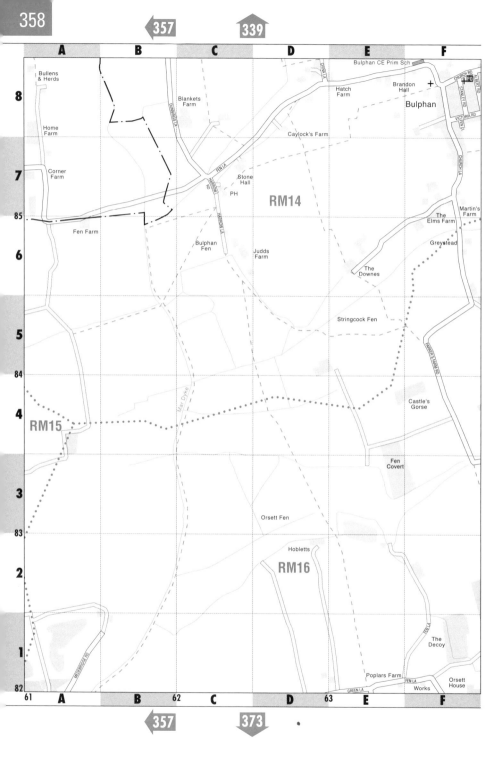

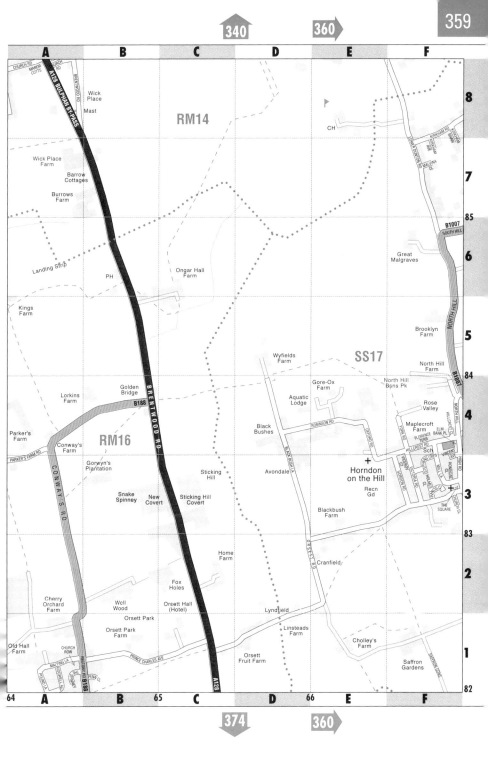

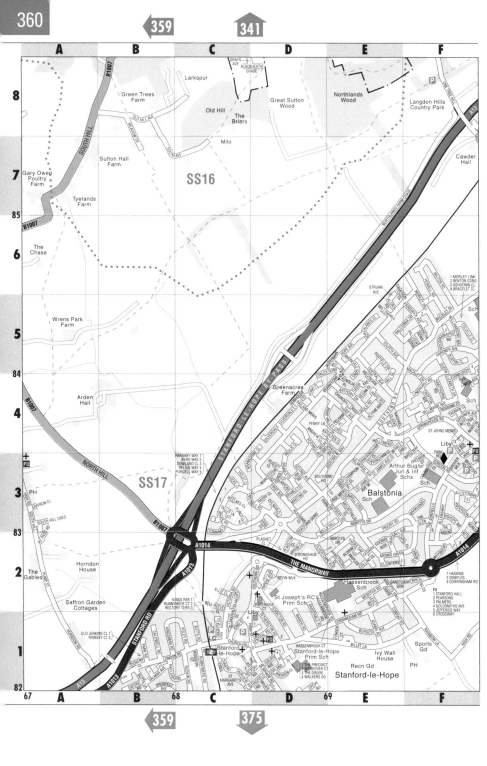

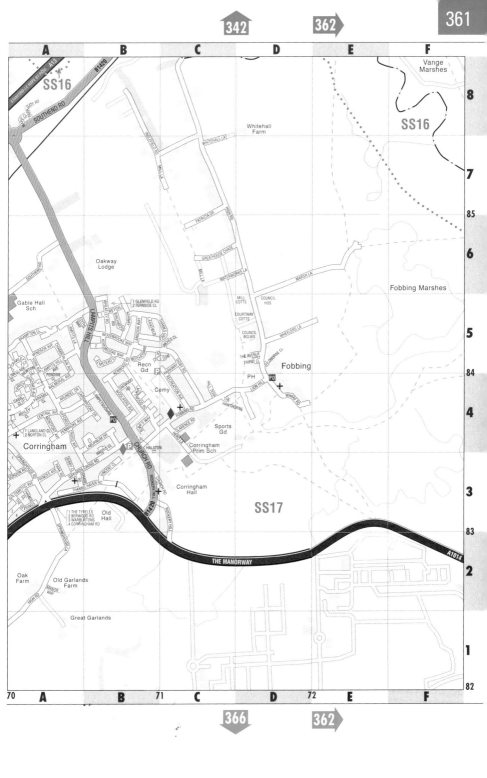

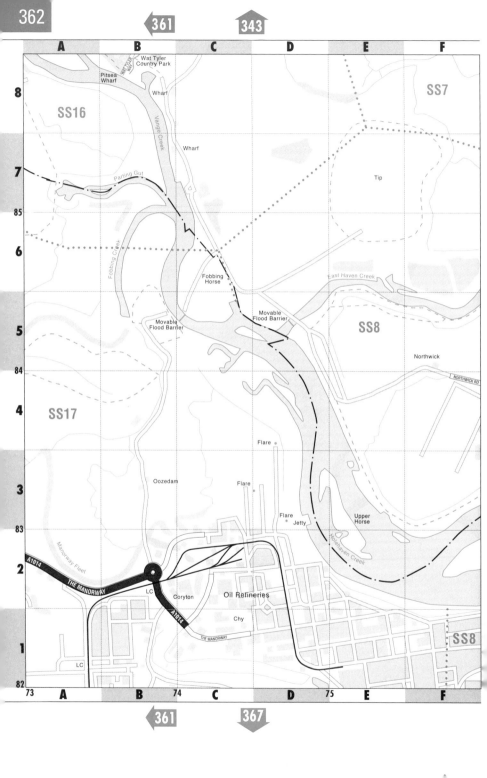

SS7

SS16

Pitsea
Wharf

Wat Tyler
Country Park

Wharf

Wharf

Vange Creek

Parting Gut

Tip

Fobbing Creek

Fobbing
Horse

East Haven Creek

Movable
Flood Barrier

Movable
Flood Barrier

SS8

Northwick

NORTHWICK RD

SS17

Oozedam

Flare

Flare

Flare

Jetty

Upper
Horse

Holehaven Creek

Manorway Fleet

A1014

THE MANORWAY

LC

Coryton

Oil Refineries

A1014

Chy

THE MANORWAY

SS8

LC

LC

73   74   75

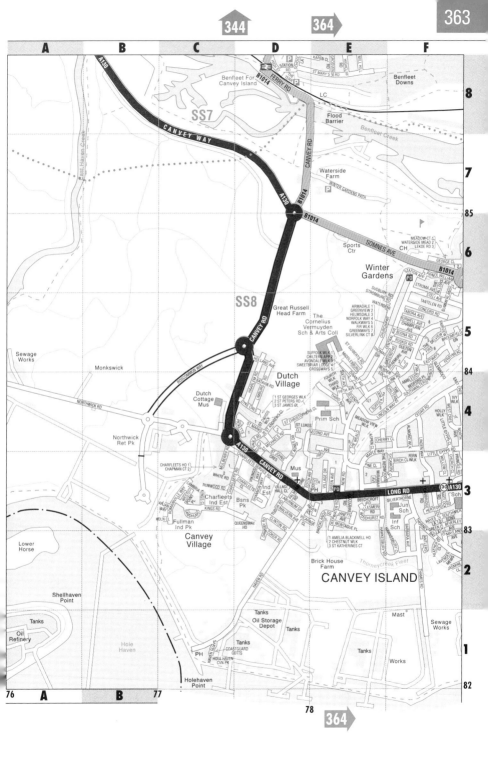

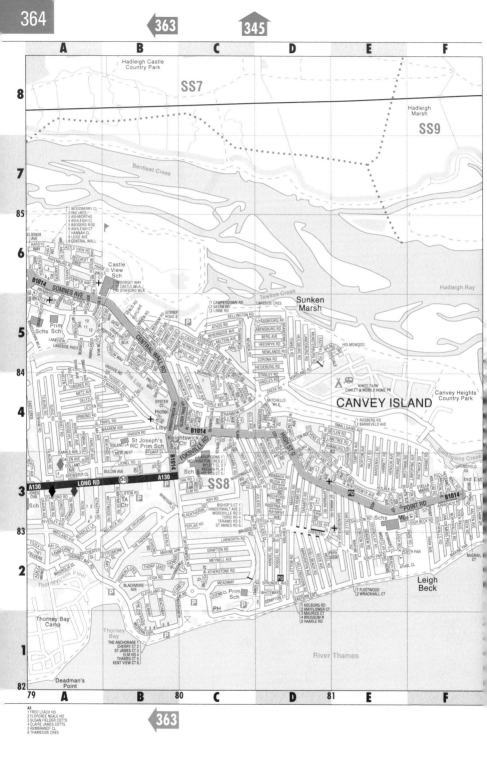

A B C D E F

Hadleigh Castle
Country Park

SS7

8

Hadleigh
Marsh SS9

Bentfleet Creek

7

85

1 WOODBERRY CL
2 THE LEES
3 ASHWORTHS
4 ASHLEIGH CL
5 BADGERS RISE
6 ASHLEIGH CT
7 HANNAH CL
8 LEIGE AVE
9 CENTRAL WALL

ELSINOR
WAY HARDYS
WAY Castle View Rd

6

B1014 SOMNES AVE

Castle
View
Sch

Hadleigh Ray

1 DORSET WAY
2 CASTLE WLK
3 STAFFORD WLK

Prim
Schs Prim
Sch

Tewkus Creek

Sunken
Marsh

1 CAMPERDOWN RD
2 GEESH RD
3 LINNE RD

Lakeside Cres

GENNEP
ROAD S

5

Lakeview
Lakeside Path

STRASBOURG RD
ABENSBURG RD
BERG AVE
HEESWYK RD
NEWLANDS RD
CORONA RD
HEIDEBERG RD

Holmswood

84

ATHOS RD
WHERNSIDE AVE
MILTSIN AVE

STANLEY RD
HINDLES RD

KINGS PARK
CHALET & MOBILE HOME PK

Canvey Heights
Country Park

CREEK RD

CANVEY ISLAND

4

St Joseph's
RC Prim Sch

OYSTER
Hotel

Liby

CENTRAL WALL RD

MITCHELLS
WLK

RAINBOW RD

1 ROSBERG RD
2 BARNEVELD AVE

Smallgains Creek

Knightswick
Ctr B1014

FOKSVILLE RD

Sch

Stuart CL

MERLIN CT

HIGH ST

3 A130 LONG RD 30 A130

DALEN AVE
DOLLANT
AVE

BULOW AVE

Sch

PO SS8

CLIFTON RD

TA
Ctr

WINDSOR

BISHOP'S CT 1
VANDERWALT AVE 2
WOODVILLE RD 3
TORSI RD 4
TERAMO RD 5
ST ANNES RD 6

ROSBACH RD
OLIUDA RD
DELGADA

ROCHFORD
RAYMENT

POINT RD B1014

Ind Est

SPRINGFIELD
RD

Schs

83

A130
JONES
CNR

Sch

BEVERLEY

THE DRIVEWAY

WESTWOOD RD

ASH RD

BLACKTHORN

POPLAR RD

ODESSA RD

WINTERSWYK AVE

PO

STELLA
RD

McGRAIL
CT

2

Thorneycreek Fleet

THE PARKWAY

MARINE APP

LABWORTH RD

GRAFTON RD

MEYNELL AVE

ATHERSTONE RD

MEADWAY

DELDERE
AVE

SPRUNDEL AVE
WHITEWAYS
COMPTON

PARK
VIEW

Leigh
Beck

1 FLEETWOOD
2 WRACKHALL CT

ATHOL CL

P

BLACKMORE
AVE

CLEVELAND

THORP LEAS

LEIGH RD

OVENS CL Prim
Sch

EASTERN
ESPL

1 KOLBURG RD
2 MAYFLOWER CT
3 MAURICE CT
4 BRUSSUM RD
5 HAARLE RD

Thorney Bay
Camp

Thorney
Bay

PH

THE ANCHORAGE 1
CHERRY CT 2
ST JAMES CT 3
ELM HO 4
THAMES CT 5
KENT VIEW CT 6

1

River Thames

82

Deadman's
Point

79 A 80 B C 80 D 81 E F

A3
1 FRED LEACH HO
2 FLORENCE NEALE HO
3 SUSAN FIELDER COTTS
4 CLAIRE JAMES COTTS
5 REMBRANDT CL
6 THAMESIDE CRES

346
366
366

SS9

Belton Hills
Belton Gardens
BELTON WAY W
CASTLE DR.
Leigh-on-Sea
Playing
Field

MARINE PAR
BELTON WAY E
BELTON GDNS

RECTORY GR
Schs
Liby

MAPLE AVE

Leigh Cliffs
Leigh Cliffs

COCKLE SHEDS
BELTON
BRIDGE
ALLEY DOCK
Leigh
Heritage
Ctr

SANS SOUCI
LEIGH PARK CT
HIGH ST
NEW RD

LEIGH
THE
GARDENS

1 BARYTA CT
2 THE TERRACE
3 PLEASANT TERR
4 NORMAN PL
5 NORMAN TERR
6 HILLSIDE RD

ESTUARY CT 1
RICHMOND CT 2
GRAND COURT W 3
SOUTHDOWN CT 4

Sewage
Works
Leigh Marsh

Two Tree Island /
Nature Reserve

SOUTHEND-ON-SEA

Slipway

Hadleigh Ray

SS8

Oyster Creek

Canvey Point

Smallgains Creek

SILVERPOINT
MARINE
POINT RD
BEVELAND RD
BOMMEL AVE
BOYCHANAN RD
MARINE PAR

Leighbeck
Point

8
85
7
6
5
84
4
3
83
2
1
82

A B C D E F

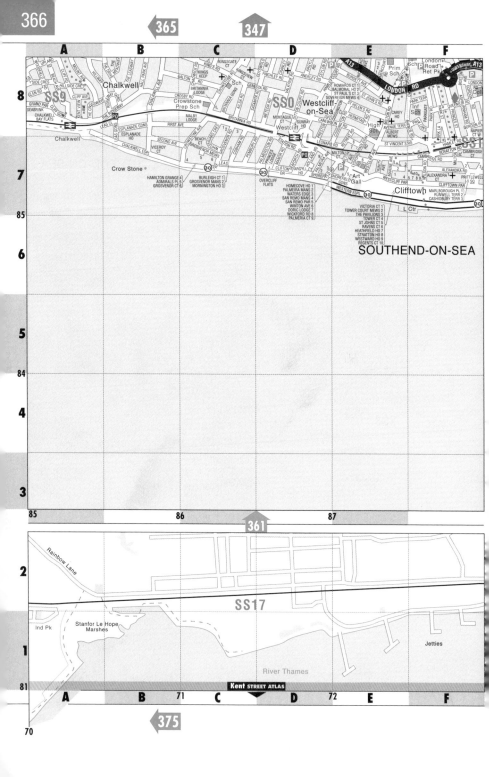

Chalkwell

SS9

Chalkwell

Crow Stone

Crowstone
Prep Sch

Westcliff

**Westcliff-
on-Sea**

SS0

SOUTHEND-ON-SEA

Clifftown

SS1

HAMILTON GRANGE 4
ADMIRALS PL 5
GROSVENOR CT 6

BURLEIGH CT 1
GROSVENOR MANS 2
MORNINGTON HO 3

OVERCLIFF
FLATS

HOMECOVE HO 1
PALMEIRA MANS 2
WATERS EDGE 3
SAN REMO MANS 4
SAN REMO PAR 5
WINTON AVE 6
DORIC LODGE 7
WICKFORD RD 8
PALMERIA CT 9

VICTORIA CT 1
TOWER COURT MEWS 2
THE PAVILIONS 3
TOWER CT 4
ST JOHNS CT 5
RAVENS CT 6
HEATHFIELD HO 7
STRATTON HO 8
WESTWARD HO 9
REGENTS CT 10

MARLBOROUGH PL 1
RUNWELL TERR 2
CASHIOBURY TERR 3

Rainbow Lane

SS17

Ind Pk

Stanfor Le Hope
Marshes

Jetties

River Thames

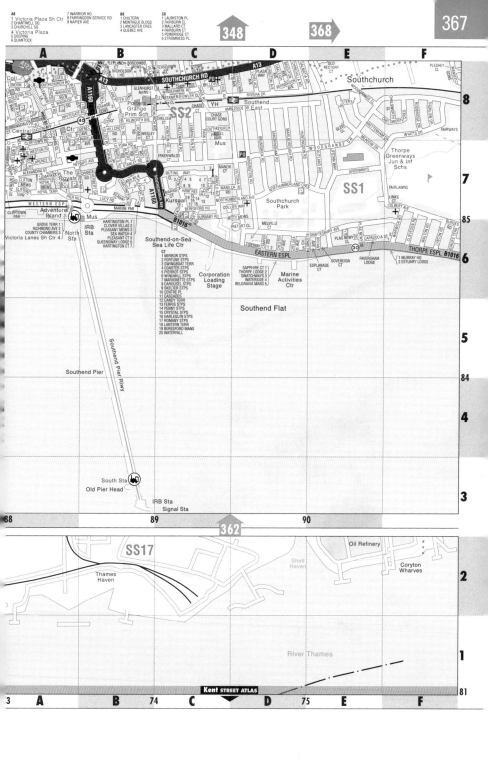

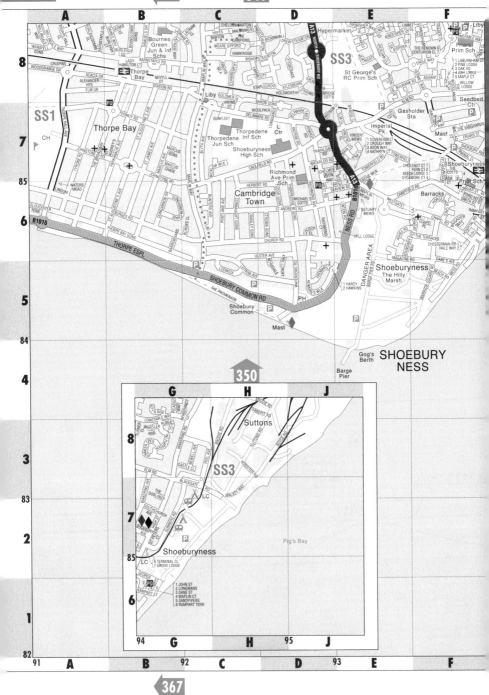

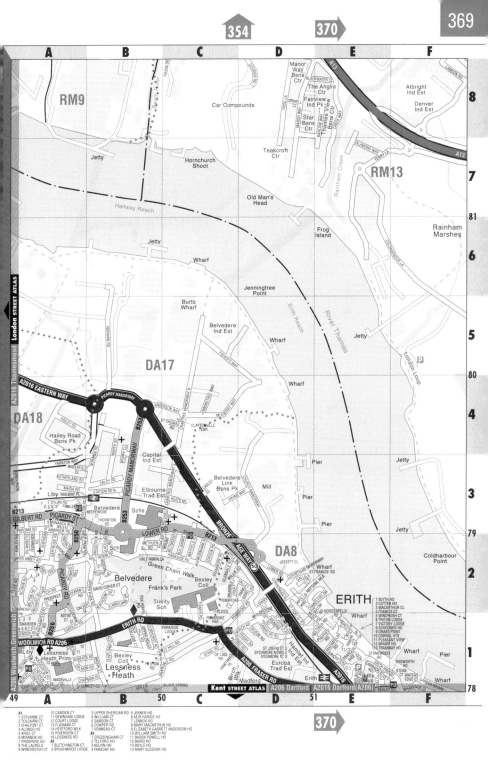

A1
1 STEVANNE CT
2 TOLCAIRN CT
3 CHALFONT CT
4 ALONSO HO
5 ARIEL CT
6 MIRANDA HO
7 PROSPERO HO
8 THE LAURELS
9 WINCHESTER CT

10 CAMDEN CT
11 NEWNHAM LODGE
12 COURT LODGE
13 FLAXMAN CT
14 HERTFORD WLK
15 RIVERVIEW CT
16 LESSNESS RD
A2
1 BLETCHINGTON CT
2 BRUSHWOOD LODGE

3 UPPER SHERIDAN RD
4 WILLIAM CT
5 SAMSON CT
6 COWPER RD
7 VENMEAD CT
A3
1 CRESSINGHAM CT
2 TELFORD HO
3 KELVIN HO
4 FARADAY HO

5 JENNER HO
6 KEIR HARDIE HO
7 LENNOX HO
8 MARY MACARTHUR HO
9 ELIZABETH GARRETT ANDERSON HO
10 WILLIAM SMITH HO
11 BADEN POWELL HO
12 BAIRD HO
13 BOYLE HO
14 MARY SLESSOR HO

1 BLYTH HO
2 CUTTER HO
3 MACARTHUR CL
4 FRANCIS CT
5 WINDRUSH CT
6 TRITON LODGE
7 VICTORY LODGE
8 SCHOONER HO
9 DRAKE POINT
10 CORRAL HTS
11 PLEASANT VIEW
12 TRAMWAY HO
13 STONEWOOD

369
355

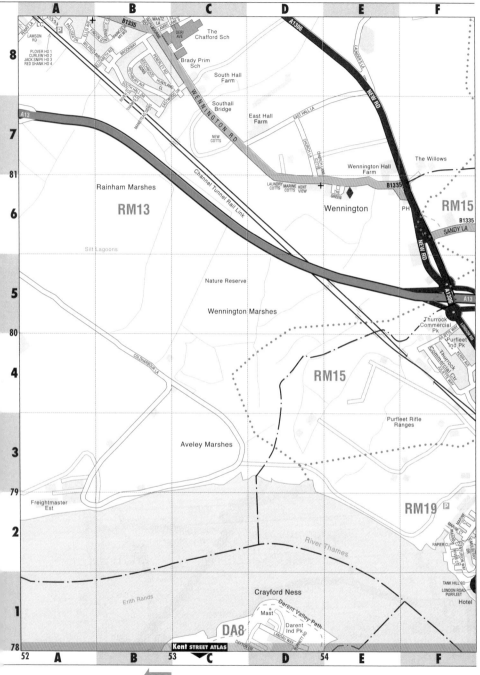

A13

LAMSON RD
PLOVER HO 1
CURLEW HO 2
JACK SNIPE HO 3
RED SHANK HO 4

B1335

The Chafford Sch

Brady Prim Sch

South Hall Farm

Southall Bridge

East Hall Farm

A1306

NEW RD

The Willows

RM13

Rainham Marshes

Wennington Hall Farm

Wennington

RM15

B1335

SANDY LA

B1335

Silt Lagoons

NEW RD

Nature Reserve

A1306

A13

Wennington Marshes

Thurrock Commercial Pk

Purfleet Ind Pk

COLDHARBOUR LA

RM15

Purfleet Rifle Ranges

Aveley Marshes

Freightmaster Est

RM19

River Thames

Erith Rands

Crayford Ness

TANK HILL RD
LONDON ROAD PURFLEET
Hotel

Darent Valley Path

Mast

Darent Ind Pk

DA8

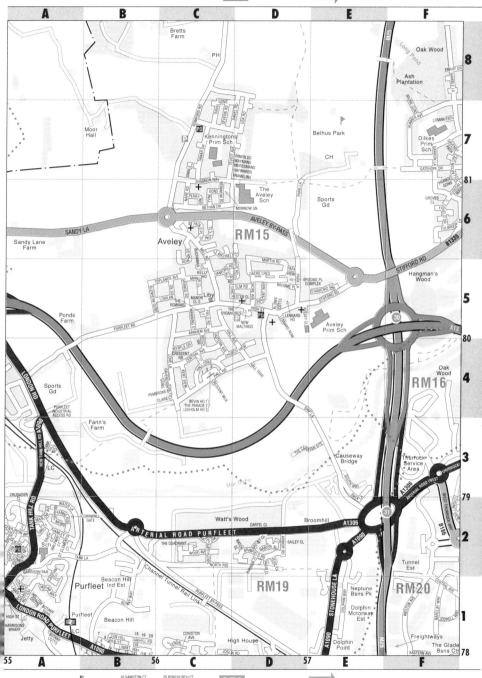

B1
1 RIVERVIEW TERR
2 SUSSEX TERR
3 SOUTHLAND TERR
4 DUNCOMBE CT
5 HEBERDEN CT
6 WINGROVE DR
7 HOWBURGH CT
8 TRAYFORD CT
9 STORAS CT
10 SAWSTON CT
11 KYRKLY CT
12 BRADFIELD CT
13 RIVERVIEW FLATS
14 WROXALL CT
15 ROOKLEY CT
16 DUNNOSE CT
17 BRANSTONE CT
18 SHORWELL CT
19 BRIGHSTONE CT
20 BONCHURCH CT

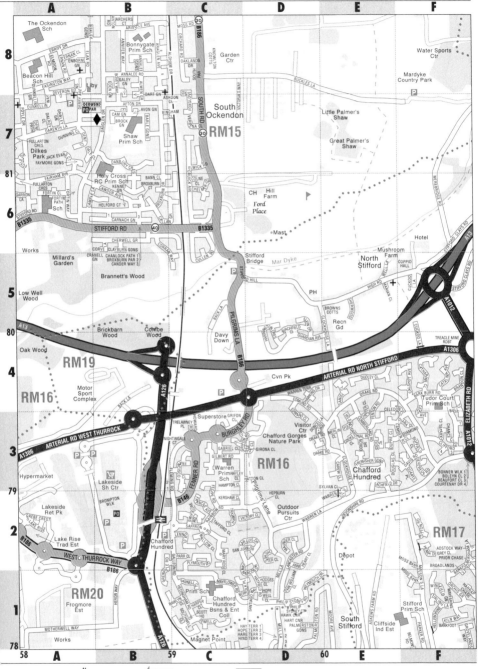

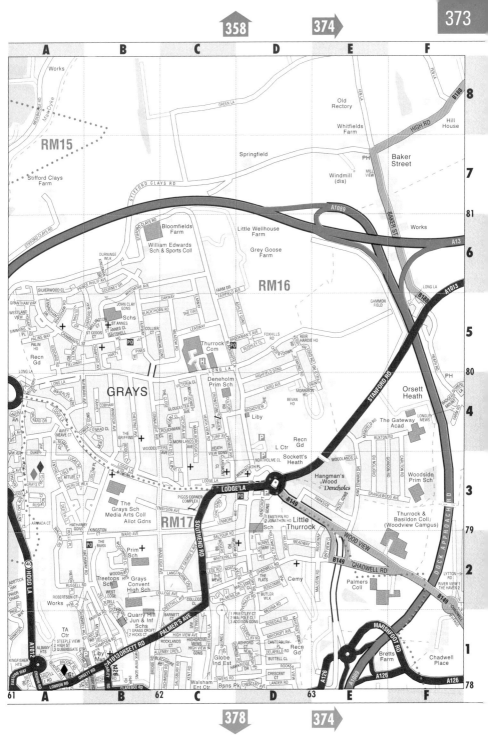

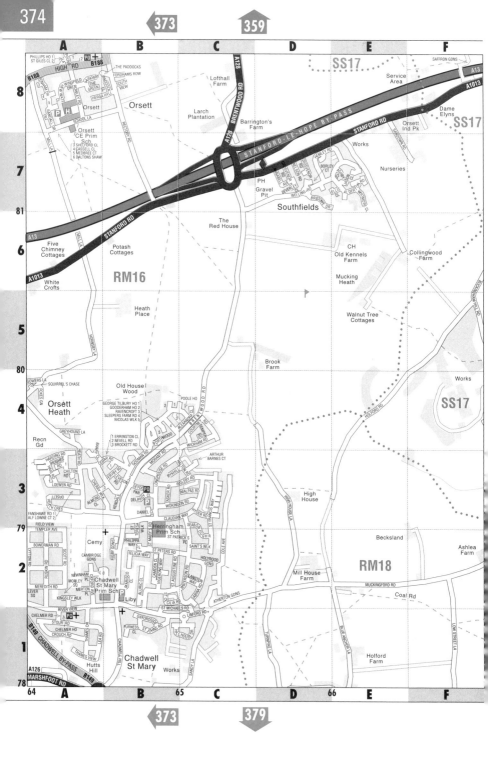

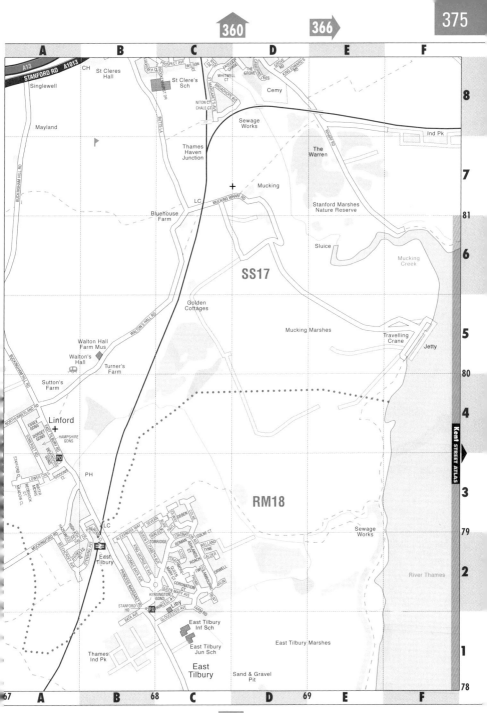

371

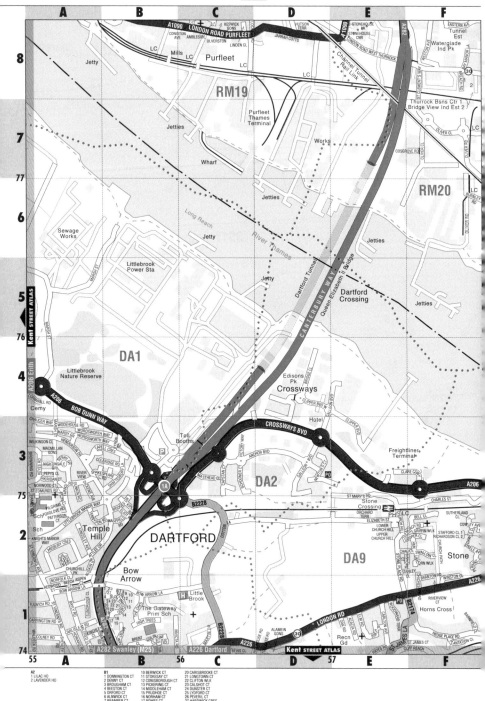

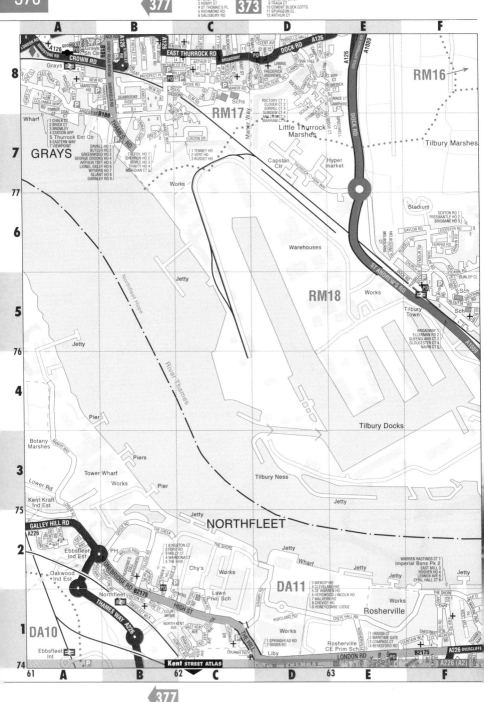

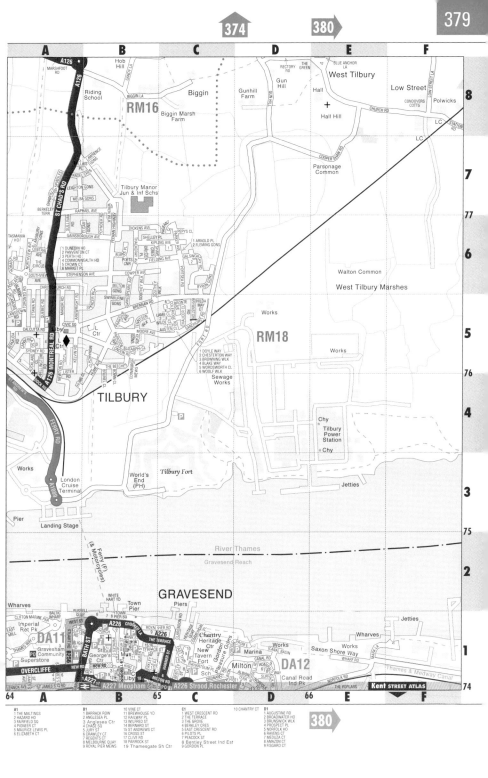

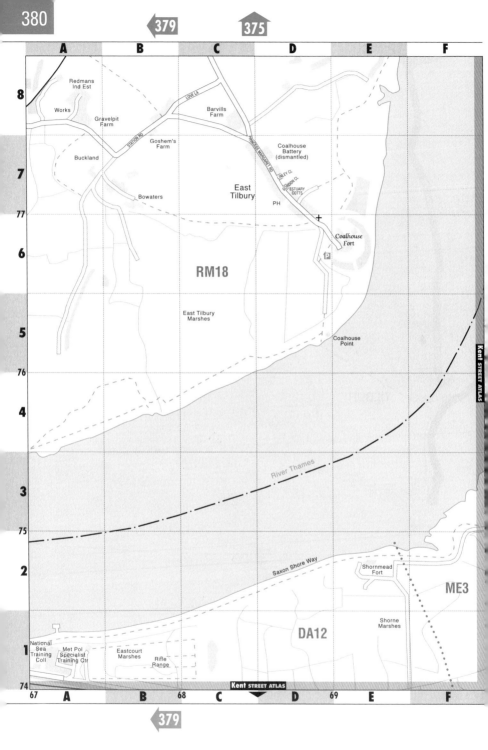

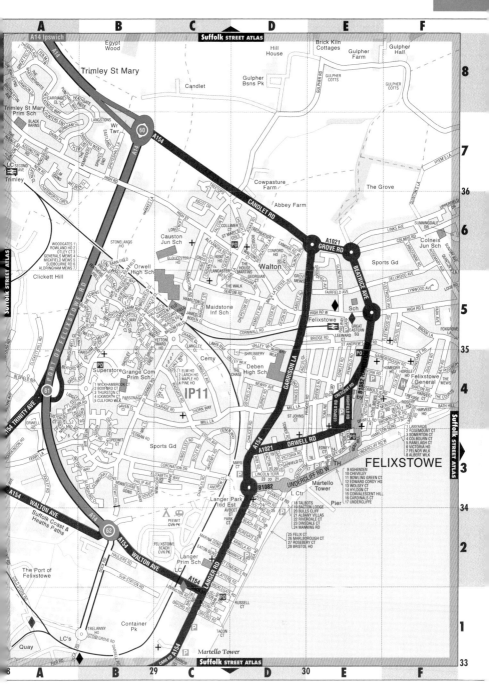

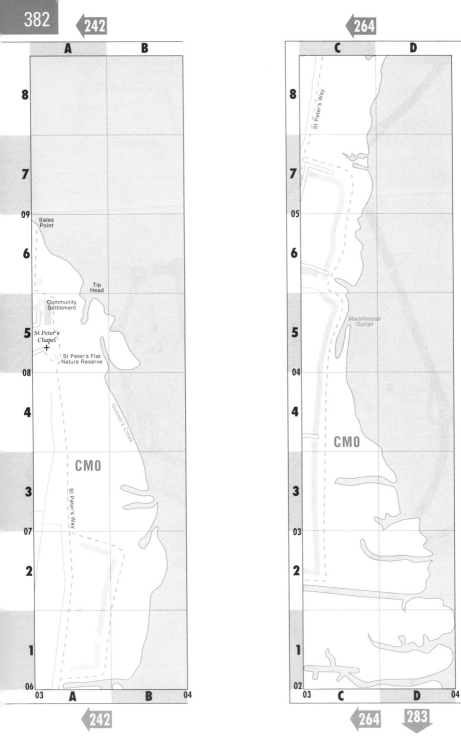

A B

C D

8

7

09
Sales
Point

6

Tip
Head

Community
Settlement

5
St Peter's
Chapel

St Peter's Flat
Nature Reserve

08

4

Gunter's Creek

CMO

3

St Peter's Way

07

2

1

06
03 A B 04

8

St Peter's Way

05

7

6

Marshhouse
Outfall

5

04

4

CMO

3

03

2

1

02
03 C D 04

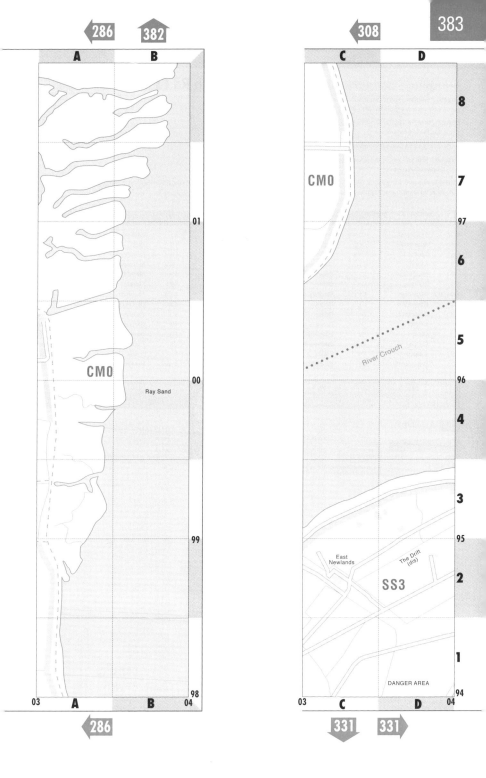

A
B

C
D

8

01

7
97

6

CMO

5

River Crouch

00

Ray Sand

96

4

3
95

CMO

99

East
Newlands

The Drift
(dis)

SS3

2

1

DANGER AREA

98

03
A
B
04

03
C
D
04

384

Index

Church Rd [6] Beckenham BR2..........53 C6

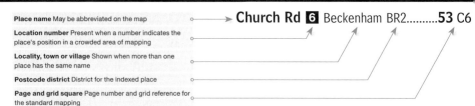

- **Place name** May be abbreviated on the map → Church Rd
- **Location number** Present when a number indicates the place's position in a crowded area of mapping → [6]
- **Locality, town or village** Shown when more than one place has the same name → Beckenham
- **Postcode district** District for the indexed place → BR2
- **Page and grid square** Page number and grid reference for the standard mapping → 53 C6

Cities, towns and villages are listed in CAPITAL LETTERS **Public and commercial buildings** are highlighted in **magenta**
Places of interest are highlighted in blue with a star★

Abbreviations used in the index

Acad	**Academy**	Comm	**Common**	Gd	**Ground**	L	**Leisure**	Prom	**Promenade**
App	**Approach**	Cott	**Cottage**	Gdn	**Garden**	La	**Lane**	Rd	**Road**
Arc	**Arcade**	Cres	**Crescent**	Gn	**Green**	Liby	**Library**	Recn	**Recreation**
Ave	**Avenue**	Cswy	**Causeway**	Gr	**Grove**	Mdw	**Meadow**	Ret	**Retail**
Bglw	**Bungalow**	Ct	**Court**	H	**Hall**	Meml	**Memorial**	Sh	**Shopping**
Bldg	**Building**	Ctr	**Centre**	Ho	**House**	Mkt	**Market**	Sq	**Square**
Bsns, Bus	**Business**	Ctry	**Country**	Hospl	**Hospital**	Mus	**Museum**	St	**Street**
Bvd	**Boulevard**	Cty	**County**	HQ	**Headquarters**	Orch	**Orchard**	Sta	**Station**
Cath	**Cathedral**	Dr	**Drive**	Hts	**Heights**	Pal	**Palace**	Terr	**Terrace**
Cir	**Circus**	Dro	**Drove**	Ind	**Industrial**	Par	**Parade**	TH	**Town Hall**
Cl	**Close**	Ed	**Education**	Inst	**Institute**	Pas	**Passage**	Univ	**University**
Cnr	**Corner**	Emb	**Embankment**	Int	**International**	Pk	**Park**	Wk, Wlk	**Walk**
Coll	**College**	Est	**Estate**	Intc	**Interchange**	Pl	**Place**	Wr	**Water**
Com	**Community**	Ex	**Exhibition**	Junc	**Junction**	Prec	**Precinct**	Yd	**Yard**

Index of towns, villages, streets, hospitals, industrial estates, railway stations, schools, shopping centres, universities and places of interest

384 Aal–Alb

A

Aalten Ave SS8 364 F3
Abacus Prim Sch SS12 321 F5
Abbas Wlk CO10 34 C5
ABBERTON 163 A3
Abberton IG8 310 C5
Abberton Rd
Fingringhoe CO5 163 D3
Layer de la H CO2 162 C5
Abberton Resr Nature Reserve★ CO2 161 F2
Abberton Wildfowl Visitor Ctr★ CO2 161 E1
Abberton Wlk RM13 354 F4
Abbess Cl CM1 231 E2
ABBESS RODING 203 E4
Abbey Cl Fyfield CM5 227 C1
Hullbridge SS5 301 D2
Romford RM1 336 A5
Abbey Cotts CO11 115 C7
Abbey Cres
Belvedere DA17 369 A2
Thorpe-le-S CO16 142 A1
Abbey Ct Colchester CO2 136 A5
[10] Ipswich IP1 17 A7
Waltham Abbey EN9 265 B5
Abbey Dale Cl CM17 224 C7
ABBEY FIELD 135 E5
Abbey Fields CM3 278 B7
Abbey Field View CO2 135 E4
Abbeygate Ho CO2 135 F6
Abbey Gate St [11] CO2 135 F6
Abbey Ho EN9 266 A5
Abbey La Coggeshall CO6 131 A1
Saffron Walden CB10 22 D1
Abbey Mdw CO9 51 D2
Abbey Mead Ind Est EN9 265 C5
Abbey Park Ind Est IG11 352 C4
Abbey Rd Barking IG11 352 B4
Barking IG11 352 C3
Billericay CM12 296 F1
Greenhithe DA9 377 C2
Hullbridge SS5 301 D1
Ilford IG2 333 D6
Sudbury CO10 15 E1
Abbey St Ickleton CB10 3 A4
Thorpe-le-S CO16 142 A1
Abbey Turning CM9 236 D4
Abbeyview EN9 265 C6
Abbey View CM6 96 E2
Abbey Wood La RM13 355 D3
Abbigail Gdns CO15 196 B4
Abbotsbury Cl IP2 17 A1
Abbots Cl Brentwood CM15 295 A1
Abbots Cl *continued*
Clacton-on-S CO15 195 E6
Rainham RM13 355 C3
Wix CO11 115 C5
Abbots Cotts CB9 10 A4
Abbots Ct SS15 319 E1
Abbotsford Gdns IG8 310 A3
Abbotsford Rd IG3 334 B2
Abbots Gdns CO16 194 C4
Abbots Hall Prim Sch SS17 360 E3
Abbotsleigh Rd CM3 301 E7
Abbotsmead CM9 236 F5
Abbot's Rd CO2 136 B3
Abbots Ride CM11 297 C2
Abbotsweld CM18 223 D5
Abbotsweld Prim Sch CM18 223 D6
Abbots Wick La CO5 188 B3
Abbots Wlk SS3 368 C8
Abbotswood SS7 345 C5
Abbotswood Gdns
Ilford IG5 333 A7
Redbridge IG5 332 F8
Abbott Rd CO12 90 F2
Abbotts Cl Romford RM7 335 B8
Southend-on-S SS9 346 E5
Abbotts Cres E4 309 D6
Abbott's Croft CB9 9 F4
Abbotts Ct Romford RM3 314 F2
Stanstead Abbotts SG12 197 D4
Sturmer CB9 9 E5
Abbotts Dr
Stanford-le-H SS17 360 D2
Waltham Abbey EN9 266 A6
Abbotts Hall Chase SS17 360 E2
Abbotts La CO6 134 A7
Abbotts Pl CM2 232 D3
Abbotts Rise SG12 197 D4
Abbotts Way
Bishop's Stortford CM23 145 E3
Stanstead Abbotts SG12 197 D4
Abbs Cross Gdns RM12 336 D3
Abbs Cross La RM12 336 C2
Abbs Cross Sch & Arts Coll RM12 336 C1
Abdy Ave CO12 90 E2
Abell Way CM2 233 B4
Abels Rd CO9 103 D8
Abenberg Way CM13 317 B8
Abensburg Rd SS8 364 D5
Abercorn Ct [11] CB9 8 F7
Abercorn Gdns RM6 334 B5
Abercorn Ho CM3 233 E8
Abercorn Way CM8 184 A2
Abercrombie Ho [17] RM3 314 D5
Abercrombie Way CM18, CM19 223 C6
Aberdare Cl IP2 17 B2
Aberdeen Gdns SS9 346 A2
Aberdour Rd IG3 334 B2
Abigail Ct CM5 249 A5
Abigail Mews RM3 314 F1
Abingdon Cl IP2 17 A1
Abingdon Ct [3] SS13 321 A1
Abinger Cl Barking IG11 353 A8
Clacton-on-S CO16 195 C6
Abington Ct RM14 337 C3
Abington Pl [2] CB9 9 A8
Abraham Cohen Ct IG1 333 A5
Abraham Ct RM14 337 A2
Abraham Dr CM8 156 E4
Abraham Fisher Ho E12 352 A7
Abram's La SG8 19 C4
Abreys SS7 345 A7
ABRIDGE 290 A6
Abridge Gdns RM5 313 A4
Abridge Mews RM4 290 B6
Abridge Pk RM4 290 A5
Abridge Rd Chigwell IG7 289 E4
Theydon Bois CM16 268 A1
Abridge Way IG11 353 B3
Acacia Ave Colchester CO4 136 E8
Hornchurch RM12 335 F2
Acacia Cl IP3 18 E1
Acacia Ct Brantham CO11 60 D1
Waltham Abbey EN9 266 A5
Acacia Dr
Great Dunmow CM6 123 C1
Maldon CM9 236 F1
Southend-on-S SS1 368 A8
Upminster RM14 356 A8
Acacia Gdns
Upminster RM14 337 F4
Witham CM8 184 B4
Acacia Rd Basildon SS13 343 E8
Greenhithe DA9 376 E1
Acacias Ct [12] EN11 221 A6
Academy Fields Rd RM2 336 B6
Academy Sq [1] RM2 336 B6
Accommodation Rd CO4 109 D7
Accrington Ho [10] RM3 314 D5
Acer Ave RM13 355 D2
Acer Gr Chelmsford CM1 232 D4
Ipswich IP8 16 C1
Achilles Way CM7 128 B5
Achnacone Dr CO4 109 C3
Acland Ave CO3 135 B7
Acland Ct CO3 135 A7
Acle Cl IG6 311 B3
Aconbury Rd RM9 353 B4
Acorn Ave Braintree CM7 127 E2
Halstead CO9 76 D1
Acorn Cl Chingford E4 309 B5
Colchester CO4 110 D4
Harwich CO12 90 F1
Ipswich IP2 16 C2
Acorn Ct IG2 333 E6
Acorn Ctr The IG6 312 B4
Acorn Mews Harlow CM18 224 A6
Acorn Mews *continued*
West Mersea CO5 218 D6
Acorn Pl Basildon SS16 341 B5
Maldon CM9 236 F5
Acorn St SG12 198 D8
Acorns The Chigwell IG7 311 E6
Hockley SS5 324 E7
Acorn Trad Ctr RM20 377 E8
Acorn Wlk CO7 166 A5
Acre Rd RM10 354 B5
Acres Ave CM5 248 F5
Acres End CM1 231 E4
Acres The SS17 360 F3
Acre View RM11 336 E7
Acton Cl CO10 33 F8
Acton Gn CO10 33 E7
Acton La CO10 33 F8
Acton Sq [4] CO10 33 E7
Ada Cole Meml Stables Horse Sanctuary★ CM19 222 E4
Adair Rd IP1 16 D8
Adalia Cres SS9 346 B3
Adalia Way SS9 346 B2
Adam Bsns Ctr SS14 320 F1
Adams Cl IP2 17 C3
Adams Ct Halstead CO9 76 D2
Saffron Walden CB11 43 C8
Adam's Elm Ho SS9 346 E2
Adams Glade SS4 325 D6
Adams Ho CM20 199 D1
Adams Maltings CO9 76 D2
Adams Rd SS17 360 E1
Adam Way SS11 321 E8
Adderley Rd CM23 145 F7
Addington Rd IP11 381 A7
Addison Ct CM16 268 A8
Addison Gdns RM17 373 C2
Addison Rd
Great Holland CO13 170 B5
Redbridge IG6 311 C2
Sudbury CO10 34 B8
Wanstead E11 332 A5
Adelaide Dr CO2 136 A1
Adelaide Gdns
Dagenham RM6 334 E6
South Benfleet SS7 344 D1
Adelaide Rd Ilford IG1 333 B2
Ipswich IP4 18 D6
Tilbury RM18 378 F6
Adelaide St CO12 90 F5
Adeliza Cl IG11 352 C5
Adelphi Cres RM12 336 B2
Adelsburg Rd SS8 364 C4
Aden Rd IG1 333 C4
Adingtons CM20 199 F2
Admiral Ct IG11 353 C3
Admiral Rd IP8 36 E8
Admirals Cl E18 332 B7
Admirals Lodge RM1 335 F6
Admirals Pl SS0 366 C7
Admirals The CO12 91 D4
Admirals Way DA12 379 D1
Admirals Wlk
Chelmsford CM1 231 F3
Greenhithe DA9 377 B2
Hoddesdon EN11 221 B4
Southend-on-S SS3 368 D5
Wivenhoe CO7 164 B8
Adnams Wlk RM12 355 A7
Adomar Rd RM8 334 E1
Adstock Way RM17 372 F2
Adult Coll of Barking & Dagenham RM9 353 F7
Advent Ct IG8 309 F5
Adventure Island★ SS1 367 A7
Advice Ave RM16 373 A4
Aerofoil Grove CO4 109 D2
Aetheric Rd CM7 127 E3
Affleck Rd CO4 136 E7
Afflets Ct SS14 342 C8
Afton Dr RM15 372 B7
Agar Rd [9] CO14 171 C8
Agar Road App [10] CO14 171 C8
Agate Rd CO15 195 F2
Agincourt Rd CO15 195 D4
Agister Rd IG7 312 A5
Agnes Ave Ilford IG1 352 B8
Southend-on-S SS9 346 B2
Agnes Gdns RM8 353 D8
Agnes Silverside Cl
Beerchurch CO2 162 F8
Colchester CO2 135 F1
Agricultural/Domestic Mus★ CM9 238 E7
Aidan Cl RM8 353 E8
Ailsa Rd SS0 366 C8
AIMES GREEN 243 F2
Ainger Rd CO12 90 E2
AINGERS GREEN 166 E5
Aingers Green Rd CO7 167 A5
Ainsley Ave RM7 335 C5
Ainslie Ho E4 309 A5
Ainslie Rd IP1 17 A6
Ainslie Wood Cres E4 309 B5
Ainslie Wood Gdns E4 309 B5
Ainslie Wood Prim Sch E4 309 B5
Ainslie Wood Rd E4 309 B5
Aintree Cres IG6 311 C1
Aintree Gr RM14 336 F1
Airborne Cl SS9 346 E5
Airborne Ind Est SS9 346 E5
Aire Dr RM15 357 B1
Aire Wlk CM8 183 E2
Airey Hos CO10 11 D1
Airey Neave Ct RM16 373 A4
Airfield Way RM12 355 C6
Airlie Gdns IG1 333 B3
Airport Ret Pk SS2 347 E6
Airthrie Rd IG3 334 B2
Aisne Rd CO2 135
Ajax Cl CM7 128
Akenfield Cl [1] CM3 301
Akersloot Pl CO5 218
Akhurst Ct CO5 218
Alamein Gdns DA2 376
Alamein Rd
Burnham-on-C CM0 306
Chelmsford CM1 231
Colchester CO2 135
Swanscombe DA10 377
Alanbrooke Rd CO2 136
Alan Cl SS9 346
Alan Dr CO16 168
Alan Gdns RM7 335
Alan Gr SS9 346
Alan Hasler Ho CM6 150
Alan Rd Ipswich IP3 17
Witham CM8 183
Alan Way CO3 134
Albany Ave SS0 347
Albany Chase CO15 196
Albany Cl Chelmsford CM1 231
West Bergholt CO6 108
Albany Ct Chingford E4 287
Epping CM16 245
Albany Gdns CO2 136
Albany Gdns E CO15 196
Albany Gdns W CO15 196
Albany Hts RM17 373
Albany Rd Dagenham RM6 334
Hornchurch RM12 336
Pilgrims Hatch CM15 294
Rayleigh SS6 324
Tilbury RM18 379
West Bergholt CO6 108
Wickford SS12 321
Albany The Ipswich IP4 17
Woodford IG8 309
Albany The, A Bsns & Ent Col… RM12 336
Albany View IG9 288
Albany Villas IP11 381
Alba Rd CM17 200
Albemarle App IG1 333
Albemarle Cl RM17 373
Albemarle Gdns
Braintree CM7 128
Ilford IG2 333
Albemarle Link CM2 232
Albemarle St CO12 91
Albert Ave E4 309
Albert Cl Grays RM16 373
Rayleigh SS6 323
Rochford SS4 325
Albert Cotts CO7 60
Albert Cres E4 309
Albert Ct CM7 128
Albert Dr SS15 341

Armonde Cl CM3 209 E1
Armond Rd CM8 183 F3
Armor Rd RM19 371 D2
Armourers Cl CM23 145 B4
Armoury Rd CO6 108 F4
Armstead Wlk RM10 354 A5
Armstrong Ave IG8 309 E4
Armstrong Cl
Dagenham RM8 334 D4
Danbury CM3 256 F8
Stanford-le-H SS17 360 E2
Armstrong Rd SS7 344 D7
Armstrong Way CO9 30 A2
Arncroft Ct 8 IG11 353 B2
Arne Cl SS17 360 D3
Arne Ct SS15 341 C6
Arne Mews SS15 341 C8
Arneways Ave RM6 334 D8
Arnheim Rd CM0 306 C4
Arnhem Ave RM15 371 C5
Arnhem Gr CM7 127 E5
Arnhem Rd CM1 231 E6
Arnold Ave Basildon SS16 341 A5
Southend-on-S SS1 367 C7
Arnold Ave E EN3 265 A1
Arnold Ct E18 309 F2
Arnold Dr CO4 136 E6
Arnold Ho CM2 232 A1
Arnold Pl RM18 379 C6
Arnold Rd
Clacton-on-S CO15 195 D1
Dagenham RM9 353 F5
Dagenham RM10 354 A5
Waltham Abbey EN9 265 C4
Arnolds Ave CM13 295 C4
Arnolds Cl CM13 295 C4
Arnolds Farm La CM13 295 E6
Arnolds Way SS4 325 D7
Arnold Villas CO5 186 C6
Arnold Way CM2 254 C3
Arnside Ho 2 RM3 315 A4
Arnstones Cl CO4 136 C8
Arodene Ho IG2 333 A5
ARP Shelter Mus* IP4 17 F5
Arran Ct SS12 321 F6
Arran Dr E12 332 D2
Arras Sq 12 IP1 17 C6
Arrow Rd CO4 136 F7
Arrowsmith Cl IG7 311 F5
Arrowsmith Path IG7 311 F5
Arrowsmith Rd IG7 311 F5
Arrowsmith Wlk CO4 110 A6
Arterial Ave RM13 355 C1
Arterial Rd
Southend-on-S SS6, SS9 346 C6
Thundersley SS6 345 B8
Arterial Rd North Stifford
RM16 372 E4
Arterial Rd West Thurrock
RM20 372 A3
Arterial Road Purfleet
RM19 371 C2
Artesian Cl RM11 335 F4
Arthur Barnes Ct RM16 374 C3
Arthur Bugler Inf Sch
SS17 360 E3
Arthur Bugler Jun Sch
SS17 360 E3
Arthur Ct Chelmsford CM1 231 F5
12 Grays RM17 378 C8
Arthur Rd RM6 334 D5
Arthur St
5 Colchester CO2 135 F6
Grays RM17 378 C8
Arthur's Terr IP4 17 E6
Arthur Toft Ho RM17 378 B8
Arthur Walls Ho 3 E12 333 A1
Arthy Cl CM3 211 A4
Artillery Cl IG2 333 D5
Artillery Dr CO12 90 D1
Artillery St CO1 136 B6
Arun RM18 375 C2
Arun Cl CM1 232 C5
Arundel Cl CM12 297 C6
Arundel Dr
Corringham SS17 361 A3
Woodford IG8 310 A3
Arundel Gdns Ilford IG3 334 A2
Rayleigh SS6 323 B5
Southend-on-S SS0 347 A3
Arundel Mews CM12 297 C6
Arundel Rd Rochford SS4 303 C1
Romford RM3 314 F2
South Benfleet SS7 344 B7
Wickford SS11 299 C1
Arundel Way
Billericay CM12 297 C6
Ipswich IP3 18 E3
Arundel Wlk 1 CB9 8 E8
Arwela Rd IP11 381 D2
Arwen Gr CM3 301 C6
Asbury Cl CO4 136 D8
Ascension Bsns Pk 2
RM16 372 B3
Ascension Rd RM5 313 C4
Ascent Pk CM20 200 B5
Ascham Dr E4 309 A3
Ascot Cl
Bishop's Stortford CM23 146 C8
Redbridge IG6 311 E4
Thundersley SS7 345 B7
Ascot Dr Felixstowe IP11 381 C6
Ipswich IP3 18 B3
Ascot Gdns Colchester CO3 134 E7
Hornchurch RM12 355 E8
Ascot Gr SS14 342 E6
Ascot Mews
Clacton-on-S CO15 196 C5
Southminster CM0 284 E4
Ashanti Cl SS3 368 F8
Ashbeam Cl CM13 316 C4
Ash Bglws CM7 127 E3
Ashbourne Ave E18 332 B7
Ashbourne Rd RM3 314 D6
Ashbrook Pl SS6 345 F8
Ashbrook Rd RM10 335 B1
Ashburnham Gdns RM14 337 C3
Ashburnham Rd
Belvedere DA17 369 C2
Southend-on-S SS1 366 F8
Ashburton Ave IG3 352 F8
Ashbury Dr CO6 132 F3
Ashbury Gdns RM6 334 D6
Ashby Cl Hornchurch RM11 337 A3
Orsett RM16 374 E7
Ashby Rd CM8 212 A7
Ashby Rise CM23 119 B1
Ash Cl Brightlingsea CO7 192 E7
Clacton-on-S CO15 195 C3
Hatfield Peverel CM3 211 A4
Ipswich IP3 18 F1
Pilgrims Hatch CM15 293 F4
Romford RM5 313 B3
Ashcombe SS4 325 D4
Ashcombe Cl SS9 346 B6
Ash Ct Chingford E4 287 D2
Harwich CO12 90 E2
Romford RM7 335 B5
Southend-on-S SS3 368 F7
Woodford E18 310 C2
Ashdale CM23 145 D4
Ashdene Cl SS5 301 E2
ASHDON 6 B1
Ashdon Cl
Brentwood CM13 295 C3
South Ockendon RM15 372 C7
Woodford IG8 310 B4
Ashdon Mus The* CB10 24 B8
Ashdon Prim Sch CB10 6 B1
Ashdon Rd Ashdon CB10 24 E3
Saffron Walden CB10 23 C3
Ashdon Road Commercial Ctr
CB10 23 A3
Ashdon Way SS16 342 A5
Ashdown Cl
Great Notley CM77 154 B8
Stanford-le-H SS17 360 F5
Ashdown Cres SS7 345 E4
Ashdown Ct IG11 352 B6
Ashdown Ho SS7 344 F6
Ashdown Way
Colchester CO4 136 D7
Ipswich IP3 18 D3
Ashdown Wlk RM7 313 B2
ASHELDHAM 285 A7
Asheldham Pits Nature
Reserve* CM0 285 A8
ASHEN 11 D1
Ashen Cl CO10 11 D1
Ashenden IP11 381 E4
Ashen Hill CO10 11 D2
Ashen La CO10 11 C3
Ashen Rd Ashen CO10 12 A1
Clare CO10 12 B5
Ridgewell CO9 29 B8
Ashes Cl CO14 170 F8
Ashes Rd Cressing CM77 155 F7
Southend-on-S SS3 368 E6
Ash Fall CM8 184 A5
Ashfield SS6 322 F3
Ashfield Cl CM6 123 C1
Ashfield Ct IP4 18 A6
Ashfield Farm Rd CM9 235 D8
Ashfields Basildon SS13 343 C8
Loughton IG10 288 F7
Ashfields Farm CM6 149 B3
Ashford Ave CM14 316 B7
Ashford Ct RM17 373 D1
Ashford Rd
Chelmsford CM1 231 E2
Wallend E6 352 A5
Woodford E18 310 B1
Ash Gn Billericay CM11 297 E2
Canewdon SS4 304 D1
Great Chesterford CB10 3 D1
Ash Gr Blackheath CO2 163 A8
Burnham-on-C CM0 306 B6
Capel St M IP9 35 A2
Chelmsford CM2 254 D7
Great Cornard CO10 34 C5
Great Dunmow CM6 150 D7
Heybridge CM9 237 C6
Wivenhoe CO7 137 C3
Ash Ground Cl CO11 86 D8
Ashgrove Rd IG3 334 A3
Ash Groves CM21 173 A2
Ash Ho IP2 16 D2
Ash Ind Est CM19 222 F7
Ashingdale Cl SS8 364 C2
ASHINGDON 325 D7
Ashingdon Cl E4 309 C7
Ashingdon Hts SS4 325 B7
Ashingdon Rd SS4 325 D6
Ashingdon Sch SS4 303 B1
Ashlands Ct RM18 375 C2
Ashlea Cl CB9 9 B6
Ashlea Rd CB9 9 B6
Ashleigh Cl SS8 364 A6
Ashleigh Ct
Canvey Island SS8 364 A6
Hoddesdon EN11 221 A5
Ingatestone CM4 274 B3
Waltham Abbey EN9 266 A5
Ashleigh Dr SS9 365 F8
Ashleigh Gdns RM14 337 D1
Ashley Ave IG6 311 B1
Ashley Cl SS17 361 A3
Ashley Ct CO12 91 B3
Ashley Gdns
Colchester CO3 135 C6
Grays RM16 373 D5
Ashley Gn CM3 278 B7
Ashley Gr IG10 288 E6
Ashley Lodge CO15 196 A3
Ashley Rd Chingford E4 309 A4
Harwich CO12 91 B3
Ashley St IP2 17 C4
Ash Lodge SS3 368 F8
Ashlong Gr CO9 76 E3
Ashlyn Gr RM11 336 D8
Ashlyns SS13 343 B7
Ashlyns La CM5 225 F2
Ashlyns Rd CM16 245 F1
Ashlyn's Rd CO13 170 E4
Ashmans Row CM3 301 D6
Ashmeads IG10 288 F6
Ashmere Gr IP4 17 F6
Ashmere Rise CO10 34 A8
Ashmole Dr CO13 170 F6
Ashmour Gdns RM1 313 D1
Ashpole Rd CM7 102 B1
Ash Rd Alresford CO7 165 B8
Canvey Island SS8 364 C3
Hadleigh SS7 345 E2
Ash Rise CO9 103 F8
Ashstead Cl CO16 195 B6
Ashton Cl IP2 16 C2
Ashton Ct E4 309 E7
Ashton Gate RM3 314 D3
Ashton Gdns RM6 334 E5
Ashton Pl Chelmsford CM2 233 A3
Thundersley SS7 345 A6
Ashton Rd RM3 314 D2
Ash Tree Cl CM1 231 F2
Ash Tree Cnr CM3 208 B6
Ash Tree Cres CM1 231 F2
Ashtree Ct EN9 266 A5
Ash Tree Ct Rochford SS4 326 D4
Romford RM1 336 A6
Ash Tree Field CM20 199 A2
Ash Tree Wlk 1 SS14 342 F5
Ashurst Ave SS2 348 F2
Ashurst Cl CO5 163 F8
Ashurst Dr
Chelmsford CM1 232 D7
Ilford IG6 333 C6
Ashvale Dr RM14 337 E2
Ashvale Gdns
Romford RM5 313 D5
Upminster RM14 337 F2
Ashway SS17 361 B4
Ash Way Colchester CO3 134 F3
Hockley SS5 324 F8
Ashwells Mdw CO6 105 B6
Ashwells Rd CM15 293 E6
Ashwin Ave CO6 133 D4
Ash Wlk Southend-on-S SS1 367 B7
South Ockendon RM15 357 D2
Ashwood SS7 344 B7
Ashwood Ave RM13 355 B1
Ashwood Cl CM0 306 B7
Ashwood Rd E4 309 D7
Ashworth Pl CM17 224 D8
Ashworths
Canvey Island SS8 364 A6
Rochford SS4 325 C6
Askews Farm Rd RM17 372 E1
Askins Rd CO7 59 C3
Askwith Rd RM13 354 D3
Aspen Cl SS8 363 E4
Aspen Ct Basildon SS15 319 C1
Brentwood CM13 317 A7
Dartford DA1 376 A1
Redbridge IG5 332 E8
Aspen Gn SS4 325 C7
Aspen Gr RM14 356 A8
Aspens EN9 266 C4
Aspens The CM23 119 B3
Aspen Way
3 Colchester CO4 136 D8
Little Oakley CO12 117 B7
South Ockendon RM15 357 D2
Aspin Mews CB10 22 E3
Asquith Ave SS7 345 B7
Asquith Cl RM8 334 C3
Asquith Dr CO4 110 C5
Asquith Gdns SS7 345 C7
Assandune Cl SS4 325 D7
Astell Ct CO13 170 F4
Aster Cl Basildon SS15 341 D5
Bishop's Stortford CM23 145 D6
4 Chelmsford CM1 232 F6
Clacton-on-S CO16 195 C4
Aster Rd IP2 16 E4
Asthall Gdns IG6 333 C7
Astley RM17 377 F8
Astley Rd CO15 195 D3
Aston Ct 10 IG8 310 A4
Aston Mews RM6 334 C4
Aston Rd SS15 341 B6
Astor Ave RM7 335 C5
Astra Cl RM12 355 B6
Astra Ct E 3 RM12 355 B6
Astra Ctr CM20 199 F4
Astra Ct W 2 RM12 355 B6
Ataka Rd IP11 381 D6
Athelstan Cl RM3 314 F1
Athelstan Ct E6 352 A3
Athelstan Gdns SS11 299 D1
Athelstan Rd
Colchester CO3 135 C5
Romford RM3 314 F1
Athena Est CM20 200 B4
Atherstone Cl SS8 364 C2
Atherstone Rd SS8 364 C2
Atherton End CM21 172 E3
Atherton Gdns RM16 374 C2
Atherton Ho
8 Romford RM3 314 E3
Woodford IG5 310 E1
Atherton Rd Ipswich IP2 16 D2
Woodford IG5 310 F1
Athol Cl SS8 364 E2
Athol Ct IG3 334 A4
Atholl Rd Chelmsford CM2 232 F5
Ilford IG3 334 A4
Athol Rd DA17 369 C1
Athos Rd SS8 364 C5
Atlanta Bvd RM1 335 E5
Atlantic Cl DA10 377 E2
Atlantic Sq CM8 184 A3
Atlantis Cl IG11 353 B2
Atlas Bglws CO6 105 A6
Atlas Ct CO6 105 A7
Atlas Ho 3 IP4 17 E6
Atlas Rd CO6 104 F7
Atlas Works CO6 105 B6
Atridge Chase CM12 297 A4
Atrium 9 IG9 310 D8
Attlee Ct RM17 373 A3
Attlee Dr DA1 376 A2
Attlee Gdns 7 CO1 136 A6
Attwood Cl CO4 110 B5
Attwoods Cl CM2 254 C3
Aubrey Buxton Nature
Reserve* CM24 94 A1
Aubrey Cl CM1 232 B7
Aubretia Cl RM3 314 E2
Auckland Ave RM13 354 F2
Auckland Cl
Chelmsford CM1 231 E5
Tilbury RM18 379 A5
Auckland Rd IG1 333 C4
Auction Pl RM4 290 B6
Audleigh Pl IG7 311 A4
Audley Cl CM77 154 B7
Audley Ct CB11 22 D1
AUDLEY END
Castle Hedingham 52 E8
Saffron Walden 43 B8
Audley End House &
Gardens* CB11 22 B1
Audley End Miniature Rly*
CB11 43 A8
Audley End Rd CB11 43 C8
Audley End Sta CB11 42 F5
Audley Gdns Ilford IG3 333 F2
Loughton IG10 289 D7
Waltham Abbey EN9 265 C5
Audley Gr IP4 18 F5
Audley Rd Colchester CO3 135 C5
Great Leighs CM3 180 F7
Saffron Walden CB11 22 E1
Audleys Cl SS2 347 E5
Audley Way Basildon SS14 342 B6
Frinton-on-S CO13 171 B6
Audrey Gdns CM23 145 F4
Audrey Rd IG1 333 B1
Audries Est CO14 171 A8
Augers 7 CM0 306 C4
Augusta Cl IP3 38 E7
Augustine Ct EN9 265 B6
Augustine Rd 1 DA12 379 D1
Augustine Way CM3 256 F2
Augustus Cl
Colchester CO4 110 B6
Haverhill CB9 9 D7
Augustus Mews CM7 127 E2
Augustus Way CM8 211 E8
Aukingford Gdns CM5 248 F5
Aukingford Gn CM5 248 F4
Aundle Ho IG8 311 A4
Auriel Ave RM10 354 D6
Aurora Ct IG8 309 F6
Austen Cl Braintree CM7 155 A8
Greenhithe DA9 377 C1
Loughton IG10 289 D6
Tilbury RM18 379 C5
Austen Dr CM4 275 D2
Austin Ave CO15 220 E6
Austin St IP2 17 C4
Austral Dr RM11 336 D4
Austral Way CM3 283 A3
Auton Croft CB11 43 D7
Autoway CO4 110 C5
Autumn Cl CO16 195 C5
Avcoca Terr SS0 347 D2
Avebury Rd SS0 347 E2
AVELEY 371 C6
Aveley By-Pass RM15 371 D6
Aveley Cl RM15 371 D5
Aveley Mans 1 IG11 352 B5
Aveley Prim Sch RM15 371 E5
Aveley Rd Romford RM1 335 E7
Upminster RM14 356 C4
Aveley Sch The RM15 371 D6
Aveley Way CM9 258 F8
Aveline Rd CO7 111 E7
Aveling Park Rd E17 309 A1
Aveling Park Sch E17 309 A1
Avelon Rd Rainham RM13 355 A4
Romford RM5 313 D4
Avenue Cl RM3 314 F3
Avenue Ct IG5 332 E8
Avenue Gate IG10 288 C3
Avenue Ind Est
Chingford E4 309 A4
Romford RM3 314 D2
Avenue Pl CM23 146 A6
Avenue Rd
Bishop's Stortford CM23 146 B6
Brentwood CM14 316 C6
Chelmsford CM2 254 D7
Hoddesdon EN11 221 D5
Ilford RM6 334 C4
Ingatestone CM4 274 B3
Romford RM3 314 F3
South Benfleet SS7 344 E3
Southend-on-S, Clifftown
SS0 366 F8
Southend-on-S, Leigh Cliffs
SS9 365 E8
Theydon Bois CM16 267 D3
Witham CM8 184 A3
Woodford IG8 310 C4
Avenue Terr Ilford IG2 333 E5
Southend-on-S SS0 366 E8
Avenue The
Billericay CM12 297 A2
Braintree CM7 127 F3
Brentwood CM13 316 F4
11 Buckhurst Hill IG9 310 C8
Canvey Island SS8 364 B2
Chingford E4 309 D5
Clacton-on-S CO15 196 B7
Colchester CO3 135 C6
Danbury CM3 256 F7
Fobbing SS17 361 D4
Great Braxted CM8 185 A3
Great Dunmow CM6 150 E8
Great Oakley CO12 116 B3
Greenhithe DA9 377 B2
Hadleigh SS7 345 E3
Hoddesdon EN11 221 A4
Hornchurch RM12 336 D2
Hullbridge SS5 301 D3
Ipswich IP1 17 C8
Kelvedon Hatch CM15 293 E8
Loughton IG10 288 E3
Lower Nazeing EN9 244 C6
North Fambridge CM3 303 A7
Romford RM1 335 D7
Trimley St M IP11 381 A7
Wanstead E11 332 B6
Washbrook IP8 35 F7
West Bergholt CO6 108 D3
Witham CM8 184 A2
Wivenhoe CO7 137 B1
Avery Gdns Ilford IG2 333 A6
Redbridge IG2 332 F6
Avey La High Beach IG10 288 A8
Waltham Abbey EN9 265 E2
Aviation Way SS2 347 B7
Avignon Cl CO2 136 B4
Avila Chase CM2 254 B1
Avington Wlk SS7 344 F6
Avitus Way CO4 110 B5
Avocet Cl
Frinton-on-S CO13 170 E6
Kelvedon CO5 158 D2
West Mersea CO5 218 D7
Avocet Ct IP11 381 D2
Avocet Way CM9 237 C5
Avon Cl SS4 325 C5
Avon Ct 10 Chingford E4 287 C1
Upminster RM14 337 E4
Avondale Cl Loughton IG10 288 F2
Rayleigh SS6 323 F2
Avondale Cres IG4 332 D6
Avondale Ct
Southend-on-S SS9 346 D1
Woodford E18 310 B2
Avondale Dr
Loughton IG10 288 F3
Southend-on-S SS9 346 F4
Avondale Gdns SS17 360 E5
Avondale Ho CO15 196 A3
Avondale Rd
Basildon SS16 343 A4
Clacton-on-S CO15 196 A3
Ipswich IP3 18 A2
Rayleigh SS6 323 F2
South Benfleet SS7 344 D3
Avondale Wlk SS8 363 E4
Avon Gn RM15 372 B7
Avon Ho RM14 337 E4
Avon House Sch IG8 310 A6
Avon Rd Canvey Island SS8 364 A3
Chelmsford CM1 231 C5
Upminster RM14 337 D5
Avontar Rd RM15 357 B1
Avon Terr IG10 288 F3
Avon Way Colchester CO4 136 F6
Southend-on-S SS3 368 E7
Wanstead E18 332 A8
Avon Way Ho CO4 136 F6
Avon Wlk CM8 183 E3
Avril Way E4 309 C5
Avro Rd SS2 347 D6
Axe St IG11 352 C4
Axial Way CO4 110 B6
Axon Pl IG1 333 C2
Aylesbeare SS3 368 D8
Aylesbury Dr
Basildon SS16 340 F5
Great Notley CM77 154 C5
Holland-on-S CO15 196 F6
Aylesbury Mews SS15 319 F2
Aylets Field CM18 223 E5
Aylett Cl SS8 364 C4
Aylett Rd RM14 337 C2
Ayletts Basildon SS14 342 F6
Broomfield CM1 208 B3
Aylmer Rd RM8 334 E1
Ayloffe Rd Colchester CO4 110 C1
Dagenham RM9 353 F6
Ayloff Prim Sch RM12 355 B8
Ayloffs Cl RM11 336 E6
Ayloff's Wlk RM11 336 E6
Aylsham La RM3 314 D6
Aylsham Rd EN11 221 C8
Aynsley Gdns CM17 224 C8
Aynsworth Ave CM23 119 B2
Ayr Gn RM1 313 E2
Ayron Rd RM15 357 B1
Ayrton Ho SS9 346 A2
Ayr Way RM1 313 E2
AYTHORPE RODING 176 B3
Azalea Ave SS12 321 C7
Azalea Ct IG1 352 B7
Azalea Ct
8 Chelmsford CM1 232 F6
Chingford IG8 309 E3
Colchester CO4 136 D8
Azalea Mews SS8 364 A2
Azalea Way CO16 195 C4

B

Baardwyk Ave SS8 364 E3
Babbacombe Gdns IG4 332 E7
Babington Rd
Dagenham RM8 353 C8
Hornchurch RM12 336 B3
Baburgh Ho CO10 33 F7
Back Hamlet IP3 17 E5
Back Hill Hadstock CB1 5 B6
Holbrook IP9 62 E4
Back La Broomfield CM1 208 D1
Buckhurst Hill IG9 310 D8
Colchester CO3 134 E7
Dagenham RM6 334 E4
East Hanningfield CM3 278 B7
Felixstowe IP11 381 D5
Ford End CM3 179 B6
Grays RM20 377 A8
Great Oakley CO12 116 C3
Ickleton CB10 3 A3
Ingatestone CM4 274 A6
Little Hallingbury CM22 173 B7
Little Waltham CM3 208 C4
Lower Nazeing EN9 222 C1
Pleshey CM3 178 E2
Purfleet RM19 371 E3
Ramsey CO12 90 A1
Rochford SS4 325 F1
Sheering CM22 173 B1
South Ockendon RM16 372 C5
Stisted CM77 129 C7
Stock CM4 275 D2
Tattingstone IP9 61 C6
Washbrook IP8 35 E8
Wickham Bishops CM8 212 F4
Back La E CO7 139 A6
Back La W CO7 138 F7
Backnang Sq 1 CM2 232 C2
Back Rd Ardleigh CO7 112 B5
Tollesbury CM9 216 C4
Writtle CM1 231 A1
Backwarden Nature Reserve*
CM3 256
Backwardens Nature Trail*
CM3 256
Back Waterside La CO7 192
BACON END 149
BACONEND GREEN 149
Bacon Link RM5 313
Bacons Chase CM0 242
Bacons Green Cotts CO7 58
Bacon's La CO6 106
Bacon Terr 3 RM8 353
Bacton Lodge IP11 381
Bacton Rd IP11 381
Badburgham Ct EN9 265
Baddeley Cl EN3 265
Baddow Cl
Dagenham RM10 354
Woodford IG8 310
Baddow Ct CM2 255
Baddow Hall Ave CM2 255
Baddow Hall Cres CM2 255
Baddow Hall Jun & Inf Sch
CM2 255
Baddow Place Ave CM2 255
Baddow Rd
Chelmsford CM2 232
Great Baddow CM2 254
Baden Powell Cl RM9 353
Baden Powell Dr CO3 135
Baden Powell Ho 11
DA17 369
Baden Rd IG1 352
Bader Cl IP3 18
Bader Way RM13 355
Badger Cl IG2 333
Badger Ct E4 309
Badger Gr CM7 128
Badger Hall Ave SS7 345
Badgers CM23 145
Badgers Bank IP2 16
Badgers Cl
Galleywood CM2 254
Southend-on-S SS0 347
Badgers Gn CO6 132
Badgers Holt CO3 134
Badgers Keep CM0 306
Badgers Mount
Chadwell St M RM16 373
Hockley SS5 324
Badgers Rise SS8 364
Badgers The SS16 341
Badgers Way SS7 345
Badley Hall Rd CO7 112
Badlis Rd E17 309
Badminton Ct CO15 220
Badminton Rd CO15 220
Badshah Ave IP3 18
Bag La CM4 273
Bagleys Spring RM6 334
Bagshaw Rd CO12 91
Bailey Bridge Rd CM7 127
Bailey Cl Chingford E4 309
Haverhill CB9 9
Ipswich IP2 16
Purfleet RM19 371
Bailey Ct 4 E4 309
Bailey Dale CO3 134
BAILEY HILL 28
Bailey La CO10 12
Bailey Rd SS9 346
Bailey The SS6 323
Baillie Cl RM13 355
Bainbridge Dr CO5 186
Bainbridge Rd RM9 353
Baines Cl CO3 135
Baird Cl IP2 16
Baird Ho 12 DA17 369
Bairny Wood App IG8 310
Baker Ave CM3 211
Baker Cl SS15 341
Baker Mews CM9 237
Baker Rd IP9 91
Bakers Almshouses IP9 61
Bakers Cl CM3 301
Bakers Cotts CM15 293
Bakers Ct
5 Bishop's Stortford
CM23 146
Colchester CO1 109
Bakers Ct RM8 334
Bakers Ct
Ramsden Heath CM11 298
Wickford SS11 321
Baker's Ct SS14 321
Bakers Farm Cl SS11 322
Bakersfield CM3 282
Bakers Field CM4 275
Bakers La Danbury CM3 256
Epping CM16 245
Felsted CM6 152
Ingatestone CM4 274
West Hanningfield CM2 276
Baker's La Colchester CO4 109
Great Notley CM77 154
Tolleshunt Major CM9 214
Bakers Mdw CM15 272
Bakers Mead CM3 207
Bakers Mews CM4 274
Baker's Rd CO10 12
Baker St Chelmsford CM2 232
Orsett RM16 373
BAKER STREET 373
Bakers Villas The CM16 245
Bakers Wlk CM21 172
Baker Way CM8 211
Bakery Cl Roydon CM19 222
Tillingham CM0 263
Bakery Ct CM24 119
Baldocks Rd CM16 267
Baldry Cl IP8 16
Baldwin Ho E6 352
Baldwin's Hill IG10 288
Baldwin's La CO6 131
Bale Cl CO3 134
Balfe Ct CO4 136
Balfour Cl SS12 321
Balfour Rd Grays RM17 373
Ilford IG1 333
Balfour Terr IP3 38
Balgonie Rd E4 287

Bla–Bra 389

Black Chapel La
North End CM6 151 E1
Pleshey CM6 178 E8
Blackdown SS0 347 E1
Blackdown Ave IP5 18 F6
Blackfriars CO10 33 D6
Blackfriars Ct 8 IP4 17 D5
Blackgate Rd SS3 368 G7
BLACKHALL 64 B4
BLACKHEATH 163 B8
Blackheath CO2 163 A8
Blackheath Chase SS16 360 D8
Blackhorse La CM16 247 D6
Black Horse La IP1 17 C6
Blackhouse La CO10 34 C3
Black La CM7 71 F2
Blacklands Cl CB11 43 C7
Blackley La Braintree CM3 153 F3
Great Notley CM77 154 A4
Black Lion Ct CM17 200 C4
Blacklock CM2 233 A3
Blackman Way CM8 184 A1
BLACKMORE 272 F8
Blackmore Ave SS8 364 B2
Blackmore Ct EN9 266 A6
BLACKMORE END 74 B2
Blackmore Mead CM4 272 F8
Blackmore Prim Sch
CM4 250 E1
Blackmore Rd
Blackmore CM1 251 D3
Buckhurst Hill IG9 288 E2
Grays RM17 373 C1
Hook End CM15 250 B2
Ingatestone CM4 273 D6
Kelvedon Hatch CM15 271 F2
Blackmores SS15 340 F6
Blackmore Wlk SS6 324 A2
BLACK NOTLEY 155 B5
Blackshots La RM16 373 C5
Blacksmith Cl
Billericay CM12 297 B5
Chelmsford CM1 232 E8
Dagenham RM6 334 C5
Blacksmiths Alley CM4 272 E8
Blacksmiths Cl CM23 145 B5
Black Smiths Cl SG12 197 A7
Blacksmith's Cnr CO6 109 B8
Blacksmith's Cnr CO4 83 D4
BLACKSMITH'S CORNER 36 C6
Blacksmiths Cotts CM17 224 F4
Blacksmiths Hill CO10 11 B4
Blacksmiths La
Bulmer Tye CO10 32 F2
Shudy Camps CB21 7 C6
Wickham Bishops CM8 212 E5
Blacksmith's La
Harwich CO12 90 F2
Rainham RM13 354 F4
Blacksmiths Way CM21 172 B1
Blackthorn Ave CO4 136 E7
Blackthorn Cl Ipswich IP3 18 E1
Writtle CM1 231 A1
Blackthorn Ct SS16 341 A4
Blackthorne Dr E4 309 D6
Blackthorne Rd SS8 364 C3
Blackthorn Rd
Barking IG1 352 D7
Grays RM16 373 B5
Harwich CO12 90 F2
Hockley SS5 324 F8
Witham CM8 183 E4
Blackthorn Way
Brentwood CM14 316 D5
Tolleshunt Knights CM9 187 A2
Blackwater SS7 344 F4
Black Water CM14 294 B1
Blackwater Ave CO4 110 E1
Blackwater Cl
Burnham-on-C CM0 306 C5
Chelmsford CM1 232 C6
Heybridge Basin CM9 237 E3
Rainham RM13 369 E8
Southend-on-S SS3 349 E1
Blackwater Cotts CM77 129 D3
Blackwater Dr CO5 218 A6
Blackwater La CM8 212 B8
Blackwater Mews CM0 261 E2
Blackwater Way CM7 128 A4
Blackwell Dr CM7 127 C4
Blackwood Chine CM3 301 E6
Bladen Dr IP4 18 F5
Bladon Cl Braintree CM7 127 E7
Tiptree CO5 186 E5
Blaine Dr CO13 170 F7
Blair Cl
Bishop's Stortford CM23 145 C7
Rushmere St A IP4 18 E5
Blair Par CB9 8 E8
Blake Ave IG11 352 F4
Blakeborough Dr RM3 314 E1
Blake Cl Lawford CO11 86 B4
Rainham RM13 354 F4
Blake Ct CM3 301 E6
Blake Dr Braintree CM7 128 C4
Clacton-on-S CO16 195 D6
BLAKE END 126 A2
Blake Hall Cres E11 332 A3
Blake Hall Dr SS11 322 A6
Blake Hall Gdns* CM5 248 E7
Blake Hall Rd
Chipping Ongar CM5 248 A5
Wanstead E11 332 A4
Blake Rd CM8 183 F5
Blakes Ct CM21 172 E2
Blakesley Ho 4 E12 333 A1
Blake Way RM18 379 C5
Blamsters Cres CO9 103 D8
Blamsters Rise CM6 97 A2
Blanchard Cl CO13 170 A7
Blanchard Gr EN3 265 B1
Blanchard Mews RM3 314 F3
Blanche St IP4 17 D6
Blandford Cl RM7 335 B7
Blandford Cres E4 287 C2
Blandford Rd IP3 18 D3
Blaney Cres E6 352 B2
Blatches Chase
Rayleigh SS2 346 F7
Southend-on-S SS2 347 A8
Blatchford Ho 8 RM10 335 A1
Blaxhall Ct 17 CB9 8 E7
Blenheim Ave IG2 333 A5
Blenheim Chase SS9 346 E3
Blenheim Cl
Bicknacre CM3 256 F2
Braintree CM7 127 E7
Brantham CO11 60 D1
Hockley SS5 324 E8
Romford RM7 335 C7
Sawbridgeworth CM21 200 C8
Upminster RM14 337 E3
Blenheim Cres SS9 346 E2
Blenheim Ct
Bishop's Stortford CM23 145 C7
Clacton-on-S CO15 195 D2
Hornchurch RM12 355 C7
4 Ipswich IP1 17 A7
4 Wickford SS11 322 A5
Woodford IG8 310 B3
Woodford IG8 310 C2
Blenheim Dr CO2 163 A8
Blenheim Gdns
Aveley RM15 371 B5
Mayland CM3 261 A1
Blenheim Mews SS9 346 E3
Blenheim Park Cl SS9 346 F4
Blenheim Prim Sch SS9 346 F3
Blenheim Rd
Clacton-on-S CO15 195 D2
Ipswich IP1 17 A7
Pilgrims Hatch CM15 294 A3
Blenheim Way
North Weald Bassett
CM16 247 A4
Tiptree CO5 186 F5
Blessing Way IG11 353 C3
Bletchington Ct 1 DA17 369 A2
Blewetts Cotts RM13 354 F2
Blickling Cl IP2 17 B2
Blickling Rd CM77 154 C8
Bligh Rd DA11 379 A1
Blind La Easthorpe CO2 160 B4
Eight Ash G CO6 134 A8
Goldhanger CM9 238 C7
Howe Green CM2 255 F4
Little Burstead CM12 318 B5
Mundon CM9 259 C2
Tolleshunt Knights CM9 187 B1
West Hanningfield CM2 276 F5
Bliss Cl CM8 211 F7
Blithbury Rd RM9 353 B6
Blithe Ct CO7 164 B8
Blockhouse Rd RM17 378 C8
Blofield Rd IP11 381 A4
Blois Meadows Bsns Ctr
CB9 27 C8
Blois Rd
Steeple Bumpstead CB9 27 D8
Sturmer CB9 9 F1
Blomville Rd RM8 334 E1
Bloom Cl CO13 170 F6
Bloomfield Ave CO13 170 E7
Bloomfield Cres IG2 333 B5
Bloomfield Ct CO10 12 B7
Bloomfield St IP4 18 B6
Bloomsbury Ho IG8 310 E4
Bloomsbury Mews IG8 310 E4
Blooms Hall La CO10 2 F8
Blossom Cl RM9 353 F4
Blossom Mews CO5 218 D6
Blott Rise CM8 211 F8
Blountswood Rd
Hockley SS5 324 A8
Hullbridge SS5 323 F6
Blower Cl SS6 323 F3
Blows Cotts RM15 371 D5
Bloyers Mews CO1 109 F1
Blue Anchor La RM18 374 E1
Bluebell Ave CO16 195 C4
Bluebell Cl Ipswich IP2 16 E4
Romford RM7 335 E2
Witham CM8 183 E3
Bluebell Gn 5 CM1 232 E7
Bluebell Way
Colchester CO4 109 C2
Ilford IG1 352 B6
Bluebell Wood CM12 296 E4
Blueberry Cl IG8 310 A4
Bluebird La RM10 354 A5
Bluebridge Cotts CO9 77 A1
Bluebridge Ind Est CO9 77 B1
Bluegate La IP9 60 B7
Bluegate Pk CM14 316 B7
Bluehouse Ave CO16 195 A4
Blue House Farm Chase
CM3 303 B7
Bluehouse Rd E4 309 E7
Bluemans CM16 247 D7
Bluemans End CM16 247 D7
Blue Mill La CM9 235 E4
Blue Mills Hill CM8 212 B7
Blue Rd CO5 186 C5
Bluestem Rd IP3 38 E8
Blunden Cl RM8 334 C3
Blundens The CO6 56 C6
Blunt's Hall Dr CM8 183 D1
Blunts Hall Rd CM8 183 D1
Blunts Wall Rd CM12 296 E1
Blyford Rd CO16 195 A4
Blyford Way IP11 381 A4
Blyth Ave SS3 368 C7
Blyth Cl IP2 17 A1
Blyth Ct CB11 43 E8
Blythe La CO7 164 B8
Blythe Rd Hoddesdon EN11 221 D5
Stanford-le-H SS17 360 E4
Blythe Way Maldon CM9 259 A8
South Benfleet SS7 344 C7
Blyth Ho DA8 369 E1
Blyth's Mdw CM7 127 F3
Blyth's Way CM77 126 F2
Blythswood Rd IG3 334 A4
Blyth Wlk RM14 337 E5
Blythwood Gdns CM24 119 D6
Blyton Cl SS12 321 D5
Boadicea Cotts CO8 79 F6
Boadicea Way CO2 135 C4
Boar Cl IG7 312 A5
Boarded Row SS4 328 A5
Boardman Ave E4 287 B4
Boars Tye Rd CM8 156 D6
Boat Ho The CO7 192 E5
Boat House Mews The
CO10 12 B7
Boatman Cl IP8 36 E8
Bobbing Cl SS4 325 F2
BOBBINGWORTH 248 D8
Bobbingworth Mill CM5 248 A7
Bobbits La IP9 36 F8
Bobbits Way CO7 164 C8
Bob Dunn Way DA1 376 A4
Bober Ct CO2 163 B7
Bob Russell Ho CO2 136 A5
BOCKING 127 F4
BOCKING
CHURCHSTREET 127 F8
Bocking Church Street Prim
Sch CM7 127 F8
Bocking End CM7 127 F3
Bockingham Gn SS13 343 A8
Bocking Pl CM7 127 F3
BOCKING'S ELM 195 B5
Bockings Elm Par CO16 195 B5
Bocking's Gr CO16 195 B5
Bocking Windmill* CM7 128 A8
Bodell Cl RM16 373 B3
Bodiam Cl Basildon SS13 343 B6
Ipswich IP3 18 D4
Bodiam Rd IP3 18 D4
Bodiam Wlk 3 CB9 8 E8
Bodle Ave DA10 377 E1
Bodley Cl CM16 245 F1
Bodmin Rd CM1 232 D5
Bogmoor Rd SG8 39 A8
Bohemia Chase SS9 346 D5
Bohun Cl CM3 180 F7
Boiler Ho The SS4 325 E2
Bois Field Terr CO9 76 E2
Bois Hall Gdns CO9 76 F3
Boley Dr CO15 196 A4
Boleyn Cl Billericay CM12 297 A5
Grays RM16 372 F3
Loughton IG10 288 E3
Southend-on-S SS9 346 C7
Boleyn Ct IG9 288 B1
Boleyn Gdns
Brentwood CM13 317 A7
Dagenham RM10 354 C5
Boleyn Ho 1 SS4 325 F2
Boleyns Ave CM7 127 F6
Boleyn Way Boreham CM3 209 F1
Clacton-on-S CO15 220 F8
Haverhill CB9 8 D7
Redbridge IG6 311 C4
Boley Rd CO6 106 A8
Bolford St CM6 69 F2
Bolingbroke Cl CM3 180 F7
Bolney Dr SS9 346 C7
Bolsin Dr CO4 109 E4
Bolton La IP4 17 D6
Boltons The IG8 310 A6
Bommel Ave SS8 365 A3
Bonchurch Ave SS9 346 D2
Bonchurch Ct 20 RM19 371 B1
Bonds Cotts CM5 204 A1
Bond St Chelmsford CM2 232 C2
Grays RM17 378 C8
Ipswich IP4 17 D5
Bonham Cl CO15 196 A5
Bonham Dr RM16 374 A8
Bonham Gdns RM8 334 D2
Bonham Rd RM8 334 D1
Bonington Chase CM1 232 E6
Bonington Rd RM12 355 D7
Bonks Hill CM21 172 D1
Bonner Wlk RM16 372 F3
Bonneting La CM23 92 B8
Bonnett Mews RM11 336 E3
Bonnington Rd IP3 17 F1
Bonningtons CM13 317 B7
Bonny Cres IP3 38 C8
Bonnygate SS14 342 D7
Bonnygate Prim Sch
RM15 372 B8
Boomes Ind Est RM13 354 F1
Boone Pl CM8 184 A2
Boons Cl CM3 233 E8
BOOSE'S GREEN 77 F2
Bootham Cl CM12 296 F1
Bootham Rd CM12 296 F1
Booth Ave CO4 136 C8
Boothby Ct E4 309 C7
Booth Pl CM0 306 C5
Booth's Ct CM13 295 B3
Borda Cl CM1 232 A5
Border Edge Ho 6 CM14 316 C6
Border's La IG10 289 B5
BOREHAM 233 E8
Boreham Cl SS11 322 B5
Boreham Ct CM1 177 D2
Borehamgate CO10 33 F7
Boreham Ind Est CM3 209 F2
Boreham Mews 1 EN11 197 A1
Boreham Pl CO9 10 B2
Boreham Prim Sch CM3 233 F8
Boreham Rd
Great Leighs CM3 181 B7
Little Waltham CM3 181 B2
Borland Cl DA9 377 A2
BORLEY 14 F3
Borley Ct RM16 374 D7
BORLEY GREEN 14 D2
Borley Rd CO10 15 B4
Borman Cl SS9 347 A6
Borough La CB11 43 D8
Borradale Ct CB9 27 B6
Borrett Ave SS8 364 A4
Borrowdale Ave IP4 17 E8
Borrowdale Cl
Redbridge IG4 332 E7
Thundersley SS7 344 F6
Borrowdale Rd
Thundersley SS7 344 F6
Thundersley SS7 344 F7
Borwick La
Crays Hill CM11 320 F4
Wickford CM11, SS12 321 A4
Bosanquet Rd EN11 221 C8
Boscawen Gdns CM7 128 C4
Boscombe Ave
Grays RM17 373 D2
Hornchurch RM11 336 D4
Boscombe Ave *continued*
Wickford SS12 320 F8
Boscombe Ct CO15 196 F6
Boscombe Mews SS2 367 B8
Boscombe Rd SS2 348 B1
Bosgrove E4 309 C8
Boss Hall Bsns Pk IP1 16 E7
Boss Hall Rd IP1 16 E7
Bostocke Cl SS15 341 D5
Bostock Rd IP2 17 C1
Boston Ave Rayleigh SS6 323 B4
Southend-on-S SS2 347 F1
Boston Lofts 2 SS2 347 F1
Boston Rd IP4 17 F7
Boswell Ave SS4 325 D5
Boswells Dr CM2 232 C2
Boswells Sch The CM1 232 D6
Bosworth Cl SS5 324 F4
Bosworth Cres RM3 314 C4
Bosworth Ho DA8 369 E1
Bosworth Rd
Dagenham RM10 335 A1
Southend-on-S SS9 346 C7
Botanical Way CO16 194 A5
Botany Cotts RM19 371 A1
Botany Dr CM7 128 D3
Botany La CO16 168 B5
Botany Terr RM19 371 A1
Botany Way RM19 371 B1
Botelers SS16 341 E4
Boteley Cl E4 309 D8
Botney Hill Rd CM12 318 D4
Bouchers Mead CM1 232 F7
Bouchiers Barn Visitors Ctr*
CO6 130 D7
Bouchiers Pl CO5 159 D2
Bouchier Wlk 2 RM13 355 A6
Boudicca Mews 5 CM2 232 B1
Boudicca Wlk CO7 137 C3
Bouldrewood Rd SS7 344 B5
Boulevard The
Greenhithe DA9 377 C3
3 Redbridge IG8 311 A3
Rochford SS4 325 F3
Boulter Gdns RM13 355 A7
Boulton Cotts CM9 237 B5
Boulton Rd RM8 334 F2
Boult Rd SS15 341 C8
Boundary Cl
Bishop's Stortford CM23 146 A5
Ilford IG3 352 E8
Boundary Ct CM16 267 D7
Boundary Dr CM13 295 E2
Boundary Rd Barking IG11 352 C3
Barking IG11 352 D4
Bishop's Stortford CM23 146 A5
Colchester CO4 136 F4
Romford RM1 336 A5
Southend-on-S SS9 346 B8
Sturmer CB9 9 D5
Upminster RM14 337 B2
Wivenhoe CO7 137 A4
Boundary Way SS3 368 E6
Bounderby Gr CM1 231 E7
Bounstead Hill CO2 162 C5
Bounstead Rd CO2 162 D7
Bourchier Ave CM7 128 D5
Bourchier Way CO9 103 D8
Bourne Ave SS15 341 A8
Bournebridge Cl CM13 295 E2
Bournebridge Hill CO9 103 B6
Bournebridge La RM4 291 B2
Bourne Cl Basildon SS15 341 A8
Halstead CO9 103 D8
Bourne Ct Braintree CM7 128 D1
Colchester CO2 136 A4
Wanstead E11 332 A6
Woodford IG8 310 D1
Bourne End RM11 337 A4
Bourne Gdns E4 309 B6
Bourne Hill IP2 17 A1
Bourne Ho IG9 310 D7
Bourne Mill* CO2 136 B4
Bournemouth Park Prim Sch
SS2 348 B2
Bournemouth Park Rd
SS2 348 B2
Bournemouth Rd CO15 196 F6
Bourne Park Residential Pk
IP2 17 B1
Bourne Rd Colchester CO2 136 B4
Haverhill CB9 9 B8
West Bergholt CO6 108 E2
BOURNES GREEN 349 B1
Bournes Green Chase
SS3 349 B1
Bournes Green Inf Sch
SS1 368 B8
Bournes Green Jun Sch
SS1 368 B8
Bourne Terr IP2 37 B8
Bourne The CM23 146 A8
Bouvel Dr CM0 306 B8
Bouverie Rd CM2 254 B8
Bovey Way RM15 372 B8
Bovills Way CO16 168 C1
Bovingdon Rd CM7 101 D2
BOVINGER 248 A7
Bovinger Way SS1 348 F1
BOW ARROW 376 B1
Bow Arrow La
Dartford DA1 376 A1
Dartford DA2 376 B1
Bowbank Cl SS3 349 F1
Bowden Dr RM11 336 E3
Bowdens La CO6 80 F7
Bower Cl RM5 313 D3
Bower Ct CM16 268 A7
Bower Farm Rd RM4 313 D7
Bower Gdns CM9 236 F3
Bower Hall Dr CB9 27 B6
Bower Hall La CO5 190 F1
Bower Hill CM16 268 A7
Bower Hill Ind Est CM16 268 A7
Bower La SS14 342 E8
Bowerman Rd RM16 374 A2
Bower Park Sch RM1 313 E4
Bowers Cl CM8 156 E3
Bowers Court Dr SS13 343 F5
BOWERS GIFFORD 343 E6
Bowers Ho 5 IG11 352 B5
Bowers Rd SS7 344 D5
Bower Vale CM16 268 A7
Bowery Ct 4 RM10 354 B6
Bowes Ct 17 DA2 376 B1
Bowes Dr CM5 249 A4
Bowes Ho CM5 249 A4
Bowes Rd Dagenham RM8 353 C8
Wivenhoe CO7 137 D1
Bowfell Ct SS16 341 A5
Bowfell Dr SS16 341 A5
Bowhay CM13 317 B8
Bowland Dr IP8 16 C1
Bowland Rd IG8 310 C4
Bowlers Croft SS14 320 F2
Bowling Cl 14 CM23 145 F6
Bowling Green Ct IP11 381 E4
Bowls The IG7 311 F7
Bowman Ave SS9 346 B6
Bowmans Pk CO9 51 E4
Bowmont Cl CM13 295 B3
Bown Cl RM18 379 B5
Bowness Way RM12 355 A7
Bowsers La CB10 5 C3
Bowthorpe Cl IP1 17 B7
Bowyer Ct 4 E4 287 C1
Box Cl SS15 319 D1
Boxford Cl SS6 322 F3
Boxford Ct Felixstowe IP11 381 A4
Haverhill CB9 8 E7
Boxhouse La CO7 84 C5
Box La IG11 353 C3
Boxley La CM22 175 D8
Box Mill La CO9 76 E3
Boxmoor Rd RM5 313 C5
Boxoll Rd RM9 334 F1
BOXTED 82 F7
Boxted Ave CO16 195 C4
Boxted Church Rd CO6 82 C5
Boxted Cl IG9 288 E1
BOXTED CROSS 83 B5
Boxted Rd Colchester CO4 109 E6
Great Horkesley CO6 82 C3
Boxted St Peter's CE Prim Sch
CO4 82 F7
Boxted Straight Rd CO4 83 A5
Boyce Gn SS7 344 D2
Boyce Hill Cl SS9 346 B7
Boyce Rd
Southend-on-S SS3 368 H8
Stanford-le-H SS17 360 C3
Boyce View Dr SS7 344 C2
Boyd Cl 1 CM23 146 B8
Boyd Ct SS12 321 F5
Boydell's Dairy Farm*
CM7 100 E8
Boyden Cl SS2 348 F2
Boydin Cl CM8 211 E8
Boydlands IP9 35 A1
Boyes Croft CM6 123 D1
Boyle Ho 13 DA17 369 A3
Boyles Court Cotts CM14 316 A3
Boyles Ct CO2 163 B7
Boyne Dr CM1 232 D6
Boyne Rd RM10 335 A1
Boysenberry Wlk IP3 38 C7
Boyton Cl SS7 345 A5
BOYTON CROSS 230 B7
BOYTON END 70 C5
Boyton Hall La CM1 230 C8
Boyton Rd IP3 18 B1
Boytons SS15 341 E6
Boytons Acre CB11 43 D8
Boyton's La CB10 26 A1
Boyton Vineyard* CO10 10 D5
Brabant Rd CM3 303 A7
Brabner Gdns CM11 298 C4
Bracelet Cl SS17 360 F5
Brace Wlk CM3 301 E5
Brackenbury Cl IP1 17 B8
Bracken Cl IG10 289 B8
Bracken Ct 1 IG6 311 F4
Brackendale CM11 297 D3
Brackendale Ave SS13 343 C4
Brackendale Cl SS5 324 E7
Brackendale Ct SS13 343 C4
Brackendale Gdns RM14 356 C8
Bracken Dell SS6 323 E2
Brackenden Dr CM1 232 D7
Bracken Dr IG7 311 C4
Brackenhayes Cl IP2 17 B3
Bracken Ind Est IG6 311 F2
Bracken Mews
Chingford E4 287 C1
Romford RM7 335 B5
Brackens Dr CM14 316 D5
Brackens The CO4 110 B3
Bracken The E4 309 C8
Bracken Way
Abberton CO5 163 B2
Thundersley SS7 345 A6
Brackley Cl IP11 381 C5
Brackley Cres SS13 343 A8
Brackley Ho 4 RM3 314 F4
Brackley Sq IG8 310 D3
Bracknell Ho 3 RM3 314 F4
Bracks La CO6 131 F3
Bradbourne Rd RM17 378 B8
Bradbourne Way SS13 343 C5
Bradbrook Cotts CO6 108 F4
Bradbury Dr CM7 127 D3
Bradd Cl RM15 357 C2
Braddock Cl RM5 313 C4
Braddy Ct CO5 158 C2
BRADFIELD 87 F2
Bradfield Ct 12 RM19 371 B1
Bradfield Dr IG11 353 A7
BRADFIELD HEATH 114 D8
Bradfield Ho IG8 311 A4
Bradfield Prim Sch CO11 87 E1
Bradfield Rd CO11 115 B7
Bradford Bury SS9 346 C6
Bradford Dr CO4 109 E2
Bradford Rd IG1 333 D3
Bradfords Ct CM7 128 A4
Bradford St Braintree CM7 128 A4
Chelmsford CM2 232 A1
Brading Ave CO15 196 A7
Brading Cres E11 332 B2
Bradleigh Ave RM17 373 C2
Bradley Ave SS7 344 F5
Bradley Cl
Canvey Island SS8 364 A5
Great Dunmow CM6 123 C2
Thundersley SS7 344 F5
Bradley Comm CM23 119 C3
Bradley Gn SS13 321 C1
Bradley Ho IG8 310 A3
Bradley Link SS7 344 F5
Bradley Mews 1 CB10 22 F2
Bradley Rd EN9 265 C4
Bradley St 6 IP2 17 C4
Bradley Way SS4 325 F1
Bradshaw Rd RM16 373 A5
BRADWELL 129 D2
Bradwell Ave RM10 335 A2
Bradwell Cl RM12 355 B6
Bradwell Ct
Braintree CM77 155 C8
3 Brentwood CM13 295 C3
Bradwell Gn 2 CM13 295 C3
Bradwell Ho SS11 321 F7
BRADWELL-ON-SEA 242 B2
Bradwell Power Sta Visitor
Ctr* CM0 242 A6
Bradwell Rd
Buckhurst Hill IG9 288 E2
Steeple CM0 262 A3
St Lawrence CM0 262 E6
Tillingham CM0 263 E6
BRADWELL WATERSIDE 241 F4
Brady Ave IG10 289 C7
Brady Ct 4 RM8 334 D3
Brady Prim Sch RM13 370 C8
Braemar Ave CM2 254 B8
Braemar Cres SS9 346 A2
Braemar Gdns RM11 337 A5
Braemar Wlk SS13 343 B6
Braemore SS8 363 F5
Braemore Cl CO4 110 D3
Braeside Sch
Buckhurst Hill IG9 288 B1
Buckhurst Hill IG9 310 C8
Bragg Cl RM8 353 B6
Braggon's Hill IP29 2 B8
Braiding Cres CM7 128 C3
Brain Rd CM8 183 E3
BRAINTREE 128 B5
Braintree Ave IG4 332 E7
Braintree Cnr CO9 75 F6
Braintree Coll CM7 128 A5
Braintree Ent Ctr CM7 127 D5
Braintree Foyer The 7
CM7 127 F2
Braintree Mus & Heritage
Ctr* CM7 127 F3
Braintree Rd
Cressing CM77 155 E7
Dagenham RM10 335 A1
Felsted CM6 152 C6
Gosfield CO9 102 E5
Great Bardfield CM7 72 B1
Great Dunmow CM6 124 A1
Shalford CM7 100 E6
Terling CM3 181 E5
Wethersfield CM7 73 D2
Witham CM8 183 F4
Braintree Sta CM7 128 A2
Braintree Town FC CM7 128 C2
Brain Valley Ave CM77 155 B6
Brairwood Cl SS9 346 D5
BRAISWICK 109 B2
Braiswick CO4 109 C2
Braiswick La CO4 109 D4
Braiswick Pl
Basildon SS15 341 B8
Colchester CO4 109 C3
Braithwaite Ave RM7 335 A4
Braithwaite Dr CO4 109 F2
Bramber Ct 7 DA2 376 B1
Bramble Cl Chigwell IG7 289 C1
Southend-on-S SS9 346 B7
Bramble Cres SS7 346 A5
Bramble Croft DA8 369 C2
Bramble Ct
2 Redbridge IG6 311 F4
Witham CM8 183 E4
Brambledown CO5 218 C7
Bramble Dr IP3 18 E1
Bramble La
Little Dunmow CM6 151 F8
Upminster RM14 356 D4
Bramble Rd
Canvey Island SS8 364 C3
Hadleigh SS7 345 F6
Southend-on-S SS9 346 B7
Witham CM8 183 E4
Bramble Rise CM20 199 C1
Brambles CO14 171 B7
Brambles The
Basildon SS15 341 A8
Bishop's Stortford CM23 145 C6
Braintree CM7 127 E3
Chigwell IG7 311 C4
Colchester CO3 134 F3
Southminster CM0 284 D3
Steeple CM0 284 A7
Bramble Tye
Basildon SS15 319 F1
Harwich CO12 90 D1
Bramblewood 1 IP8 16 C2
Bramblings The E4 309 D6
Bramerton Rd SS5 324 D6
Bramfield Rd E SS6 324 A2
Bramfield Rd W SS6 323 F2
Bramford La IP1 16 F8
Bramford Rd IP1 16 E8
Bramhall Cl IP2 16 D1
Bramley Chase IP4 18 B7
Bramley Cl Alresford CO7 165 B8
Braintree CM7 128 A1
Colchester CO3 135 B7
Woodford IG8 310 C3
Bramley Cotts CM3 182 B2
Bramley Cres IG2 333 A5
Bramley Ct
7 Chingford E4 287 C1
Hadleigh SS7 345 E2
Bramley Gdns SS15 341 C8

Church La *continued*
Copdock IP8............... 35 F7
Crays Hill CM11........... 320 B6
Dagenham RM10.......... 354 C5
Debden CB11.............. 68 A7
Doddinghurst CM15...... 272 B2
East Mersea CO5......... 191 E1
Elsenham CM22........... 120 E8
Felixstowe IP11........... 381 D6
Ford End CM3............. 179 B6
Great Henny CO10....... 54 D8
Great Holland CO13...... 170 B3
Great Leighs CM3........ 180 D7
Great Tey CO6............ 132 C4
Great Warley CM13....... 338 D5
Great Wigborough CO5... 188 F4
Harkstead IP9............. 63 B3
Henny CM12............... 91 E6
Little Totham CM9........ 214 B1
Manningtree CO11....... 288 F6
Margaretting CM4........ 274 E6
Marks Tey CO6............ 133 A4
Mistley CO11.............. 86 E4
Neuby CO4................ 53 A1
North Ockendon RM14... 357 B7
North Weald Bassett CM16 247 A6
Purfleet RM19............. 371 A1
Ridgewell CO9............ 29 B6
Romford RM1............. 335 E7
Sheering CM22............ 201 D7
Stapleford Abbotts RM4.. 291 C5
Stow Maries CM3......... 280 D3
Takeley, Brewer's End
CM22..................... 148 B2
Takeley, Little Canfield CM6 149 B7
Toppesfield CO9.......... 50 B2
Washbrook IP8............ 35 D6
Weeley Heath CO16...... 168 A7
Wennington RM13........ 370 D2
West Hanningfield CM2.. 277 A4
White Roothing or White Roding
CM6....................... 203 C3
Widdington CB11......... 67 C4
Writtle CM1................ 231 E6
Church Lane Cotts
Chelmsford CM1.......... 272 B2
Rainham RM13............ 370 D2
CHURCH LANGLEY..... 224 D6
Church Langley Com Prim Sch
CM17..................... 224 D6
Church Langley Way
CM17..................... 224 D8
Church Leys CM18...... 223 F6
Church Manor CM23.... 146 B8
Church Manorway DA8. 369 D3
Churchmans Ho IP1..... 17 B5
Church Mdw CO10...... 32 E6
Church Mdws CM7...... 127 F6
Church Mead
Roydon CM19............. 198 B3
White Notley CM8........ 155 F7
Church Mews
Basildon SS15............. 341 B6
Nayland CO6.............. 56 B7
Church Mill Grange
CM7....................... 200 E6
Church Par SS8......... 363 F4
Church Park Rd SS13... 343 B8
Church Path
Greenhithe DA9.......... 376 F1
Hadstock CB1............. 5 D8
Northfleet DA11.......... 378 C6
Saffron Walden CB10.... 22 D1
Wanstead E11............. 332 A1
Church Pk CO10......... 11 C1
Churchponds CO9....... 51 E8
Church Rd
Alphamstone CO10....... 54 C5
Ashdon CO7.............. 165 A7
Barking IG2............... 352 D2
Barling SS3............... 349 E1
Basildon, Barstable SS14,
SS15..................... 342 C7
Basildon, Bowers Gifford
SS13..................... 343 D4
Basildon, Great Berry RM14 340 D2
Basildon, Lee Chapel SS15 341 F4
Basildon, Pipps Hill SS15. 341 E6
Bentley IP9................ 60 F1
Black Notley CM77....... 155 A4
Boxted CO4............... 82 F1
Bradwell CM77........... 129 F1
Brightlingsea CO7........ 192 E8
Buckhurst Hill IG9........ 288 B2
Bulmer CO10............. 32 F7
Bulphan RM14............ 358 F4
Burnham-on-C CM0...... 306 A5
Capel St M IP9............ 35 A1
Chrishall SG8............. 19 D1
Clacton-on-S CO15....... 196 A1
Copford CO6.............. 133 B4
Cressing CM77........... 156 E7
Elmstead Market CO7... 138 A5
Erith DA8.................. 369 C2
Fingringhoe CO5......... 164 B4
Fordham CO6............. 107 F4
Frating Green CO7........ 138 C1
Gosfield CO9.............. 77 D2
Great Cornard CO10...... 34 B1
Great Hallingbury CM22. 146 E4
Great Leighs CM3........ 173 A7
Great Totham CM9....... 211 F3
Great Yeldham CO9...... 30 C4
Greenhithe DA9.......... 376 E2
Hadleigh SS7............. 344 F4
Harlow CM17............. 200 E3
Hatfield Peverel CM3..... 211 A2
High Beach IG10.......... 288 D6
Hockley SS5............... 324 A6
Ilford IG2................. 333 C3
Kelvedon Hatch CM14... 271 F8
Layer de la H CO2........ 161 C5
Little Baddow CM3....... 243 B4
Little Bentley CO7....... 113 F6
Little Bromley CO11...... 113 A5

396 Col–Cou

Colebrook Path IG10 289 B7
Cole Ct RM3 314 D5
COLE END 44 D6
Cole End La CB10 44 D5
Coleford Ho 7 RM3 314 E4
Cole Gn CO10 13 A1
Cole Hill CM3 181 B5
Colehills CB11 65 C4
Colehills Cl CB11 65 C4
Coleman Ct CO15 195 F3
Coleman Rd
 Belvedere DA17 369 A2
 Dagenham RM9 353 E6
Colemans Ave SS0 347 D4
Colemans La CM3 256 D7
Coleman's La EN9 243 E5
Coleman St SS2 348 A1
Cole Ness Rd IP3 38 A8
Colenso Rd IG2 333 E4
Coleridge Rd Dartford DA1 376 B3
 Maldon CM9 237 A1
 Romford RM3 314 B3
 Tilbury RM18 379 C5
Coleridge Wlk CM13 295 D2
Coles Cl CM5 249 A5
Coles Gn IG10 289 A8
COLES GREEN 35 C8
Coles La CO14 144 A1
Coles Oak La CO7 84 C6
Colet Cres CO2 135 F4
Colet Rd CM13 295 D4
Coley Ct SS7 344 B4
Colgate Pl EN3 265 A2
Colin Cl DA2 376 B1
Colin Pond Ct RM6 334 D8
Colinton Rd IG3 334 B2
Collard Ave IG10 289 C7
Collard Gn IG10 289 C7
College Ave RM17 373 C2
College Cl
 Bishop's Stortford CM23 145 D7
 Grays RM17 373 C2
College Ct
 Manningtree CO11 86 C4
 5 Romford RM2 336 B6
College Gdns Chingford E4 287 B2
 Redbridge IG4 332 E6
College Ho CM7 127 E2
College Pl DA9 377 C3
College Rd Braintree CM7 127 E2
 Clacton-on-S CO15 196 A3
 Grays RM17 373 C2
 Northfleet DA11 378 B2
College Sq CM20 223 D8
College St IP4 17 C5
College Way SS1 367 A8
Coller Rd CO12 90 F5
Colles Brook Rd CO7 166 F4
Colletts Chase CO6 80 F4
Colley Rd CM2 255 A6
Collier Ct RM16 373 B5
COLLIER ROW 313 B2
Collier Row CB10 6 B1
Collier Row La RM5 313 C1
Collier Row Rd
 Dagenham RM5 312 F2
 Romford RM5 313 B3
COLLIERS HATCH 247 C1
Colliers The CM9 237 E3
Collier Way SS1 367 D7
Collimer Cl IP9 63 E7
Collimer Ct IP11 381 C6
Collindale Cl SS8 364 D4
Collindale Gdns CO15 196 C5
Collingwood SS7 344 E4
Collingwood Ave IP3 18 B3
Collingwood Cl CM7 128 C5
Collingwood Fields CO7 59 B4
Collingwood Gn CO15 195 D1
Collingwood Ho
 Greenhithe DA9 377 D2
 Southend-on-S SS0 347 D2
Collingwood Prim Sch
 CM3 301 E6
Collingwood Rd
 Basildon SS16 342 D4
 Clacton-on-S CO15 195 D1
 Colchester CO3 134 E6
 Rainham RM13 355 A3
 South Woodham Ferrers
 CM3 301 F6
 Witham CM8 184 A2
Collingwood Terr SS16 342 D5
Collingwood Way SS3 349 E1
Collingwood Wlk SS16 342 D5
Collins Cl
 10 Braintree CM7 127 F2
 Stanford-le-H SS17 360 E2
COLLINS CROSS 146 B8
Collins Cross CM23 119 B1
Collins Ct 5 IG10 288 D4
Collins Ho 8 IG11 352 B5
Collins Mdw CM19 223 B7
Collinson's IP2 16 D5
Collins Rd CO9 53 D1
Collins Way
 Brentwood CM13 295 F4
 Southend-on-S SS9 347 A6
Collinwood Gdns
 Ilford IG5 333 A7
 Redbridge IG5 332 F6
Collops Villas CM6 125 A4
Collyers Ct CO1 136 B7
Colman Cl SS17 360 D3
Colne RM18 375 C3
Colne Bank Ave CO3 135 D8
Colne Chase CM8 183 E2
Colne Cl
 South Ockendon RM15 372 C6
 South Woodham Ferrers
 CM3 301 E7
Colne Com Sch & Coll The
 CO7 192 E8
Colne Cswy CO2 136 D5
Colne Ct Braintree CM7 128 C1
 East Tilbury RM18 375 C2
 Rowhedge CO5 164 A8
Colne Dr Romford RM3 314 F4
Colne Dr *continued*
 Southend-on-S SS3 349 E1
COLNE ENGAINE 77 F2
Colne Engaine CE Prim Sch
 CO6 78 A2
Colneford Hill CO6 105 D7
Colne Ho 5 IG11 352 B6
Colneis Jun Sch IP11 381 F6
Colneis Rd IP11 381 F6
Colne Park Rd CO6 105 D7
Colne Pl SS16 342 C5
Colne Rd Brightlingsea CO7 192 E6
 Bures CO8 79 E8
 Clacton-on-S CO15 195 F2
 Coggeshall CO6 131 A6
 Halstead CO9 77 A2
 Sible Hedingham CO9 75 E8
Colne Rise CO5 163 F8
Colne Springs CO9 29 B6
Colne Terr CO7 164 B8
Colne The CO7 192 E5
Colne Valley RM14 337 E5
Colne Valley Cl CO9 76 D2
Colne Valley Farm Pk*
 CO9 51 D5
Colne Valley Railway*
 CO9 51 C5
Colne Valley Rd CB9 9 A7
Colne View
 Colchester CO2 136 D2
 Point Clear B CO16 193 A2
Colne View Cotts CO5 163 D3
Colne View Ret Pk CO1 110 A1
Colne Way CO16 192 F4
Colne Wlk CM7 128 D1
Colney Rd DA1 376 A1
Colneys Cl CO10 15 D1
Colombo Rd IG1 333 C4
Colson Gdns IG10 289 B5
Colson Gn IG10 289 B4
Colson Path IG10 289 A5
Colson Rd IG10 289 B5
Colt Hatch CM20 199 B1
Colthorpe Rd CO15 195 F8
Colthurst Gdns EN11 221 D8
Coltishall Cl SS11 322 B6
Coltishall Rd RM12 355 C6
Colt Mews EN3 265 A2
Coltsfield CM24 119 E8
Coltsfoot Ct
 Colchester CO4 109 C2
 Grays RM17 378 D8
Coltsfoot Path RM3 314 D4
Coltsfoot Rd IP2 16 E4
Colts The CM23 145 E4
Columbia Wharf Rd
 RM17 378 A8
Columbine Gdns
 Ipswich IP2 16 E5
 Walton-on-t-N CO14 171 B7
Columbine Mews CO3 134 C7
Columbines The CO10 1 E2
Columbine Way RM3 314 E2
Colvers CM17 202 C2
Colville Cl
 Corringham SS17 360 F5
 Great Notley CM77 154 C7
Colville Mews CM12 296 F5
Colvin Chase CM2 254 B1
Colvin Cl CO3 134 F7
Colvin Gdns Chingford E4 309 C7
 Redbridge IG6 311 C3
 Wanstead E11 332 B7
Colwall Gdns IG8 310 A5
Colworth Cl SS7 345 D4
Colyers Reach CM2 233 A2
Colyn Pl CB10 22 E3
Comac Yd CO15 195 E5
Combes Rd RM9 353 F5
Comet Cl RM19 371 A2
Comet Way SS2 347 B6
Comfrey Ct RM17 378 D8
Comma Cl CM7 127 E1
Commerce Est E18 310 C1
Commerce Pk CO2 136 D4
Commerce Way
 Colchester CO2 136 D4
 Lawford CO11 86 C5
Commercial Ho IG2 333 A5
Commercial Pl DA12 379 C1
Commercial Rd Ipswich IP1 17 B4
 Southend-on-S SS0 347 D4
Commercial Way SS15 340 E7
Commodity Ctr CM8 184 F4
Commodore Ho SS14 342 E6
Common App SS7 345 A7
Commonfields CM20 199 E1
Commonhall La SS7 345 D3
Common Hill CB10 22 D2
Common La
 Duddenhoe End SG8 40 B7
 Little Baddow CM3 234 E2
 Stock CM4 275 E2
 Thundersley SS7 345 B7
 Woodham Walter CM9 235 B3
Common Quay IP2 17 D5
Common Rd
 Great Wakering SS3 350 B4
 Harlow EN9 222 E2
 Ingrave CM13 317 C5
 Stock CM4 275 E3
Commonside Rd CM18 223 F4
Common St CO10 12 B8
Commons The CO3 135 A5
Common The
 Danbury CM3 256 E6
 East Hanningfield CM3 278 B7
 Thundersley SS7 345 A7
Commonwealth Ho RM18 379 A5
Como St RM7 335 D7
Compass Ct
 Gravesend DA11 378 E1
 16 Manningtree CO11 86 D4
Compasses Rd CM77 129 F5
Compass Gdns CM0 306 A6
Compton Ave
 Brentwood CM13 295 C1
 Romford RM2 336 C8
Compton Ct
 Canvey Island SS8 364 D2
 Southend-on-S SS9 346 B1
Compton Ct *continued*
 Wickford SS11 321 E7
Compton Mews 5 CO4 136 C8
Compton Rd CO4 136 C8
Compton Terr SS11 321 E7
Compton Wlk SS15 341 B7
Comroston 13 EN11 221 A6
Comyns Cl CO4 110 A6
Comyns Pl CM1 231 B1
Comyns Rd RM9 354 A5
Conan Doyle Cl CM7 155 A8
Concorde Ho 1 RM12 355 B6
Concord Rd SS8 363 F5
Conder Way CO2 136 D4
Condor Wlk RM12 355 B5
Condovers Cotts RM18 379 F8
Conduit La
 Hoddesdon EN11 221 A6
 Woodham Mortimer CM9 257 E6
Conduit La E EN11 221 B6
Coney Acre CB11 93 D8
Coney Burrows E4 309 E8
Coney Gree CM21 172 D3
Conference Cl 3 E4 309 C8
Conford Ho IP11 381 D6
Congregation Ho 5 CO9 76 F2
Congreve Rd EN9 265 E6
Conies Rd CO9 103 D7
Conifer Ave RM5 313 B5
Conifer Cl Alresford CO7 164 F7
 Colchester CO4 136 E8
Conifer Ct
 7 Bishop's Stortford
 CM23 145 F8
 Ilford IG1 352 B6
Conifer Dr CM14 316 D5
Conifers SS7 345 E3
Conifer Way CM6 123 C1
Coningsby Gdns E4 309 B4
Conisborough Ct 12 DA2 376 B1
Coniston SS2 347 A7
Coniston Ave Barking IG11 352 E5
 Purfleet RM19 371 C1
 Upminster RM14 356 C8
Coniston Cl Barking IG11 352 E5
 Great Notley CM77 154 D6
 Rayleigh SS6 323 E2
Coniston Ct CM16 268 A8
Coniston Gdns IG4 332 E7
Coniston Rd
 Canvey Island SS8 364 A3
 Ipswich IP3 18 B2
 South Benfleet SS7 344 E8
Coniston Sq IP3 18 B2
Coniston Way RM12 355 A7
Connaught Ave
 Chingford E4 287 D2
 Frinton-on-S CO13 170 F4
 Grays RM16 373 C3
 Loughton IG10 288 D5
Connaught Cl
 Clacton-on-S CO15 196 B3
 Colchester CO1 136 C6
Connaught Ct
 Chingford E4 287 E2
 Clacton-on-S CO15 196 B3
Connaught Dr CM3 301 C7
Connaught Gdns
 Braintree CM7 128 B4
 Southend-on-S SS3 368 C6
Connaught Gdns E CO15 196 B4
Connaught Gdns W CO15 196 B3
Connaught Hill IG10 288 D5
Connaught Ho
 Clacton-on-S CO15 196 B4
 Frinton-on-S CO13 170 F5
Connaught La IG1 333 D2
Connaught Mews
 2 Frinton-on-S CO13 170 F5
 Ilford IG1 333 D2
 Loughton IG10 288 E5
Connaught Rd
 Chingford E4 287 E1
 Haverhill CB9 8 E7
 Hornchurch RM12 336 D1
 Ilford IG1 333 D2
 Little Clacton CO16 168 C5
 Rayleigh SS6 346 A8
Connaught Way CM12 297 A5
Connaught Wlk SS6 346 A8
Connect La IG6 311 C1
Connington Cres E4 309 D7
Connor Cl IG6 311 C2
Connor Rd RM9 353 F8
Conqueror Ct RM3 314 D3
Conquerors Cl CM3 211 B3
Conrad Cl RM16 373 B4
Conrad Gdns RM16 373 B4
Conrad Rd
 Stanford-le-H SS17 360 E1
 Witham CM8 183 F5
Consort Cl CM14 316 C5
Constable Ave CO16 195 C6
Constable Cl Lawford CO11 86 B4
 West Mersea CO5 218 D7
Constable Ct
 Brightlingsea CO7 192 F7
 Colchester CO2 135 B3
Constable Ho CM7 127 E3
Constable Mews 3 RM8 353 B8
Constable Rd
 Felixstowe IP11 381 F4
 Ipswich IP4 17 D8
 Sudbury CO10 33 E8
Constable View CM1 232 F6
Constable Way
 Black Notley CM77 155 B5
 Southend-on-S SS3 368 G8
Constance Cl
 Broomfield CM1 208 A3
 Witham CM8 212 B8
Constantine Rd
 Colchester CO3 135 D5
 Ipswich IP1 17 B5
 Witham CM8 211 E8
Constitution Hill
 Ipswich IP1 17 B8
 South Benfleet SS7 344 D3
 Sudbury CO10 33 F8
Consul Ave RM13 354 D2
Convalescent Hill IP11 381 E3
Convent Cl SS15 341 C6
Convent Hill CM7 128 A5
Convent La CM7 128 A5
Convent Rd SS8 364 B3
Con Way SS7 344 D3
Conway Ave SS3 350 B3
Conway Cl Halstead CO9 103 D8
 Haverhill CB9 8 E8
 Ipswich IP2 17 B2
 Rainham RM13 355 A5
 Wivenhoe CO7 164 C8
Conway Cres RM6 334 C5
Conway Gdns RM17 378 B7
Conway's Rd RM16 359 A3
Conybury Cl EN9 266 A7
Conybury Ct EN9 266 A7
Conyer Cl CM9 258 F8
Conyers CM20 199 C2
Conyers Cl IG8 309 E4
Conyers Way IG10 289 B6
Cook Cl CO12 90 F1
Cook Cres CO4 136 E7
Cooke Cl RM16 372 E3
Cooke St 3 IG11 352 C4
Cookham Ct SS3 349 E2
Cook Pl CM2 232 F3
Cooks Cl CO9 103 F8
Cook's Cl RM5 313 C2
Cook's Cnr CO11 88 E2
Cooks Gn SS13 321 C1
Cook's Gn CO8 55 B1
COOK'S GREEN 169 B2
Cook's Hall Rd CO6 108 C3
Cooks Hill CO4 83 B6
Cook's La Colchester CO3 134 F7
 Great Bardfield CM7 71 E4
 West Bergholt CO3 134 E8
COOKSMILL GREEN 229 F1
Cooks Spinney CM20 200 A2
Coolgardie Ave
 Chigwell IG7 311 A7
 Chingford E4 309 D5
Coolyne Way CO15 196 B7
Coombe Dr SS16 341 C1
Coombe Lodge CO6 105 B6
Coombe Rd Romford RM3 336 F8
 Southminster CM0 284 D5
Coombe Rise
 Chelmsford CM1 232 B7
 Shenfield CM15 294 F1
 Stanford-le-H SS17 360 E2
Coombes Cl CM12 296 F4
Coombes Gr SS4 326 B3
Coombes Rd RM9 353 F4
Coombewood Dr
 Dagenham RM6 334 F5
 Thundersley SS7 344 F5
Cooper Cl DA9 376 F2
Cooper Dr CM7 127 D4
Cooper Pk CM7 127 D4
Coopers CM3 233 E8
COOPERSALE 246 C2
Coopersale Cl 3 IG8 310 C3
Coopersale Comm CM16 246 D3
Coopersale Hall Sch
 CM16 268 B5
Coopersale La CM16 268 B3
Coopersales SS15 341 A6
Coopersale St CM16 268 D7
COOPERSALE STREET 268 C8
Coopersale & Theydon
 Garnon CE Prim Sch
 CM16 246 D2
Coopers Ave CM9 237 D5
Coopers Cl
 Bishop's Stortford CM23 145 B4
 Chigwell IG7 312 B8
 Dagenham RM10 354 B6
Coopers' Company & Coborn
 Sch The RM14 337 D2
Coopers Cres
 Great Notley CM77 154 C8
 West Bergholt CO6 108 F4
Coopers Ct RM2 336 C8
Coopers Dr CM11 319 C6
COOPER'S END 41 A5
Coopers End Rd CM24 121 A2
Coopers End Rdbt CM24 121 B3
Cooper Shaw Rd RM18 379 E7
Coopers Hill CM5 249 A1
Coopers La
 Clacton-on-S CO15 195 C3
 Great Leighs CM3 180 F7
Cooper's La CO7 84 F5
Coopers Mews CM5 249 A2
Cooper's Row CM1 232 A5
Coopers Villas CM22 121 B2
Coopers Way SS2 348 A5
Cooper Wlk CO4 136 D8
Coote Gdns 2 RM8 334 F1
Coote Rd RM8 334 F1
COPDOCK 35 F7
Copdock Prim Sch IP8 35 F8
Copdoek SS14 342 C7
Copeland Ho 7 CM14 316 C6
Copelands SS4 325 D6
Copeman Rd CM13 295 D2
COPFORD 133 D4
Copford Ave SS6 323 F1
Copford CE Prim Sch
 CO6 133 D2
Copford Cl Billericay CM11 297 C2
 Woodford IG8 310 E4
Copford Ct CO6 133 C4
COPFORD GREEN 133 C2
Copford Rd CM11 297 C2
Copingford End CO6 133 D5
Copland Cl
 Broomfield CM1 208 A1
 Great Baddow CM2 254 F8
Copland Rd SS17 360 D1
Copleston High Sch IP4 18 C5
Copleston Rd IP4 18 B5
Coploe Rd CB10 3 A2
Coploe Rise CB10 3 A3
Coppen Rd RM8 334 F4
Coppens Gn SS12 321 E6
Copperas Rd CO7 192 F5
Copper Beech Cl IG5 311 A2
Copper Beech Ct IG10 289 A8
Copper Beeches
 Brentwood CM14 316 C6
 Colchester CO3 134 D5
 Thundersley SS7 345 B7
Copper Beech Rd RM15 357 C2
Copper Ct Braintree CM7 127 E1
 Sawbridgeworth CM21 172 E2
Copperfield
 Billericay CM11 319 D6
 Chigwell IG7 311 D4
Copperfield Ct IG6 333 C8
Copperfield Gdns CM14 294 C1
Copperfield Rd
 Chelmsford CM1 231 E7
 Ipswich IP2 16 E5
Copperfields
 Basildon SS15 341 C7
 Saffron Walden CB11 43 C8
Copperfields Way RM3 314 D2
Coppergate Ct EN9 266 A5
Copper Gr IP8 36 E8
Coppice Cl CM6 123 D1
Coppice End CO4 110 B3
Coppice Hatch CM18 223 D6
Coppice La Basildon SS15 319 F1
 Pleshey CM6 178 E8
Coppice Path IG7 312 B6
Coppice Prim Sch IG7 312 A5
Coppice Rd CO7 165 B8
Coppice Row CM16 267 D3
Coppice The
 Bishop's Stortford CM23 145 D5
 Clacton-on-S CO15 195 D1
 Kelvedon Hatch CM15 271 E2
Coppid Hall RM16 372 F5
Coppings The EN11 197 A1
Coppins Cl CM2 232 E4
Coppins Green Prim Sch
 CO15 195 E5
Coppins Rd CO15 195 D4
Coppins The 2 RM6 334 B4
Coprolite St IP3 17 E5
Copse Hill CM19 223 B5
Copse The Billericay CM12 297 B4
 Bishop's Stortford CM23 146 C8
 Chingford E4 287 F1
 Colchester CO4 109 F3
 Felsted CM6 152 F6
Copsfield Ct E18 332 A8
Copshall Cl CM18 223 E4
Coptfold Cl SS1 348 F1
Coptfold Rd CM14 316 D8
Copthall Cl CM22 146 F4
COPTHALL GREEN 266 E6
Copthall La CM6 70 B3
Copt Hall La CO5 189 C3
Copt Hill CM3 256 E6
Copthorne Ave IG6 311 B4
Copthorne Gdns RM11 337 A6
Copy Hill CB9 8 E3
Coral Cl Ilford RM6 334 D8
 South Woodham Ferrers
 CM3 301 C8
Coral Dr IP1 16 D8
Coral Ho CM20 199 A1
Coralin Wlk CO3 134 C6
Coram Gn CM13 295 D4
Coraway SS7 345 C5
Corbets Ave RM14 356 B7
CORBETS TEY 356 B7
Corbets Tey Rd RM14 356 B8
Corbets Tey Sch RM14 356 C7
Corbett Rd E11 332 C5
Corbett Villas RM8 334 C3
Corbridge Mews 6 RM1 335 F6
Corcorans CM15 294 C3
Cordelia Cres SS6 323 C3
Cordell Cl CO10 15 D8
Cordell Pl CO10 15 D8
Cordell Rd CO10 15 D8
Corder Rd IP4 17 D8
Cordwainers The SS2 348 A5
Cordwinders CO7 59 F1
Corfe Cl 2 SS13 343 B5
Coriander Rd CO5 186 C4
Cories Cl RM8 334 D2
Corinda Ho CO13 170 F4
Corinth Ho IG3 334 A4
Corinthian Manorway
 DA8 369 D2
Corinthian Rd DA8 369 D2
Coriolanus Cl CO2 135 A3
Cormorant Wlk
 Chelmsford CM2 254 C5
 8 Hornchurch RM12 355 B6
Cornard Mere Nature Trail*
 CO10 34 B3
Cornard Rd CO10 33 F7
CORNARD TYE 34 E7
Cornec Ave SS9 346 B6
Cornec Chase SS9 346 C6
Cornel Cl CM8 183 D4
Cornelius Vale CM2 233 B4
Cornelius Vermuyden Sch &
 Arts Coll The SS8 363 E5
Cornells La CB11 67 E3
Cornell Way RM5 313 B5
Corner Ho CM18 223 F6
Corner Mdw CM18 224 A4
Corner Pk CB10 22 E3
Corner Rd CM11 320 D6
Cornerth Cres CO10 34 B6
Cornfields CM3 301 C8
Cornflower Cl
 Colchester CO3 134 C7
 Ipswich IP2 16 E4
Cornflower Dr CM1 232 F6
Cornflower Gdns CM12 296 F4
Cornflower Rd CO15 220 G7
Cornflower Way RM3 314 E2
Cornford Way CO11 86 B4
Cornhill
 4 Chelmsford CM1 232 B2
 16 Ipswich IP1 17 C6
Cornhill Ave SS5 324 E7
Cornhouse Bldgs SS6 345 C8
Corniche The CM7 72 B1
Cornish Ct CO10 34 A7
Cornish Gr CM3 301 E6
CORNISH HALL END 48 C5
Cornish Hall End Rd
 Stambourne CO9 28 A1
 Steeple Bumpstead CM7, CO9 48 E8
Cornmill EN9 265 B6
Corn Mill Ct CB11 43 E8
Cornshaw Rd RM8 334 D3
Cornsland CM14 316 D7
Cornsland Cl RM14 337 C8
Cornsland Ct 10 CM14 316 C7
Cornwall Cl Barking IG11 352 F6
 Hornchurch RM11 337 A7
 Lawford CO11 86 B3
Cornwall Cres CM1 232 A7
Cornwall Gate RM19 371 A2
Cornwall Gdns
 Braintree CM7 128 B4
 Rochford SS4 325 C5
Cornwall Ho CM23 145 E4
Cornwallis Dr
 Marks Tey CO6 132 F3
 South Woodham Ferrers
 CM3 301 F7
Cornwallis Ho SS14 342 A8
Cornwallis Pl CB10 22 E3
Cornwallis Rd
 Dagenham RM9 353 E8
 Haverhill CB9 8 F6
Cornwallis Terr IP4 17 F6
Cornwall Rd Basildon SS13 343 F7
 Dartford DA1 376 A4
 Felixstowe IP11 381 D5
 Pilgrims Hatch CM15 294 B4
Cornwell Cres SS17 360 E3
Cornworthy SS3 368 C8
Cornworthy Rd RM8 353 C7
Corona Rd Basildon SS16 341 B3
 Canvey Island SS8 364 D5
Coronation Ave
 Braintree CM7 127 F2
 Colchester CO2 136 A2
 East Tilbury RM18 375 C2
Coronation Cl
 Great Wakering SS3 349 F4
 Ilford IG6 333 C7
Coronation Cotts CM15 316 E8
Coronation Ct RM18 375 C2
Coronation Dr
 Felixstowe IP11 381 C3
 Hornchurch RM12 355 B7
Coronation Hill CM16 245 F2
Coronation Rd
 Bishop's Stortford CM23 145 E5
 Burnham-on-C CM0 306 B4
 Clacton-on-S CO15 195 C3
 Ipswich IP4 18 B5
Coronation Villas CO16 141 F7
Coronation Way CM77 155 D6
Corporal Lillie Cl CO10 33 E6
Corporation Ave IP2 37 A8
Corporation Rd CM1 232 A4
Corral Hts DA8 369 E1
Corran Way RM15 372 B6
Corriander Dr CM22 94 D2
CORRINGHAM 361 A4
Corringham Prim Sch
 SS17 361 C3
Corringham Rd
 Corringham SS17 361 A2
 Stanford-le-H, Balstonia
 SS17 360 F2
 Stanford-le-H SS17 360 E1
Corry Ct 7 CO4 136 D8
Corsellis Ho CO7 137 B1
Corsel Rd SS8 364 E3
Cortina Dr RM13 354 C3
Cortoncroft Cl CO13 170 F7
Corton Rd IP3 18 B1
Corton Trad Est SS7 344 D7
Corve La RM15 372 B6
Cory Dr CM13 295 B2
Cosgrove Ave SS9 346 B3
Cosgrove Rd RM20 376 F7
Cossington Ct SS0 366 E8
Cossington Rd SS0 366 E8
Costead Manor Rd CM14 294 B1
Coteford Cl IG10 289 B7
Cotelands SS16 342 F3
Cotesmore Gdns RM8 353 C8
Cotleigh Rd RM7 335 D5
Cotman Ave CO11 86 B4
Cotman Lodge CM1 232 F6
Cotman Mews RM8 353 B7
Cotman Rd
 Clacton-on-S CO16 195 D6
 Colchester CO3 135 A5
 Ipswich IP3 18 A1
Cotswold Ave SS6 323 D4
Cotswold Cres CM1 231 D6
Cotswold Ct
 Clacton-on-S CO15 196 A3
 Colchester CO4 110 C4
Cotswold Dr CO10 15 C6
Cotswold Gdns
 Brentwood CM13 295 E2
 Ilford IG2 333 D4
Cotswold Rd
 Clacton-on-S CO15 195 F5
 Romford RM3 314 F3
 Southend-on-S SS0 347 D1
Cottage Dr CO2 136 D3
Cottage Gn CO16 195 C6
Cottage Gr CO16 195 C6
Cottage Pl
 Chelmsford CM1 232 B3
 3 Ipswich IP1 17 B6
Cottages The SS3 368 F
Cottage Wlk CO16 195 C6
Cottesmore Ave IG5 311 A
Cottesmore Cl SS8 364 B
Cottesmore Ct SS9 346 A
Cottesmore Gdns SS9 346 A
Cottey Ho CM2 254 B
Cottingham Rd IP8 16 B
Cottis Cl SS16 341 A
Cotton Cl RM9 353 C
Cotton La DA2, DA9 376 C
Cottons App RM7 335 D
Cottons Ct 3 RM7 335 D
Cottonwood Cl CO2 135 D
Couchmore Ave IG5 310 F
Coulde Dennis CM3 278 B

Coulsdon Cl CO16 195 C6
Coulson Cl RM8 334 C3
Coulter Ho DA9 377 C2
Coulter Mews CM11 297 B3
Council Ave DA11 378 C1
Council Bglws
Braintree CM7 127 F7
Fobbing SS17 361 D4
Council Cotts
Great Holland CO13 169 F3
Helions Bumpstead CB9 8 E1
Council Hos
Bicknacre CM3 256 F1
Bradwell on S CM0 263 E8
Corringham SS17 361 D4
Finchingfield CM7 72 C6
Great Bromley CO7 139 A6
Hadstock CB1 5 B6
Holbrook IP9 62 D6
Peldon CO5 189 E5
Shudy Camps CB21 7 B6
Thorington Street CO6 57 B3
Thorpe-le-S CO16 141 E2
Tolleshunt Major CM9 214 D3
Wakes Colne CO6 79 C1
Wix CO11 115 B5
Wrabness CO11 88 F2
Council Houses
Cressing CM77 156 A4
Great Bentley CO7 166 F5
COUNTESS CROSS 78 D3
Counting House La CM6 123 D1
County Chambers SS1 367 A7
County Pl CM2 232 B1
Coupals Cl CB9 9 C6
Coupals Com Prim Sch CB9 9 D7
Coupals Ct CB9 9 C6
Coupals Rd CB9 9 E6
Courage Cl RM11 336 C5
Courage Ct 7 CM13 295 C3
Courage Wlk CM13 295 D3
Courtauld Cl CO9 76 F1
Courtauld Homes of Rest
CO9 76 E3
Courtauld Mews 1 CM7 127 F2
Courtauld Rd
Basildon SS13 321 C2
Braintree CM7 128 A4
Court Ave RM3 315 A3
Court Cl CM23 145 E5
Court Eight CM8 183 F5
Court Eighteen CM8 183 F5
Court Eleven CM8 183 F5
Courtenay Cl CO10 15 D2
Courtenay Dr RM16 372 F3
Courtenay Gdns RM14 337 C3
Court Farm CO11 61 A1
Courtfield SS7 344 D1
Courtfield Cl EN10 221 A3
Court Fifteen CM8 183 F5
Court Five CM8 183 E5
Court Four CM8 183 F5
Court Fourteen CM8 183 F5
Court Gdns RM3 315 A3
Court Ind Est CM2 232 C2
Courtland Ave
Chingford E4 309 F8
Ilford IG1 333 A3
Redbridge IG1 332 F2
Courtland Dr IG7 311 C7
Courtland Mews CM9 258 F8
Courtland Pl CM9 258 F8
Courtlands Billericay CM12 296 E2
Chelmsford CM1 232 A6
Halstead CO9 103 D8
Southend-on-S SS9 346 B7
Court Lodge 12 DA17 369 A1
Court Mews DA11 378 B1
Court Needham EN3 265 A2
Courtney Park Rd SS16 341 B5
Courtney Rd RM16 374 C4
Courtney Twrs IG2 333 D5
Court Nine CM8 183 F5
Court Nineteen CM8 183 F5
Court One CM8 183 F5
Court Rd CM1 208 B3
COURTSEND 330 F8
Court Seven CM8 183 F5
Court Seventeen CM8 183 F5
Court Six CM8 183 F5
Court Sixteen CM8 183 F5
Court St CO6 56 A1
Courts The
Felixstowe IP11 381 F4
Rayleigh SS6 323 E3
Court Ten CM8 183 F5
Court The CO7 59 B2
Court Thirteen CM8 183 F5
Court Three CM8 183 F5
Court Twelve CM8 183 F5
Court Twenty CM8 183 F5
Court Two CM8 183 F5
Court View CM4 273 F1
Courtway IG8 310 C5
Court Way Ilford IG6 333 C8
Romford RM3 314 E1
Courtway Cotts SS17 361 D4
Courtyard Mews 1 DA9 377 A1
Courtyard Offices CM8 185 B3
Courtyard The
Basildon SS14 342 D7
Billericay CM11 297 C1
Braintree CM7 128 A4
Brentwood CM15 294 B2
Harlow CM17 200 D4
Ipswich IP1 17 B7
Maldon CM9 236 F2
Mayland CM3 260 F1
Coval Ave CM1 232 A3
Coval La CM1 232 A2
Coval Wells CM1 232 A2
Covehite Ct 3 CB9 8 E6
Covenbrook CM13 317 B7
Coventry Cl
Colchester CO1 136 A8
Hullbridge SS5 301 F1
Coventry Rd IG1 333 B3
Coverdale CM8 183 E4
Coverdales The IG11 352 D3
Coverley Cl CM13 316 C4
Covert Rd IG6 311 F4
Coverts The
Brentwood CM13 295 A1
West Mersea CO5 218 D6
Writtle CM1 231 B1
Cowan Lodge 1 IG8 310 C4
Cowbridge La IG11 352 B5
Cowdray Ave CO1 109 F1
Cowdray Cres CO1 135 F7
Cowdray Ctr The CO1 110 A1
Cowdray Way RM12 355 A8
Cowdrie Way CM2 233 B4
Cowell Ave CM1 231 E5
Cowell Lodge IG8 309 F5
Cowell St IP2 17 C3
Cowels Farm La CM6 97 E5
COW GREEN 294 A5
Cow La
Great Chesterford CB10 4 A5
Point Clear B CO16 193 C3
Cowley Ave DA9 377 A2
Cowley Ct 3 E18 310 A1
Cowley Rd Felixstowe IP11 381 E4
Ilford IG1 333 A4
Redbridge IG1 332 F4
Romford RM3 314 B3
Wanstead E11 332 B6
Cowlins CM17 200 D4
Cowpar Mews CM7 155 A8
Cowper Ave RM18 379 B6
Cowper Rd
6 Belvedere DA17 369 A2
Rainham RM13 355 A1
Cowper St IP4 18 B6
Cowslip Cl IP2 16 E4
Cowslip Ct CO3 134 C7
Cowslip Mead SS14 342 B6
Cowslip Rd E18 310 B1
Cow Watering La CM1 230 E2
Coxbridge Ct CM12 297 A2
Coxes Cl SS17 360 D3
Coxes Farm Rd CM11 319 E7
Coxhall Rd IP9 36 E1
Cox La IP4 17 D5
Cox Ley CM22 174 A3
Coxon Dr RM16 372 E3
Cox Rd CO7 165 B8
Coxs Cl Haverhill CB9 8 D7
South Woodham Ferrers
CM3 301 E8
Cox's Ct CO12 91 E5
Cox's Gdns CM23 145 E5
Cox's Hill CO11 86 B4
COXTIE GREEN 293 C4
Coxtie Green Rd
Pilgrims Hatch CM14 293 C5
South Weald CM14 293 A2
Coytes Gdns 2 IP1 17 C5
Crabbe St IP4 18 A6
Crabbs Gn CM22 148 C1
Crabb's Hill CM3 210 F2
Crabs Croft CM7 128 D3
Crabtree CO13 170 C8
Crabtree Ave RM6 334 D7
Crabtree Hill CB11 67 C3
Crabtree La CO6 81 C1
Crabtree Manorway N
DA17 369 C5
Crabtree Manorway S
DA17 369 C3
Crabtrees CB11 43 E8
Cracknell Cl CO7 137 B2
Crafton Gn CM24 119 E7
Craftsmans Sq SS2 348 A5
Craig Ct CO2 135 B3
Craigdale Rd RM11 335 F4
Craigfield Ave CO15 196 A6
Craig Gdns E18 309 F1
Craig Ho CM7 128 A3
CRAIG'S END 49 D8
Craig's Hill CO8 79 E6
Craigs La CO8 79 E6
Craiston Way CM2 254 F5
Crammavill St RM16 373 A5
Crammerville Wlk 2
RM13 355 B1
Cramphorn Wlk CM1 231 F3
Cramswell Cl CB9 8 E6
Cranberry Sq IP3 38 C7
Cranborne Cl CO4 109 F2
Cranborne Gdns RM14 337 B2
Cranborne Rd
Barking IG11 352 D4
Hoddesdon EN11 221 C7
Cranbourne Ave E11 332 B7
Cranbourne Ct E18 332 B7
Cranbourne Dr EN11 197 C2
Cranbourne Gdns IG6 333 C8
Cranbourne Ho EN11 197 C2
Cranbourne Prim Sch The
EN11 197 B2
Cranbrook Ave SS7 345 C4
Cranbrook Coll (Boys)
IG1 333 A2
Cranbrook Dr RM2 336 C7
Cranbrook La CO10 2 F1
Cranbrook Lodge SS7 345 C4
Cranbrook Rd IG1, IG2 333 A5
Cranbrook Rise Ilford IG1 333 A4
Redbridge IG1 332 F5
Crane Ave CO3 134 B4
Crane Cl RM10 354 A6
Crane Hill IP2 16 E4
Cranell Gn RM15 372 B5
CRANES 320 F2
Cranes Cl SS13 320 F1
Cranes Ct SS14 342 C8
Cranes Farm Rd SS14 320 D1
Cranes La SS14 342 C8
Crane's La CO5 157 F1
Cranfield Ct
4 Wickford SS12 321 C8
2 Woodford IG8 310 A6
Cranfield Park Ave SS12 321 F2
Cranfield Park Ct 5
SS12 321 D5
Cranfield Park Rd SS12 321 D4
Cranford Cl CO13 170 E5
CRANHAM 337 E4
Cranham Gdns RM14 337 F4
Cranham Hall Cvn Pk
CM3 208 F6
Cranham Pl RM14 357 A7
Cranham Rd Broxted CM6 95 F3
Hornchurch RM11 336 B5
Cranleigh Cl CO16 195 B6
Cranleigh Dr SS9 346 E1
Cranleigh Gdns
Barking IG11 352 D6
Hullbridge SS5 301 D1
Loughton IG10 288 F3
Cranley Ave SS0 347 D1
Cranley Dr IG2 333 C4
Cranley Gdns SS3 368 C6
Cranley Rd Ilford IG2 333 C4
Southend-on-S SS0 347 D1
Cranmer Cl CM12 297 B6
Cranmer Ct RM14 337 C2
Cranmere Ct CO1 136 A7
Cranmer Gdns RM10 354 C8
Cranmer Ho CM2 253 F7
Cranmer's La CO6 131 E6
Cranmore Cl CM22 94 C2
Cranmoregreen La CO10 2 F3
Cranston Ave SS0 347 D5
Cranston Gdns E4 309 B4
Cranston Park Ave RM14 356 C8
Cranwell Cres IP3 18 C1
Cranwell Gdns CM23 119 C1
Cranworth Cres 7 E4 287 D1
Craven Ave SS8 364 A3
Craven Cl SS4 325 D5
Craven Ct RM6 334 E5
Craven Dr CO4 110 C3
Craven Gdns Barking IG11 352 E3
Ilford IG6 333 D8
Redbridge IG6 311 D1
Romford, Harold Park RM3 315 C4
Romford, Willoughby's Hill
RM5 313 A5
Crawford Ave RM16 373 B5
Crawford Chase SS12 321 E5
Crawford Cl CM12 297 C5
Crawford Compton Cl
RM12 355 C6
Crawley Cl SS17 361 A4
Crawley Ct 6 DA11 379 B1
CRAWLEY END 19 D4
Crawley End SG8 19 D4
Crayfields CM6 123 E1
Crayford Cl CM9 258 E8
Crayford Rd CO10 15 D2
Craylands SS14 342 F7
Craylands La DA10 377 D2
Craylands Sch The DA10 377 D2
Craylands Sq DA10 377 D2
CRAYS HILL 320 D5
Crays Hill CM11 320 C5
Crayshill Pk CM11 320 C5
Crays Hill Prim Sch
CM11 320 D6
Crays Hill Rd CM11 320 D4
Crays View CM12 319 B8
Crealock Gr IG8 309 F5
Creance Ct CM2 232 A2
Creasen Butt Cl CM9 237 A4
Creasey Cl RM11 336 B2
Creasy Ct SS14 342 E6
Crediton Ho 4 RM3 314 D4
Credon Cl CO15 195 F7
Credon Dr CO15 195 F7
Credo Way RM20 377 B8
Creeds Cotts CM16 267 E7
Creeds Farm CM16 267 E7
Creek Cotts CO14 144 E4
Creekhurst Cl CO7 193 A6
Creekmouth Ind Pk IG11 352 F1
Creek Rd Barking IG11 352 F2
Canvey Island SS8 364 D4
CREEKSEA 305 F5
Creeksea Ferry Rd SS4 305 C2
Creeksea La CM0 305 F6
Creekside RM13 354 F1
Creek The DA11 378 B2
Creek View Basildon SS16 342 E3
Great Wigborough CO5 188 F2
Creek View Ave SS5 301 D3
Creekview Rd CM3 301 F7
Creek Way RM13 369 E8
Creephedge La CM3 278 E5
Cree Way RM1 313 E3
Creffield Rd CO3 135 D6
Crepping Hall Dr IP9 61 F1
Crescent Ave Grays RM17 378 D8
Hornchurch RM12 335 F2
Crescent Cl CM12 296 F4
Crescent Ct
Billericay CM12 297 A2
Grays RM17 373 D1
Heybridge CM9 236 F5
Crescent Dr CM15 294 E1
Crescent Gdns CM12 296 F4
Crescent Rd Aveley RM15 371 C4
Billericay CM12 296 F4
Bishop's Stortford CM23 146 A6
Brentwood CM14 316 B6
Canvey Island SS8 364 D2
Chingford E4 287 E2
Dagenham RM10 335 B1
Felixstowe IP11 381 E4
Great Baddow CM2 255 A7
Heybridge CM9 236 F5
Ipswich IP1 17 B6
South Benfleet SS7 344 D2
Southend-on-S SS9 346 B1
Tollesbury CM9 216 E1
Walton-on-t-N CO14 171 C8
Woodford E18 310 C2
Crescent The
Clacton-on-S CO15 196 B7
Colchester CO4 110 C7
Epping CM16 267 F7
Frinton-on-S CO13 170 F4
Gestingthorpe CO9 31 F2
Great Holland CO13 170 A4
Great Horkesley CO6 82 B1
Great Leighs CM3 180 E5
Greenhithe DA9 377 C2
Hadleigh SS7 345 F3
Harlow CM17 200 C6
Ilford IG2 333 A5
Loughton IG10 288 D3
Marks Tey CO6 133 A3
Crescent The *continued*
Steeple Bumpstead CB9 27 B7
Thorpe-le-S CO16 141 F2
Upminster RM14 337 F4
West Bergholt CO6 108 D5
Crescent View IG10 288 D4
Crescent Way RM15 371 D5
Crescent Wlk RM15 371 C4
Cressages Cl CM6 152 F6
Cress Croft CM7 128 D1
Cressells SS15 341 F6
Cresset Cl SG12 197 C3
CRESSING 156 A6
Cressingham Ct 1 DA17 369 A3
Cressing Prim Sch CM77 155 E6
Cressing Rd
Braintree CM7 128 C2
Witham CM8 183 D6
Cressing Sta CM77 155 D5
Cressing Temple Barns*
CM77 156 B2
Crest Ave Basildon SS13 343 C6
Grays RM17 378 B7
Cresthill Ave RM17 373 C2
Crestlands CO7 165 B7
Crest The
Sawbridgeworth CM21 172 D2
Southend-on-S SS9 346 D6
Crest View DA9 377 A3
Creswick Ave SS6 323 C3
Creswick Ct SS6 323 C3
Crete Hall Rd DA11 378 E1
Crick Ct 3 IG11 352 C3
Cricket Ct E6 352 A2
Cricketers Cl
Broomfield CM1 208 C1
Erith DA8 369 E1
Sudbury CO10 33 E6
Cricketers La CM13 317 D3
Cricketers Ret Pk SS13 321 A2
Cricketers Row CM13 317 D3
Cricketers Way SS13 321 A2
Cricketfield Gr SS9 346 F2
Cricketfield La CM23 145 E8
Cricket Hill Rd IP11 381 B5
Crickhollow CM3 301 C5
Cricklade Ave RM3 314 D4
Cringle Lock CM3 301 E5
CRIPPLE CORNER 54 B2
Cripplegate CM0 284 E5
Cripsey Ave CM5 248 F5
Crispe Ho 4 IG11 352 D3
Crispin Cl CB9 8 D7
Crispins SS1 368 A8
Crispin Terr IG8 310 D4
Critchett Terr 1 CM1 232 A3
Crittal Ct CM7 127 D4
Crittall Cl CM8 156 E4
Crittall Ct CM8 184 A3
Crittall Dr CM7 127 D4
Crittall Rd CM8 184 B3
CRIX GREEN 153 D6
Crix Green Villas CM6 153 D6
Croasdaile Rd CM24 119 E8
Croasdale Cl CM24 119 E8
Crocklands CO9 104 A5
CROCKLEFORD HEATH 111 C2
Crocus Cl
Clacton-on-S CO16 195 C4
Ipswich IP2 16 F4
Crocus Fields CB10 22 E3
Crocus Way CM1 232 E7
Croft Cl Braintree CM7 128 A3
South Benfleet SS7 344 C5
Southend-on-S SS9 346 E4
Croft Ct Chelmsford CM1 232 E8
20 Sudbury CO10 33 E7
Crofters CM21 172 E3
Crofters End CM21 172 E3
Crofters Wlk CM77 154 D8
Croft Ho 4 CO9 76 F2
Croft La CB9 9 B6
Croft Lodge Cl IG8 310 B4
Crofton Ave SS17 360 F4
Crofton Cl IP4 18 B7
Crofton Gr E4 309 D6
Crofton Ho 6 CO10 33 E8
Crofton Rd Grays RM16 373 E3
Ipswich IP4 18 B7
Croft Rd Clacton-on-S CO15 195 D4
Kelvedon CO5 158 B2
South Benfleet SS7 344 C5
Sudbury CO10 33 E8
Croftside CO8 55 F1
Croft St IP2 17 C3
Crofts The SS3 349 E4
Croft The Bures CO8 55 F1
Chingford E4 309 E8
Earls Colne CO6 105 A6
Elsenham CM22 94 C1
Glemsford CO10 2 C4
Great Yeldham CO9 30 A2
Loughton IG10 289 A7
Rayleigh SS6 345 F8
Croft Villas CO10 2 C3
Croft Way CM8 184 A3
Cromarty Ho CM14 316 D6
Cromarty Rd IP4 18 B8
Cromar Way CM1 231 F1
Crombie Cl IG4 332 F6
Crome Cl CO3 135 A5
Cromer Ave SS15 341 B8
Cromer Cl SS15 341 B8
Crome Rd CO16 195 D5
Cromer Mews CO4 109 E3
Cromer Rd Dagenham RM6 334 E5
Hornchurch RM11 336 D4
Ipswich IP1 16 F8
Romford RM7 335 C5
Southend-on-S SS1 367 B8
Woodford IG8 310 A6
Cromer Terr 3 RM6 334 B6
Crompton Cl SS14 341 F8
Crompton Pl 8 EN3 265 A1
Crompton Rd IP2 16 F7
Crompton St CM1 231 F1
Cromwell Ave CM12 297 A3
Cromwell Cl
Bishop's Stortford CM23 145 B7
Boreham CM3 233 D8
Cromwell Ct
Brentwood CM14 316 B6
11 Ipswich IP1 17 C5
Maldon CM9 237 A3
Cromwell Ctr
Barking IG11 353 A2
Redbridge IG6 312 B5
Witham CM8 184 B2
Cromwell Ctr The RM8 334 F4
Cromwell Hill CM9 236 F3
Cromwell Ho CO4 109 F4
Cromwell La CM9 236 F3
Cromwell Lodge IG11 352 E7
Cromwell Pk CM6 152 B5
Cromwell Rd
Brentwood CM14 316 B6
16 Colchester CO2 135 F6
Grays RM17 373 A1
Hockley SS5 324 E6
Little Dunmow CM6 151 E6
Saffron Walden CB11 43 E7
Southend-on-S SS2 348 B3
Cromwells Mere RM5 313 D4
Cromwell Sq 8 IP1 17 C5
Cromwell Trad Ctr IG11 352 E2
Cromwell Way CM8 183 F2
Crondon Park La CM4 275 E4
Crooked La DA11, DA12 379 B1
Crooked Mile
Waltham Abbey EN9 265 C6
Waltham Abbey EN9 265 C7
Crooked Way EN9 221 E1
Cropenburg Wlk SS8 364 B5
Croppath Rd RM10 354 A8
Croquet Gdns CO7 137 C1
Crosby Ct IG7 312 A7
Crosby Rd
Dagenham RM10 354 B4
Southend-on-S SS0 366 C8
Cross Ave SS12 321 C6
Crossbow Ct CM5 249 A2
Crossbow Rd IG7 311 F5
Crossby Cl CM15 295 E8
Cross Cotts CO4 83 B6
Crosse Cts SS15 341 C5
CROSS END 78 C8
Crossfell Rd SS7 344 F7
Crossfield Rd
Clacton-on-S CO15 195 E3
Hoddesdon EN11 221 B8
Southend-on-S SS2 348 D2
Crossfields Halstead CO9 103 F8
Loughton IG10 289 B4
Stoke-by-N CO6 56 C5
Crossfield Way CO13 170 B6
Cross Field Way CO4 83 B5
Crossgate Field IP11 381 C5
Cross Gn SS16 341 F5
Cross Hill CO12 116 D1
Crossing Rd CM16 268 A6
Cross La CO5 218 F7
Crossley Ave CO15 220 E7
Crossley View CO15 196 B3
Crossness Rd IG11 352 F2
Cross Rd Basildon SS13 343 F7
Chingford E4 287 E1
Dagenham RM6 334 C4
Gravesend DA11 378 F1
Hadleigh SS7 345 B4
Maldon CM9 237 A1
Romford RM7 335 B8
Witham CM8 183 F5
Woodford IG8 310 F4
Crossroads CO9 31 E2
Cross Roads IG10 288 C7
Cross St Felixstowe IP11 381 C6
16 Gravesend DA11 379 B1
Saffron Walden CB10 22 D1
Sudbury CO10 33 D7
Cross The
West Mersea CO5 218 E7
Wivenhoe CO7 137 B2
Crosstree Wlk CO2 136 A3
Crossway Dagenham RM8 334 C1
6 Stanford-le-H SS17 360 F3
Woodford IG8 310 C6
Cross Way
3 Harlow CM17 200 D1
West Mersea CO5 218 E7
CROSSWAYS 376 D4
Crossways
Canvey Island SS8 363 E4
Chelmsford CM2 254 C7
Clacton-on-S CO15 220 G8
Colne Engaine CO6 77 F1
Loughton IG10 289 A4
Romford RM2 336 B8
Shenfield CM15 295 A3
Crossways Bvd DA2 376 C3
Crossways The SS0 366 A8
Crossway The CM11 297 D3
Crotchets Cl IP9 35 A1
Crouch Ave Barking IG11 353 B3
Hullbridge SS5 301 E1
Crouch Beck CM3 301 E7
Crouch Ct Braintree CM7 128 D1
Harlow CM20 199 C3
Crouch Dr Wickford SS11 321 D8
Witham CM8 183 E2
CROUCH GREEN 51 C4
Crouchman Cl RM16 373 C4
Crouchmans Ave SS3 350 A4
Crouchman's Farm Rd
CM9 235 C7
Crouch Mdw SS5 301 E4
Crouch Pk SS5 301 E4
Crouch Rd
Burnham-on-C CM0 306 C5
Grays RM16 374 A1
Crouch St Basildon SS15 319 E2
Colchester CO3 135 E6
Crouch Valley RM14 337 E4
Crouchview Cl SS11 322 B7
Crouch View Cotts CM3 300 C5
Crouch View Cres SS5 325 A8
Crouch View Gr SS5 301 D3
Crouch View Villas SS4 304 E2
Crouch Way SS3 368 E7
Crough Rd CM3 303 A7
Croutel Rd IP11 381 F5
Crowborough Rd SS2 348 A2
Crowe Hall La IP9 62 A1
Crow Gn CM15 294 A5
Crow Green La CM15 294 A4
Crow Green Rd CM15 294 A5
Crowhall La CO11 87 E1
Crowhurst Ct CO3 135 E7
Crowhurst Rd CO3 135 E7
Crow La Romford RM7 335 B4
Tendring CO16 141 A3
Crowland Cl 7 IP2 17 A2
Crowland Rd CB9 8 F8
Crowlands Ave RM7 335 B5
Crowlands Jun & Inf Schs
RM7 335 C5
Crown Ave SS13 343 C7
Crown Bays Rd CO4 136 C8
Crown Bldgs 4 E4 287 D1
Crown Cl Basildon SS13 343 C6
Sheering CM22 201 C8
Crown Ct RM18 379 A5
Crownfield EN10 221 A2
Crownfield Ave IG2 333 E6
Crownfield Jun & Inf Schs
RM7 313 A1
Crownfield Rd CO10 2 B6
Crownfields CO7 84 F6
Crown Gate
Colchester CO4 110 D6
Harlow CM20 223 D8
Crown Gdns SS6 323 C2
Crown Hill Ashdon CB10 6 B1
Loughton CM16 267 A5
Rayleigh SS6 323 C2
Waltham Abbey EN9, CM20 266 F6
Crownhill Rd IG8 310 E3
Crown Hts SS6 323 D2
Crown La Harwich CO12 91 D4
Tendring CO16 140 D3
Crown La N CO7 110 F7
Crown La S CO7 111 A4
Crown Mdw CM7 128 D4
Crownmead Way RM7 335 B7
Crown Par RM13 355 B1
Crown Rd Billericay CM11 297 B2
Clacton-on-S CO15 195 C1
Cold Norton CM3 280 F6
Grays RM17 378 A8
Hockley SS5 324 B5
Ilford IG6 333 D7
Kelvedon Hatch CM14 293 D8
Crown St Brentwood CM14 316 C8
Castle Hedingham CO9 51 E4
Dagenham RM10 354 C6
Dedham CO7 84 F6
Felixstowe IP11 381 C6
Great Bardfield CM7 72 B2
Ipswich IP1 17 C6
Crown Terr CM23 146 A7
Crown Way CM0 284 C4
Crow Pond Cotts CM3 182 C3
Crow Pond Rd CM3 182 C3
Crowsfield Cotts CM2 276 F4
CROW'S GREEN 125 E8
Crowsheath La CM11 298 E6
Crows La CM3 279 D5
Crowsnest The CM0 306 C3
Crows Rd Barking IG11 352 B6
Epping CM16 245 F1
Crow St CM22 94 F5
Crowstone Ave SS0 366 C8
Crowstone Cl SS0 347 D1
Crowstone Prep Sch SS0 366 C8
Crowstone Rd
Grays RM16 373 C4
Southend-on-S SS0 366 C8
Crowstone (Sutton) Prep Sch
SS4 348 B8
Croxall Ct CM8 183 F2
Croxford Way RM7 335 D3
Croxon Way CM0 306 B7
Crozier Ave CM23 145 C8
Crozier Mews IP4 18 B6
Crozier Terr CM2 233 B4
Cruce Way CO16 192 F3
Crucible Cl RM6 334 B5
Cruick Ave RM15 372 C6
Crummock Cl CM77 154 C6
Crunch Croft CB9 9 E5
Crusader Cl RM19 371 A2
Crusader Way CM7 128 D2
Crushes Cl CM13 295 E3
Crushton Pl CM1 231 F6
Crusoe Rd DA8 369 D1
Crystal Ave RM12 336 E1
Crystal Ct 1 RM13 355 A1
Crystal Stps 15 SS1 367 C7
Crystal Way RM8 334 C3
Cuckfield Ave IP3 18 E3
Cuckoo Cnr SS2 347 E4
Cuckoo Farm Bsns Pk
CO4 110 A7
Cuckoo Hill Bures CO8 55 F1
Sible Hedingham CO9 75 B8
Cuckoo La RM16 372 F5
Cuckoos La
Great Canfield CM6 149 A3
Takeley CM6 148 F2
Cuckoo Way CM77 154 C7
Cudmore Grove Ctry Pk*
CO5 192 A1
Culford Pl IP3 17 F4
Culford Rd RM16 373 C4
Culford Wlk IP11 381 A3
Cullen Sq RM15 372 C5
Cullingham Rd IP1 17 A5
Cullings Ct EN9 265 F6
Culpeper Cl IG6 311 B4
Culverdown SS14 342 A6
Culver Rise CM3 301 E6
Culver St E CO1 135 F7
Culver St W CO1 135 F7
Culvert Cl CO6 130 F1
Culver Wlk 21 CO1 135 F7
Cumberland Ave
Hornchurch RM12 336 E1
Maldon CM9 236 E1
South Benfleet SS7 344 C3
Southend-on-S SS2 348 D2

East End La CO7 60 C2
East End Rd
Bradwell on S CM0 242 C3
East Bergholt CO7 60 A3
Easten Greene CO6 80 E4
East Entrance RM10 354 B3
Easterford Rd CO5 158 C2
Easterling Cl CO12 91 A4
Eastern App IG11 353 A3
Eastern App CM2 232 F5
Eastern Ave Aveley RM15 371 C4
Grays RM20 376 F8
Haverhill CB9 8 F8
Ilford IG2 333 D5
South Benfleet SS7 344 C5
Southend-on-S SS2 348 B3
Wanstead E11 332 C5
Eastern Ave E RM1, RM2, RM3 313 E1
Eastern Avenue Ret Pk RM7 335 C7
Eastern Avenue W RM7 335 B7
Eastern Cl
Rushmere St A IP4 18 F4
Southend-on-S SS2 348 A3
Eastern Cres CM1 231 F5
Eastern Espl
Canvey Island SS8 364 D2
Southend-on-S SS1 367 D6
Eastern Prom CO16 192 F3
Eastern Rd
Brightlingsea CO7 192 E6
Burnham-on-C CM0 306 C5
Grays RM17 373 D2
Rayleigh SS6 323 B1
Romford RM1 335 F6
Easternville Gdns IG2 333 C5
Eastern Way
Belvedere DA18 369 A4
Grays RM17 373 A1
East Essex Aviation Mus* CO16 192 E4
Eastfield Gdns RM10 354 A8
Eastfield Rd Basildon SS15 319 F2
Brentwood CM14 316 D8
Canvey Island SS8 364 D5
Dagenham RM9 353 F8
Dagenham RM9, RM10 354 A8
Eastgate Basildon SS14 342 B5
Great Chesterford CB10 3 D2
Eastgate 13 IP4 17 D6
East Gate CM20 199 D1
Eastgate Bsns Ctr 2 SS14 342 B6
East Gates Ind Est CO1 136 B7
Eastgate St CO12 91 D6
EAST GORES 132 A4
East Gores Farm CO6 131 F4
East Gores Rd CO6 131 F5
East Hall La RM13 370 D7
Eastham Cres CM13 317 A7
EAST HANNINGFIELD 278 B7
East Hanningfield CE Prim Sch CM3 278 B7
East Hanningfield Ind Est CM3 278 C6
East Hanningfield Rd
Howe Green CM2 255 E2
Rettendon CM3 278 C4
East Haven CO15 195 E5
East Hill CO1 136 A7
EAST HORNDON 339 E7
EASTHORPE 160 B7
Easthorpe Rd Feering CO5 159 D7
Messing CO5 159 F5
East Kent Ave DA11 378 C1
East La CO7 85 B5
Eastland Ct IP11 381 B7
East Lawn IP4 18 C8
Eastleigh Rd SS7 344 E1
Eastley SS16 341 F4
East Mayne SS13 321 A2
Eastmead IG3 334 A4
EAST MERSEA 191 F1
East Mersea Rd CO5 190 E1
East Mill Gravesend DA11 379 A1
Halstead CO9 76 F2
East Mill Gn IP9 60 E6
Easton End SS15 341 A6
Easton Farm CM6 122 E6
Easton Rd CM8 184 A3
Easton Way CO13 171 B6
East Park Cl RM6 334 E6
East Pk Harlow CM17 200 C3
Sawbridgeworth CM21 172 E1
East Rd
Bishop's Stortford CM23 146 B7
Dagenham, Chadwell Heath RM6 334 E6
East Mersea CO5 191 D1
Harlow CM20 200 B4
Romford RM7 335 D4
West Mersea CO5 218 E7
East Row Holbrook IP9 62 D6
Wanstead E11 332 A5
East Side CO4 83 A4
East Sq SS14 342 B6
East St Barking IG11 352 C5
Braintree CM7 128 A3
Coggeshall CO6 131 A2
Colchester CO1 136 B7
Grays RM17 378 C8
Grays, West Thurrock RM20 377 E8
Harwich CO12 91 D4
Rochford SS4 325 F2
Saffron Walden CB10 22 E1
Southend-on-S, Leigh Cliffs SS9 365 E8
Southend-on-S SS2 347 F2
Sudbury CO10 33 F8
Tollesbury CM9 216 D1
Wivenhoe CO7 164 B8
East Stockwell St CO1 135 F7
East Terr Gravesend DA12 379 C1
Walton-on-t-N CO14 144 D1
East Thorpe SS14 342 C6
East Thurrock Rd RM17 378 C8
EAST TILBURY 375 C1
East Tilbury Inf Sch RM18 375 C1
East Tilbury Jun Sch RM18 375 C1
East Tilbury Rd SS17 375 A4
East Tilbury Sta RM18 375 B2
East View Chingford E4 309 C5
Takeley CM22 148 C8
Writtle CM1 230 F1
East View Cl CB10 45 F8
Eastview Dr SS6 323 E5
East Ward Mews CO1 136 C7
Eastway E11 332 B6
Eastway Ent Ctr IP1 16 D8
Eastways
Canvey Island SS8 363 F5
Witham CM8 184 B4
Eastways Ind Est CM8 184 B4
EASTWICK 199 A4
Eastwick Hall La CM20 199 A5
Eastwick Rd
Eastwick CM20 199 B4
Gilston CM20 199 E6
East Wlk Basildon SS14 342 B6
Harlow CM20 199 D1
EASTWOOD 346 E5
Eastwoodbury Cl SS2 347 E6
Eastwoodbury Cres SS2 347 E6
Eastwoodbury La SS2 347 C6
Eastwood Bvd SS0 347 A2
Eastwood Cl E18 310 A1
Eastwood Dr
Colchester CO4 110 B3
Rainham RM13 370 B7
Eastwood Ind Est SS9 346 C6
Eastwood La S SS0 347 B2
Eastwood Old Rd SS9 346 B6
Eastwood Park Cl SS9 346 E6
Eastwood Park Dr SS9 346 E7
Eastwood Prim Sch SS9 346 F6
Eastwood Rd Ilford IG3 334 A4
Rayleigh SS6 323 E1
Southend-on-S SS9 346 D3
Woodford E18 310 A1
Eastwood Rd N SS9 346 D4
Eastwood Rise
Rayleigh SS9 324 C1
Southend-on-S SS9 346 C8
Eastwood Sch The SS9 346 F5
Eaton Cl Billericay CM12 297 A5
Trimley St M IP11 381 A7
Eaton Cotts CO5 186 D7
Eaton Ct RM10 354 C6
Eaton Dr RM5 313 B3
Eaton Gdns
Dagenham RM9 353 E5
Felixstowe IP11 381 C2
Eaton Ho 5 CM23 146 B8
Eaton Mews CO2 136 B3
Eaton Rd
Southend-on-S SS9 346 C2
Upminster RM14 337 E2
Eaton Rise E11 332 C6
Eatons Mead E4 309 A8
Eaton Way CM9 213 E7
Ebbsfleet Ind Est DA11 378 A2
Ebbsfleet Int Sta DA10 378 A1
Ebbsfleet Wlk DA11 378 B1
Ebenezer Cl CM8 183 E5
Ebenezer Terr CM2 254 F7
Ebony Cl CO2 135 D2
Eccles Ho 2 RM3 314 D4
Eccles Rd IP2 16 D1
Eccleston Cres RM6 334 B4
Eccleston Gdns CM12 297 A5
Echo Hts E4 287 B1
Eckersley Rd CM1 232 C3
Eddy Cl RM7 335 B5
Eden Cl Holdbrook EN3 265 A1
Witham CM8 183 E3
Eden Gn RM15 372 B8
Edenhall Cl RM3 314 C5
Edenhall Glen RM3 314 C5
Edenhall Rd RM3 314 C5
Eden Rd Haverhill CB9 9 A7
Ipswich IP4 18 B5
Edens Cl CM23 146 B7
Edenside CO13 170 E7
Edens Mount CM21 172 F4
Eden Way CM1 231 C5
Edgar Ho E11 332 A4
Edgar Rd RM6 334 D4
Edgecotts SS16 341 E4
Edgefield Ave
Barking IG11 352 F5
Lawford CO11 86 B3
Edgefield Ct 3 IG11 352 F5
Edgehill Gdns RM10 354 A8
Edgeworth Rd IP2 16 E2
Edgware Rd CO16 195 D5
Edgworth Rd CO10 33 E7
Edinburgh Ave
Corringham SS17 360 F4
Southend-on-S SS9 346 B2
Edinburgh Cl Rayleigh SS6 323 B5
Witham CM8 212 A8
Edinburgh Gate CM20 199 D3
Edinburgh Gdns
Bishop's Stortford CM23 145 E6
Braintree CM7 128 C4
Edinburgh Ho 1 RM2 336 C7
Edinburgh Mews RM18 379 B5
Edinburgh Pl CM20 200 A4
Edinburgh Way
Basildon SS13 343 B6
Harlow CM20 199 E3
Edison Ave RM12 335 F3
Edison Cl
3 Braintree CM7 127 F1
Hornchurch RM12 335 F3
Edison Gdns CO4 110 C1
Edison Rd CO15 196 F6
Edisons Pk DA2 376 D4
Edith Borthwick Sch The CM7 127 F8
Edith Cavell Way CB9 27 C6
Edith Cl SS8 363 E3
Edith Rd Canvey Island SS8 363 D3
Clacton-on-S CO15 195 E2
Dagenham RM6 334 D4
Kirby-le-S CO13 170 D8
Edith Rd *continued*
Southend-on-S SS2 347 F2
Edith Way SS17 361 A4
Edmund Cl CB9 8 F8
Edmund Gn CO9 102 E8
Edmund Rd Grays RM16 372 D4
Rainham RM13 354 E2
Witham CM8 211 E8
Edmunds Ho CM16 267 F8
Edmund's Twr CM19 223 C8
EDNEY COMMON 252 D5
Edney Ct IP11 381 E3
Edridge Cl RM12 355 D7
Edward Ave
Brightlingsea CO7 192 F7
Chingford E4 309 B4
Edward Bowden Ct CB10 22 D1
Edward Bright Cl CM9 237 A2
Edward Cl Billericay CM12 296 F5
Grays RM16 372 D3
Ipswich IP1 16 F8
Little Clacton CO16 168 E5
Rochford SS4 325 C6
Romford RM2 336 C8
Edward Cordy Ho IP11 381 E3
Edward Ct EN9 265 F6
Edward Dr CM2 254 C7
Edward Francis Jun Sch SS6 323 E3
Edward Gdns SS11 321 D8
Edward Ho CB10 22 E3
Edward Mans 8 IG11 352 F5
Edward Marke Dr CO5 163 B3
Edward Paxman Gdns 10 CO1 136 C6
Edward Rd Dagenham RM6 334 E5
Thorpe-le-S CO16 168 F7
Edwards Cl CM13 295 E3
Edwards Hall Prim Sch SS9 346 C7
Edwards Rd DA17 369 A2
Edward St CO12 90 E5
Edwards Way CM13 295 E4
Edwards Wlk CM9 236 F3
Edward Terr CO16 168 E5
Edwina Gdns IG4 332 E6
Edwin Ave E6 352 A3
Edwin Cl RM13 354 F2
Edwin Hall View CM3 279 C1
Edwin Lambert Sch RM11 336 A4
Edwin's Hall Rd CM3 279 D3
Edwin St DA12 379 B1
Egbert Gdns SS11 299 D1
Egerton Dr SS16 340 E5
Egerton Gdns IG3 333 F1
Egerton Green Rd CO2 135 A3
Egg Hall CM16 246 A2
Egglestone Cl IP2 16 F1
Eggshell La CM7 27 E2
Eglington Rd E4 287 D2
Eglinton Dr CM2 233 B4
Eglinton Rd DA10 377 F1
Egremont St CO10 2 B3
Egremont Way CO3 134 C4
Egret Cres CO4 137 A8
Ehringshausen Way CB9 9 B7
Eider Ct CM23 146 A6
Eight Acre La CO2 135 C2
EIGHT ASH GREEN 134 B8
Eight Ash Green & Aldham CE Prim Sch CO3 107 F1
Eisenhower Rd SS15 341 A6
Elan Rd RM15 372 A8
Elbourne Trad Est DA17 369 B3
Elbury Ct IG8 310 E3
Eldan Ho RM4 313 E7
Eldbert Cl SS2 348 E2
Eldeland SS15 341 E7
Elder Ave SS12 321 C6
Elderberry Cl
Basildon SS16 341 B5
Redbridge IG6 311 B3
Elderberry Gdns CM8 184 B4
Elderfield CM17 200 D3
Elder Field CM77 154 B5
Elderfield Wlk E11 332 B6
Elderstep Ave SS8 364 E3
ELDER STREET 44 E1
Elderton Rd SS0 347 D1
Elder Tree Rd SS8 364 C4
Elder Way Rainham RM13 355 D2
Wickford SS12 321 C6
Eld La CO1 135 F7
Eldon Cl CO4 110 E1
Eldon Rd EN11 221 D4
Eldonwall Est RM8 334 F3
Eldon Way SS5 324 E6
Eldon Way Ind Est SS5 324 D6
Eldred Ave CO2 135 B3
Eldred Cl IP1 16 D8
Eldred Ct CO10 34 C4
Eldred Dr CO10 34 C4
Eldred Gdns RM14 337 E4
Eldred Rd IG11 352 E4
Eldridge Ct 2 RM10 354 B6
Eleanor Chase SS12 321 C7
Eleanor Cl CO5 186 D6
Eleanor Cross Rd EN8 265 A5
Eleanor Ct RM11 336 D4
Eleanor Gdns RM8 334 F2
Eleanor Way CM14 316 E5
Eleanor Wlk
3 Greenhithe DA9 377 C3
Tiptree CO5 186 D6
Electric Ave SS0 347 C2
Electric Ho 9 E4 287 D1
Electric Par Ilford IG3 333 F2
Woodford E18 310 A1
Eleven Acre Rise IG10 288 F6
Eleventh Ave CM24 120 B2
Elfrida Ho CO2 135 B3
Elgar Cl Basildon SS15 341 D8
Buckhurst Hill IG9 310 D8
South Benfleet SS7 344 B6
Elgar Dr CM8 211 F7
Elgar Gdns RM18 379 B6
Elgin Ave Chelmsford CM1 232 A2
Romford RM3 315 B4
Elgin Ho CM14 316 D6
Elgin Rd IG3 333 E4
Elham Dr SS13 343 C6
Elianore Rd CO3 135 B7
Eliot Cl SS12 321 C5
Eliot Mews SS2 348 A2
Eliot Rd Dagenham RM9 353 D8
Dartford DA1 376 B2
Eliot Way CM9 237 A1
Elizabeth Ave Ilford IG1 333 D2
Rayleigh SS6 323 C1
Witham CM8 212 A8
Elizabeth Cl
Colchester CO4 110 C4
Hockley SS5 324 E4
Lower Nazeing EN9 243 D8
Romford RM7 313 B2
Saffron Walden CB10 22 F2
Tilbury RM18 379 B5
Elizabeth Ct
Buckhurst Hill IG9 288 B1
6 Gravesend DA11 379 A1
Harwich CO12 91 A3
Ipswich IP3 17 F5
4 Sudbury CO10 33 F8
Walton-on-t-N CO14 144 E3
6 Woodford E18 310 A2
2 Woodford IG8 310 C3
Elizabeth Dr
Theydon Bois CM16 267 E3
Wickford SS12 321 B8
Elizabeth Garrett Anderson Ho 9 DA17 369 A3
Elizabeth Ho
Pilgrims Hatch CM15 294 B3
3 Romford RM2 336 C7
Southend-on-S SS9 346 D7
Elizabeth Rd
Bishop's Stortford CM23 145 E5
Grays RM16 372 F4
Harwich CO12 91 A3
Pilgrims Hatch CM15 294 B3
Rainham RM13 370 B8
Southend-on-S SS1 367 D6
Elizabeth St DA9 376 E2
Elizabeth Twr 6 SS2 347 F1
Elizabeth Villas CO5 187 A2
Elizabeth Way
Basildon SS15 341 D5
Brightlingsea CO7 192 F6
Felixstowe IP11 381 C3
Hadleigh SS7 345 C4
Halstead CO9 76 E2
Harlow CM20 199 B2
Hatfield Peverel CM3 211 A4
Heybridge CM9 237 A5
Saffron Walden CB10 22 F2
Sudbury CO10 33 C5
Wivenhoe CO7 137 C3
Eliza Cook Cl DA9 377 B3
Elkins The RM1 313 E1
Ellenborough Cl CM23 145 D5
Ellenbrook Cl SS9 346 E3
Ellenbrook Gn IP2 16 D1
Ellenbrook Rd IP2 16 D1
Ellen Ct 5 E4 287 C1
Ellen Way CM77 154 D7
Ellen Wilkinson Ho 12 RM10 335 A1
Ellerman Rd RM18 378 F5
Ellerton Gdns RM9 353 C5
Ellerton Rd RM9 353 C5
Ellesmere Gdns IG4 332 E5
Ellesmere Rd
Canvey Island SS8 363 E3
Rochford SS4 303 C1
Ellie Cl SS17 360 C2
Elliot Cl
South Woodham Ferrers CM3 301 F6
Woodford IG8 310 D4
Elliot Pl CM7 128 C3
Elliots Dr CO14 171 B8
Elliott Ct CM23 146 A8
Elliott Gdns RM3 314 B3
Elliott St IP1 17 A6
Ellis Ave RM13 370 A8
Ellis Cl RM16 374 E7
Ellis Rd Boxted CO4 82 F3
Bradfield CO11 114 D8
Clacton-on-S CO15 195 E2
Ellmore Cl RM3 314 B2
Ellswood SS15 319 D1
Elm Ave Heybridge CM9 237 C5
Upminster RM14 356 B8
Elm Bank Pl SS17 359 F4
Elm Bglws CM7 127 D4
Elmbourne Dr DA17 369 B2
Elmbridge CM17 200 F3
Elmbridge Hall CM5 227 C1
Elmbridge Rd IG6 312 A4
Elmbrook 3 E18 332 A8
Elmbrook Dr CM23 145 E3
Elm Cl Alresford CO7 165 B8
Brantham CO11 60 D1
Buckhurst Hill IG9 310 D8
Chelmsford CM1 232 A8
Elsenham CM22 94 C2
Epping Green CM16 245 B7
Great Baddow CM2 254 F6
Great Bentley CO7 166 E8
Haverhill CB9 8 F8
Rayleigh SS6 323 D3
Romford RM7 313 B1
Sible Hedingham CO9 51 D2
Southend-on-S SS3 368 E7
Takeley CM22 148 C7
Tiptree CO5 186 C7
Waltham Abbey EN9 265 D5
Wanstead E11 332 B5
Elm Close Extension CM22 148 C7
Elm Cotts Billericay CM11 319 E7
Southend-on-S SS2 347 F2
Waltham Abbey EN9 265 D1
Elm Court Pk CM4 250 F1
Elm Cres CO4 136 D7
Elmcroft CO7 138 A6
Elmcroft Ave E11 332 B7
Elmcroft Cl E11 332 B7
Elm Ct Chingford E4 309 C4
Elmdon CB11 20 B4
Sturmer CB9 9 E5
Elm Ct *continued*
Theydon Bois CM16 267 E2
Woodford IG8 310 F4
Elmdale Dr CO11 86 D3
Elmden Ct CO15 195 E5
Elmdene Ave RM11 336 F6
ELMDON 20 B4
Elmdon Pl 1 CB9 9 B8
Elmdon Rd RM15 372 A8
Elm Dr Brightlingsea CO7 192 D7
Halstead CO9 76 F1
Harwich CO12 91 B3
Rayleigh SS6 323 D3
Elmer App SS1 367 A8
Elmer Ave Romford RM4 313 E7
Southend-on-S SS1 367 A8
Elmer Cl RM13 355 A5
Elmer Gdns RM13 355 A5
Elm Est CO7 59 C3
Elm Farm Cvn Pk CO16 142 A1
Elmfield Cl CO15 196 E7
Elmfield Rd E4 309 D8
Elm Gdns
North Weald Bassett CM16 247 B5
Trimley St M IP11 381 A7
Elm Gn Basildon SS13 343 A5
Billericay CM11 297 E2
Elm Gr
Bishop's Stortford CM23 146 B7
Clacton-on-S CO15 195 F6
Hornchurch RM11 336 E5
Hullbridge SS5 301 D2
Kirby Cross CO13 170 D6
Saffron Walden CB10 22 D1
Southend-on-S SS1 368 A8
Wivenhoe CO7 137 B1
Woodford IG8 309 F5
Elm Green La CM3 256 C8
Elm Green Prep Sch CM3 234 D3
Elm Hall Gdns E11 332 B5
Elm Ho Canvey Island SS8 364 B1
Felixstowe IP11 381 C4
Elmhurst
2 Greenhithe DA9 377 B1
Hoddesdon EN10 221 A4
Elmhurst Ave SS7 344 B4
Elmhurst Cl CB9 9 B7
Elmhurst Dr
Hornchurch RM11 336 C4
Ipswich IP3 17 F3
Woodford E18 310 A1
Elmhurst Rd CO12 91 C3
Elmhurst Way IG10 288 F2
Elm La Capel St M IP9 35 A1
Marks Tey CO5, CO6 132 B2
Washbrook IP8 35 E8
Elmores IG10 289 A6
Elm Par RM12 355 B8
ELM PARK 355 B7
Elm Park Ave
Hornchurch RM12 355 A8
Rainham RM12 354 F8
Elm Park Sta RM12 355 A8
Elm Rd Aveley RM15 371 D5
Basildon SS13 321 E1
Bishop's Stortford CM23 145 F8
Canvey Island SS8 364 C3
Chelmsford CM2 254 A8
East Bergholt CO7 59 C3
Grays RM17 378 C8
Great Dunmow CM6 123 C2
Greenhithe DA9 376 E1
Hadleigh SS7 345 D2
Little Clacton CO16 168 C3
Romford RM7 313 B1
Rushmere St A IP5 18 F7
Southend-on-S, Leigh-on-S SS9 346 E1
Southend-on-S, Shoeburyness SS3 368 E8
South Woodham Ferrers CM3 301 C8
Sudbury CO10 34 A7
Wickford SS11 321 D8
Elm Rise CM8 184 A5
Elms EN9 266 C4
Elms Dr CM1 232 A4
Elms Farm Rd RM12 355 C7
Elms Gdns RM9 353 F8
Elms Hall Rd CO6 104 E8
Elms Ind Est RM3 315 B3
Elmsleigh Dr SS9 346 E3
Elmslie Cl IG8 310 F4
Elmslie Lodge IG6 333 C8
Elms Rd CM1 229 F6
Elm St IP1 17 C6
Elmstead Cl SS17 361 B4
ELMSTEAD HEATH 138 A2
ELMSTEAD MARKET 138 A6
Elmstead Prim Sch CO7 137 F6
Elmstead Rd
Colchester CO4 136 E5
Ilford IG3 333 F2
Wivenhoe CO7 137 D4
Elms The
Chipping Ongar CM5 249 A1
East Bergholt CO7 60 C3
Frinton-on-S CO13 170 F6
Great Chesterford CB10 3 E3
Elmswood IG7 311 D4
Elm Terr RM20 377 B8
Elmtree Ave CM15 271 F2
Elm Tree Ave CO13 170 F7
Elm Tree Cl CO13 170 F7
Elmtree Rd SS16 343 A4
Elm View Rd SS7 344 B3
Elmway RM16 373 C5
Elm Way Boreham CM3 209 E1
Brentwood CM14 316 A6
Elm Wlk Rayne CM77 126 F2
Romford RM2 336 A8
Elmwood Colchester CO3 134 D6
Sawbridgeworth CM21 172 F1
Woodford E18 310 B2
Elmwood Ave
Colchester CO2 135 B2
Hockley SS5 324 F4
Elmwood Ct SS5 324 E6
Elmwood Dr CO5 218 D7
Elmwood Prim Sch CM3 301 D7
Elounda Ct SS7 344 D4
Elrington Rd IG8 310 A5
Elronds Rest CM3 301 C6
Elsden Chase CM0 284 D4
ELSENHAM 94 C
Elsenham CE Prim Sch CM22 94 D
Elsenham Cres SS14 342 F6
Elsenham Cross CM22 94 D
Elsenham Ct SS6 323 B3
Elsenham Hall CM22 120 E
Elsenham Mews SS14 342 F6
Elsenham Rd E12 352 A
Elsenham Sta CM22 94 C3
Elsham Dr CM77 154 B6
Elsinor Ave SS8 364 A6
Elsmere Rd IP1 17 C8
Elstar La CO6 109 B8
Elstow Gdns RM9 353 E4
Elstow Rd RM9 353 E4
Elstree Cl RM12 355 B5
Elstree Gdns IG1 352 C7
Elthorne Pk CO16 195 D4
Eltisley Rd IG1 352 B8
Elton Park Bsns Ctr IP2 16 E
Elton Pk IP2 16 D
Elton Wlk CO5 186 D
Elverston Cl SS15 341 D
Elvet Ave RM2 336 C
Elvina Ho CO15 220 F
Elvin Ct RM2 336 B
Elvin Dr RM16 372 D
Elwes Cl CO4 110 D
Elwick Rd RM15 372 C
Elwin Rd CO5 186 D
Elwood CM17 224 E
Ely Cl CM0 284 D
Ely Gdns Colchester CO1 136 A
Dagenham RM10 335 C
Redbridge IG1 332 E
Ely Pl IG8 311 A
Ely Rd SS2 348 C
Elysian Gdns CM9 216 C
Ely Way Basildon SS14 342 E
Rayleigh SS6 323 C
Emanuel Rd SS16 341 E
Embassy Ct Maldon CM9 237 A
8 Wanstead E18 332 A
Emberson Ct CM2 232 F
Emberson Way CM16 247 C
Ember Way CM0 306 A
Emblems CM6 123 C
Embra Ct CO2 136 B
Emerald Gdns RM8 335 A
Emerald Ho 2 RM13 355 A
Emerson Dr RM11 336 D
Emerson Ho RM11 336 D
EMERSON PARK 336 E
Emerson Park Ct RM11 336 D
Emerson Park Sch RM11 337 B
Emerson Park Sta RM11 336 E
Emerson Rd IG1 333 A
Emerson Terr IG8 310 D
Emily Bray Ho IP4 17 F
Emily May Ct CO12 91 A
Emily White Ct SS11 321
Emlen St IP1 17 A
Emmanuel Cl IP2 16 E
Emma's Cres SG12 197
Emmaus Way IG7 311 A
Emmerson Ho CM23 146 A
Emmott Ave IG6 333 C
Emperor Circ IP3 38
Empire Bsns Pk CO15 195
Empire Ct
Clacton-on-S CO15 195
3 Frinton-on-S CO13 170
Empire Rd CO12 91
Empire Wlk
2 Chelmsford CM2 232 C
Greenhithe DA9 377 C
Empress Ave Chingford E4 309 B
Ilford IG1 333 A
Redbridge IG1 332
Wanstead E12 332 D
West Mersea CO5 218
Woodford IG8 309
Empress Dr CO5 218 D
Empress Par E4 309 A
Emson Cl CB10 22
Emsworth Rd IG6 311
Enborne Gn RM15 372 A
Endean Ct CO7 137 A
Endeavour Cl CM9 216
Endeavour Dr SS14 320
Endeavour Sch The CM15 316
Endeavour Way IG11 353
Endey Wood CM1 252
Endlebury Ct E4 309
Endlebury Rd E4 309
Endsleigh Ct CO3 135
Endsleigh Gdns IG1 332
Endway SS7 345
End Way Cotts CM0 285
Endways Ct CM15 294
Endway The
Great Easton CM6 122
Mayland CM3 283
Steeple Bumpstead CB9 27
Enfield Ho 6 RM3 314
ENFIELD ISLAND VILLAGE 265
Enfield Rd SS11 322
Engaines Prim Sch CO16 168
Engayne Gdns RM14 337
Engayne Prim Sch RM14 337
Engineers Sq CO4 109
England's La IG10 289
Englefield Cl SS5 325
Englefields CM0 263
Engleric SG8 19
Enid Way CO4 109
Ennerdale Ave
Great Notley CM77 154
Hornchurch RM12 355
Ennerdale Ct E11 332
Ennismore Gdns SS2 348
Enoch Ho CO4 136
Ensign Cl SS9 347
Ensign Ct DA11 378
Ensign Ho RM17 377

Fern Ct Chingford E4 . . . . . 309 C4
Romford RM5 . . . . . 313 A3
Southend-on-S SS3 . . . . . 368 F7
Stanford-le-H SS17 . . . . . 360 D3
Ferndale Cl Basildon SS15 341 B6
Clacton-on-S CO15 . . . . . 195 F7
Ferndale Cres SS8 . . . . . 364 B2
Ferndale Rd Harwich CO12. 91 D5
Rayleigh SS6 . . . . . 323 E5
Romford RM5 . . . . . 313 C1
Southend-on-S SS2 . . . . . 348 C2
Fernden Way RM7 . . . . . 335 B5
Ferndown
Hornchurch RM11 . . . . . 336 F5
7 Wanstead E18 . . . . . 332 A8
Ferndown Cl SS2 . . . . . 367 C8
Ferndown Rd CO13 . . . . . 170 E5
Ferndown Way CM3 . . . . . 211 B4
Fern Gr CB9 . . . . . 8 E8
Fernhall Dr IG4 . . . . . 332 D6
Fernhall La EN9 . . . . . 266 D8
Fernhayes Cl IP2 . . . . . 17 A2
Fern Hill Basildon SS16 . . 341 C4
Glemsford CO10 . . . . . 2 B7
Fernhill Ct E17 . . . . . 309 D1
Fern Hill La CM18 . . . . . 223 F3
Fernie Cl IG7 . . . . . 312 A5
Fernie Rd CM7 . . . . . 127 D2
Fernlea CO4 . . . . . 109 C2
Fernlea Rd
Burnham-on-C CM0 . . . . . 306 B5
Harwich CO12 . . . . . 91 D5
South Benfleet SS7 . . . . . 344 E3
Fernleigh Ct Romford RM7 335 C6
Southend-on-S SS0 . . . . . 347 A1
Fernleigh Dr SS9 . . . . . 347 A1
Ferns The IG9 . . . . . 288 B1
Fernside Cl SS17 . . . . . 361 B4
Fern Way CO15 . . . . . 220 F7
Fernways IG1 . . . . . 352 B8
Fern Wlk Basildon SS16 . . . 340 E4
Canvey Island SS8 . . . . . 363 F3
Fernwood SS7 . . . . . 345 E4
Fernwood Ave CO15 . . . . . 196 F5
Ferrers Rd CM3 . . . . . 301 D6
Ferris Ave CM3 . . . . . 280 F5
Ferris Stps 13 SS1 . . . . . 367 C7
Ferro Rd RM13 . . . . . 355 A1
Ferry La Felixstowe IP11 . . 381 A3
Rainham RM13 . . . . . 369 E7
Ferrymead SS8 . . . . . 363 F5
Ferry Rd
Burnham-on-C CM0 . . . . . 305 E6
Fingringhoe CO5 . . . . . 164 B6
Hullbridge SS5 . . . . . 301 D2
North Fambridge CM3 . . . . . 303 A6
South Benfleet SS7 . . . . . 363 D8
Tilbury RM18 . . . . . 379 A4
Feryby Rd RM16 . . . . . 374 B3
Feryngs Cl CM17 . . . . . 200 D4
Fesants Croft CM20 . . . . . 200 B3
Festival Gdns CM9 . . . . . 215 D4
Festival Link SS14 . . . . . 342 B8
Festival Way SS14 . . . . . 320 B1
Fetherston Ct RM6 . . . . . 334 F5
Fetherston Rd SS17 . . . . . 360 D1
Fetcham Ct 5 IG11 . . . . . 352 C3
Feverills Rd CO16 . . . . . 168 D4
Fews Lodge RM6 . . . . . 334 D7
Fiat Ave CO15 . . . . . 220 D6
Fiddlers Cl DA9 . . . . . 377 B3
Fiddlers Folly CO3 . . . . . 107 E1
FIDDLERS HAMLET 268 C7
Fiddlers Hill CO3 . . . . . 107 E2
Fiddlers La CO7 . . . . . 59 C3
Field Cl Abridge RM4 . . . . . 290 B6
Buckhurst Hill IG9 . . . . . 310 C7
Chingford E4 . . . . . 309 B4
Field Ct CO4 . . . . . 136 E8
Fielders Ct 14 CM14 . . . . . 316 C8
Fielders The SS8 . . . . . 364 A2
Fieldfare CM11 . . . . . 319 C8
Fieldgate Dock CO7 . . . . . 192 E5
Field Gate La CM22 . . . . . 94 A3
Fieldhouse Cl E18 . . . . . 310 B2
Fielding Ave RM18 . . . . . 379 C6
Fielding Way
Brentwood CM13 . . . . . 295 C3
Southend-on-S SS0 . . . . . 347 D2
Field Rd RM15 . . . . . 371 C5
Fields Cl CO16 . . . . . 167 F6
Fields Farm Rd CO2 . . . . . 162 B4
Fieldside CB11 . . . . . 43 E7
Fields Park Cres RM6 . . . . . 334 D6
Field View Grays RM16 . . . . . 374 A3
Sudbury CO10 . . . . . 33 F8
Fieldview Cl CO4 . . . . . 109 F4
Field View Cl RM7 . . . . . 335 A8
Field View Dr CM9 . . . . . 214 C4
Fieldway Basildon SS13 . . . 343 C4
Dagenham RM8 . . . . . 353 C8
Grays RM16 . . . . . 373 A5
Stanstead Abbotts SG12 . . . 197 B4
Wickford SS12 . . . . . 321 D3
Field Way
Hoddesdon EN11 . . . . . 197 C2
Wivenhoe CO7 . . . . . 137 C2
Field Wlk CO14 . . . . . 171 A8
Fiennes Cl RM8 . . . . . 334 C3
Fiesta Dr RM9, RM13 . . . . . 354 C1
Fifth Ave
Canvey Island SS8 . . . . . 363 E4
Chelmsford CM1 . . . . . 232 B6
Frinton-on-S CO13 . . . . . 170 E5
Grays RM20 . . . . . 377 A8
Halstead CO9 . . . . . 77 B1
Stansted Mountfitchet CM24 120 B2
Thundersley SS7 . . . . . 345 A6
Wickford SS11 . . . . . 322 A6
Fifth Ave / Allende Ave
CM20 . . . . . 199 C3
Filey Rd CM0 . . . . . 284 A3
Fillebrook Ave SS9 . . . . . 347 A2
Fillebrook Ct SS9 . . . . . 347 A2
Filliol Cl CM3 . . . . . 278 B6
Filston Rd DA8 . . . . . 369 C1
Finbars Wlk IP4 . . . . . 17 F5
Finborough Cl IP4 . . . . . 18 F6
Finch Ct CM5 . . . . . 249 A5
Finchdale CO15 . . . . . 195 F6
Finch Dr Braintree CM7 . . 127 D4
Great Bentley CO7 . . . . . 139 D1
Finches Cl SS17 . . . . . 361 C4
Finches The SS7 . . . . . 345 A7
Finchfield SS6 . . . . . 323 D1
Finch Gdns E4 . . . . . 309 A5
Finch Hill CO10 . . . . . 33 A7
FINCHINGFIELD 72 C5
Finchingfield Ave IG8 . . 310 C3
Finchingfield CE Prim Sch
CM7 . . . . . 72 D6
Finchingfield Guildhall Mus*
CM7 . . . . . 72 D6
Finchingfield Rd
Stambourne CO9 . . . . . 49 C7
Steeple Bumpstead CB9 . . . . . 27 C6
Finchingfields The CM15. 271 E2
Finchingfield Way
Blackheath CO2 . . . . . 163 A8
7 Wickford SS12 . . . . . 321 C5
Finchland View CM3 . . . . . 301 D6
Finchley Ave CM2 . . . . . 254 A8
Finchley Cl DA1 . . . . . 376 A1
Finchley Rd Grays RM17 . . 378 B8
Ipswich IP4 . . . . . 17 E6
Southend-on-S SS0 . . . . . 366 D8
Finchmoor CM18 . . . . . 223 D5
Finch's CM8 . . . . . 212 F6
Findley Cl IP9 . . . . . 61 F2
Findon Gdns RM13 . . . . . 370 B8
Finer Cl CO16 . . . . . 195 C5
FINGRINGHOE 163 F5
Fingringhoe CE Prim Sch
CO5 . . . . . 163 F5
Fingringhoe Rd
Abberton CO5 . . . . . 163 B3
Colchester CO2, CO5 . . . . . 136 D1
Fingringhoe Wick
Conservation Ctr* CO5 164 D3
Fingringhoe Wick Nature
Reserve & Visitor Ctr*
CO5 . . . . . 164 D3
Fingrith Hall Cotts CM4. . 250 F3
Fingrith Hall La CM4 . . . . . 250 F3
Finham Cl CO4 . . . . . 136 F7
FINKLE GREEN 28 A5
Finnymore Rd RM9 . . . . . 353 E5
Finsbury Pl CO9 . . . . . 76 F2
Finucane Gdns RM13 . . . . . 355 A6
Firbank Rd RM5 . . . . . 313 B5
Fir Ct SS15 . . . . . 319 C1
Firebronds Rd IP9 . . . . . 62 D5
Firecrest Rd CM2 . . . . . 254 C5
Firefly Way IP3 . . . . . 38 B8
Firfield Rd SS7 . . . . . 345 C6
Firham Park Ave RM3 . . . 315 A3
Firlands CM23 . . . . . 145 E6
Firlands Ho CM23 . . . . . 145 E6
Firle The SS16 . . . . . 341 C3
Firlie Wlk CO2 . . . . . 136 A2
Firmans SS16 . . . . . 341 B3
Firmin Cl IP1 . . . . . 17 A6
Firmins Ct CO6 . . . . . 108 D4
Fir Pk CM19 . . . . . 223 B5
Firs EN9 . . . . . 266 C4
Firs Chase CO5 . . . . . 218 A6
Firs Chase Cvn Pk CO5 . . 218 A7
Firs Ct SS16 . . . . . 342 F4
Firs Cvn Pk CO16 . . . . . 168 D2
Firs Dr Loughton IG10 . . . . . 289 A8
Writtle CM1 . . . . . 231 B1
Firsgrove Cres CM14 . . . . . 316 B6
Firsgrove Rd CM14 . . . . . 316 C6
Firs Hamlet CO5 . . . . . 218 A6
Firs Rd Tiptree CO5 . . . . . 186 D4
West Mersea CO5 . . . . . 218 B7
First Ave
Basildon RM14, SS16 . . . . . 340 E4
Billericay CM12 . . . . . 318 F7
Canvey Island SS8 . . . . . 363 E4
Chelmsford CM1 . . . . . 232 B5
Clacton-on-S CO15 . . . . . 196 B4
Dagenham RM10 . . . . . 354 B3
Frinton-on-S CO13 . . . . . 170 E4
Glemsford CO10 . . . . . 2 C5
Grays RM20 . . . . . 377 A8
Halstead CO9 . . . . . 77 B1
Harwich CO12 . . . . . 91 C3
Hook End CM15 . . . . . 272 C5
Hullbridge SS5 . . . . . 301 F1
Ilford RM6 . . . . . 334 C6
Seawick CO16 . . . . . 220 C6
Southend-on-S SS0 . . . . . 366 B8
Stanford-le-H SS17 . . . . . 360 D3
Stansted Mountfitchet CM24 120 B2
Walton-on-t-N CO14 . . . . . 144 E3
Weeley CO16 . . . . . 140 F1
Wickford SS11 . . . . . 322 A6
First Ave / Mandela Ave
CM20 . . . . . 199 F2
Firs The Canvey Island SS8 363 F5
Gosfield CO9 . . . . . 102 E8
Grays RM16 . . . . . 373 C5
Layer de la H CO2 . . . . . 162 A6
Pilgrims Hatch CM15 . . . . . 294 A3
Woodford IG8 . . . . . 310 C3
Firstore Dr CO3 . . . . . 134 E7
Firs Wlk IG8 . . . . . 310 A5
Fir Tree Cl Colchester CO4. 110 B4
Grays RM17 . . . . . 378 D8
Romford RM1 . . . . . 335 D8
Fir Tree Hill IP9 . . . . . 62 E4
Fir Tree La CM3 . . . . . 234 E1
Fir Tree Rise
Chelmsford CM2 . . . . . 254 B6
Ipswich IP8 . . . . . 16 C2
Fir Trees Abridge RM4 . . . . . 290 B6
Epping CM16 . . . . . 246 B2
Fir Tree Wlk
Dagenham RM10 . . . . . 335 C1
Heybridge CM9 . . . . . 237 C5
Fir Way CO15 . . . . . 220 G6
Fir Wlk SS8 . . . . . 363 F5
Firwood's Rd CO9 . . . . . 103 E8
Fisgard Ct 9 DA12 . . . . . 379 D1
Fishbane Cl IP3 . . . . . 38 B8
Fisher Cl Haverhill CB9 . . . . . 9 D8
Holdbrook EN3 . . . . . 265 B2
Fisher Ct CM14 . . . . . 316 B5
Fishermans Way EN11 . . . 221 D8
Fishermen's Hill DA11 . . . 378 B2
Fishers Cl EN8 . . . . . 265 A5
Fishers Hatch CM20 . . . . . 199 E1
Fisher's La CO7 . . . . . 60 C3
Fisher's Way DA17 . . . . . 369 C5
Fisher Way CM7 . . . . . 128 C4
Fishmarket St CM6 . . . . . 70 A2
Fish Pond Hill IP9 . . . . . 63 C3
Fishponds Hill CO6 . . . . . 81 F4
Fishponds La IP9 . . . . . 62 E5
Fish St CM9 . . . . . 238 E6
Fisin Wlk CO3 . . . . . 134 E3
Fiske Ct Barking IG11 . . . . . 352 D3
Clacton-on-S CO15 . . . . . 195 F2
Fitches Cres CM9 . . . . . 237 B1
Fitches Croft CO6 . . . . . 133 C4
Fitches Mews CM9 . . . . . 237 B1
Fitzgerald Cl CO11 . . . . . 86 B4
Fitzgerald Cotts CO12 . . . . . 90 F2
Fitzgerald Ct IP4 . . . . . 18 A5
Fitzgerald Rd E11 . . . . . 332 A6
Fitzgilbert Rd CO2 . . . . . 135 C4
Fitzilian Ave RM3 . . . . . 314 F2
Fitzmaurice Rd IP3 . . . . . 18 B3
Fitzpiers CB10 . . . . . 22 E2
Fitzroy Cl CM12 . . . . . 297 A4
Fitzroy St 2 IP1 . . . . . 17 C6
Fitzstephen Rd RM8 . . . . . 353 C7
Fitzwalter La CM3 . . . . . 256 D6
Fitzwalter Pl
Chelmsford CM1 . . . . . 231 E3
Great Dunmow CM6 . . . . . 150 D8
Fitzwalter Rd
Boreham CM3 . . . . . 233 F8
Colchester CO3 . . . . . 135 B6
Little Dunmow CM6 . . . . . 151 E7
Fitzwarren SS3 . . . . . 349 D1
Fitzwilliam Cl IP2 . . . . . 16 F2
Fitzwilliam Rd CO3 . . . . . 135 B7
Fitzwilliams Ct CM17 . . . . . 200 E4
Fitzwimarc Sch The SS6 . 323 E3
Five Acres Bicknacre CM3 . 256 F3
Harlow CM18 . . . . . 223 E5
Holbrook IP9 . . . . . 62 D5
Stansted Mountfitchet CM24 119 E8
Walton-on-t-N CO14 . . . . . 171 B8
Fiveash La CM77 . . . . . 129 E1
Five Elms Prim Sch RM8 334 F1
Five Elms Rd RM9 . . . . . 334 F1
Five Fields CO4 . . . . . 136 E7
Five Gables Chase CO5 . . 218 D5
Five Oaks SS7 . . . . . 345 B4
Five Oaks La IG7 . . . . . 312 E5
Five Ways CO3 . . . . . 134 D4
Fiveways Ret Pk CO3 . . . . 134 D4
FLACKS GREEN 182 B2
Flag Hill CO7 . . . . . 193 F8
Flagstaff Cl EN9 . . . . . 265 B6
Flagstaff Rd
Colchester CO2 . . . . . 135 F6
Waltham Abbey EN9 . . . . . 265 B6
Flail Cl CO7 . . . . . 137 F6
Flambird's Chase
Purleigh CM3 . . . . . 280 A7
Stow Maries CM3 . . . . . 279 F6
Flamboro Cl SS9 . . . . . 346 D6
Flamboro Wlk SS9 . . . . . 346 D6
Flamingo Wlk 4 RM13 . . 355 A6
Flamstead Gdns RM9 . . . . . 353 C5
Flamstead Rd RM9 . . . . . 353 C5
Flanders Cl CM7 . . . . . 127 E5
Flanders Field CO2 . . . . . 136 B3
Flanders Rd E6 . . . . . 352 A3
Flandrian Cl EN3 . . . . . 265 B1
Flatford Dr CO16 . . . . . 195 B5
Flatford La CO7 . . . . . 85 D7
Flatford Mill (Field Ctr)*
CO7 . . . . . 85 D7
Flatford Rd
East Bergholt CO7 . . . . . 85 C8
Haverhill CB9 . . . . . 8 C8
Flats The Grays RM17 . . . . . 373 D2
Greenhithe DA9 . . . . . 377 C2
Flavian Cl CB9 . . . . . 9 D7
Flavius Way CO4 . . . . . 110 A6
Flaxen Cl E4 . . . . . 309 B7
Flaxen Rd E4 . . . . . 309 B7
Flax La CO10 . . . . . 2 C3
Flaxman Ct 13 DA17 . . . . . 369 A1
Fleet Ave RM14 . . . . . 337 D5
Fleet Cl RM14 . . . . . 337 D5
Fleet Hall Cotts SS4 . . . . . 348 B8
Fleethall Gr RM16 . . . . . 373 A5
Fleethall Rd SS4 . . . . . 348 A8
Fleet Rd SS7 . . . . . 344 D1
Fleetway SS16 . . . . . 342 F4
Fleetwood SS8 . . . . . 364 E2
Fleetwood Ave
Felixstowe IP11 . . . . . 381 F5
Holland-on-S CO15 . . . . . 196 E7
Southend-on-S SS0 . . . . . 347 C2
Fleetwood Cl CO15 . . . . . 196 E7
Fleetwood Rd IP11 . . . . . 381 F5
Fleming Cl 7 CM7 . . . . . 127 F1
Fleming Gdns
Romford RM3 . . . . . 314 D1
Tilbury RM18 . . . . . 379 C6
Fleming Ho RM3 . . . . . 314 E1
Fleming Rd Grays RM16 . . 372 C3
Waltham Abbey EN9 . . . . . 265 B4
Flemings CM13 . . . . . 316 C4
Flemings Farm Rd SS9 . . 346 D8
Flemish Cotts The CO7 . . . 84 F6
Flemish Ct CO1 . . . . . 135 F8
Flemming Ave SS9 . . . . . 346 D3
Flemming Cres SS9 . . . . . 346 D4
Fletcher Ct CM11 . . . . . 297 D2
Fletcher Dr SS12 . . . . . 321 E6
Fletcher Rd Chigwell IG7 . 311 F5
Ipswich IP3 . . . . . 18 A1
Fletchers SS16 . . . . . 341 E3
Fletchers Sq SS2 . . . . . 348 A5
Flex Mdw CM19 . . . . . 222 F7
Flint Cl Basildon SS16 . . . . . 340 F5
Ipswich IP2 . . . . . 17 B2
Flint St RM20 . . . . . 377 B8
Flintwich Manor CM1 . . . . . 231 E7
Flitch Ind Est The CM6 . . . 150 D7
Flitch La CM6 . . . . . 150 E7
Flixton Cl CO16 . . . . . 195 A4
Flood La CO4 . . . . . 110 C6
Flora Gdns RM6 . . . . . 334 C5
Flora Rd CM8 . . . . . 183 D4
Florence Cl Grays RM20 . . 377 E8
Hadleigh SS7 . . . . . 345 D3
Harlow CM17 . . . . . 224 C6
Hornchurch RM12 . . . . . 336 E2
Florence Cotts CO7 . . . . . 192 F6
Florence Ct E11 . . . . . 332 C7
Florence Elson Cl E12 . . 352 A8
Florence Gdns
Dagenham RM6 . . . . . 334 C4
Hadleigh SS7 . . . . . 345 D3
Florence Ho RM3 . . . . . 314 E1
Florence Neale Ho 2
SS8 . . . . . 364 A3
Florence Rd
Canvey Island SS8 . . . . . 364 D3
Walton-on-t-N CO14 . . . . . 144 E2
Florence Root Ho 3 IG4 332 F6
Florence Terr SS17 . . . . . 359 F4
Florence Way SS16 . . . . . 341 B5
Florence Wlk 8 CM23 . . . 145 F8
Florentine Ho 3 IG1 . . . 333 B2
Florie's Rd CO6 . . . . . 131 F8
Flowers Way CO15 . . . . . 220 G7
Flux's La CM16 . . . . . 268 A6
FOBBING 361 D5
Fobbing Farm Cl SS16 . . . 342 A3
Fobbing Rd SS17 . . . . . 361 C3
Fodderwick 1 SS14 . . . . . 342 A5
Fogerty Cl EN3 . . . . . 265 B2
Foksville Rd SS8 . . . . . 364 C4
Fold Croft CM20 . . . . . 199 A1
Fold The SS14 . . . . . 342 B6
Foley Cotts CM7 . . . . . 102 D3
Folkards La CO7 . . . . . 192 F8
Folkes La RM14, CM13 . . . . . 337 F7
Folkestone Rd E6 . . . . . 352 A2
Folley The CO3 . . . . . 134 D5
Folly Chase SS5 . . . . . 324 B6
FOLLY GREEN 103 D1
Folly La Capel St M IP8 . . . 35 D4
Hockley SS5 . . . . . 324 C6
Folly Mill La CM6 . . . . . 96 E6
Folly The
Layer de la H CO2 . . . . . 162 A5
Tiptree CO5 . . . . . 186 F2
Wivenhoe CO7 . . . . . 164 C7
Folly View SG12 . . . . . 197 B4
Fonnereau Rd IP1 . . . . . 17 C6
Fontayne Ave
Chigwell IG7 . . . . . 311 C6
Rainham RM13 . . . . . 354 E5
Romford RM1 . . . . . 313 E1
Font Cl SS15 . . . . . 341 C6
Fonteyn Cl SS15 . . . . . 341 C8
Fonteyne Gdns IG8 . . . . . 310 D1
Fontwell Park Gdns
RM12 . . . . . 355 E8
Forbes Cl RM11 . . . . . 336 B3
Ford Cl Basildon SS15 . . . . . 341 A6
Rainham RM13 . . . . . 354 F5
FORD END Clavering 64 E4
Felsted 179 B7
Ford End IG8 . . . . . 310 B4
Ford End CE Prim Sch
CM3 . . . . . 179 B6
FORDHAM 107 D5
Fordham All Saints CE Prim
Sch CO6 . . . . . 107 D4
Fordham Cl RM11 . . . . . 337 A4
FORDHAM HEATH 107 F2
Fordham Pl IP4 . . . . . 18 F5
Fordham Rd Bures CO6, CO8 79 F2
Wormingford CO6 . . . . . 80 E2
Fordhams Row RM16 . . . . . 374 B8
Ford Ho SS3 . . . . . 368 F6
Ford La Alresford CO7 . . . . . 165 A5
Rainham RM13 . . . . . 354 F5
Ford Rd Clacton-on-S CO15 195 D3
Dagenham RM10 . . . . . 354 A5
Northfleet DA11 . . . . . 378 B2
Fords La CO4 . . . . . 109 D5
Fordson Rd CM2 . . . . . 233 B6
Ford St CO6 . . . . . 107 C2
FORDSTREET 107 C3
Fordstreet Hill CO6 . . . . . 107 C2
Fordview Ind Est RM13 . . 354 D2
Fordwater Cl CO9 . . . . . 10 B3
Fordwich Rd CO7 . . . . . 165 E1
Fordyce Cl RM11 . . . . . 337 A4
Fordyke Rd RM8 . . . . . 334 F2
Forebury Ave CM21 . . . . . 172 F2
Forebury Cres CM21 . . . . . 172 F2
Forebury The CM21 . . . . . 172 F2
Fore Field CM7 . . . . . 128 D3
Forefield Gn CM1 . . . . . 232 F7
Fore Hamlet IP3 . . . . . 17 E5
Forelands Pl CM21 . . . . . 172 E2
Foremans CM1 . . . . . 231 E3
Foremark Cl IG6 . . . . . 311 F4
Foresight Rd CO2 . . . . . 136 D2
Fore St Basildon SS15 . . . . . 319 E2
Harlow CM17 . . . . . 200 C4
Ipswich IP4 . . . . . 17 D5
Forest App Chingford E4 . . 287 E2
Woodford IG8 . . . . . 310 A3
Forest Ave Chigwell IG7 . . 311 A5
Chingford E4 . . . . . 287 E2
Forest Cl
Waltham Abbey EN9 . . . . . 266 B2
Wanstead E11 . . . . . 332 A6
Woodford IG8 . . . . . 310 B6
Forest Ct Chingford E4 . . . . . 287 F1
Loughton IG10 . . . . . 288 D6
Forest Dr Chelmsford CM1 231 E1
Chingford IG8 . . . . . 309 E3
Fyfield CM5 . . . . . 227 C1
Theydon Bois CM16 . . . . . 267 E3
Wanstead E12 . . . . . 332 D1
Forest Edge IG9 . . . . . 310 D7
Forester Cl IP8 . . . . . 36 E8
Forester Ct CM12 . . . . . 296 F3
Foresters Ct
Loughton IG10 . . . . . 289 A7
Wivenhoe CO7 . . . . . 137 B1
Forest Farm Cotts IG6 . . . 311 E2
Forest Glade
Basildon SS16 . . . . . 340 F4
Chingford E4 . . . . . 309 E5
Forest Glade *continued*
Epping CM16 . . . . . 246 E4
Forest Gr CM16 . . . . . 246 C5
Foresthall Rd CM24 . . . . . 119 E4
Forest Ho E4 . . . . . 287 E2
Forest Hts IG9 . . . . . 310 A8
Forest Ind Pk IG6 . . . . . 311 E2
Forest La IG7 . . . . . 311 A5
Forest Mount Rd IG8 . . . . . 309 D3
Forest Park Ave CO15 . . . . . 195 F7
Forest Rd Chingford E17 . . 309 D1
Colchester CO4 . . . . . 136 D7
Loughton IG10 . . . . . 288 E5
Redbridge IG6 . . . . . 312 B4
Romford RM7 . . . . . 335 B8
Witham CM8 . . . . . 184 A5
Woodford IG8 . . . . . 310 A7
Forest Side
Buckhurst Hill IG9 . . . . . 288 C1
Chingford E4 . . . . . 287 F1
Epping CM16 . . . . . 267 D6
Forest Terr IG7 . . . . . 311 A5
Forest View E4 . . . . . 287 D2
Forest View Dr SS9 . . . . . 346 A3
Forest View Rd
Chingford E17 . . . . . 309 C2
Loughton IG10 . . . . . 288 D5
Forest Way Loughton IG10 288 E6
Woodford IG8 . . . . . 310 B6
Forfar Cl Ipswich IP4 . . . . . 18 B8
Southend-on-S SS9 . . . . . 346 B2
Forfields Way CM77 . . . . . 155 E6
Forge Cotts
Hatfield Heath CM22 . . . . . 173 F3
Pentlow CO10 . . . . . 13 E6
Forge Cres CM77 . . . . . 129 D3
Forge Ct CO7 . . . . . 111 E7
Forges Cnr CO10 . . . . . 13 E6
Forges Rd E12 . . . . . 332 D2
Forge St CO7 . . . . . 85 A6
Former Horsehair Factory
CO10 . . . . . 2 C5
Fornham Ho IP4 . . . . . 18 B6
Forres CO13 . . . . . 170 F4
Forres Cl EN11 . . . . . 221 A8
Forres Ho CM14 . . . . . 316 D6
Forres Prim Sch EN11 . . . 197 B1
Forrest Cl CM3 . . . . . 301 C7
Forrest Ct IP4 . . . . . 18 A7
FORRY'S GREEN 75 B6
Forster Cl E4 . . . . . 309 D3
Forsters Cl RM6 . . . . . 334 F5
Forsyth Ct 1 RM10 . . . . . 354 B6
Forsyth Dr CM7 . . . . . 155 A8
Forsythia Cl
Chelmsford CM1 . . . . . 232 E7
Ilford IG1 . . . . . 352 B7
Forterie Gdns IG3 . . . . . 353 A8
Fortescue Chase SS1 . . . . . 348 F1
Forth Rd RM14 . . . . . 337 D5
Forties Cl CB9 . . . . . 9 D8
Fortinbras Way CM2 . . . . . 254 B8
Fortin Cl RM15 . . . . . 372 A6
Fortin Path RM15 . . . . . 372 A6
Fortin Way RM15 . . . . . 372 A6
Fortis CM8 . . . . . 211 E8
Fortis Ho 4 CM8 . . . . . 211 E8
Fort Rd RM18 . . . . . 379 C5
Fortune Cl CM3 . . . . . 181 A7
Fortune Ct IG11 . . . . . 353 C3
Fortunes The CM18 . . . . . 223 F6
Fortune Stps 2 SS1 . . . . . 367 C7
Fort William Rd SS16 . . . . . 342 B2
Forum The SS2 . . . . . 348 A5
Fosbery Ct EN3 . . . . . 265 A2
Fossetts La CO6 . . . . . 107 F4
Fossetts Way SS2 . . . . . 348 C4
Fossway RM8 . . . . . 334 C2
Fostal Cl SS9 . . . . . 346 E3
Foster Ct 2 CM8 . . . . . 184 A2
Foster Rd
Canvey Island SS8 . . . . . 364 C4
Great Totham CM9 . . . . . 213 A4
Harwich CO12 . . . . . 90 E5
Fosters Cl Woodford E18 . . 310 B2
Writtle CM1 . . . . . 230 F1
Foster's Cotts CM77 . . . . . 129 D2
Foster St CM17 . . . . . 225 A7
FOSTER STREET 224 F7
Fougar Cl CM3 . . . . . 301 E8
FOULNESS ISLAND 330 C5
Foundation St 13 IP4 . . . . . 17 C5
Founders Rd EN11 . . . . . 197 B1
Foundry SS5 . . . . . 324 E6
Foundry Bsns Pk SS5 . . . . . 324 E6
Foundry La
Burnham-on-C CM0 . . . . . 306 B5
Copford CO6 . . . . . 133 D5
Earls Colne CO6 . . . . . 105 B6
Ipswich IP2 . . . . . 17 C5
Founes Dr RM16 . . . . . 372 E3
Fountain Ct Harwich CO12 . . 91 E5
West Mersea CO5 . . . . . 218 D7
Fountain Farm CM18 . . . . . 223 F6
Fountain La Copford CO6 . . 134 A1
Easthorpe CO6 . . . . . 160 F8
Hockley SS5 . . . . . 324 B6
Fountain Pl EN9 . . . . . 265 C5
Fountain Rd CM1 . . . . . 205 C4
Fountains Rd IP2 . . . . . 16 F1
Fountains The IG10 . . . . . 288 D2
Fountain Wlk DA11 . . . . . 378 F1
Four Acres
Great Chesterford CB10 . . . . . 3 E3
Saffron Walden CB11 . . . . . 22 E1
Four Acres The CM21 . . . . . 173 A2
Four Ashes CM7 . . . . . 74 C1
Four Ash Hill CO9 . . . . . 10 E1
Four Sisters CO7 . . . . . 59 B5
Four Sisters Cl SS9 . . . . . 346 F5
Four Sisters Way SS9 . . . . . 346 F5
Fourth Ave Basildon SS16 . 340 E3
Chelmsford CM1 . . . . . 232 B5
Clacton-on-S CO15 . . . . . 196 C4
Frinton-on-S CO13 . . . . . 170 F4
Glemsford CO10 . . . . . 2 B5
Grays RM20 . . . . . 377 A8
Halstead CO9 . . . . . 77 B1
Harlow CM19 . . . . . 223 B8
Romford RM7 . . . . . 335 D3
Seawick CO16 . . . . . 220 B6
Fourth Ave *continued*
Stanford-le-H SS17 . . . . . 360 E5
Stansted Mountfitchet CM24 120 B2
Thundersley SS7 . . . . . 345 A6
Wickford SS11 . . . . . 322 A6
Fourth Wlk SS8 . . . . . 363 E4
Four Wantz The CM5 . . . . . 249 A4
Fourways CM22 . . . . . 94 C1
Fourways Ct 1 EN11 . . . . . 221 A7
Four Wents The E4 . . . . . 309 D8
Fowe's La CO10 . . . . . 31 B8
Fowey Ave IG4 . . . . . 332 D6
Fowler Cl SS1 . . . . . 367 C8
Fowler Ct CM2 . . . . . 254 A4
Fowler Rd IG6 . . . . . 312 C5
Fowlers Arc CO13 . . . . . 170 F4
Fowley Mead Pk EN8 . . . . . 265 A5
Fowlmere Rd SG8 . . . . . 19 A6
Foxberry Gdns IP3 . . . . . 18 D5
Foxborough Chase CM4 . 276 B5
Foxburrow Rd IP3 . . . . . 18 F1
Fox Burrow Rd IG7 . . . . . 312 D6
Fox Burrows La CM1 . . . . . 231 B2
Fox Cl Romford RM5 . . . . . 313 B5
Thundersley SS7 . . . . . 344 F6
Fox Cres CM1 . . . . . 231 F4
Foxdells La CM23 . . . . . 118 F2
Foxden CM8 . . . . . 184 D6
FOXEARTH 14 C6
Foxendale Folly CO3 . . . . . 134 C7
Foxes Cnr CO6 . . . . . 107 D1
Foxes Gn RM16 . . . . . 374 A4
Foxes Gr CM13 . . . . . 296 C2
Foxes La Aldham CO3, CO6 133 D8
Ashen CO10 . . . . . 11 D
Foxes Par EN9 . . . . . 265 C6
Foxes Rd CO10 . . . . . 11 E
Foxfield Chase CM3 . . . . . 283 A8
Foxfield Cl SS5 . . . . . 325 A6
Foxfield Dr SS17 . . . . . 360 E5
Foxglove Cl
Bishop's Stortford CM23 . . . 145 C6
Clacton-on-S CO15 . . . . . 195 F7
Hoddesdon EN11 . . . . . 197 C
Witham CM8 . . . . . 183 D
Foxglove Cres IP3 . . . . . 18 E
Foxglove Ct SS15 . . . . . 341 C
Foxglove Gdns E11 . . . . . 332 C
Foxglove Ho DA1 . . . . . 376 A
Foxglove Rd Romford RM7 335 E
South Ockendon RM15 . . . . . 372 C
Foxgloves The CM12 . . . . . 296 F
Foxglove Way CM1 . . . . . 232 F
Foxglove Wlk 4 CO4 . . . . . 136 E
Foxgrove La IP11 . . . . . 381 F
Foxhall Cl CO7 . . . . . 59 C
Foxhall Fields CO7 . . . . . 59 C
Foxhall Rd Ipswich IP3, IP4 18 D
Mayland CM0 . . . . . 283 E
Steeple CM0 . . . . . 284 B
Upminster RM14 . . . . . 356 C
Foxhatch SS12 . . . . . 321 F
Fox Hatch CM15 . . . . . 271 E
Foxhills Rd RM16 . . . . . 373 D
Foxholes Rd CM2 . . . . . 254 F
Fox House Rd DA17 . . . . . 369 B
Foxhunter Wlk CM11 . . . . . 297 D
Foxlands Cres RM10 . . . . . 354 C
Foxlands Rd RM10 . . . . . 354 C
Foxleigh CM12 . . . . . 319 A
Foxleigh Cl CM12 . . . . . 319 A
Foxley Cl Ipswich IP3 . . . . . 18 D
Loughton IG10 . . . . . 289 B
Foxley Dr CM23 . . . . . 146 B
Fox Manor Way RM20 . . . . . 377 B
Foxmead CM8 . . . . . 184 D
Foxmeadows SS7 . . . . . 344 F
Fox St CO7 . . . . . 110 F
FOX STREET . . . . . 110 F
Foxtail Rd IP3 . . . . . 38 E
Foxton Rd Grays RM20 . . . 377 D
Hoddesdon EN11 . . . . . 221 A
Foxwood Chase EN9 . . . . . 265 C
Foxwood Cl CO11 . . . . . 85 C
Foxwood Cres IP4 . . . . . 18 F
Foxwood Ct SS9 . . . . . 346 D
Foxwood Pl SS9 . . . . . 346 D
Fox Yd CO9 . . . . . 53 C
Foyle Dr RM15 . . . . . 372 A
Foys Wlk CM11 . . . . . 319 C
Frambury La CB11 . . . . . 66 F
Frame The SS15 341
Framlingham Ct
5 Ilford RM6 334
5 Ipswich IP1 17
Rayleigh SS6 323
Framlingham Way CM77 . 154
Frampton Rd
5 Basildon SS13 321
Epping CM16 246
Ipswich IP3 38
Frances Ave RM16 372
Frances Bardsley Sch for Girls
The RM1 336
Frances Cl CO7 137
Frances Cottee Lodge
SS6 346
Frances Ct E4 309
Frances Gdns RM15 371
Frances Gn CM1 233
Frances Rd E4 309
Francis Ave IG1 333
Franciscan Way IP1 17
Francis Cl Haverhill CB9 8
Horndon on t H SS17 359
Tiptree CO5 186
Francisco Cl RM16 372
Francis Ct
3 Basildon SS14 342
Copford CO6 133
Erith DA8 369
Francis Ct CM20 199
Francis Ct CM8 156
Francis Green Ho 7 EN9 265
Francis Kellerman Wlk
CO3 135
Francis Mews CM9 259
Francis Rd Braintree CM7 . 127
Ilford IG1 333
14 Sudbury CO10 33

Ingatestone Rd
Blackmore CM4 272 F7
Edney Common CM4 252 A1
Roxwell CM1 251 F2
Stock CM4 275 B1
Wanstead E12 332 C3
Woodford IG8 310 B3
Ingatestone Sta CM4 274 B3
Ingaway SS16 341 F5
Ingelow Gdns IP4 18 B6
Ingelrica Ave CM3 211 B3
Ingels Mead CM16 245 F2
Ingestre St CO12 91 D4
Ingham Rd CB9 9 B8
Ingleby Gdns IG7 312 B7
Ingleby Rd
Dagenham RM10 354 B6
Grays RM16 374 C3
Ilford IG1 333 B3
Inglefield Rd SS17 361 B6
Ingleglen RM11 337 A4
Inglehurst Gdns IG4 332 F6
Inglenook CO15 196 B7
Ingleside Ct CB10 22 D1
Ingleton Ho
4 Ingatestone CM4 274 C4
11 Romford RM3 314 D4
Inglewood Cl
Hornchurch RM12 355 D8
Redbridge IG6 311 F4
Inglis Rd CO3 135 D6
Ingram Cotts CM1 251 F4
Ingram Mews CM7 155 B8
Ingram Rd RM17 373 C2
Ingram's Piece CO7 111 E8
Ingram's Well CO10 33 F7
Ingram's Well Rd CO10 33 F7
INGRAVE 317 D5
Ingrave Cl SS12 321 E6
Ingrave Ho RM9 353 B4
Ingrave Johnstone CE Prim Sch CM13 317 C4
Ingrave Rd
Brentwood CM13, CM15 316 E7
Romford RM1 335 E7
Ingrebourne Ct E4 309 B8
Ingrebourne Gdns RM14 337 D3
Ingrebourne Prim Sch RM3 314 C6
Ingrebourne Rd RM13 355 B1
Ingrebourne Valley* RM13 355 E7
Ingress Gdns DA9 377 D2
Ingress Park Ave DA9 377 C3
Ingreway RM3 315 C4
Inkerman Row 3 CO10 33 E8
Inkerpole Pl CM2 232 F4
Inks Gn E4 309 C5
Inmans Row IG8 310 A6
Innes Cl SS12 321 E5
Innes End 4 IP8 16 C2
Innham Hill CO9 75 C6
Innova Way EN3 265 A3
Inskip Dr RM11 336 E3
Inskip Rd RM8 334 D3
Institute Rd CM16 246 D2
Integrated Support Ctr, PRU CM18 223 F4
International Bsns Pk SS8 363 D3
Inverclyde Gdns RM6 334 D7
Invermay Ct CM15 294 C1
Inverness Ave SS0 347 D2
Inverness Cl CO1 136 A8
Inverness Dr IG6 311 E4
Invicta Ct CM12 296 E3
Invicta Ctr The IG11 353 A4
Invicta Rd DA2 376 B1
INWORTH 185 F8
Inworth La CO6 79 D2
Inworth Rd CO5 158 E3
Inworth Wlk
5 Colchester CO2 136 A1
Wickford SS11 322 A8
Io Ctr IG11 352 F1
IO Ctr EN9 265 A5
Iona Way SS12 321 F6
Iona Wlk CO5 164 A8
IP Central 20 IP4 17 D5
IPSWICH 17 C7
Ipswich High Sch IP9 38 C2
Ipswich Hospl IP4 18 C6
Ipswich Mews SS16 340 F5
Ipswich Mus* IP1 17 C6
Ipswich Prep Sch IP1 17 B7
Ipswich Rd Ardleigh CO7 83 F1
Brantham CO11 60 E2
Colchester CO4 110 C3
Dedham CO7 84 B6
Harkstead IP9 63 B3
Holbrook IP9 62 E6
Holland-on-S CO15 196 D6
Ipswich IP10 38 F6
Stratford St M CO7 58 E2
Ipswich Sch IP1 17 C7
Ipswich Sta IP2 17 B4
Ipswich Transport Mus* IP3 18 C2
Ireland Rd IP3 17 F1
Ireton Ho CO4 109 F4
Ireton Pl RM17 373 A2
Ireton Rd CO3 135 D5
Iris Cl Chelmsford CM1 232 F5
Ipswich IP2 16 F5
Pilgrims Hatch CM15 294 B4
Iris Ct IG11 353 B5
Iris Mews SS15 341 C5
Iris Path RM3 314 C3
Irlam Rd IP2 16 D1
Iron Latch La CO3 134 C8
Ironside Wlk CO11 86 C4
Irons Way RM5 313 C3
Iron View CM7 128 C2
Ironwell La Hockley SS5 325 A3
Rochford SS4 325 E2
Irvine Gdns RM15 371 F7
Irvine Pl SS12 321 F5
Irvine Rd CO3 135 C5
Irvine Way CM12 297 A1
Irving Cl
Bishop's Stortford CM23 145 D4
Hockley SS5 324 E5
Irvington Cl SS9 346 D4
Irvon Hill Rd SS12 321 C7
Isaac Sq CM2 255 B6
Isabel Ct EN11 221 B8
Isabella Ho EN8 265 A5
Isbell Gdns RM1 313 E3
Isbourne Rd CO4 136 F7
Isham Pl IP3 17 E4
Ishams Chase CM8 212 C7
Isis Dr RM14 337 A5
Island Centre Way EN3 265 A2
Island Ct CM23 146 A5
Island La CO13 143 E1
Island Rd CO14 143 E4
Italstyle Bldg The CM20 200 C6
Ivanhoe CO13 170 E3
Iver Rd CM15 294 B3
Ives Gdns RM1 335 F7
Ivinghoe Rd RM8 353 B7
Ivor Brown Ct CO4 110 B4
Ivry St IP1 17 B7
Ivy Barns La
Ingatestone CM4 274 A8
Margaretting CM4 252 C1
Ivy Bower Cl 2 DA9 377 B2
Ivybridge EN10 221 A4
IVY CHIMNEYS 267 E7
Ivy Chimneys CM16 267 E7
Ivy Chimneys Prim Sch CM16 267 F7
Ivy Chimneys Rd CM16 267 E7
Ivy Cl DA1 376 A1
Ivy Cotts
Great Dunmow CM6 123 B4
Steeple CM0 262 A3
Ivy Gate Cl SS11 321 E8
Ivyhouse Rd RM9 353 E6
Ivy La CO5 192 B3
Ivy Lodge La RM3 315 B1
Ivy Lodge Rd CO6 109 C8
Ivy Rd SS7 344 A6
Ivy Terr Hoddesdon EN11 221 C8
3 Ilford IG2 333 C5
Ivy Todd Hill CB11 68 A8
Ivy Wlk Canvey Island SS8 363 F4
Dagenham RM9 353 E6
Ixworth Rd CB9 8 E6

J

Jacaranda Cl CM1 233 A6
Jack Andrews Dr CO4 110 C5
Jack Branch Ct CO15 195 E2
Jack Cook Ho 9 IG11 352 B5
Jack Cornwell St E12 352 A8
Jackdaw Cl
Billericay CM11 319 C8
Southend-on-S SS3 368 E8
Jack Evans Ct RM15 372 A7
Jack Hatch Way CO7 137 A3
Jacklin Gn IG8 310 A6
Jacks Cl SS11 321 F7
JACK'S HATCH 223 A2
Jack's La CM22 148 D7
Jack Snipe Ho RM13 370 A8
Jackson Cl
Greenhithe DA9 377 A2
Hornchurch RM11 336 F7
Jackson Ct
1 Dagenham RM10 354 A6
Wanstead E11 332 B3
Jackson Ho CO4 110 B6
Jackson Pl CM2 254 D6
Jackson Rd Barking IG11 352 D4
Clacton-on-S CO15 195 E2
Jacksons Cl CM5 249 A2
Jacksons La CM11 297 C2
Jackson's La CB10 3 D3
Jacksons Mews CM11 297 C2
Jackson Sq 10 CM23 145 F7
Jackson's Sq CB10 3 D3
Jackson Wlk CO2 136 B3
Jack Stevens Cl CM17 224 C6
Jacob Ct EN3 265 A2
Jacobs Ave RM3 314 E1
Jacobs Cl Dagenham RM10 354 B8
Great Cornard CO10 34 B5
Jacobs Ct CO7 192 F6
Jacquard Way 6 CM7 128 A2
Jacqueline Ct CO3 135 A7
Jacqueline Gdns CM12 297 B5
Jacques Hall Sch CO11 88 A3
Jade Cl RM8 334 C3
Jade Ho 6 RM13 355 A1
Jaffe Rd IG1 333 D3
Jaggard's Rd CO6 131 A3
James Alexander Ho SS5 301 D3
James Ave RM8 334 F3
James Boden Cl IP11 381 C5
James Carter Rd CO3 134 F3
James Cl Romford RM2 336 A6
Wivenhoe CO7 137 C3
James Croft CM2 254 B2
James Ct Chingford E4 309 D8
3 Woodford E18 310 B1
James Gdns CO16 194 B5
James Hatfield Ho IP2 17 D4
James Hornsby High Sch The SS15 341 D7
James Lee Sq EN3 265 A1
James Oglethorpe Prim Sch The RM14 337 F2
Jameson Pl 5 CO10 33 E8
Jameson Rd CO15 195 C3
James Parnell Dr CO2 135 F1
James Rd CO15 195 C2
James Sq CM11 297 E2
James St Barking IG11 352 C5
Brightlingsea CO7 192 F6
Colchester CO1 136 A6
Epping CM16 246 A3
James Wicks Ct CO3 135 E7
Janebrook Rd IP2 16 E2
Jane Ct 7 RM1 335 F6
Janet Duke Inf Sch SS15 341 D6
Janet Duke Jun Sch SS15 341 D6
Janette Ave SS8 363 E3
Janice Mews 3 IG1 333 B1
JANKE'S GREEN 106 E8
Janmead Brentwood CM13 295 B2
Witham CM8 184 A3
Janus Cl CB9 9 D6
Japan Rd RM6 334 D5
Japonica Ct CO15 196 C4
Jaques Cl CO10 2 C5
Jardine Rd SS13 343 C8
Jarmin Rd CO1 135 F8
Jarndyce CM1 231 F6
Jarrah Cotts RM19 376 D8
Jarrow Rd RM6 334 C5
Jarvis Cl 1 IG11 352 D4
Jarvis Field CM3 234 D5
Jarvis Rd
Canvey Island SS8 364 A6
South Benfleet SS7 344 E4
Jarvis Way RM3 314 E1
Jasmin Cl CM23 145 C6
Jasmine Cl Basildon SS16 340 F4
Canvey Island SS8 363 F2
2 Chelmsford CM1 232 E7
Colchester CO4 136 E8
Ilford IG1 352 B7
Ipswich IP2 16 F3
Jasmine Rd RM7 335 E2
Jasmine Way CO15 220 G7
Jason Cl Brentwood CM14 315 F6
Canvey Island SS8 364 B5
Orsett RM16 374 E7
Jason Ct CM14 315 F6
JASPER'S GREEN 100 E2
Jay Cl Great Notley CM77 154 D8
Haverhill CB9 9 C7
Jaymar Ct 9 CM7 127 F2
Jayrest Ctr CO3 134 E4
Jays La CO6 132 F3
Jays The CO4 110 C3
JAYWICK 220 F7
Jaywick La CO15, CO16 195 A3
Jaywick Rd CB9 9 A8
J Ct CM20 199 F1
Jeans La CM23 145 E7
Jeffcut Rd CM2 232 E2
Jefferies Rd IP4 17 E6
Jefferies Way 5 SS17 360 F3
Jefferson Ave 3 SS15 341 A6
Jefferson Cl
Colchester CO3 134 E5
Ilford IG2 333 B6
Jeffery Rd CM2 255 A7
Jeffrey Cl CO3 134 F5
Jeffreys Ct CM77 155 E6
Jeffrey's Rd CM77 155 E6
Jekylls La CM7 48 D4
Jellicoe Ct E4 309 D4
Jellicoe Way CM7 128 C4
Jena Cl SS3 368 E7
Jenkins Dr CM22 94 C3
Jenkins Hill CO11 87 C3
Jenkins La
Bishop's Stortford CM22 146 C5
Wallend IG11 352 C2
Jenner Cl CM7 127 F1
Jenner Ho
5 Belvedere DA17 369 A3
Romford RM3 314 E1
Jenner Mead CM2 233 A3
Jenningham Dr RM16 373 A5
Jennings Cl 1 CO1 136 C6
Jennings Pl CM4 275 A8
Jenningtree Way DA17 369 C4
Jenny Path RM3 314 D3
Jericho Pl CM4 272 E8
Jermayns SS15 341 E6
Jermyns Cl IP9 35 B2
Jerningham Ave IG5 311 B1
Jerounds CM19 223 B6
Jerounds Com Jun & Inf Sch CM19 223 B5
Jersey Cl EN11 221 A7
Jersey Gdns SS11 321 D8
Jersey Rd Ilford IG1 352 B8
Maldon CM9 237 B1
Rainham RM13 355 A5
Jersey Way CM7 127 D2
Jervis Cl IP9 62 D5
Jervis Ct 14 RM10 354 B6
Jervis Rd CM23 145 F6
Jesmond Rd
Canvey Island SS8 364 B2
Grays RM16 373 D5
Jessel Dr IG10 289 C7
Jessett Cl DA8 369 D2
Jessica Cl CO4 136 F7
Jessop Cl CO15 196 A8
Jessop Ct EN9 265 F5
Jetty Mews SS1 367 D7
Jetty Wlk RM17 378 A8
Jim Desormeaux Bglws CM20 199 E2
Jimmy's La CO11 60 F2
Joan Gdns RM8 334 E2
Joan Rd RM8 334 E2
Joan Villas IG2 333 C4
Jocelyns CM17 200 C4
Jodrell Way RM20 371 F1
Joes Rd CO10 34 F6
John Ball Wlk 2 CO1 135 F7
John Barker Ho IG1 333 D2
John Barr Ho CM7 127 B7
John Bird Ct CO1 109 F1
John Bramston Prim Sch IG6 312 A4
John Bramston Sch The CM8 183 F1
John Bunyan Inf Sch CM7 127 E4
John Bunyan Jun Sch CM7 127 E4
John Burns Dr IG11 352 E5
John Chadwick Ho IG3 333 E3
John Childs Way SS6 323 E2
John Clay Gdns RM16 373 B5
John Cornwell VC Ho 6 E12 352 A8
John Crouch Ct CO12 91 C3
John Ct EN11 197 A1
John Dane Player Ct 5 CB10 22 E1
John Dyde Cl CM23 146 A6
John Eliot Cl EN9 221 E2
John English Ave CM7 127 E4
John Hammond Cl CO2 162 F8
John Harper St 4 CO1 135 E8
John Henry Keene Meml Homes CM1 232 A4
John Kavanagh Ct 1 CO1 136 A6
John Kent Ave CO2 135 B2
John King Ct CO7 192 F6
John Lawrence Wlk CO2 135 F1
John Parker Cl RM10 354 B5
John Perry Prim Sch RM10 354 D6
John Raven Ct CO5 158 D3
John Ray Gdns CM77 155 B5
John Ray Inf Sch CM7 154 F8
John Ray Jun Sch CM7 154 F8
John Ray St CM7 128 A3
Johnson Cl Braintree CM7 155 A7
Ipswich IP2 17 C3
Rochford SS4 325 D5
Wickford SS12 321 D5
Johnson Ct SS4 325 F2
Johnson Rd
Great Baddow CM2 255 A5
St Osyth CO16 194 B4
Johnson's Dr CO7 138 A6
Johnsons Way DA9 377 C1
Johnsons Yd CB11 22 D2
Johns Rd CM23 119 A1
John St Brightlingsea CO7 192 F6
Grays RM17 378 C8
Ipswich IP3 17 E4
Southend-on-S SS3 368 G6
John's Terr RM3 315 C4
Johns The CM5 249 A4
Johnston Cl Halstead CO9 103 F8
Holland-on-S CO15 196 E5
Johnstone Rd SS1 368 A7
Johnston Rd IG8 310 A5
Johnston Way CM9 259 A8
John Tibauld Ct CB9 27 B6
John Warner Sch The EN11 197 B1
John Weston Nature Reserve* CO14 144 D6
John William Cl RM16 372 D1
Jollyboys La N CM6 152 C6
Jollyboys La S CM6 152 C4
Jonathan Feedham Ct CO7 137 B1
Jonathans RM11 336 E3
Jonathon Ho RM17 373 D2
Jones Cl SS2 347 E3
Jones Cnr SS8 364 A3
Jonquil Way CO4 109 C2
Jordan Cl CB11 43 E8
Jordans Cl RM10 354 B8
Jordans The SS2 348 A2
Jordans Way RM13 355 D3
Jo Richardson Com Sch RM9 353 D4
Joscelyn's Yd 11 CM23 146 A7
Joseph Clarke Sch E4 309 D4
Joseph Ct CM14 316 B5
Joseph Gdns CM8 156 E4
Joseph Lister Lodge E11 332 B3
Joshua Wlk EN8 265 A5
Josling Cl RM17 377 F8
Joslin Rd RM19 371 D1
Joslyn Cl EN3 265 A1
Josselin Cl CO6 105 B7
Josselin Ct SS13 321 C2
Josselin Rd SS13 321 C2
Josselyns The IP11 381 A8
Jotmans Hall Prim Sch SS7 344 B4
Jotmans La
South Benfleet SS7 343 F2
South Benfleet SS7 344 A3
Journeymans Way SS2 348 A5
Jovian Way
Colchester CO4 110 B6
Ipswich IP1 16 D7
Joyce Brooks Ho CO3 135 D6
Joyce Ct EN9 265 D5
Joyce's Chase CM9 239 A8
Joydon Dr RM6 334 B5
Joyes Cl RM3 314 D6
Joyners Cl RM9 353 F8
Joyners Field CM18 223 C4
Jubilee Ave
Broomfield CM1 208 B2
Chingford E4 309 C4
Clacton-on-S CO16 195 E8
Romford RM7 335 C6
Jubilee Cl Colchester CO3 134 D6
Greenhithe DA9 377 C1
Harwich CO12 90 E2
Hockley SS5 324 E5
Romford RM7 335 B6
Jubilee Cott 12 CM23 146 A7
Jubilee Cotts SS4 327 D6
Jubilee Ct
Great Dunmow CM6 123 C1
Sible Hedingham CO9 75 E8
Tiptree CO5 186 D4
Waltham Abbey EN9 265 F6
Walton-on-t-N CO14 171 C7
Jubilee Dr SS11 321 C8
Jubilee End CO11 86 C5
Jubilee La CO7 111 C3
Jubilee Par IG8 310 C4
Jubilee Rd Crays Hill CM11 320 C4
Grays RM20 377 B8
Rayleigh SS6 323 E2
Sudbury CO10 33 F8
Jubilee Rise CM3 257 A6
Jubilee Terr
Chelmsford CM1 232 A4
Woodham Ferrers CM3 279 B4
Jubilee Villas 8 E4 287 D1
Jubilee Way CO13 170 F6
Jubilee Wks CB11 65 E6
Jubilee Wlk 3 CB9 9 A7
Judge Rd CM2 233 B4
Judith Anne Ct RM14 337 E2
Judith Ave RM5 313 B4
Julia Gdns IG11 353 D3
Julian Ave CO4 110 B6
Julian Cl Broomfield CM1 208 B1
Haverhill CB9 9 D7
Julie Ho EN11 221 C8
Julien Court Rd CM7 128 A4
Juliers Cl SS8 364 D3
Juliers Rd SS8 364 D3
Juliette Way RM15 370 F5
Junction Rd Basildon SS13 343 B4
Brentwood CM14 316 C6
Cold Norton CM3 281 A6
Romford RM1 335 F6
Junction Rd E RM6 334 E4
Junction Rd W RM6 334 E4
Junction The CM13 295 B3
Juniper Cl Billericay CM11 297 D4
Halstead CO9 103 D8
Juniper Cres CM8 184 A4
Juniper Ct
Brentwood CM13 316 F7
Great Dunmow CM6 123 B1
Ilford RM6 334 C5
Juniper Dr
Chelmsford CM2 254 B6
South Ockendon RM15 357 E2
Juniper Rd Boreham CM3 233 F8
Colchester CO3 134 D5
Ilford IG1 352 B8
Southend-on-S SS9 346 F4
Juniper Way
Colchester CO4 136 D8
Romford RM3 314 E2
Juno Mews CO2 135 C1
Jupes Hill CO7 85 C4
Jupe's Hill CO6 79 D1
Jupiter Cl CB9 9 D6
Jupiter Rd IP4 18 B7
Jury St 5 DA11 379 B1
Justinian Cl CB9 9 D6
Jutland Ct CO10 33 F7
Jutsums Ave RM7 335 B5
Jutsums Ct RM7 335 B5
Jutsums La RM7 335 B5
Juvina Cl 3 CM8 211 F7

K

Kale Croft CO3 134 D5
Kale Rd SS7 344 E4
Kamerwyk Ave SS8 364 C4
Kandlewood CM13 295 B2
Kangels The CB11 40 D2
Karen Cl Brentwood CM15 294 C2
Rainham RM13 354 E3
South Benfleet SS7 363 E8
Stanford-le-H SS17 360 C1
Wickford SS12 321 C6
Karen Terr IG2 333 D6
Karina Cl IG7 311 E5
Kate Daniels Ho CO16 140 F1
Katella Trad Est IG11 352 E2
Katemon Ct SG12 197 D4
Kate's La CB10 24 C8
Katherine Cl SS6 324 A1
Katherine Gdns IG6 311 C3
Katherine Rd SS13 343 E7
KATHERINES 222 F5
Katherine Semar Inf Sch CB11 43 E6
Katherine Semar Jun Sch CB11 43 E6
Katherines Hatch CM19 223 A6
Katherines Ho CM19 223 A6
Katherines Prim Sch CM19 223 A6
Katherine's Way CM19 223 A6
Kathleen Cl SS17 360 E4
Kathleen Dr SS9 346 F2
Kathleen Ferrier Cres SS15 341 D8
Kathryn Ct SS3 368 E7
Katonia Ave CM3 260 F1
Kavanaghs CM14 316 B7
Kavanaghs Rd CM14 316 B7
Kavanaghs Terr CM14 316 B7
Kay Cl CM3 181 A7
Kayla Ct 6 CO3 135 E6
Keable Rd CO6 132 E3
Keary Rd DA10 377 F1
Keating Cl CO11 86 B4
Keats Ave Braintree CM7 154 F8
Romford RM3 314 B3
Keats Cl Chigwell IG7 311 C4
Maldon CM9 259 A8
Wanstead E11 332 B6
Keats Gdns RM18 379 B5
Keats Rd Belvedere DA17 369 C3
Colchester CO3 134 F6
Keats Sq CM3 301 E6
Keats Way SS12 321 C7
Keats Wlk
Brentwood CM13 295 D2
Rayleigh SS6 324 A2
Kebbles CO10 2 B6
Keble Cl CO3 135 D6
Kecksy's CM21 172 F4
Kedington Hill CO10 34 B2
Keeble Cl CO5 186 E5
Keeble Ct CO7 166 E7
Keeble Pk CM9 258 F8
Keeble's Yd 7 CB9 9 A8
Keeble Way CM7 128 A3
Keefield CM19 223 B3
Keegan Pl SS8 364 C4
Keelan Ct IG1 333 B1
Keelars La CO7 137 E2
Keel Cl IG11 353 C3
Keelers Way CO6 109 B7
Keelings La CM0 285 E8
Keelings Rd CM0 285 F8
Keene Cl CO5 218 D7
Keene Way CM2 254 B3
Keepers Gn CO4 109 B3
Keep The 3 CB9 8 E7
Keer Ave SS8 364 D2
KEERES GREEN 176 D1
Keighley Mews SS3 349 D2
Keighley Rd RM3 314 E3
Keir Hardie Ho
6 Belvedere DA17 369 A3
Grays RM16 373 D5
Keir Hardie Way IG11 353 A5
Keith Ave SS11 299 D2
Keith Cl CO15 196 B8
Keith Rd IG11 352 D3
Keith Way
Hornchurch RM11 336 E4
Southend-on-S SS2 347 E5
Kelburn Way RM13 355 A2
Kellington Rd SS8 364 C5
Kelly Ho RM15 371 C5
Kelly Rd Basildon SS13 343 E6
Ipswich IP2 16 E5
Kelly Way RM6 334 E5
Kelsie Way IG6 311 E4
Kelso Cl
Great Horkesley CO6 109 C6
Rayleigh SS6 323 C6
Kelso Lodge E18 310 B1
Kelston Rd IG6 311 B1
KELVEDON 158 D2
Kelvedon Cl
Billericay CM11 297 C2
Brentwood CM13 295 E3
Chelmsford CM1 232 A6
Rayleigh SS6 323 A3
Kelvedon Dr IP4 18 F5
Kelvedon Gn CM15 271 F2
Kelvedon Hall La
Kelvedon Hatch CM14 271 B4
Tiptree CO5 185 E5
KELVEDON HATCH 271 E2
Kelvedon Hatch Com Prim Sch CM15 271 E2
Kelvedon Hatch Nuclear Bunker* CM14 271 C4
Kelvedon Ho IG9 288 E2
Kelvedon Rd
Billericay CM11 297 C2
Coggeshall CO6 158 A8
Kelvedon CO5 158 F2
Messing CO5 159 C2
Tiptree CO5 186 B7
Tolleshunt D'arcy CM9 215 C6
Wickham Bishops CM8 212 F5
Kelvedon St Mary's CE Prim Sch CO5 158 C2
Kelvedon Sta CO5 158 C3
Kelvedon Way IG8 310 F4
Kelvedon Wlk RM13 354 F4
Kelvin Ct CO13 170 F3
Kelvin Ho 3 DA17 369 A3
Kelvin Rd
South Benfleet SS7 344 D7
Tilbury RM18 379 A5
Kelvinside SS17 360 E4
Kemball St IP4 18 A5
Kembles SS6 323 E4
Kempe Rd CM7 72 D6
Kemp Ho E6 352 A6
Kempley Ct RM17 378 D8
Kemp Rd RM8 334 D3
Kempson Dr CO10 34 C5
Kempsters The IP11 381 B7
Kempton Ave RM12 336 F1
Kempton Cl SS7 345 B7
Kempton Pk CO16 168 B5
Kempton Rd E6 352 A4
Kemsley Cl DA9 377 B1
Kemsley Rd
Earls Colne CO6 105 A6
Felixstowe IP11 381 D5
Ken Cooke Ct 4 CO1 135 F7
Kendal RM19 371 C1
Kendal Ave Barking IG11 352 E4
Epping CM16 268 A8
Kendal Cl Hullbridge SS5 301 E1
Rayleigh SS6 323 E2
Woodford IG8 309 F8
Kendal Croft RM12 355 A7
Kendal Ct 9 Chingford E4 287 C1
Wickford SS11 322 A5
Kendale RM16 374 B3
Kendall CE Prim Sch CO1 136 C4
Kendall Rd CO1 136 A6
Kendall's Almshouses 3 CO1 136 A6
Kendall Terr CO1 136 A6
Kendal Rd EN9 265 C4
Kendal Way SS9 346 E7
Kendon Cl E11 332 B6
Kenholme SS9 346 E4
Kenilworth Ave
Chingford E17 309 A1
Romford RM3 315 B4
Kenilworth Cl CM12 296 E2
Kenilworth Ct
7 Chingford E4 309 C8
8 Dartford DA2 376 B1
Kenilworth Gdns
Hornchurch RM12 336 D1
Ilford IG3 333 F2
Loughton IG10 288 F3
Rayleigh SS6 323 C3
Southend-on-S SS0, SS9 347 A3
Kenilworth Gr CO16 142 A2
Kenilworth Pl SS15 319 E1
Kenilworth Rd CO15 196 E6
Kenley Cl SS11 322 B6
Kenley Gdns RM12 336 F2
Kenmar Cl SS6 346 A8
Kenmore Cl SS8 364 E2
Kennedy Ave SS15 340 F6
Kennedy Cl Ipswich IP4 18 A6
Rayleigh SS6 346 A8
South Benfleet SS7 344 B7
Kennedy Rd IG11 352 E4
Kennedy Way CO15 196 A5
Kennel La CM12, CM11 319 C7
Kennels The CO6 104 F6
Kennet Cl RM14 337 E5
Kennet Gn RM15 372 B6
Kenneth Ave IG1 352 B8
Kenneth Chambers Ct IG8 310 E4
Kenneth Gdns SS17 360 F5
Kenneth More Rd 4 IG1 333 B1
Kenneth Rd Basildon SS13 343 C7

Mill Cotts *continued*
Great Baddow CM2 255 C8
Mill Crn CM19 198 A1
Millcroft CM23 119 A1
Millcroft Mews CO5 218 C7
Mill Cswy SG8 19 C5
Mill Ct Braintree CM7 128 B2
Harlow CM20 199 D3
St Osyth CO16 193 F4
Takeley CM6 149 B7
Milldene Prim Sch CO5 186 D6
MILL END Gt Dunmow CM6 123 B4
Tillingham CM0 263 E8
Mill End CM6 70 A2
MILLEND GREEN 97 B1
Millennium Way CM7 155 D8
Millennium Wlk CM14 316 D8
Miller Ave EN3 265 A1
Miller Cl RM5 313 A3
Miller Ct RM2 336 A8
Miller's Barn Rd CO15 195 A1
Millers Cl
Bishop's Stortford CM23 145 C5
Braintree CM7 128 A8
Chigwell IG7 312 B8
Colchester CO3 134 C6
Great Horkesley CO6 109 B7
Miller's Cl CM6 151 A4
Millers Croft
Great Baddow CM2 254 F6
Great Dunmow CM6 123 E1
Millersdale CM19 223 B4
Millers Dr CM77 154 C7
MILLER'S GREEN 228 C4
Millers Green Rd CM5 228 B3
Millers Ho The SG12 197 D4
Millers La Colchester CO3 134 D6
Stanstead Abbotts SG12 197 C4
Miller's La IG7 290 B1
Millers Mead CO5 158 E4
Millers Mews 3 CM4 274 C4
Millers Reach CO11 87 A4
Millers Row CM7 48 C6
Millers View IP1 16 F7
Millfield
Burnham-on-C CM0 306 B4
High Ongar CM5 249 D3
Mill Field Barnston CM6 151 A4
Chelmondiston IP9 63 E8
Harlow CM17 200 C4
Millfield Cl SS6 323 E3
Millfield Gdns IP4 18 A6
Millfields Danbury CM3 257 A6
Sawbridgeworth CM21 172 F3
Stansted Mountfitchet CM24 119 E6
Tiptree CO5 186 C6
Writtle CM1 231 A1
Millfields Prim Sch CO7 137 D1
Millfields Way CB9 9 B8
Mill Gn Basildon SS13 343 A7
Burnham-on-C CM0 306 B4
Mill Gr CM5 249 D4
Mill Grange CM0 306 B7
MILL GREEN Haverhill 7 D7
Ingatestone CM4 273 F7
Little Bentley 140 A8
Mill Green Ct SS13 343 B7
Mill Green Pl SS13 343 B7
Mill Green Rd CM4 273 F7
Mill Hatch CM20 200 A4
Millhaven Cl RM6 334 B5
Millhead Way SS4 326 B1
Mill Hill Braintree CM7 128 B2
Chelmsford CM2 253 F2
Farnham CM23 118 E5
Harwich CO12 91 C3
Haverhill CB9 9 A7
Lawford CO11 85 D4
Manningtree CO11 86 C4
Purleigh CM3 258 C1
Shenfield CM15 294 F2
South Benfleet SS7 363 E8
Stansted Mountfitchet CM24 119 E6
Sudbury CO10 33 D7
Wormingford CO6 80 E6
Mill Hill Dr CM12 297 B5
Mill Ho 7 Rochford SS4 325 F2
Woodford IG8 309 F5
Millhoo Ct EN9 265 F5
Mill House Cotts CO12 116 D4
Millhouse Inf Sch SS15 341 C8
Millhouse Jun Sch SS15 341 C8
Millhouse Villas CM6 151 A4
Millhurst Mews CM17 200 E4
Millicent Preston Ho 4
IG11 352 D4
Milligans Chase CM2 254 B1
Milliners Way CM23 145 C4
Mill La Ardleigh CO7 112 B4
Birch CO2 161 A3
Bradfield CO11 87 D2
Brent Pelham SG9 64 A5
Broomfield CM1 208 C1
Cavendish CO10 13 B8
Chelmondiston IP9 63 F7
Clavering CB11 65 B6
Coggeshall CO5 131 F1
Colne Engaine CO6 105 B8
Corringham SS17 361 C7
Cressing CM77 155 D5
Dagenham RM6 334 E5
Danbury CM3 257 A6
Dedham CO7 84 F7
Felixstowe IP11 381 C4
Finchingfield CM7 48 F3
Fobbing SS17 361 C6
Ford End CM3 179 D7
Grays RM16 372 D1
Great Dunmow CM6 123 D1
Great Holland CO13 169 E3
Great Leighs CM3 181 B7
Great Leighs CM77 154 C1
Great Maplestead CO9 76 E8
Great Yeldham CO9 30 A3
Harlow CM17 200 E4
Harwich CO12 91 D3
Hatfield Heath CM22 173 F3
High Ongar CM5 249 D2
Hinxton CB10 3 A7
Hoddesdon EN10 221 A2
Horndon on t H SS17 359 F3
Mill La *continued*
Ickleton CB10 3 B4
Ingatestone CM4 274 A6
Kelvedon Hatch CM15 271 E2
Layer de la H CO2 162 B5
Little Baddow CM3 234 E3
Littlebury CB11 21 F4
Maldon CM9 237 A3
Manningtree CO11 86 D4
Moreton CM5 226 C5
Navestock Heath RM4 292 B8
Orsett RM16 374 A7
Pebmarsh CO9 78 A7
Purleigh CM3 258 C1
Ramsden Heath CM11 298 B5
Rayne CM7 153 E8
Rochford SS4 326 B2
Saffron Walden CB10 22 F2
Salcott-c-V CM9 216 B8
Sawbridgeworth CM21 172 F3
Sewardstone E4 287 B6
Stebbing CM6 124 E5
Stock CM4 275 F2
Stoke-by-N CO6 56 D7
Sudbury CO10 33 D7
Terling CM3 182 A3
Thorington Street CO6 57 C4
Thorpe-le-S CO16 141 F1
Tolleshunt Major CM9 214 E3
Toot Hill CM5 247 E2
Walton-on-t-N CO14 171 C8
Washbrook IP8 16 A1
Weeley Heath CO16 168 A6
Witham CM8 183 F1
Woodford IG8 309 F5
Wyatts Green CM15 272 D4
Mill Lane Cl CO16 168 A6
Mill Lodge SS3 368 E6
Millom Ho 1 RM3 314 D4
Mill on the Green CO7 166 E8
Mill Park Ave RM12 336 E2
Mill Park Dr CM7 128 B1
Mill Race SG12 197 D4
Mill Rd Aveley RM15 371 C6
Billericay CM11 319 D6
Birdbrook CO9 10 E2
Boxted CO4 82 F4
Burnham-on-C CM0 306 C7
Clare CO10 12 C7
Colchester CO4 109 F4
Debden CB11 68 B8
East Bergholt CO7 59 E2
Elder Street CB10 45 B3
Felsted CM6 152 A4
Finchingfield CM7 72 D5
Fordham CO6 107 D4
Foxearth CO10 14 C5
Great Bardfield CM7 72 B2
Great Totham CM9 213 D7
Haverhill CB9 9 A7
Helions Bumpstead CB9 26 C8
Henham CM22 94 E4
Ilford IG1 333 A1
Maldon CM9 237 B2
Margaret Roding CM1 205 D5
Marks Tey CO6 133 C4
Mayland CM3 283 B8
North End CM6 151 F2
Ridgewell CO9 29 B6
Stambourne CO9 28 C3
Stock CM4 275 F2
Tillingham CM0 263 E4
West Mersea CO5 218 D7
Mill Rise IP9 62 D5
Mill Road Cotts CB10 45 B3
Mill Road Dr IP3 18 C1
Mill Side CM24 119 E6
Millside Ind Est CM23 146 A5
Mills La CO10 15 C4
Millsmead Way IG10 288 F7
Millson Bank CM2 233 A4
Mills Rd CO10 34 A8
Mill St
Bishop's Stortford CM23 146 A5
Brightlingsea CO7 193 A6
Colchester CO1 136 A6
Harlow CM17 224 F5
Nayland CO6 56 B1
Stoke-by-N CO6 56 D8
St Osyth CO16 193 F4
Mills The IP4 18 E8
MILL STREET 56 D8
Mill Tye CO10 34 A4
Mill Vale Lo CM8 183 F2
Mill View Bradwell CM77 129 D3
Great Chesterford CB10 3 C2
Orsett RM16 373 E7
Mill View Ct CM1 230 A5
Millview Mdws SS4 325 F1
Mill Vue Rd CM2 232 F2
Millways CM9 213 B4
Millwell Cres IG7 311 B5
Mill Wlk CO5 186 C6
Millwrights CO5 186 C6
Milner Ct 4 E18 310 A2
Milner Pl CM12 296 F5
Milner Rd Dagenham RM8 334 C2
Sudbury CO10 34 B8
Milner St IP4 17 E5
Milnrow IP2 16 C2
MILTON 379 D1
Milton Ave Basildon SS16 340 F4
Braintree CM7 155 A8
Hornchurch RM12 335 F2
Southend-on-S SS0 366 E7
Milton Cl Colchester CO3 134 F6
Rayleigh SS6 324 A2
Southend-on-S SS2 348 A1
Milton Cres
Chipping Ongar CM5 248 F5
Ilford IG2 333 C5
Milton Ct Dagenham RM6 334 C4
Holland-on-S CO15 196 E6
Southend-on-S SS0 366 E7
Waltham Abbey EN9 265 C5
Milton Gdns RM18 379 B6
Milton Hall Cl SS3 350 A3
Milton Hall Prim Sch SS0 366 E8
Milton Pl Chelmsford CM1 232 A5
Gravesend DA12 379 C1
Milton Pl *continued*
Southend-on-S SS1 366 F7
Milton Rd Belvedere DA17 369 A2
Brentwood CM14 316 C6
Corringham SS17 360 F6
Gravesend DA12 379 C1
Grays RM17 373 B1
Harwich CO12 91 D4
Lawford CO11 86 B2
Maldon CM9 259 A8
Romford RM1 336 A5
Southend-on-S SS0 366 E8
Swanscombe DA10 377 E1
Witham CM8 183 F5
Milton St Ipswich IP4 18 B6
Southend-on-S SS2 348 A1
Swanscombe DA10 377 D1
Waltham Abbey EN9 265 C5
Miltsin Ave SS8 364 C5
Milverton Gdns IG3 333 F2
Milwards CM19 223 B4
Milwards Prim Sch CM19 223 B4
Mimosa Cl Basildon SS16 340 F4
Chelmsford CM1 232 F6
Pilgrims Hatch CM15 294 B4
Romford RM3 314 C3
Mimosa Ct CO4 136 E8
Minchen Rd CM20 200 A1
Minden Rd CO10 33 F7
Minehead Ho 6 RM3 314 E5
Minerva Cl Harwich CO12 90 F1
Haverhill CB9 9 D6
Minerva End CO2 135 C1
Minerva Rd E4 309 B3
MINNOW END 208 A6
Minos Way IP1 16 D8
Minsmere Dr CO16 195 C6
Minsmere Rd IP3 38 D8
Minsmere Way CO10 34 C6
Minster Cl SS6 324 A1
Minster Ct RM11 337 A3
Minster Rd SS15 341 C6
Minster Way
Hornchurch RM11 337 A3
Maldon CM9 258 E8
Minters Cotts CO11 115 C5
Minton Hts SS4 325 C6
Minton La CM17 224 C8
Miramar Ave SS8 363 E3
Miramar Way RM12 355 D7
Miranda Ho 6 DA17 369 A1
Miranda Wlk CO4 136 E7
Mirosa Dr CM9 237 B1
Mirosa Reach CM9 259 A8
Mirravale Ct 7 IG9 310 C8
Mirravale Trad Est RM6 334 E4
Mirror Stps 1 SS1 367 C7
Mission La CO7 60 B3
Mistleigh Ct CM15 294 F2
MISTLEY 86 F4
Mistley End SS16 342 C5
MISTLEY HEATH 87 B2
Mistley Norman CE Prim Sch
CO11 87 A4
Mistley Path SS16 342 C5
Mistley Place Park* CO11 86 E4
Mistley Rd CM20 200 A2
Mistley Side SS16 342 C5
Mistley Sta CO11 86 F4
Mistley Thorn IG1 333 A4
Mistley Towers* CO11 86 F5
Mistral Ct E4 309 B7
Mitchell Ave CO9 76 E1
Mitchell Circ CM7 73 C6
Mitchell Cl Erith DA17 369 C3
Rainham RM13 355 C3
Mitchells Ave SS8 364 D4
Mitchells Wlk SS8 364 D4
Mitchell Way CM3 301 D8
Mitre Bldgs 3 CM20 199 C1
Mitre Ct Belvedere DA17 369 A2
1 Dagenham RM6 334 B4
9 Woodford E18 310 A2
Mitre Gdns CM23 146 A4
Mitre Ho RM7 335 B7
Mitre Way IP3 17 F4
Mitton Vale CM2 232 F2
Moat Cl
Doddinghurst CM15 272 C3
Ramsden Heath CM11 298 C3
Moat Edge Gdns CM12 297 A4
Moat End SS1 349 B1
Moat Farm CO9 28 B7
Moat Farm Chase CM8 183 F3
Moat Farm Cl IP4 17 F8
Moat Field SS14 342 C8
Moat Fields CO6 107 D6
Moat Ho CM19 222 E7
Moat La CO8 55 A4
Moat Lodge Ho 2 SS14 342 C7
Moat Rd Birdbrook CO9 28 C7
Fordham CO6 107 D6
Moat Rise SS6 323 D1
Moat The CM5 247 F2
Moat Wlk CB9 8 E8
Moby Dick RM6 334 F7
Modlen Rd CO14 171 B7
Moffat Ave IP4 18 B8
Mole Hall La CB11 67 F3
Mole Hall Wildlife Pk*
CB11 67 F3
MOLEHILL GREEN
Elsenham 121 D6
Great Notley 153 C4
Molehill Green Cotts
CM22 121 C6
Molehill Green Rdbt
CM22 121 C5
Molesworth EN11 197 A2
Mollands SS16 342 F4
Mollands Ct RM15 357 E1
Mollands La RM15 357 D1
Mollison Ave EN3 265 A3
Molrams La CM2 255 B6
Molyneaux Ct CM12 297 A3
Momples Rd CM20 200 B1
Monarch Cl Haverhill CB9 8 C8
Rainham RM13 355 A3
Tilbury RM18 379 B5
Monarch Pl IG9 310 C8
Monarch Rd DA17 369 A3
Monarch Way Ilford IG2 333 D5
Ipswich IP8 36 D8
Monastery Rd SS15 341 C6
Monkchester Cl IG10 289 A8
Monkdowns Rd CO6 131 B3
Monken Hadley CM7 128 B8
Monkham's Ave IG8 310 B5
Monkham's Dr IG8 310 B5
Monkhams Hall EN9 243 C2
Monkham's La IG8 310 B6
Monklands Ct 2 CO9 76 D1
Monksbury CM18 224 A5
Monks Chase CM13 317 C5
Monks Cl EN10 221 A3
Monk's Cnr CB10 47 B4
Monks Ct CM8 183 E3
Monksford Dr SS5 301 D1
Monks Gate IP8 16 A6
Monksgrove IG10 289 A4
Monks Haven SS17 360 E2
Monks Hill CB11 43 F8
Monkside SS14 342 D7
Monk's La CO7 84 D4
Monks Lodge Rd CO9 52 D2
Monks Mead CM3 256 F2
Monks Rd CO6 105 B7
MONK STREET 97 B6
Monks Well DA9 377 C3
Monk's Well 1 DA9 377 C3
Monkswick Rd CM20 199 F1
Monks Wlk CM9 240 E8
Monkswood Ave EN9 265 D6
Monkswood Dr CM23 145 D6
Monkswood Gdns IG5 333 A8
Monkwick Ave CO2 135 F1
Monkwick Jun & Inf Schs
CO2 136 A2
Monkwood Cl RM1 336 A6
Monmouth Ave E18 332 B8
Monmouth Cl IP2 17 B1
Monmouth Mews SS16 340 F5
Monmouth Rd RM9 353 F7
Monnow Gn RM15 371 C6
Monnow Rd RM15 371 C6
Monoux Cl CM11 297 D1
Monoux Gr E17 309 A2
Mons Ave CM11 297 D2
Mons Rd CO2 135 D4
Montague Ave SS9 346 D2
Montague Bldgs 2 SS1 367 B8
Montague Ct SS0 366 D8
Montague Ho 13 IG8 311 A3
Montague Pl SS8 363 E3
Montague Rd IP11 381 F4
Montague Way CM12 297 A4
Montagu Gdns CM1 232 F7
Montalt Ho IG8 309 F6
Montalt Rd IG8 309 F5
Montbazon Ct CM14 294 B1
Montbretia Cl CO3 134 D6
Montbretia Ct CO16 195 C4
Monteagle Ave IG11 352 C6
Monteagle Ct IG11 352 C5
Monteagle Prim Sch RM9 353 B4
Montefiore Ave SS6 323 D8
Montfort Ave SS17 361 A3
Montfort Ct 8 CB9 8 F7
Montfort Gdns IG6 311 C4
Montgomerie Ct E4 287 D2
Montgomerie Inf Sch
SS7 344 B7
Montgomerie Jun Sch
SS7 344 B7
Montgomery Cl
Chelmsford CM1 232 E7
Colchester CO2 136 B4
Grays RM16 373 C4
Montgomery Cres RM3 314 D5
Montgomery Ct
2 Dagenham RM10 354 A6
Southend-on-S SS3 349 E1
Montgomery Jun & Inf Schs
CO2 135 D2
Montgomery Rd IP2 17 B1
Monton Rise IP2 16 D2
Montpelier Cl CM12 297 A5
Montpelier Ct 4 CM14 316 C7
Montpelier Gdns RM6 334 C4
Montpellier Ho IG7 311 C5
Montreal Rd Ilford IG1 333 C4
Tilbury RM18 379 A5
Montrose Ave RM2 314 C1
Montrose Cl IG8 310 A6
Montrose Ct IP3 17 F4
Montrose Ho IG2 333 A5
Montrose Rd CM2 233 A4
Montsale SS13 343 C8
Montserrat Ave IG8 309 D3
Moonhall Bsns Pk CB9 9 A5
Moon Hall La CB9 9 A6
Moons Cl SS4 325 D7
Moorcroft SS4 325 D6
Moorcroft Ave SS7 345 E6
Moore Ave Grays RM20 372 E1
Tilbury RM18 379 B5
Moore Cl CM11 297 D5
Moore Cres RM9 353 B4
Moore Ho RM11 336 A5
Moore Rd DA10 377 E1
Moores Ave SS17 342 C1
Moorescroft CM15 271 E2
Moore's Pl CM14 316 D8
Moore Twr CM18 223 F7
Moorfield Ct CM8 183 F1
Moorfields CM18 223 C4
Moor Hall La
Bishop's Stortford CM23 145 C3
Bishop's Stortford, Thorley
CM23 145 B3
Danbury CM3 256 E2
Moor Hall Rd CM17 201 A4
Moorhen Ave CM0 262 C8
Moorhen Way CM19 198 A1
Moorhouse Gn CO7 111 E8
Moorings The CM23 146 A5
Moor La RM14 337 F4
Moorland Cl RM5 313 B2
Moorlands Reach CM21 173 A1
Moor Park Cl SS9 346 C5
Moor Park Gdns SS9 346 C5
Moor Rd Great Tey CO6 132 C8
Langham CO4 83 D4
Moors Cl Feering CO5 158 E5
Great Bentley CO7 139 E1
Moors Croft CM7 128 D3
Moor's Farm Chase CM9 214 A3
Moorsfield CO10 34 B4
Moorside CO1 136 B7
Moors La
Little Dunmow CM6 151 D7
Rayne CM77 126 D3
Moor's La CO7 139 E1
Moors The CM6 151 D7
Mope La CM8 212 D6
Mopsies Rd SS14 342 E6
Moran Ave CM1 232 B7
Morant Gdns RM5 313 B5
Morant Rd Colchester CO1 136 B5
Grays RM16 374 B3
Moray Cl RM1 313 E3
Moray Way RM1 313 E3
Mordaunt Gdns RM9 353 E5
Morden Rd RM6 334 E4
Mordon Rd IG3 333 F4
Morebarn Rd CO7 112 E2
Morecambe Cl RM12 355 B7
Morecambe Ho 5 RM3 314 E5
Morecombe Ct IP4 18 A7
Moreland Ave SS7 344 C7
Moreland Cl
Great Wakering SS3 350 A4
South Benfleet SS7 344 C6
Moreland Rd SS11 299 C2
Morelands Ave RM16 373 C4
Moreland Way E4 309 C7
Morella Cl CO7 166 E8
Morello Ct CO2 163 A7
Moremead EN9 265 D6
Mores La CM14 293 D5
MORETON 226 C2
Moreton Bay Ind Est
RM2 314 D1
Moreton Bridge CM5 226 D1
Moreton CE Prim Sch
CM5 226 C3
Moreton Gates CM5 226 C2
Moreton Gdns IG8 310 E5
Moreton Rd
Chipping Ongar CM5 248 F7
Fyfield CM5 227 B2
Moreton CM5 248 B8
Moretons Basildon SS13 343 A6
Galleywood CM2 254 B2
Moretons Ct SS13 343 A6
Moretons Mews SS13 343 A6
Moretons Pl SS13 343 A6
Morgan Cl RM10 354 A5
Morgan Cres CM16 267 E3
Morgan Terr RM6 334 C6
Morgan Way
Rainham RM13 355 C2
Woodford IG8 310 E4
Morland Ct CO6 82 B1
Morland Prim Sch IP3 38 A8
Morland Rd
Dagenham RM10 354 A5
Ilford IG1 333 B2
Ipswich IP3 37 F8
Morley Ave E4 309 D3
Morley Gr CM20 199 C2
Morley Hill SS17 360 F5
Morley Link SS17 360 F5
Morley Rd Barking IG11 352 D4
Dagenham RM6 334 E6
Halstead CO9 76 F2
Tiptree CO5 186 D4
Morley Sq RM16 374 A2
Morleys Rd CO6 105 A6
Mornington Ave
Ilford IG1 333 A4
2 Ipswich IP1 17 A8
Rochford SS4 326 A2
Mornington Cl IG8 310 A6
Mornington Cres
Canvey Island SS8 364 C4
Hadleigh SS7 345 F3
Mornington Ho SS0 366 C8
Mornington Rd
Canvey Island SS8 364 C4
Chingford E4 287 D2
Loughton IG10 289 C6
Woodford IG8 309 F6
Morningtons CM19 223 C4
Morpeth Ho 8 RM3 314 D4
Morrab Gdns IG3 333 F1
Morrells SS16 341 F4
Morrin's Chase SS3 350 D3
Morrins Cl SS3 350 D3
Morris Ave Billericay CM11 297 D1
Clacton-on-S CO15 220 E8
Morris Ct Basildon SS15 341 B7
Chingford E4 309 B7
Holdbrook EN3 265 A2
Waltham Abbey EN9 265 F5
Morris Gdns DA1 376 A2
MORRIS GREEN 74 C8
Morris Harp CB10 22 E3
Morris Ho CM18 223 C5
Morrison Ave E4 309 A4
Morrison Dr CM8 211 F7
Morrison Ho RM16 373 D4
Morrison Rd IG11 353 E3
Morris Rd Chelmsford CM2 232 D2
Dagenham RM8 334 F2
Romford RM3 314 B3
Morrow La CO7 112 A6
Mors End CO7 58 D2
Morses La CO7 165 F1
Morten Rd CO1 135 E8
Mortimer Gdns CO4 110 B6
Mortimer Rd
Hatfield Peverel CM3 211 A4
Rayleigh SS6 323 E5
Mortimer Way CM8 211 E7
Mortlake Rd IG1 352 D8
Morton Rd CM9 213 A4
Morton Way CO9 77 A3
Mosbach Gdns CM13 317 B8
Moseley St SS2 348 D1
Moss Bank RM17 372 F2
Moss Cl SS16 342 E3
Mossdown Cl DA17 369 A2
Moss Dr SS16 342 E3
Mossfield Cl CO3 135 C6
Mossford Ct Ilford IG6 333 B8
Redbridge IG6 311 B1
Mossford Gn IG6 333 C8
Mossford Green Prim Sch
IG6 311 C1
Mossford La IG6 311 C1
Moss La Hornchurch RM11 336 A5
Romford RM1 335 F5
Moss Path CM2 254 C3
Moss Rd Colchester CO3 134 E4
Dagenham RM10 354 A5
South Ockendon RM15 372 C8
Witham CM8 184 B3
Moss Way CO6 108 E3
Moss Wlk CM2 254 B6
Motehill SS16 341 C4
Motherwell Way RM20 372 A1
Mottram Cl 9 IP2 16 C2
Motts Cl CM7 127 E4
MOTT'S GREEN 173 D6
Motts La CM8 184 B4
Mott's La CO6 132 D4
Mott St High Beach IG10 288 A8
Sewardstone IG10 287 E8
Motts Yd CM6 124 E5
Moules La CB1 5 C6
MOULSHAM 254 A8
Moulsham Chase CM2 254 C8
Moulsham Dr CM2 254 B8
Moulsham Hall La
Braintree CM3 153 F2
Great Leighs CM3 154 A1
Moulsham High Sch CM2 254 B7
Moulsham Jun & Inf Schs
CM2 254 B7
Moulsham St
Chelmsford CM1 232 B2
Chelmsford, Moulsham CM2 232 B1
Moulsham Thrift CM2 254 A6
Moulton Cl CO10 33 F8
Moultrie Way RM14 337 E5
Mountain Ash Ave SS9 346 B6
Mountain Ash Cl
Colchester CO4 110 C2
Southend-on-S SS9 346 B6
Mountain's Farm Rd CM6 150 C3
Mountains Rd CM8, CM9 213 C7
Mount Ave
Brentwood CM13 295 B2
Chingford E4 309 B7
Hockley SS5 324 E7
Rayleigh SS6 323 C3
Romford RM3 315 C4
Southend-on-S SS0 366 A8
Mountbatten Cl CO10 15 F2
Mountbatten Ct
Braintree CM7 128 B4
Buckhurst Hill IG9 310 D8
7 Ipswich IP1 17 A7
Mountbatten Dr
Colchester CO2 136 B4
Southend-on-S SS3 349 E1
Mountbatten Ho 4 RM2 336 C7
Mountbatten Rd
Braintree CM7 128 C4
Sudbury CO10 15 F2
Mountbatten Way CM1 232 E7
Mount Bovers La SS5 324 E3
MOUNT BURES 79 F5
Mount Cl Rayleigh SS6 323 C2
Wickford SS11 321 E8
Mount Cres
Brentwood CM14 316 D6
Hockley SS5 324 D6
South Benfleet SS7 344 E4
Moundale Gdns SS9 346 F4
Mount Dr Ipswich IP3 18 F1
Stansted Mountfitchet CM24 119 E5
Mount Echo Ave E4 287 B1
Mount Echo Dr E4 287 B1
MOUNT END 268 F7
Mountfield Cl SS17 360 E3
Mountfield Rd E6 352 A2
Mountfields SS13 343 C4
Mountfitchet Castle & Norman
Village* CM24 119 F6
Mountfitchet Mathematics &
Computing Coll The
CM24 119 F4
Mountfitchet Rd CM24 119 E5
Mount Hill CO9 76 D1
Mounthill Ave CM2 232 D3
Moutier Ct 12 E11 332 A6
Mount Lodge Chase CM9 213 E6
MOUNTNESSING 295 D8
Mountnessing SS7 345 D2
Mountnessing CE Prim Sch
CM15 295 E7
Mountnessing La CM15 272 E1
Mountnessing Rd
Billericay CM12 296 E4
Blackmore CM4 272 F6
Mountnessing CM15, CM4 273 A4
Mountney Cl CM4 273 F1
Mount Pleasant
Great Totham CM9 213 E6
Halstead CO9 76 E1
Ilford IG1 352 C7
Maldon CM9 236 F2
Mount Pleasant Ave
CM13 295 E4
Mount Pleasant Cotts
Brentwood CM15 295 A4
Saffron Walden CB11 43 D8
Mount Pleasant Rd
Chigwell IG7 311 D6
Romford RM5 313 D4
Saffron Walden CB11 43 E8
South Woodham Ferrers
CM3 301 D7
Mount Rd Braintree CM7 128 A3
Coggeshall CO6 131 B2
Dagenham RM8 334 F3
Epping CM16 268 E6
Haverhill CB9 9 B7

Norfolk Ave
Clacton-on-S CO15 196 E7
Southend-on-S SS9 346 F3
West Mersea CO5 218 D7
Norfolk Cl Basildon SS15 341 A6
Canvey Island SS8 364 A5
Dartford DA1 376 A1
Maldon CM9 236 E1
Norfolk Cres CO4 110 B1
Norfolk Ct 4 Ilford RM6 334 B6
Rochford SS4 325 D5
Norfolk Dr CM1 232 A7
Norfolk Gdns CM7 128 B4
Norfolk Ho
5 Gravesend DA12 379 D1
Romford RM7 313 A2
Norfolk Pl RM16 372 C1
Norfolk Rd Barking IG11 352 E5
Dagenham RM10 354 B7
Gravesend DA12 379 E1
Ilford IG3 333 E4
Ipswich IP4 17 D6
Maldon CM9 236 E1
Romford RM7 335 C5
Upminster RM14 337 A2
Wallend E6 352 A4
Norfolk Way
Bishop's Stortford CM23 145 F5
Canvey Island SS8 363 F5
Norham Ct 16 DA2 376 B1
Norman Ave CM23 145 D6
Norman Cl Marks Tey CO6 132 E3
Romford RM5 313 B1
St Osyth CO16 194 A4
Waltham Abbey EN9 265 D6
Norman Cres
Brentwood CM13 317 A7
Ipswich IP3 18 A2
Rayleigh SS6 323 E5
Norman Ct Ilford IG1 333 D4
Stansted Mountfitchet CM24 119 E7
Woodford IG8 310 B5
Normandie Way CO8 79 E8
Normandy Ave
Burnham-on-C CM0 306 C5
Colchester CO2 136 A3
Normandy Way EN11 221 D8
Norman Hill CM3 182 B2
Normanhurst CM13 295 C3
Normanhurst Sch E4 287 D2
Norman Pl SS9 365 E8
Norman Rd
Belvedere DA17 369 B3
Clacton-on-S CO15 196 E6
Hornchurch RM11 336 B4
Ilford IG1 352 B7
Manningtree CO11 86 D4
Normansfield CM6 150 E7
Normanshire Dr E4 309 B6
Normans Rd SS8 364 D4
Norman's Way CM24 119 E7
Norman Terr SS9 365 E8
Normanton Pk E4 309 E8
Norman Way
Colchester, Lexden CO3 135 B6
Colchester, Shrub End CO3 135 B4
Point Clear B CO16 192 F3
Norris Cl
Bishop's Stortford CM23 146 C7
Braintree CM7 128 C5
Norris La EN11 221 A7
Norris Rd EN11 221 A6
Norris Rise 4 EN11 221 A7
Norseman Cl 3 IG3 334 B3
Norsey Cl CM11 297 B3
Norsey Dr CM11 297 D3
Norsey Rd CM11 297 C4
Norsey View Dr CM12 297 B6
Norsey Wood Nature Reserve* CM11 297 D4
Northallerton Way 15 RM3 314 D5
Northampton Cl CM7 128 D5
Northampton Gr SS16 340 F4
Northampton Ho 4 RM3 314 E6
Northampton Mdw CM7 72 B2
North Ave
Canvey Island SS8 364 A3
Chelmsford CM1 231 F5
Haverhill CB9 8 E8
Southend-on-S SS2 348 C2
Northbank Rd E17 309 C1
North Barn EN10 221 B1
NORTH BENFLEET 343 F8
North Benfleet Hall Rd
Basildon SS12 322 A1
North Benfleet SS12 321 F1
North Boundary Rd E12 332 D2
Northbourne Rd CO15 195 F4
Northbrook Rd IG1 333 A2
Northbrooks CM19 223 C7
Northbury Jun & Inf Schs IG11 352 C6
North Circular Rd
Chingford E17 309 B2
Ilford IG1, E12 333 A1
Wallend E6, E12 352 A5
Wanstead IG1 332 D5
Woodford E18 310 C1
North Cl Dagenham RM10 354 A4
Ipswich IP4 17 E8
Redbridge IG7 312 A5
North Colne SS16 342 D4
North Court Rd CM1 208 A3
North Cres
Southend-on-S SS2 347 D5
Steeple Bumpstead CB9 27 B7
Wickford SS12 321 D7
North Crescent Prim Sch SS12 321 D7
North Crockerford SS16 342 E4
Northcroft CO10 33 E7
North Cross Rd IG6 333 C7
North Dell CM1 232 E7
North Dene IG7 311 D5
Northdown Gdns IG2 333 E6
Northdown Rd RM11 336 B4
North Dr Brentwood CM13 296 C2
Great Baddow CM2 254 F7
Mayland CM3 260 F1
Romford RM2 336 C8
NORTHEND
Saffron Walden CB11 22 A3
Southminster CM0 284 E5
NORTH END Felsted 151 F2
Great Yeldham 30 F3
Northend CM14 316 C5
North End
Buckhurst Hill IG9 288 C2
Romford RM3 314 C8
Southminster CM0 284 E5
North End Rd
Gestingthorpe CO9, CO10 31 C2
Hinxton CB10 3 B8
Little Yeldham CO9 30 E2
Northern App CO4 109 E3
Northern Ave SS7 344 C5
Northern Rd CO10 34 B8
Northern Relief Rd IG11 352 C5
Northfalls Rd SS8 364 F3
NORTH FAMBRIDGE 303 A8
North Fambridge Sta CM3 303 B8
Northfield
Great Bardfield CM7 72 B3
Loughton IG10 288 D5
Northfield Cl CM11 297 C2
Northfield Cres SS3 350 B4
Northfield Gdns
Colchester CO4 110 A4
Dagenham RM9 353 F8
Northfield Path RM9 353 F8
Northfield Rd
Dagenham RM9 353 F8
Saffron Walden CB11 43 E8
Sawbridgeworth CM21 172 E4
Northfields Grays RM17 373 D2
Stansted Mountfitchet CM24 119 E7
NORTHFLEET 378 C2
Northfleet Ind Est DA10 377 F3
Northfleet Sta DA11 378 B1
North Gate CM20 199 C1
Northgate End CM23 145 F8
Northgate Ind Pk RM5 312 F1
Northgate Prim Sch CM23 145 E8
Northgate St
Colchester CO1 135 F8
Ipswich IP1 17 C6
North Gr CM18 224 A7
North Hall Rd
Henham CM22 94 B7
Rickling Green CB11 67 A2
North Hill Colchester CO1 135 E7
Horndon on t H SS17 360 A3
Little Baddow CM3 234 D5
North Hill Bsns Pk SS17 359 F4
North Hill Dr RM3 314 D6
North Hill Gdns 1 IP4 17 E6
North Hill Gn RM3 314 D6
North Hill Rd IP4 17 E6
North Ho
Frinton-on-S CO13 170 F4
Harlow CM18 223 F6
North Kent Ave DA11 378 C1
North La CO6 133 B5
Northlands App SS16 341 C1
Northlands Cl SS17 360 E5
Northlands Farm Chase SS17 360 E7
Northlands Jun & Inf Sch SS13 343 B6
Northlands Pavement 3 SS13 343 B5
North Lawn IP4 18 C8
North Mill Pl CO9 76 E3
NORTH OCKENDON 357 B6
Northolme Cl RM16 373 C3
Northolt Ave CM23 119 B1
Northolt Way RM12 355 C7
North Pl Harlow CM20 200 B5
4 Waltham Abbey EN9 265 B6
North Prim Sch CO1 135 E8
North Rd
Belchamp Walter CO10 31 F6
Belvedere DA17 369 B4
Brightlingsea CO7 192 F7
Clacton-on-S CO15 195 F6
Crays Hill CM11 320 D5
Dagenham RM6 334 E6
Great Yeldham CO9 30 A2
Havering-atte-B RM4 291 F1
Hoddesdon EN11 221 A7
Ilford IG3 333 E2
Purfleet RM19 371 C2
Romford RM4 313 E7
Southend-on-S SS0 347 E1
South Ockendon RM15 357 D4
Takeley CM22 148 C8
Tollesbury CM9 216 C2
North Residence IG3 334 B6
North Rise CO10 34 A6
North Road Ave CM14 316 C8
North Sea View CO12 90 F2
North Service Rd 6 CM14 316 C8
NORTH SHOEBURY 349 F1
North Shoebury Rd SS3 349 D1
North St Barking IG11 352 C5
4 Bishop's Stortford CM23 145 F7
Great Dunmow CM6 123 D1
Great Wakering SS3 350 B4
Hornchurch RM11 336 D4
Lower Nazeing EN9 221 E1
Maldon CM9 237 B2
Manningtree CO11 86 D4
Rochford SS4 325 F2
Romford RM1 335 D7
Southend-on-S SS9 365 E8
Southminster CM0 284 D4
Steeple Bumpstead CB9 27 B7
Sudbury CO10 33 E8
Tillingham CM0 263 E4
Tolleshunt D'arcy CM9 215 E5
Walton-on-t-N CO14 171 C8
North Sta* SS1 367 A6
North Station Rd CO1 135 E8
NORTH STIFFORD 372 E5
North Street Par 1 CO10 33 E7
North Terr 5 CM23 145 F8
Northumberland Ave
Basildon SS15 341 C5
Northumberland Ave *continued*
Hornchurch RM11 336 C6
Southend-on-S SS1 367 D7
Wanstead E12 332 C3
Northumberland Cl CM7 128 B4
Northumberland Cres
SS1 367 D7
Northumberland Ct 1
CM2 232 F4
Northumberland Ho 11
IG8 311 A3
Northumberland Rd SS17 375 A4
Northview Ave RM18 379 A6
North View Cotts CO6 109 B7
North View Cvn Site IG6 312 A3
Northview Dr
Southend-on-S SS0 347 D2
Woodford IG8 310 D1
Northville Dr SS0 347 C4
North Wall CO16 193 A3
NORTH WEALD BASSETT 247 C5
North Weald Cl
Hornchurch RM12 355 C5
Wickford SS11 322 B6
North Weald Sta* CM16 247 B4
Northwick Park Prim Sch SS8 363 E4
Northwick Rd SS8 363 B4
Northwick Ret Pk SS8 363 B4
Northwood RM16 374 B4
Northwood Ave RM12 355 A8
Northwood Dr 2 DA9 377 A1
Northwood Gdns IG5 333 A7
Norton Ave SS8 364 E3
Norton Cl Chingford E4 309 A5
Corringham SS17 361 A3
Norton Ct IG2 333 E5
NORTON END 42 E4
NORTON HEATH 250 D5
Norton Heath Rd CM5 250 E8
Norton La High Ongar CM5 249 D5
High Ongar, Norton Mandeville CM4, CM5 250 C6
NORTON MANDEVILLE 249 F6
Norton Pl CM11 298 C5
Norton Rd Chelmsford CM1 232 A3
Dagenham RM10 354 D6
Haverhill CB9 8 E6
Ingatestone CM4 274 B4
Norway Cres CO12 90 F3
Norway Wlk RM13 355 C1
Norwich Ave SS2 348 C2
Norwich Cl
Clacton-on-S CO16 195 E6
Colchester CO1 136 A8
Southend-on-S SS2 348 C2
Norwich Cres Ilford RM6 334 B6
Rayleigh SS6 323 C5
Norwich Ct 2 IP1 17 A7
Norwich Ho SS4 325 D5
Norwich Mews IG3 334 A3
Norwich Rd IP1 17 A7
Norwich Wlk SS14 342 F7
Norwood Ave
Clacton-on-S CO15 196 B5
Romford RM7 335 E4
Norwood Ct DA1 376 A3
Norwood Dr SS7 344 E1
NORWOOD END 227 D5
Norwood End
Basildon SS14 342 D7
Fyfield CM5 227 D5
Norwood Way CO14 171 A7
NOSTERFIELD END 7 F5
Notcutts CO7 59 E1
Notley Gn CM77 154 B6
Notley Green Prim Sch CM77 154 C8
Notley High Sch CM7 154 F8
Notley Rd CM7 154 F8
Nottage Cl
Corringham SS17 360 F4
Wivenhoe CO7 164 C8
Nottage Cres CM7 127 E3
Nottidge Rd IP4 17 E6
Nottingham Rd CO15 196 E6
Nottingham Way SS16 340 F5
NOUNSLEY 211 B1
Nounsley Rd CM3 211 B1
Nounsley Terr CM3 211 B1
Nuneaton Rd RM9 353 E5
Nunnery St CO9 51 D4
Nunns Cl CO6 131 A2
Nunn's Rd CO1 135 E7
Nunns Way RM17 373 D2
Nun's Mdw CO9 102 E7
Nuns Wlk CO9 29 F1
Nunty's La
Greenstead Green CO9 104 A1
Pattiswick CM77 129 F8
NUPER'S HATCH 291 E2
Nursery Cl
Bishop's Stortford CM23 145 F6
Colchester CO3 134 C5
Ilford RM6 334 D5
Rayleigh SS6 323 D1
South Ockendon RM15 357 C1
Woodford IG8 310 B5
Nursery Dr CM7 128 A5
Nursery Fields CM21 172 D2
Nursery Gdns SS15 341 D8
Nursery La CM3 256 F8
Nursery Rd
Bishop's Stortford CM23 145 F6
Chelmsford CM2 254 B8
Great Cornard CO10 34 B5
Hoddesdon EN11 197 B1
Hook End CM15 272 C5
Loughton IG10 288 D5
Lower Nazeing EN9 221 D2
Stanford-le-H SS17 360 E3
Wanstead E12 332 E2
Nursery Rise CM6 150 D7
Nursery Wlk
Felixstowe IP11 381 D5
Romford RM7 335 D5
Nutberry Ave RM16 373 B4
Nutberry Cl RM16 373 A4
Nutbrowne Rd RM9 354 A4
Nutcombe Cres SS4 325 D4
Nutfield Gdns IG3 334 A2
NUTHAMPSTEAD 39 A2
Nuthatch Cl CM11 319 C8
Nutter La E11 332 C6
Nuxley Rd DA17 369 A1
Nyall Ct RM2 336 D8
Nyssa Cl IG8 310 F4
Nyth Cl RM14 337 D5

O

Oakapple Cl CO2 135 D1
Oak Ave Crays Hill CM11 320 C4
Jaywick CO16 195 A2
Upminster RM14 356 B8
Wickford SS11 322 C7
Oakbank CM13 295 E4
Oak Bglws CM7 127 E3
Oak Bsns Pk CO16 141 F8
Oak Chase SS12 321 A7
Oak Cl Clacton-on-S CO15 195 E6
Felixstowe IP11 381 C4
Maldon CM9 259 B8
Rushmere St A IP4 18 E7
Thorpe-le-S CO16 142 A1
Waltham Abbey EN9 265 D5
West Bergholt CO6 108 E4
Oak Cnr Beaumont CO16 141 F8
Woodham Mortimer CM9 257 D6
Oak Cotts CM3 233 E8
Oak Ct Chingford E4 309 B4
Hadleigh SS7 345 E2
South Ockendon RM15 357 C3
Oakdale Ct E4 309 C5
Oakdale Gdns E4 309 C5
Oakdale Inf Sch E18 310 B1
Oakdale Jun Sch E18 310 B1
Oakdale Rd E18 310 B1
Oakdene RM3 314 F1
Oak Dene Cl RM11 336 B5
Oakdene Rd SS13 343 C8
Oakdown Ho IG7 311 F5
Oak Dr CM21 200 C8
Oak Eggar Chase IP8 36 D8
Oak End CM18 223 F6
Oaken Grange Dr SS2 347 E5
Oak Fall CM8 184 A5
Oak Farm Rd CM9 235 E1
Oakfield Chingford E4 309 B5
Stebbing CM6 125 A4
Oakfield Cl SS7 344 C3
Oakfield Dr CO4 83 A5
Oakfield Ho 2 IG1 333 B1
Oakfield La CM3 182 A2
Oakfield Lodge 9 IG1 333 B1
Oakfield Prim Sch SS12 321 E5
Oakfield Rd Belstead IP8 36 A7
Ilford IG1 333 B1
Rochford SS4 303 A1
South Benfleet SS7 344 C3
Washbrook IP8 35 F6
Oakfields Chigwell IG7 311 C5
Loughton IG10 289 A4
Oakfield Wood Nature Reserve* CO11 88 D4
Oak Glade CM16 246 D2
Oak Glen RM11 336 E8
Oak Gn CM11 297 D1
Oak Gr IP8 16 A6
Oak Hall CM23 145 E8
Oakhall Ct E11 332 B5
Oak Hall Rd E11 332 B5
Oakham Cl SS16 340 F5
Oakham Ct SS9 346 E2
Oakhaven CO12 90 F1
Oak Hill Beazley End CM7 101 A8
Chingford IG8 309 E3
Wethersfield CM7 73 F1
Oak Hill Cl IG8 309 D3
Oak Hill Cres IG8 309 E3
Oak Hill Ct IG8 309 E3
Oak Hill Gdns IG8 309 F2
Oak Hill La IP2 17 B3
Oakhill Prim Sch IG8 309 E4
Oakhill Rd RM19 371 B1
Oak Hill Rd RM4 291 E1
Oak Ho Ipswich IP2 16 D2
Southend-on-S SS3 368 F8
Stutton IP9 61 F2
Oakhurst Cl Redbridge IG6 311 C2
Wickford SS12 321 C6
Oakhurst Dr SS12 321 C5
Oakhurst Gdns E4 287 F1
Oakhurst Rd Rayleigh SS6 345 F8
Southend-on-S SS2 348 A2
Oak Ind Pk CM6 150 F6
Oak La Crays Hill CM11 320 C3
Woodford IG8 309 F3
Oakland Farm Ind Est CM4 297 F6
Oakland Gdns CM13 295 C4
Oakland Pl IG9 310 A8
Oakland Rd CO12 91 C3
Oaklands Ave
Colchester CO3 134 E5
Romford RM1 335 F7
Oaklands Cl
Bishop's Stortford CM23 119 B2
Great Notley CM77 154 D8
Oaklands Cres CM2 254 B8
Oaklands Dr
Bishop's Stortford CM23 119 B2
Harlow CM17 224 C7
South Ockendon RM15 372 C8
Oaklands Inf Sch CM2 254 B8
Oaklands Mews SS4 325 C4
Oaklands Park Ave IG1 333 C2
Oaklands Pk
Bishop's Stortford CM23 119 B2
Brentwood CM15 295 B1
Oaklands Sch IG10 288 D4
Oaklands Way CM3 234 E2
Oaklea Ave CM2 232 E3
Oakleafe Gdns IG6 333 B8
Oaklee IP2 17 A1
Oakleigh Ave
Hullbridge SS5 301 E2
Southend-on-S SS1 367 D8
Oakleigh Ct CM23 145 D8
Oakleigh Lodge IG3 334 A1
Oakleigh Park Dr SS9 346 E1
Oakleigh Rd CO15 195 F8
Oakleigh Rise CM16 268 A7
Oakleighs SS7 344 C4
Oakley Ave Barking IG11 352 F5
Rayleigh SS6 322 F3
Oakley Cl Chingford E4 309 C7
Grays RM20 377 C8
Oakley Cross CO12 117 B7
Oakley Ct IG10 289 A7
Oakley Dr Billericay CM12 296 F5
Romford RM3 315 A5
Oakley Rd Braintree CM7 127 F7
Harwich CO12 90 D1
Wix CO11 115 E5
Oak Lodge E11 332 A4
Oak Lodge Ave IG7 311 D5
Oak Lodge Tye CM1 233 A6
Oak Manor View CM3 180 F7
Oakmead Rd CO16 193 B3
Oakmoor Way IG7 311 E5
Oak Piece CM16 247 C6
Oak Rd Canvey Island SS8 364 C3
Chappel CO6 106 B3
Crays Hill CM11 320 C4
Epping CM16 245 F1
Grays RM17 378 C8
Great Cornard CO10 34 B6
Greenhithe DA9 376 E1
Halstead CO9 103 D7
Heybridge CM9 237 B6
Little Maplestead CO9 77 A8
Pebmarsh CO9 77 F8
Ramsden Heath CM11 298 D5
Rivenhall CM8 184 C6
Rochford SS4 325 E2
Romford RM3 314 F2
Tiptree CO5 186 C7
Oak Rd N SS7 345 E2
Oak Rd S SS7 345 E2
Oak Ridge CO12 117 B7
Oak Rise IG9 310 D7
Oakroyd Ave CM6 150 E8
Oakroyd Ho CM6 150 E8
Oaks EN9 266 C4
Oaks Ave RM5 313 C1
Oaks Com Prim Sch The IP2 16 E3
Oaks Dr CO3 135 D7
Oaks End CO2 162 A5
Oaks Gr E4 309 E8
Oaks Hospl The CO4 109 E3
Oakside Ct Redbridge IG6 311 D1
Wanstead E11 332 A7
Oaks La IG2 333 E7
Oaksmere Gdns IP2 17 A2
Oaks Park High Sch IG2 333 E6
Oaks Pl CO4 109 E2
Oaks Ret Pk CM20 199 F3
Oak St
Bishop's Stortford CM23 145 F6
Romford RM7 335 C6
Oakstead Cl IP4 18 A6
Oaks The Billericay CM11 319 C6
Chingford IG8 309 E3
Dartford DA2 376 B1
Frinton-on-S CO13 170 F6
Oaktree Cl
14 Bishop's Stortford CM23 145 F7
Brentwood CM13 316 F7
Oak Tree Cl IG10 289 C8
Oak Tree Cotts CO6 133 B8
Oaktree Gdns CM17 224 D7
Oaktree Gr IG1 352 D7
Oak Tree Rd CO7 165 B8
Oaktrees CM9 214 B5
Oakview CO12 90 F1
Oakview Cl SS9 346 E3
Oak View Cvn Pk CM24 120 A4
Oak View Sch IG10 289 A6
Oakway RM16 373 C5
Oak Wlk Hockley SS5 324 E7
Sible Hedingham CO9 51 D2
South Benfleet SS7 344 B8
Southend-on-S SS9 346 D4
Oakwood EN9 265 E5
Oakwood Ave
Brentwood CM13 295 E3
Clacton-on-S CO15 196 E7
Southend-on-S SS9 346 E5
West Mersea CO5 218 D7
Oakwood Bsns Pk CO15 169 A1
Oakwood Chase RM11 336 F4
Oakwood Cl
Kirby Cross CO13 170 E6
South Benfleet SS7 344 B5
Woodford IG8 310 E4
Oakwood Ct Althorne CM3 283 A3
Chingford E4 287 E2
Romford RM2 336 C8
Southend-on-S SS9 346 E5
Oakwood Dr
Billericay CM12 297 C5
West Mersea CO5 218 D7
Oakwood Est CM20 200 B4
Oakwood Gdns Ilford IG3 333 F2
West Mersea CO5 218 D7
Oakwood Gr SS13 343 B6
Oakwood Hill IG10 289 B4
Oakwood Hill Ind Est IG10 289 B4
Oakwood Ind Est DA11 378 A2
Oakwood Inf Sch CO15 195 D2
OakWood Mews 5 CM17 200 C4
Oakwood Rd
Corringham SS17 361 B3
Rayleigh SS6 323 C4
Oakwood Villas SS9 346 C7
Oak Yd CO9 76 E2
Oasis Ct CM1 232 F5
Oast Ct 3 SS4 325 F2
Oasthouse Ct CB10 22 D1
Oast House Spinney CM7 127 F6
Oast Way SS4 325 F2
Oates Rd RM5 313 B5
Oatfield Cl CO3 134 D6
Oatlands CO7 137 F6
Oban Ct SS11 322 B5
Oban Ho 5 IG11 352 D3
Oban Rd SS2 348 C1
Oban St IP1 17 B7
Oberon Cl CO4 136 F7
Obrey Way CM23 145 E3
Observation Ct IP1 17 B5
Observer Way CO5 158 C4
Occasio Ho CM20 223 C8
Ocean View CO14 171 D8
Ockelford Ave CM1 231 F5
Ockendon Rd RM14 357 B7
Ockendon Sch The RM15 372 A8
Ockendon Sta RM15 357 B2
Ockendon Way CO14 171 A8
Octave Ho CM16 267 E3
Octavia Dr CM8 211 E7
Oddcroft CO6 77 F1
Odell Cl IG11 352 F5
Odeon The IG11 352 D5
Odessa Rd SS8 364 D3
Odin Lodge CM9 258 F8
O'Donoghue Ho SS17 360 E2
Office La CM9 214 A4
Ogard Rd EN11 221 C8
Ogilvie Ct SS12 321 E5
Oglethorpe Rd RM10 335 A1
Okehampton Rd RM3 314 C4
Okehampton Sq RM3 314 C4
Old Barn La CM3 277 F2
Old Barn Rd CO8 80 A6
Old Barns La CM4 251 C3
Old Bell Cl CM24 119 D6
Old Bell La CM3 278 B1
Old Brickworks The RM3 315 A3
Oldbury Ave CM2 254 F8
Oldbury Cotts SS3 349 D3
Old Burylodge La CM24 120 A4
Old Camps Castle CB21 7 E3
Old Cattle Market 5 IP4 17 C5
Oldchurch Gdns RM7 335 D4
Old Church Hill SS16 341 A1
Old Church La Bulmer CO10 32 F3
Bulmer Tye CO10 32 F2
Mountnessing CM13 296 B6
West Bergholt CO6 108 D5
Oldchurch Rd RM7 335 E4
Old Church Rd
Basildon SS13 343 F5
Chingford E4 309 A7
East Hanningfield CM3 278 B6
Oldchurch Rise RM7 335 E4
Old Clements La CB9 8 F7
Old Coach Rd CO1 136 B7
Old Coastguard Cotts
CM0 241 E4
Old College Ct DA17 369 B1
Old Convent The CO5 158 B1
Old Court Ho 2 CM24 119 E6
Old Court Rd CM2 232 D3
Old Croft Cl CM1 205 D5
Old Crown La CM14 293 D7
Old Ct Chelmsford CM2 232 D3
Long Melford CO10 15 D8
Olde Forge CO7 165 E1
Old Farm Ct CM12 297 A4
Old Farm Yd CM22 201 C8
Old Ferry Rd CO7 164 B8
Oldfield Rd IP8 16 B1
Oldfields CM14 316 C6
Old Forge CO7 137 C2
Old Forge Rd
Boreham CM3 233 E8
Layer de la H CO2 161 F5
Old Forge The SS6 323 C3
Old Foundry Rd IP4 17 D6
Old Hall Cl CB9 27 C7
Old Hall Ct SS3 350 A4
Old Hall La Capel St M IP9 35 F3
Tollesbury CM9 216 C5
Walton-on-t-N CO14 144 E3
Old Hall Rise CM17 224 E8
OLD HARLOW 200 D4
OLD HEATH 136 C3
Old Heath Com Prim Sch CO2 136 D3
Old Heath Rd
Colchester CO1, CO2 136 C4
Southminster CM3, CM0 284 A2
Old Highway EN11 221 C8
Old Hill Ave SS16 360 B8
Oldhouse Croft CM20 199 E2
Old House La Boxted CO4 83 B2
Lower Nazeing EN9 243 F8
Roydon CM19 222 E6
Old House Rd CO6 109 A8
Oldhouse Villas CM22 148 C8
Old Ipswich Rd CO7 110 E7
Old Jenkins Cl SS17 360 B1
Old Leigh Rd SS9 347 A1
Old Library The 15 CO11 86 D4
Old London Rd
Capel St M IP9 59 F7
Rawreth SS11 322 D6
Woodham Walter CM9 235 E1
Old Macdonald's Educational Farm Pk* CM14 292 F1
Old Maltings Ct The 3
EN11 221 A6
Old Maltings The 2
CM23 146 A7
Old Market Ct 3 CO10 33 E7
Old Market Pl 2 CO10 33 E7
Old Market Ret Pk 10
SS13 343 B5
Old Market Terr 11 CM14 316 C8
OLD MEAD 94 D4
Old Mead SS2 347 A7
Oldmead Ho 13 RM10 354 B6
Old Mead La CM22 94 D4
Old Mead Rd CM22 94 C5
Old Mill Chase CM7 73 C3
Old Mill Ct E18 332 C8
Old Mill La Coggeshall CO5 158 D7
Little Hallingbury CM22 173 B6
Old Mill Par 2 RM1 335 E5
Old Mill Pl RM7 335 D5
Old Mill Rd Langham CO4 83 D5
Saffron Walden CB11 43 E8
Old Moors CM3 180 F7
Old Nazeing Rd EN10 221 C1

Philmead Rd SS7 344 B2
PHILPOT END 150 A2
Philpot End La CM6 150 B4
Philpott Ave SS2 348 E2
Phoenix Bldgs 1 RM13 355 B1
Phoenix Cl CO5 218 B6
Phoenix Ct E4 309 B7
Phoenix Ct CO2 136 D5
Phoenix Ct 21 CO10 33 E7
Phoenix Gr CM2 254 A8
Phoenix Hospl SS0 347 E2
Phoenix Ind Pk CO12 91 A4
Phoenix Pavilions CO12 91 C2
Phoenix Prim Sch SS15 341 C6
Phoenix Rd IP4 18 A7
Phoenix Sq CO4 110 C5
Phoenix Way SS7 345 C7
Picador Ho 6 RM10 354 B6
Picardy Manorway DA17 369 B4
Picardy Rd DA17 369 A2
Picardy St DA17 369 A3
Picasso Way SS3 350 A1
Piccotts La CM7 126 B8
Pickering Ave E6 352 A2
Pickering Ct 13 DA2 376 B1
Pickering Rd IG11 352 C6
Pickers Way CO15 196 E7
Picketts SS8 363 D4
Picketts Ave SS9 346 E4
Picketts Cl SS9 346 E4
Pickford Wlk CO4 136 F7
Pick Hill EN9 266 A7
Pickpocket La CM77 154 D6
Pickwick Ave CM1 231 D6
Pickwick Cl SS15 341 D7
Pickwick Rd IP2 16 E5
Picton Cl SS6 323 E1
Picton Gdns SS6 323 E1
Pier App CO14 171 C8
Pier Ave CO15 195 E2
Pierce Glade CO5 186 C5
Piercing Hill CM16 267 D4
Piercys SS13 343 B5
Pier Gap CO15 195 F2
Pier Hill SS1 367 A7
Pier Rd Felixstowe IP11 381 A1
Gravesend DA11 378 F1
Greenhithe DA9 377 B3
Pierrefitte Way CM7 127 E3
Pierrot Stps 5 SS1 367 C7
Pigeon Ct E4 309 C4
Pigeon's La IP8 16 A3
Piggs Corner Complex
RM17 373 C3
Pightle The Capel St M IP9 35 B2
Finchingfield CM7 72 D6
Haverhill CB9 9 A8
Pightle Way CO14 171 A7
Pig La CM22 146 A3
Pigotts Way CM23 145 E5
PIG STREET 168 E6
Pigstye Green Rd CM5 251 A8
Pike La RM14 356 F7
Pike Way CM16 247 A4
Pilborough Way CO3 134 E3
Pilcox Hall La CO16 140 D8
Pilgrim Cl CM7 127 F5
Pilgrims Cl Billericay CM11 297 B2
Great Chesterford CB10 3 D2
Pilgrims Hatch CM15 293 F4
Southend-on-S SS2 348 E1
Pilgrims Ct Bures CO8 55 F1
Dartford DA1 376 A2
PILGRIMS HATCH 294 A4
Pilgrims La RM16 372 C5
Pilgrim's La
Pilgrims Hatch, Bentley
CM14 293 D5
Pilgrims Hatch CM14 293 E4
Pilgrims' Rd DA10 377 E3
Pilgrims View DA9 377 C1
Pilgrims Way SS7 345 F3
Pilgrims Wlk 4 CM11 297 B2
Pilgrim Way SS15 341 C6
Pilkingtons CM17 224 D8
Pilot Cl SS11 322 A5
Pilots Pl 6 DA12 379 C1
Pimblett Row CM22 94 F5
Pimpernel Rd IP2 16 F3
Pimpernel Way RM3 314 D4
Pinceybrook Rd CM18 223 C4
Pincey Mead SS13 343 A5
Pincey Rd CM24 120 F3
Pincey Rdbt CM24 121 A3
Pinchpools Rd CM23 93 A3
Pindar Rd EN11 221 C7
Pine Ave
Great Dunmow CM6 123 B1
Ipswich IP1 17 B8
Pine Cl Brantham CO11 86 D8
Canvey Island SS8 363 E3
Great Bentley CO7 166 F8
Ingatestone CM4 274 C4
Southend-on-S SS9 346 B5
6 Wickford SS12 321 C5
Pine Cres CM13 295 D5
Pinecroft Brentwood CM13 295 B2
Romford RM2 336 C7
Pinecroft Gdns CO4 110 B3
Pinecroft Rise CO10 33 D5
Pine Ct RM14 356 B8
Pine Dr Ingatestone CM4 274 C4
Ipswich IP3 18 F1
Pine Gr
Bishop's Stortford CM23 146 B6
West Mersea CO5 218 B7
Witham CM8 184 A5
Pine Ho IP11 381 C4
Pinelands CM23 118 F1
Pine Lodge SS3 368 F8
Pine Rd SS7 345 D2
Pines Hill CM24 119 D5
Pines Rd CM1 231 D5
Pines The Basildon SS15 319 C1
Grays RM16 373 B5
Hatfield Peverel CM3 211 A5
Woodford IG8 310 A7
Pinetree Cl IP5 18 F7
Pine Tree Ct CO4 136 E8
Pine Tree Pl SS4 325 E2
Pinetrees SS7 345 C3
Pineview Ct E4 287 C1
Pine View Manor CM16 246 A1
Pine View Rd IP1 17 A8
Pinewood Ave
Rainham RM13 355 B1
Southend-on-S SS9 346 D5
Pinewood Cl
Clacton-on-S CO15 195 E7
Harlow CM17 224 C7
Hullbridge SS5 301 E2
Kirby Cross CO13 170 D6
Stanford-le-H SS17 375 B3
Pinewood Prim Sch RM5 313 B5
Pinewood Rd RM4 313 D6
Pinewood Way CM13 295 D4
Pinfolds RM15 371 D7
Pinhoe Dr CB9 8 C8
Pinkeneys SG8 19 D5
Pinkham Dr CM8 211 F8
Pink La CM3 182 D7
Pinkney Cl CB10 44 E2
Pinkuah La CO10 13 F6
Pinley Gdns RM9 353 B4
Pin Mill Cl IP2 16 C1
Pinmill Rd IP9 63 F8
PINNACLES 223 A8
Pinnacles EN9 265 E5
Pinnacle The RM6 334 E5
Pinners Cl CM0 305 F7
Pinner's Cross SG8 39 A7
Pintail Cl IP2 16 E3
Pintail Cres CM77 154 C6
Pintail Rd IG8 310 B3
Pintails 4 SS13 343 C6
Pintolls CM3 301 D6
Pioneer Ct 4 DA11 379 A1
Pioneer Pl 8 CO1 136 A6
Pioneer Sch Basildon SS14 342 C7
Basildon SS14 342 C8
Pipchin Rd CM1 231 E5
Piperell Way CB9 9 A5
Piperell Way Units CB9 9 A5
Piper Rd CO3 135 B7
Pipers Cl CB9 9 C6
Piper's Tye CM2 254 D3
Pipers Vale Cl IP3 17 E1
Piper's Vale Com Prim Sch
IP3 17 F1
Piper Way IG1 333 D3
Pippin Ct SS11 321 F8
Pippins Rd CM0 306 C6
Pippins The
Colchester CO4 136 C8
Glemsford CO10 2 C4
Halstead CO9 76 D2
PIPPS HILL 319 F1
Pipps Hill Rd N CM11 320 B3
Pirie Rd CO6 108 E3
Pishiobury Dr CM21 200 D8
Pitcairn Cl RM7 335 A7
Pitcairn Rd IP1 16 E8
Pitfield Ho CM7 127 D4
Pit La CO5 186 C6
Pitmans Cl SS1 367 A8
Pitmire La CO8 55 B6
PITSEA 343 B5
Pitsea Hall La SS16 343 B3
Pitsea Jun Sch SS13 343 A5
Pitsea Rd SS14 343 A5
Pitsea Sta SS13 343 B4
Pitsea View Rd CM11 320 D4
Pitseaville Gr SS16 342 E5
Pitt Ave CM8 212 A8
Pitt Chase CM2 254 E5
Pittfields SS16 341 B5
Pitt Gn CM8 212 A8
Pittman Cl CM13 317 C5
Pittman Gdns IG1 352 C7
Pittman's Field CM20 199 F1
Pitts End CO7 59 D3
Place Cotts CM3 300 C5
Place Farm Com Prim Sch
CB9 8 F8
Place Farm Ct CO2 136 D2
Place Farm La CM15 272 A2
Pladda Mews SS12 321 F5
Plains Farm Cl CO7 110 D6
Plains Field CM7 128 D1
Plains Rd
Great Totham CM9 213 F6
Little Totham CM9 214 A6
Plains The E4 287 E2
Plain The CM16 246 B3
Plaistow Cl SS17 360 D2
PLAISTOW GREEN 103 D5
Plaistow Green Rd CO9 103 C5
Plaiters Way CM7 128 D3
Plane Tree Cl
Burnham-on-C CM0 306 B6
Chelmsford CM2 254 B6
Plane View Cl CO16 195 B2
Plantaganet Pl 3 EN9 265 B6
Plantagenet Gdns RM6 334 D4
Plantagenet Pl RM6 334 D4
Plantation Cl
Greenhithe DA9 376 F1
Saffron Walden CB11 43 E6
Plantation Rd CM3 209 F1
Planton Way CO7 192 E6
Plashet Cl SS17 360 D2
Plashet Gdns CM13 317 A6
Plashets CM22 173 D1
Plashetts SS14 342 D7
Plas Newydd SS1 367 E6
Plas Newydd Cl SS1 367 E6
Platford Gn RM11 336 E7
Platinum Ct RM7 335 B8
Platters Cl IP3 38 B7
Platters Rd IP11 381 C2
Plaw Hatch Cl CM23 146 B8
Plaw Hatch Cnr CM23 146 D8
Players Ct CM6 152 C6
Playfield Ave RM5 313 C2
Playfield Rd IP9 35 B1
Playford Ct 2 CO10 33 E8
Playford Rd IP4 18 E8
Playhouse Sq CM20 223 C8
Playle Chase CM9 213 B4
Plaza Way SS1 367 D8
Pleasant Ct SS1 367 B7
Pleasant Dr CM12 296 E3
Pleasant Mews
Southend-on-S SS1 367 B7
West Mersea CO5 218 C6
Pleasant Rd
Bishop's Stortford CM23 145 E8
Southend-on-S SS1 367 B7
Pleasant Row 13 IP4 17 D5
Pleasant Terr SS9 365 E8
Pleasant Valley CB11 43 D7
Pleasant View DA8 369 E1
PLEDGDON GREEN 95 C3
PLESHEY 178 E2
Pleshey Cl
Southend-on-S SS1 367 F8
6 Wickford SS12 321 E6
Pleshey Rd CM3 179 B5
Plomer Ave 2 EN11 197 A1
Plotlands Mus* SS16 340 E3
Plotters Ct 7 EN11 221 D8
Plough Cnr CO16 168 C4
Plough Dr CO3 135 A5
Plough La CO10 33 D7
Ploughmans Cl CM23 145 C5
Ploughmans Headland
CO3 134 E5
Ploughmans La CM77 154 C8
Plough Rd CO7 166 E6
Plough Rise RM14 337 E4
Plough St IP3 17 E4
Plover Cl CO13 170 E6
Plover Gdns RM14 337 F3
Plover Ho RM13 370 A8
Plover Rd IP2 16 E2
Plovers Barron CM15 272 D3
Plovers Mead CM15 272 D3
Plovers The CM0 262 D7
Plover Wlk CM2 254 B5
Plowmans SS6 323 E4
Plowman Way RM8 334 C3
Plowright Ho 5 CO1 135 E8
Ployters Rd CM18 223 C4
Plumberow SS15 341 E6
Plumberow Ave SS5 324 E7
Plumberow Mount Ave
SS5 324 E8
Plumberow Prim Sch
SS5 324 E7
Plume Ave Colchester CO3 135 A4
Maldon CM9 236 F1
Plume Sch (Lower) CM9 237 A2
Plume Sch (Upper) CM9 236 F2
Plumleys SS13 343 B7
Plummers Rd CO6 107 E7
Plumpton Ave RM12 336 B2
Plumpton Rd EN11 221 C8
Plumptre La CM3 256 D5
Plums La CM7 99 E4
Plum St CO10 2 A6
Plumtree Ave CM2 254 F6
Plumtree Cl RM10 354 C6
Plumtree Mead IG10 289 A6
Plymouth Ho 10 IG11 353 A5
Plymouth Rd
Chelmsford CM1 232 E5
Clacton-on-S CO15 220 J8
Felixstowe IP11 381 D6
Grays RM16 372 C2
Plymtree SS1 349 C1
Pochard Way CM77 154 C5
Pocklington Cl CM2 233 A3
Podsbrook Ho CM8 183 F2
Pod's Brook Rd CM7 127 D2
Pods La CM77 126 D2
Poets Cnr RM18 379 B6
Point Cl SS8 364 F3
POINT CLEAR 193 A3
POINT CLEAR BAY 192 F3
Point Clear Bay Holiday Cvn
Pk CO16 192 F3
Point Clear Rd CO16 193 D3
Point Rd SS8 364 F3
Pointwell La CO6 158 A8
Pole Barn La CO13 170 F5
Polecat Rd CM77 155 F5
Polegate Cotts RM17 377 E8
Pole Hill Rd E4 287 C2
Pole La CM8 155 C3
Polesworth Rd RM9 353 D5
Poley Rd SS17 360 C1
Pollard Cl IG7 312 A5
Pollard Ct IP2 16 D2
Pollard Hatch CM19 223 B5
Pollards Cl Loughton IG10 288 C4
Rochford SS4 325 F2
Pollards Ct SS4 325 E2
Pollard's Gn CM2 232 F2
Pollards Villas CM7 99 D2
Pollard Wlk CO16 195 C5
Polley Cl CO13 170 E7
Polstead Cl SS6 323 A3
Polsteads SS16 342 E3
Polstead St CO6 56 D5
Polstead Way CO16 195 B4
Polsten Mews EN3 265 A2
Pomfret Mead SS14 342 A6
Pompadour Cl CM14 316 C5
Pond Chase CO3 135 B4
Pond Cl Felixstowe IP11 381 B5
Hullbridge SS5 301 E3
Pond Cotts IP9 61 E2
Pond Cross Cotts CB11 67 A8
Pond Cross Farm CB11 67 A8
Pond Cross Way CB11 67 A8
Ponders Rd CO6 107 C4
Pondfield La CM13 317 A7
Pondfield Rd
Colchester CO4 110 D1
Dagenham RM10 354 B7
Pondfields CM6 123 D1
Pondholton Dr 2 CM8 211 F7
Pond House La CO15 196 D8
Pond La
Hatfield Heath CM22 174 A2
Stansted Mountfitchet
CM24 119 D7
Pond Lees Cl RM10 354 D5
Ponds Rd CM2 254 B1
Pondtail Ct CO13 170 C6
Pond Wlk RM14 337 E2
Poney Chase CM8 212 F5
Poney's CM8 212 F5
Pontisbright Cotts CO6 106 E6
Pontypool Wlk RM3 314 C4
Poole Cl IP3 18 D3
Poole Ho RM16 374 C4
Poole Rd RM11 337 A4
Pooles Ct IG3 334 A1
Pooles La SS5 301 E3
Poole St Cavendish CO10 1 C1
Great Yeldham CO9 51 B6
Pooley's Yard IP2 17 B4
Poolhurst Wlk SS5 301 E4
Pool's La CM1 251 F4
Poore St CB11 65 F8
Poors La SS7 345 E4
Poors La N SS7 346 A5
Poors' Piece Nature Trail*
CM3 234 F1
Poperinghe Rd CO2 135 F4
Popes Cres SS13 343 B5
Popes Ct CB9 9 E5
Pope's La CO3 135 E7
Pope's Rd CO6 106 D4
Popes Wlk SS6 324 A2
Poplar Cl Blackmore CM4 272 E8
Chelmsford CM2 254 C6
Clacton-on-S CO15 195 B2
Great Yeldham CO9 30 A1
Halstead CO9 103 F8
Ingatestone CM4 274 A2
South Ockendon RM15 357 D1
South Woodham Ferrers
CM3 301 C8
Witham CM8 184 A5
Poplar Cotts
Birch Green CO5 160 C1
Hastingwood CM17 224 E5
Poplar Ct Chingford E4 309 B4
Great Cornard CO10 34 B7
Hockley SS5 324 E6
Poplar Dr CM13 295 C3
Poplar Gr CM0 306 B5
Poplar Grove Chase CM9 237 B8
Poplar Hall Cl CO1 109 E1
Poplar La IP8 16 B3
Poplar Mount DA17 369 C2
Poplar Rd
Canvey Island SS8 364 C3
Great Cornard CO10 34 B7
Rayleigh SS6 345 F8
Wanstead E12 332 E2
Poplar Row CM16 267 E2
Poplars EN9 266 C4
Poplars Ave SS5 324 F4
Poplars Cl CO7 165 B7
Poplar Shaw EN9 265 F6
Poplar St RM7 335 C7
Poplars The Abridge RM4 290 B6
12 Basildon SS13 343 C6
Brantham CO11 60 D2
Colchester CO3 134 E5
Gravesend DA12 379 E1
Great Dunmow CM6 123 C2
Great Hallingbury CM22 146 F4
Poplar Way Ilford IG6 333 C7
Kirby Cross CO13 170 D6
Poppy Cl Erith DA17 369 B3
Ipswich IP2 16 F4
Pilgrims Hatch CM15 294 B4
Poppyfield Cl SS9 346 D6
Poppy Gdns Basildon SS15 341 C5
Colchester CO2 136 C3
Poppy Gn CM1 233 A6
Porchester Cl RM11 336 E5
Porchester Rd CM12 297 A5
Pork La CO13 169 E5
Porlock Ave SS0 347 A4
Portal Prec CO1 135 F7
Port Ave DA9 377 B1
Portchester Ct SS9 346 F1
Porter Cl RM20 377 C8
Porter Rd IP3 18 F1
Porters SS13 343 C8
Porters Ave RM8 353 C7
Porters Brook Wlk CO4 110 C2
Porters Cl CM14 294 A1
Porter's Cl CO3 107 F2
Porter's Cotts CO3 107 F1
Porters Field CM7 127 D4
Porters Grange Prim Sch
SS1 367 B8
Porter's La CO3 107 F2
Porters Pk CM3 210 A2
PORTERS TOWN 348 B1
Porter Way CO16 195 B3
Portia Ct 12 IG11 353 A5
Port La
Bishop's Stortford CM22 146 B2
Colchester CO1 136 B5
Portland Ave Harwich CO12 91 C3
Southend-on-S SS1 367 B8
Portland Cl Braintree CM7 128 B3
Dagenham RM6 334 E6
Portland Commercial Est
IG11 353 C3
Portland Cres CO12 91 C3
Portland Gdns RM6 334 D6
Portland Ho CO13 170 F5
Portland Pl
17 Bishop's Stortford
CM23 145 F7
Greenhithe DA9 377 C3
Portland Rd
Bishop's Stortford CM23 145 F7
15 Colchester CO2 135 F6
Northfleet DA11 378 D1
Portlight Cl CO11 87 A4
Portmadoc Ho 2 RM3 314 E6
Portman Dr
Billericay CM12 297 B5
Woodford IG8 310 D1
Portman Rd IP1 17 B6
Portman Road (Ipswich Town
FC) IP1 17 B5
Portmans Walk Ind Ctr
IP1 17 A5
Portman's Wlk IP1 17 A5
Portmore Gdns RM5 313 A5
Portnoi Cl RM1 313 D1
Portobello Rd CO14 171 C8
Port Of Felixstowe Rd
IP11 381 A4
Portreath Pl CM1 232 A7
Portsea Rd RM18 379 C6
Portsmouth Rd CO15 220 J8
Portway Chelmsford CM2 233 B4
Rainham RM13 355 A4
Portway Ct CO9 76 F3
Poseidon Ct 1 IG11 353 B2
Posford Ct CO4 109 F4
Postman's La CM3 234 E3
Post Mdw CM11 319 D6
Post Mill Cl IP4 17 F6
Post Office Cnr IP9 61 F2
Post Office Cotts CM22 173 C8
Post Office La
Glemsford CO10 2 B5
Little Totham CM9 214 B4
Post Office Rd
Chelmsford CM1 232 B8
Harlow CM20 199 D1
Ingatestone CM4 274 B3
Woodham Mortimer CM9 257 E6
Postway Mews 1 IG1 333 B1
POTASH 60 E8
Potash Cotts IP9 60 E8
Potash La IP9 60 E8
Potash Rd Billericay CM11 297 D6
Matching Green CM17 202 D4
Potiphar Pl CM14 316 B6
Pot Kiln Chase CO9 31 F2
Pot Kiln Prim Sch CO10 34 B6
Pot Kiln Rd CO10 34 B6
Pot Kilns The CO10 34 C6
Potteries The EN9 266 C5
Potters Cl Danbury CM3 257 A6
Loughton IG10 288 F7
Potters Field CM17 224 D6
Potters La CM3 278 D2
Potter St
Bishop's Stortford CM23 145 F7
Harlow CM17 224 C6
Sible Hedingham CO9 75 E7
POTTER STREET 224 D6
Potter Street Prim Sch
CM17 224 C6
Potters Way SS2 347 F5
Pottery La
Castle Hedingham CO9 51 F3
Chelmsford CM1 232 A5
Potton Dr SS12 321 F6
Poulteney Rd CM24 119 E8
Poulton Cl CM9 259 B8
Pound Cl EN9 243 E8
Pound Farm Dr CO12 91 A3
Poundfield Cl CO7 165 B7
Poundfield Ho CO7 138 A5
Poundfield Rd IG10 289 A4
Pound Fields CM1 253 B8
Pound Gate CM6 124 D6
Pound Hill Villas CM6 151 E8
Pound La
Basildon, Laindon SS15 341 D8
Basildon, North Benfleet
SS12 343 F7
Capel St M IP9 59 F8
Orsett RM16 359 A1
Pound La N SS15 319 D1
Pound Lane Central SS15 319 D1
Pound Wlk CB10 22 E2
Powdermill La EN9 265 B6
Powdermill Mews 2 EN9 265 B6
Powdermill Way EN9 265 B6
Powell Cl CO5 186 E5
Powell Ct SS4 325 F1
Powell Gdns RM10 354 B8
Powell Rd Basildon SS15 341 B7
Buckhurst Hill IG9 288 C2
POWERS HALL END 183 D3
Powers Hall End CM8 183 E3
Powers Hall Inf Sch CM8 183 D3
Powers Hall Jun Sch
CM8 183 D3
Powle Terr IG1 352 D7
Powling Rd IP3 18 A2
Pownall Cres CO2 135 F4
Pownall Rd IP3 17 E4
Pownsett Terr IG1 352 C7
Poynder Rd RM18 379 B6
Poynings Ave SS2 348 E2
Poynings Way RM3 314 E2
Poyntens SS6 323 C1
Poynter Pl CO13 170 E7
Poynters La SS3 350 B2
Prail Ct CO6 130 F2
Pratts Farm La CM3 208 D4
Pratt's La IP9 38 A2
Preaching Cross CM4 297 F6
Precinct The SS17 360 D1
Premier Ave RM16 373 C4
Prentice Cl SS4 325 F2
Prentice Hall La CM9 240 B8
Prentice Mews IP3 38 C8
Prentice Pl CM17 224 C6
Prentice Way IP3 18 B4
Prescott SS16 341 C3
Prescott Gn IG10 289 C6
President Rd CO3 134 E5
Presidents Ct SS15 340 F6
Preston Ave E4 309 D4
Preston Dr E11 332 C6
Preston Gdns
Rayleigh SS6 323 D4
Redbridge IG1 332 E5
Preston Ho 3 RM10 335 A1
Preston Rd
Clacton-on-S CO15 196 D5
Romford RM3 314 D6
Southend-on-S SS0 366 D8
Prestwick Dr CM23 119 B1
Prestwood Cl SS7 344 F7
Prestwood Dr
Romford RM5 313 C5
Thundersley SS7 345 A7
Pretoria Ave SS15 319 F1
Pretoria Cres E4 287 C1
Pretoria Rd Chingford E4 287 D1
Halstead CO9 76 F2
Ilford IG1 352 B7
Pretoria Rd *continued*
Romford RM7 335 C6
Prettygate Inf Sch CO3 135 B4
Prettygate Jun Sch CO3 135 B4
Prettygate Rd CO3 135 A4
Pretyman Rd
Felixstowe IP11 381 C1
Ipswich IP3 18 B3
Priestley Ct RM17 373 C2
Priestley Gdns RM6 334 B5
Priests Ave RM1 313 D1
Priests Field CM13 317 C5
Priest's La
Brentwood CM15 316 F8
Shenfield CM15 294 F1
Prime's Cl CB10 22 D1
Primley La CM22 173 C1
Primrose Ave RM6 334 B4
Primrose Cl Basildon SS16 341 B4
Bishop's Stortford CM23 145 C6
Canvey Island SS8 364 A6
Primrose Ct 2 CM14 316 C7
Primrose Field CM18 223 F5
Primrose Glen RM11 336 E7
Primrose Hill
Brentwood CM14 316 C7
Chelmsford CM1 231 F3
Haverhill CB9 8 F7
Holbrook IP9 62 D4
Ipswich IP2 16 F4
Primrose La Ramsey CO12 89 A1
Tiptree CO5 186 C6
Primrose Pl CM8 183 E4
Primrose Rd
Clacton-on-S CO15 196 E6
Woodford E18 310 B1
Primrose Wlk
Colchester CO4 136 E7
Maldon CM9 237 B1
Southminster CM0 284 C3
Primula Cl CO16 195 C4
Primula Ct SS15 341 D5
Primula Way CM1 233 A6
Prince Albert Rd CO5 218 D6
Prince Ave SS2, SS0 347 C4
Prince Avenue Prim Sch
SS0 347 D5
Prince Charles Ave RM16 359 B1
Prince Charles Cl
Clacton-on-S CO15 195 C1
Sudbury CO10 33 F8
Prince Charles Rd CO2 136 A2
Prince Cl SS0 347 C5
Prince Edward Rd CM11 297 C2
Princel La CO7 84 F7
Princel Mews CO7 84 F7
Prince Of Wales Dr IP2 17 B2
Prince of Wales Ind Est
CO6 133 B4
Prince Of Wales Rd CM8,
CM9 213 A3
Prince of Wales Rdbt
CO6 133 B4
Prince Philip Ave
Clacton-on-S CO15 195 C1
Grays RM16 373 B6
Prince Philip Rd CO2 136 A1
Princes Ave
Corringham SS17 361 A2
Mayland CM3 283 A8
Southminster CM0 284 D4
Thundersley SS7 344 F6
Woodford IG8 310 C6
Princes Cl Basildon SS15 341 E8
Billericay CM12 297 C6
North Weald Bassett CM16 247 C6
Princes Ct Billericay CM12 297 C6
Bishop's Stortford CM23 145 C7
Southend-on-S SS2 347 E4
Prince's Espl CO14 144 D1
Princesfield Rd EN9 266 B6
Princes Gate CM23 145 C7
Princes Gate CM20 199 E3
Princes Gate CM0 284 D4
Princes Gdns IP11 381 D4
Princes Lodge SS0 366 D7
Princes Mews CM12 297 C6
Princes Pk RM13 355 A5
Princes Rd
Buckhurst Hill IG9 310 C8
Burnham-on-C CM0 306 C6
Canvey Island SS8 363 F3
Chelmsford CM2 254 B7
Clacton-on-S CO15 196 D5
Felixstowe IP11 381 E4
Harwich CO12 91 B3
Ilford IG6 333 D7
Maldon CM9 237 A2
Romford RM1 336 A6
Prince's Rd
Navestock Heath CM14,
RM4 292 F8
Navestock Side CM14 293 A7
Princess Alexandra Hospl
CM20 199 C1
Princess Anne Cl CO15 195 C1
Princess Ave RM18 375 C2
Princess Ct SS11 322 A8
Princess Dr CO4 110 C5
Princess Gdns SS4 325 D5
Princess Margaret Rd
RM18 380 D
Princess Par RM10 354 A
Princess Rd SS6 323 F
Princess St CO12 90 F
Princes St Gravesend DA11 379 B
Ipswich IP1 17 B
Southend-on-S SS1 366 F
Princess Way CB9 8 E
Prince St CO10 33 E
Princes Way
Brentwood CM13 295 A
Buckhurst Hill IG9 310 C
Princes Well CB10 45 F
Princethorpe Rd IP3 18 C
Princeton Mews CO4 110 B
Prince William Ave SS8 363 F
Printers Way CM20 200 A
Prior Chase RM17 372 F
Prior Cl CO9 103 D
Prioress Cres DA9 377 C

Roberts Cl RM3 314 B2
Roberts Ct CM2 254 E7
Robert's Hill CO8 79 F3
Roberts Ho RM10 354 B5
Robertson Ct RM17 373 B2
Robertson Dr SS12 321 E5
Roberts Pl RM10 354 A6
Roberts Rd Basildon SS15 341 E7
Belvedere DA17 369 A1
Chingford E17 309 B2
Colchester CO1, CO2 136 A5
North Fambridge CM3 303 A7
Robert Suckling Ct CB9 27 B6
Robert Wallace Cl CM23 118 F1
Robert Way Wickford SS11 321 F6
Wivenhoe CO7 137 C3
Robin Cl Billericay CM12 297 C6
Great Bentley CO7 166 D8
Haverhill CB9 9 C7
Romford RM5 313 D3
Stanstead Abbotts SG12 197 C3
Robin Cres CO3 134 B4
Robin Dr IP2 16 D3
ROBINHOOD END 49 B6
Robin Hood Rd
Brentwood CM15 294 C2
Elsenham CM22 94 C1
Robinia Cl Basildon SS15 319 D1
Redbridge IG6 311 E4
Robinia Ct 1 CO4 136 E7
Robin Jeffrey Ct 18 CM23 145 F6
Robinsbridge Rd CO6 130 F2
Robinsdale CO15 195 F6
Robin's La CM16 267 C3
Robinson Cl
Bishop's Stortford CM23 145 F5
Hornchurch RM12 355 B5
Robinson Rd
Brightlingsea CO7 193 A7
Dagenham RM10 354 A8
Horndon on t H SS17 359 E4
Robinsons Cl CM0 284 D3
Robinson Way DA11 378 A2
Robins The CM15 272 D4
Robinsway EN9 265 E5
Robin Way
Chelmsford CM2 254 B5
Sudbury CO10 33 C5
Robjohns Rd CM1 253 E8
Robletts Way CO6 80 E4
Roborough Wlk RM12 355 C6
Roca Ct E11 332 A6
Rochdale Way CO4 136 E6
Roche Ave SS4 325 E2
Roche Cl SS4 325 F2
Rochefort Dr SS4 347 F8
Rochehall Way SS4 348 B8
Rochelle Cl CM6 70 A3
Rochester Cl CM7 128 D4
Rochester Ct CB10 22 F2
Rochester Dr SS0 347 C4
Rochester Gdns IG1 332 F4
Rochester Mews SS0 347 C4
Rochester Rd RM12 355 B5
Rochester Way
Basildon SS14 342 F7
6 Basildon SS14 342 F8
Sudbury CO10 15 D2
Rocheway SS4 326 A2
ROCHFORD 325 E1
Rochford Ave
Brentwood CM15 295 A4
Ilford RM6 334 C6
Loughton IG10 289 C6
Southend-on-S SS0 347 E1
Waltham Abbey EN9 265 D5
Rochford Cl
Hornchurch RM12 355 B6
Stansted Mountfitchet CM24 119 E8
Wickford SS11 321 F6
Rochford Garden Way
SS4 325 E3
Rochford Gn IG10 289 C6
Rochford Hall Cl SS4 325 D1
Rochford Hall Cotts SS4 325 D1
Rochford Ho
Waltham Abbey EN9 265 D6
Walton-on-t-N CO14 144 E2
Rochford Prim Sch SS4 325 E2
Rochford Rd
Bishop's Stortford CM23 119 C1
Canvey Island SS8 364 D3
Chelmsford CM2 232 C1
Southend-on-S SS2 347 E5
St Osyth CO16 194 B4
Rochford Sta SS4 325 E1
Rochford Way
Frinton-on-S CO13 170 F7
Walton-on-t-N CO14 171 A7
Rochforte Cl SS4 325 F2
Rockall SS2 347 A7
Rockall Cl CB9 9 D7
Rockchase Gdns RM11 336 E5
Rockells Farm* CB11 41 B5
Rock Gdns RM10 354 B7
Rockhampton Wlk 10
CO2 136 A1
Rockingham Ave RM11 336 B4
Rockingham Cl CO4 110 D3
Rocklands Ct RM17 373 C1
Rockleigh Ave SS9 347 A1
Rockleigh Ct CM15 295 A2
Rockwell Rd RM10 354 B7
Rockwood Gdns IG10 289 C6
RODBRIDGE CORNER 15 C4
Rodbridge Dr SS1 367 F8
Rodbridge Hill CO10 15 B5
Rodbridge Nature Reserve*
CO10 15 B4
Roddam Cl CO3 135 C6
Roden Cl CM17 200 F4
Roden St IG1 333 A1
Roden Terr CM5 204 A1
Roding CM14 294 B1
Roding Ave IG8 310 E4
Roding Cl Fyfield CM5 227 D2
Great Wakering SS3 350 B4
Roding Ct CM7 128 D1
Roding Dr CM15 271 F2
Roding Gdns IG10 288 E3
Roding Hall RM4 290 B6
Roding Hospl (BUPA)
IG4 332 D8
Roding La
Buckhurst Hill IG9, IG7 288 E1
Chigwell IG7 289 A1
Roding La N IG8 310 E2
Roding La S IG4 332 D7
Roding Leigh CM3 301 E7
Roding Lodge IG1 332 D5
Roding Prim Sch
Barking RM8 353 C7
Woodford IG8 310 E3
Roding Rd IG10 288 F3
Rodings Ave SS17 360 D4
Rodings Ct E4 309 D5
Rodings Prim Sch CM6 204 C8
Rodings The
Southend-on-S SS9 346 D7
Upminster RM14 337 D5
5 Woodford IG8 310 C4
Roding Valley High Sch
IG10 288 E4
Roding Valley Sta IG9 310 D6
Roding View
Buckhurst Hill IG9 288 D1
Chipping Ongar CM5 249 B4
Roding Way
Rainham RM13 355 D3
Wickford SS12 321 E7
Rodney Cres EN11 221 A8
Rodney Gdns CM7 128 C4
Rodney Rd
Chipping Ongar CM5 248 F2
Wanstead E11 332 B7
Rodney Way
Chelmsford CM1 253 E7
Romford RM7 313 B2
Rodwells SS3 349 E4
Roebuck Ct E4 309 C3
Roebuck Hts IG9 288 C2
Roebuck La IG9 288 C1
Roebuck Rd IG6 312 B4
Roebuck Trad Est IG6 312 B4
Roedean Cl SS2 348 F1
Roedean Dr RM1 335 E7
Roedean Gdns SS2 348 F2
Rogation Cl CO3 134 D6
Roger Browning Ho 25
CO1 135 F7
Roger Reede's Almshouses
RM1 335 E7
Rogers Cl IP11 381 D6
ROGERS END 6 B1
Rogers Gdns RM10 354 A7
Rogers Ho 9 RM10 335 A1
Rogers Rd
Dagenham RM10 354 A7
Grays RM17 373 C2
Roggel Rd SS8 364 D2
Rohan Ct SS6 301 D6
Rohan Pl 4 IG4 332 F6
Rokeby Gdns IG8 310 A2
Rokells SS14 342 A7
Rokell Way CO13 170 F6
Rokescroft SS13 343 A5
Roland La SS8 364 B4
Rolands Cl CM1 232 B7
Roles Gr RM6 334 E7
Rollason Way CM14 316 C7
Rollerworld* CO1 136 B7
Rollestons CM1 252 F8
Rolley La CO5 158 C2
Roll Gdns IG2 333 A6
Rolls Ct The E4 309 C5
Rolls Park Ave E4 309 B5
Rolls Park Rd E4 309 B5
Rolph CE Prim Sch CO16 141 F1
Rolph Cl CO16 142 A2
Rolphs Cotts CM8 156 D5
ROLPHY GREEN 179 A4
Romagne Cl SS17 359 F3
Romainville Way SS8 363 C3
Roman RM18 375 C2
Roman Cl Maldon CM9 236 F4
Mountnessing CM15 295 E8
Rainham RM13 354 D3
Roman Ct Braintree CM7 128 C1
Saffron Walden CB11 43 E7
3 Wickford SS11 322 A5
Roman Hill CO2 163 B7
Roman Ho
3 Chelmsford CM2 232 B1
Rainham RM13 354 D3
Roman La CM24 120 B2
Roman Lodge IG9 288 C1
Roman Mews 7 EN11 221 A7
Roman Rd Colchester CO1 136 A7
Ilford IG1 352 B6
Ingatestone CM4 273 F1
Little Waltham CM3 208 B5
Mountnessing CM15 295 E8
Roman Rise CM21 172 D2
Romans Farm Chase
CM0 306 C7
Romanshurst CM9 237 A4
Romans Pl CM1 231 B1
Roman St 8 EN11 221 A7
Romans Way CM1 231 B1
Roman Vale CM17 200 C5
Roman Way
Billericay CM12 319 A8
Burnham-on-C CM0 306 B8
Colchester CO2 135 E3
Haverhill CB9 9 D7
Littlebury CB11 21 F4
Long Melford CO10 15 C6
Point Clear B CO16 193 A3
Waltham Abbey EN9 265 B4
Romany Stps 17 SS1 367 C7
Rom Cres RM7 335 F4
Romeland EN9 265 C6
ROMFORD 335 D7
Romford Cl CO4 136 B8
Romford Rd Aveley RM15 371 C7
Chipping Ongar CM5 270 F7
Ilford E12 333 A1
Redbridge IG6 312 C5
Upminster RM15 356 C1
Romford Sta RM1 335 E5
Romney Chase RM11 337 A5
Romney Cl Braintree CM7 127 E6
Romney Cl *continued*
Brightlingsea CO7 165 E1
Clacton-on-S CO16 195 D5
Kirby Cross CO13 170 E7
Romney Ho SS4 325 F2
Romney Rd
Billericay CM12 296 F1
Ipswich IP3 38 A8
Romsey Cl Hockley SS5 324 D6
South Benfleet SS7 344 B5
Stanford-le-H SS17 360 B1
Romsey Cres SS7 344 B5
Romsey Dr SS7 344 B5
Romsey Gdns RM9 353 D4
Romsey Rd
Dagenham RM9 353 D4
South Benfleet SS7 344 A5
Romsey Way SS7 344 B5
Romside Pl 4 RM7 335 D7
Romulus Cl CO4 109 F5
Rom Valley Way RM7 335 E4
Ronald Dr SS6 323 A4
Ronald Hill Gr SS9 346 D1
Ronald Park Ave SS0 347 C2
Ronald Rd Halstead CO9 103 E8
Romford RM3 315 A2
Roneo Cnr RM12 335 F3
Roneo Link RM12 335 F3
Ronnie La E12 352 A8
Ron Todd Cl RM10 354 A4
Ronver Lodge E4 309 E7
Roodegate SS14 342 A6
Rook Cl RM13 355 A5
ROOK END 68 A5
Rook End La CB11 68 B5
Rookeries The CO6 133 B4
Rookery Chase CO7 84 E2
Rookery Cl
Great Chesterford CB10 3 D3
Hatfield Peverel CM3 211 A5
Rayleigh SS6 323 C2
Stanford-le-H SS17 360 B1
Rookery Cres RM10 354 B5
Rookery Ct RM20 377 A8
Rookery Hill SS17 361 C2
Rookery La
Great Totham CM9 213 E7
North Fambridge CM3 280 E1
Tiptree CO5 186 C7
Wendens Ambo CB11 42 E4
Rookery Rd CM4 250 D3
Rookery The Grays RM20 377 A8
Lawford CO11 86 C4
Stansted Mountfitchet CM24 119 E8
Rookery View RM17 373 D1
Rookes CB10 22 D3
Rookes Cres CM1 253 F8
Rookley Ct 15 RM19 371 B1
Rook Lodge IG1 332 D5
Rookwood Ave IG10 289 C6
Rookwood Cl
Clacton-on-S CO15 195 D7
Grays RM17 373 B2
Rookwood Gdns E4 309 F8
Rookwood Ho 2 IG11 352 D3
Rookwood Way CB9 9 A6
Rookyards SS16 342 E5
Roosevel Ave SS8 364 A4
Roosevelt Rd 1 SS15 341 A6
Roosevelt Way
Colchester CO2 136 B4
Dagenham RM10 354 D6
Roos Hill Debden Rd CB11 43 E5
Roothings The CM9 237 B5
Roots Hall Ave SS2 347 F2
Roots Hall Dr SS2 347 E2
Roots Hall (Southend United
F.C.) SS2 347 E2
Roots La CM8 212 E5
Roper Cl CO4 110 B6
Roper Ct IP4 18 C5
Ropers Ave E4 309 C5
Roper's Chase CM1 253 A7
Ropers La CO10 15 B5
Ropers Yd 12 CM14 316 C8
Rope Wlk Ipswich IP4 17 E5
Maldon CM9 237 A1
Rosabelle Ave CO7 137 B1
Rosalind Cl CO4 136 F7
Rosalind Ct 6 IG11 353 A5
Rosary Ct CM15 316 E8
Rosary Gdns SS0 347 B4
Rosbach Rd SS8 364 D3
Rosberg Rd SS8 364 E3
Roscommon Way SS8 363 C4
Rose Acre Basildon SS14 342 F6
Stratford St M CO7 58 F6
Roseacre Cl RM11 336 F4
Roseacres
Sawbridgeworth CM21 172 D3
Takeley CM22 148 C7
Rose Allen Ave CO2 162 F8
Rose Ave Colchester CO3 134 C4
Woodford E18 310 B1
Rosebank Harwich CO12 91 A3
Waltham Abbey EN9 265 E6
West Mersea CO5 218 B6
Rose Bank CM14 316 D7
Rosebank Ave RM12 355 C7
Rosebank Ct CO15 196 A2
Rosebank Rd CO5 218 B6
Rosebay Ave CM12 296 F5
Rosebay Cl CM8 183 D3
Roseberry Ave
Basildon SS16 341 B4
South Benfleet SS7 344 C7
Roseberry Cl RM14 337 F5
Roseberry Ct SS7 344 C7
Roseberry Gdns RM14 337 F5
Roseberry Wlk SS7 344 C7
Rosebery CM23 146 C6
Rosebery Ave CO1 136 A7
Rosebery Ct IP11 381 D2
Rosebery Rd
Chelmsford CM2 254 B8
Felixstowe IP11 381 F4
Grays RM17 377 E8
Ipswich IP4 17 F5
Rosebury Ct CM3 295 D3
Rosebury Sq 2 IG8 311 A3
Rose Cl 10 SS12 321 E5
Rose Cotts
Brent Pelham SG9 64 A5
Great Sampford CM7 47 E5
Harlow CM17 224 F5
Willingale CM5 228 D3
Rose Cres CO4 109 D2
Rosecroft Cl
Basildon SS16 341 A4
Clacton-on-S CO15 195 E6
Rose & Crown Mews
CM0 284 D4
Rose & Crown Wlk CB10 22 D2
Rose Ct Blackheath CO2 163 B8
Ilford IG1 352 B6
Rosedale Cotts CO3 133 F5
Rosedale Dr RM9 353 B5
Rosedale Gdns RM9 353 B5
Rosedale Rd
Dagenham RM9 353 B5
Grays RM17 373 D1
Romford RM1 335 C8
Rosedene Gdns IG2 333 A7
Rose Dr CM0 284 D3
Rosefinch Cl CB9 9 C7
Rose Gdns Braintree CM7 128 A2
Seawick CO16 220 B6
Rose Glen Chelmsford CM2 254 C7
Romford RM7 335 E3
ROSE GREEN 106 E5
Rose Green Cotts CO6 106 E5
Rosehatch Ave RM6 334 D8
ROSE HILL 18 A4
Rose Hill CM7 128 A2
Rosehill Cres IP3 17 F4
Rose Hill Prim Sch IP3 18 A4
Rosehill Rd IP3 17 F4
Rose Ho 12 CO1 136 A6
Rose La Billericay CM12 297 A2
Dagenham RM6 334 E7
Great Chesterford CB10 3 E2
Ipswich IP1, IP4 17 C5
Salcott-c-V CM9 216 B8
Wivenhoe CO7 164 B7
Roselaine SS14 342 B7
Roseland Ct CO15 195 F3
Roselands Ave EN11 197 A1
Roselawn Fields CM1 232 B8
Roseley Cotts CM20 199 B4
Rosemary Ave
Braintree CM7 127 F4
Felixstowe IP11 381 F6
Romford RM1 335 F8
Rosemary Cl
Great Dunmow CM6 123 C1
1 Harlow CM17 200 C4
South Ockendon RM15 357 C2
Tiptree CO5 186 C5
Rosemary Cotts CM3 209 E1
Rosemary Cres
Clacton-on-S CO15 195 F2
Great Dunmow CM6 123 C1
Tiptree CO5 186 C5
Rosemary Ct
2 Colchester CO4 136 D8
Tiptree CO5 186 C5
Rosemary Dr IG4 332 D6
Rosemary Gdns
Dagenham RM8 334 F3
Sudbury CO10 15 F2
Rosemary La
Castle Hedingham CO9 52 A5
Great Dunmow CM6 123 C1
Halstead CO9 76 E2
Stebbing CM6 124 C7
Thorrington CO7 166 B5
Rosemary Lodge SS2 347 F1
Rosemary Rd CO15 195 F2
Rosemary Rd W CO15 195 E2
Rosemary Way CO15 220 G7
Rosemead SS7 344 C7
Rosemead Gdns CM13 295 D5
Rosemount CM19 223 A5
Rosemount Cl IG8 310 F4
Rosemount Ct IP11 381 F4
Rose Park Ct IG5 310 F1
Rose Rd SS8 364 A3
Roserna Rd SS8 364 D3
Rosery Ho IP11 381 F4
Rosery Mews CO13 170 A4
Rose St DA11 378 B1
Roses The IG8 309 F3
Rose Tree Mews IG8 310 E4
Rosetta Cl CO7 137 B2
Rosetti Terr 4 RM8 353 B8
Rose Vale EN11 221 A6
Rose Valley CM14 316 D7
Rose Valley Cres SS17 360 E4
Rose Way SS4 348 A8
Rose Wlk CO9 29 B6
Rosewood Ave RM12 355 A7
Rosewood Cl
Colchester CO4 110 A4
South Ockendon RM15 357 E2
Rosewood Ct RM6 334 C6
Rosewood Ho 8 CM14 316 C7
Rosewood La SS3 368 F7
Rosher Ho DA11 378 F1
ROSHERVILLE 378 E1
Rosherville CE Prim Sch
DA11 378 E1
Rosherville Way DA11 378 E1
Rosilian Dr SS5 302 C1
Roslings Cl CM1 231 D5
Roslyn Gdns RM2 313 F1
Rossall Cl RM11 336 A5
Ross Ave RM8 334 F3
Ross Cl Haverhill CB9 9 D7
Saffron Walden CB11 43 E6
Rossdene Gdns CM6 204 D7
Rossendale CM1 231 E1
Rossendale Cl CO4 110 D3
Rosshill Ind Pk SS2 348 A4
Rossiter Rd SS3 368 H8
Rosslyn Ave Chingford E4 309 F8
Dagenham RM8 335 A4
Romford RM3 314 F1
Rosslyn Cl SS5 324 E7
Rosslyn Ct SS17 360 C1
Rosslyn Rd Barking IG11 352 D5
Billericay CM12 296 F2
Hockley SS5 324 E7
Rosslyn Terr CO5 158 C3
Ross Way SS16 341 B3
Rotary Way CO3 135 E8
Rothbury Ave RM13 370 B8
Rothbury Ho 5 RM3 314 D4
Rothbury Rd CM1 231 D1
Roth Dr CM13 317 B8
Rothesay Ave CM2 254 A8
Rothmans Ave CM2 254 E6
Rothwell Cl SS9 346 C6
Rothwell Gdns RM9 353 C4
Rothwell Rd RM9 353 C4
ROTTEN END 101 A7
Rotunda The 1 RM7 335 D6
Rough Hill Farm Cotts
CM3 278 C7
Roughtallys CM16 246 F4
Roughtons CM2 254 C3
Roundacre Basildon SS14 342 A6
Halstead CO9 103 E8
Roundaway Rd IG5 310 F1
ROUNDBUSH 281 B8
Roundbush Bglws CM9 281 C8
Roundbush Cnr
Birch Green CO5 160 D3
Great Totham CM9 213 D6
ROUNDBUSH GREEN 176 C2
Roundbush Rd
Birch Green CO5 160 D2
Mundon CM9 281 A8
Round Cl CO3 135 B7
Round Coppice Rd
Great Hallingbury CM24 147 A8
Stansted Mountfitchet CM24 120 B1
Rounders Ct 12 RM10 354 B6
Round Hill Rd SS7 345 A2
Roundhills EN9 265 E4
Roundmead Ave IG10 289 A6
Roundmead Cl IG10 289 A7
Roundridge Rd IP9 35 B2
Roundwood Ave CM13 295 B2
Roundwood Gr CM13 295 B2
Roundwood Lake CM13 295 B2
Roundwood Rd IP4 18 A7
Rounton Rd EN9 265 E6
Rous Chase CM2 254 B1
Rouse Way CO1 136 B7
Rous Rd IG9 288 E1
Routh Ave IP3 18 F1
Rover Ave
Clacton-on-S CO15 220 E6
Redbridge IG6 311 F4
Rowallan Cl CO3 135 A3
Rowallen Par RM8 334 C3
Rowan Chase CO5 186 C6
Rowan Cl
Clacton-on-S CO15 195 C3
Colchester CO3 134 D4
Great Bentley CO7 166 F8
Harwich CO12 91 B3
Ilford IG1 352 D7
Ipswich IP3 18 D2
Rayleigh SS6 323 B6
Rowan Dr CM9 237 C5
Rowan Gr RM15 371 C6
Rowan Green E CM13 316 F7
Rowan Green W CM13 316 F7
Rowanhayes Cl IP2 17 B3
Rowan Ho
4 Basildon SS13 343 B8
Ilford IG1 352 D7
Rowan Pl CO1 109 E1
Rowans EN9 266 C4
Rowans The Aveley RM15 371 C5
Billericay CM11 319 D8
Rayleigh SS9 346 B6
Rowans Way
Loughton IG10 288 F5
Wickford SS11 321 E8
Rowan Way Canewdon SS4 304 E1
Great Dunmow CM6 123 C1
Hatfield Peverel CM3 211 A3
Ilford RM6 334 C8
South Ockendon RM15 357 C1
Witham CM8 184 A5
Rowan Wlk
Hornchurch RM11 336 D7
Sawbridgeworth CM21 172 E2
Southend-on-S SS9 346 D6
Rowden Par E4 309 A4
Rowden Park Gdns E4 309 A4
Rowden Rd E4 309 B4
Rowdowns Rd RM9 353 F5
Rowe Gdns IG11 353 A3
Rowenhall SS15 340 F6
ROW GREEN 154 D6
ROW HEATH 167 F4
ROWHEDGE 163 F8
Rowhedge CM13 317 B7
Rowhedge Cl SS13 321 D2
Rowhedge Ct CO7 136 F4
Rowhedge Ferry Rd CO7 164 A8
Rowhedge Rd CO2, CO5 136 E1
Rowherns La CO7 139 F4
Rowland Cres IG7 311 E6
Rowland Ho IP11 381 B5
Rowlands Rd RM8 334 F2
Rowlands The SS7 344 E3
Rowland's Yd CO12 90 E2
Rowland Wlk RM4 313 E7
Rowley Cl CO11 86 D8
Rowley Cotts The CO6 56 D5
Rowley Ct CB9 9 E5
Rowley Hill CB9 9 E5
Rowley Mead CM16 246 C6
Rowley Rd RM16 374 A8
Rowney Ave CB10 44 E2
Rowney Gdns
Dagenham RM9 353 C6
Sawbridgeworth CM21 200 C8
Rowney Rd RM9 353 B6
Rowney Wood CM21 172 C1
Rowntree Way CB11 43 D7
Rows The 1 CM20 199 D1
Row The Hadstock CB1 5 B7
Stratford St M CO7 58 C2
Roxborough Cl CO6 132 E3
Roxburgh Ave RM14 337 C1
Roxburghe Rd CO16 167 F6
ROXWELL 230 B6
Roxwell Ave CM1 231 D3
Roxwell CE Prim Sch
CM1 230 A6
Roxwell Cres SS12 321 E6
Roxwell Gdns CM13 295 C4
Roxwell Ho IG10 288 E2
Roxwell Rd Barking IG11 353 A3
Chelmsford CM1 231 C4
Roxwell CM1 230 E5
Writtle CM1 231 A4
Roxwell Way IG8 310 C3
Roxy Ave RM6 334 C4
Royal Artillery Way SS2 348 F2
Royal Cl Ilford IG3 334 A4
Rochford SS4 325 D5
Royal Cres IG2 333 D5
Royal Ct Basildon SS15 341 B7
3 Brentwood CM14 316 C7
Colchester CO4 110 E1
Maldon CM9 237 A1
Rayleigh SS9 346 B8
Southend-on-S SS2 348 A1
Royal Docks Rd E6 352 B1
Royal Gunpowder Mills*
EN9 265 B7
Royal Hospital Sch IP9 62 D3
Royal Jubilee Ct RM2 336 A8
Royal Liberty Sch The
RM2 336 C8
Royal Mews SS1 367 A7
Royal Oak Chase SS15 341 E8
Royal Oak Ct RM8 334 C2
Royal Oak Dr SS11 322 A8
Royal Oak Gdns 6 CM23 145 F6
Royal Par 16 RM10 354 B6
Royal Pier Mews 9 DA11 379 B1
Royal Pier Rd DA12 379 C1
Royal Sq CO7 84 F7
Royals The SS1 367 A7
Royal Terr SS1 367 A7
Roy Ave IP3 18 B5
Roycraft Ave IG11 352 F3
Roycroft Cl E18 310 B2
ROYDON 198 B1
Roydon Bridge SS14 342 D8
Roydonbury Ind Est CM19 222 E8
Roydon Cl IG10 288 E2
ROYDON HAMLET 222 C4
Roydon Lodge Chalet Est
CM19 198 C1
Roydon Mill Leisure Pk
CM19 198 A1
Roydon Prim Sch CM19 222 B8
Roydon Rd Harlow CM19 198 E1
Stanstead Abbotts SG12 197 E4
Roydon Sta CM19 198 B2
Roydon Way CO13 170 F6
Royer Cl SS5 325 A4
Roy Gdns IG2 333 F6
Royle Cl RM2 336 B6
Royston Ave
Basildon SS15 319 D1
Chingford E4 309 B5
Southend-on-S SS2 348 B3
Royston Ct IG1 332 D5
Royston Dr IP2 16 D2
Royston Gdns IG1 332 D5
Royston La CB11 20 C6
Royston Par IG1 332 D5
Royston Rd Romford RM3 315 A3
Wendens Ambo CB11 42 C5
Ruaton Dr CO16 195 C4
Rubens Cl SS3 368 G8
Rubens Gate CM1 232 F7
Rubens Rd IP3 18 A1
Rubicon Ave SS11 321 F8
Rubin Pl EN3 265 A2
Ruby Ct 5 Rainham RM13 355 A1
Southend-on-S SS9 346 E5
Rudd Ct CO4 110 F1
Rudkin Rd CO4 109 F5
Rudlands IP8 16 C1
RUDLEY GREEN 258 C2
Rudsdale Way CO3 134 F5
Rudyard Ct CM14 316 B5
Rue De Jeunes 6 CM7 127 F2
Rue De St Lawrence EN9 265 C5
Ruffels Field CM6 124 E4
Ruffles Cl SS6 323 E3
Ruffles Rd CB9 9 C7
Rugby Gdns RM9 353 C6
Rugby Rd Dagenham RM9 353 C6
Great Cornard CO10 34 B4
Rugosa Cl CO3 134 C7
Rumballs Ct CM23 145 C4
Rumbold Rd EN11 221 C8
Rumbullion Dr CM12 296 F3
Rumford Sh Hall The
RM1 335 E7
Rumsey Fields CM3 256 F7
Rumsey Row CM1 231 B1
Runcorn Ho 5 RM3 314 E4
Rundells CM18 224 A4
Rundells Wlk SS14 342 E7
Rundels Cotts SS7 345 A6
Rundels The SS7 345 A6
Runnacles St CM8 156 C5
Runnacles Way IP11 381 B5
Runnel Ct 7 IG11 352 C3
Running Mare La CM2 254 A3
Running Waters CM13 317 A6
Runnymede Chase SS7 345 A5
Runnymede Ct SS17 360 C1
Runnymede Rd
Canvey Island SS8 364 B3
Stanford-le-H SS17 360 C1
Runsell Cl CM3 256 F7
RUNSELL GREEN 257 B7
Runsell La CM3 256 F8
Runsell View CM3 257 A7
RUNWELL 299 E1
Runwell Chase SS11 300 A3
Runwell Gdns SS11 299 D2
Runwell Hospl SS11 300 A5
Runwell Prim Sch SS11 299 D2
Runwell Rd SS11 300 B3
Runwell Terr SS1 366 F7
Runwood Rd SS8 363 C3
Rupert Rd CM0 284 C4

Springett's Hill CO8 ...... **55** D2
Springfarm Cl RM13 ..... **355** D2
SPRINGFIELD **232** E6
Springfield
Brentwood CM15 .... **294** C1
Epping CM16 .... **267** F7
Hadleigh SS7 .... **345** D4
Springfield Ave
Brentwood CM13 .... **295** E2
Felixstowe IP11 .... **381** E5
Springfield Basin CM2 ... **232** C2
Springfield Cl CM5 ...... **248** F5
Springfield Cotts CM9 ... **237** B5
Springfield Ct
Bishop's Stortford CM23 ... **145** E8
Clacton-on-S CO15 .... **195** C3
2 Ilford IG1 .... **352** B7
Rayleigh SS6 .... **323** A4
Upminster RM14 .... **337** B1
Springfield Dr Ilford IG2 . **333** C5
Southend-on-S SS0 .... **347** D3
Springfield Gdns
Upminster RM14 .... **337** C1
Woodford IG8 .... **310** C3
Springfield Gn CM1 ...... **232** E4
Springfield Ind Est CM0 . **306** A5
Springfield Inf Sch IP1 .... **16** F8
Springfield Jun Sch IP1 ... **16** F8
Springfield La IP1 .... **16** F8
Springfield Lyons App
CM2 .... **233** A5
Springfield Mdws CO16 .. **168** C4
Springfield Nursery Est
CM0 .... **306** A6
Springfield Park Ave
CM2 .... **232** E2
Springfield Park Hill
CM2 .... **232** D2
Springfield Park La CM2 . **232** E2
Springfield Park Par
CM2 .... **232** D2
Springfield Park Rd CM2 **232** E2
Springfield Pl CM1 ...... **232** E5
Springfield Rd
Billericay CM12 .... **297** B5
Burnham-on-C CM0 ...... **306** A6
Canvey Island SS8 .... **364** F3
Chelmsford CM1 .... **232** E4
Chingford E4 .... **287** E2
Grays RM16 .... **373** E4
Sudbury CO10 .... **15** E1
Wickford SS11 .... **321** F8
Springfields Basildon SS16 **342** F4
Braintree CM77 .... **127** C2
Brightlingsea CO7 .... **192** F7
Great Dunmow CM6 ...... **150** D8
Waltham Abbey EN9 ...... **265** E5
Springfields Dr CO2 ..... **135** A3
Springfield Terr 2 CO10 ... **33** F8
Spring Gardens Ind Est
RM7 .... **335** C5
Spring Gardens Rd CO6 . **106** E6
Spring Gdns
Hornchurch RM12 .... **355** B8
Long Melford CO10 .... **15** C8
Rayleigh SS6 .... **323** C2
Romford RM7 .... **335** C5
Woodford IG8 .... **310** C3
Spring Gr IG10 .... **288** D3
Springhall Ct CM21 ...... **172** E2
Springhall La CM21 ...... **172** E1
Springhall Rd CM21 ..... **172** E2
Springham Dr CO4 ...... **110** A6
Springhead Rd DA11 .... **378** D1
Spring Hill CB11 .... **22** A1
Springhill Cl CO7 .... **138** E8
Springhill Rd CB11 .... **43** D8
Spring Hills CM20 .... **199** B1
Spring Hills Twr CM20 ... **199** A1
Springhouse La SS17 .... **361** A2
Springhouse Rd SS17 .... **360** F4
Springhurst Cl IP4 .... **17** F6
Spring La Colchester CO3 . **135** A7
Colchester, Lexden CO3 ... **135** A8
Eight Ash G CO3 .... **108** B1
Great Totham CM9 .... **213** D7
Hatfield Peverel CM3, CM9 . **211** F2
Maldon CM9 .... **237** B4
West Bergholt CO6 ...... **108** E3
Wivenhoe CO7 .... **137** B2
Springland Cl IP4 .... **18** A6
Springlands Way CO10 .... **15** F2
Spring Lane Rdbt CO3 ... **135** A7
Springleigh Pl SS0 ...... **347** D2
Spring Mdw CO10 .... **2** B6
Springmead CM77 .... **154** D7
Spring Meadow Prim Sch
CO12 .... **91** A3
Spring Mews CM21 ...... **172** E2
Spring Pl 2 IG11 .... **352** C3
Spring Pond Cl CM2 ..... **254** E8
Spring Pond Mdw CM15 . **272** C4
Springpond Rd RM9 ..... **353** E7
Spring Rd
Brightlingsea CO7 .... **192** F7
Ipswich IP4 .... **18** A6
St Osyth CO16 .... **194** A3
Tiptree CO5 .... **186** C4
Spring Rise
Galleywood CM2 .... **254** C2
Haverhill CB9 .... **9** C6
Spring Sedge Cl CO3 .... **134** C7
Springtail Rd IP8 .... **36** E8
Spring Vale DA9 .... **377** C1
Springvalley La CO7 ..... **111** C4
Springwater Cl SS9 ...... **346** C7
Springwater Gr SS9 ..... **346** C7
Springwater Rd SS9 ..... **346** C8
Spring Way CO9 .... **51** E1
SPRINGWELL **22** A7
Springwell Ct SG12 ...... **197** C3
Springwell Rd CB10, CB11 . **22** A5
Springwood Ct CM7 ...... **127** D3
Springwood Dr CM7 ...... **127** C4
Springwood Ind Est CM7 **127** D3
Springwood Way RM1 ... **336** A6
Sprites End IP11 .... **381** B7
Spriteshall La IP11 ...... **381** B7
Sprites La IP8, IP2 .... **16** C2
Sprites Prim Sch IP2 ..... **16** C2
SPROUGHTON **16** A6
Sproughton Bsns Pk IP1 . **16** C8
Sproughton CE Prim Sch
IP8 .... **16** B6
Sproughton Ct IP8 .... **16** A6
Sproughton Rd IP1 .... **16** D7
Spruce Ave
Colchester CO4 .... **136** E8
Great Dunmow CM6 ...... **123** B1
Spruce Cl Basildon SS15 .. **319** C1
West Mersea CO5 .... **218** B7
Witham CM8 .... **184** A4
Spruce Hill CM18 .... **223** E3
Spruce Hills Rd E17 ..... **309** C1
Sprundel Ave SS8 .... **364** D2
Spur Cl RM4 .... **290** B6
Spurgate CM13 .... **295** B1
Spurgeon Cl
11 Grays RM17 .... **378** C8
Sible Hedingham CO9 ...... **51** E1
Spurgeon Pl CO5 .... **158** C2
Spurgeon St CO1 .... **136** C6
Spurling Rd RM9 .... **353** F6
Spurling Wks EN11 ...... **221** C7
Spur Rd IG11 .... **352** C2
Spurway Par 2 IG2 ...... **332** F6
Squadrons App RM12 .... **355** D6
Square St 3 CM17 .... **200** C1
Square The
10 Brentwood CM14 ...... **316** C8
Colchester CO2 .... **135** B3
Heybridge CM9 .... **237** A5
Horndon on t H SS17 ...... **359** F3
Ilford IG1 .... **333** A4
Sawbridgeworth CM21 .... **172** E2
Stansted Mountfitchet CM22 . **93** F3
Stock CM4 .... **275** E2
Tillingham CM0 .... **263** E4
West Mersea CO5 .... **218** B6
Widdington CB11 .... **67** D4
Woodford IG8 .... **310** A5
Squires Cl CM23 .... **145** C8
Squires Ct Earls Colne CO6 **105** B6
Hoddesdon EN11 .... **221** A5
Squire's Ct 1 CB9 .... **8** E7
Squire St CM3 .... **301** E7
Squires The RM7 .... **335** B5
Squirrells Ct CM1 .... **231** F5
Squirrells SS16 .... **341** B3
Squirrel's Chase RM16 ... **374** A4
Squirrels Cl 2 CM23 ..... **145** F8
Squirrels Ct RM2 .... **336** C7
Squirrels Field CO4 ...... **109** F5
Squirrel's Heath Ave RM2 **336** B8
Squirrels Heath Inf Sch
RM2 .... **336** B6
Squirrels Heath Jun Sch
RM2 .... **336** B6
Squirrels Heath La RM11,
RM2 .... **336** D7
Squirrels Heath Rd RM3 . **314** F1
Squirrel's La IG9 .... **310** D7
Squirrels The IP9 .... **35** A2
Stable Cl Colchester CO3 .. **134** E6
West Mersea CO5 .... **218** E7
Stablecroft CM1 .... **232** E8
Stablefield Rd CO14 ..... **171** A7
Stable Mews
Southend-on-S SS2 .... **347** F2
West Mersea CO5 .... **218** E8
Stables The
Buckhurst Hill IG9 .... **288** C2
Sawbridgeworth CM21 .... **173** B3
Stable Yard Cotts CM6 ... **122** C4
Stacey Ct 9 CM23 .... **145** F6
Stacey Dr SS16 .... **341** C2
Stacey's Mount CM11 .... **320** C5
Stackfield CM20 .... **200** A3
Stackyard The CB10 .... **3** A3
Stacy Ct CM6 .... **123** C1
Staddles CM22 .... **173** B8
Stadium Rd SS2 .... **348** A1
Stadium Trad Est SS7 .... **345** C7
Stadium Way
Harlow CM19 .... **198** F1
Thundersley SS7 .... **345** C7
Staffa Cl SS12 .... **321** F5
Stafford Ave RM11 .... **336** D8
Stafford Cl Grays RM16 ... **372** C2
Greenhithe DA9 .... **376** F2
Kirby Cross CO13 .... **170** E6
Linford SS17 .... **375** A3
Southend-on-S SS9 .... **347** A6
Stafford Cres CM7 .... **128** D4
Stafford Ct EN10 .... **221** A3
Stafford Dr EN10 .... **221** A3
Stafford Gn SS16 .... **340** F4
Stafford Ho
Bishop's Stortford CM23 ... **145** F5
Hoddesdon EN10 .... **221** A3
Stafford Ind Est RM11 ... **336** D8
Staffords CM17 .... **200** E4
STAFFORD'S CORNER ... **188** E5
Stafford Wlk SS8 .... **364** A5
Stagden Cross SS14 ...... **342** F5
Stagden Cross Villas
CM1 .... **177** E2
Staggart Gn IG7 .... **311** F4
Stag Hts IG9 .... **310** B8
Stag La IG9 .... **310** B8
Stainer Cl 1 CM8 .... **211** F7
Stainers CM23 .... **145** C5
Staines Rd IG1 .... **352** D8
Stainforth Rd IG2 .... **333** D5
Stairs Rd SS3 .... **350** F4
Stalham Way IG6 .... **311** B2
Stalin Rd CO2 .... **136** B4
Stallards Cres CO13 ..... **170** E6
STAMBOURNE **28** D3
STAMBOURNE GREEN ... **28** A1
Stambourne Rd
Great Yeldham CO9 .... **29** D3
Ridgewell CO9 .... **28** F5
Toppesfield CO9 .... **50** B8
Stambridge Prim Sch
SS4 .... **326** C2
Stambridge Rd
Clacton-on-S CO15 .... **195** C4
Rochford SS4 .... **326** C2
Stamford Cl IP2 .... **36** F8
Stamford Gdns RM9 ..... **353** C5
Stamford Rd RM9 .... **353** C5
Stammers Ct CM0 .... **284** D4
Stammers Rd CO4 .... **109** F4
STANBROOK **96** E7
Standard Ave CO15 ...... **220** D6
Standard Rd
Belvedere DA17 .... **369** A1
9 Colchester CO1 .... **136** C6
Standen Ave
Hornchurch RM12 .... **336** E1
South Woodham Ferrers
CM3 .... **301** C5
Standfield Gdns RM10 ... **354** A6
Standfield Rd RM10 ...... **354** A7
Standingford CM19 ...... **223** B3
Standley Rd CO14 .... **144** D1
Standrums CM6 .... **150** D8
Stane Cl CM23 .... **118** F1
Stane Field CO6 .... **132** E3
Stanes Rd CM7 .... **127** F6
Stanetta Ct 3 RM6 ...... **334** B4
Staneway SS16 .... **341** D3
Stanfield Cl CO3 .... **134** E3
Stanfield Mdw CM8 ...... **155** F1
Stanfield Rd SS2 .... **348** A1
Stanfields Ct CM20 ...... **199** E1
Stanford Cl Romford RM7 . **335** B5
Woodford IG8 .... **310** E5
Stanford Ct EN9 .... **266** A6
Stanford Gdns RM15 ..... **371** E5
Stanford Hall 1 SS17 .... **360** F3
Stanford Ho
3 Barking IG11 .... **353** B3
East Tilbury RM18 .... **375** B2
STANFORD-LE-H **360** E1
Stanford-le-Hope By-Pass
Basildon SS16, SS17 ...... **342** B1
Orsett RM16 .... **374** D8
Stanford-le-H SS17 .... **360** D4
Stanford-le-Hope Prim Sch
SS17 .... **360** D1
Stanford-le-Hope Sta
SS17 .... **360** C1
Stanford Marshes Nature
Reserve* SS17 .... **375** E7
Stanford Rd
Canvey Island SS8 .... **364** A3
Grays RM16 .... **373** E4
Orsett SS17, RM16 .... **374** E8
Stanford-le-H SS17 .... **360** B1
STANFORD RIVERS **270** C6
Stanford Rivers Rd CM5 . **271** A8
Stanhope Gdns
1 Dagenham RM8 .... **334** F1
Redbridge IG1 .... **332** F3
Stanhope Rd
Dagenham RM8 .... **334** F1
Rainham RM13 .... **355** A3
Swanscombe DA10 .... **377** F1
Stanier Cl SS1 .... **367** C8
Stanley Ave Barking IG11 . **352** F3
Brightlingsea CO7 .... **193** A7
Dagenham RM8 .... **334** F3
Ipswich IP3 .... **18** A4
Romford RM2 .... **336** A7
Stanley Cl Greenhithe DA9 **376** E2
Hornchurch RM12 .... **336** C2
Romford RM2 .... **336** A7
Stanley Drapkin Prim Sch
CB9 .... **27** B6
Stanley Pl CM5 .... **249** A2
Stanley Rd Bulphan RM14 . **358** F8
Canvey Island SS8 .... **364** D4
Chingford E4 .... **287** D1
Clacton-on-S CO15 .... **195** C2
Felixstowe IP11 .... **381** E3
Grays RM17 .... **378** B8
Great Chesterford CB10 ..... **3** E3
Halstead CO9 .... **76** D2
Hornchurch RM12 .... **336** D2
Ilford IG1 .... **333** D2
Rochford SS4 .... **325** C7
South Benfleet SS7 ...... **344** D6
Southend-on-S SS1 .... **367** B7
Sudbury CO10 .... **33** E8
Swanscombe DA10 .... **377** F1
Wivenhoe CO7 .... **137** C1
Woodford E18 .... **309** F2
Stanley Rd N RM13 ...... **354** E4
Stanley Rd S RM13 ...... **354** F3
Stanley Rise CM2 .... **232** F3
Stanleys Farm Rd CB11 ... **43** F8
Stanley Terr CM12 .... **297** A1
Stanley Wood Ave CO10 ... **15** F1
Stanley Wooster Way
CO4 .... **136** E7
Stanmore Cl CO16 .... **195** D5
Stanmore Rd
Belvedere DA17 .... **369** C2
Wickford SS11 .... **322** B6
Stanmore Way
Loughton IG10 .... **289** A8
St Osyth CO16 .... **194** B4
Stannard Way CO10 .... **34** A6
Stannetts SS15 .... **341** B8
Stansfield Ct SS7 .... **344** B7
Stansfield Rd SS7 .... **344** B7
Stansgate Rd
Dagenham RM10 .... **335** A1
Steeple CM0 .... **261** F5
STANSTEAD **2** F7
STANSTEAD ABBOTTS ... **197** E4
Stanstead Dr EN11 ...... **221** B8
Stanstead Pl CO9 .... **103** F8
Stanstead Rd
Halstead CO9 .... **103** F8
Hoddesdon EN11 .... **197** B1
Wanstead E11 .... **332** B6
Stansted Airport Sta
CM24 .... **121** B4
Stansted Cl
Billericay CM11 .... **297** D2
Chelmsford CM1 .... **231** E1
Hornchurch RM12 .... **355** B6
Stansted Ctyd CM24 ..... **121** B1
**STANSTED
MOUNTFITCHET** **119** C8
Stansted Mountfitchet Sta
CM24 .... **119** E6
Stansted Rd
Birchanger CM23 .... **119** C4
Bishop's Stortford CM23 ... **119** B2
Colchester CO2 .... **136** A1
Elsenham CM22 .... **94** C1
Stansted Way CO13 ..... **171** A6
Stanstrete Field CM77 ... **154** B5
Stanton Ct 4 RM10 ...... **354** A6
Stanton Gate RM7 ...... **335** D6
Stanton Pl 9 CB9 .... **9** B8
Stantons CM20 .... **199** B1
STANWAY **134** C5
Stanway Cl
2 Chigwell IG7 .... **311** E5
Glemsford CO10 .... **2** C5
Stanway Ctr The CO3 .... **134** E4
Stanway Fiveways Prim Sch
CO3 .... **134** D5
STANWAY GREEN **134** D3
Stanway Prim Sch CO3 .. **134** C6
Stanway Rd
South Benfleet SS7 ...... **344** C5
Waltham Abbey EN9 ...... **266** A6
Stanway Sch The CO3 .. **134** D5
Stanwell St 9 CO2 ...... **135** F6
Stanwyck Dr IG7 .... **311** C5
Stanwyck Gdns RM3 ..... **314** B5
Stanwyn Ave CO15 ...... **195** E3
STAPLEFORD ABBOTTS . **291** C3
Stapleford Abbotts Prim Sch
RM4 .... **291** C4
Stapleford Ave IG2 ...... **333** E6
Stapleford Cl
Chelmsford CM2 .... **232** A1
Chingford E4 .... **309** C7
Stapleford End SS11 .... **322** B5
Stapleford Gdns RM5 .... **313** A4
Stapleford Rd RM4 ...... **291** B5
STAPLEFORD TAWNEY .. **269** C3
Stapleford Way IG11 .... **353** B2
Staplegrove SS3 .... **368** D8
Staplers Cl CM9 .... **213** B4
Staplers Heath CM9 ..... **213** B4
Staplers Wlk CM9 .... **213** B4
Staples Rd IG10 .... **288** E6
Staples Road Jun & Inf Sch
IG10 .... **288** E6
Stapleton Cres RM13 .... **355** A6
Staple Tye CM18 .... **223** D5
Staple Tye Sh Mews
CM18 .... **223** C5
Stapley Rd DA17 .... **369** A1
Starboard Ave DA9 ...... **377** B1
Starboard View CM3 ..... **301** E6
Star Bsns Ctr RM13 ..... **369** D8
Starch House La IG6 .... **311** D1
Starfield Cl IP4 .... **18** B6
Star La Epping CM16 ..... **246** A1
Great Dunmow CM6 ...... **123** D1
Great Wakering SS3 ...... **349** E3
Ingatestone CM4 .... **274** C4
Ipswich IP4 .... **17** D5
Star Lane Ind Est SS3 ... **349** E3
Starling Cl
Buckhurst Hill IG9 .... **288** A1
Thundersley SS7 .... **345** B7
Starling Ct 17 CM23 ..... **145** F6
STARLING'S GREEN **64** F3
Starling's Hill CO9 .... **75** E4
Starmans Cl RM9 .... **353** E4
Star Mead CM6 .... **70** A2
Starr Rd CM22 .... **94** F5
START HILL **147** A7
State Mans IG6 .... **311** C1
State Par IG6 .... **311** C1
Station App
Basildon, Laindon SS15 ... **341** C5
Basildon, Pitsea SS16 .... **343** B4
Braintree CM7 .... **128** A2
Buckhurst Hill IG9 .... **310** D6
Burnham-on-C CM0 ...... **306** B5
Canvey Island SS8 .... **363** F6
Frinton-on-S CO13 .... **170** F5
Grays RM17 .... **378** A8
Harlow CM20 .... **200** C5
Hockley SS5 .... **324** E6
North Fambridge CM3 .... **303** B8
Southend-on-S, Prittlewell
SS2 .... **347** F2
Southend-on-S SS1 .... **367** A8
South Woodham Ferrers
CM3 .... **301** C8
Theydon Bois CM16 ...... **267** E3
Upminster RM14 .... **337** C2
Wanstead E11 .... **332** A6
Wickford SS11 .... **321** D8
Woodford IG8 .... **310** B4
2 Woodford, Snaresbrook
E18 .... **310** B1
Station Ave Rayleigh SS6 .. **323** C3
Southend-on-S SS2 .... **348** A3
Wickford SS11 .... **321** D8
Station Cres
Cold Norton CM3 .... **280** F5
Rayleigh SS6 .... **323** D3
Station Ct
Chipping Ongar CM5 ...... **249** A3
Wickford SS11 .... **321** D8
Station Est 1 E18 .... **310** B1
Station Gate SS15 .... **341** C5
Station Hill CO8 .... **79** E8
Station Ind Est CM0 .... **306** B5
Station La Basildon SS13 .. **343** B5
Harwich CO12 .... **91** C4
Hornchurch RM12 .... **336** E2
Ingatestone CM4 .... **274** B3
Station Par Barking IG11 . **352** C5
Dagenham RM10 .... **354** A6
Hornchurch RM12 .... **355** B8
3 Romford RM1 .... **335** E5
2 Wanstead E11 .... **332** A6
Woodford IG9 .... **310** D6
Station Pas E18 .... **310** B1
Station Rd Alresford CO7 . **165** A8
Althorne CM3 .... **282** F1
Ardleigh CO7 .... **111** E7
Belvedere DA17 .... **369** A3
Bentley IP9 .... **60** E6
Billericay CM12 .... **296** F2
Birdbrook CO9 .... **10** D1
Bishop's Stortford CM23 ... **146** A7
Station Rd *continued*
Bradfield CO11 .... **87** E3
Braintree CM7 .... **127** F2
Brightlingsea CO7 .... **192** E6
Burnham-on-C CM0 ...... **306** B5
Canvey Island SS8 .... **364** E2
Chigwell IG7 .... **311** B7
Chingford E4 .... **287** D1
Clacton-on-S CO15 .... **195** F3
Clare CO10 .... **12** C7
Cold Norton CM3 .... **281** A5
Colne Engaine CO6 .... **77** F1
Cressing CM8 .... **156** A3
Earls Colne CO6 .... **105** A7
East Tilbury RM18 .... **380** B7
Elsenham CM22 .... **94** C2
Epping CM16 .... **268** A8
Felsted CM6 .... **151** F6
Great Bentley CO7 .... **166** E8
Great Dunmow CM6 ...... **150** E8
Greenhithe DA9 .... **377** A2
Greenhithe DA9 .... **377** A3
Harlow CM17 .... **200** C4
Harwich, Bath Side CO12 ... **91** E5
Harwich CO12 .... **90** F5
Harwich, Dovercourt CO12 .. **91** D4
Hatfield Peverel CM3 ...... **210** F5
Haverhill CB9 .... **9** A8
Hockley SS5 .... **324** E6
Hoddesdon EN10 .... **221** A3
Holdbrook EN9 .... **265** A5
Ilford, Barkingside IG6 .... **333** D8
Ilford IG1 .... **333** B1
Kelvedon CO5 .... **158** C3
Kirby Cross CO13 .... **170** B6
Long Melford CO10 .... **15** C5
Loughton IG10 .... **288** E4
Maldon CM9 .... **237** A3
Manningtree CO11 .... **86** C5
Marks Tey CO6 .... **133** B4
Newport CB11 .... **67** A8
Northfleet DA11 .... **378** B1
North Weald Bassett CM16 . **247** B4
Rayleigh SS6 .... **323** C3
Rayne CM77 .... **126** F1
Romford, Chadwell Heath RM6,
RM8 .... **334** D4
Romford, Harold Wood RM3 **314** F2
Romford RM2 .... **336** C7
Saffron Walden CB11 ...... **22** D1
Sawbridgeworth CM21 .... **172** F3
Sible Hedingham CO9 ...... **51** E2
South Benfleet SS7 ...... **363** D8
Southend-on-S, Eastwood
SS9 .... **346** E3
Southend-on-S, Leigh-on-S
SS9 .... **346** E1
Southend-on-S, Thorpe Bay
SS1 .... **368** B8
Southend-on-S, Westcliff-on-S
SS0 .... **366** D7
Southminster CM0 .... **284** E4
Stanstead Abbotts SG12 .. **197** C4
Stansted Mountfitchet CM24 **119** E6
Sudbury CO10 .... **33** E7
Takeley CM22 .... **148** C7
Thorpe-le-S CO16 .... **168** F8
Thorrington CO7 .... **166** A6
Tiptree CO5 .... **186** C4
Tollesbury CM9 .... **216** D2
Tolleshunt D'arcy CM9 .... **215** E5
Trimley St M IP11 .... **381** A7
Upminster RM14 .... **337** C2
Wakes Colne CO6 .... **106** D6
Wendens Ambo CB11 ...... **42** F5
West Horndon CM13 ...... **339** D5
White Notley CM8 .... **155** F2
Wickford SS11 .... **299** C2
Wickham Bishops CM8 .... **212** C4
Witham CM8 .... **184** A3
Wivenhoe CO7 .... **164** B8
Wrabness CO11 .... **88** F3
Station Rd N DA17 .... **369** B3
Station Road Ind Est
Great Dunmow CM6 ...... **150** E7
Tolleshunt D'arcy CM9 .... **215** E5
Station Sq RM2 .... **336** B7
Station St Ipswich IP2 ..... **17** C3
Saffron Walden CB11 ...... **22** D1
Walton-on-t-N CO14 ..... **171** C8
Station Terr CM3 .... **210** F5
Station Way
Basildon SS14, SS16 ...... **342** A5
Buckhurst Hill IG9 .... **310** D6
Station Yd IP2 .... **17** B4
Staveley Ct 4 E11 .... **332** A6
Staverton Rd RM11 ...... **336** D5
Stays La CM5 .... **229** A3
Steadman Ho 4 RM10 .... **335** A1
Steamer Terr 2 CM1 ..... **232** A3
Steam Mill Rd CO11 ..... **114** B8
STEBBING **124** E5
STEBBING GREEN **125** C3
Stebbing Prim Sch CM6 . **124** E5
Stebbing Rd CM6 .... **152** B7
Stebbings SS16 .... **341** C4
Stebbings Ct 5 CM0 ..... **306** C4
Stebbing Way IG11 ...... **353** A3
Stedman Ct CO15 .... **220** D6
Steed Cl RM11 .... **336** B2
Steed Cres CO2 .... **136** A5
Steeds Mdw CO10 .... **15** C8
Steeds Way IG10 .... **288** E6
Steel App IG11 .... **353** B3
Steele Ave DA9 .... **377** A2
Steele Cl CO6 .... **132** F3
Steen Cl CM4 .... **274** B4
STEEPLE **261** E3
STEEPLE BUMPSTEAD **27** B8
Steeple Bumpstead Rd
CB9 .... **26** E7
Steeple Cl Heybridge CM9 . **237** D5
Rochford SS4 .... **325** D3
Steeplefield SS9 .... **346** E6
Steeple Gate SS7 .... **345** E2
Steeplehall SS13 .... **343** A5
Steeple Hts SS7 .... **344** B6
Steeple Mdws CM0 ...... **284** B4
Steeple Rd
Latchingdon CM3 .... **282** D7
Steeple CM0 .... **262** C4
Steeple Rd *continued*
Steeple CM0 .... **284** B7
STEEPLE VIEW **319** B1
Steeple View
Bishop's Stortford CM23 ... **145** F8
Grays RM17 .... **373** A1
Steeple Way CM15 ...... **272** B2
Steerforth Cl CM1 .... **231** D7
Steli Ave SS8 .... **363** F5
Stella Maris IP2 .... **16** D5
Stella Maris Cl SS8 ...... **364** F3
Sten Cl EN3 .... **265** A2
Stenning Ave SS17 ...... **375** B2
Stepfield CM8 .... **184** B2
Stephen Ave RM13 ...... **355** A6
Stephen Cl Haverhill CB9 .... **8** F8
Long Melford CO10 .... **15** B5
Stephen Cranfield Cl
CO5 .... **164** A7
Stephen Marshall Ave
CM7 .... **72** C6
Stephen Neville Ct CB11 .. **43** D8
Stephens Cl RM3 .... **314** C5
Stephens Cres SS17 ..... **359** F3
Stephen's Ct IP4 .... **18** B6
Stephenson Ave RM18 ... **379** A6
Stephenson Cl
Hoddesdon EN11 .... **221** C6
Hoddesdon EN11 .... **221** D6
Stephenson Rd
Braintree CM7 .... **128** A1
Clacton-on-S CO15 .... **196** B8
Colchester CO4 .... **110** D6
North Fambridge CM3 .... **303** A8
Southend-on-S SS9 .... **346** C6
Stephenson Rd W CO15 . **169** A1
Sterling Cl CO3 .... **134** E5
Sterling Complex IP1 ..... **16** D7
Sterling Ind Est RM10 ... **354** B8
Stern Cl IG11 .... **353** C3
Sterry Cres RM10 .... **354** A7
Sterry Gdns RM10 .... **354** A6
Sterry Ho RM13 .... **355** B2
Sterry Rd Barking IG11 ... **352** F4
Dagenham RM10 .... **354** A7
Stevanne Ct 1 DA17 ..... **369** A1
Stevenage Rd E6 .... **352** A6
Stevens Cl
Canvey Island SS8 .... **364** D4
Colchester CO4 .... **109** E3
Stevens La CM6 .... **152** F6
Stevenson Rd IP1 .... **17** B6
Stevenson Way SS12 .... **321** C5
Stevens Rd
Dagenham RM8 .... **334** C1
Witham CM8 .... **183** E1
Stevens Way IG7 .... **311** E6
Stevens Wlk CO4 .... **136** F7
STEVENTON END **6** C2
STEWARDS **223** E3
Stewards Cl Epping CM16 . **268** A6
Frinton-on-S CO13 .... **170** F7
Stewards Elm Farm La
SS4 .... **326** D4
STEWARD'S GREEN **268** B7
Stewards Green Rd CM16 **268** B6
Stewards Sch CM18 ..... **223** D4
Stewards Wlk RM1 ...... **335** E6
Stewart Ave RM14 ...... **337** B1
Stewart Pl SS12 .... **321** F5
Stewart Rainbird Ho 1
E12 .... **352** A7
Stewart Rd CM2 .... **254** A6
Stewarts The CM23 ..... **145** E6
Stewarts Way CM23 ...... **92** F2
Steyning Ave SS2 .... **348** E1
Stickland Rd DA17 ...... **369** A2
STICKLING GREEN **65** C6
Stifford Clays Inf Sch
RM16 .... **373** B5
Stifford Clays Jun Sch
RM16 .... **373** B5
Stifford Clays Rd
Grays RM16 .... **373** B6
Orsett RM16 .... **373** B7
Stifford Hill RM16 .... **372** C5
Stifford Prim Sch RM17 .. **372** F1
Stifford Rd Aveley RM15 .. **371** E5
South Ockendon RM15 .... **372** B6
Stile Croft CM18 .... **224** A6
Stile La SS6 .... **323** D2
Stilemans SS11 .... **321** D8
Stilemans Wood CM7 .... **128** D1
Stiles Cl DA8 .... **369** B1
Stiles The CM9 .... **237** E3
Stillwells SS4 .... **326** A2
Stirling Ave SS9 .... **346** B2
Stirling Cl Rainham RM13 . **355** B2
Rayleigh SS6 .... **323** B5
Stirling Dr CB9 .... **8** E8
Stirling Pl SS13 .... **343** B8
Stirrup Cl CM1 .... **232** E7
Stirrup Mews CO3 .... **134** E6
STISTED **129** C6
Stisted CE Prim Sch
CM77 .... **129** B6
Stivvy's Rd CM9 .... **235** C3
St. Michael's Chase CO6 . **133** D2
STOCK **275** F3
Stock CE Prim Sch CM4 . **275** D3
Stock Chase CM9 .... **237** B5
Stock Cl SS2 .... **347** F4
Stockdale Rd RM8 .... **334** F2
Stocker Gdns RM9 .... **353** C5
Stockfield Ave EN11 ..... **221** B8
Stockhouse Cl CM9 ...... **187** B2
Stockhouse Rd CO5 ...... **187** B7
Stock Ind Pk SS2 .... **348** A4
STOCKING GREEN **24** C1
Stocking La SG8 .... **39** C1
Stock La CM4 .... **274** D3
Stockland Rd RM7 .... **335** D5
Stockley Cl CB9 .... **9** C7
Stockman Terr CM77 ..... **154** C8
Stockmen Field CM23 .... **145** C5
Stockmers End 1 IP9 ...... **35** A1
Stock Park Ct SS9 .... **346** E6
Stock Rd Billericay CM12 .. **297** C5
Galleywood CM2 .... **254** B2
Southend-on-S SS2 .... **347** F4
Stock CM4 .... **275** D1